WITHDRAWN
OWENS LIBRARY
N.W.M.S.U.

ANNUAL REVIEW OF
INFORMATION
SCIENCE AND
TECHNOLOGY

VOLUME **27** 1992

ISBN: 0-938734-66-0
ISSN: 0066-4200
CODEN: ARISBC
LC No. 66-25096

Annual Review of Information Science and Technology

Volume 27, 1992

Edited by

Martha E. Williams
University of Illinois
Urbana, Illinois, USA

asis

Published on behalf of the
American Society for Information Science
by Learned Information, Inc.

1992

Learned Information, Inc.
Medford, New Jersey

©American Society for Information Science, 1992

All rights reserved. No part of this publication may be reproduced, stored in a retrieval system or transmitted in any form or by any means, electronic, mechanical, photocopy, recording or otherwise, without the prior written permission of the copyright owner, the American Society for Information Science.

Special regulations for readers in the United States: This publication has been registered with the Copyright Clearance Center Inc. (CCC), Salem, Massachusetts. Please contact the CCC about conditions under which photocopies of parts of this publication may be made in the U.S.A. All other copyright questions, including photocopying outside of the U.S.A., should be referred to the copyright owner, unless otherwise specified.

Neither the publisher nor the American Society for Information Science assumes responsibility for any injury and/or damage to persons or property that may result from the use or operation of any methods, products, instructions, or ideas contained in this publication.

ISBN: 0-938734-66-0
ISSN: 0066-4200
CODEN: ARISBC
LC No. 66-25096

Published and distributed by:
Learned Information, Inc.,
143 Old Marlton Pike
Medford, NJ 08055-8750

for the
American Society for Information Science
8720 Georgia Avenue, Suite 501
Silver Spring, MD 20910-3602, U.S.A.

Distributed outside North America by:
Learned Information Ltd.
Woodside, Hinksey Hill
Oxford OX1 5AU
England

The opinions expressed by contributors to publications of the American Society for Information Science do not necessarily reflect the position or official policy of the American Society for Information Science.

ARIST Production staff, for ASIS:
Charles & Linda Holder, Graphic Compositors
Cover design by Sandy Skalkowski Brock
Printed in the U.S.A.

Contents

Preface vii
Acknowledgments xi
Advisory Committee for *ARIST* xii
Contributors xiii
Chapter Reviewers xiv

I
Planning Information Systems and Services   1

1   The Impact of Information Technology on the Individual
Ruth A. Palmquist   3

2   Social Equity and Information Technologies: Moving toward Information Democracy
Ronald D. Doctor   43

II
Basic Techniques and Technologies   97

3   Parallel Information Processing
Edie M. Rasmussen   99

III
Applications   131

4   Data Representations for Geographic Information Systems
Clifford A. Shaffer   135

5 Environmental Research: Communication Studies and Information Sources
Zorana Ercegovac — 173

6 The Information Environment of Managers
Jeffrey Katzer and Patricia T. Fletcher — 227

IV The Profession — 265

7 Education and Training for Information Science in the Soviet Union
Pamela Spence Richards — 267

8 Ethical Considerations of Information Professionals
Thomas J. Froehlich — 291

Introduction to the Index — 325

Index — 327

Introduction to the Keyword and Author Index — 383

Keyword and Author Index of *ARIST* Titles for Volumes 1-27 — 385

About the Editor — 429

Preface

PUBLISHING HISTORY

This is the 27th volume of the *Annual Review of Information Science and Technology* (*ARIST*). It was produced for the American Society for Information Science (ASIS) and published by Learned Information, Inc. ASIS initiated the series in 1966 with the publication of Volume 1 under the editorship of Carlos A. Cuadra, who continued as Editor through Volume 10. Martha E. Williams has served as Editor starting with Volume 11. ASIS is the owner of *ARIST*, maintains the editorial control, and has the sole rights to the series in all forms.

Through the years several organizations have been responsible for publishing and marketing *ARIST*. Volumes 1 and 2 were published by Interscience Publishers, a division of John Wiley & Sons. Volumes 3 through 6 were published by Encyclopaedia Britannica, Inc. Volumes 7 through 11 were published by ASIS itself. Volumes 12 through 21 were published by Knowledge Industry Publications, Inc. Volumes 22 through 25 were published by Elsevier Science Publishers B.V., Amsterdam, The Netherlands. With Volume 26 Learned Information, Inc., assumed the role of publisher of *ARIST* for ASIS.

POLICY

ARIST is an annual publication that reviews numerous topics within the broad field of information science and technology. The contents vary from year to year; no single topic is treated on an annual basis. Inasmuch as the field is dynamic, the contents (chapters) of the various *ARIST* volumes must change to reflect this dynamism. *ARIST* chapters are scholarly reviews of specific topics as substantiated by the published literature. Some material may be included, even though not backed up by literature, if it is needed to provide a balanced and complete picture of the state of the art for the subject of the chapter. The time period covered varies from chapter to chapter, depending on whether the topic has been treated previously by *ARIST* and, if so, on the length of the interval from the last treatment to the current one. Thus, reviews may cover a one-year or a multiyear period. The reviews aim to be critical in that they provide the author's expert opinion regarding developments and activities within the chapter's subject area. The review guides the reader to or from specific publications. Chapters aim to be scholarly, thorough within the scope defined by the chapter author, up to date, well written, and readable by an audience that goes beyond the author's immediate peer group to researchers and practitioners in information science and technology, in general, and ASIS members, in particular.

PURPOSE

The purpose of *ARIST* is to describe and to appraise activities and trends in the field of information science and technology. Material presented should be substantiated by references to the literature. *ARIST* provides an annual review of topics in the field. One volume is produced each year. A master plan for the series encompasses the entire field in all its aspects, and topics for each volume are selected from the plan on the basis of timeliness and an assessment of reader interest.

REFERENCES CITED IN TEXT AND BIBLIOGRAPHY

The format for referring to bibliographic citations within the text involves use of the cited author's name instead of reference numbers. The cited author's surname is printed in upper case letters. The reader, wishing to find the bibliographic references, can readily locate the appropriate reference in the bibliography (alphabetically arranged by first author's last name). A single author appears as SMITH; coauthors as SMITH & JONES; and multiple authors as SMITH ET AL. If multiple papers by the same author are cited, the distinction is made by indicating the year of publication after the last name (e.g., SMITH, 1986), and if a further distinction is required for multiple papers within the same year, a lower case alpha character follows the year (e.g., SMITH, 1986a). Except for the fact that all authors in multi-authored papers are included in bibliographic references, the same basic conventions are used in the chapter bibliographies. Thus, the reader can easily locate in the bibliography any references discussed in the text.

Because of the emphasis placed on the requirement for chapter authors to discuss the key papers and significant developments reported in the literature, and because *ARIST* readers have expressed their liking for comprehensive bibliographies associated with the chapters, more references may be listed in the bibliographies than are discussed and/or cited in the text.

The format used for references in the bibliographies is based on the *American National Standard for Bibliographic References*, ANS Z39.29. We have followed the ANSI guidelines with respect to the sequence of bibliographic data elements and the punctuation used to separate the elements. Adoption of this convention should facilitate conversion of the references to machine-readable form as need arises. Journal article references follow the ANSI guide as closely as possible. Conference papers and microform publications follow an *ARIST* adaptation of the format.

STRUCTURE OF THE VOLUME

In accordance with the *ARIST* master plan, this volume's eight chapters fit within a basic framework: I. Planning Information Systems and Services; II. Basic Techniques and Technologies; III. Applications; and IV. The Profession. Chapter titles are provided in the Table of Contents, and an Introduction to each section highlights the events, trends, and evaluations given by the chapter authors. An Index to the entire volume is provided to help the user locate material relevant to the subject content, authors, and organizations cited in the book. An explanation of the guidelines employed in the Index is provided in the Introduction to the Index. A Keyword and Author Index to this and all prior volumes follows the Index.

DATABASES AND ABSTRACTING AND INDEXING SERVICES COVERING *ARIST*

ARIST as a whole and/or individual chapters are included in a number of abstracting and indexing (A&I) journals both within the United States and internationally. Databases that both cover *ARIST* and are available through major online services in the United States are:

> INSPEC (Computer and Control Abstracts)
> Social SciSearch (Social Sciences Citation Index)
> LISA (Library and Information Science Abstracts)
> Information Science Abstracts
> BIOSIS (Biological Abstracts)
> Library Literature
> Current Contents
> CompuMath Citation Index

Publishers of other A&I journals and databases who would like to include *ARIST* in their coverage are encouraged to contact the publisher for a review copy and notify the editor who will add the database name(s) to this list when appropriate.

Acknowledgments

Appreciation is expressed to many individuals and organizations for their roles in creating this volume. First and foremost are the authors of the individual chapters who have generously contributed their time and efforts in searching, reviewing, and evaluating the large body of literature on which their chapters are based. The *ARIST* Advisory Committee Members and *ARIST* Reviewers provided valuable feedback and constructive criticism of the content. DIALOG Information Services generously provided the authors with online access to databases. Appreciation is expressed to all of the members of the editorial staff and *ARIST* technical support staff who are listed on the Acknowledgments page.

Martha E. Williams

Acknowledgments

The American Society for Information Science and the Editor wish to acknowledge the contributions of the three principals on the editorial staff and the technical support staff.

Mary W. Rakow, Copy Editor

Debora Shaw, Index Editor

Linda C. Smith, Bibliographic Editor

Technical Support Staff

El-Siddig At-Taras, Technical Advisor

Laurence Lannom, Technical Advisor

Scott E. Preece, Technical Advisor

Linda C. Smith, Technical Advisor

Sheila Carnder, Word Processing

Joy Ligon, Word Processing

Linda Holder, Compositor

Advisory Committee for *ARIST*

Nicholas J. Belkin

Martin Dillon

Raya Fidel

Jeffrey Katzer

Jessica L. Milstead

John Regazzi

Linda C. Smith

Fran Spigai

Carol Tenopir

Contributors

Ronald D. Doctor
University of Alabama
School of Library and
   Information Studies
536 Main Library/Box 870252
Tuscaloosa, AL 35487

Zorana Ercegovac
University of California at
   Los Angeles
Graduate School of Library
   and Information Science
300 Circle Drive North
Los Angeles, CA 90024

Patricia T. Fletcher
Syracuse University
School of Information Studies
Syracuse, NY 13244

Thomas J. Froehlich
Kent State University
School of Library and
   Information Science
P.O. Box 5190
Kent, OH 44242

Jeffrey Katzer
Syracuse University
School of Information Studies
Syracuse, NY 13244

Ruth A. Palmquist
University of Tennessee
Graduate School of Library
   and Information Science
804 Volunteer Blvd.
Knoxville, TN 37996

Edie M. Rasmussen
University of Pittsburgh
School of Library and
   Information Science
135 North Bellefield Avenue
Pittsburgh, PA 15260

Pamela Spence Richards
Rutgers University
School of Communication,
   Information and Library
   Studies
4 Huntington Street
New Brunswick, NJ 08903

Clifford A. Shaffer
Virginia Polytechnic Institute
   and State University
Department of Computer
   Science
562 McBryde Hall
Blacksburg, VA 24061

Chapter Reviewers

David Becker

Nicholas J. Belkin

Christine Borgman

Walter M. Carlson

Bonnie Carroll

Martin Dillon

Raya Fidel

José-Marie Griffiths

Glynn Harmon

Peter Hernon

Lee A. Hollaar

Michael E.D. Koenig

Lois F. Lunin

Jessica L. Milstead

John Regazzi

Peter Schipma

Elliot Siegel

Linda C. Smith

Fran Spigai

Carol Tenopir

Mickie A. Voges-Piatt

I
Planning Information Systems and Services

Section I includes two chapters, both of which deal with the social aspects of information. Ruth A. Palmquist of the University of Tennessee explores "The Impact of Information Technology on the Individual," and Ronald D. Doctor of the University of Alabama discusses "Social Equity and Information Technologies: Moving toward Information Democracy."

Ruth A. Palmquist tells us that access to information creates changes in a society that is based on information as a resource, and we, as information scientists, must be aware of these changes as they are experienced at all levels of society. Information technologies are change agents and have an impact on the lives of individuals. Her chapter focuses on the way computer-based technologies affect the environments in which individuals function. She looks at the individual within a cultural context, a work context, and a citizenship or governance context. Among the considerations in the home (cultural) context are leisure activities, "smart" homes with various monitoring and alarm systems, and the effect of the media on family structure. Among the considerations in the work context are job satisfaction, fear of technological change, and geographical dispersion of workers (working at home, the electronic cottage industry or telecommuting). Among the considerations in the citizenship context are teledemocracy and the use of information technology by government.

Ronald D. Doctor explores the concept of information democracy, noting that it has roots in several fields—political science, sociology, social work, communication science, and library and information studies—but that it is explicitly recognized only in library and information studies. He focuses on the interplay between information technologies and society and on the theme of social equity in the distribution and use of information resources. When dealing with information democracy there is a focus on the information poor—a population that goes beyond the economically poor to include the aged, the disabled, those in rural areas, and those in school.

Ronald Doctor traces the historical origins leading to the concerns for social equity and information technologies. There is power associated with the control of knowledge resources as well as with the control of economic and political resources. Ron discusses technology and society, including the information age, societal constraints, and predicting the future. He covers the issues of power and control in a democracy in terms of the roots of a democratic government and the principles of a democratic society. Doctor looks at social equity and information technology in several broad areas: (1) relationships between societal and technological developments; (2) concepts of democracy and power and control relationships in democracies; (3) concepts of social justice and social equity, including poverty and its amelioration; (4) information needs, sources, and uses, including research on how and where people seek information to meet everyday needs; and (5) applications in the form of mass information delivery systems.

1 The Impact of Information Technology on the Individual

RUTH A. PALMQUIST
University of Tennessee, Knoxville

INTRODUCTION

Society today abounds with electronic information that is available to nearly all individuals through a bewildering array of information technologies. So rapid has the development of these technologies been that more change has occurred within one generation than formerly occurred over many generations. Information technology has been felt in most of the areas of an individual's private and work life. Forecasts of the future, brought to us largely through the application of improved information technologies, fill the shelves of local bookstores (NAISBITT & ABURDENE; TOFFLER; TURKLE; ZUBOFF). Many more forecasts appear in the business section of the bookstore, helping to introduce the notion that our work lives will be constantly evolving in a newly emerging "information society." However, few of these best-selling forecasts are based on an empirical examination of gathered evidence. The impetus to write this chapter originally came from a concern that among these predictions of the future, there seemed few attempts to examine the impact of information technology empirically.

There is a growing awareness within the information science community that the improved access to information for which our research strives may fuel some of the change our society is experiencing. While the societal changes represent a fascinating and complex research challenge, information scientists must bear some responsibility to anticipate

---

The assistance of Eunice M. Schroeder is gratefully acknowledged.

Annual Review of Information Science and Technology (ARIST), Volume 27, 1992
Martha E. Williams, Editor
Published for the American Society for Information Science (ASIS)
By Learned Information, Inc., Medford, N.J.

the impact that improved access to information will have on the individual. The technologies used to transport and to organize information are equally influential and are often characterized in the literature as the "new" information technologies; this distinction essentially draws a vague line between older broadcast technologies (e.g., radio, television) and newer computer-based technologies (e.g., video games, multimedia, fax). The following chapter concentrates primarily on these newer technologies.

The last attempt to look at such an audaciously broad area of literature was in 1983, when KOCHEN examined several intellectual issues that stemmed from growing societal changes. He states in his introduction that the topic of "information and society" is "not a scientific one" and that "there are no discoveries resulting from scientific research to be reviewed" (p. 277). His concern was with such issues as national security and commercial competitive advantage and the implications for policy decision making. Since 1983, many of the issues he discussed became the focus for additional *ARIST* reviews. For example, T.H. MARTIN provided a chapter on office automation and how it affects the organization of work; BROADBENT & KOENIG examined information technology management; and STEINFIELD explored computer-mediated communication such as electronic mail (e-mail) and electronic bulletin boards. Today we need to look at how information technologies affect the life of the individual.

Scope

The focus of this chapter is on recent research on or forecasts about how computer-based technologies affect the environments in which the individual functions. These environments are those that support the society of which the individual is a part. Society is supported by activities that provide cultural knowledge, activities that allow the individual to know the society as a whole. Society also needs its individual members to be productive so that they sustain themselves and therefore sustain society. Finally, society needs power to protect its members from the perceived threats of those who live outside society. Consequently, this review looks at the individual within a cultural context, a work context, and a citizenship or governance context. It focuses on the most recent years, 1988–1991. For an older survey, see the 1987 overview by PERROLLE. Some special environments (e.g., medicine, health, safety) are given little or no coverage due to space constraints.

A quick look at the bibliography shows that few of the articles come from the information science literature. As information science becomes more interdisciplinary, its literature becomes increasingly difficult to define. Nevertheless, many authors within information science and in other related fields have expressed concern for a better understanding of the potential impact of information technology on the life of the individual. Until recently, the primary focus for information technology has been to speed up existing processes or make them less costly, with little concern for related influences that might arise. This review can begin to broaden our understanding of those influences.

Value of Technology to Society

The concept of technological change has been widely discussed and debated, and the debate seems to be increasing as we near the end of the century. For each argument that information technology provides for greater prosperity (see STRASSMANN), there is a counter argument that it can enslave the individual and degrade the quality of life (see POSTMAN, 1992). Although such insights are not dismissed, they are beyond the scope of this review and are included only if they are exceptional.

THE INDIVIDUAL'S NEED FOR SOCIAL EXPERIENCE

Human Culture

Computers now share the human environment, and inevitably they may affect our sense of identity and our ability to relate to one another. In the following section, the literature describing the general changes in human culture is examined first, followed by those efforts to examine the individual living alone, the individual at home and at leisure, and finally, the individual in community groups.

Much recent scholarship has tried to assess the cultural shifts caused by social, political, economic, and technological change. It is extremely difficult to measure technologically induced change without also considering the concomitant changes in the social, political, and economic arenas. A particularly ambitious effort by INGLEHART draws on two decades of surveys, the Euro-Barometers, carried out by the Commission of the European Communities, which regularly measured the attitudes, values, and behaviors of 12 Western nations. Also included are the data from a World Value Survey done in the early 1980s by the European Value System Study Group. Inglehart concludes that "throughout the advanced industrial societies, what people want out of life is changing" (p. 3). He finds that economic growth as a dominant goal of the individual has been replaced by the aim of a better quality of life. The individual is more likely to live alone than ever before in human history, so it is not surprising that Inglehart's data reveal a growing need for a sense of belonging, esteem, and self-realization. The search for self-realization often dictates movement to work environments in which the individual can find more fulfilling employment. As the individual moves to new surroundings, knowledge about other members of the society increases. A belief is fostered that it is possible to create a lifestyle slightly different from the one the individual left behind. This widened scope brings a relaxation of traditional religious, social, and sexual norms, and with greater economic security comes a toleration of difference and less class conflict. Among the less well-educated respondents, Inglehart reports that these shifts in traditional norms are less comfortably tolerated or understood. Thus, some class conflict will occur, according to Inglehart, as long as there are strong differences in the degree of education achieved by members of the society.

The use of electronic technologies such as television to acquire synthetic cultural experiences is explored by MEYROWITZ. His remarkable effort has been applauded by some as a masterful study and criticized by others for its limited focus on television, possibly overestimating television's communicative impact. However, his work enlightens information science in several ways. He presents three case studies that illustrate the blurring of public and private behaviors as we move from a time when we experienced largely "print situations" to the present when we can more easily sample "electronic situations" in a wide variety of social roles. Children, for example, were once traditionally shielded from exposure to certain "adult" situations they were not yet allowed to experience because the printed documents through which such experience were retold were carefully restricted. Today such exposure is available "electronically" and is almost impossible to restrict. As a result, argues Meyrowitz, there is a blurring for the child of the contextual clues needed to choose appropriate behaviors and a resulting sense of isolation when the wrong behaviors emerge and are censored by adults.

The individual's identity is strongly influenced by the various roles he or she assumes within his or her social and work experience. These vary for most adults from parent, spouse, child of aging parents, and employee to more trivial roles within our recreational lives (e.g., softball player, Star Trek fan). These roles can become less defined in an environment in which all information is readily available to all members of a society. GERGEN, in his fascinating monograph, argues persuasively that the technology actually encourages the individual to accept and to perpetuate roles that previously might have been discarded. Today's individual can maintain many more relationships and roles of varying types and intensities through the electronic media than could his or her grandparents, who may have lived most of their lives in the same neighborhood with little to connect them to a larger geographically diverse social group. The answering machine, cellular phone, fax machine, and e-mail all provide an avenue for perpetuating relationships with an ever-widening collection of semiformal acquaintances. This process of social saturation, argues Gergen, has changed our understanding of self by eroding standard social arrangements. We all have friends who live at a distance, and many long-distance relationships are sustained through electronic media.

POSTMAN (1992) agrees that the computer has become an "ecological" technology, capable of influencing life so massively as to generate total societal change, but he also points out that modern society is very skeptical of the status quo. In addition, whether due to immigrant beginnings, a frontier mentality, abundant natural resources, or unprecedented political and religious freedoms, Americans fight any and all constraints, pushing constantly toward change. Postman, Gergen, and Meyrowitz would urge their readers to recognize that our electronic technologies have strong disadvantages as well as advantages. More specifically, these technologies may help us sustain relationships with distant acquaintances, but they can also isolate and confuse our social identities.

Finally, a strong recommendation is warranted for an excellent theoretical text that puts much of the present technological environment into a context of evolving human activity. BENIGER traces what he calls the present "control revolution" of the information society from early standardizing and systematizing activities that originated more than a century ago as the industrial revolution became more complex. From the production of the spinning jenny in 1786 to the standardizing of railroad gauges in 1886 to the various innovations for stabilizing air travel in the early 1900s, Beniger demonstrates how the increasing reliance on the market to control production led directly to the need for computer technologies. His strong theoretical approach is coupled with the presentation of chronologies of innovation in such commercial realms as retail trade and transportation. He shows how many major impacts on modern life can be predicted from those early activities, and he believes that the current information age is not a revolution but a continuation of efforts to cope with growing complexities.

A less theoretically satisfying attempt to place the information society into a historical context is the essay by ROBERTSON, who examines the evolution of civilization as a sequence of the major innovations for recording and recalling information. His effort begins with the earliest tools for recording language, continues through the printing press, and ends with a discussion of electronic text as a recording medium.

The Isolated Individual

Electronic technologies have removed the individual's need to experience personally how his environment works. Several authors provide compelling reviews that verify this assertion. QUILLING, in a rather thin and shallow review of educational research, nevertheless makes an elegant argument for educators to be aware of the shift in our Western humanist culture from a tradition of strong, mutual obligation to one of the individual as an isolated part of the natural world—one who is not necessarily able to exert dominion over it. The empirical efforts marshalled by FUNKHOUSER & SHAW make a stronger argument that this awareness of limited dominion is both created by and compensated for with electronically produced synthetic experience. Their most persuasive essay uses older communications research to support the ever-declining tolerance of boredom and inactivity. This declining tolerance is compensated by the heightened sense of excitement derived from the electronically produced experience. It satisfies the expectation of quick, effective solution to problems, but it also contributes to the misperception of many physical and societal events, thus leading to a superficial understanding of environment. The authors argue that although we have a broader view of the world than any previous generation, we stand ready to be more ignorant of the natural world than our preelectronic ancestors.

POSTMAN (1985) and BRYANT both argue that the individual's search for entertainment is eroding his or her attention span and negatively influencing a variety of societal strengths, such as the political process. DONOHUE ET AL. agree and argue that computers and telecommunications technologies have encouraged the individual to avoid the cognitive processes involved in searching out all sides of an issue to become a truly informed citizen. To many media communications researchers this fear surfaced with the advent of television.

WHITNEY & WARTELLA present the only evidence available to counter the argument that the public grows continuously more ignorant of public issues. They examine various efforts in communications research on public ignorance and note that what is measured is media exposure rather than media attention. They argue that exposure and attention measures, while highly correlated for print messages, such as newspaper articles, are far less correlated for visual messages from a video display device. They believe that television requires much less attention than print media and that comparison of exposure times to each generates an inaccurate picture of what the individual may know.

Again INGLEHART provides the strongest demographic evidence for the individual's growing isolation. The number of individuals in industrial societies who are living alone has increased dramatically over the past decade. Inglehart's longitudinal survey data identify factors such as changing social and sexual norms and the improved economic opportunities for working women as reasons for the growing number of single adults. QUILLING believes that factors such as smaller family size, increasing divorce and separation rates, and workplace mobility mean less time to devote to strong personal associations. GERGEN also offers a view of technology's role in sustaining geographically dispersed relationships.

The communications literature provides the strongest efforts to examine this phenomenon by looking at television and radio. In a fascinating content–analysis study, LARSON & ORAVEC explore the tremendous popularity of the National Public Radio program "A Prairie Home Companion," which they see as a possible synthetic community for its 5–10 million weekly radio listeners. Despite its satiric humor, the program emphasizes strong traditional values such as the nuclear family, marriage, and religion, a strong distrust of urban life and its attendant technologies, and a strong distrust of different social groups.

Similarly, CERULO ET AL. and CARPIGNANO ET AL. provide illuminating examinations of the formats for various mass media products, particularly talk shows, that promote synthetic approximations of a meaningful membership group for their audiences. They explain the techniques used to create a social audience bound together by common interests, beliefs, and feelings, and they argue that these shows comfort the disconnected by ensuring a feeling of being "bound together" with others. They argue that such shows are specifically tailored to certain populations and provide a way to enjoy social interactions that substitute for real contact with friends, family, and neighbors.

Mate-seeking via electronic media is a newer phenomenon. Empirical evidence of its effectiveness is very difficult to find. At best, some descriptive articles recount experiences of popular communication patterns. For example, the French Minitel system marketed by Telecom has experienced heavy use of an electronic videotex messaging service. Users post messages to a community bulletin board and may withhold their identity or use a pseudonym. As somewhat superficially reported by DELACY, this activity is seen as "the emotional equivalent of safe sex in an age when physical contact is often associated with contamination" (p. 228).

In much the same vein but on a more scholarly level, ADELMAN & AHUVIA look at the growth of "marriage market intermediaries." They discuss various formats from video-based dating services to computer networks that enable singles to search for, match with, and interact with potential marriage partners. They make an argument, supported with only anecdotal evidence, for the possibility that these artificial environments foster inappropriate disclosures that ultimately hinder rather than facilitate the processes they wish to serve. For example, computer profiles are created that specify the criteria for an ideal partner. Such profiles can be drawn so specifically that they produce few if any matches.

Some would argue that the telecomputing technologies provide a comfortable "playground" for those who believe they are detached from society. TURKLE and more recently HAFNER & MARKOFF present case studies of young men and women who describe themselves as computer hackers. Hafner and Markoff, using personal interviews, court transcripts, and newspaper accounts, attempt to describe the information age "cowboy" or "urban terrorist" who enjoys living outside the law and has mastered the new electronic corridors that allow access to protected environments that are potentially damaging to society when entered illegally. They describe this personality as being both economically and politically motivated, beginning with the desire to circumvent fees levied on services by large corporate and governmental providers. They point out that the microcomputer was spawned by the desire of hackers like Steven Jobs and Steven Wozniak, co-inventors of the Apple computer, to bring computing technology into the hands of the individual so that the average citizen could know as much about large corporations and government agencies as those agencies and corporations knew about him or her. The success of Jobs and Wozniak, founders of the microcomputer revolution, has removed them from the ranks of the isolated hackers. Their creation may have a large historical role to play in our national economic health as information technology opens up new areas of trade, particularly in the service sector. However, the tool they created and the "electronic cowboy" for whom it was originally intended have provided science fiction with "cyberpunk."

The Individual at Home

Leisure time has traditionally been spent in the home. Today various technologies used in the home alleviate burdensome tasks and generate additional leisure. MILES provides an excellent inventory of several "smart home" technologies, such as the answering machine or coded phone register, alarms and warning mechanisms on heating and cooling systems as well as on windows and doors, and thermostats and feedback mechanisms that monitor the home environment. All these devices make home life easier, safer, and more efficient.

In a similar review of "smart home" technologies, PETRIE surveys the videotext and teletex systems in Britain, along with increasing multimedia options such as a graphical user interface to select options without prior computer training. Although he provides little beyond what is currently used in Britain, Petrie concludes by stating that "ultimately the users/private citizens will expect their information needs to be satisfied with utmost convenience by an in-home, integrated, multimedia response" (p. 136).

Media use within the home offers an increasing array of choices. In a study of children and the media environment, DORR & KUNKEL found that in most of the homes they sampled the phrase "using computers" was judged to mean "playing video games." They state that the use of both personal computers and video games promoted rather than retarded social interaction in the home. They also make a useful distinction between television and computer-mediated entertainment, noting that the information processing activities for the latter are quite different from those required for television viewing since the individual user must supply much of the meaningful context. This theme was reiterated in a communications study of the cognitive effects of computer use by SALOMON.

In the case of television viewing, Dorr and Kunkel describe the phenomenon called "grazing"—i.e., the use of remote controls to sample multiple programs and maintain a sense of plot for each. The authors provide a useful review of the research on children and media use in the home, stating that the relationships between the new computer-based media and family structure are consistent with those found for older television-based media. Parents' participation in media use is particularly influential, and it is essential to the use of computer-aided instruction in the home.

The Individual in the Community

Computers have become integral to the organization of community information in many U.S. and European cities. RUBINYI reports on a qualitative study of 72 small community-oriented nonprofit organizations and their adoption of computer technology. Assisted by Apple Computer Inc. and a community affairs council, participating organizations used e-mail, computer conferencing, and community bulletin boards to share and collectively build community resource materials. Most group members had little prior experience with computing, but within most of the successful groups there emerged some individual, an "early adopter," who had some experience and who could serve as a catalyst for others. Rubinyi found that in general three to five organizations would form a network on the basis of some shared interest. Similarly, in Britain, HARTLEY & WILLIAMS describe the use of computer database technologies to supply individuals with a range of welfare, legal rights, and community resources information. They describe a particularly innovative expert system called PLEXUS, developed at the University of London, to provide gardening advice to the public.

Computing technology applications for the elderly have been particularly well reported, offering information on health care, retirement, social interaction, and economic issues (OGOZALEK). SCHIFFMAN & SHERMAN use demographic surveys to present the "new-age" elderly, who are more willing to embrace innovation than their traditional counterparts. The new-age elder is less interested in possessions and yet possesses more discretionary income than traditional elders, choosing to spend more money on new and exciting experiences. CHATMAN provides an excellent ethnographic approach to studying the information channels of the elderly within a retirement community. She examined how 55 retirees used various media and found that they tend to view television for large periods of the day, often preferring a particular program over social interaction. Elders report that television is a way of staying in touch and involved in the social world.

The use of electronic media to provide health care for the elderly and others has been extensively reported. For an examination of "telemedicine" and other electronic delivery systems for the elderly see FURLONG and GREENBERGER & PUFFER. In addition, information technologies are used in noninvasive procedures to present medical data graphically.

Perhaps the most ambitious application is the Human Genome Project. As reported by FRENKEL, this effort aims to determine the location of the estimated 100,000 human genes that comprise the entire human genome and thus provide a complete analysis of the structure of DNA. The Human Genome Project will require the ability to store and retrieve huge quantities of interrelated biological data, an extremely complex task, especially since the entire scope of the analysis can only emerge as work progresses. Since genetic code is self-modifying, many of the elements are dynamic and require a database that can keep track of such changing relationships.

In summary, there has been a rapid proliferation of personal computers. *Statistical Abstract of the United States* reports that by 1988 more than 22 million personal computers were in use in American homes; the figure for 1983 was 7.6 million. Nevertheless, there is little consensus that information technology is creating systematic differences in the individual's daily life. The optimist finds that information technology helps in forming social relationships and assists isolated members of society, particularly the elderly, in becoming connected to daily events. The pessimist claims that information technology removes the individual from a personal knowledge of the environment. By experiencing different cultures and attitudes synthetically, the individual's sense of the world is extended but a sense of his or her place in that world may be lost. Information technology may create more isolation. Clearly it holds great promise in the home as a safety aid, and it has been useful in health care. It seems to be a growing component in the entertainment choices in the home but seems unlikely soon to alleviate the stresses and strains already present in the family. It can increase interactions within the home, but it can also introduce children to adult situations that blur the child's understanding of acceptable roles and behaviors.

INFLUENCES ON THE INDIVIDUAL'S WORK LIFE

The workplace is the arena in which information technology has been the most influential. DRUCKER provides an excellent overview of the world of work since World War II and documents the evolution of business from an industrial-based environment to a knowledge-based one. He demonstrates that the blue collar worker, who made spectacular advances in the first 75 years of this century, is now becoming the "social problem" of today's high-skill, high-tech work environment. For further evidence, one need only examine the business section in bookstores. Both management and workers need new skills to cope with this rapidly changing environment (CORNFIELD; KEEN; KERR; VINCENT).

The future labor force is now viewed with a much more geographically global perspective. JOHNSTON provides a demographically well-supported examination of the labor market as we move toward the year 2000. He describes massive relocation as skilled workers become the capital of the future. The greatest shift will be among the young, well educated who will flock to the cities of the developed world. He believes that this global movement of workers will create a gradual standardization of labor practices among industrialized countries; for example, he predicts that the standard European five-week vacation will be common in the United States by the end of the decade. Women will be an increasingly prized proportion of this global workforce, especially in the less-developed nations where their entrance into the workforce will change social and work conditions. Child care and in-home services will also have to increase to lure women into the world's workforce. Women currently hold more than one-third of the world's jobs. Educational levels are increasing worldwide, and by the year 2000 the developed countries will produce only 21% of the world's high school graduates.

WALLACE admits that "it is impossible to offer a simple account of technological change in the American work force of today" (p. 363). He provides an excellent overview of several currents of change that have been examined by those who study work and the changing workforce. His concerns are quite similar to those described by KRAEMER & DANZIGER and revolve around three major areas: (1) social interaction—the frequency and effectiveness of interpersonal communications among various elements of the work environment; (2) job enhancement—the skills required and the domains in which the worker can apply those skills; and (3) quality-of-work issues, which center on worker control and flexibility.

Social Interactions

One of the most studied impacts of information technology is how it affects the organization of work. If we examine the studies that focus on the individual worker, the amount of literature decreases. Technologies such as e-mail, fax, teleconferencing, and the recent group-decision support systems (GDSS) are often discussed for their influence on the speed or efficiency of work performance. The human impacts are more difficult to assess.

In his 1980 *ARIST* chapter, RICE offers an excellent tutorial for examining research on computer-mediated social interactions in organizational settings. A more recent article by RICE & AYDIN provides an excellent, critical introduction to the theoretical components of social information processing theory. Essentially, the theory postulates that individual perceptions of an information system are influenced by the opinions, information, and behavior of those who exert social influence on the individual worker. These authors propose operationalizations of the type of social influence by using the characteristic of proximity. The organization is viewed as a communications network and proximity is examined according to whether interactions are relational, positional, or spatial.

Relational proximity is determined when people choose those co-workers with whom they relate or communicate most often. Positional proximity is determined by equating positions within the structural hierarchy of the organization. Spatial proximity arises from the physical structures in the work environment that position individuals together. These proximity types were explored in the context of explaining attitudes toward a new hospital information system. This work follows an earlier study by AYDIN that examined the changes in interpersonal communications patterns in two hospitals using a computerized medical information system. She found that the system increased rather than decreased face-to-face communications between departments because of an increased interdependence of tasks.

In another effort to examine social influence, SCHMITZ & FULK studied a network composed of an individual, his or her supervisor, and five close communication partners. The setting was a large R&D organization where 636 employees had e-mail access through a personal PROFS terminal in their work area. PROFS is a mainframe-based product and provides a menu-driven e-mail system, a document-sharing and archiving facility, "read only" bulletin board information, and an e-mail directory. The authors used survey techniques and in-depth interviews to explore how individuals develop perceptions of the richness of various message media (e.g., numeric text, hand-written text, e-mail, telephone, and face-to-face) that are useful for reducing information ambiguity. Supervisors who were proactive in encouraging e-mail use had a strong influence on their groups' adoption of e-mail, but co-worker use was the most consistent and strongest predictor of an individual's use and assessment of e-mail. Although the authors cautioned about the generalizability of their sample, they make an effective case for considering social influence as an aid to understanding how individuals perceive and use information technology.

The influences on an individual's psychological behavior by computer-mediated social interaction concern several researchers. MATHESON & ZANNA hypothesize that workers who use computer-mediated communication differ in their level of private and public self-awareness from those who use face-to-face communication since computers facilitate the loss of a user's public self through which the overt aspects of communication are made sensitive to evaluation by others. Despite some methodological and measurement problems, they assert that the differences they found between face-to-face and computer-mediated communication are a strong indication that the latter intensifies private self-awareness. Their findings support some of the ethnographic reports of TURKLE—viz., the individual's increased rather than reduced private self-awareness.

In an ambitious and well-executed field study of a Fortune 500 company, SPROULL & KIESLER (1986) tested 13 hypotheses using an e-mail environment in two divisions of the company—an R&D division and an administrative division. During an eight-week period, they examined actual message attributes such as length, opening, closing, politeness, and topic. Participants also assessed their perceived sense of these attributes. Subjects were asked to indicate which medium (face-to-face, e-mail, telephone, or hard-copy mail) they would use to present messages to subordinates and to superiors. They found few gender or hierarchical differences for items such as number of messages sent and received but considerable differences between the administrative and research divisions in their use and volume of messages. Social and organizational context clues were both reduced when e-mail was used. In addition, e-mail messages showed that the users were relatively self-absorbed; they focused more on themselves (high use of the pronouns "I" and "my") than on others or on work; people also behaved rudely more often on e-mail than they did in face-to-face conversations. Employees preferred sending e-mail messages more often to superiors than to subordinates. Finally, approximately 62% of the e-mail messages received contained information that respondents believed they could not have gotten any other way. SPROULL & KIESLER (1991) provide an excellent overview of their research findings together with their view of how networking affects organizational structure.

Group Work Influences

The current work environment in corporations has focused heavily on "managed interdependence." ZUBOFF and ROCKART & SHORT argue that in the new information-based organization considerable interdependence is needed to maintain competitive advantage. Computer-mediated techniques have been the approach chosen to create and monitor such interdependence, and, as FINHOLT & SPROULL maintain, it is groups, not individuals, that form the fundamental unit of work in modern organizations. An explicit focus on computer-mediated effects on groups by organizational researchers has been much less common than predictions and research about how computing will affect work and work life for the individual. Electronic work groups are a relatively new phenomenon, one that managers do not necessarily understand. Finholt and Sproull propose a framework for analyzing groups formed by e-mail distribution lists. These lists are proposed as a reflection of various electronic groups operating within the corporation and as a mechanism to augment or change patterns of coordination and performance in small face-to-face work groups. In a small study of a Fortune 500 company, the extensive scope and diversity of the distribution lists were surprising to the researchers (less so, perhaps, to those of us who have dipped into the world of computer-based discussion groups available nationally through Internet). The liveliness of participants, the diversity of interests, and the fact that at least some of these communication groups behave like real social groups—despite the fact that they share no physical space, their members are invisible, and their interaction is asynchronous—can all be heavily influenced by management policies of the organization. The authors argue convincingly that these electronic groups provide "windows on the organization" and show the importance of play at work, play that perhaps was always present in social activity and is now visible through electronic communication.

The group-decision support system (GDSS), a new technology, has emerged to improve organizational decision making and ensure that organization members will feel that they are part of decision-making efforts and therefore will support resulting changes. Essentially, a GDSS functions as a real-time, electronic brainstorming session among members of a decision-making work group. It uses the computer to conceal the contributors' identities so that ideas can be suggested and selected according to merit rather than the contributor's organizational role. A comprehensive review of progress in creating and evaluating GDSS is provided by KRAEMER & KING. Created to redress some of the shortcomings of computer conferencing, teleconferencing, and e-mail, GDSS units are growing in use but at a rate far below what could be expected, given their need and promise. The primary benefits believed to be derived from GDSS are an improved sense of group cohesion and an increase in the individual's interest in group activities. Such systems are believed to transfer some of the protocol of decision making to the system and appear to reduce the amount of intragroup tension in difficult decision-making situations.

Job-Enhancement Impacts

De-skilling is the chief concern among those who study how information technology affects job enhancement. As WALLACE recounts it, the debate has two sides. First, for those who believe that changes in job skills have generally enhanced jobs, the skills needed to use technology are an improvement since the worker must use more judgment and discretion and have a broader understanding of the total process. For those who believe that technology has de-skilled the worker and downgraded jobs, the effect has been to make work more routine, requiring closer supervision. A third camp sees both an upgrading and a downgrading, with no net change in the skill distribution of the workforce in the long run.

This scenario is supported by an extensive survey sponsored by the Organization for Economic Cooperation and Development (OECD) in 1986. The results of various OECD-sponsored studies (BRAINARD & FULLGATE) indicate that technology has had the greatest impact on the occupational structure of the workforce and its required skills. These studies reinforce a shift to white-collar occupations and to a growth in professional and technical employment (DRUCKER). The impacts on job skills are felt mainly in particular regions, firms, and occupations and not uniformly within the workforce of the OECD nations (Europe, the United States, Turkey, and Japan). The highest net decline in jobs occurred in manufacturing, where there is integrated central control of groups of machines or processes. The summary by BRAINARD & FULLGATE provides an excellent overview of the impacts of technology on the major economic industrial and service sectors. These authors separate, for example, the service industries into social services including government, education, and health, on the one hand, and personal and distributional service sectors, on the other. Information technology has served to shift job skills "toward diagnosis, problem solving, and interface between systems" (p. 40).

ATTEWELL provides a well-grounded study of de-skilling using U.S. Bureau of Labor Statistics data. He also uses several insurance industry case studies to examine the controversy more closely than statistics would allow. His data do not support the de-skilling hypothesis and show instead an upgrading of the insurance workforce from 1960 to 1980.

In support of the de-skilling position, another study of the insurance industry by KRAUT ET AL. found strong evidence that automation of the record system made jobs less complex and less interesting. In addition, the skills gained by service representatives who went on to become service managers became less relevant. MILLMAN & HARTWICK examined the impact of an automated office system on middle managers in Montreal. While the sample is poorly defined, the mailed survey drew responses from 75 of the 151 middle managers contacted from 14 different organizations. Respondents were asked to state whether automation had increased, decreased, or not affected 15 aspects of work. The aspects were derived from previous work and covered added elements about work interest, freedom, and responsibility. The middle managers felt that automation had led to changes that, without exception, demanded more skills and accuracy but also increased work enrichment and satisfaction.

Cheney and colleagues and Davenport and Cronin make valuable contributions to the understanding of skills for information management professionals. CHENEY ET AL. provide empirical evidence of the skill changes needed for future employment in information systems management, predicting a clearer division in the work of information systems professionals created by both innovation and complex and ill-structured problem environments. DAVENPORT & CRONIN argue for the designation of "virtual apprentice" for a newcomer to a complex work environment. They see hypertext as an ideal technology to allow the virtual apprentice to explore the organizational labyrinth and acquire the social understandings needed to be successful. These understandings have traditionally come from a human mentor, but Davenport and Cronin argue that in today's complex organizations such understandings are beyond the scope of a single individual mentor. Using the widest range of information from political histories to organizational and personal gossip, apprentices can "make their own sense of what they do in the organization, and should be encouraged, within reason, to write their own script, trying out moves with other colleagues. A hypertext which offers simple and unified access to as wide a range of information as is feasible (total intelligence) can support such play" (p. 68).

Another aspect of job enhancement is occupational structure, the study of which examines the links among various work divisions or occupational groups. The notion of occupation and the ability to define an occupational group are becoming complex. ABBOTT effectively outlines changes that influence occupational study and provides a brief but substantive introduction to the definitional and theoretical concerns. He points out, for example, that the boundaries among professions are becoming blurred. A dying cancer patient may ask the same question of both his physician and his cleric. Each professional may see the question differently, according to what is deemed a unique professional view, however the patient may find the different views confusing and his question poorly answered. Abbott sees a good deal of restructuring of the divisions of labor among those professions dealing with large-scale problems like design and information.

To argue their respective theoretical scenarios for the shift of power in today's work world, TOFFLER and ZUBOFF both provide popularized accounts, enlivened with examples from industry, of the changing structure of competitive organizations. The political and economic consequences of the changes in occupational structures are not yet well understood. Most analysts—e.g., TOFFLER, DRUCKER, and especially ZUBOFF—generally agree that the organizational structure is flatter and more democratic, but EVANS argues from a Marxist perspective against Zuboff's democratizing view. Zuboff's position is that the ability to access a company's database by multiple levels of the organization will flatten the stratification between upper management and worker, thus empowering the worker and making him or her feel equal to management. Evans argues from the Marxist camp that the alienation once felt by the worker toward management will now be directed toward the activity of his or her own labor. Alienation is an issue of power that resides not simply in a worker's occupational role but also in social relations between work roles. The need for an equal voice in decision making within the workplace is essential in changing the more alienating, traditional workplace relationships.

Quality of Work Life

Embedded in the issue of social influence is the concern about control; both the workers' sense of being controlled by technology and their sense of mastery afforded by technology. While few studies cited by KRAEMER & DANZIGER found managers or professionals who were concerned about being controlled by technology, there is a growing concern about control among clerical/administrative workers. In a strongly pessimistic, somewhat less-than-scholarly view of control of clerical and administrative workers, GARSON characterizes large organizational settings as exerting conditions of control similar to early industrial sweatshops. For example, quotas for a day's production for airline reservationists can be set quite high and monitored easily using transaction logs. Her ethnographic approach and her fictional writing style create a strong sense of workers' real, visceral objections to the structure placed on work environments using computer-mediated technologies. She believes that the "underlying premise of modern automation is a profound distrust of thinking human beings" (p. 261). ABBOTT also believes that the use of computerized control and surveillance will increase in the workplace, but he believes that the decentralization or flattening of the organizational hierarchy may help to offset the alienation felt by such surveillance.

A more scholarly examination by KRAUT ET AL. studied supervisors and customer service representatives in a large public utility. Since managers were promoted solely from the ranks of customer service representatives, and thus knew the job of their subordinates, they had a strong sense of control or mastery. However, the introduction of a new computerized system rendered their previous knowledge obsolete. Customer representatives experienced increased control over their jobs while supervisors experienced some loss of control over the interaction between themselves and the customer representatives.

Throughout the 1970s and 1980s many case studies showed that information technology can improve productivity, but it can also degrade the user's quality of work life. The tension between an industry's need to be competitive and the worker's need to be committed to and enjoy work spawned efforts to humanize the workplace. Quality of work life (QWL) is the term under which much of this research has been done. An excellent critique of QWL research is provided by ALIC, who believes that few of the efforts to improve QWL have been carefully evaluated and the results publicized. Nevertheless, he acknowledges that QWL has affected corporate culture because it aims to give workers a greater say in work organization decisions and therefore serves to alter traditional hierarchies in which decisions are made at the top.

Job Satisfaction and Fear of Technological Change

Although the introduction of computing technologies has improved productivity, it has also caused loss of job satisfaction. Computers have made work cleaner and less physically demanding, but they can also intensify the pace of work, render the human contribution more mechanical, and provide supervisors with feedback that deprives the worker of a sense of autonomy (e.g., GARSON; SHAIKEN, 1989; ZUBOFF).

CUNNINGHAM ET AL. surveyed 298 telecommunications workers to identify their common concerns about the changing technologies in their workplace. The workers were too young to retire and were experiencing very low morale. A capable literature review used to guide this survey showed that two common fears have emerged in similar studies:

(1) the fear of loss of interest in the job due to the way work is organized, and (2) the fear of job loss and the inability of the labor unions to oppose such threatened losses. In their sample, Cunningham and co-workers found that of 11 identifiable fears about technology, the overwhelming fear was that the job would change drastically. This fear accounted for 33% of the responses given. Only a few (8%) believed that their jobs would actually be lost due to technological changes. The authors conclude that the fears about job future, industry future, and societal future consume much employee energy and conversation.

Others have explored the different expectations between the new information worker and his older counterpart. In a complex study, MANZ & GROTHE surveyed 4,000 employees of a large, American-based computer manufacturer, concentrating on those who will be in their late thirties to fifties by the year 2000. This group was compared with three other age ranges to assess the differences in job satisfaction and many other QWL issues. The younger workers scored consistently and significantly lower than their counterparts in 73% of the 31 QWL issues assessed. For example, the younger workers were significantly less personally motivated, felt less personal investment in the jobs they held, and found work much less meaningful than their older counterparts. While the study concentrated only on a single organization, the authors summarized the younger workers as prone to being more restless and more dissatisfied with job choices. The authors believe that their study strongly supports the case that the workforce is experiencing changing attitudes and expectations. Without making specific recommendations, the authors urge the movement toward a reorganization of work that will allow these younger workers to satisfy their need to have their individuality recognized.

Insurance service representatives liked their jobs significantly less after a computerized information system was introduced. In the study by KRAUT ET AL., contact with colleagues became less frequent, and even though their overall work loads decreased, these workers experienced less interest and enjoyment on the job. KRAEMER & DANZIGER, who provide an excellent overview of studies in this area, state that overall the impacts of computing on how workers feel about their quality of work life depend on how the technology affects the workplace and how much input the workers have in the process. There is as yet no indication that impacts exist that extend across task or technological domains.

Geographical Dispersion of Workers

The notion of working at home via computing technology has been discussed for several years. FORESTER believes that various psychological factors render an "electronic cottage" industry unlikely. He cites studies that show that at-home workers lack motivation and discipline and experience loneliness and time-management problems. On the other hand, in a study with a disappointingly small sample ($n = 17$), OLSON found that the productivity of home-based workers was about the same as office-based workers but that the managers were uncomfortable in dealing with remote workers because the managers had to be better organized, do more planning, and spend more time in formal communication than with on-site workers. Olson followed her field study with a large ($n = 1,615$) survey of professionals who use computers in their work. The sample was obtained using the subscriber lists of two major computer journals. Of the respondents a group was identified that said they did some work at home; of this group only 10% reported that the work they did at home was the "only paid work" (group A). Another group worked "at home after work hours" (group B), and a third group "did no work at home" (group C). The results of an attitudinal survey of the three groups showed that group A had a lower need for social interaction and dominance and a higher need for autonomy than did groups B and C; no differences were found among the groups in need for achievement, but group A had lower job satisfaction and a lower commitment to the organization. Olson believes that certain attitudes predispose workers to prefer telecommuting over physical commuting. She does not believe, however, that telecommuting will become common for most bureaucratic organizations. Acceptance of telecommuting comes largely from the corporate culture, specifically the willingness of management.

BUSH looks specifically at telecommuting work done in software development. He developed seven case histories over 15 years and found that the reasons for telecommuting work could be categorized as task-based, structural, and social. The primary task-based reason for telecommuting is efficiency. Work can be done more quickly because interruption and socializing are reduced. The single biggest disadvantage is the loss of help that is available in an office from co-workers. The structural effect is the reduced need for office space with its overhead costs. An organization can access expertise more effectively through telecommuting. The advantage of good, well-planned worker–manager communications becomes a serious disadvantage if the relationship between them is vague or intermittent. Finally, the social effects are increased worker motivation, job satisfaction, and job enrichment. Telecommuting demonstrates trust and gives the worker more autonomy and family time.

Bush's case studies seem to reinforce earlier work showing that effective telecommuters are independent, persistent, and well organized, with little fear of failure. The worst candidates for telecommuting are socially active, gregarious, and dependent and see their jobs as simply a part of office society. Bush argues that the high-tech company of the future will need the remote expertise that telecommuting provides on an as-needed basis. In general, however, face-to-face contact will continue to be essential for ill-defined tasks. Telecommuting is likely to be most successful in large, thriving entrepreneurial organizations where corporate culture is clearly conveyed, where failure is tolerated, and where shared experience can be relied on more heavily than rules for the coordination of work.

KRAUT provides detailed data on telecommuting among bookkeepers, accountants, sales supervisors, secretaries, mathematicians, engineers, management analysts, advertisers, lawyers, and physicians. He presents a far darker picture of the potential impacts of telecommuting. For him the growth of telecommuting is a potential source of worker exploitation, but one that is very difficult to determine empirically. Several other efforts are worthy of note but are not described in much detail because they deal with special populations.

SNIZEK examines the effects of microcomputers on the productivity of university scientists. He considers how access to networks such as BITNET and Internet affects scientists' use of data, their colleagues, and their ability to extend their work day to include work from home.

A fascinating discussion of the potential effects of international telecommuting is presented by BLAKE & SURPRENANT. "Electronic immigrants" would live in one nation and use computer-based telecommunications technology to transport their skills and knowledge to another nation. Of particular interest is the discussion of the threats to national sovereignty that such telecommuting in lesser-developed nations might create. The authors describe the overlapping spheres of influence that already exist between multinational corporations and national governments in the countries where such corporations operate. This relationship is further strained if the international telecommuter develops a strong, dependent tie with other employer nation(s). The strength of such ties can enhance power relationships with the worker's own national government (employer). The result, the authors say, may be the creation of "telecolonies" whose finances and political power are heavily controlled from outside their national borders. A "telecolony" would give a less-developed nation a continuous flow of money and sustained expertise that would have been lost through emigration. An example from our own field is found in the recent interview with the president of Information Access Co., Morris Goldstein. He suggests that just such a possibility exists for obtaining indexing and abstracting skills abroad. IAC already uses some indexers who work at home, and the interview suggests that through satellite transmission of data there is no reason why such an arrangement could not be extended to workers outside the United States (PEMBERTON).

Clearly information technology has and continues to exert a strong influence on the individual and his work. It may well be central to our future understanding of the structure and function of work organization for human productivity, but for the individual it holds the power to enhance a job or render human labor unnecessary. There seems to be evidence that while computers provide a degree of "democracy" in the workplace by allowing more levels of the organization to have access to information for decision making, there is also a tendency for the technology to restrict human freedom in some industries through the monitoring of transaction data. Clearly in those work environments where participation is facilitated by information technology, there is a need for more committed and competent employees and managers to meet the requirement for such individuals with new kinds of worker incentives.

CITIZENSHIP

The least empirical evidence for information technology's impact on the individual is in the area of citizenship, yet it is an area that is extremely important to policy analysts, many of whom are information scientists. Contemporary politics and the role of the individual in governance can be viewed, perhaps somewhat simplistically, as a sharing of power. The individual as a voting citizen selects others who will carry out activities and services for his and "the public good." Information and the technology that brings it to our attention have provided enough evidence of society to provide many competing views of "the public good." For example, there is sufficient knowledge about farming to create very different perceptions about the needs of the dairy farmer vs. the needs of the tobacco or produce farmer. So when the good of the farmer is at issue, the "good" for one type of farmer may not be the "good" for all farmers. The result, well discussed by DRUCKER, is our issue-based political environment.

It seems prudent to recognize the importance of the many organizations for policy analysis that have developed in response to the government's increasing need to understand society and be informed. WEISS has collected in a single source descriptions of 15 policy advisory organizations, ranging from national "think tanks" like the RAND Corp. to smaller organizations for state government legislative advice. She reminds us that such organizations depend heavily on techniques of empirical data gathering and analysis.

The House Committee on Energy and Commerce, for example, requested the Office of Technology Assessment (OTA) (U.S. CONGRESS. OFFICE OF TECHNOLOGY ASSESSMENT) to evaluate the impacts of new communication technologies. The result is a good overview of the concerns that government must address. However, for this chapter, such policy advisory publications have not been sought because they often lack specific detail concerning the data analysis used to arrive at the overview.

CLEVELAND, in his 1985 essay, argued insightfully that the informatization of society was essentially changing the established hierarchies, hierarchies that were based on traditions of control and secrecy, ownership and location. The arrangement of the final section of this *ARIST* chapter is based on Cleveland's ideas. First to be examined is the issue of privacy as stemming from the changing relationship between information control and secrecy. The second section looks at the fading importance of location or geography in the individual's ability to realize political power. Finally, a general discussion of the emerging idea of "teledemocracy" is provided to explore the notion that information technologies can provide a new degree of political responsiveness.

Control over Information

Information technology has had a profound impact on individual privacy. Two giants, the commercial credit industry and the federal government, are the principal holders of massive data about the individual. Each use of a credit card or application for credit permits the gathering of widely separated electronic transactions of private activities, such as shopping or travel, which can be easily brought together to form a personal information profile of an individual's spending history. Likewise, the government, through a series of required records (birth, work, marriage, taxes), has created extensive data banks on the American population. Additionally, PRITCHARD states that the National Security Agency (NSA) maintains the ability to monitor every single communication in the nation, whether by phone, modem, or telegram. She also points out that the government has begun to compare its own information with that of commercial sources. For example, actual spending can be checked against income tax files to identify candidates for tax evasion. So far, these data banks have been used in the interests of the American public: identifying welfare fraud, locating students who have defaulted on student loans, and the like. (For an excellent treatment of the issues of privacy protection along with a comparative view of the legislative efforts made to ensure data protection in the United States, Germany, Sweden, and France, see the book by FLAHERTY.)

A 1991 survey by Louis Harris and Associates for Equifax, a large credit-reporting bureau, found that Americans have mixed feelings about threats to privacy. Seventy-nine percent are concerned; 71% believe that consumers have lost control over personal information, but only 30% have decided not to apply for a job, credit, or insurance to avoid disclosing information. When asked about more specific aspects of privacy, the respondents show that other priorities come first. For example, 96% believe that credit checks for loan applicants are appropriate; 83% support preemployment drug testing; 78% say they would be upset if they could not get credit based on credit reports; and 44% say they would be upset if they could not use credit cards to purchase goods and services (WALLICH). Some evidence exists that the individual who uses credit cards understands that some loss of privacy is the price paid for the convenience of the card (LAVER).

The potential for intrusion through the possible misuse of this personal information has seldom formed the basis for legal action. Most right-of-privacy cases in state courts are concerned with abortion rights, freedom of speech and press, and drug testing (PRESSMAN). It is far from clear just how great the individual's concern is for this potentially intrusive aspect of computing technology. Much of the public concern that is expressed centers on corporate misuse of technology. Indeed, the marketing industry seems to be well aware of the potential for such personal information profiles to serve as a "dialog" between the customer and the marketer, as opposed to the "monolog" that television advertising permits. Marketers see such efforts as a tailoring of market offerings to suit the tastes of the individual, saving time and effort for the consuming public (BLATTBERG & DEIGHTON).

GANDY provides a thoughtful discussion of the current trends toward more surveillance. He marshals some OTA studies that point to the workplace as the arena most monitored. He cites recent Roper polls that found that 28% of those polled said that "polls and research surveys are an invasion of privacy," but in a 1986 study 40% agreed that "the research industry serves a useful purpose." GANDY believes, as does PRITCHARD, that it is possible to establish standards about information we do not want passed on without our permission. However, both admit that the United States has been slower than Europe to develop laws to control the abuse of data on the individual.

DUNCAN & PEARSON offer a good overview of what the near future holds for resolving the privacy issue in four areas: statistical, computer, legal, and administrative. They describe masking techniques that can limit disclosure of parts of an individual's record. In addition, electronic gatekeepers and monitors will detect remote access and keep masking techniques secure.

There has been recent evidence of attempts to remove or circumvent control over information. According to CLEVELAND, one characteristic that makes information an amazingly versatile resource is its diffusiveness; it tends to leak, and the more it leaks, the more information there is. KING describes the collaboration between Equifax and Lotus Technology to produce a CD-ROM product that holds detailed economic and demographic information from Equifax's extensive data banks of credit information. This MarketPlace software could allow users to create a tailored list of potential clients using certain social and economic criteria. MarketPlace uses Equifax data on households combined with census and postal information so that it is possible, for example, to identify a list of teenage boys in New England whose parents are college graduates and have a combined income of more than $100,000 (KING, p. 103). Almost as soon as Lotus announced its intention to produce MarketPlace, the criticism started. Through the encouragement of PACS-L (Public Access Computer Services Listserv) participants and others within the academic and library communities, thousands of people objected by telephone, fax, and e-mail to Lotus chairman, Jim Manzi. Lotus countered that it had built in privacy safeguards; an individual could not be directly accessed by name since information could only be gathered on an individual who fell into a specific target group; but privacy advocates were not dissuaded. On January 23, 1991, Lotus announced cancellation of its MarketPlace CD-ROM products.

During August 1991, the attempted coup in the Soviet Union was heavily reported through international e-mail networks. These networks redistributed many political messages sent from Moscow (GOODMAN). Communication satellites, telephones, and fax machines were also used during the Tiananmen Square crisis in China during the summer of 1989. Messages via these technologies were again used by private citizens to keep the world informed (J. F. COATES). In addition, remote-sensing technology can detect human rights infringements from secret prisons to weapons deployment to environmental pollution hazards.

Corporations can also be scrutinized by the public. PRITCHARD provides a detailed demonstration of the avenues available to examine corporate public records. PAUL describes various state and local government records on individuals that are available commercially.

The Fading Importance of Geography

For centuries societies have formed into effective groups largely by virtue of physical proximity. Large urban areas evolved as effective organizing units for the governance and production required by our present social structure. However, the combination of telecommunications and computer technology has made the physical proximity of worker and work much less important. Further, with the shift from a society based largely on industrial capital to one based on knowledge, the physical proximity of raw material to work site is no longer a reason for urban areas to function as they have. CLEVELAND identifies many of the properties of information that make it a vastly different resource from those of the industrial age. Two important characteristics of information are its ability to be widely shared and its easy transportability. Thus, the physical location of an information worker is largely a matter of choice. The evidence for and against the value of telecommuting has already been discussed, but the evidence of a real movement of citizens away from urban centers is more difficult to identify. There is evidence that city governments recognize that the city's role is changing and that a telecommunications network structure must take the place of older pathways to serve the needs of urban citizens (CASTELLS; GRAHAM & DOMINY; NEWSTEAD).

Two recent studies attempt to bring some demographic data to bear on the question of a shift away from metropolitan areas. Using the March annual demographic file of the Current Population Survey for 1980 and 1987, COOK & BECK examine the occupational distribution of the civilian labor force to see if managerial–professional occupations are moving to less-populated metropolitan areas. Because some occupations were reclassified by the U.S. government in 1983, there are problems in analyzing the data. Nevertheless, during the 1980s, Cook and Beck generally found more, not fewer, managerial and professional workers in large metropolitan areas. DILLMAN & BECK had previously found evidence of a movement into rural areas in the 1970s, but the follow-up efforts by Cook and Beck do not support the continuation of the trend. They believe that this activity in the 1970s may have been a movement of lower-skilled and clerical jobs away from the cities.

Dillman and Beck present a demographic analysis that emphasizes the absence of a rural information infrastructure, seen by the authors as a barrier to rural development. They argue that today's younger worker, not likely to have had any experience with rural life, may not be comfortable in rural environments. They also present an insightful argument for the limitations of agricultural development when it is seen as a mass production industry rather than one that can be more heterogeneously responsive to the consumer.

Teledemocracy

Could the new information technologies, particularly satellite-based telecommunications technology, enable a geographically dispersed citizenry to function like a small town meeting? Instead of employing expensive policy analysis organizations to survey a sample of the citizens affected by a policy under discussion, couldn't government request a poll of those citizens through some electronic means, such as toll-free 800 phone numbers? These questions represent the notions of teledemocracy.

CLEVELAND points out that with an information-rich polity, the definition of control changes: "Decision making proceeds not by the flow of recommendations up and orders down, but by development of a shared sense of direction among those who must form the parade if there is going to be a parade" (p. 62). As mentioned previously, the enormity of information available to all citizens creates many special public groups within the society. The government's need to respond to each of these groups creates a new crisis of complexity. A strong possibility exists, argues Cleveland and most recently BANKES & BUILDER, that the informatization of society may destabilize American society. Information technology allows citizens to see and hear how a government responds to their needs and provides a channel for feedback. The possibility of bias is extremely high, and the ability of communications technologies in particular to affect the perceptions of citizens is clearly seen by many as a danger.

More recently there has been a fascinating effort to examine the more decentralizing media like videotext, cable, and satellite-based transmission. These new media are portrayed by ABRAMSON ET AL. as "democratizing" because they decentralize decisions about media content. They provide the viewer with more choice and expand the range of producers to include citizens with a gripe, candidates with a plea for votes, public officials with a message for constituents, and interest-group leaders as well as entertainment options. Thus, the new media create a less mediated environment from which the citizen can choose desired messages.

Advocates for teledemocracy are usually more interested in politics than ordinary citizens are, but teledemocracy's appeal is effectively described in Abramson's book. Officials cannot claim ignorance about what constituents want as individuals use the technology so cheaply available to gain a greater voice in government. Greater participation by citizens could improve the efficiency with which government responds to societal needs. Such ideas have been explored by ARTERTON, who has conducted research on various citizen-participation projects. He describes, for example, an Alaskan teleconferencing network that allows legislative committees to take testimony from citizens throughout the state. Electronic mail, available with the system, can be used to send messages to legislators in Juneau. In Pennsylvania, city and county officials use cable television to provide "electronic office hours." Arterton finds that information technologies can effectively mitigate the inequalities of participation among different societal groups. However, he adds that his research does not support an inevitable shift toward greater direct participation in governance by citizens.

The notion of the democratizing use of information technology is not new; it has been one of the central themes in library and information science since the 1960s. CASE provides an excellent review of current experiences of standardizing and marketing videotext applications, such as the British Prestel system and the French Minitel system. PFAFFENBERGER, in his recent book, recounts the development of the present online bibliographic technology as a response to early information and library science visions of reducing the information inequalities of society through improved public access. He develops an exploration of online searching as a technological system, one that has a social context as part of its development. He examines the physical expressions (organizations) of this social context as well as the knowledge and legislative artifacts (regulatory laws) that have evolved as the online industry became the complex web of participants it is today. His point, effectively made, is that because the goal of democratizing access was constructed within the library and information science communities, bibliographic retrieval systems provide not a well-ordered set of ranked information but an unjudged, non-ranked set of "all there is." This, he points out, is unlikely to appeal to the information poor.

DOCTOR has developed a plan that would address the societal gap between information rich and information poor. In addition to exploring the reasons behind the gap and demonstrating them with recent socioeconomic research, he creates an intriguing institutional framework for developing an earlier idea of public information utilities. He argues for the development of national and regional institutes for information democracy that could target local needs and still be sensitive to the larger national agenda. These institutes would ensure that the information technologies exert a democratizing influence.

A number of interesting studies have focused on the use of information technology in governing. Since this process affects those who are governed, the impact on the individual makes the topic relevant. BIMBER reviews the empirical studies of congressional information use. Many such efforts have focused on the information-dissemination activities before and during election campaigns, but several of the studies address the norms of information specialization that underlie the committee system. Political scientists have often been divided over the importance of information and expertise in congressional decision making, some describing how ill informed certain decisions are and others showing the efforts made to establish assessment and collection policies that bring more and better information to the legislator's desk.

MOONEY presents a sound investigation of the written information used by a sample of members in the legislatures of Massachusetts, Oregon, and Indiana. Using an interview setting, Mooney asked legislators to sort documents from their files pertaining to 12 human services bills that came before their houses. The sorting categories were established according to the number of subprocesses involved in law making, to which each document had made a contribution toward informing the legislator. The median number of documents was nine. The use of information was greatest when a bill was being written and least when a roll-call vote was impending for which the determination was simple and the time short. In studies like Mooney's and a similar one by LEVIN to look at local government officials, the recommendation is often that information technology could add greatly to the efficiency with which government officials find and organize information about impending decisions. (See also CAUDLE & MARCHAND, HJORTDAL, and KRUEGER ET AL.)

ABRAMSON ET AL. note that there is a growing body of evidence that the U.S. Congress relies heavily on C-SPAN, a public access cable channel, to inform members about current issues of interest. He also describes the Member Information Network (MIN), a computer-based full-text information system that was developed to provide status reports on pending legislation, brief descriptions of bills' contents and intent of floor amendments, roll-call vote results, summaries of debates, and so forth (p. 151).

Finally, in the general area of political reform through the application of technology, two recent books are of interest. A fascinating collection of essays ("thought experiments," as the authors call them), edited by BECKER, provides effective visions of politics as possibly redefined through the laws of quantum physics. While none of the essayists is a physicist, the contributors believe that the paradigm shift of societal change is exposing the inadequacies of representative government derived from the finite world of Newtonian physics and that there is a need to reexamine the process of government according to the major scientific paradigm shift of the 20th century—namely, quantum theory. They seek to demonstrate that true democracies are self-organizing systems and that Marxism is an ambitious notion of the Newtonian age.

The second book, by EZRAHI, although extremely dense in style, is a full analysis of the interaction between the transformation of democracy through science. Inspired by Bertrand Russell, the author attempts to examine the changes in the knowledge content of human existence throughout the 20th century and assess the likelihood that science can succeed, where government has not, in freeing the individual from chance, prejudice, and arbitrariness. Ezrahi builds his case by examining the cultural foundation of the political uses of technology and argues that the preeminence of science is now appropriately declining while greater, more responsive systems of democratic action emerge.

CONCLUSION

Of all of the research done to examine the new information technologies, the impact on the individual is one area least addressed. A partial explanation for this is that the impacts can only be felt over time, and since many of the technologies discussed here are still relatively novel to most people, the importance of their impact is still some time away. Also the spread of the technologies is largely in accordance with business and industrial needs and is seldom addressed in terms of their impact on the general public. However, J. F. COATES asserts that "technology causes trouble. As a major agent of change it intrinsically, not accidentally, dislocates and distresses established relationships and forces economic, political or social change" (p. 389). To a large extent, because the United States leads in the application of information technologies, it will be the first to realize such change. Thus, it will become more and more important for researchers to examine the impacts of information technology on all aspects of an individual's life.

The chapter represents a look at the individual's relationship with the new information technologies from the living room to the work site to the voting booth. There is evidence that computer technology helps in the management and maintenance of the household, but it does less to change the quality of home life for most Americans than do the more traditional broadcast media such as television and radio. The use of the new technologies to establish interpersonal relationships also points to the problems of loneliness and social integration being felt by a more mobile society. More significant empirical evidence is found in the work environment, where the impact has been felt in how work is organized. There is evidence that information technology can both enhance and detract from job satisfaction, social interaction among workers, and quality of work life. In the activities of citizenship and the information gathering that prevails in political decision making, there is much speculation about the possibility for "teledemocracy," but there is very little evidence that would point to its success except in remote locations like Alaska.

Information science and its related technologies, in their role to improve the individual's access to information, seem to be major potential contributors to the comfort with which the individual functions in a more complex, information-rich life. As such, they have a responsibility to continue to monitor the impact of information and the technologies available to access it. It is not our responsibility alone, but one that is shared with other social science research disciplines. A large proportion of the research efforts described in this chapter were qualitative in nature. Such efforts, when well executed, hold the potential for more clearly discerning patterns of information technology use. However, the area to be covered is vast, and researchers are faced with a host of questions that will require both quantitative and qualitative work. Finally, it is critical to broaden the interdisciplinary discussions that must occur to provide information science with the appropriate tools and insights for the work ahead.

BIBLIOGRAPHY

ABBOTT, ANDREW. 1989. The New Occupational Structure: What Are the Questions? Work and Occupations. 1989 August; 16(3): 273-291. ISSN: 0730-8884.

ABRAMSON, JEFFREY B.; ARTERTON, F. CHRISTOPHER; ORREN, GARY R. 1988. The Electronic Commonwealth: The Impact of New Media Technologies on Democratic Politics. New York, NY: Basic Books, Inc.; c1988. 331p. ISBN: 0-465-01878-5; LC: 87-47783.

ADELMAN, MARA B.; AHUVIA, AARON C. 1991. Mediated Channels for Mate Seeking: A Solution to Involuntary Singlehood? Critical Studies in Mass Communication. 1991; 8: 273-289. ISSN: 0739-3180.

ALIC, JOHN A. 1990. Who Designs Work?: Organizing Production in an Age of High Technology. Technology in Society. 1990; 12: 310-317. ISSN: 0160-791X.

APPELBAUM, EILEEN; SCHETTKAT, RONALD, eds. 1990. Labor Market Adjustments to Structural Change and Technological Progress. New York, NY: Praeger Publishers; 1990. 247p. ISBN: 0-275-93376-8.

ARTERTON, F. CHRISTOPHER. 1989. Teledemocracy Reconsidered. See reference: FORESTER, TOM, ed. 438-450.

ATTEWELL, PAUL. 1987. The Deskilling Controversy. Work and Occupations. 1987 August; 14(3): 323-346. ISSN: 0730-8884.

AYDIN, CAROLYN E. 1989. Occupational Adaptation to Computerized Medical Information Systems. Journal of Health and Social Behavior. 1989 June; 30(2): 163-179. ISSN: 0022-1465.

BANKES, STEVE; BUILDER, CARL. 1992. Seizing the Moment: Harnessing the Information Technologies. The Information Society. 1992 January-March; 8(1): 1-59. ISSN: 0197-2243.

BASCH, REVA. 1991. Annual Review of Database Developments. Database. 1991 October; 14(5): 13-19. ISSN: 0162- 4105.

BECKER, THEODORE L., ed. 1991. Quantum Politics: Applying Quantum Theory to Political Phenomena. New York, NY: Praeger Publishers; 1991. 232p. ISBN: 0-275-93310-5; LC: 90-49219.

BENIGER, J.R. 1986. The Control Revolution: Technological and Economic Origins of the Information Society. Cambridge, MA: Harvard University Press; 1986. 493p. ISBN: 0-674-16985-9.

BIMBER, BRUCE. 1991. Information as a Factor in Congressional Politics. Legislative Studies Quarterly. 1991 November; 16(4): 585-605. ISSN: 0362-9805.

BLAKE, VIRGIL L.; SURPRENANT, THOMAS T. 1990. Electronic Immigrants in the Information Age: Public Policy Considerations. The Information Society. 1990; 7: 233-244. ISSN: 0197-2243.

BLATTBERG, ROBERT C.; DEIGHTON, JOHN. 1991. Interactive Marketing: Exploiting the Age of Addressability. Sloan Management Review. 1991 Fall; 33(1): 5-14. ISSN: 0019-848X.

BRAINARD, ROBERT; FULLGATE, KYM. 1986. Technology and Jobs. STI Review. 1986 Autumn; (1): 10-43. Also available from: OECD Publication Service, Sales and Distribution Division, 2 Rue Andre-Pascal, 75775 Paris Cedex 16, France.

BROADBENT, MARIANNE; KOENIG, MICHAEL E.D. 1988. Information and Information Technology Management. In: Williams, Martha E., ed. Annual Review of Information Science and Technology: Volume 23. Amsterdam, The Netherlands: Elsevier Science Publishers B.V.; c1988. 237-270. ISSN: 0066-4200; ISBN: 0-444-70543-0; CODEN: ARISBC.

BRYANT, JENNINGS. 1989. Message Features and Entertainment Effects. In: Bradac, James J., ed. Message Effects in Communication Science. Newbury Park, CA: Sage Publications; 1989. 231-262. ISBN: 0-8039-3224-3; ISBN: 0-8039-3225-1 (pbk); LC: 89-5928.

BUSH, WILLIAM R. 1990. Telecommuting: The Case of Research Software Development. Technological Forecasting and Social Change. 1990; 37: 235-250. ISSN: 0040-1625.

CARPIGNANO, PAOLO; ANDERSEN, ROBIN; ARONOWITZ, STANLEY; DIFAZIO, WILLIAM. 1990. Chatter in the Age of Electronic Reproduction: Talk Television and the "Public Mind". Social Text. 1990; 25/26: 33-55. ISSN: 0164-2472.

CASE, DONALD OWEN. 1991. An Example of the Social Construction of Information Technologies: Videotex in the United States and Europe. In: Griffiths, José-Marie, ed. ASIS '91: Proceedings of the American Society for Information Science (ASIS) 54th Annual Meeting: Volume 28; 1991 October 27-31; Washington, DC. Medford, NJ: Learned Information, Inc. for ASIS; c1991. 139-149. ISSN: 0044-7870; ISBN: 0-938734-56-3; CODEN: PAISDQ.

CASTELLS, MANUEL. 1989. The Informational City: Information Technology, Economic Restructuring and the Urban-Regional Process. Cambridge, MA: Basil Blackwell; 1989. 402p. ISBN: 0-631-15988-6.

CAUDLE, SHARON L.; MARCHAND, DONALD A. 1990. Managing Information Resources: New Directions in State Government. Information Management Review. 1990 Winter; 5(3): 9-30. ISSN: 8756-1557.

CERULO, KAREN A.; RUANE, JANET M.; CHAYKO, MARY. 1992. Technological Ties That Bind: Media-Generated Primary Groups. Communication Research. 1992 February; 19(1): 109-129. ISSN: 0093-6502.

CHARAN, RAM. 1991. How Networks Reshape Organizations—For Results. Harvard Business Review. 1991 September/October; 69(5): 104-115. ISSN: 0017-8012.

CHARTRAND, ROBERT LEE. 1986. Information Technology in the Legislative Process: 1976-1985. In: Williams, Martha E., ed. Annual Review of Information Science and Technology: Volume 21. White Plains, NY: Knowledge Industry Publications, Inc.; c1986. 203-239. ISSN: 0066-4200; ISBN: 0-86729-209-1; LC: 66-25096; CODEN: ARISBC.

CHATMAN, ELFREDA A. 1991. Channels to a Larger Social World: Older Women Staying in Contact with the Great Society. Library and Information Science Research. 1991; 13(3): 281-300. ISSN: 0740-8188.

CHENEY, PAUL H.; HALE, DAVID P.; KASPER, GEORGE M. 1990. Knowledge, Skills and Abilities of Information Systems Professionals: Past, Present, and Future. Information and Management. 1990 November; 19: 237-247. ISSN: 0378-7206.

CHURCHER, P.R. 1991. The Impact of Artificial Intelligence on Leisure. AI & Society. 1991 April-June; 5(2): 147-155. ISSN: 0951-5666.

CLEVELAND, HARLAN. 1985. The Twilight of Hierarchy: Speculations on the Global Information Society. In: Guile, Bruce R., ed. Information Technologies and Social Transformation. Washington, DC: National Academy Press; 1985. 55-80. ISBN: 0-309-03529-5.

COATES, JOSEPH F. 1991. Science, Technology, and Human Rights. Technological Forecasting and Social Change. 1991; 40: 389-391. ISSN: 0040-1625.

COATES, VARY T. 1992. Technology and U.S. Stock Markets: Social and Institutional Change. Technological Forecasting and Social Change. 1992; 41: 1-12. ISSN: 0040-1625.

COLLINS, H.M. 1990. Artificial Experts: Social Knowledge and Intelligent Machines. Cambridge, MA: The MIT Press; c1990. 266p. ISBN: 0-262-03168-X.

COOK, ANNABEL KIRSCHNER; BECK, DONALD M. 1991. Metropolitan Dominance versus Decentralization in the Information Age. Social Science Quarterly. 1991 June; 72(2): 284-298. ISSN: 0038-4941.

CORNFIELD, DANIEL B., ed. 1987. Workers, Managers, and Technological Change: Emerging Patterns of Labor Relations. New York, NY: Plenum Press; c1987. 326p. ISBN: 0-306-42450-9; LC: 87-2327.

CUNNINGHAM, J. BARTON; FARQUHARSON, JOHN; HULL, DENIS. 1991. A Profile of the Human Fears of Technological Change. Technological Forecasting and Social Change. 1991; 40: 355-370. ISSN: 0040-1625.

DAVENPORT, ELISABETH; CRONIN, BLAISE. 1991. The Virtual Apprentice. Journal of Information Science. 1991; 17(1): 65-70. ISSN: 0165-5515.

DELACY, JUSTINE. 1989. The Sexy Computer. See reference: FORESTER, TOM, ed. 228-236.

DEMING, CAREN J.; BECKER, SAMUEL L. 1988. Media in Society: Readings in Mass Communication. Glenview, IL: Scott, Foresman and Company; c1988. 435p. ISBN: 0- 673-15820-9; LC: 88-730.

DESHPANDE, ROHIT; KOHLI, AJAY K. 1989. Knowledge Disavowal: Structural Determinants of Information-Processing Breakdown in Organizations. Knowledge: Creation, Diffusion, Utilization. 1989 December; 11(2): 155-169. ISSN: 0164-0259.

DILLMAN, DON A.; BECK, DONALD M. 1988. Information Technologies and Rural Development in the 1990s. The Journal of State Government. 1988 January/February; 61(1): 29-38. ISSN: 0039-0097.

DOCTOR, RONALD D. 1991. Information Technologies and Social Equity: Confronting the Revolution. Journal of the American Society for Information Science. 1991; 42(3): 216-228. ISSN: 0002-8231.

DONOHUE, GEORGE A.; OLIEN, CLARICE N.; TICHENOR, PHILLIP J. 1987. Media Access and Knowledge Gaps. Critical Studies in Mass Communication. 1987 March; 4(1): 87- 92. ISSN: 0739-3180.

DORR, AIMEE; KUNKEL, DALE. 1990. Children and the Media Environment: Change and Constancy Amid Change. Communication Research. 1990 February; 17(1): 5-25. ISSN: 0093-6502.

DRUCKER, PETER F. 1989. The New Realities: In Government and Politics, in Economics and Business, in Society and World View. New York, NY: Harper and Row; 1989. 276p. ISBN: 0-06-091699-0 (pbk); LC: 89-1992.

DUNCAN, GEORGE T.; PEARSON, ROBERT W. 1989. Improving Access to Data While Protecting Confidentiality: Prospects for the Future. Paper presented at: 1989 Joint Statistical Meetings; 1989 August 14-19; Washington, DC. 16p. ERIC: ED 317169.

EARLY, STEVEN; WILSON, RAND. 1986. Do Unions Have a Future in High Technology? Technology Review. 1986 October; 89(7): 56-65, 79. ISSN: 0040-1692.

EVANS, FRED. 1991. To "Informate" or "Automate": The New Information Technologies and Democratization of the Workplace. Social Theory and Practice. 1991 Fall; 17(3): 409-439. ISSN: 0037-802X.

EZRAHI, YARON. 1990. The Descent of Icarus: Science and the Transformation of Contemporary Democracy. Cambridge, MA: Harvard University Press; c1990. 354p. ISBN: 0-674-19828-X; LC: 90-4197.

FINHOLT, TOM; SPROULL, LEE S. 1990. Electronic Groups at Work. Organization Science. 1990 February; 1(1): 41-64. ISSN: 1047-7039.

FLAHERTY, DAVID H. 1989. Protecting Privacy in Surveillance Societies. Chapel Hill, NC: University of North Carolina Press; c1989. 483p. ISBN: 0-8078-1871-2; LC: 89-4762.

FORESTER, TOM, ed. 1989. Computers in the Human Context: Information Technology, Productivity, and People. Cambridge, MA: The MIT Press; 1989. 548p. ISBN: 0-262-06124-4; ISBN: 0-262-56050-X (pbk); LC: 89-2331.

FRENKEL, KAREN A. 1991. The Human Genome Project and Informatics. Communications of the ACM. 1991 November; 34(11): 41-51. ISSN: 0001-0782.

FUNKHOUSER, G. RAY; SHAW, EUGENE F. 1990. How Synthetic Experience Shapes Social Reality. Journal of Communication. 1990 Spring; 40(2): 75-87. ISSN: 0021-9916.

FURLONG, MARY S. 1989. An Electronic Community for Older Adults: The SeniorNet Network. Journal of Communication. 1989 Summer; 39(3): 137-144. ISSN: 0021-9916.

GANDY, OSCAR H. 1989. The Surveillance Society: Information Technology and Bureaucratic Social Control. Journal of Communication. 1989 Summer; 39(3): 61-76. ISSN: 0021-9916.

GARSON, BARBARA. 1989. The Electronic Sweatshop: How Computers Are Transforming the Office of the Future into the Factory of the Past. New York, NY: Penguin Books, Inc.; c1988, 1989. 288p. ISBN: 0-14-012145-5.

GERGEN, KENNETH J. 1991. The Saturated Self: Dilemmas of Identity in Contemporary Life. New York, NY: Basic Books; 1991. 295p. ISBN: 0-465-07186-4; LC: 90-55597.

GILLESPIE, ANDREW; ROBINS, KEVIN. 1989. Geographical Inequalities: The Spatial Bias of the New Communications Technologies. Journal of Communication. 1989 Summer; 39(3): 7-18. ISSN: 0021-9916.
GOODMAN, S.E. 1992. Inside Risks. Communications of the ACM. 1992 February; 35(2): 174. ISSN: 0001-0782.
GRAHAM, S.D.N.; DOMINY, G.R. 1991. Planning for the Information City: The U.K. Case. Progress in Planning. 1991; 35: 169-248. ISSN: 0305-9006.
GREENBERGER, MARTIN; PUFFER, JAMES C. 1989. Telemedicine: Toward Better Health Care for the Elderly. Journal of Communication. 1989 Summer; 39(3): 137-144. ISSN: 0021-9916.
HAFNER, KATIE; MARKOFF, JOHN. 1991. Cyberpunk: Outlaws and Hackers on the Computer Frontier. New York, NY: Simon and Schuster; 1991. 368p. ISBN: 0-671-68322-5.
HARTLEY, R.J.; WILLIAMS, JOHN. 1991. Legal Information for Living: The Role of Information Technology. In: Meadows, Arthur Jack, ed. Information Technology and the Individual. London, England: Pinter Publishers Ltd.; 1991. 26-53. ISBN: 0-86187-877-9.
HEYDEBRAND, WOLF V. 1989. New Organizational Forms. Work and Occupations. 1989 August; 16(3): 323-357. ISSN: 0730-8884.
HJORTDAL, HELGE. 1991. Report on the Introduction of New Technology in Parliaments. Constitutional and Parliamentary Information. 1991; 1(161): 1-13. ISSN: 0010-6623.
INGLEHART, RONALD. 1990. Culture Shift in Advanced Industrial Society. Princeton, NJ: Princeton University Press; 1990. 484p. ISBN: 0-691-02296-8.
JOHNSON, HAYNES B. 1991. Social and Human Factors in the Information Age. In: Chartrand, Robert Lee, ed. Critical Issues in the Information Age. Metuchen, NJ: The Scarecrow Press, Inc.; 1991. 105-109. ISBN: 0-8108-2402-7; LC: 91-8790.
JOHNSTON, WILLIAM B. 1991. Global Work Force 2000: The New World Labor Market. Harvard Business Review. 1991 March-April; 69(2): 115-127. ISSN: 0017-8012.
KANTER, ROSABETH MOSS. 1991. Transcending Business Boundaries: 12,000 World Managers View Change. Harvard Business Review. 1991 May/June; 69(3): 151-164. ISSN: 0017-8012.
KEEN, PETER G.W. 1991. Shaping the Future: Business Design through Information Technology. Boston, MA: Harvard Business School Press; c1991. 264p. ISBN: 0-87584-237-2; LC: 90-49732.
KERR, JAMES M. 1991. The IRM Imperative: Strategies for Managing Information Resources. New York, NY: John Wiley & Sons, Inc.; c1991. 282p. ISBN: 0-471-52434-4; LC: 90-39806.
KING, ALAN. 1991. Revisited: The Rise and Fall of Lotus MarketPlace. Online. 1991 July; 15(4): 102-104. ISSN: 0146-5422.
KOCHEN, MANFRED. 1983. Information and Society. In: Williams, Martha E., ed. Annual Review of Information Science and Technology: Volume 18. White Plains, NY: Knowledge Industry Publications, Inc. for the American Society for Information Science (ASIS); 1983. 277-304. ISSN: 0066-4200.

KRAEMER, KENNETH L.; DANZIGER, JAMES N. 1990. The Impacts of Computer Technology on the Worklife of Information Workers. Social Science Computer Review. 1990 Winter; 8(4): 592-613. ISSN: 0894-4393.

KRAEMER, KENNETH L.: KING, JOHN LESLIE. 1988. Computer-Based Systems for Cooperative Work and Group Decision Making. ACM Computing Surveys. 1988 June; 20(2): 115-146. ISSN: 0360-0300.

KRAUT, ROBERT E. 1989. Telecommuting: The Trade-Offs of Home Work. Journal of Communication. 1989 Summer; 39(3): 19-47. ISSN: 0021-9916.

KRAUT, ROBERT; DUMAIS, SUSAN; KOCH, SUSAN. 1989. Computerization, Productivity, and Quality of Work-Life. Communications of the ACM. 1989 February; 32(2): 220-238. ISSN: 0001-0782.

KRUEGER, RICK; KITCHEN, WILL; KITCHEN, KAREN. 1989. Using Information Technology. The Journal of State Government. 1989 November/December; 62(6): 207-209. ISSN: 0039-0097.

LARSON, CHARLES U.; ORAVEC, CHRISTINE. 1987. A Prairie Home Companion and the Fabrication of Community. Critical Studies in Mass Communication. 1987 September; 4(3): 221-244. ISSN: 0739-3180.

LASH, SCOTT; FRIEDMAN, JONATHAN, eds. 1992. Modernity and Identity. Cambridge, MA: Blackwell Publishers; 1992. 379p. ISBN: 0-631-17585-7; LC: 90-27629.

LAVER, MURRAY. 1989. Information Technology: Agent of Change. Cambridge, England: Cambridge University Press; 1989. 189p. ISBN: 0-521-35035-2; ISBN: 0-521-35925-2 (pbk); LC: 88-21412.

LEEBAERT, DEREK, ed. 1991. Technology 2001: The Future of Computing and Communications. Cambridge, MA: The MIT Press; 1991. 392p. ISBN: 0-262-12150-6; LC: 90-40022.

LEEBAERT, DEREK; DICKINSON, TIMOTHY. 1991. A World to Understand: Technology and the Awakening of Human Possibility. In: Leebaert, Derek, ed. Technology 2001: The Future of Computing and Communications. Cambridge, MA: The MIT Press; c1991. 293-321. ISBN: 0-262-12150-6.

LEVIN, MARC A. 1991. The Information-Seeking Behavior of Local Government Officials. The American Review of Public Administration. 1991 December; 21(4): 271-286. ISSN: 0275-0740.

MANN, PATRICIA S. 1990. Representing the Viewer. Social Text. 1990; 9(2): 177-184. ISSN: 0164-2472.

MANZ, CHARLES C.; GROTHE, ROGER. 1991. Is the Work Force Vanguard of the 21st Century a Quality-of-Work-Life Deficient-Prone Generation? Journal of Business Research. 1991; 23: 67-82. ISSN: 0148-2963.

MARTIN, THOMAS H. 1988. Office Automation. In: Williams, Martha E., ed. Annual Review of Information Science and Technology: Volume 23. Amsterdam, The Netherlands: Elsevier Science Publishers B.V.; c1988. 217-235. ISSN: 0066-4200; ISBN: 0-444-70543-0; CODEN: ARISBC.

MARTIN, WILLIAM J. 1988. The Information Society. London, England: Aslib; 1988. 174p. ISBN: 0-85142-219-5.

MATHESON, KIMBERLY; ZANNA, MARK P. 1990. Computer-Mediated Communications: The Focus Is on Me. Social Science Computer Review. 1990 Spring; 8(1): 1-13. ISSN: 0894-4393.

MCLUHAN, MARSHALL; POWERS, BRUCE R. 1989. The Global Village: Transformations in World Life and Media in the 21st Centry. New York, NY: Oxford, England: Oxford University Press; 1989. 220p. ISBN: 0-19-505444-X; LC: 88-22718.

MEADOWS, ARTHUR JACK, ed. 1991. Information Technology and the Individual. London, England: Pinter Publishers Ltd.; 1991. 147p. ISBN: 0-86187-877-9; LC: 90-27685.

MEYROWITZ, JOSHUA. 1985. No Sense of Place: The Impact of Electronic Media on Social Behavior. Oxford, England: Oxford University Press; 1985. 416p. ISBN: 0-19-503474-0.

MILES, IAN. 1989. From IT in the Home to Home Informatics. See reference: FORESTER, TOM, ed. 198-212.

MILKMAN, RUTH; PULLMAN, CYDNEY. 1991. Technological Change in an Auto Assembly Plant: The Impact on Workers' Tasks and Skills. Work and Occupations. 1991 May; 18(2): 123-147. ISSN: 0730-8884.

MILLMAN, ZEEVA; HARTWICK, JON. 1987. The Impact of Automated Office Systems on Middle Managers and Their Work. MIS Quarterly. 1987 December; 11(4): 479-491. ISSN: 0276-7783.

MOONEY, CHRISTOPHER Z. 1991. Information Sources in State Legislative Decision Making. Legislative Studies Quarterly. 1991 August; 16(3): 445-455. ISSN: 0362-9805.

MURDOCK, GRAHAM; GOLDING, PETER. 1989. Information Poverty and Political Inequality: Citizenship in the Age of Privatized Communications. Journal of Communication. 1989 Summer; 39(3): 180-195. ISSN: 0021-9916.

NAISBITT, JOHN; ABURDENE, PATRICIA. 1990. Megatrends 2000: Ten New Directions for the 1990's. New York, NY: William Morrow and Company, Inc.; 1990. 384p. ISBN: 0-688-07224-0; LC: 89-13301.

NEWSTEAD, ANTHONY. 1989. Future Information Cities. Futures. 1989 June; 21(3): 265-278. ISSN: 0016-3287.

NIELSEN, BRIAN. 1991. Intellectual Freedom in an Electronic Age. Online. 1991 May; 15(3): 88-90. ISSN: 0146-5422.

OGOZALEK, VIRGINIA Z. 1991. The Social Impacts of Computing: Computer Technology and the Graying of America. Social Science Computer Review. 1991 Winter; 9(4): 655-667. ISSN: 0894-4393.

OLSON, MARGRETHE H. 1989. Work at Home for Computer Professionals: Current Attitudes and Future Prospects. ACM Transactions on Office Information Systems. 1989 October; 7(4): 317-338. ISSN: 0734-2047.

PARSONS, CHARLES K.; LIDEN, ROBERT C.; O'CONNOR, EDWARD J.; NAGAO, DENNIS H. 1991. Employee Responses to Technologically-Driven Change: The Implementation of Office Automation in a Service Organization. Human Relations. 1991 December; 44(12): 1331-1356. ISSN: 0018-7267.

PAUL, NORA. 1991. For the Record: Information on Individuals. Database. 1991 April; 14(2): 15-23. ISSN: 0162-4105.

PEMBERTON, JEFFERY K. 1989. Database Interviews Morris Goldstein, President of Information Access Company. Database. 1989 October; 14(5): 29-38. ISSN: 0162-4105.

PERROLLE, JUDITH A. 1987. Computers and Social Change: Information, Property, and Power. Belmont, CA: Wadsworth Publishing Company; c1987. 297p. ISBN: 0-534-07464-2; LC: 86-18979.

PETRIE, HOWARD. 1991. Technology in and outside the Home: Its Effects on the Provision of Personal Information for Living. In: Meadows, Arthur Jack, ed. Information Technology and the Individual. London, England: Pinter Publishers, Ltd.; c1991. 117-137. ISBN: 0-86187-877-9.

PFAFFENBERGER, BRYAN. 1990. Democratizing Information: Online Databases and the Rise of End-User Searching. Boston, MA: G.K. Hall & Co.; c1990. 191p. ISBN: 0-8161-1860-4; ISBN: 0-8161-1872-8 (pbk).

POSTMAN, NEIL. 1985. Amusing Ourselves to Death: Public Discourse in the Age of Show Business. New York, NY: Viking Press; 1985. 184p. ISBN: 0-670-80244-1.

POSTMAN, NEIL. 1992. Technopoly: The Surrender of Culture to Technology. New York, NY: Alfred A. Knopf; 1992. 222p. ISBN: 0-394-58272-1.

PRESSMAN, STEVEN. 1988. Protecting Rights in State Courts. In: Rosenbaum, Marcus D., ed. Editorial Research Reports: Volume 1. Washington, DC: Congressional Quarterly Inc.; 1988. 274-279. ISSN: 0013-0958; ISBN: 0-87187-492-X.

PRITCHARD, TERESA. 1991. Databases, Individual Privacy and 747's. Database. 1991 April; 14(2): 6-8. ISSN: 0162-4105.

PRITCHARD, TERESA; HUTCHENS, SUSAN. 1991. Remote Access to Corporate Public Records: Scanning the Field. Database. 1991 April; 14(2): 24-27. ISSN: 0162-4105.

QUILLING, JOAN. 1990. Organizations, Individuals, and Families in a Technological Society. Journal of Studies in Technical Careers. 1990 Spring; 12(2): 115-121. ISSN: 0163-3252.

RAKOW, LANA F. 1988. Gendered Technology, Gendered Practice. Critical Studies in Mass Communication. 1988 March; 5(1): 57-70. ISSN: 0739-3180.

RICE, RONALD E. 1980. The Impacts of Computer-Mediated Organizational and Interpersonal Communication. In: Williams, Martha E., ed. Annual Review of Information Science and Technology: Volume 15. White Plains, NY: Knowledge Industry Publications, Inc.; 1980. 221-249. ISSN: 0066-4200; ISBN: 0-914236-65-2.

RICE, RONALD E.; AYDIN, CAROLYN. 1991. Attitudes toward New Organizational Technology: Network Proximity As a Mechanism for Social Information Processing. Administrative Science Quarterly. 1991 June; 36: 219-244. ISSN: 0001-8392.

ROBERTSON, DOUGLAS S. 1990. The Information Revolution. Communication Research. 1990 April; 17(2): 235-254. ISSN: 0093-6502.

ROCKART, JOHN F.; SHORT, JAMES E. 1991. The Networked Organization and the Management of Interdependence. In: Morton, Michael S. Scott, ed. The Corporation of the 1990s: Information Technology and Organizational Transformation. New York, NY: Oxford, England: Oxford University Press; 1991. 189-219. ISBN: 0-19-506358-9; LC: 90-37886.

ROTHSCHILD, JOAN, ed. 1983. Machina Ex Dea: Feminist Perspectives on Technology. New York, NY: Pergamon Press; c1983. 233p. ISBN: 0-08-029404-9; ISBN: 0-08-029403-0 (pbk); LC: 83-8353.

RUBINYI, ROBERT M. 1989. Computers and Community: The Organizational Impact. Journal of Communication. 1989 Summer; 39(3): 110-123. ISSN: 0021-9916.

SALOMON, GAVRIEL. 1990. Cognitive Effects with and of Computer Technology. Communication Research. 1990 February; 17(1): 26-44. ISSN: 0093-6502.

SCHIFFMAN, LEON G.; SHERMAN, ELAINE. 1991. Value Orientations of New-Age Elderly: The Coming of an Ageless Market. Journal of Business Research. 1991; 22: 187-194. ISSN: 0148-2963.

SCHMITZ, JOSEPH; FULK, JANET. 1991. Organizational Colleagues, Media Richness, and Electronic Mail: A Test of the Social Influence Model of Technology Use. Communication Research. 1991 August; 18(4): 487-523. ISSN: 0093-6502.

SHAIKEN, HARLEY. 1985. Work Transformed: Automation and Labor in the Computer Age. New York, NY: Holt, Rinehart, and Winston; 1985. 306p. ISBN: 0-03-042681-2.

SHAIKEN, HARLEY. 1989. The Automated Factory: Vision and Reality. See reference: FORESTER, TOM, ed. 291-300.

SHATTUCK, JOHN; SPENCE, MURIEL MORISEY. 1989. The Dangers of Information Control. See reference: FORESTER, TOM, ed. 451-461.

SIMONDS, A.P. 1989. Ideological Domination and the Political Information Market. Theory and Society. 1989 March; 18: 181-211. ISSN: 0304-2421.

SLACK, JENNIFER DARYL. 1984. Communication Technologies and Society: Conceptions of Causality and the Politics of Technological Intervention. Norwood, NJ: Ablex Publishing Corp.; c1984. 166p. ISBN: 0-89391-124-0; LC: 83-15693.

SMITH, H.A.; MCKEEN, J.D. 1992. Computerization and Management: A Study of Conflict and Change. Information and Management. 1992 January; 22: 53-64. ISSN: 0378-7206.

SNIZEK, WILLIAM E. 1987. Some Observations on the Effects of Microcomputers on the Productivity of University Scientists. Knowledge: Creation, Diffusion, Utilization. 1987 June; 8(4): 612-624. ISBN: 0164-0259.

SPROULL, LEE; KIESLER, SARA. 1986. Reducing Social Context Cues: Electronic Mail in Organizational Communication. Management Science. 1986 November; 32(11): 1492-1512. ISSN: 0025-1909.

SPROULL, LEE; KIESLER, SARA. 1991. Computers, Networks and Work. Scientific American. 1991 September; 265(3): 116-123. ISSN: 0036-8733.

STEINFIELD, CHARLES W. 1986. Computer-Mediated Communication Systems. In: Williams, Martha E., ed. Annual Review of Information Science and Technology: Volume 21. White Plains, NY: Knowledge Industry Publications, Inc.; 1986. 167-202. ISSN: 0066-4200; ISBN: 0-86729-209-1; LC: 66-25096; CODEN: ARISBC.

STRASSMANN, PAUL A. 1985. Information Payoff: The Transformation of Work in the Electronic Age. New York, NY: The Free Press; c1985. 298p. ISBN: 0-02-931720-7; LC: 84-24737.

TAILBY, STEPHANIE; WHITSON, COLIN, eds. 1989. Manufacturing Change. Cambridge, MA: Basil Blackwell; 1989. 226p. ISBN: 0-631-15983-5.

THOMAS, ROBERT J. 1992. Organizational Politics and Technological Change. Journal of Contemporary Ethnography. 1992 January; 20(4): 442-477. ISSN: 0891-2416.

TOFFLER, ALVIN. 1990. Powershift: Knowledge, Wealth, and Violence at the Edge of the 21st Century. New York, NY: Bantam Doubleday, Inc.; 1990. 585p. ISBN: 0-553-05776-6; LC: 90-1068.

TURKLE, SHERRY. 1984. The Second Self: Computers and the Human Spirit. New York, NY: Simon & Schuster, Inc.; 1984. 362p. ISBN: 0-671-46848-0; ISBN: 0-671-60602-6 (pbk); LC: 83-27102.

U.S. CONGRESS. OFFICE OF TECHNOLOGY ASSESSMENT (OTA). 1990. Critical Connections: Communication for the Future. Washington, DC: Government Printing Office; 1990. 395p. (OTA-CIT-407). LC: 90-010386; GPO: 052-003-01143-3. Available from: Superintendent of Documents, U.S. Government Printing Office, Washington, DC 20402-9325.

VINCENT, DAVID R. 1990. The Information-Based Corporation: Stakeholder Economics and the Technology Investment. Homewood, IL: Dow Jones-Irwin; c1990. 298p. ISBN: 0- 87094-684-6; LC: 89-11964.

WALLACE, MICHAEL. 1989. Brave New Workplace: Technology and Work in the New Economy. Work and Occupations. 1989 November; 16(4): 363-392. ISSN: 0730-8884.

WALLICH, PAUL. 1991. Of Two Minds about Privacy. Scientific American. 1991 June; 264(6): 27. ISSN: 0036-8733.

WEINBERG, NATHAN. 1990. Computers in the Information Society. Boulder, CO: Westview Press, Inc.; 1990. 183p. ISBN: 0-8133-0986-7; ISBN: 0-8133-0985-9 (pbk); LC: 90-11981.

WEISS, CAROL H., ed. 1992. Organizations for Policy Analysis: Helping Government Think. Newbury Park, CA: Sage Publications, Inc.; 1992. 289p. ISBN: 0-8039-4359-8; ISBN: 0-8039-4360-1 (pbk); LC: 91-12233.

WHITNEY, D. CHARLES; WARTELLA, ELLEN. 1988. The Public as Dummies: Comments on American Ignorance. Knowledge: Creation, Diffusion, Utilization. 1988 December; 10(2): 99-110. ISSN: 0164-0259.

WILLIAMS, FREDERICK, ed. 1988. Measuring the Information Society. Newbury Park, CA: Sage Publications, Inc.; 1988. 286p. ISBN: 0-8039-3155-7; ISBN: 0-8039-3156-5 (pbk); LC: 87-27701.

YOUNG, ELIZABETH L. 1991. Information Services and Education for the Community and the Individual. In: Chartrand, Robert Lee, ed. Critical Issues in the Information Age. Metuchen, NJ: The Scarecrow Press, Inc.; 1991. 110-117. ISBN: 0-8108-2402-7; LC: 91- 8790.

ZIMMERMAN, JAN, ed. 1983. The Technological Woman: Interfacing with Tomorrow. New York, NY: Praeger Publishers; 1983. 296p. ISBN: 0-03-062829-6; LC: 82-14033.

ZUBOFF, SHOSHANA. 1988. In the Age of the Smart Machine: The Future of Work and Power. New York, NY: Basic Books, Inc.; 1988. 468p. ISBN: 0-465-03212-5; ISBN: 0-465-03211-7 (pbk); LC: 87-47777.

2 Social Equity and Information Technologies: Moving toward Information Democracy

RONALD D. DOCTOR
University of Alabama

INTRODUCTION

This chapter is about information democracy in America. It focuses on the interplay between information technologies and society and on social equity in the distribution and use of information resources. These themes recently achieved recognition as one of four major topics of the 1991 White House Conference on Library and Information Services (NATIONAL COMMISSION ON LIBRARIES AND INFORMATION SCIENCE). The Congressional Office of Technology Assessment also recognized these issues:

> The opportunity for people to participate in economic, political, and cultural life depends on their ability to access and use communication and information services. Individuals need skills and tools to locate the communication pathways, information, and audiences in a timely fashion and in an appropriate form. Unequal access to communication resources leads to unequal advantages, and ultimately to inequalities in social and economic opportunities. (U.S. CONGRESS. OFFICE OF TECHNOLOGY ASSESSMENT)

The aphorism by FRANCIS BACON, "Knowledge itself is power," is widely known. Less widely known are the views of James Madison:

> Popular government without popular information, or the means of acquiring it, is but a prologue to a farce or tragedy, or perhaps both. Knowledge will forever govern ignorance,

and a people who mean to be their own governors must arm themselves with the power which knowledge gives. (PADOVER, p.337)

I define information democracy as a sociopolitical system in which *all* people are guaranteed the right to benefit from access to information resources. Information democracy deals with empowerment, with ensuring that people have the tools they need to participate in the decision-making structures that affect their daily lives.

When we deal with information democracy issues, we generally focus on the "information poor." CHILDERS & POST examined the "culture of information poverty" in America. In their schema, the information poor include the disadvantaged (including the economically poor), the elderly, the undereducated, the racially/ethnically oppressed, the unemployed and underemployed, the physically handicapped, and the imprisoned.

Using 1990 data from the U.S. Bureau of the Census, the ALLIANCE FOR PUBLIC TECHNOLOGY reports that of 240 million Americans, the following populations are potentially among the information poor:

- The 64.8 million who live in rural areas (27%);
- The 32.4 million who are below the poverty level (14%);
- The 58.4 million who are in school (24%);
- The 31 million who are over age 65 (12.5%, one of every eight Americans); and
- The 27 million over age 16 who are disabled (11%).

These groups are not mutually exclusive; people in one group tend also to be in other groups.

Since information democracy involves empowerment, we must be concerned with the sources of societal power: money (or wealth), authority (or political resources), and knowledge. Later we show that problems associated with the information poor seem to correlate with the distribution of these resources. We also show that the gap between the economically rich and poor seems to be growing. Such disparities in economic resources have concerned political thinkers from ARISTOTLE to JOHN ADAMS to LORD MACAULAY, all of whom believed that extreme differences in wealth make democracies unstable (HOCHSCHILD, 1981, p. 8).

The mechanisms that society uses to mediate contention for control of economic, political, and knowledge resources affect the relative stability and success of democracies, including American democracy. There is great power associated with control of those mediating mechanisms, and that control is increasingly important as we move into the information age. These issues of power and control in democratic societies are discussed later.

Organization of the Chapter

This chapter consists of five major sections, each of which focuses on a body of literature that deals with the major themes of information democracy. These literatures concern:

- Relationships between society and technology;
- Concepts of democracy and its implementations, including power and control relationships;
- Concepts of social justice and social equity, including redistribution of societal resources;
- Information needs, sources, and uses, including how and where people seek information to meet everyday needs; and
- Applications in the form of mass information delivery systems. These include information and referral and community information services, technology-based education systems, and high-capacity computer networks linking people all over the nation.

These areas are interdependent, but each literature is distinct and vast. No attempt has been made to be comprehensive; rather, the key literature in each area is pointed out, with the hope that readers will use this information to locate other items of interest.

Throughout this chapter, the focus is on the United States. Nevertheless, much of the discussion of democracy and social justice and some of the discussion of implementation activities also are relevant outside the United States. Some equity-related topics are notably absent from this chapter. Equitable distribution and use of information technologies in our public schools are barely touched on. In addition, although information policy in general is discussed, specific policy discussion or recommendations are not included. Each deserves a chapter in its own right.

For the most part the emphasis is on the recent literature, writings, and activities during the past 20 years, although specific coverage varies with subject matter. The discussions of theoretical and conceptual topics use the literature of the past two decades, occasionally reaching further back. The discussion of implementation activities draws on more recent sources, many published within the past five years.

TECHNOLOGY AND SOCIETY

Kranzberg (KRANZBERG, 1967, 1985; KRANZBERG & PURSELL, 1967a, 1967b) has written extensively about the history of technology–society interactions. CHERRY wrote about sociocultural relationships involving society and telecommunications technologies. Both focused on the idea that technology has no meaning outside its social context. Robins and Webster (ROBINS & WEBSTER, 1979, 1983; WEBSTER & ROBINS) explored how technology and society interact and the dangers and potentials of those interactions. BENIGER, DUTTON ET AL., and DANZIGER described recent sociological research involving people and computers. Sackman developed innovative proposals for social experimentation via experimental mass information utilities (SACKMAN; SACKMAN & BOEHM; SACKMAN & NIE).

A common thread through all this research is the notion that technology and society interact; no specific technology is foreordained and invulnerable to societal pressures. Technology and society develop cojointly, each affecting the development of the other. This notion of interdependence is important if we are to understand how today's information technologies relate to American concepts of social equity. We begin this exploration of the literature by reviewing some of the mechanisms by which these interactions occur.

The Information Age: Cultural Lag

We are in the midst of what some social commentators call the information age. CHERRY describes this age as "a social movement of enormous scale, stemming from 'explosive' developments in the electronics industry. . .based upon the 'technology of information.'" KRANZBERG (1967; 1985) notes that the technologies and social structures of the information age evolved from earlier developments. That is, the transformation of society that we characterize as an information age is evolutionary rather than revolutionary. BENIGER documents more than 75 names that have been applied to this information age by various writers.[1] MACHLUP, PORAT & RUBIN, PORAT, and RUBIN have analyzed one of the key characteristics of this age—viz., the shift from an industrial economy based on manufactured goods to an information-based, service-oriented economy.

Although this shift is based on evolutionary changes in technology and society, it has revolutionary impacts. KRANZBERG (1985) believes that we are facing a social revolution driven by rapid evolutionary changes in computer, communications, and information technologies and by the interaction of those technologies with our social institutions. These impacts change where and how people work, live, play, and pray. They bring new social patterns and cultural values. They change and modify the direction of technological development. New social

---

[1] Among the more common names attached to the changes we are witnessing are: information revolution, second industrial revolution, age of access, post-industrial era, and communications age.

patterns, changing cultural values, and disarray in existing institutions all produce resistance to the technological progenitors of change, slowing the social dislocations inherent in revolutionary activity. In this way, society gains the time needed to adapt to, or change, the technological forces acting on it. This societal interaction with changing technology is what OGBURN calls "cultural lag." In the view of KRANZBERG (1967), cultural lag is evidence that society imposes its will, however unconscious and disorganized, on technology.

Social equity concerns are a manifestation of cultural lag, an integral and necessary part of our evolution to an information society. If the history described by Cherry and Kranzberg is a guide, the expression of and action on these concerns will affect how information technologies develop and the role they will play in shaping future society.

The "gateway concept" of MAYO describes how technology and society interact and how the interactions produce cultural lag. Mayo identified four factors that affect the "flow of innovations into society": (1) the push of technology, (2) the technology gate, (3) the social gate, and (4) the pull of society. The "gates" are subject to myriad technological, social, economic, and political forces.

The forces acting at the social gate, for example, include: (1) economic (marketplace and national economic) forces, (2) a need to serve the common good, (3) public receptivity, and (4) regulation and legislation. These are the very forces that affect and are affected by social equity concerns.

The various technological possibilities present in society at any given time are filtered by these gateways. Some are modified as they pass through the gateways; others are blocked by one or more of the forces acting at the gateway. Those that successfully pass become integrated into society's structure. This filtering process is a manifestation of Ogburn's cultural lag.

Technology-based equity issues and evidence of cultural lag also arise in the workplace. ZUBOFF observes that information technologies can be used to replace and extend human activities either by automating them or by "informating" them. A technology informates as well as automates when it generates new information about the activities to which it applies. Informating properties are what distinguish information technologies from earlier generations of machine technologies. If properly applied, informating can increase "intellective" skills, thus compensating for the loss of control that people feel when computerized processes are introduced. At the same time, the nature of work changes, from dependence on physical (or "acting on") processes to intellective (or "acting with") processes that require more abstract, thinking skills. Both employee and employer can benefit by choosing an informating rather than an automating approach when introducing information technologies. Cultural lag effects and perpetuation of social inequities in the workplace are more prominent in the automating scenario than the informating one.

Shaping the Future

What the literature tells us then is that technological changes are not deterministic. We can use the forces that create technological and social gateways and cultural lag to shape the way technology and society develop. By explicit policies and actions, we can minimize undesirable inequities in the distribution and use of information resources.

CHERRY noted that we cannot foresee what impacts the information age will have on society. However, we know from history that the impacts will be significant, unevenly distributed and diffused, and assimilated and modified at uneven rates. Such differences across socioeconomic groups are at the root of information democracy equity issues. To lay a foundation for exploring these issues, we first must examine how changing information environments might affect power and control relationships in America.

DEMOCRACY—POWER AND CONTROL ISSUES

Providing access to information resources and the means for people to use that access effectively in their daily lives is fundamental to the concept of information democracy. This is an empowerment issue. It concerns how and to whom power and control are allocated in our society. These power and control issues are increasingly critical as we move into the information age. To understand their importance, we must understand some of the concepts that underlie American democracy.

DAHL (1989) traces the evolution of American democracy from the Greek city-states of the 5th century B.C. through the representative democracies that arose from the monarchies and aristocracies of England and Sweden in the 17th and 18th centuries. He contends that American democracy is a pluralistic system, based on a dynamic balance among groups with competing interests in a variety of sociopolitical arenas. The shifting points of balance among these groups are affected by how society's resources are distributed.

DAHL (1989; 1990) analyzed the principles that define democracies and thereby identified conditions of individual equality that must be met in democratic decision making. He expressed these conditions as operational criteria that require "adequate and equal opportunities": (1) to participate effectively in preference formulation and decision-making processes, (2) to discover and validate the choices available, and (3) to "decide how matters to be decided by means of the democratic process are to be placed on the agenda" (DAHL, 1989, p. 115).

Adequate and equal opportunity derives from Dahl's recognition that influence is a function of the resources available to individuals and groups and that those resources are unequally distributed. MARCH (p. 62) extended Dahl's analysis, noting that each citizen "must have the opportunity to be fully informed of the implications of alternative policies." Further, political institutions must function in a way that discovers, comprehends, and shapes "the sharing of citizen interests." Thus an information system that facilitates these processes of preference discovery through "enlightened understanding" is necessary.

In the context of information democracy, our concern is how far we must move toward "adequate and equal opportunity" in the distribution and use of information resources to maintain a functioning democracy. How we respond to this concern depends in part on our perception of how political and economic power is distributed in America and on the extent to which that distribution introduces a critical imbalance in democratic processes. It also depends on our notions of social justice and where on the spectrum of social justice norms we place information democracy issues. The subsections that follow deal with these power and control issues. We examine social justice considerations in the next major section.

Democracy, Power, and Equality

There seems to be general agreement that power derives from three interrelated resources: money, authority, and knowledge. The presence or absence of these sources in various combinations determines whether an individual or group is empowered. As long as these sources of power are distributed equitably, democratic societies tend to be stable.

Much of the political science literature in this area deals with one resource or another. A few deal with two (R.E. LANE; SCHWARTZ; SHAPIRO & REEHER, 1988b); fewer deal with all three (MARCH; NAGEL, 1988; RAE).

SCHWARTZ begins with Marx's concepts of property rights and the notion of power as appropriation of property by controlling pre-ownership attitudes. He notes that modern political science theorists start by defining power in terms of centralized control, but eventually they move to concepts based on "shared attitudes and mutual relations."

SHAPIRO & REEHER (1988b, p. 2) observe that an examination of power relations requires a consideration of the "economic and social resources that empower and disempower political agents." DAHL (1990) explores the links between political democracy and economic inequality, concluding that "democracy can only be achieved by democratizing aspects of the economy and the workplace directly."

Rae is pragmatic, defining power in terms of possible actions within known regimes. He defines a regime as "a socially created constellation of rules that delimit the range of electable futures for some persons or classes of persons" (RAE, p. 38). He notes that LASSWELL asks: "Who gets what, when, how?" In contrast, Rae asks: "Who can do what, when, how?" (RAE, p. 39). To Rae, power and knowledge go hand-in-hand:

> Power is the knowing capacity to determine some aspect(s) of the future, or to determine the range of available futures from which such choices are made...Power always requires knowledge; power without knowledge is not power. (RAE, p. 40)

Thus, Rae focuses on power as a knowledge-based action phenomenon.

He looks to the predicaments of ordinary people for revelations about the nature of power. The first requisite to exercising power in everyday situations is to know what is possible, to know what the range of alternate and available regimes is. (Later we will see that Rae's approach is similar to Dervin's.)

Like Dahl these political theorists conclude that democracy requires individuals to have adequate and equal opportunities to participate in the decisions of their government. Such opportunities in turn require adequate and equal distribution of information resources as well as the ability to use those resources effectively.

Information-Based Power—Alternative Visions

The literature of political science theorists is supplemented by a growing body of literature concerning empirical manifestations of information-based societal power issues. This literature focuses more explicitly on how information technologies affect the distribution of power in the United States and other nations. DOCTOR reviewed this literature and found that it is characterized by vast differences of opinion regarding "how our political and economic systems will change as we move into the Information Age. The extremes are represented by technological optimism on the one hand and neo-Luddite reaction on the other" (DOCTOR, p. 217). Commentators from one extreme to the other make impassioned and reasonable arguments for their points of view. They support their arguments with a wealth of anecdotal empirical evidence but with little systematic data. The situation is characteristic of a new policy research area that is striving for definition.

CLEVELAND and CHERRY argue that by their nature the new information technologies distribute and disperse information capabilities, tending to decentralize control of information and its concomitant power. Cleveland, in particular, focuses on the redistribution of power and reorganization of society as a consequence of changes induced by the inevitable spread of information and communication technologies.

If knowledge is power, then the "wider the spread of knowledge, the more power gets diffused" (CLEVELAND, p. 68). Both Cleveland and Cherry believe openness and participatory democracy will spread and that the new technologies will enhance democracy.

Robins and Webster (ROBINS & WEBSTER, 1979, 1983; WEBSTER & ROBINS), however, argue that we are witnessing an intensified centralization of the tools of control, that increased power is being vested in an oligopoly, and that there is a growing disparity between the affluent, who are able to access the new technologies, and the economically disadvantaged, who are effectively denied access. MOSCO (1988a; 1988b; 1989a; 1989b; 1990) has written extensively about concentration of power in the telecommunications industry and how that concentration diminishes access to information resources. H.I. SCHILLER (1981; 1989; 1991) and SCHILLER & SCHILLER, like LASSWELL and RAE, are concerned with "who gets what." Their emphasis is on the concentration and use of information resources by corporate America and on the impact of restrictive government policies on access to information. GANDY (1988; 1989) focuses on the increased power that accrues to private firms and government as a result of the enhanced surveillance and privacy intrusions that new information technologies enable. He argues that without adequate social controls these capabilities could dramatically shift the distribution of societal power in America. D. SCHILLER (1982; 1988) is primarily concerned with the economics of information. He views information resources as commodities and notes that control of these resources through the economic system may significantly affect the distribution of political and economic power. SIEFERT ET AL. have collected various essays that deal with the social distribution of power, focusing on policy issues affecting information-based power distribution in the United States.

The middle ground between technological optimists and pessimists is occupied by writers who are somewhat less pessimistic about our ability to control shifting power relationships. Here we find works by BRAND and by TOFFLER, both oriented to less technical audiences.

BRAND seems fully aware of the incipient power struggle. In *The Media Lab*, he provides a remarkable account of the advanced technologies being developed at and around MIT, and he warns of the growing inability of our political institutions to guide and control these technologies. He notes that the Media Lab operates at the intersection of three major industries, each a significant economic power: (1) the broadcast and motion picture industry, (2) the print and publishing industry, and (3) the computer industry. Over time, Brand argues, the area of intersection will grow until it is difficult to distinguish one industry from another. In an emerging megacorporate society, information is the dominant medium for creating wealth, and the principal information technologies are telecommunications and computing. As these developments occur, economic and political power tend to become more highly concentrated.

Considering the powerful economic and political forces at work, Brand foresees the need for a new principle as fundamental as freedom of speech and press: the right of access (BRAND, p. 219). DOCTOR observes that Brand's call for a new "right to access" is critically important but will probably be insufficient: "Access will be of little benefit to large portions of the population, unless it is accompanied by equipment and training that allow effective use of that access." He argues instead for a "right to benefit from access"—i.e., information democracy.

All of these social commentators and analysts agree on one point: great power is associated with access to and use of information resources. They also agree that we are likely to see increased contention for control of information resources and that the "information poor" may be unable to reap the benefits available to groups that are better endowed. Where they diverge is in their views of how successful we are likely to be in affecting the outcome of this struggle for control.

If information policies and activities designed to reinforce democratic principles are to succeed, they must conform to American beliefs about social justice and social equity. The next section provides a framework for thinking about social equity. We then review more deeply the basis of information age social equity concerns and consider the state of research on the nature and magnitude of differential socioeconomic effects.

SOCIAL JUSTICE AND SOCIAL EQUITY

Because a democracy requires an informed and empowered people, any developments that threaten to shift the balance of power to an elite and away from the people threaten that democracy. Some scholars and political commentators believe that this shift is occurring as we move deeper into the information age. Thus we are led to consider social equity, or social justice, in the distribution of information resources and to explore the potential for redistributing those resources and the means to use them effectively among a broader base of the population. Equity embodies the idea of justice according to natural law or right as opposed to equality which means identical in value. We begin with a brief look at an economist's approach to social equity.

Economics and Social Equity

A traditional argument in economics against explicit governmental intervention to redistribute resources is that the free market will ensure an adequate and efficient distribution over time. Many economists, however, do not agree. SAMUELSON & NORDHAUS note that even a perfectly functioning market system would not meet social equity objectives, because "goods follow the dollar. A rich man's cat may receive the milk that a poor child needs to remain healthy. Distribution of income and goods in a market economy often is a consequence of accidents of technology or birth. Economic efficiency is not the sole objective of democratic societies. Democracies, pursuing social goals other than economic efficiency, opt to achieve equity through redistributive policies" (SAMUELSON & NORDHAUS, p. 49).

Redistributive policies may use (1) *taxation* (e.g., progressive income tax), (2) *income support* (e.g., unemployment insurance) and (3) *subsidies* (e.g., food stamps) (SAMUELSON & NORDHAUS). Economists cannot say how far such redistribution should go, but they *can* analyze the costs and benefits of such programs which affect the acceptability of proposed programs. Individual attitudes also affect the feasibility and acceptance of redistribution activities as well as the perceived magnitude of societal disparities.

HOCHSCHILD (1981) analyzed American attitudes toward the redistribution of wealth, and discovered a broad spectrum of views. Her findings can be applied to the redistribution of information resources.

Disparities in Wealth and the Information Gap

Both government actions and personal wealth affect the distribution of, access to, and life cycle of information resources. Whether the *income gap* between the rich and the poor is growing or diminishing affects growth of the *information gap* between information "haves" and "have-nots." HOCHSCHILD (1981; 1988), using almost 50 years of U.S. census data, concluded that claims of a diminishing gap between rich and poor are "at best ambiguous, and much evidence suggests that they are simply false" (1981, p. 2). She also found that data on property and possessions suggest much greater differences between the richest and poorest than income data indicate (HOCHSCHILD, 1981, p. 6).

Hochschild's conclusions are supported by recent data from the Congressional Budget Office (CBO) (NASAR; U.S. CONGRESS. CONGRESSIONAL BUDGET OFFICE; U.S. CONGRESS. HOUSE. COMMITTEE ON THE BUDGET).[2] Four illustrative points from the CBO's 1992 report are:

- Two-thirds of the growth in pre-tax income of all American families between 1977 and 1989 went to the wealthi-

---

[2]CBO data are based on income tax returns, whereas Current Population Surveys data are obtained from the Bureau of the Census.

est 600,000 families. Only 1% of America's families got two-thirds of the growth in income.
- These wealthiest families each had an annual income of at least $310,000, with a per capita income exceeding $75,000 per year.
- The top 1% of America's 60 million families had 17% of total income, up from 9% in 1977.
- Average income of families in the top 1% increased from $310,000 to $560,000, a 77% increase. But average income of the median family was up only 4%, to $36,000. And income of people at the low end of the scale declined.

THUROW also believes that the middle class (approximately $15,000–$25,000 in 1982) is disappearing as families with incomes both above and below the middle class increase and decrease respectively. He blames technology-induced losses in middle-income jobs and the rise in female-headed households (almost always low-income).

LINDEN, of the Conference Board, does not agree that there is a bipolar trend in wages. He emphasizes instead the 10-year doubling in the number of low-income households headed by persons under 35 and the large increase in the number of single-person homes and families headed by women. He contends that the share of income available to the middle-fifth of the population has remained almost constant.

Despite their disagreement about the middle class, Thurow and Linden seem to be saying the same thing about growth of the lower and higher income groups (Thurow's bipolarization effect). That is, the gap between the wealthiest people in America and the poorest is increasing. Disparities in income, and therefore in the ability to acquire information resources, are worsening.

Egalitarian vs. Differentiating Norms in America

We need to understand not only how information resources currently are distributed in the United States but also the types of redistribution activities that might be effective and acceptable. A major part of Hochschild's work concerns this issue.

It is difficult to identify what redistribution activities might be acceptable. With regard to income, we commonly assume that the poor would favor redistribution of societal assets, and the rich would oppose it. Hochschild, however, has found that one's attitude toward redistribution activities depends more on the domain into which the activity falls than on the person's economic class. She identifies three domains—socializing, economic, and political—as well as a set of norms (widely held social values) that people apply to these domains.

Hochschild found that we tend toward equality, or egalitarian norms, in the socializing domain (home, family, schools, and neighborhoods) (HOCHSCHILD, 1981, Chap. 4). We also tend to be egalitarian in the political (or social justice) domain where we deal with tax and social policies, political rights and authorities, and "visions of utopia" (HOCHSCHILD, 1981, Chap. 5). However, in the economic domain we do not insist on equality, but rather accept economic differences (HOCHSCHILD, 1981, Chap. 6).

These are tendencies, not hard and fast rules. When confronted with a distributive issue, we draw on internal norms that express these tendencies. We are not always consistent in applying these norms because sometimes our internal norms conflict with reality. Consequently, there is overlap among the three domains.

HOCHSCHILD (1981) focuses on six internal norms that affect decisions about distributive justice: (1) strict equality, (2) need, (3) investments, (4) results, (5) ascription, and (6) procedures.

Our internal norms range from egalitarian (strict equality) to differentiating (ascriptive; distribution according to need or merit).[3] We also use procedures norms, but these can lie any place on the continuum depending on the procedure used. And we apply a whole range of discrete norms between these two extremes (rewards for effort, charity for the poor).

People, whether rich or poor, tend to make allocative decisions by starting from egalitarian norms (redistribution based on strict equality, need, and investment) in the socializing and political domains. However they start from differentiating norms (redistribution based on investment, results, or ascriptive differences) in the economic domain. "Justice, then, requires differentiation in economic matters, but equality in personal and political matters" (HOCHSCHILD, 1981, p. 48).

Of course the situation is not quite this clear-cut. As we noted, there is much variation among people, and there is significant overlap of norms from one domain to the next. Nevertheless, information resource redistribution activities are more likely to be approved if they are designed to fall within the socializing or political domain rather than the economic.

The distribution of information resources concerns the political and social distribution of economic goods—a mixed norm area where people are likely to have mixed views about government activities to distribute information resources equitably. If we view information resources as

---

[3]Equality assumes "that all people may legitimately make the same claims on social resources." It is a subset of, not a synonym for, justice. Differentiation assumes that "people may legitimately make varying claims on social resources." Differentiation may be based on gender, race, hereditary position, etc. It also is a subset of justice (HOCHSCHILD, 1981, p. 46).

primarily political (e.g., information we need to vote), as an issue of political rights, or social policies, we tend to favor redistribution policies oriented toward strict equality. If we view information resources as socializing (e.g., distributing computers to schools), we tend to support governmental actions designed to achieve equality, or equity. However, if we view information resources as economic goods, we tend to oppose equalizing activities.

These considerations are being applied in the development of community-based information delivery systems. With these concepts in mind then, we now consider how a key information resource, namely computers, is distributed across socioeconomic groups.

Computers and Education

DOCTOR (p. 219) examined data available in 1990 and found significant disparities in the distribution of computing resources (e.g., computer hardware, software, training). Evidence from studies between 1970 and 1985 analyzed by DUTTON ET AL. and surveys reported by KOMINSKI and the Educational Testing Service (ETS) (MARTINEZ & MEAD) indicates that computer ownership and availability of school instruction determine computer competence in school. These studies included surveys by LOUIS HARRIS & ASSOCIATES, LAUTENBERG, and TICHENOR ET AL. They indicate that ethnic differences in computer competence are linked to ownership of and access to computers at home and at school. MARTINEZ & MEAD, DILLMAN, and LAROSE & METTLER also report significant rural-urban differences in computer ownership and computer competence.

The differences found in computer accessibility favor white students over blacks and hispanics, and urban students over rural. The differences are strongly correlated to family income and affluence. The U.S. BUREAU OF THE CENSUS noted that lack of access to computers by poor children during their school years could limit their employment opportunities as adults.

Evidence is lacking as to whether these disparities are growing, diminishing, or remaining stable. However, if changes in income and wealth across socioeconomic class are any indication, we may reasonably hypothesize that the computer gap, like the gap between the information rich and information poor, is widening.

Distribution of Telephone Service

Socioeconomic differences in access to information resources are not limited to computers. Although more than 95% of all U.S. households have telephone service, 25% of households below the poverty line do not have telephones (U.S. GENERAL ACCOUNTING OFFICE). Disparities in urban–rural communication system infrastructure also were apparent in a survey of the 32 telephone companies serving Alabama cities and rural areas. SINGLETON & QUINN found that rural areas tend to have lower quality service and fewer advanced features than urbanized areas, and the per capita income in 74% of the local service areas (primarily rural) was less than $10,000 (the 1986 state average was $11,315).

Distribution of Public Library Service

Equity problems also exist in the distribution of public library service (SHAVIT; see also studies by the AMERICAN LIBRARY ASSOCIATION. LIBRARY ADMINISTRATION DIVISION and by INTERNATIONAL RESEARCH ASSOCIATES, L. MARTIN, BENSON & LUND). RICH points out that equitable service delivery can't be equated with provision of equal service. LUCY & MLADENKA discuss how to apply concepts of equity in service distribution. BLANK ET AL. found that inequalities in New York City library service could not be explained by demographic characteristics. LEVY ET AL. attributed the inequalities they found in Oakland to a "circulation-allocation cycle" prevalent in low income areas (deteriorated buildings are uninviting; thus, circulation is low, resulting in low budgets, and the cycle—the circulation-allocation cycle—repeats). A similar pattern afflicts middle class neighborhoods as well (ASTRID & WOLFF).

So, we see that historical evidence confirms the persistent gap between services to the rich and the poor. If the information gap is widening, and can destabilize our democracy, then corrective action is necessary. However, any information resource redistribution activity should be structured to conform to Hochschild's (1981) findings, and must meet the real and perceived needs of people.

INFORMATION NEEDS AND USES

This section points to some relevant research on information needs and uses. It is not comprehensive because past *ARIST* chapters have covered the subject exceptionally well. Our emphasis here is on literature that identifies the everyday information needs of ordinary people. Thus, much of this work centers on the use of libraries.

The first significant studies of users in libraries were developed by sociologists in the 1930s and focused on the demographics of library users. These were supplemented by empirical studies centered on library statistics (e.g., circulation counts) and by studies on the uses of libraries. Library use research led to a paradigm shift, away from the library as an institution and toward the user as an adapting, changing person with needs that differed according to context and situation (CHEN).

Several hundred useful articles and books have been written about information needs and uses, and about user and use studies. One of the most useful is the recent review article by DERVIN & NILAN, in the 1986 volume of *ARIST*. DERVIN & NILAN emphasize that user needs and uses should be central to information system operation, and should be user defined. To identify these needs, one must ask how people define needs in different situations, how they present these needs to systems, and how they use what the systems provide.

DERVIN & FRASER found that what "predicted how users were helped best were not library characteristics per se (e.g., kind of library) or experience with libraries (e.g., recency of use), but rather the context that led to the use and the materials/services obtained" (DERVIN & FRASER, p. 31).

In this connection, DERVIN notes that information needs arise when a person's cognitive structure is not adequate to a task or a person wishes to resolve a problem in his or her state of knowledge or a person's state of knowledge is insufficient, uncertain or in conflict.

To deal with these situations she developed her "sense-making approach" which "assesses how people make sense of their worlds and how they use information and other resources in the process" (DERVIN & NILAN, p. 20).

Other researchers also have attempted to define everyday citizen information needs by identifying and categorizing the social developments that lead to daily information needs (VICKERY & VICKERY) and by examining the needs of coherent communities (DONOHUE, p. 81).

CHILDERS & POST defined 11 broad areas of information needs of the poor: health, home and family, consumer affairs, housing, employment, welfare programs, law, the political process, transportation, education, and recreation. Each area was further subdivided and the subcategories classified into five major types of information: factual, legal, directional, financial, and counseling. As shown below a similar classification system is used in many of today's computerized community information systems.

The studies of opinion leaders and information needs in low-income communities by CHATMAN (1983; 1987) illustrate recent work in this area. She found that low-income people are likely to look to their opinion leaders for: (1) events that occur in the neighborhood (factual information); (2) where to go to buy things (directional and financial information); (3) information about health problems and what to do when people are sick and need health care (counseling, legal and directional information); and (4) bringing up children (factual and counseling information).

Radio and print media (newspapers and books) were primary sources of information for both opinion leaders and isolates. Job information was the most useful type of information received, and the library was an important source for both groups. Both sought information on: (1) ways to cope with life's problems, (2) family relationships, and (3) employment and career opportunities.

CHATMAN (1987) notes that the type of information required (e.g., employment information) "precludes extensive diffusion." That is, since opinion leaders compete with their followers for job information, they are compromised in that area. Thus, what is most needed from libraries, community information systems, and other outreach programs is objective information and referral services focused on job search and career information. The situation is similar in other countries, such as Finland (SUOMINEN).

Dervin (DERVIN ET AL.; DERVIN) applied her Information-Needs Content Analysis Scheme to a random sample of the general population in two cities and found that consumer problems, education and schooling, health and neighborhood concerns were the top-rated problems for which people needed information but she cautioned that identifying needs is not enough. If the service does not deliver the resources people are really after, they may consider it a failure. It is very important, then, to separate information from "help" or "service."

Still, some services mix information and advocacy, and sometimes people who are seeking information really are seeking help or advocacy (BERNARD ET AL.; NATIONAL CITIZENS' ADVICE BUREAUX COMMITTEE; OGG). About 40% of the cases of the British Citizens' Advice Bureaux involve advocacy (ZUCKER). Advocacy may be essential for an information service to succeed (BUNDY; VOOS). It may take several forms: consumer advice or dealing with complaints due to a perceived error or injustice.

Like other researchers (CROWLEY & CHILDERS; HILTZ; PARKER & PAISLEY; RIEGER & ANDERSON; SPITZER & DENZIN; TICHENOR ET AL.; ZWEIZIG) before her, DERVIN found a strong correlation between education level and information use. Educated (and affluent) citizens are more likely to seek information, to be exposed to print media, to use more professional sources, and to experience less trouble securing information than their less educated counterparts.

In examining the extensive literature dealing with information sources, Dervin noted that much of the evidence, although indirect, indicates:

- Television is the most used (and believed) mass medium for the average adult, but it lacks the kind of information needed to solve everyday problems;
- Peer-kin relationships (friends, family, relatives) are the most used sources on most topics for most people;

- Awareness of potential information sources is low (BLOCK);
- Use of professionals and nonprofit agencies is limited to the highly educated elite (LEVINE & PRESTON); and
- A law of least effort is a strong factor in source use. Most people tend to use sources and services that are close to home rather than comparison shop (ALEXANDER ET AL.; UDELLET; ZWEIZIG).

The latter and the role of gatekeepers are particularly important when considering home-based computerized information services, the next topic.

MASS INFORMATION SYSTEMS

As information technologies become more pervasive, more democratic distribution of information resources becomes a pressing societal need. This section examines current mechanisms for distributing information resources and approaches for integrating market and government-sponsored activities.

We focus on *interactive* information delivery systems and *new* information technologies. We do not address non-interactive media (print media, radio and TV). Our concern is primarily with *delivery* systems rather than the technologies. For the most part, these delivery systems use computers and extensive computer networks. This section does not delve into computer technologies or the esoteric but essential mechanics of networks; it concerns the services these computers and networks deliver to the information user.

Attempts to develop equitable interactive information delivery mechanisms have been sporadic over the past 30 years (DOCTOR). Many of these attempts were spurred by federal funding during the 1960s and 1970s (BENSON & LUND; DEAHL; DONOHUE; DONOHUE & KOCHEN; LEVY ET AL.; LIPSMAN; NATIONAL BOOK COMMITTEE; STUEART). This funding helped community-based agencies, including libraries, to experiment with information and referral systems (BLACK ET AL.; BROWN; DURRANCE; LONG; LUKE; W. MARTIN; MEDNICK; NEW YORK UNIVERSITY) and other community information services (FORSMAN; HESS; KAHN ET AL.; KIDD; PEPPI). Some of these experiments evolved into mature systems, which in turn spawned additional services as new delivery technologies became available.

During the last half of this period, computer technologies have developed rapidly, and personal computers are now affordable by the masses. As business and individual access to microcomputers expanded, some computer technology developers shifted their attention to new mechanisms for delivering large volumes of information to this new community of prospective patrons. The new delivery mechanisms meant developing large computerized databases and information files, and national networks over which these databases and files could be accessed. Early efforts were government sponsored (e.g., ARPANET (KARRAKER)), but these were followed quickly by commercial services (e.g., CompuServe, DIALOG, and BRS). This movement to large-scale, networked, computerized information sources was essentially independent of the earlier library and community-based information movements.

Over the past few years, there has been some merging of these two independent movements and the development of new hybrid systems, many of which are oriented toward information delivery to middle- and upper-income groups; some provide low-cost delivery to public schools and libraries. Some are library based, but generally libraries are just one component of the delivery system.

Today's information delivery systems are consumer based or specialist based. Specialist-based systems include Internet and NREN; CompuServe, DIALOG, BRS and others; information and referral (I&R) systems; and libraries and library-based systems. Consumer-based information systems include: library-based community information systems; local and state government sponsored community systems; independent not-for-profit networks (e.g., NPTN); independent for-profit networks (e.g., Prodigy); campus-wide information systems (CWIS); telephone company (RBOC) gateway systems; and audiotex systems.

Specialist-based systems are characterized by (1) information that is designed for a special class of clientele or is highly technical, (2) a complex user-system interface and syntax that require training for effective use, or (3) need for an intermediary to make effective use of the system. Consumer-based systems are designed for direct use by patrons, with only minimal assistance from an intermediary, and offer information to meet everyday needs. We now look briefly at current developments in each area except audiotex.

Specialist-Based Information Systems

Internet and NREN. Internet is a U.S. based, worldwide complex of computer networks (KARRAKER). NSFNET, the backbone of the Internet, connects super- and mainframe computers serving academic and governmental purposes. Educators and researchers in universities, government personnel and government contractors are able to communicate and share information and computing resources. Since its origin more than 30 years ago, the Internet has become a rich resource for those who have access to it (e.g., NSF NETWORK SERVICE CENTER, 1992a, 1992b; ST. GEORGE & LARSEN). During the past few years, the Net has been opened to private sector organizations as long as their use conforms to the Internet's general purposes. In the next several years, the network will become a major element of the newly authorized National Research and Education Network (NREN).

Currently, the Internet and NSFNET (MARKUSON) interconnect more than 600 colleges and universities and about 400 other organizations worldwide, support more than 3 million workstations, and have traffic growing at about 15%-20% per month.

KARRAKER provides a useful history of the Internet. The Internet originated in the 1960s as ARPANET, a project of the Department of Defense's Advanced Research Projects Agency (ARPA). Electronic message traffic increased rapidly, and the network was upgraded with higher speed, higher-capacity lines. Administration of the network's "backbone" shifted from ARPA to the National Science Foundation (NSF) as non-defense users proliferated. The new backbone, to which a whole variety of regional and special-purpose networks were connected, became known as NSFNET. The entire complex is known as the Internet.

Growth continued to accelerate (NSF NETWORK NEWS, 1987; 1991; 1992). The need for a major overhaul of the network and expanded public purposes was recognized by congressional and executive branch action in the passage of the High Performance Computing Act of 1991 (U.S. CONGRESS). That act calls for spending more than one billion dollars over the next five years to greatly increase the speed and capacity of the network. The act also creates NREN, which is intended to provide for connections to public libraries and K-12 schools. MCCLURE ET AL. detail the issues surrounding development of NREN.

KARRAKER notes that the higher speed of the upgraded network means:

- In medicine, we can transmit 100 three-dimensional x-rays or CAT scans in one second;
- In the space program, we can send 1,000 satellite photographs across the network in one second; and
- In libraries, we can transmit the equivalent of the entire *Encyclopaedia Britannica* in one second, more than 100,000 typed pages per second.

Additional speed, or capacity, also means that many more computers can be connected to the network if the political system allows for it. Thus, NREN *could* be a national turning point for achieving information democracy.

NREN's potential has raised the hopes of those concerned with information access, but the legislation creating NREN is ambiguous and raises important policy issues (DOCTOR & TURNER): (1) universal access to information systems; (2) public vs. private and nonprofit ownership and operation; (3) who decides what services will be available; (4) who sets rates or fees for access; and (5) who uses, who pays, and who benefits.

Proponents of NREN have likened it to an information superhighway. The highway metaphor, however, has negative as well as positive aspects, and those negative aspects involve social equity considerations. DOCTOR & TURNER observed that when a highway is built through the middle of a community, it may have a divisive, isolating effect. To carry the metaphor further, we could examine the increased "gap" that a new highway creates between those who own vehicles and can use the highway effectively and those who are "vehicle poor"; and we could consider the usage and demographic effects of pay-per-mile toll highways.

These "social equity" aspects of the interstate highway metaphor are critically important as we move along the political path that will create the new superhighways of information, but they have not been an essential part of the rhetoric surrounding the NREN legislation. These aspects of NREN very likely will receive greater attention as NSF and others begin to implement the bill.

DOCTOR & TURNER identified four social equity actions to be considered as part of NREN implementation:

- Incorporate the concept of universal service;
- Develop explicit provisions for free or very low-cost local access to the network through public and school libraries, K-12 classrooms, and nonprofit organizations. Provisions for physical access to the network should ensure that the cost of using the network is within the means of schools and library patrons. Development of fee schedules for use of the network should include special provisions for affordable access for small schools and libraries, rural areas and the economically disadvantaged;
- Develop interfaces and applications that are useful to and usable by nontechnical patrons; and
- Include training and assistance programs to help the general public learn how to use the network effectively. Access, even low cost access, will provide greater benefits if the targeted patron is sufficiently motivated and knows how to use the network effectively. Training programs and programs that demonstrate how the system can be useful for dealing with important problems should accompany network implementation.

The concept of universal access is important and was a key aspect of the development of the telephone system because it was congressionally mandated by the Communications Act of 1934 (DORDICK). It stipulated that telephone service be available to everyone, regardless of income or location, and that rates for local service be affordable.

As a result 94% of American households have telephones today, and most states require some sort of "lifeline rates" for low-income households. A telecommunications network built along the lines of the "telephone metaphor" would extend the principle of universal service to computer-based telecommunications (ALLIANCE FOR PUBLIC TECHNOLOGY; BRYANT).

CompuServe, DIALOG, BRS, and others. Information utilities such as DIALOG and BRS offer a wealth of bibliographic, financial, and full-text data. Their costs are high, and they require extensive training or intermediaries for effective use. Until their use is greatly simplified and access/use costs are reduced, they are not likely to meet the information needs of most people.

Commercial online services like CompuServe, Genie, and America Online have greater mass appeal but cater to fewer than 1.5 million U.S. households, less than 1% of the computer-owning public. Nevertheless, these members have pioneered a dynamic new electronic medium that provides discussion and help forums, news, business/financial information, and electronic communication. These services require no intermediaries and are available for as little as $5 to $10 per month. Information available on these services tends to be specialized and they do not offer local information. There is some evidence that these services are restructuring to increase their mass appeal, but whether they will provide information helpful in the daily lives of the lower income groups, the "bottom third of our population" (the B3), is problematical.

Information and referral systems. Information and referral (I&R) systems are the only information services on our list that effectively serve the B3. Most of these are still "low-tech" systems, just beginning to move into computerization, and almost all use a trained intermediary. Very few allow direct patron access to their information resource files. Still, there is much we can learn from the history and operations of these I&R centers (DONOHUE & KOCHEN, p. 12).

The idea of such public information systems is not new (KOCHEN). Their roots can be traced to 18th and 19th century social service traditions of England (HIMMELFARB, 1984; 1991), which led to the private sector charity organizations of the 1870s (LONG) and then the social service exchanges of late 19th and early 20th-century America. These pioneering agencies were organized not to help people obtain services, but to avoid duplication of services (WILLIAMS). By the end of World War II, however, I&R centers were oriented toward helping people in need. More than 3,000 community-based veteran's information centers, modeled after the British Citizens' Advisory Bureaux, sprang up and flourished in the late 1940s (U.S. DEPARTMENT OF LABOR, 1946; 1947), but by 1949 most had closed (KAHN, 1969). Beginning in the 1960s, federal sponsorship associated with President Johnson's War on Poverty programs led to considerable community I&R activity. Today the ALLIANCE OF INFORMATION AND REFERRAL SYSTEMS (AIRS) lists more than 950 systems in its directory.

FORSMAN classifies today's I&R systems in three "crisis intervention" categories:

- Hotlines (emergency, anonymous telephone services for people in crisis, providing a "listening ear" and referral to agencies and professional backup when necessary);
- Switchboards (telephone I&R services as well as message centers sometimes including a walk-in or message-drop facility); and
- Free clinics (walk-in centers providing direct medical services and counseling, both medical and non-medical).

Switchboards and free clinics arose out of the counterculture of white alienated youths in the late 1960s. The prototype for switchboards was the old "central" switchboard in American communities, which was a source of information for solving human problems.

The charity origin of I&R service is reflected in today's private sector nonprofit organizations like United Way of America. In 1972, about 60 I&R centers operated under United Way auspices in the United States and Canada. Today, United Way plays a role in most of the centers listed in the AIRS directory.

ACTIVITIES OF I&R CENTERS. KOCHEN argued that to be useful a general information system must meet the needs of low-income people and that people will not use an information system if they believe their needs are not understood. This occurs if the person feels the counselor is "listening from a different frame of reference or cognitive map" (p. 153). Thus it is important to identify the *cognitive maps* of the target population.

Cognitive maps are determined in part by gossip, grapevines, or peer-kin relationships, as well as gatekeeper activities and cultural and social conditioning. This cognitive approach is the basis of current research on information needs and uses.

These ideas led KOCHEN & DONOHUE (p. 5) to formulate three key concepts for I&R centers, which also apply to current technology-based information delivery systems:

- Educating and assisting people in making wise choices;
- Making information available to those in need at affordable prices; and

- Making people at various levels of sophistication aware of the available community resource options.

Long (LONG, p.13; LONG ET AL., 1971, 1973) identified eight activities of I&R centers that are necessary for meeting the information needs of individuals. These activities apply to computerized information delivery systems as well as to I&R centers, although some of these activities are absent from some information centers:

- Community Education. Alert potential users to the existence of available services.
- Resource files. Develop and update resource files about community resources in human service areas.
- Information and referral. Provide telephone information about resources and formal referrals to service agencies.
- Systematic follow-up. Follow up with clients and agencies to determine if the service was obtained and provide advocacy if necessary.
- Counseling. Provide counseling or casework services, escort services, and outreach or case-finding services. Operate holiday clearinghouses and volunteer bureaus.
- Outreach. Participate in community education.
- Reporting. Prepare statistical reports on service requests for other agencies and undertake research on community needs to help planners.
- Advocacy. Help people who would have difficulty making effective contact unaided. Prod helping agencies where this appears needed. Engage in advocacy for developing new service programs by documenting and lobbying for needed services that are unavailable.

There is an abundant literature in the I&R subfield dealing with day-to-day information needs of the general population. LEVINSON and LEVINSON & HAYNES provide a good introduction to the literature. MEDNICK (p. 107), also useful, cites six broad I&R subject areas: (1) income maintenance; (2) emergency assistance; (3) housing; (4) health services; (5) child and family services; and (6) legal services.

These are *"survival services"* and conform to Dervin's sense-making "helps." Many I&R systems also offer information on employment, education, and government, but typically they do not provide information like community events and news.

I&R services usually are available free. They are subsidized by charitable organizations or by government. Many public libraries cooperate with local I&R agencies, but only a few act as I&R centers (e.g., Detroit Public Library, with its TIP program) (MAAS & DE SANTIS; YATES).

In the United States, most I&R clients contact the service by telephone. A trained worker takes the call and tries to determine the person's underlying information need (similar to a reference interview). Once the need is identified, the center helps the client contact the appropriate agency or simply provides a referral.

Until recently, I&R resource files were not computerized, but as computer costs have decreased, more and more agencies have computerized their files and made them available to I&R workers, but seldom to the clients. Experimentation with direct client access is beginning.

BRITISH CITIZENS' ADVICE BUREAUX (CABs) AND INDEPENDENT CENTERS. The British National Association of Citizens' Advice Bureaux (NACAB, or CAB) (KAHN ET AL.; PEPPI) and the various U.K. independent advice centers are probably the most successful systems in existence today for delivering day-to-day information to the general population. KAHN ET AL. examined the CAB operations to see if American systems could learn from them. He concluded that not much could be transferred because of cultural and structural differences in our governmental and social systems. Over the past 25 years, however, cultural changes and new technological opportunities are cause for a reexamination.

The aims of the CAB Service (NATIONAL CITIZENS' ADVICE BUREAUX) are:

> To ensure that individuals do not suffer through ignorance of their rights and responsibilities or of the services available, or through an inability to express their needs effectively.
>
> To exercise a responsible influence on the development of social policies and services, both locally and nationally.

The Bureaus provide "free, confidential and impartial information and advice on all subjects" responding to about seven million questions annually (NATIONAL CITIZENS' ADVICE BUREAUX). About 23,000 people work for the CABs; 90% of them are volunteers. Local bureaus are funded by local authorities, with minor assistance from the NACAB, which is funded by the national Department of Trade and Industry. They also obtain revenue from "membership fees" and sales of publications. Expenditures total about £10 million per year (about $18 million). One significant function of CABs is to provide two-way communication between bureaucratic government and the general populace (KAHN ET AL., p. 32). The CABs also provide early feedback on local problems to local government.

The National CAB Council is a voluntary autonomous coordinating body of the National Council of Social Service. It includes representatives of county and regional CABs and is the central policy body. The council's secretary is, in effect, CAB's executive director.

CABs receive secretariat and headquarters subsidies from the national office and from two government departments. Most funding comes from local government grants. Local government also may provide space, utilities, and telephone.

Each CAB operates independently in a voluntary relationship with the national office, but all adhere to common standards and patterns of operation. The national office provides training, information manuals, expert consultation, and channels to the national government.

The CABs offer a very wide range of services (KAHN ET AL., p. 20-21). Local CABs provide detailed reports in a standard format to the NACAB. The seven million annual queries center on social security (22.9%); consumer debt and related issues (20.2%); housing, property and land (11.6%); employment (10.2%); family and personal (9.9%); administration of justice (7.5%); taxes and duties (4.2%); local information (3.0%); health (2.6%); and other (7.9%) (NATIONAL CITIZENS' ADVICE BUREAUX, p. 6). Specific data on users by class are not available (KAHN ET AL., p. 28) so it is not clear whether the type of people who are underserved or unserved in the United States are served any better by the CAB system.

Consumer-Based Information Systems

Many consumer-based information systems operate in the United States and most are highly computerized. Some are small, local operations, but many are linked to larger networks, and a few are international. Examples are the National Public Telecomputing Network (NPTN) and the Free-Net system; Community Memory's coinbox-operated community messaging centers; HandsNet's national citizens network to support the homeless; SeniorNet's national online network for elderly citizens; and PeaceNet and EcoNet services of the Institute of Global Communications, which link 4,000 peace, environmental and social justice groups. These services are in their infancy but will likely become a permanent feature of daily life.

The key questions are, *who* will they serve, *how well* will they serve, *when* will they be available, and at *what cost*? The reader should keep these questions in mind as we examine the Free-Nets and NPTN, and other consumer-based utilities.

The Free-Nets and NPTN. The National Public Telecomputing Network (NPTN) began as Cleveland Free-Net in 1986 under Tom Grundner, then at Case Western Reserve University (GRUNDNER, 1990a). Today, Case Western operates Cleveland Free-Net as a "free, open-access, community computer system" that is available via public terminals or a computer-modem link 24 hours a day, every day. Cleveland Free-Net began with over "7,000 registered users and averaged 500-600 calls per day on ten incoming phone lines." By 1989, Free-Net had more than "23,000 registered users in the Cleveland area and around the world," 86% of whom "are over age 20 (average age 35.5 years) with a very deep 'middle class' socio-economic penetration." Today there are 3,500 calls each day on 48 incoming phone lines (CLEVELAND FREE-NET). Volunteers provide most of the staffing, and significant corporate funding comes from AT&T and Ohio Bell Telephone Co.

The Free-Nets are organized around an electronic city model. Users dial in and can access services in such "city centers" as the administration building, post office, government center, schoolhouse, medical arts building, library, courthouse, college circle, business and industrial park, NPTN/UPI newswire, international center, teleport, cafe, and "What's New in the Electronic City."

Interest in the Free-Net has gradually spread. Currently, seven Free-Net affiliates are operating, and more than a dozen others are being organized in the United States and internationally. This system of Free-Nets is modeled after National Public Radio and is called the National Public Telecomputing Network (NPTN), a nonprofit, 501(c)(3) tax-exempt corporation (GRUNDNER, 1990b; 1992). NPTN has six objectives: (1) assist in developing free and open access to community information systems; (2) establish electronic mail services among NPTN affiliates; (3) establish "cybercasting" services to all NPTN affiliates; (4) establish a national news organization to serve the community telecomputing public; (5) establish international connections between NPTN affiliates and overseas information resources; and (6) establish network-wide special services and programs.

NPTN offers three special programs:

- Academy One (a national online educational community);
- A K-12 school network program; and
- The Teledemocracy Project.

The Teledemocracy Project provides links to information from the outside world as well as communication with local elected officials. It includes:

- The Congressional Memory Project (in association with the Washington Times Corporation). This project cybercasts six congressional bills each week. The bills are searchable by subject and keyword.
- Project Hermes, a trial project of the U.S. Supreme Court, which distributes court decisions electronically within

minutes of their release to nodes. A similar project distributes 8th Circuit Court of Appeals and Ohio Supreme Court decisions.
- Distribution of U.S. Department of Commerce weekly economic data and other information.

NPTN also is developing an interactive electronic press room for political candidates during election periods, and several affiliates have created interactive electronic office space for public officials in city, county, state, and federal governments.

As presently conceived, NPTN, like the other technology-based systems we are examining, is very much a middle- and upper-class activity. Except for involvement of the public schools and libraries, the bottom third of our population is almost entirely left out. Still, of all the systems we are examining, the Free-Net/NPTN concept seems to hold the greatest promise for realizing information democracy objectives.

Library-based community information systems. Libraries appear in both specialist-based and consumer-based systems. Traditional library systems are specialist-based. Especially in reference services, a librarian serves as an intermediary between the patron and the source of information. The advent of computerized systems, however, gives the patron greater control and responsibility.

As with I&R services, significant library involvement in nontraditional information services and in serving the disadvantaged dates to the 1960s and 1970s. The community information service movement was an extension of the 1960s' concern for helping the underserved. The literature on this subject is abundant and of reasonably high quality (see, for example, AMERICAN LIBRARY ASSOCIATION (1969), BECKER, CASEY, CHILDERS, W. MARTIN, SHERRILL, and WINSOR & BURROWS).

Significant library-based community information systems currently are operating in Detroit (MAAS & DE SANTIS), Santa Monica, California *(AMERICAN LIBRARIES,* 1989b; GUTHRIE ET AL.; MACIUSZKO), Colorado Springs (DE LURY; LARSEN; MACGRATH; MALYSHEV; NELSON), and Cleveland *(AMERICAN LIBRARIES,* 1989a). A major library-backed system is under joint public-private development in St. Louis (HOLT).

C.S. JONES was the motivating force behind the Detroit Public Library's The Information Place (TIP). TIP is perhaps the longest-lived of public library community information systems. It began service in 30 branches in 1974 and is still active today. Maggie's Place III in the Pikes Peak Public Library District (Colorado Springs) is one of the best known of the current set of library-based community information systems. It is accessible via the CARL system on the Internet. Santa Monica's PEN system is discussed below.

The St. Louis system expects to provide significant benefits to the community by supporting regional economic development, helping to develop human capital in the region, and helping more citizens become comfortable with electronic information (HOLT). Similar benefits are claimed for the nonlibrary-based community information systems described below.

Despite the difficulties cited earlier, libraries are uniquely positioned to meet the information needs of all local people, especially as automation becomes commonplace in libraries and more libraries explore use of their computers for community information services (DOWLIN, 1984, 1985; EDELMAN; ESTABROOK; NELSON; U.S. DEPARTMENT OF EDUCATION). The question is, how quickly and effectively will libraries adapt to such new roles.

Library experiences in the 1960s and 1970s indicate that sustained funding and a commitment to a broader information dissemination role are necessary, yet experience also indicates difficulty in maintaining support for activities aimed at lower economic groups. Although there are hopeful signs in the innovative activities of public and academic libraries, it is not yet clear that either commitment or budget will be forthcoming. In addition, other players offer competition to libraries.

Local/state government sponsored systems. This section focuses on two notable governmental activities, a local government-sponsored community information system in Santa Monica, California, and a state government-operated system in Hawaii. Both are innovative and well supported but oriented to middle- and upper-middle income people.

SANTA MONICA'S PUBLIC ELECTRONIC NETWORK (PEN). PEN (SANTA MONICA, 1990) is one of the most successful of the nonlibrary municipal systems. It began operations in 1989 to provide greater access to city information and services. A free electronic bulletin board system connects users with each other and with city hall. Free handbooks help people learn how to navigate the system (SANTA MONICA, 1989a; 1989b; 1990).

About 4,000 of the city's 96,000 residents have registered to use PEN. They access the network more than 10,000 times per month. Access is free via microcomputers and through public terminals located in city buildings, including the library. About one-third of Santa Monica's citizens own personal computers (YARNALL). In the first two years, city departments responded to more than 4,700 messages from the public (*ALLIANCE FOR PUBLIC TECHNOLOGY QUARTERLY NEWSLETTER*).

The city's budget to run the system is $75,000 per year. This covers one full-time and one part-time staff person. Hardware and software valued at $350,000 were donated by corporations (MORAN).

PEN has five main purposes:

- To provide easy electronic access to public information;
- To provide alternative means of communication for residents to convey their needs, preferences, and intentions to their local government and to other residents;
- To enhance delivery and awareness of public services, and facilitate the public service inquiry;
- To provide an electronic forum for residents to discuss issues and concerns thereby enhancing a sense of community; and
- To offer Santa Monica residents the opportunity to understand computer technology and to provide access to the hardware and software needed to learn to communicate via an electronic information network.

Services on PEN include, among others: parks and recreation schedules; city job-line; recycling tips; police, fire, and earthquake safety tips; library news; city council agendas, minutes, and staff reports, both current and historical; e-mail between citizens, city departments, and city council members; and electronic conferencing.

PEN, like the Free-Nets, is organized on a "city buildings" concept. It provides interactive access to city officials and the area's Congressman through electronic mail, computer conferences, and online forms. The library is accessible under the Community Center. It includes a variety of information services in addition to the online catalog.

GUTHRIE & DUTTON (1992) have evaluated the PEN system, along with two other municipally sponsored public information utilities (Glendale and Pasadena, California). They speculate that local political orientations will determine the development directions of public information systems, particularly with regard to teledemocracy. Although their results do not seem to conform to what would be expected from Hochschild's model, they know that it is too early in the technology diffusion process to predict success or failure.

HAWAII FYI. Hawaii FYI is an interactive information and communication system operated by the State of Hawaii through Hawaii Information Network Corporation (Hawaii INC) (HAWAII INC). Hawaii INC was created in 1988 by the Hawaii Telecommunications and Information Industries Act (HAWAII, 1988). The University of Hawaii is involved in running the program.

Hawaii FYI is freely available via toll-free telephone numbers on each island and at terminals in state government offices, public schools and public libraries. Most services are free. Since the University of Hawaii is a CARL member, users of Hawaii FYI have direct access to all CARL facilities.

The Hawaii system is important because it is the only state-wide, state-sponsored system of such wide scope, and it was created with significant cooperation from private-sector firms such as US West and France Telecom. Since access is through microcomputers and a few public terminals, the system does not reach Hawaii's low-income population effectively. The state government, however, plans to remedy this.

Campus-Wide Information Systems (CWISs). Campus-wide information systems are unique in that they serve a well-defined and relatively homogeneous community, university faculty, students, and staff. Partly because these systems meet a large underserved information need, their numbers have expanded rapidly. "About 60% of the nation's colleges and universities have some kind of campuswide information system or are in the process of installing one," according to a recent CAUSE survey (WATKINS, 1992a). HALLMAN (1992a) lists more than 50 active CWISs accessible via the Internet. Princeton University's PNN, one of the more advanced CWIS operations, offers 300 to 400 different information items on its menus. As we'll see later, this compares favorably with commercial community service offerings by the Regional Bell Operating Companies.

HALLMAN's (1992b) report on CWIS structure, issues, and services indicates great diversity among currently operating CWISs. (See also FOLEY (1987; 1989; 1991), FOLEY ET AL. and NIELSEN). Most CWISs are operated by the campus computing center, not by the library. Some CWISs require a university computer account with an ID and password for access. Others are at least partly accessible to anyone with a microcomputer, a modem and a telephone line.

Most universities gather some sort of usage statistics, but not always in the detail required for management analysis. Where data have been collected, CWIS managers have found that once students, faculty, and staff become aware of their local CWIS, usage grows rapidly.

Case Western Reserve University's FreePort system has been in operation for three years. The system grew more than 100% per year to 45,000 logins per week by February 1992.[4] E. Jones, Director of Computer Services at Appalachian State, reports that their CWIS logged about 75,000 accesses in November 1991.[5]

Although CWIS services are heavily oriented to academic matters, the most popular services are nonacademic: advice, help, directory information, sports, dance and music events, and jobs (WORK). In short, information needs on the campus are not too different from those in the wider community.

---

[4]Raymond K. Neff, personal communication, February 19, 1992.
[5]Ernest Jones, personal communication, February 14, 1992.

For the most part, CWISs serve a limited and upscale clientele, but some make at least part of their system accessible to the surrounding community, and some are considering placing community information on their systems (WATKINS, 1992b). Case Western Reserve University, for example, is home to Cleveland Free-Net, and the University's CWIS is coordinated with Free-Net operations. Discussion on the Internet forum CWIS-L indicates that this type of extension to the community is likely to grow in the near future, and that many CWISs will use their resources to help provide community information services in their locales.

Independent for-profit networks. The mass market videotex ventures of the 1970s and early 1980s were notable failures (BRAND, p. 25-26; N.D. LANE; NYHAN ET AL.). Thus, the private sector has moved only tentatively toward mass market information services in recent years. The French national telecommunications company, France Telecom, with its Teletel system and Minitel terminals is an exception. Teletel is arguably the only large-scale implementation of information democracy in the world today. Whether we can adapt a Teletel-like system to our very different social, political and economic conditions is the question.

We begin with a look at Teletel, then move on to America's latest flirtation with videotex, the Prodigy System. Finally we examine the RBOC gateway experiments, a hybrid of NPTN and Teletel.

FRANCE TELECOM'S TELETEL SYSTEM. France Telecom initiated its Teletel service in 1982. By 1992, it had installed more than six million Minitel terminals in France (CONHAIM, 1990b), about one million of which were rentals (CONHAIM, 1990b; FOSSIER & STECKEL). Teletel adds 800,000 new French users a year. The system delivers 15,000 different services worldwide, 50–100 times more services than the experimental RBOCs, their U.S. associates (CONHAIM, 1990b). It handles over 1.5 billion calls per year, logging around 100 million hours on the various services. About 20% of France Telecom subscribers have a Minitel terminal (FRANCE TELECOM). More than 40% of France's population has access to a Minitel either at home or at the office (FOSSIER & STECKEL, p. 37). Teletel offers services in: finance and banking; transportation information and reservations; teleshopping and mail order; public utility billing and information; local weather, sports scores and classified ads; chat services; and online games. About half of Minitel's services and daily usage are professional (*WALL STREET JOURNAL*).

It is important to note what Teletel is not. It is not a community-based information system like a Free-Net; it is a generic computerized telecommunications system that offers nonlocal information and services to meet daily needs.

France Telecom operates the world's most digitized phone system, the largest packet switching data network, and the world's first nationwide ISDN (*WALL STREET JOURNAL*). The company has active ventures in the United States, United Kingdom, Italy, Japan, and Hungary. The U.S. ventures include operating agreements with several of the Regional Bell Operating Companies (RBOCs) as well as an independent gateway to Teletel in France (CONHAIM, 1989b).

U.S. access to the gateway is free. Customers use credit cards to pay online fees for the various services accessed. Minitel USA also provides communications software and will rent Minitel terminals to its customers.

Until 1990, France Telecom's budget was part of the French government budget, but in 1990 France Telecom became financially autonomous with an independent management structure (although it remains a government corporation).

Teletel is considered the only clear success in a history of videotex failures (CONHAIM, 1989a; FOSSIER & STECKEL, p. 38; HOUSEL & DAVIDSON). With an investment of $1.8 billion, Teletel generated more than $900 million in direct revenue in 1990, and created more than 12,000 jobs. Teletel reached "balanced operation" in 1990, and it expects to show profitability of 10% to 12% by 1995 (FOSSIER & STECKEL, pp. 38-39). Nevertheless French videotex users would return their Minitels immediately if they were not free but rather cost as little as $4 per month (CONHAIM, 1989b).

PRODIGY. Prodigy is a Sears-IBM joint venture videotex service. After one-half billion dollars of startup investment, Prodigy began operations in 1989 in more than a dozen U.S. cities and is now available nationwide. Prodigy is well financed and offers consumer marketing and shopping services as well as e-mail, discussion forums, and financial and news services.

Users pay a flat monthly subscription fee of $9.95–$13.95 plus additional fees for excess e-mail and for premium services. The bottom of the Prodigy screen carries two lines of advertising, revenue from which allows Prodigy to offer low-cost services.

As of mid-1991 Prodigy claimed more than 400,000 customers and more than 200 national advertisers (CONHAIM, 1990a). Profit data are not available.

Prodigy's services, like Teletel's and CompuServe's, are oriented toward middle- and upper-middle income households and businesses. It does not offer local information services.

Telephone Company (RBOC) "Gateway" Systems. The Regional Bell Operating Companies (RBOCs) are the "wild cards" in the movement toward information democracy. They seem intent on entering the information services arena, and they will likely become a major force in the distribution of information services. BRIMMER outlines much of their history and the regulatory environment in which they operate.

For most of this century, American Telephone and Telegraph Company (AT&T) operated as a legal monopoly, providing both long distance and local telephone service, as well as equipment. In return, AT&T agreed to the principle of universal service as embodied in the 1934 Communications Act and submitted to regulation by the Federal Communications Commission and corresponding state regulatory agencies.

By the late 1950s however, the "economies of providing telecommunications facilities and services" had changed, and there was increasing dissatisfaction with AT&T's monopoly power (BRIMMER). In addition, as AT&T continually sought to expand into new business areas, the U.S. Department of Justice (with some pressure from MCI) became concerned about the possible extension of AT&T's monopoly power. After considerable sparring and a series of court and regulatory decisions diluting AT&T's monopoly, the U.S. Department of Justice and AT&T reached a compromise. AT&T would be permitted to enter new businesses but its monopoly organization would be dismantled; local telephone operations would be permanently split off as independent operating companies.

In 1982, Judge Harold Greene accepted the divestiture agreement, but retained oversight authority regarding its implementation. As part of the agreement, seven Regional Bell Operating Companies (known as RBOCs, or Baby Bells) were formed.[6] The RBOCs are responsible for providing local and regional telephone service. AT&T and other long-distance carriers (e.g., Sprint and MCI) provide long-distance service.

Out of fear of their monopoly power, the AT&T divestiture order prohibited the RBOCs from originating information services, i.e., they could not develop and offer an electronic version of the Yellow Pages, a service they had long claimed as theirs.

In March 1988 Judge Greene relaxed the restrictions and allowed the Bells to transmit information provided by others and to serve as a central billing agency for independent computer-based information services. However, he still prohibited them from originating information services that would compete with nonregulated companies.

This ruling enabled the RBOCs to develop "gateway" experiments with independent information providers. These gateway experiments provided local community information to subscribers through modem-equipped computer terminals. The information was originated by independent information providers, and was carried over the RBOC gateway system to homes and businesses. By mid-1990, five of the seven RBOCs (BellSouth, Nynex, US West, Southwestern Bell and Bell Atlantic) plus Bell Canada had created gateways in seven locations. They ran the gateways either directly or through their local operating companies.

The RBOCs were still dissatisfied with the 1988 restrictions, and they appealed Judge Greene's ruling. In April 1990 an appeals court upheld

---

[6]The seven RBOCs are: Ameritech, Bell Atlantic, BellSouth, Nynex, Pacific Telesis, Southwestern Bell, and US West.

Greene's restrictions on long-distance services, but indicated that Greene should rethink his restrictions on Bell-originated information services.

The American Newspaper Publishers Association and the cable TV industry strongly opposed any Bell entry into information service development, especially entry into anything resembling electronic publishing (CARNEVALE). Despite these objections, in 1991 the courts released the RBOCs from all information service restrictions. Now, several RBOCs are preparing to commercialize their experimental gateways in selected markets. However, they are moving slowly and cautiously because they are under a threat of congressional action that would again restrict their activities.

Nevertheless, US West—a forward-looking RBOC—is considering expansion of its original Omaha, Neb. gateway to Minneapolis-St. Paul, Seattle, and Denver. Bell Canada (not subject to U.S. regulation) also has moved aggressively to commercialize ALEX, its information gateway.

The types of service available, the number of customers, and the number of service providers varies only slightly from one RBOC to another. LASKOWSKI reports that each RBOC gateway experiment offers several hundred services, typically serving 3,000 to 25,000 customers, about 0.2% to 2.0% of their customers. US West, however, expects an 18% penetration within several years. If achieved, this would compare favorably with the 5.4% first-year penetration for cellular telephones, which is considered a successful business venture (CONHAIM, 1990b).

Services are similar to those on Teletel but are not as complete as those of the Free-Nets. Some services are generic, but many are tailored to local needs. Most of the gateways offer discussion and help forums, local directory information, shopping, cultural, recreational, and political calendar information, and access to local government officials. Some, like US West's Omaha gateway, involve the public school system and provide access to the public library online catalog. The RBOCs and their information providers seem to have targeted upper-middle income households.

Pricing arrangements vary considerably from one RBOC to another and can be complex (sign-up fees, usage fee schedules, surcharged services, terminal rental fees), with a variety of billing options. Unfortunately, the fees (at least $15-$25 per month) are well out of the range of the poor.

Some RBOCs have run into significant problems, chiefly fewer subscriptions and lower profitability than expected (SMITH). Some RBOCs blame excessive regulation for low enrollments. They claim that their rates are specified by their information providers and before the Court's most recent rulings they were prohibited by regulation from originating information services that they might offer at lower rates. This meant that they could not offer essential, attractive services (e.g., electronic

Yellow Pages and other Bell-originated services), so their costs were too high for mass use. Critics argue that "they don't have [information service] products people want, and they don't know how to market them" (Massoud Saghafi as quoted by SMITH).

Southwestern Bell is an important case in point. After an initial six-month free-trial offer period, Southwestern Bell's customers had to pay full rates ($.12 per minute). Most either dropped or drastically scaled back their use of the service, yet many customers would have continued using the service if it were offered at a flat rate (SMITH). At the end of the one-year trial, Southwestern Bell's gateway system didn't meet its profitability objectives. It generated only $2 million in revenues for a $10 million investment. (Net profit was lower, of course.) Alternative investments (e.g., cellular telephones) offered greater returns on investment, so the company suspended the gateway experiment (SMITH).

But experiences differed at other Bell companies. Bell Canada offered "ALEX", a Minitel-like videotex service, on an experimental basis in Montreal and Toronto. It began in December 1988 in Montreal and April 1990 in Toronto. Within the first six months, ALEX exceeded its two-year goal with 25,000 users and 300 services (goal was 20,000 users and 150 services in 2 years). In 1990 the initial test was so successful it was cut short and full commercial service was begun. By November 1990, ALEX had almost 30,000 customers, and 170 information providers offered 650 services in Montreal and 350 services in Toronto (CONHAIM, 1990b).

US West also took an aggressive approach (LASKOWSKI). Like Southwestern Bell, it found that flat fees boosted usage and customer satisfaction, so it moved away from time-based charges. In its Omaha gateway, US West also found that customer usage responded to advertising and promotional activities. Marketing has been aggressive, including direct mail, mass media, shopping mall promotions, free weekends and rotating free services offered each week.

US West's systematic exploration of the variables affecting profitability resulted in the greatest assortment of services and one of the highest customer penetration rates (2%) among the RBOC gateways. The company's target was to have at least 50 services online at the start of operations in February 1990. By March, 400 offerings were online. By November, more than 700 services were available, 40% of which were local. Ninety percent of the services are interactive (CONHAIM, 1990b).

As a result, US West is moving from experiment to full commercialization with new gateways in larger markets (Seattle, Minneapolis-St. Paul, and Denver). It arranged with Minitel USA to make Mintel terminals available to its customers.

The RBOCs have the incentive and the resources to make a major impact on the community information service world. Whether it will be structured to serve all the people or only an elite will be a matter of profitability objectives and public policy.

A CONCLUDING NOTE

Free-market advocates will observe that the marketplace is working. The broad diversity of mass information systems currently available is a good portent. The operation of free-market forces will determine which systems survive and which do not; those that survive will do so because they provide needed services at acceptable costs.

Let us keep in mind the cautionary words of Samuelson and Nordhaus. Even a perfectly functioning market system would not meet social equity objectives because "...goods follow the dollar...Economic efficiency is not the sole objective of democratic societies. Democracies, pursuing social goals other than economic efficiency, opt to achieve equity through redistributive policies" (SAMUELSON & NORDHAUS, p. 49).

Except for I&R systems, which are just beginning to use computer technologies, few of the current systems serve the daily information needs of the poor. They are designed to serve upper and upper-middle income groups; only incidentally do some effectively reach down to middle- and lower-income groups.

Nevertheless, these systems can serve as models for other systems that can be designed to serve the poor. These market-based systems bear the brunt of financial risks, and in doing so, they provide a useful service to society (OETTINGER).

But the question remains: how can we improve distribution of information resources to *all* the people in a timely manner? In the 1970s, Sackman (SACKMAN; SACKMAN & BOEHM; SACKMAN & NIE) suggested creating Experimental Mass Information Utilities to deliver information resources to large numbers of people. DOCTOR elaborated on Sackman's idea and proposed a system of National and Regional Institutes for Information Democracy (NIID) supplemented by community-based information utilities.

Many of the individual elements of the NIID concept are in place or are being developed. What is lacking is a coordinating mechanism that would ensure development and garner acceptance of appropriate equity objectives. And of course the ubiquitous problem of providing adequate funding to implement and meet these objectives has not yet been addressed.

Moving toward information democracy in the United States will require a coordinated program of research, large-scale experimentation, and assurance of some government support. That means recognition that information equity is important and requires governmental action. Although coordinated and effective federal action is noticeably missing, local and state governments have begun to act, and local information utilities have been successfully created. Perhaps we need to be reminded again of Cherry's wisdom:

> ... [The powers of invention] for change lie in the hands of those who have the imagination and insight to see that the new invention has offered them new liberties of action, that old constraints have been removed, that their political will, or their sheer greed, are no longer frustrated, and that they can act in new ways...Such realization does not come easily, quickly, or even "naturally"...Realization of new liberties and creation of new institutions means (sic) social change, new thought, and new feelings. The invention alters society, and eventually is used in ways that were at first quite unthinkable. (CHERRY, p. 51)

Thus, we have come full circle. There are positive signs of change in the burgeoning activity of public and private organizations and in the recognition that broad access to information resources is essential for the vitality of our democratic institutions. Our challenge is to develop programs that ensure distribution of these resources to the one-third of our population that is information poor.

Let us recap the messages in the literature of information democracy:

- Society and technology are interdependent. New technologies change society, and society affects the pace of development and shape of new technologies. Rather than being subject to technological determinism, we can shape our technological futures through explicit policies and social actions;
- These policies and actions should be consistent with the nature and requirements of American democracy and should reinforce democratic principles;
- To be acceptable and successful, policies and activities designed to achieve equitable distribution of information resources should conform to American beliefs about social equity and social justice;
- Existing data provide warning signals about significant disparities in the distribution and use of information resources. Studies over the past 30 years also indicate that the "information poor" do not have access to the information resources they need in their daily lives. In the absence of explicit policies to correct these disparities, they are likely to worsen; and

- Current activities to spread the benefits of information technologies focus on the upper-middle income population and above. Few of these activities reach middle- and lower-income households. Consequently, new policy initiatives and perhaps even new institutions are needed to achieve information democracy in America.

What we need now is a national debate and consensus on how to achieve information democracy.

BIBLIOGRAPHY

ADAMS, JOHN. 1851. The Works of John Adams: Volume 6. (Edited by Charles Francis Adams). Boston, MA: Little, Brown; 1851. 550p. LC: 8-19755.

ALEXANDER, CHRISTOPHER A.; ISHIKAWA, SARA; SILVERSTEIN, MURRAY. 1968. Pattern Language Which Generates Multi-Service Centers. Berkeley, CA: Center for Environmental Structure; 1968. 283p.

ALLIANCE FOR PUBLIC TECHNOLOGY. 1990. Public Telecommunication Technologies in the 1990s: Achieving Universal Service. Washington, DC: Alliance for Public Technology; July 15. Available from: The Alliance for Public Technology, 901 15th St. NW, Ste. 230, Washington, DC 20005.

ALLIANCE FOR PUBLIC TECHNOLOGY QUARTERLY NEWSLETTER. 1991. Electronic Link for Santa Monica's Citizens. Alliance for Public Technology Quarterly Newsletter. 1991 May; 4(5): 3, 12. Available from: Alliance for Public Technology, 901 15th St. NW, Ste. 230, Washington, DC 20005-2301.

ALLIANCE OF INFORMATION AND REFERRAL SYSTEMS. 1992. Directory of Information and Referral Services in the United States and Canada, 1992-1993. Joliet, IL: Alliance of Information and Referral Systems; 1992. Available from: Alliance of Information and Referral Systems, P.O. Box 3546, Joliet, IL 60434.

AMERICAN LIBRARIES. 1989a. PC Access to Cleveland PL: A "Large, Urban PL First". American Libraries. 1989 January; 20(1): 17. ISSN: 0002-9769.

AMERICAN LIBRARIES. 1989b. "Phone-First" Fever Spreads as Libraries Add Dial-Up Access. American Libraries. 1989 October; 20(9): 839. ISSN: 0002-9769.

AMERICAN LIBRARY ASSOCIATION. 1969. Library Service to the Disadvantaged: A Study Based on Responses to Questionnaires from Public Libraries Serving Populations of Over 15,000. Chicago, IL: American Library Association; 1969. 60p.

AMERICAN LIBRARY ASSOCIATION. LIBRARY ADMINISTRATION DIVISION. 1964. Report on the Study of Access to Public Libraries. ALA Bulletin. 1964 April; 58(4): 299-304. ISSN: 0364-4006.

ARISTOTLE. 1946. The Politics of Aristotle. (Translated and edited by Ernest Barker). London, England: Oxford University Press; 1946. 411p. ISBN: 0-19-500306-3.

ASTRID, E. MERGET; WOLFF, WILLIAM M., JR. 1976. The Law and Municipal Services: Implementing Equity. Public Management. 1976 August; 58(8): 5-6. ISSN: 0033-3611.

BACON, FRANCIS. 1889. Bacon's Novum Organum. 2nd edition. (Edited by Thomas Fowler). Oxford, England: Clarendon Press; 1889. 629p. (Aphorism i). LC: 4-223.

BECKER, CAROL A. 1974. Community Information Service: A Directory of Public Library Involvement. College Park, MD: University of Maryland, College of Library and Information Services; 1974. 92p. ERIC: ED 100325.

BENIGER, JAMES R. 1986. The Control Revolution: Technological and Economic Origins of the Information Society. Cambridge, MA: Harvard University Press; 1986. 493p. ISBN: 0-674-16985-9.

BENSON, CHARLES S.; LUND, PETER B. 1969. Neighborhood Distribution of Local Public Services. Berkeley, CA: University of California, Institute of Governmental Studies; 1969. 181p. LC: 68-65796.

BERNARD, S.E.; KURTAGH, E.; JOHNSON, H.R. 1968. The Neighborhood Service Organization: Specialist in Social Welfare Innovation. Social Work. 1968; 13: 76-84. ISSN: 0037-8046.

BLACK, D.V.; SEIDEN, H.; LUKE, A.W. 1973. Evaluation of LSCA Services to Special Target Groups: Final Report. Santa Monica, CA: System Development Corporation; 1973. 257p. ERIC: ED 098919.

BLANK, BLANCHE D.; IMMERMAN, RITA J.; RYDELL, C. PETER. 1969. A Comparative Study of Urban Bureaucracy. Urban Affairs Quarterly. 1969 March; 4(3): 343-354. ISSN: 0042-0816.

BLOCK, E. 1970. Communicating with the Urban Poor: An Exploratory Inquiry. Journalism Quarterly. 1970; 47: 3-11. ISSN: 0022-5533.

BRAND, STEWART. 1987. The Media Lab: Inventing the Future at M.I.T. New York, NY: Penguin Books; 1987. 285p. ISBN: 0-670-81442-3.

BRIMMER, KARL W. 1982. U.S. Telecommunications Common Carrier Policy. In: Williams, Martha E., ed. Annual Review of Information Science and Technology: Volume 17. White Plains, NY: Knowledge Industry Publications, Inc. for the American Society for Information Science; 1982. 33-81. ISSN: 0066-4200; ISBN: 0-86729-032-3.

BROWN, ELEANOR FRANCES. 1971. Library Service to the Disadvantaged. Metuchen, NJ: Scarecrow Press; 1971. 560p. ISBN: 0-8108-0437-9.

BRYANT, JENNINGS. 1991. Alabama Information Age Task Force: Founding a First-World Alabama: The Report of the Alabama Information Age Task Force. Birmingham, AL: BellSouth Services, Corporate and Community Affairs; 1991 October. 98p. Available from: the author, College of Communication, The University of Alabama, Tuscaloosa, AL 35487.

BUNDY, M.L. 1972. Urban Information in Public Libraries. Library Journal. 1972; 97: 161-169. ISSN: 0363-0277.

CARNEVALE, MARY LU. 1990. Bell Firms Get Data-Services Opening, But Long-Distance, Gear Curbs Upheld. Wall Street Journal. 1990 April 4; 122(66): A3. ISSN: 0099-9660.

CASEY, GENEVIEVE M. 1972. Public Library Service for the Urban Disadvantaged. Detroit, MI: Wayne State University; 1972. 168p. ERIC: ED 075058.

CHATMAN, ELFREDA A. 1983. The Diffusion of Information among the Working Poor. Berkeley, CA: University of California-Berkeley; 1983. 279p. (Ph.D. dissertation). Available from: University Microfilms International, Ann Arbor, MI. (UMI order no. 83-28818).

CHATMAN, ELFREDA A. 1987. Opinion Leadership, Poverty, and Information Sharing. RQ. 1987 Spring; 26(3): 341-353. ISSN: 0033-7072.

CHEN, CHING-CHIH. 1982. Citizens' Information Needs: A Regional Investigation. In: Stueart, Robert D., ed. Information Needs of the 80s: Libraries and Information Services Role in "Bringing Information to People," Based on the Deliberations of the White House Conference on Library and Information Services. Greenwich, CT: JAI Press; 1982. 77-94. ISBN: 0-89232-164-4.

CHERRY, COLIN. 1985. The Age of Access: Information Technology and Social Revolution: Posthumous Papers of Colin Cherry. (Edited by W. Edmundson). London, England: Croom Helm; 1985. 192p. ISBN: 0-7099-3458-0.

CHILDERS, THOMAS. 1984. Information and Referral: Public Libraries. Norwood, NJ: Ablex; 1984. 307p. ISBN: 0-89391-147-X.

CHILDERS, THOMAS; POST, JOYCE A. 1975. The Information-Poor in America. Metuchen, NJ: Scarecrow Press; 1975. 182p. ISBN: 0-8108-0775-0.

CLEVELAND FREE-NET. 1990. Cleveland Free-Net Community Computer System: General Information Sheet. Cleveland, OH: Cleveland Free-Net; 1990. 4p. Available from: T.M. Grundner, National Public Telecomputing Network, Box 1987, Cleveland, OH 44106.

CLEVELAND, HARLAN. 1985. The Twilight of Hierarchy: Speculations on the Global Information Society. In: Guile, Bruce R., ed. Information Technologies and Social Transformation. Washington, DC: National Academy Press; 1985. 55-80. (Series on Technology and Social Priorities). ISBN: 0-309-03529-5.

CONHAIM, WALLYS W. 1989a. Local Services Begin to Develop on RBOC Gateways. Information Today. 1989 May; 6(5): 43-45. ISSN: 8755-6286.

CONHAIM, WALLYS W. 1989b. Videotex Leaders Call for Cooperation and Consistency. Information Today. 1989 September; 6(8): 32-34. ISSN: 8755-6286.

CONHAIM, WALLYS W. 1990a. Developing Videotex As a Consumer Medium. Information Today. 1990 March; 7(3): 31. ISSN: 8755-6286.

CONHAIM, WALLYS W. 1990b. RBOC Update: The Opening Gateways. Link-Up. 1990 November/December; 7(6): 18-19, 34-35. ISSN: 0739-988X.

CROWLEY, TERENCE; CHILDERS, THOMAS. 1971. Information Service in Public Libraries: Two Studies. Metuchen, NJ: Scarecrow Press; 1971. 210p. ISBN: 0-8108-0406-9.

DAHL, ROBERT A. 1957. The Concept of Power. Behavioral Science. 1957; 2: 201-205. ISSN: 0005-7940.

DAHL, ROBERT A. 1989. Democracy and Its Critics. New Haven, CT: Yale University Press; 1989. 397p. ISBN: 0-300-04409-7.

DAHL, ROBERT A. 1990. After the Revolution? Authority in a Good Society. Revised ed. New Haven, CT: Yale University Press; 1990. 145p. ISBN: 0-300-04964-3.

DANZIGER, JAMES N. 1985. Social Science and the Social Impacts of Computer Technology. Social Science Quarterly. 1985 March; 66(1): 3-21. ISSN: 0038-4941.

DE LURY, N.A. 1985. Maggie's Place III: The Second Generation of an Advanced Library Computer System. Library Hi Tech News. 1985; 22: 1, 7-9. ISSN: 0741-9058.

DEAHL, THOMAS F. 1976. The Model Cities Community Information Center: The Philadelphia Experiment in Automating an Information and Referral Program. See reference: KOCHEN, MANFRED; DONOHUE, JOSEPH C., eds. 114-132.

DERVIN, BRENDA. 1976. The Everyday Information Needs of the Average Citizen: A Taxonomy for Analysis. See reference: KOCHEN, MANFRED; DONOHUE, JOSEPH C., eds. 19-38.

DERVIN, BRENDA; FRASER, BENSON. 1985. How Libraries Help. Sacramento, CA: California State Library; 1985 October. 33p.

DERVIN, BRENDA; NILAN, MICHAEL. 1986. Information Needs and Uses. In: Williams, Martha E., ed. Annual Review of Information Science and Technology: Volume 21. White Plains, NY: Knowledge Industry Publications, Inc. for the American Society for Information Science; 1986. 3-33. ISSN: 0066-4200; ISBN: 0-86729-209-1.

DERVIN, BRENDA; ZWEIZIG, DOUGLAS; BANISTER, MICHAEL; GABRIEL, MICHAEL; HALL, EDWARD P.; KWAN, COLLEEN. 1976. The Development of Strategies for Dealing with the Information Needs of Urban Residents: Phase I—The Citizen Study. Seattle, WA: University of Washington, School of Communications; 1976. 968p. (Final report on project number L0035JA to the U.S. Office of Education). ERIC: ED 125640.

DILLMAN, D. 1986. The Social Impacts of Information Technologies in Rural North America. Rural Sociology. 1985; 50: 1-26. ISSN: 0036-0112.

DOCTOR, RONALD D. 1991. Information Technologies and Social Equity: Confronting the Revolution. Journal of the American Society for Information Science. 1991 April; 42(3): 216-228. ISSN: 0002-8231.

DOCTOR, RONALD D.; TURNER, PHILIP M. 1991. NREN and Information Democracy: A Presentation to the Continuing Education Program for NASA Librarians. Tuscaloosa, AL: University of Alabama, Graduate School of Library Service; 1991 May 23. 75p. ERIC: ED 338243.

DONOHUE, JOSEPH C. 1976. The Public Information Center Project. See reference: KOCHEN, MANFRED; DONOHUE, JOSEPH C., eds. 79-93.

DONOHUE, JOSEPH C.; KOCHEN, MANFRED. 1976. Community Information Centers: Concepts for Analysis and Planning. See reference: KOCHEN, MANFRED; DONOHUE, JOSEPH C., eds. 7-18.

DORDICK, HERBERT S. 1991. Toward a Universal Definition of Universal Service. In: Institute for Information Studies. Universal Telephone Service: Ready for the 21st Century? Falls Church, VA: The Institute; 1991. 109-140. ISBN: 0-89843-108-5.

DOWLIN, KENNETH E. 1984. The Electronic Library: The Promise and the Process. New York, NY: Neal-Schuman; 1984. 199p. ISBN: 0-918212-75-8.

DOWLIN, KENNETH E. 1985. The Integrated Library System. The Electronic Library. 1985 December; 3(5): 340-345. ISSN: 0264-0473.

DURRANCE, JOAN C. 1984. Armed for Action: Library Response to Citizen Information Needs. New York, NY: Neal-Schuman; 1984. 190p. ISBN: 0-918212-71-5.
DUTTON, WILLIAM H.; ROGERS, EVERETT M.; JUN, SUK-HO. 1987. Diffusion and Social Impacts of Personal Computers. Communication Research. 1987 April; 14(2): 219-250. ISSN: 0093-6502.
EDELMAN, HENDRIK, ed. 1986. Libraries and Information Science in the Electronic Age. Philadelphia, PA: ISI Press; 1986. 177p. ISBN: 0-89495-058-4.
ESTABROOK, LEIGH. 1979. Emerging Trends in Community Library Services. Library Trends. 1979; 28(2): 151-164. ISSN: 0024-2594.
FOLEY, TIMOTHY J. 1987. The Design, Implementation, and Evaluation of a Campus-Wide Electronic Information System. Bethlehem, PA: Lehigh University; 1987. 163p. (Ph.D. dissertation). Available from: University Microfilms International, Ann Arbor, MI. (UMI order no. 88-06578).
FOLEY, TIMOTHY J. 1989. Managing Campus-Wide Information Systems. In: Proceedings of the 17th Association for Computing Machinery (ACM) SIGUCCS User Services Conference; 1989 October 1-4; Bethesda, MD. New York, NY: ACM; 1989. 169-174. ISBN: 0-89791-330-2.
FOLEY, TIMOTHY J. 1991. Developing a Campus Computing and Information Policy: Issues and Concerns. Cause/Effect. 1991 Winter; 14(4): 25-29. ISSN: 0164-534X.
FOLEY, TIMOTHY J.; LUCIA, JOE; WEINER, KEVIN R. 1992. Lehigh's Second Generation Campus-Wide Information System. Paper presented at: IBM Informa '92; 1992 May 10; Hilton Head, SC. 16p. Available from: the authors, Lehigh University, Computer Center, Bethlehem, PA 18105.
FORSMAN, CAROLYN. 1976. Crisis Information Services to Youth. See reference: KOCHEN, MANFRED; DONOHUE, JOSEPH C., eds. 133-143.
FOSSIER, MARC; STECKEL, MARIE-MONIQUE. 1991. France Telecom: An Insiders Guide. 2nd edition. Chicago, IL: Intertec Publishing Corp.; 1991 May. 78p. ISBN: 0-91745-14-5.
FRANCE TELECOM. 1991. 1990 Annual Report. Paris, France: France Telecom; 1991. 51p. Available from: France Telecom, Inc., Rockefeller Center, Ste. 2703, 1270 Avenue of the Americas, New York, NY 10020.
GANDY, OSCAR H., JR. 1988. The Political Economy of Communications Competence. In: Mosco, Vincent; Wasko, Janet, eds. The Political Economy of Information. Madison, WI: University of Wisconsin Press; 1988. 108-124. ISBN: 0-299-11570-4.
GANDY, OSCAR H., JR. 1989. The Surveillance Society: Information Technology and Bureaucratic Social Control. In: Siefert, Marsha; Gerbner, George; Fisher, Janice, eds. The Information Gap: How Computers and Other New Communication Technologies Affect the Social Distribution of Power. New York, NY: Oxford University Press; 1989. 61-76. ISBN: 0-19-506468-2.
GOLDMAN, ALVIN L. 1972. Toward a Theory of Social Power. Philosophical Studies. 1972; 23: 221-268. ISSN: 0031-8116.
GRUNDNER, T.M. 1990a. Free-Netting: The Development of Free, Public Access Community Computer Systems. In: Parkhurst, Carol A., ed. Li-

brary Perspectives on NREN. Chicago, IL: Library and Information Technology Association; 1990 June. 51-52. ISBN: 0-8389-9477-5.

GRUNDNER, THOMAS M. 1990b. The Bluebook: A Guide to the Development of Free-Net Community Computer Systems. Cleveland, OH: The National Public Telecomputing Network; 1990 June. 31p. Available from: the author, National Public Telecomputing Network, Box 1987, Cleveland, OH 44106.

GRUNDNER, THOMAS M. 1992. Community Computing and the National Public Telecomputing Network. Cleveland, OH: The National Public Telecomputing Network; 1992 May. 5p. Available from: the author, National Public Telecomputing Network, Box 1987, Cleveland, OH 44106.

GUTHRIE, K. KENDALL; DUTTON, WILLIAM H. 1992. The Politics of Citizen Access Technology: The Development of Public Information Utilities in Four Cities. Paper presented at: 42nd Annual International Communication Conference; 1992 May 21-25; Miami, FL. 30p. Available from: William H. Dutton, Annenberg School for Communication, University of Southern California, University Park, Los Angeles, CA 90089-0281.

GUTHRIE, K. KENDALL; SCHMITZ, JOSEPH; RYU, DAEHEE; HARRIS, JOHN; ROGERS, EVERETT M.; DUTTON, WILLIAM H. 1990. Communication Technology and Democratic Participation: The PEN System in Santa Monica. Paper presented at: Computers and the Quality of Life; 1990 September 13-16; Washington, DC. 45p. Available from: Annenberg School for Communication, University of Southern California, Los Angeles, CA 90089-0281.

HALLMAN, JUDY. 1992a. List of Campus-Wide Information Systems (CWIS). 1992 April 7. Available as "cwis-l" on the Internet via Anonymous FTP to ftp.oit.unc.edu in subdirectory pub/docs or contact HALLMAN@ UNC.BITNET.

HALLMAN, JUDY. 1992b. Campus-Wide Information Systems. Chapel Hill, NC: University of North Carolina; 1992 April 29. (Unpublished paper). Available from: the author, University of North Carolina, Chapel Hill, NC 27599.

HAWAII. 1988. Hawaii Telecommunications and Information Industries Act. Act 1 (H.B. No. 2032), SpSLH 1988.

HAWAII INC. 1992. Hawaii FYI: Your Quick and Easy Way to Information. Honolulu, HI: State of Hawaii; 1992. 37p. Available from: Hawaii, Inc.

HESS, KARL. 1979. Community Technology. New York, NY: Harper & Row; 1979. 107p. ISBN: 0-06-011874-1.

HILTZ, S.R. 1971. Black and White in the Consumer Financial System. American Journal of Sociology. 1971; 76: 987-998. ISSN: 0002-9602.

HIMMELFARB, GERTRUDE. 1984. The Idea of Poverty: England in the Early Industrial Age. New York, NY: Alfred A. Knopf; 1984. 596p. ISBN: 0-394-53062-4.

HIMMELFARB, GERTRUDE. 1991. Poverty and Compassion: The Moral Imagination of the Late Victorians. New York, NY: Alfred A. Knopf; 1991. 475p. ISBN: 0-679-40119-9.

HOCHSCHILD, JENNIFER L. 1981. What's Fair: American Beliefs about Distributive Justice. Cambridge, MA: Harvard University Press; 1981. 345p. ISBN: 0-674-95086-0.

HOCHSCHILD, JENNIFER L. 1988. The Double-Edged Sword of Equal Opportunity. See reference: SHAPIRO, IAN; REEHER, GRANT, eds. 1988a. 168-200.

HOLT, GLEN E. 1991. A Community Information System for the City of St. Louis. St. Louis, MO: St. Louis Public Library; 1991 July 17. 21p. (Unpublished paper). Available from: the author, St. Louis Public Library, 1301 Olive St., St. Louis, MO 63103.

HOUSEL, THOMAS J.; DAVIDSON, WILLIAM H. 1991. The Development of Information Services in France: The Case of Public Videotex. International Journal of Information Management. 1991; 11: 35-54. ISSN: 0268-4012.

INTERNATIONAL RESEARCH ASSOCIATES. 1963. Access to Public Libraries: A Research Project Prepared for the Library Administration Division, American Library Association. Chicago, IL: American Library Association; 1963. 160p.

JONES, CLARA STANTON, ed. 1978. Public Library Information & Referral Service. Syracuse, NY: Gaylord; 1978. 265p. ISBN: 0-915794-06-3.

KAHN, ALFRED J. 1969. Theory and Practice of Social Planning. New York, NY: Russell Sage Foundation; 1969. 348p. LC: 79-81406.

KAHN, ALFRED J.; GROSSMAN, LAWRENCE; BANDLER, JEAN; CLARK, FELICIA; GALKIN, FLORENCE; GREENAWALT, KENT. 1966. Neighborhood Information Centers: A Study and Some Proposals. New York, NY: Columbia University School of Social Work; 1966. 150p.

KARRAKER, ROGER. 1991. Highways of the Mind. Whole Earth Review. 1991; 70: 4-11. ISSN: 0749-5056.

KIDD, JERRY S. 1976. Determining Information Needs of Civic Organizations and Voluntary Groups. See reference: KOCHEN, MANFRED; DONOHUE, JOSEPH C., eds. 39-54

KOCHEN, MANFRED. 1976. What Makes a Citizen Information System Used and Useful. See reference: KOCHEN, MANFRED; DONOHUE, JOSEPH C., eds. 149-170.

KOCHEN, MANFRED; DONOHUE, JOSEPH C., eds. 1976. Information for the Community. Chicago, IL: American Library Association; 1976. 282p. ISBN: 0-8389-0208-1.

KOMINSKI, ROBERT. 1988. Computer Use in the United States: 1984. Washington, DC: Government Printing Office; 1988 March. 29p. (Current Population Reports, Special Studies, Series P-23 No. 155). OCLC: 17827733.

KRANZBERG, MELVIN. 1967. Prerequisites for Industrialization. In: Kranzberg, M.; Pursell, C.W., Jr., eds. Technology in Western Civilization. New York, NY: Oxford University Press; 1967. Volume 1: 217-230. LC: 67-15129.

KRANZBERG, MELVIN. 1985. The Information Age: Evolution or Revolution? In: Guile, Bruce R., ed. Information Technologies and Social Transformation. Washington, DC: National Academy Press; 1985. 35-54. (Series on Technology and Social Priorities). ISBN: 0-309-03529-5.

KRANZBERG, MELVIN; PURSELL, CARROLL W., JR., eds. 1967a. Technology in Western Civilization. Volume 1: The Emergence of Modern Industrial Society: Earliest Times to 1900. New York, NY: Oxford University Press; 1967. 802p. LC: 67-15129.

KRANZBERG, MELVIN; PURSELL, C.W., JR., eds. 1967b. Technology in Western Civilization. Volume 2: Technology in the Twentieth Century. New York, NY: Oxford University Press; 1967. 772p. LC: 67-15129.

LANE, NANCY D. 1991. Teletext and Videotex. In: Lane, Nancy D.; Chisholm, Margaret E., eds. Information Technology: Design and Applications. Boston, MA: G.K. Hall & Co.; 1991. 119-139. ISBN: 0-8161-1908-2

LANE, ROBERT E. 1988. Experiencing Money and Experiencing Power. See reference: SHAPIRO, IAN; REEHER, GRANT, eds. 1988a. 80-105.

LAROSE, ROBERT; METTLER, JENNIFER. 1989. Who Uses Information Technologies in Rural America. Journal of Communication. 1989 Summer; 39(3): 48-60. ISSN: 0021-9916.

LARSEN, GITTE. 1988. Maggie's Place III: An Electronic Library Revisited. The Electronic Library. 1988 December; 6(6): 404-406. ISSN: 0264-0473.

LASKOWSKI, LINDA J. 1990. Videotex & the Regional Bell Operating Companies: What Works and What Doesn't Work. Paper presented at: BUS-03 session, Gateways & Emerging Information Services, NCF90: National Communications Forum; 1990 October 8-10; Rosemont, IL. Available from: the author, US West Communications, 1801 California St., Room 1620, Denver, CO 80202.

LASSWELL, HAROLD. 1936. Politics: Who Gets What How? New York, NY: McGraw-Hill; 1936. 264p.

LAUTENBERG, F.R. 1984. Equity in Computer Education. Computing Teacher. 1984 April; 11(8): 13-14. ISSN: 0278-9175.

LEVINE, F.J.; PRESTON, E. 1970. Community Resource Orientation among Low-Income Groups. Wisconsin Law Review. 1970; 80: 80-113. ISSN: 0043-650X.

LEVINSON, RISHA W. 1988. Information and Referral Networks: Doorways to Human Services. New York, NY: Springer; 1988. 227p. ISBN: 0-8261-4820-4.

LEVINSON, RISHA W.; HAYNES, KAREN S., eds. 1984. Accessing Human Services: International Perspectives. Beverly Hills, CA: Sage Publications; 1984. 320p. ISBN: 0-8039-2388-0.

LEVY, FRANK S.; MELTSNER, ARNOLD J.; WILDAVSKY, AARON. 1974. Urban Outcomes: Schools, Streets and Libraries. Berkeley, CA: University of California Press; 1974. 278p. ISBN: 0-520-02546-6.

LINDEN, FABIAN. 1984. (Letter to the Editor, Response to Thurow Article). New York Times. 1984 March 4; Section 3, p. 14, Col. 3.

LIPSMAN, CLAIRE K. 1972. The Disadvantaged and Library Effectiveness. Chicago, IL: American Library Association; 1972. 197p. ISBN: 0-8389-0129-8.

LONG, NICHOLAS. 1976. Information and Referral Services: A Short History and Some Recommendations. See reference: KOCHEN, MANFRED; DONOHUE, JOSEPH C.; eds. 55-73.

LONG, NICHOLAS; ANDERSON, JACQUELINE; BURD, REGINALD; MATHIS, MARY ELIZABETH; TODD, SELDON P. 1971. Information and Referral Centers: A Functional Analysis. Washington, DC: Government Printing Office; 1971. 47p. (DHEW Publication No. (OHD) 75-20235).

LONG, NICHOLAS; REINER, STEVEN; ZIMMERMAN, SHIRLEY. 1973. Information and Referral Services: The Resource File. 3rd edition. Washington, DC: U.S. Department of Health, Education and Welfare, Administration on Aging; 1973. 115p. (OHD/AOA 73-20111). SUDOC: HE17.308/2:R31.
LOUIS HARRIS & ASSOCIATES. 1984. Highlights of the Road after 1984: Study of the Impact of Technology on Society. In: Privacy and 1984: Public Opinions on Privacy Issues. Hearing before the Government Information, Justice, and Agriculture Subcommittee of the House Committee on Government Operations, 98th Congress, 1st Session, 1984 April 4. Washington, DC: Government Printing Office; 1984. 25-75. OCLC: 11228782.
LUCY, WILLIAM H.; MLADENKA, KENNETH R. 1978. Handbook for Analyzing the Distribution of Library Services. Washington, DC: The Urban Management Curriculum Development Project, The National Training and Development Service; 1978. Available as part of ERIC: ED 194671.
LUKE, A.W. 1974. Bringing the Library to the Unserved. Santa Monica, CA: System Development Corporation; 1974.
LUKES, STEVEN. 1974. Power: A Radical View. London, England: Macmillan Press, Ltd.; 1974. 64p. ISBN: 0-333-16672-8.
MAAS, NORMAN; DE SANTIS, MAGGIE. 1982. Building Constituent Bases: Support and Growth for Community I&R. Information and Referral: The Journal of the Alliance of Information and Referral Systems. 1982 Winter; 4(2): 42-60. ISSN: 0278-2383.
MACAULAY, LORD T.B. 1877. Lord Macaulay on American Institutions. Harper's New Monthly Magazine. 1877 February; 54: 460-462.
MACHLUP, FRITZ. 1962. The Production and Distribution of Knowledge in the United States. Princeton, NJ: Princeton University Press; 1962. 416p. LC: 63-7072.
MACIUSZKO, KATHLEEN. 1990. A Quiet Revolution: Community Online Systems. Online. 1990 November; 14(6): 24-32. ISSN: 0146-5422.
MAGRATH, LYNN L. 1989. The Public and the Computer: Reactions to a Second Generation Online Catalog. Library Trends. 1989 Spring; 37(4): 532-537. ISSN: 0024-2594.
MALYSHEV, NINA ALEXIS. 1986. Converting Pikes Peak Library District's Community Databases. In: Williams, Martha E.; Hogan, Thomas H., comps. Proceedings of the 7th National Online Meeting; 1986. May 6-8; New York, NY. Medford, NJ: Learned Information; 1986. 275-280. ISBN: 0-938734-12-1.
MARCH, JAMES G. 1988. Preferences, Power and Democracy. See reference: SHAPIRO, IAN; REEHER, GRANT, eds. 1988a. 50-66.
MARKUSON, BARBARA EVANS. 1991. Networks for Networkers II Conference. Washington, DC: The Library of Congress; 1991 March. 30p. OCLC: 23728092.
MARTIN, LOWELL. 1969. Library Response to Urban Change: A Study of the Chicago Public Library. Chicago, IL: American Library Association; 1969. 313p.
MARTIN, WILLIAM, ed. 1975. Library Services to the Disadvantaged. Hamden, CT: Linnet Books; 1975. 185p. ISBN: 0-208-01372-5.

MARTINEZ, MICHAEL E.; MEAD, NANCY A. 1988. The Nation's Report Card. Computer Competence: The First National Assessment. Princeton, NJ: Educational Testing Service; 1988 April. 85p. ERIC: ED 341375.

MAYO, JOHN S. 1985. The Evolution of Information Technologies. In: Guile, Bruce R., ed. Information Technologies and Social Transformation. Washington, DC: National Academy Press; 1985. 7-34. (Series on Technology and Social Priorities). ISBN: 0-309-03529-5.

MCCLURE, CHARLES R.; BISHOP, ANN P.; DOTY, PHILIP; ROSENBAUM, HOWARD. 1991. The National Research and Education Network (NREN): Research and Policy Perspectives. Norwood, NJ: Ablex; 1991. 744p. ISBN: 0-89391-813-X.

MEDNICK, RUTH W. 1976. Staffing and Training Patterns for an Information and Referral Service: The Baltimore Experience. See reference: KOCHEN, MANFRED; DONOHUE, JOSEPH C., eds. 102-113.

MORAN, JULIO. 1990. Computers Forge PEN Pal Link. Los Angeles Times. 1990 February 25; J5-J6.

MOSCO, VINCENT. 1988a. Introduction: Information in the Pay-Per Society. In: Mosco, Vincent; Wasko, Janet, eds. The Political Economy of Information. Madison, WI: University of Wisconsin Press; 1988. 3-26. ISBN: 0-299-11570-4.

MOSCO, VINCENT. 1988b. Whose Computer Revolution Is It? Information Technology and Libraries. 1988 December; 7(4): 341-348. ISSN: 0730-9295.

MOSCO, VINCENT. 1989a. Deja Vu All Over Again? Society. 1989 July 1; 26(5): 31-38. ISSN: 0147-2011.

MOSCO, VINCENT. 1989b. The Pay-Per Society: Computers and Communication in the Information Age. Essays in Critical Theory and Public Policy. Norwood, NJ: Ablex; 1989. 247p. ISBN: 0-89391-604-8.

MOSCO, VINCENT. 1990. The Mythology of Telecommunications Deregulation. Journal of Communication. 1990 Winter; 40(1): 36-49. ISSN: 0021-9916.

NAGEL, JACK H. 1975. The Descriptive Analysis of Power. New Haven, CT: Yale University Press; 1975. 200p. ISBN: 0-300-01729-4.

NAGEL, JACK H. 1988. The Marriage of Normative Values and Empirical Concepts: Mutual Integrity or Reciprocal Distortion? See reference: SHAPIRO, IAN; REEHER, GRANT, eds. 1988a. 73-79.

NASAR, SYLVIA. 1992. Rich Keep Getting Richer, Latest Figures Disclose. Tuscaloosa News (Alabama). 1992 March 5; 8A.

NATIONAL BOOK COMMITTEE. 1967. Neighborhood Library Centers and Services. 2nd edition. New York, NY: National Book Committee; 1967. 60p. ERIC: ED 019093.

NATIONAL CITIZENS' ADVICE BUREAUX (NACAB). 1990. NACAB Annual Report 1989/90: Answers for the Nineties. London, England: NACAB; 1990. 24p. Available from: NACAB, Myddelton House, 115-123 Pentonville Rd., London, NI-9LZ, England.

NATIONAL CITIZENS' ADVICE BUREAUX COMMITTEE. 1961. Advising the Citizen. London, England: National Council of Social Service; 1961. 56p. LC: 66-50169.

NATIONAL COMMISSION ON LIBRARIES AND INFORMATION SCIENCE. 1991. Information 2000: Library and Information Services for the 21st Century: Summary Report of the 1991 White House Conference on Library and Information Services (WHCLIS); 9-13 July 1991; Washington, DC. Washington, DC: Government Printing Office; 1991. 77p. ISBN: 0-16-035978-3.

NELSON, NANCY MELIN. 1989. Library Technology: Uncover, OPACs, NeXT, Kids, and More. Information Today. 1989 May; 6(5): 37-38. ISSN: 8755-6286.

NEW YORK UNIVERISTY. 1969. A Study of Library Services for the Disadvantaged in Buffalo, Rochester and Syracuse. New York, NY: New York University, Center for Field Research and School Services, School of Education; 1969. 360p. ERIC: ED 033734.

NIELSEN, BRIAN. 1992. Campus-Wide Information Systems: Leadership Roles for Libraries, Early Planning and Implementation Issues. Paper presented at: IBM Informa '92; 1992 May 10; Hilton Head, SC. 16p. Available from: the author, Northwestern University Library, Evanston, IL 60208.

NSF NETWORK NEWS. 1987. NSF-Sponsored IP Networks. NSF Network News. 1987 July; 1: 6. Available from: NSF Network Service Center, BBN Systems and Technologies, 10 Moulton St., Cambridge, MA 02138.

NSF NETWORK NEWS. 1991. NSFNET Mid-Level Wide Area Networks. NSF Network News. 1991 February; 9: 4-5. Available from: NSF Network Service Center, BBN Systems and Technologies, 10 Moulton St., Cambridge, MA 02138.

NSF NETWORK NEWS. 1992. Networks Connected to the NSFNET Backbone. NSF Network News. 1992 March; 11: 6-10. Available from: NSF Network Service Center, BBN Systems and Technologies, 10 Moulton St., Cambridge, MA 02138.

NSF NETWORK SERVICE CENTER. 1992a. FYI on Where to Start: A Bibliography of Internetworking Information. Cambridge, MA: NSF Network Service Center (NNSC). Available on Internet from info-server@nnsc.nsf.net, as userdoc-bibliography.

NSF NETWORK SERVICE CENTER. 1992b. Internet Resource Guide. Cambridge, MA: NSF Network Service Center. (Updated periodically). Available on Internet from resource-guide-request@nnsc.nsf.net.

NYHAN, MICHAEL; JOHANSEN, ROBERT; PLUMMER, ROBERT. 1981. The USA. In: Winsbury, Rex, ed. Viewdata in Action: A Comparative Study of Prestel. New York, NY: McGraw-Hill; 1981. 211-219. ISBN: 0-07-084548-4.

OETTINGER, ANTHONY. 1992. Information Democracy: Is the Free Market Failing Us? Paper to be presented at: Annual Meeting of the American Society for Information Science; 1992 October 26-29; Pittsburgh, PA. Available from: the author, Program on Information Resources Policy, Harvard University, 200 Aiken Computation Lab., 33 Oxford St., Cambridge, MA 02138.

OGBURN, WILLIAM F. 1964. On Culture and Social Change: Selected Papers. (Edited by O.D. Duncan). Chicago, IL: University of Chicago Press; 1964. 360p. LC: 64-23418.

OGG, ELIZABETH. 1969. Tell Me Where to Turn: The Growth of Information and Referral Services. New York, NY: Public Affairs Committee; 1969. 28p. LC: 77-2121.

PADOVER, SAUL K., ed. 1953. The Complete Madison: His Basic Writings. New York, NY: Harper; 1953. 361p. LC: 53-5445. (The quote originally appeared in a letter from Madison to W.T. Barry, August 4, 1822).

PARKER, EDWIN B.; PAISLEY, WILLIAM J. 1966. Patterns of Adult Information Seeking. Stanford, CA: Stanford University, Institute of Communications Research; 1966. 1 volume (discontinuous paging). ERIC: ED 010294.

PEPPI, CAROLE E. 1976. The Citizens' Advice Bureaux. See reference: KOCHEN, MANFRED; DONOHUE, JOSEPH C., eds. 94-101.

PORAT, MARC URI. 1978. Communication Policy in an Information Society. In: Robinson, Glen O., ed. Communications for Tomorrow: Policy Perspectives for the 1980s. New York, NY: Praeger; 1978. 3-60. ISBN: 0-030-46546-X.

PORAT, MARC URI; RUBIN, MICHAEL ROGERS. 1977. The Information Economy. Washington, DC: U.S. Department of Commerce, Office of Telecommunications; 1977. 9 volumes. (OT Special Publication 77-12). OCLC: 3075693.

RAE, DOUGLAS W. 1988. Knowing Power: A Working Paper. See reference: SHAPIRO, IAN; REEHER, GRANT, eds. 1988a. 17-49.

REYNOLDS, T.S. 1984. Medieval Roots of the Industrial Revolution. Scientific American. 1984 July; 251(1): 122-130. ISSN: 0036-8733.

RICH, RICHARD C. 1977. Equity and Institutional Design in Urban Service Delivery. Urban Affairs Quarterly. 1977 March; 12(3): 383-410. ISSN: 0042-0816.

RIEGER, J.H.; ANDERSON, R.C. 1968. Information Sources and Need Hierarchies of an Adult Population in Five Michigan Counties. Adult Education Journal. 1968; 18: 155-177. ISSN: 0001-8481.

ROBINS, K.; WEBSTER, F. 1979. Mass Communications and Information Technology. In: Miliband, R.; Saville, J., eds. Socialist Register. London, England: Merlin; 1979. 285-316. ISBN: 0-85036-252-0.

ROBINS, K.; WEBSTER, F. 1983. The Mis-Information Society. Universities Quarterly. 1983; 37(4): 344-355. ISSN: 0041-9230.

RUBIN, MICHAEL ROGERS. 1989. The Size and Shape of the Information Economy: An Historical Overview. In: Information: A Strategy for Economic Growth. Washington, DC: Special Libraries Association; 1990. 1-6. ISBN: 0-87111-050-3.

SACKMAN, HAROLD. 1971. Mass Information Utilities and Social Excellence. Princeton, NJ: Auerbach; 1971. 284p. ISBN: 0-87769-065-0.

SACKMAN HAROLD; BOEHM, BARRY, eds. 1972. Planning Community Information Utilities. Montvale, NJ: AFIPS Press; 1972. 501p. ISBN: 0-88283-000-7.

SACKMAN, HAROLD; NIE, NORMAN, eds. 1970. The Information Utility and Social Choice: Papers Prepared for a Conference Sponsored Jointly by the University of Chicago, Encyclopedia Britannica and the American Federation of Information Processing Societies; 1969 December 2-3; Chicago, IL. Montvale, NJ: AFIPS Press; 1970. 299p. LC: 78-129364.

SAMUELSON, PAUL A.; NORDHAUS, WILLIAM D. 1985. Economics. 12th edition. New York, NY: McGraw-Hill; 1985. 950p. ISBN: 0-07-054685-1.
SANTA MONICA. 1989a. Public Electronic Network: Getting Started on PEN. Santa Monica, CA: City of Santa Monica; 1989. 2p. Available from: PEN, City of Santa Monica, Information Systems Dept., 1685 Main St., P.O. Box 2200, Santa Monica, CA 90407-2200.
SANTA MONICA. 1989b. Public Electronic Network: PEN Basics, A Handbook for the PEN System. Santa Monica, CA: City of Santa Monica; 1989. 37p. Available from: PEN, City of Santa Monica, Information Systems Dept., 1685 Main St., P.O. Box 2200, Santa Monica, CA 90407-2200.
SANTA MONICA. 1990. PEN, Public Electronic Network: Electronic Democracy in Santa Monica. Santa Monica, CA: City of Santa Monica; 1990. 22p. Available from: PEN, City of Santa Monica, Information Systems Dept., 1685 Main St., P.O. Box 2200, Santa Monica, CA 90407-2200.
SCHILLER, DAN. 1982. Telematics and Government. Norwood, NJ: Ablex Publishing; 1982. 237p. ISBN: 0-89391-106-2.
SCHILLER, DAN. 1988. How to Think about Information. In: Mosco, Vincent; Wasko, Janet, eds. The Political Economy of Information. Madison, WI: University of Wisconsin Press; 1988. 27-43. ISBN: 0-299-11570-4.
SCHILLER, HERBERT I. 1981. Who Knows: Information in the Age of the Fortune 500. Norwood, NJ: Ablex; 1981. 187p. ISBN: 0-89391-069-4.
SCHILLER, HERBERT I. 1989. Culture, Inc.: The Corporate Takeover of Public Expression. New York, NY: Oxford University Press; 1989. 201p. ISBN: 0-19-505005-3.
SCHILLER, HERBERT I. 1991. Public Information Goes Corporate. Library Journal. 1991 October 1; 116(16): 42-45. ISSN: 0363-0277.
SCHILLER, HERBERT I.; SCHILLER, ANITA R. 1988. Libraries, Public Access to Information, and Commerce. In: Mosco, Vincent; Wasko, Janet, eds. The Political Economy of Information. Madison, WI: University of Wisconsin Press; 1988. 146-166. ISBN: 0-299-11570-4.
SCHWARTZ, NANCY L. 1988. Disparate and Shared Preferences. See reference: SHAPIRO, IAN; REEHER, GRANT, eds. 1988a. 67-72.
SHAPIRO, IAN; REEHER, GRANT, eds. 1988a. Power, Inequality, and Democratic Politics: Essays in Honor of Robert A. Dahl. Boulder, CO: Westview Press; 1988. 308p. ISBN: 0-8133-0762-7.
SHAPIRO, IAN; REEHER, GRANT. 1988b. Power, Inequality, and Schumpeter's Challenge: An Introductory Essay. See reference: SHAPIRO, IAN; REEHER, GRANT, eds. 1988a. 1-11.
SHAVIT, DAVID. 1984. The Distribution of Public Library Service. Public Library Quarterly. 1984 Summer; 5(2): 59-68. ISSN: 0161-6846.
SHERRILL, LAURENCE L., ed. 1970. Library Service to the Unserved: Papers presented at a Library Conference; 1967 November 16-18; University of Wisconsin-Milwaukee, School of Library and Information Science, Milwaukee, WI. New York, NY: R.R. Bowker; 1970. 116p. ISBN: 0-8352-0396-4; LC: 79-627940.
SIEFERT, MARSHA; GERBNER, GEORGE; FISHER, JANICE, eds. 1989. The Information Gap: How Computers and Other New Communication Technologies Affect the Social Distribution of Power. New York, NY: Oxford University Press; 1989. 232p. ISBN: 0-19-506468-2.

SINGLETON, LOY A.; QUINN, CATHY J. 1991. Alabama's Telecommunication Infrastructure: Overview of the State Local Exchange Industry. Report on a Joint Research Project by the University of Alabama Telecommunication and Film Department and the Telecommunication Division, Alabama Public Service Commission. Tuscaloosa, AL: The University of Alabama, Telecommunication and Film Dept.; 1991. 38p. (Unpublished report). Available from: the authors, Dept. of Telecommunication and Film, College of Communication, University of Alabama, Tuscaloosa, AL 35487.

SMITH, RANDOLPH B. 1990. Future Shock: People Got Hooked But Then Abandoned Telephone "Gateways". Wall Street Journal. 1990 March 15; 122(52): 1, A6. ISSN: 0099-9660.

SPITZER, S.F.; DENZIN, N.K. 1966. Levels of Knowledge in an Emergent Crisis. Social Forces. 1966; 44: 234-237. ISSN: 0037-7732.

ST. GEORGE, ART; LARSEN, RON. 1992. Internet-Accessible Library Catalogs and Databases. Albuquerque, NM: University of New Mexico. Available on Internet with the command GET INTERNET LIBRARY from listserv@unmvm.bitnet. (Updated several times each year).

STUEART, ROBERT D., ed. 1982. Information Needs of the 80s: Libraries and Information Services Role in "Bringing Information to People," Based on the Deliberations of the White House Conference on Library and Information Services. Greenwich, CT: JAI Press; 1982. 192p. ISBN: 0-89232-164-4.

SUOMINEN, ELINA. 1976. Who Needs Information and Why. Journal of Communication. 1976 Autumn; 26(4): 115-119. ISSN: 0021-9916.

TAWNEY, RICHARD HENRY. 1931. Equality. New York, NY: Harcourt, Brace; 1931. 280p. LC: 31-8502.

THUROW, LESTER C. 1984. The Disappearance of the Middle Class. New York Times. 1984 February 5; Section 3, p. 3, col. 1.

TICHENOR, P.J.; DONOHUE, G.A.; OLIEN, C.N. 1970. Mass Media Flow and Differential Growth and Knowledge. Public Opinion Quarterly. 1970; 34: 159-170. ISSN: 0033-362X.

TOFFLER, ALVIN. 1990. Powershift: Knowledge, Wealth and Violence at the Edge of the 21st Century. New York, NY: Bantam Books; 1990. 585p. ISBN: 0-553-05776-6.

U.S. BUREAU OF THE CENSUS. 1988. Who Uses a Computer? Washington, DC: U.S. Department of Commerce, Bureau of the Census; 1988 March. 2p. (Statistical Brief from the Current Population Survey, SB-288).

U.S. CONGRESS. 102ND CONGRESS, 1ST SESSION. 1991. High-Performance Computing Act of 1991: Public Law 102-194, 102nd Congress, 1st Session. 1991 December 9.

U.S. CONGRESS. CONGRESSIONAL BUDGET OFFICE. 1992. Measuring the Distribution of Income Gains. Washington, DC: Congressional Budget Office; 1992 March. 8p. (Unpublished staff working paper). Available from: Congressional Budget Office, Washington, DC.

U.S. CONGRESS. HOUSE. COMMITTEE ON THE BUDGET. 102ND CONGRESS, 1ST SESSION. 1991. The Challenging Distribution of Taxes and Income of Working People. Hearing before the Committee on the Budget.

House of Representatives, 102nd Congress, 1st Session, 1991 July 17. Washington, DC: Government Printing Office; 1991. 71p. ISBN: 0-16-035487-0.

U.S. CONGRESS. OFFICE OF TECHNOLOGY ASSESSMENT. 1990. Critical Connections: Communication for the Future. Washington, DC: Government Printing Office; 1990. 395p. (OTA-CIT-407). LC: 89-600713.

U.S. DEPARTMENT OF EDUCATION. OFFICE OF EDUCATIONAL RESEARCH AND IMPROVEMENT. 1989. Rethinking the Library in the Information Age. Volume 2: Issues in Library Research: Proposals for the 1990s. Washington, DC: Government Printing Office; 1989. 224p. OCLC: 18820533.

U.S. DEPARTMENT OF LABOR. RETRAINING AND REEMPLOYMENT ADMINISTRATION. 1946. To Organize, to Operate Your Community Advisory Center for Veterans and Others. Washington, DC: U.S. Department of Labor, Retraining and Reemployment Administration; 1946. 40p. LC: L46-26.

U.S. DEPARTMENT OF LABOR. RETRAINING AND REEMPLOYMENT ADMINISTRATION. 1947. Community Advisory Centers Face the Future. Washington, DC: U.S. Department of Labor, Retraining and Reemployment Administration; 1947. 22p. LC: L46-158.

U.S. GENERAL ACCOUNTING OFFICE. 1987. Telephone Communications: Cost and Funding Information on Lifeline Telephone Service. Washington, DC: U.S. General Accounting Office; 1987. 32p. (RCED-87-189). Available from: U.S. General Accounting Office, P.O. Box 6015, Gaithersburg, MD 20877.

UDELL, J.G. 1966. Prepurchase Behavior of Buyers of Small Electrical Appliances. Journal of Marketing. 1966; 30: 50-52. ISSN: 0022-2429.

VICKERY, BRIAN; VICKERY, ALINA. 1987. Information Science in Theory and Practice. Boston, MA: Butterworths; 1987. 384p. ISBN: 0-408-10684-0.

VOOS, HENRY. 1969. Information Needs in Urban Areas: A Summary of Research in Methodology. New Brunswick, NJ: Rutgers University Press; 1969. 90p. LC: 68-66113.

WALL STREET JOURNAL. 1990. 5,000,000 Frenchmen, Frenchwomen, French (and American) Business Can't Be Wrong. Wall Street Journal. Western edition. 1990 February 15; 122(33): A5. (France Telecom International Advertisement). ISSN: 0099-9660.

WATKINS, BEVERLY T. 1992a. University Hopes Campuswide Network Will Help Give It a Competitive Edge: Case Western Reserve Banks on System as a Major Factor in Diversifying Student Body. Chronicle of Higher Education. 1992 April 29; 38(34): A18-A20. ISSN: 0009-5982.

WATKINS, BEVERLY T. 1992b. Virginia Tech Forms Partnership to Study an "Electronic Village". Chronicle of Higher Education. 1992 May 6; 38(35): A26. ISSN: 0009-5982.

WEBSTER, FRANK; ROBINS, KEVIN. 1986. Information Technology: A Luddite Analysis. Norwood, NJ: Ablex Publishing; 1986. 387p. ISBN: 0-89391-343-X.

WILLIAMS, K.I. 1964. Social Service Exchanges. Social Work Year Book. 1964; 15: 731-734. ISSN: 0071-0237.

WINSOR, CHARLOTTE B.; BURROWS, LODEMA. 1967. A Study of Four Library Programs for Disadvantaged Persons. New York, NY: Bank Street College of Education; 1967. 88p. ERIC: ED 021592.

WORK, COLIN. 1992. Report of a Survey: Establishing a Core Information Set for Campus-Wide Information Systems (CWIS). Paper presented at: IBM Informa '92; 1992 May 10; Hilton Head, SC. Available from: the author, c.k.work@mail.southampton.ac.uk.

YARNALL, LOUISE. 1989. The New, Improved Government Input Device. CIO. 1989 November; 26-30, 34-35. ISSN: 0894-9301.

YATES, ROCHELLE. 1986. A Librarian's Guide to Telephone Reference Service. Hamden, CT: Library Professional Publications; 1986. 136p. ISBN: 0-208-02083-7.

ZUBOFF, SHOSHANA. 1988. In the Age of the Smart Machine: The Future of Work and Power. New York, NY: Basic Books; 1988. 496p. ISBN: 0-465-03212-5.

ZUCKER, M. 1965. Citizens' Advice Bureaux: The British Way. Social Work. 1965; 10: 85-91. ISSN: 0037-8046.

ZWEIZIG, DOUGLAS. 1973. Predicting Amount of Library Use: An Empirical Study of the Role of the Public Library in the Life of the Adult Public. Syracuse, NY: Syracuse University; 1973. 378p. (Ph.D. dissertation). Available from: University Microfilms International, Ann Arbor, MI. (UM order no. 74-08327).

II

Basic Techniques and Technologies

The chapter that comprises the section on basic techniques and technologies is "Parallel Information Processing" by Edie M. Rasmussen of the University of Pittsburgh. Parallel processing was covered in 1979 in Volume 14 of *ARIST* as a part of Lee Hollaar's chapter on computer architecture ("Unconventional Computer Architectures for Information Retrieval"). The increased importance of this technology, especially as it is the basis for supercomputers (now more correctly referred to as computers with massively parallel architectures), make the Rasmussen chapter particularly timely.

Over the past decade or so, significant progress in computer hardware has led to, among other things, the emergence of several kinds of parallel processing architectures (PPAs), some with thousands of processing nodes. Although these PPAs can be effectively used to solve problems in general computing, they have special advantages in areas such as weather forecasting, image processing, and product engineering, where heavy computation must be independently applied to separate parts of the problem (i.e., weather cells, pixel image elements, and CAD-CAM product elements). Here Rasmussen reviews their relevance to information storage and retrieval (IS&R) problems. Current activities include many research projects and some practical implementations. Her chapter focuses on the use of these parallel processors for processing text, primarily documents and document surrogates. Research on parallel processing of text has developed in two areas: (1) a hardware approach involving the development of special-purpose machines for text processing, and (2) a software approach in which data structures and algorithms are developed for text searching using general-purpose parallel computers. While the design of special-purpose architectures for text was a well-developed field when Lee Hollaar reviewed it for *ARIST*, the use of parallel processors for information processing developed only in the mid- to late 1980s as commercial general-purpose parallel machines became available. Over the past decade, parallel algorithms for the traditional access methods for text (pattern matching, signature files, inverted lists, and clustering) have been developed and implemented, and prototypes and a few commercial systems have emerged. IS&R applications that are especially advantageous for PPAs include clustering and other methods of automatic classification wherein one record or a record pair is processed simultaneously on each node. For the usual class of Boolean retrieval, the PPAs are particularly suited to data sets requiring partitioning because they are too big to be processed by a single processor, even one using industry standard inverted term/index methods.

3 Parallel Information Processing

EDIE M. RASMUSSEN
University of Pittsburgh

INTRODUCTION

Conventional serial architectures, based on the von Neumann paradigm, in which one instruction acts on one datum at a time, have continually improved in speed due to developments in very large-scale integration (VLSI), increased word size, cache memory, and floating point hardware. However, such machines are approaching the fundamental limit in speed imposed by the physical nature of signal transmission (DECEGAMA). At the same time, the demand for computer processing capability continually outstrips the capability of computer architectures to provide it. An obvious solution to the limitation of serial architecture is parallelism, in which tasks, such as data transfer and arithmetic, or logical operations are overlapped or performed simultaneously. In their review of the history of parallelism and supercomputing, HOCKNEY & JESSHOPE point out that parallelism was proposed in Babbage's original design for the analytic engine and was implemented in the first general-purpose electronic digital computer, the ENIAC. Functional parallelism, in which independent units perform different functions, and low-level parallelism at the bit level contribute to the performance of inherently serial architectures.

As PARKINSON (1985, p. 29) has pointed out, "all computers are parallel, but some computers are more parallel than others." Increases in processing speed brought about by functional or bit-level parallelism are still limited by the speed of the central processor, and further improvement requires replicated processing units, allowing parallel

Annual Review of Information Science and Technology (ARIST), Volume 27, 1992
Martha E. Williams, Editor
Published for the American Society for Information Science (ASIS)
By Learned Information, Inc., Medford, N.J.

processing at the task or problem level. The development of vector or pipelined computers in the early 1970s, coupled with improvements in VLSI technology and the development of concurrent programming techniques and experience with experimental machines, led in the late 1970s and early 1980s to the construction of parallel machines with various architectures (GILDER; WILSON).

The focus of this chapter is on the use of these parallel processors for processing text, primarily documents and document surrogates. Research on parallel processing of text has developed in two areas: (1) a hardware approach that involves the development of special-purpose machines for text processing, and (2) a software approach, in which data structures and algorithms are developed for text searching using general-purpose parallel computers. As a general topic, parallel processing of text has not been addressed in *ARIST*. Text retrieval and cluster analysis on one machine, the Distributed Array Processor, have been summarized by WILLETT & RASMUSSEN, and parallel algorithms for the Connection Machine are discussed by STANFILL (1992). An *ARIST* chapter by HOLLAAR (1979) dealt with the design of nonconventional computer architectures for text and database management. Because special-purpose parallel architectures for text processing have also been reviewed by HOLLAAR (1992), HURSON ET AL. (1990), and OZKARAHAN (1986), they are covered here only briefly.

There has been considerable research on the development of parallel processors for operations on formatted databases, in which attributes are associated with specific fields in the record. These database machines (DBMs) have been extensively reviewed (HSAIO; HURSON ET AL., 1989; OZKARAHAN, 1986; SU). However, unformatted data, such as that found in bibliographic or full-text databases, present different problems—i.e., very large databases, unpredictable and complex search patterns that may be located anywhere in the record, and the need to move large amounts of data from secondary storage for processing. With one or two exceptions DBMs have not been used for unformatted text, and thus are not treated here.

The rest of the chapter is organized as follows. Because it is a relatively new area, an overview of parallel processing and a general taxonomy are given, followed by a discussion of parallel processors and parallel algorithms along with an evaluation of parallel performance. Within this context the rationale for parallel processing of text is discussed. Relevant work on parallel data structures and algorithms for searching text and their use in parallel and distributed information retrieval systems are covered. Parallel hardware for text is surveyed briefly. Finally, the parallel component of some new approaches to information retrieval is examined.

PARALLEL PROCESSING

HWANG & BRIGGS identify four levels of parallel processing: (1) at the job or program level, (2) at the task or procedure level, (3) at the interinstruction level, and (4) at the intrainstruction level. For this review, parallel processing is defined as processing that involves simultaneous operations within a program or task by multiple interconnected processors. Distributed processing using a computer network that is physically dispersed and loosely coupled is closely related and is also considered.

The concept of a supercomputer, defined as the most advanced computer architecture of its time, suggests that there is a class of problems demanding the highest performance available. To meet the computational demands of tasks such as structural analysis, weather forecasting, remote sensing, aerodynamic simulations, and high-energy physics, high-performance computing is required. Moreover, as some problems are solved by high-performance computing, new problems arise, which by virtue of their scale or detail require still greater computing power, so that there is a continual demand for increased processing speed. For instance, HWANG & BRIGGS suggest that "weather and climate researchers will never run out of their need for faster computers" (p. 42). In these high-performance areas, parallel processing seems to offer the best hope of meeting the voracious demands for processing power.

The limitation that fundamental physics imposes on the processing potential of a serial processor is a major argument for parallel processing. WILSON plots number of processors against megaflops (millions of floating-point operations per second) per processor to show that there are different routes to the same performance but that to achieve teraflops (trillions of floating-point operations per second) performance, "the only practical approach is to use a very large number (at least tens of thousands) of very fast processors (at least tens of mflops each)" (p.5). However, absolute processing speed is not the only argument for parallel processing. Wilson also points out that due to the economies of scale in VLSI technology, several small processors with a total performance equivalent to a large processor almost invariably cost less than the large processor. SHARP describes other benefits that argue in favor of distributed and parallel processing: high availability, high reliability (graceful degradation), high adaptability through upgrades and incremental growth, consistent response, sharing of resources, and automatic load sharing.

Given the variety of designs that are possible within the general concept of parallel processing, it is not surprising that various attempts have been made to develop a taxonomy to aid in discussion and comparison. The most widely used is the system developed by FLYNN (1966; 1972), who categorized computer architectures according to the nature of the instruction stream (sequence of instructions as performed by the machine) and the data stream (sequence of data called for by the instruction stream). His taxonomy recognized four categories: (1) SISD (single instruction stream, single data stream); (2) SIMD (single instruction stream, multiple data stream); (3) MISD (multiple instruction stream, single data stream); and (4) MIMD (multiple instruction stream, multiple data stream). SISD characterizes the sequential von Neumann machine. A MISD machine would apply multiple instructions to each item of data, and it is difficult to see how such a machine would operate; unless one considers that pipelined machines or pattern-matching hardware fit this definition, there are no examples of this class. According to Flynn's taxonomy, therefore, parallel machines are either SIMD or MIMD. Pipelined vector processors, such as the CRAY Y-MP, and array processors, such as the Connection Machine (CM) and the Distributed Array Processor (DAP), comprise the SIMD class. The MIMD class is more varied and includes both loosely and tightly coupled multiprocessor designs.

Although it is useful and widely recognized, Flynn's classification fails to differentiate the many possible architectures in the MIMD class. Other, more complex taxonomies have been proposed (notably by FENG and by HANDLER) as well as attempts to introduce subclasses into Flynn's scheme (see, for example, HOCKNEY & JESSHOPE as well as SKILLICORN). Hockney and Jesshope present broad structural subdivisions of the MIMD class: pipelined, switched, and network systems. Switched systems are further subdivided into shared-memory and distributed-memory systems, and network systems are divided by topology (e.g., mesh, cube, reconfigurable). Taxonomies such as these are useful mechanisms for thinking about parallelism and for considering the suitability of a parallel architecture for a particular application. Both QUINN and GILDER consider the relative merits of large numbers of simple processors and fewer, more powerful processors.

PARALLEL PROCESSORS

While a wide variety of parallel architectures is available, particularly in the MIMD class, most of the work in parallel text processing has used only a few general-purpose parallel machines or special-purpose hardware devices designed specifically for text. In the SIMD class, some early work was done on the Massively Parallel Processor (MPP), an experimental machine with a 132 x 128 processor grid developed by Goodyear Aerospace Corp. (HOCKNEY & JESSHOPE), but the Distributed Array Processor (DAP) and the Connection Machine (CM) have been the main platforms. In the MIMD class, networks of transputers (reconfigurable microprocessors) in various configurations have been used in a number of studies.

SIMD array processors are comprised of large numbers (4K to 64K in current machines) of simple processing elements (PEs). The large number of PEs is possible because they are relatively simple devices (usually bit-serial) that act synchronously; each PE maintains its own data in a local memory and carries out instructions that are broadcast by a master processor. Through the use of a logical mask, processors may be disabled, so that processing is done only on data that meet programmed conditions. Data and instructions may be broadcast to all PEs, or data may be transferred between PEs through planar shifts or (in some machines) more complex routing.

The first commercial array processor was the DAP, originated by International Computers Ltd. (ICL) and now produced by Active Memory Technology. It is currently available in a range of sizes; a DAP with 4K bit-serial PEs is organized as a 64 x 64 grid. Each PE has a local memory. Communication between processors is via the orthogonal grid, and there are also direct links to the nearest neighbors, allowing both broadcasts and data shifts. In later models a high-speed input–output (I/O) facility was added. Access is via a host Sun or Vax workstation, and the DAP may be programmed in FORTRAN PLUS, a parallel FORTRAN, or APAL, an assembly-level language (TREW).

The Connection Machine CM-2 series produced by Thinking Machines Corp., is available in configurations with 2K to 64K processors, each with a local memory (up to 32 kB in the CM-2 for a total of 2 GB). The system is connected as a hypercube of processor chips, each containing 16 physical processors, allowing efficient methods of interprocessor communication. Although the processors are bit-serial, a floating-point accelerator is available for every 32 processors. The Connection Machine is accessed via a front end such as a Sun workstation. It can be programmed in parallel versions of FORTRAN, C, and LISP. High-speed I/O is provided by the DataVault, a disk configuration with 30 to 60 GB of storage and a transfer rate of 25 MB/second, which may be increased to 100 MB/second by the use of multiple units (THINKING MACHINES CORPORATION). (The latest model Connection Machine, the CM-5 just produced, has MIMD capabilities, with fewer, far more powerful processors (GILDER).)

A third SIMD array processor, the MP-1 from MasPar Computer Corp., is also commercially available but has not been reported as a platform for text processing. TREW compares and evaluates the three major products—DAP, CM, and MP-1.

MIMD computers generally use more powerful processors, often conventional microprocessors, which can act independently. If there are only a few processors, they can share a global memory, but as more processors are added, the possibility of contention increases, and an architecture that provides a local memory for each processor may be preferable. Data communication between processors may be significant, and various approaches for interconnecting the processors have been used, including buses, switching mechanisms, and networks. Multiprocessors are characterized by a shared memory, either global (tightly coupled) or local with shared addressing (loosely coupled). Multicomputers have CPUs with local memory and communicate via message passing (QUINN). MIMD computers have been designed in many configurations, including a hypercube; some systems, such as the Meiko Computing Surface, offer a reconfigurable topology, so that a tree, mesh, or hypercube can be made available (WILSON). TREW & WILSON survey various commercial MIMD architectures. The use of a MIMD architecture introduces additional complexity into the processing environment since the program must be broken down into tasks that are assigned to processors (real or virtual). Factors such as the number of processes created and their assignment to processors, synchronization, the amount of sequential processing, contention for shared data structures, distribution of workload, and efficiency of the parallel algorithm must be considered (QUINN).

Various studies in text processing have used MIMD transputer networks (CRINGEAN ET AL., 1990a; WALDEN & SERE). Transputers are programmable 32-bit RISC (reduced instruction set chip) microprocessors that pass messages via four communications channels that operate independently of processing. Each transputer has on-chip memory, and later models added a floating-point unit. Networks of transputers can be configured using the four available links. OCCAM, an architecture-specific programming language, was designed to be used with transputer systems (BARRON).

PARALLEL ALGORITHMS

While the ideal parallel processor would identify the inherent parallelism in a problem and assign data and tasks to processors in a manner transparent to the user, current parallel processing is under programmer control and requires that the user know the architecture in order to assign data structures and distribute data and/or tasks. JAMIESON distinguishes between the virtual algorithm (the computational steps to be performed for a given task), the ideal algorithm (a parallel algorithm without architectural constraints), and the architecture-dependent algorithm, which results from the binding of the algorithm steps to a particular architecture as data and tasks are assigned to processors. A parallel algorithm to solve a problem can be found by exploiting inherent parallelism in an existing sequential algorithm, creating a new parallel algorithm, or adapting an existing parallel algorithm (QUINN). In fact, parallel algorithms are often designed as a theoretical exercise whether there is an appropriate architecture to implement them or not. The literature on parallel algorithms is extensive (for reviews, see KUNG, MOITRA & IYENGAR, and QUINN).

The SIMD/MIMD classification for parallel processors is also useful in classifying algorithms (KUNG). A typical SIMD algorithm requires synchronous operations under central control and statically partitioned data as well as broadcast rather than routed communications. A MIMD algorithm usually has asynchronous instructions, distributed tasks, static or dynamic partitioning of data, and a relatively high processing-to-communication ratio.

JAMIESON has identified a set of attributes that more fully characterizes parallel algorithms and their relationship to parallel architectures. The first of these, the nature of the parallelism, distinguishes between data parallelism (dividing data among processors, which is often amenable to SIMD processing) and function parallelism (decomposing the algorithm into tasks that are assigned to different processors, implying a MIMD operation). Another feature of the parallelism is the granularity; data granularity refers to the size of the data items processed, while module granularity refers to the amount of processing that can be done independently. Fine-module granularity suggests SIMD execution, while large-grain algorithms suggest MIMD. For example, KUNG classifies image processing as a SIMD algorithm and concurrent database algorithms as MIMD algorithms. The degree of parallelism, uniformity of operations, synchronization requirements, static/dynamic nature of the algorithm, and data dependencies also feature in the choice of a SIMD or MIMD architecture. Although the characteristics of an algorithm may indicate whether it will perform better on a SIMD or MIMD architecture, SIMD algorithms can be performed on a MIMD machine, even if less efficiently by distributing the data over independent processors, but MIMD algorithms are generally not amenable to SIMD operation if they require concurrent independent tasks.

Many text processing operations have characteristics that make them viable candidates for SIMD operations. String searching, or pattern matching, for instance, is fine grained in terms of both data (a single character) and modularity (a single character comparison before communication is required). For other information retrieval problems the identification of a document with a single processor and the large size of the databases to be searched seem to imply a massively parallel processor. HILLIS & STEELE suggest that a massively parallel processor such as the Connection Machine is suitable for a data parallel algorithm, in which the parallelism comes primarily from simultaneous operations across large data sets. However a data parallel algorithm may also be accommodated by a MIMD machine by distributing data over fewer processors and increasing the modular granularity of the processing.

PERFORMANCE EVALUATION

Since most computing environments are largely serial, there is an added cost in software and hardware in implementing and running a parallel application. Therefore, it is desirable to have some way to determine whether a particular problem should be implemented in parallel. Two measures of the performance of parallel algorithms are commonly used: speed-up and efficiency. The speed-up, S_p, with p processors is defined as: $S_p = T_1/T_p$, where T_1 and T_p are the times with 1 and p processors. This measure is more appropriate for a MIMD architecture, where the same problem can usually be run on a varying number of processors. For SIMD machines, T_1 is difficult to measure because the processor is simple and the local memory is limited. A better comparison is: $S_p = T_S/T_p$, where T_S is the time for the best serial algorithm on a conventional processor. Linear speed-up implies a speed-up of p with p processors—i.e., $S_p = p$. (Superlinear speed-up—i.e., $S_p > p$—is controversial and seems to rely on the way the problem is defined (QUINN)). A related measure, the efficiency E_p attained with p processors is defined as: $E_p = S_p/p$, and a value close to unity indicates an effective use of parallel resources. Efficiency is a useful measure in MIMD machines where it can be plotted against number of processors to identify the point of diminishing marginal return for incremental processors and help to identify bottlenecks. PARKINSON (1986) has argued that speed-up and efficiency are less significant for SIMD machines because timing a single bit-serial processor is not meaningful, and even if an inexact match between number of processors and problem size or the nature of the algorithm results in idle processors, it is not significant with large numbers of cheap processors. Measurement of efficiency and speed-up require that the same application be programmed in both serial and parallel environments, which is not always practical. These measures have also been criticized for their failure to take account of other variables, such as the cost to attain a given level of performance (KARP & FLATT; PARKINSON, 1986).

Various methods have been used to measure the performance of parallel information retrieval applications. In addition to comparative measures, such as speed-up and efficiency (in operational systems or simulations), absolute measures, such as mips (millions of instructions per second), average response time per query, and scan rate (document-query comparisons over time) (POGUE & WILLETT, 1987), have been reported. STANFILL (1990) discusses the relative merits of complexity analysis, performance modeling, benchmarks, and timing for parallel performance evaluation. Complexity analysis is complicated by the parallel element. The relative amounts of serial and parallel processing and the speed of certain kinds of operations in a particular environment may make a seemingly efficient algorithm parallelize poorly. Performance modeling adds timing data to the complexity analysis and perhaps a simulation, but the necessary simplifications limit reliability in predicting system behavior. There are no standard benchmarks for information retrieval performance (at least in terms of efficiency), although STANFILL & THAU describe a synthetic database with variable parameters that could be replicated by other researchers. Timing figures can represent a realistic measure of parallel efficiency, but they must be interpreted cautiously because processor speed improves with new technical developments so that published figures do not indicate present potential for a particular parallel application. Moreover, many published timing figures are for a subsystem, and may measure processing time on locally stored data, eliminating I/O costs, which are a major factor in operational systems.

An indication of the speed-up that may be obtained by a parallel algorithm is given by a consideration of Amdahl's law, which states that the maximum speed-up that can be obtained in a problem in which a fraction s of the total work is sequential is given by:

$$S_p \leq \frac{1}{s + (1-s)/p}$$

This implies that a few sequential operations can significantly limit the speed-up obtained by parallel computation (QUINN). For example, if 10% of the operations are necessarily sequential, Amdahl's law indicates that the maximum attainable speed-up is 10 no matter how many processors are used. Recently, however, the relevance of Amdahl's law to practical applications has been questioned (GUSTAFSON; KARP & FLATT). In many applications s is a function of problem size, and an effective parallel algorithm is one in which the value of s decreases and maximum attainable speed-up increases as the problem is scaled up.

Processor speed is often measured in terms of attainable performance (mips or flops), but other hardware factors also affect performance. HWANG & BRIGGS discuss the problem of balancing the bandwidth—the number of operations performed per unit time—over the system. In general, for a processor cycle time t_p, a main memory cycle time t_m, and an average access time t_a for I/O devices, t_p and t_m are measured in nanoseconds and t_a in milliseconds, and $t_a \gg t_m > t_p$. Therefore, processing bandwidths must be matched to avoid a bottleneck in the system. For information retrieval where the amount of I/O may be significant, high-speed data transfer or efficient data filtering will be needed to avoid bottlenecks. Recent models of the DAP and the CM have introduced improved data transfer methods to handle this problem.

PARALLEL INFORMATION PROCESSING

The tasks for which many parallel processors were designed (artificial intelligence (AI), image processing, and scientific calculations) are particularly computationally intensive. The typical numeric application requires large amounts of computational time with minimal use of secondary storage and I/O. Nonnumeric applications, on the other hand, tend to be less computationally intensive and to rely more on I/O and large amounts of secondary storage. Therefore, the rationale for using parallel processors in text processing differs from that for scientific computing. AGOSTI relates the file characteristics and functionality of an information retrieval system to the development of special-purpose devices such as associative memories. These devices incorporate information processing functions, such as file searching in hardware, in order to improve performance. Agosti suggests that because of the special characteristics of text files and processing, conventional computer systems are less suitable than these special-purpose devices.

Most nonnumeric processing has been carried out on conventional sequential architectures, but it can also be adapted to general-purpose parallel architectures. Unlike the hardware devices mentioned above, these architectures are not designed with text processing in mind. STANFILL (1990) suggests that the fundamental reason to use a parallel computer for an information retrieval system is speed. The increased computational power can be used to improve response time, to search larger databases, to use improved algorithms, and to reduce search costs. Cost analysis has not been a major consideration in the literature of parallel information retrieval. Most work has concentrated on providing response times to databases of a realistic size consistent with an interactive system while using access methods not commonly used in current commercial systems. In many cases the speed of a parallel processor has been used to eliminate index-based access to a document collection, thus eliminating storage and update overheads.

Information retrieval has been seen as a natural application for parallel processing because of the obvious parallelism in many commonly used algorithms. Data parallelism, for instance, occurs naturally in searching a body of text for a query pattern or in searching a large document collection for occurrences of a particular combination of index terms. Ranking or clustering algorithms can be viewed as a series of repeated nearest-neighbor searches, with the same calculation repeated for every document–document or document–query pair. Depending on the way in which data are assigned to processors, these tasks can be characterized as fine-grained data-parallel operations or coarse-grained asynchronous operations, so that both SIMD and MIMD architectures can be used, although the implementations will be quite different.

While the inherent parallelism in information retrieval makes it a suitable candidate for implementation on a parallel processor, it is not a typical parallel application because its complexity is a linear rather than an exponential function of the size of the database: $O(N)$ or $O(\log N)$ depending on the data structure used. Moreover, as the size of the database increases, the amount of data that is transferred to primary memory increases, so that data transfer rather than processing speed may be the limiting factor. COCKSHOTT, in an article on "Disadvantages of Parallelism in Text Retrieval," argues that an indexed approach is always better than a brute-force approach since the former is linear in the number of terms in the query or the size of the answer set rather than the size of the database. He also argues that the problem should be "squeezed. . .down to an algorithm of minimal complexity" before parallelism is invoked as a last resort. However, the indexed approach has limitations and overheads associated with it, and for large databases a parallel, unindexed approach may be preferable. Problems such as document or term clustering, which are $O(N^2)$ or greater are obvious choices for parallel implementation. In practice, of course, aside from the fact that serial processing of indexed databases has been the norm, there is no reason *not* to implement a problem in parallel unless it is economically indefensible.

The above discussion assumes that what is being parallelized is some aspect of text processing or information retrieval that has traditionally been performed on a serial architecture. However, one could also justify the use of parallel processing to implement techniques that have not been possible because of processing restrictions or to develop new ways of processing text that are based on a parallel environment, such as the incorporation of network models for information retrieval. Innately parallel areas that are developing rapidly in other fields are neural-network and spreading-activation models and the use of genetic algorithms for heuristic solutions to complex problems (RASMUSSEN). Novel parallel applications to information retrieval are discussed later.

PARALLEL ACCESS METHODS FOR TEXT

In his survey of access methods for text, FALOUTSOS identifies four classes: (1) full-text scanning, (2) inversion of terms, (3) multi-attribute retrieval methods (signature files), and (4) clustering methods. Parallel algorithms for all of these methods have been developed and studied, and SIMD and MIMD machines have been used. On a SIMD architecture, data-parallel algorithms and fine-grained data structures, which assign a single character, document number, or text signature to each processor, are suitable. On a MIMD architecture, individual tasks or segments of the document database or index have been assigned to individual processors. Previous descriptions of parallel information retrieval techniques have focused on specific platforms. WILLETT & RASMUSSEN describe parallel algorithms for searching and clustering databases on the Distributed Array Processor, and STANFILL (1992) describes and provides pseudocode, complexity analysis, and performance modeling for a number of parallel algorithms for information retrieval on the Connection Machine. In the sections that follow, SIMD and MIMD implementations of parallel algorithms for access methods for text are summarized.

Pattern Matching

SIMD. One of the earliest applications of parallel array processors to text was pattern matching (string searching): the identification of a target string or pattern within a body of text. Since string searching is a serial character-by-character examination of a file, it avoids the storage and update overheads associated with indexes while allowing the identification of patterns with left- and right-hand truncation, and variable- and fixed-length "don't care" characters at a cost of requiring many more processing cycles. A serial search of a large file is a relatively slow operation, but if many characters can be searched simultaneously, pattern matching is a small-grained highly parallel operation. Since array processors can have thousands of simple processors, the storage of a single character of text in each processor suggests that with an appropriate algorithm, an efficient way to scan a large body of text could be found.

An early report of a pattern-matching algorithm implemented on the Massively Parallel Processor (MPP) (MEILANDER) is typical. Text was organized as a contiguous string of 16,384 characters, one character for each of the MPP's 16K processors. As a target character was broadcast to all processors, a logical bit map was generated to show the processors where a match was found, then it was shifted to the next character until the target pattern was complete. Logical operators could also be applied, and the system could determine whether words were in the same sentence, paragraph, or document; the system could also handle initial and final as well as variable-length internal "don't care" conditions. For simple queries, the limitation in throughput was the input data rate of

1.28 x 10^9 bits/sec, but with more complex queries, the processing capability was the limiting factor. A composite 100-character query would take about 3½ min in a 30-GB full-text source.

The effectiveness of a Distributed Array Processor with 4K PEs for string matching was shown in work on protein and nucleic acid sequences, which, like text, can be represented as one-dimensional character strings (COULSON ET AL.; LYALL ET AL.). The rate of sequence comparisons is said to match that of a CRAY-1 while being considerably more cost effective. Early in its development there was considerable interest in nonnumeric applications for the DAP (HOUSE), and text applications were developed by OLDFIELD and CARROLL ET AL. Oldfield used the DAP to prepare abstracts of legal text. To use the parallel capability of the machine, he broadcast words from the lexicon to the processors containing the text in order to identify all occurrences simultaneously, rather than identifying text words in the lexicon (a serial process).

CARROLL ET AL. used the DAP to identify keywords in the natural-language queries for 2,472 titles and abstracts from the INSPEC test collection. For a performance evaluation they implemented a serial version of the same searches on a minicomputer running the Aho-Corasick algorithm and found that the parallel processor gave a speed-up of one to two orders of magnitude. The relative speed depended on the number of patterns matched (for the parallel algorithm) and the number of characters per pattern (for the serial algorithm), illustrating the difficulty of comparing serial and parallel performances. Since the entire data set was held in memory, the performance evaluation compares processing time only. A later version of the DAP addressed the I/O problem by incorporating a Fast Input Output facility capable of transferring 40 MB/sec. PAGE & REDDAWAY used this 32 x 32 DAP-2 to measure search rates for text that ranged from 80 to 700 MB/sec, exceeding the disk transfer capability.

MIMD. While the projects described above have treated pattern matching as a fine-grained data-parallel problem suitable for an array processor, CRINGEAN ET AL. (1988) carried out a simulation that suggested that pattern matching was also an appropriate problem for a MIMD network of transputers. This result was verified when CRINGEAN ET AL. (1990b; 1991) implemented Horspool's modification of the Boyer-Moore algorithm on a transputer network. In their system, pattern matching is the second stage of a document retrieval system providing ranked output. In the first stage, queries are matched against text signatures to eliminate those for which a match could not occur, and documents for signatures that pass this screening are passed to a processor pool where work is assigned to processors as they become available. A root transputer is assigned the tasks of input, processing the query, and comparing the text signatures; it passes possible matches to an 8-MB mass storage transputer, which distributes data to and collects results from a triple chain of transputers. These chained transputers constitute a processor pool or farm to which data are dynamically allocated when a processor is available for work. The mean time to search a query on a database of 6,004 titles and abstracts was 11.0 sec using a 15-processor pool, representing a speed-up S_{15} of 12.4.

Text Signatures

SIMD. Array processors are particularly efficient at handling bit-level formatted data. If the memory associated with the processors is viewed as a series of planes across the processor array, then formatted data allow each processor to address the same respective location in its associated memory when searching for a value in a particular field. Text signatures, which reduce variable-length unformatted data to a fixed-length bit-string representation indicating the content of the text, are thus well suited to processing by SIMD machines such as the Connection Machine and the Distributed Array Processor.

POGUE & WILLETT (1987) used text signatures to search standard test collections of up to 27,361 documents on the Distributed Array Processor and reported scan rates large enough to suggest that a viable search system could be supported. Such a system was reported by STANFILL & KAHLE, who tested a signature-based retrieval system incorporating query term weights and relevance feedback on a memory-resident database of 31,994 Reuters news releases (18 MB) on a 16K processor prototype of the Connection Machine (the CM-1). They reported a search time of 4 msec for a 25-term Boolean query and estimated a search time of 2 minutes for the same query in a 15-GB database, including I/O time. In discussing this work, WALTZ compared a parallel search time of 40 msec for 40 MB of text to a serial machine operating at 6,645 mips.

The CM system proved controversial. SALTON & BUCKLEY (1988b) critiqued both its effectiveness and efficiency. They compared the results obtainable on a set of document test collections using binary document weights (as in the CM implementation) with those using "tfxidf" (term-frequency, inverse-document frequency) weights and found a significant improvement if document terms were weighted. They also pointed out that a direct comparison with a serial search is misleading because large document collections are not searched serially but use indexes to reduce the portion of the file that must be examined. On this basis they suggested that a Sun-3 workstation operating at 3.5 mips could approach the performance of the CM for the text retrieval operations. STONE used the CM system as the basis for considering the effect of processor parallelism and I/O operations on system performance. He based his analysis on two idealized machines, one similar to the CM, the other having the same memory size and I/O subsystem but a single processor. Because the parallel machine scans much more data than necessary, he calculated the effective speed-up for 64K processors exclusive of I/O effects to be about 64; in the case study, the parallel algorithm required two to 2,000 times as much I/O activity, so Stone concluded that for realistic parameters of the problem, the single processor operating an algorithm with indexing would be faster than the 64K processors running the parallel algorithm without indexing. Stone recommended the implementation of a parallel version of the indexed algorithm. STANFILL (1988) reexamined the data based on a 64K processor Connection Machine (the CM-2) that would allow a database up to 2 GB and calculated a speed-up of 80 times over a 10-mips serial machine in an interactive system and 50 times in a batch system.

MIMD. WALDEN & SERE showed that a MIMD architecture can also be used for signature-based retrieval. Their implementation was developed on Hathi-2, a multiprocessor system of reconfigurable IMS T800 transputers. Documents represented by text signatures (512 bits for each word of text) were distributed over the network of slave transputers; a master process communicated each encoded query word to the slave processes, which carried out a serial scan of their stored documents and returned the results to the master process. Tree and ring configurations were tested, and speed-up close to linear was found for a 10-MB database with 15 processors.

The two-stage transputer-based system developed by CRINGEAN ET AL. (1990b; 1991), described in the previous section, used a text-signature search for a screening mechanism to identify potential document-query matches for the second-stage pattern-matching operation. A full system description is given in CRINGEAN ET AL. (1990a).

Inverted Index Algorithms

SIMD. STANFILL ET AL. responded to the criticisms of their signature-based retrieval system by SALTON & BUCKLEY (1988b) and STONE by developing a parallel version of the inverted index algorithm. Their mailbox algorithm allows ranking of documents against queries and permits interactive searching of databases on secondary storage. The optimal number of processors for cost effectiveness depends on database size and processor and storage costs. For a 100-GB database, 32 disks and 8K processors are suggested. However, with this algorithm data must be transferred between processors in processing a query, and data transfer is slower than computation. Therefore,

STANFILL (1990) modified the algorithm to use partitioned posting files, in which the postings list for each term is stored within specified row boundaries in memory. This method requires more processing when the database is constructed but eliminates the large amount of data transfer in the mailbox algorithm. The parallel algorithm was tested on a synthetic 64-GB database on a 4K processor CM and compared with the serial inverted file algorithm on a Sun-4/280 for a calculated speed-up of approximately 400. Further work (STANFILL & THAU) suggests three possible hardware configurations and I/O strategies, indicating that databases of up to 8192 GB could be searched with response times between milliseconds and seconds, depending on the configuration and database size.

ASOKAN ET AL. also implemented an indexed algorithm on the Connection Machine, based on a hash table that pointed to a list of document numbers for each word. Clusters of processors handled each query word and called for its associated list of document numbers, which were then combined in a modified bitonic sort, duplicates were deleted after scoring for multiple occurrences, and the documents were than ranked. Term weights do not appear to have been used. The system was tested on a database of 512 documents. Using the Distributed Array Processor, REDDAWAY combined an index of document numbers for rare terms with a bit-map representation for common terms; proximity data allow the identification of index phrases. Recent documents were DAP resident while older documents were held on disk. Because of compression, the inverted files require from 7.5% to 18% of the text file. Calculated access time to a 20-GB database was 35 queries/sec.

MIMD. HARDWICKE ET AL. developed a transputer-based system for index-lookup of text words, which is similar to inverted file processing, a method for parallel access to a version of the *Collins English Dictionary*. Each transputer stored an alphabetically ordered subsection of the dictionary (one to four transputers were used for this purpose). High-frequency words were removed and were accessed via a trie structure on the root transputer. Words not filtered by this process passed along a chain to the transputer containing the appropriate subdictionary. A binary search was then performed, both with and without an index, and morphological analysis was done if necessary. With four transputers, lookup times were from 0.8 to 2.00 msec/word when the index was used.

Other Vector-Based Methods

SIMD. POGUE & WILLETT (1984) used document vectors without indexing to perform a nearest-neighbor search of several test collections on the Distributed Array Processor. This work illustrates several limitations associated with SIMD architectures. First, parallelism is limited by the number of processors available; in this case, 4,096 documents could be searched simultaneously; for larger collections, several documents were assigned to each processor and searched in multiples of 4,096. Second, the relatively efficient serial algorithm for comparing a query vector with a document vector, in which a pointer is moved along the two ordered lists (terms in the document and terms in the query arranged in alphabetic or numeric-code order), could not be implemented on the parallel architecture since all processors were required to address the same relative memory location simultaneously. Therefore, every query term had to be compared with every document-vector term, giving an $O(NM)$ parallel algorithm vs. an $O(N+M)$ serial algorithm (where N and M are the lengths of the document and query vectors). With these limitations, speed-up factors of eight to 60 were reported over a serial mainframe. However no comparison was made with the still more efficient inverted-file serial algorithm.

MIMD. Another system that used document vectors to produce ranked output to a query was a simulation study of a binary search tree, with each document stored in a bucket forming one of the leaves of the tree (STEWART & WILLETT). The work is based on an algorithm for nearest-neighbor searching of a tree structure in high dimensional space, which was developed by EASTMAN & WEISS. A backtracking search of the tree identified the document most similar to the query. Simulation of three parallel searching techniques showed a sublinear speedup; it was most marked after about ten processors were used and depended on query length and the characteristics of the document collection.

Clustering Methods

Cluster analysis, or automatic classification, has been used to create groups of documents based on the terms they contain or to create groups of terms based on the documents in which they co-occur. It is computationally intensive, particularly for the rigorous methods (such as the hierarchical agglomerative methods) in which the similarity between all document–document pairs must be calculated. This gives a computational requirement of minimally $O(N^2)$ and up to $O(N^5)$ for some methods, thus limiting the size of data set that can be processed. The high degree of parallelism in cluster processing was noted by SALTON & BERGMARK, who used the FPS 190-L, an attached array processor to compare query vectors with centroid and document vectors in searching a clustered document collection, showing a speed-up of 2.5 for host plus array processor over the host alone.

SIMD. RASMUSSEN & WILLETT (1987) used the Distributed Array Processor for nonhierarchic clustering of three test collections of up to 27,361 documents and compared the processing times with those of a serial algorithm based on an inverted file. They found that the parallel algorithm performed substantially less efficiently than a conventional processor using a serial algorithm. One reason was the limited ability of the parallel processor to handle the variable-length document records; another was the efficiency of the serial algorithm, which eliminated calculation of all zero-valued similarities (for pairs that had no common terms). Because the DAP could not address different memory locations in different PEs simultaneously, or handle parallel PE to PE communication, the choice of parallel algorithm was limited. These restrictions do not apply to all SIMD machines, however. This emphasizes the importance of matching the data structure to the hardware and using the best possible serial algorithm when evaluating speed-up. Clustering problems for which the data structure was formatted, such as the use of the Jarvis-Patrick method for bit strings representing chemical structures (RASMUSSEN ET AL.) and hierarchical agglomerative methods for real-valued records, such as survey and census data (RASMUSSEN & WILLETT, 1989), were better suited to the DAP architecture and showed significant speed-up over a serial processor.

MIMD. SHARMA considered the suitability of a hypercube architecture for distributing clusters across processors and searching the clusters in parallel. Clustering the database provided a basis for assigning documents to clusters, thus reducing idle time in the processors. Two mechanisms for allocating documents were proposed, one favoring efficiency and the other effectiveness. Sharma performed a timing analysis, which indicated the point at which the relationship between I/O and computational costs results in diminishing marginal returns as processors are added. The analysis was based on a hypothetical "typical" document collection and published specifications for hypercube architectures.

FRIEDER & SIEGELMANN also considered a clustered database as a basis for allocating documents to a multiprocessor system. Since the problem of mapping documents to processors to achieve an optimal mapping (even distribution and minimal interprocessor communication) is NP complete, they proposed a genetic algorithm to assign documents to processor nodes; the "goodness" of each generation of document allocations was evaluated on the basis of the sum of the cluster diameters it defined. A simulation examined various partitioning schemes and multicomputer architectures (a 16-node hypercube and three mesh configurations) on a small (64 document) database and found that the genetic algorithm provided a better allocation than the best of 100,000 random permutations.

PARALLEL AND DISTRIBUTED INFORMATION RETRIEVAL SYSTEMS

The work described above on data structures and algorithms established that parallel algorithms could be found to implement traditional access methods for text. Recent work has focused on the incorporation of these algorithms in operational information retrieval systems.

The prototype signature-based system developed on the Connection Machine (STANFILL & KAHLE) was implemented as DowQuest, a commercial service offering access to 1 GB of full-text news stories to subscribers of the Dow Jones News/Retrieval Service (WEYER). DowQuest is operated on a 32K processor machine (with a second machine available as backup). From Weyer's perspective as a user, the novelty of the system is not its parallel operation (which is, after all, meant to be transparent to the user) but the underlying retrieval model (which provides natural-language queries, ranked output, and relevance feedback). Since commercial services have been reluctant to offer these features on existing services, it is interesting that the innovative step of mounting the system on a parallel processor has encouraged innovation in this area as well.

AALBERSBERG & SIJSTERMANS designed InfoGuide, a full-text retrieval system implemented on POOMA, a parallel object-oriented MIMD machine; in its prototype version, it has 100 processing nodes and 1.6 GB of internal memory. Each node has 16 MB of local storage and four communications links to other nodes. Every fifth node is connected to a Sun network. The system supports both Boolean and weighted free-text queries as well as browsing of word lists. The inverted files and documents are distributed over the nodes but can be addressed by each interface node. Reported scan rates and response times compare favorably with published data for earlier DAP and CM machines.

Distributed systems have also been seen as a way to improve performance through concurrency. By partitioning data across a number of machines, improved access times, capacity for incremental system growth, and improved reliability and availability can be achieved (MACLEOD ET AL.). Moreover, many identical small machines may be more cost effective than a single large one. Macleod et al. describe the basic facilities required for a distributed information retrieval system: (1) remote operations calls so that functions on a remote node can be invoked; (2) a communications protocol; and (3) a directory system to provide information about objects and their location. By simulating a number of strategies for distributing documents across nodes, a configuration to optimize performance can be found. MARTIN ET AL. examined caching strategies to offset degradation of performance resulting from high volumes of network traffic. Clustering has been proposed as a mechanism for dividing a set of documents across the nodes of a distributed system (FRIEDER & SIEGELMANN; SHARMA).

An early use of a distributed system to search a large file of chemical structures was reported by Chemical Abstracts Service (DITTMAR ET AL.). The database was segmented over a number of minicomputers, each of which searched a portion of the database using a sequential file operation. The search itself was also divided into two functions: one set of minicomputers did an initial screen search to identify potential matches, and a second set carried out the slower atom-by-atom searches to identify true matches (operations that are comparable with a text-signature search followed by a pattern-matching operation for text). By adjusting database segment size and the number of minicomputers for each function, an acceptable response time for online searching could be maintained.

KAPALEASWARAN & RAJARAMAN used four PCs on a local area network (LAN) to provide a selective-dissemination-of-information (SDI) service to a database update of about 8,000 abstracts. The file was partitioned for preprocessing; two methods were used for searching, one by which an index sequential file is stored on each PC and the user profiles are distributed, and another by which the database is partitioned into four subject areas and profiles are assigned to the appropriate partition. Since the processors were not very powerful (AT computers), processing times are reported in hours rather than minutes but compare favorably with a sequential processor in price and performance.

At the other end of the spectrum is another LAN-based system in which a database of MEDLINE and medical records is distributed over a LAN to provide real-time response (YOUNT ET AL.). Each of 32 servers has a 600-MB hard disk; the network links a mix of 386-processor PCs, DEC stations, Microvax IIs, and Sun-3/60s. The system contains 850,000 medical reports and 2,500,000 references and serves over 1,500 users. Reported response times range from 1 to 7 sec for simple high-posting queries. DANZIG ET AL. propose an information retrieval system based on distributed indexing, in which document databases are distributed across an international network.

PARALLEL HARDWARE FOR TEXT

Relatively early in the development of parallel processors, it was suggested that the conventional von Neumann architecture was not particularly suitable for text processing (HOLLAAR, 1979) because it was designed for computational tasks rather than comparing data and because it required that data be moved from secondary to primary memory for processing, which is a relatively slow operation.

STELLHORN proposed a back-end processor to handle the list-merging operations associated with Boolean retrieval. However, index structures that allow more efficient processing of text bring their own problems in the form of storage overheads and the additional processing needed to create and update the indexes. Many designs for hardware solutions to text processing have been proposed; somewhat fewer prototypes have been developed, and a few systems have reached commercial status. Because these systems have been reviewed elsewhere (HOLLAAR, 1979, 1992; HURSON ET AL., 1990; OZKARAHAN, 1986), only a few major ones are mentioned here.

The general hardware solution proposed for pattern matching is a back-end machine that accepts queries and performs a search on data from storage, then reports the results to the front-end machine. The components of such a system are: (1) the search controller, which accepts queries and controls the search; (2) the term comparator, which examines the data as they come off the disk and checks for a match with query terms; and (3) the query resolver, which applies the query logic to the search results (HURSON ET AL., 1990). Designs for the most complex component, the term comparator, include parallel comparators and associative memories, cellular logic, and hardware versions of a finite-state automaton. Parallel comparators have hard-wired registers where search keys are stored and searched as data are streamed through a buffer. Associative memories provide a parallel capability to access memory by content. Cellular comparators provide dynamic reconfigurability so that single cells are programmed to recognize a single character and to generate a match signal. Finite-state machines implement, in hardware, state tables that record transitions between a set of states that indicate a pattern match. OZKARAHAN (1986) discusses the relative advantages and disadvantages of these approaches. Text processors that use these methods include CAFS, RAP.3, a PFSA version of URSA, GESCAN 2, and TRW.

ICL's CAFS (Content-Addressable Filestore) is a search engine that scans material stored on disk at the effective disk-transfer rate. Key channels operate in parallel to match search criteria, while a search-evaluation unit applies the logical constraints in the query. Multiple CAFS units can operate on a single host (CARMICHAEL). RAP.3, originally a DBM, has been augmented with text retrieval capabilities (OZKARAHAN, 1985; 1991). URSA (Utah Retrieval System Architecture) is a full-text retrieval system, which incorporated a variation of the finite-state automata called the partitioned finite-state automata (PFSA) (HOLLAAR, 1985; HOLLAAR ET AL.). Based on his early experience with URSA and recent advances in processor speed and storage capacity, HOLLAAR (1991) suggests a balanced approach using a low-cost searcher on each disk and a small surrogate (such as a partially inverted list with one entry per term per document) to allow initial screening.

Optical technology has been considered as an alternative to magnetic and electronic media for information storage and processing (BERRA & TROULLINOS). MITKAS ET AL. propose a full-text search system on an optical back-end processor. High-speed data transfer would be provided by multiple laser beams for reading data or the use of transmissive optical discs, and optical data processing would allow high-speed comparisons. If feasible, such a system would solve the problem of data-transfer speed and processor limitations in high-speed pattern matching.

NETWORK MODELS FOR INFORMATION RETRIEVAL

Network models for information processing, such as artificial neural networks (ANNs) and spreading-activation models, comprise an active research area. In these models, information is represented as a network of weighted nodes and directed links, and activation and learning rules are applied to generate desired outcomes from entered data. The term "parallel distributed processing" indicates the parallel nature of network models: rules fire and nodes are activated simultaneously across the network. Much of the developmental work in this area has been done on serial processors, but the computation required makes them slow and difficult to scale up, and their implementation on parallel computers is a matter of practical as well as theoretical significance. SINGER compares five reports of ANNs on the Connection Machine and discusses the general issues involved in parallel ANNs. DOSZKOCS ET AL. explore the relationship between network models and the features and goals of information retrieval. They provide a history and tutorial for connectionist models and review applications to information retrieval. A growing body of research considers the use of neural networks (BELEW; KWOK; MACLEOD & ROBERTSON; WILKINSON & HINGSTON) and spreading-activation techniques (COHEN & KJELDSEN; CROFT ET AL.; SALTON & BUCKLEY, 1988a) for information retrieval.

Although there is some research on implementations of connectionist models on parallel hardware and research on connectionist models applied to information retrieval, there is relatively little intersection between these two subsets of the connectionist literature. The study of parallel implementation of network models for information retrieval merits further research.

One study that does combine parallel processing and network models is an interesting implementation of a network model for information retrieval on a 32K Connection Machine (ODDY & BALAKRISHNAN).

This system, PThomas, is related to network-processing techniques such as spreading activation and neural networks. In this study the database consisted of a network of documents, titles, author names, and index terms, with nodes and edges assigned to sets of CM processors. User interaction involved a form of relevance feedback, in which document citations, author names, and index terms were displayed for user reaction. Nodes in the network were selected or inhibited according to the information provided by the user in each iteration. A small database (15 documents) was used and no performance data were given, but the implementation introduces a less traditional approach to information retrieval. Tests on larger databases are needed to evaluate both the machine and retrieval performance. Oddy and Balakrishnan point out that a database of even 10,000 documents could generate a million nodes and edges, thus requiring virtual processors; practical problems would clearly arise with very large databases, and the use of a partitioned network would be necessary.

CONCLUSIONS

Although the design of special-purpose architectures for text was a well-developed field when HOLLAAR (1979) reviewed it for *ARIST*, the use of parallel processors for information processing developed only in the mid- to late 1980s as commercial general-purpose parallel machines became available. Over the past ten years, parallel algorithms for the traditional access methods for text (pattern matching, signature files, inverted lists, and clustering) have been developed and implemented, and prototypes and a few commercial systems have been developed. Valuable lessons have been learned: the need to match the parallel algorithm with the appropriate data structure and architecture, the need to use the best possible serial algorithm when comparing serial and parallel performance, the danger of sacrificing retrieval effectiveness in order to create a high-speed parallel search system, the importance of matching I/O bandwidth with processing speed, and the desirability of balancing cost effectiveness against novelty. Problems remain: the optimum assignment of tasks and data to processors, the appropriate ratio of processors to database size, and ways to minimize the impact of data transfer. Comparisons among systems are difficult, and benchmarks or other standard performance measures are needed, particularly for cost/performance ratios.

With the design of large-scale parallel systems, STANFILL & THAU suggest that although the technology now allows the searching of very large databases, it has outstripped our knowledge of how to apply it. Thus, new methods and algorithms for information processing are needed that will use the increased computational power available to provide more effective and efficient retrieval to large, full-text databases.

BIBLIOGRAPHY

AALBERSBERG, IJSBRAND JAN; SIJSTERMANS, FRANS. 1990. InfoGuide: A Full-Text Document Retrieval System. In: Tjoa, A.M.; Wagner, R., eds. DEXA 90: Database and Expert System Applications: Proceedings of the International Conference; 1990 August 29-31; Vienna, Austria. Vienna, Austria: Springer-Verlag; 1990. 12-21. ISBN: 3-21182-234-8.

AGOSTI, MARISTELLA. 1984. Special-Purpose Hardware and Effective Information Processing. Information Technology. 1984 January; 3(1): 3-14. ISSN: 0144-817X.

ASOKAN, N.; RANKA, SANJAY; FRIEDER, OPHIR. 1990. A Parallel Free-Text Search System with Indexing. In: Rishe, N.; Navathe, S.; Tal, D., eds. Parbase-90: International Conference on Databases, Parallel Architectures, and Their Applications; 1990 March 7-9; Miami Beach, FL. Los Alamitos, CA: IEEE Computer Society Press; 1990. 519-521. ISBN: 0-81862-035-8; LC: 89-80524; IEEE catalog no.: 90CH2728-4.

BARRON, IANN M. 1986. The Transputer and OCCAM. In: Kugler, H.-J., ed. Information Processing 86: Proceedings of the IFIP World Computer Congress; 1986 September 1-5; Dublin, Ireland. New York, NY: Elsevier Science Publishers; 1986. 259-265. ISBN: 2-444-70077-3.

BELEW, RICK. 1989. Adaptive Information Retrieval: Using a Connectionist Representation to Retrieve and Learn about Documents. In: Belkin, N.J.; van Rijsbergen, C.J., eds. SIGIR '89: Proceedings of the Association for Computing Machinery Special Interest Group on Information Retrieval (ACMSIGIR) 12th Annual International Conference on Research and Development in Information Retrieval; 1989 June 25-28; Cambridge, MA. New York, NY: ACM; 1989. 11-20. (Special issue of the SIGIR Forum). ISBN: 0-89791-321-3; OCLC: 22731311.

BERRA, P. BRUCE; TROULLINOS, NIKOS B. 1987. Optical Techniques and Data/Knowledge Base Machines. Computer. 1987 October; 20(10): 59-70. ISSN: 0018-9162.

CARMICHAEL, J.W.S. 1984. The Application of ICL's Content Addressable Filestore to Text Storage and Retrieval. In: Miller, J.J.H., ed. Protext I: Proceedings of the 1st International Conference on Text Processing Systems; 1984 October 24-26; Dublin, Ireland. Dublin, Ireland: Boole; 1984. 3-11. ISBN: 0-906783-39-9; 0-906783-40-2.

CARROLL, DAVID M.; POGUE, CHRISTINE A.; WILLETT, PETER. 1988. Bibliographic Pattern Matching Using the ICL Distributed Array Processor. Journal of the American Society for Information Science. 1988; 39(6): 390-399. ISSN: 0002-8231; CODEN: AISJB6.

COCKSHOTT, PAUL. 1989. Disadvantages of Parallelism in Text Retrieval. In: Colloquium on Parallel Techniques for Information Retrieval; 1989 April 10; London, England. London, England: Institution of Electrical Engineers; 1989. 7/1-7/3. (Digest No.: 189/54). Available from: Institution of Electrical Engineers, Savoy Place, London WC2R OBL.

COHEN, PAUL R.; KJELDSEN, RICK. 1987. Information Retrieval by Constrained Spreading Activation in Semantic Networks. Information Processing & Management. 1987; 23(4): 255-268. ISSN: 0306-4573; CODEN: IPMADK.

COULSON, A.F.W.; COLLINS, J.F.; LYALL, A. 1987. Protein and Nucleic Acid Sequence Database Searching: A Suitable Case for Parallel Processing. Computer Journal. 1987; 30(5): 420-424. ISSN: 0010-4620.

CRINGEAN, JANEY K.; ENGLAND, ROGER; MANSON, GORDON A.; WILLETT, PETER. 1990a. Best Match Searching in Document Retrieval Systems Using Transputer Networks. Report for the Period May 1988 to November 1990 to the British Library Research and Development Department on Project SI/G/814. Sheffield, England: Department of Information Studies and National Transputer Support Centre; 1990 November. (Report No. 6043). Available from: British Library Research and Development Department, 2 Sheraton Street, London W1V 4BH.

CRINGEAN, JANEY K.; ENGLAND, ROGER; MANSON, GORDON A.; WILLETT, PETER. 1990b. Parallel Text Searching in Serial Files Using a Processor Farm. In: Vidick, Jean-Luc, ed. SIGIR '90: Proceedings of the 13th International Conference on Research and Development in Information Retrieval; 1990 September 5-7; Brussels, Belgium. New York, NY: Association for Computing Machinery; 1990. 429-453. ISBN: 0-89791-408-2.

CRINGEAN, JANEY K.; ENGLAND, ROGER; MANSON, GORDON A.; WILLETT, PETER. 1991. Network Design for the Implementation of Text Searching Using a Multicomputer. Information Processing & Management. 1991; 27(4): 265-283. ISSN: 0306-4573; CODEN: IPMADK.

CRINGEAN, JANEY K.; MANSON, GORDON A.; WILLETT, PETER; WILSON, GEORGE A. 1988. Efficiency of Text Scanning in Bibliographic Databases Using Microprocessor-based, Multiprocessor Networks. Journal of Information Science. 1988; 14: 335-345. ISSN: 0165-5515.

CROFT, W.B.; LUCIA, T.J.; CRINGEAN, J.; WILLETT, P. 1989. Retrieving Documents by Plausible Inference: An Experimental Study. Information Processing & Management. 1989; 25(6): 599-614. ISSN: 0306-4573; CODEN: IPMADK.

DANZIG, PETER B.; AHN, JONGSUK; NOLL, JOHN; OBRACZKA, KATIA. 1991. Distributed Indexing: A Scalable Mechanism for Distributed Information Retrieval. In: Bookstein, A.; Chiaramella, Y.; Salton, G.; Raghavan, V.V., eds. SIGIR '91: Proceedings of the Association for Computing Machinery Special Interest Group on Information Retrieval (ACMSIGIR) 14th Annual International Conference on Research and Development in Information Retrieval; 1991 October 13-16; Chicago, IL. New York, NY: ACM; 1991. 220-229. (Special issue of the SIGIR Forum). ISBN: 0-89791-448-1.

DECEGAMA, ANGEL L. 1989. Parallel Processing Architectures and VLSI Hardware: Volume I. Englewood Cliffs, NJ: Prentice Hall; 1989. 478p. ISBN: 0-13-902206-6.

DITTMAR, P.G.; FARMER, N.A.; FISANICK, W.; HAINES, R.C.; MOCKUS, J. 1983. The CAS ONLINE Search System. 1. General System Design and Selection, Generation, and Use of Search Screens. Journal of Chemical

Information and Computer Sciences. 1983; 23: 93-102. ISSN: 0095-2338; CODEN: JCISD8.

DOSZKOCS, TAMAS E.; REGGIA, JAMES; LIN, XIA. 1990. Connectionist Models and Information Retrieval. In: Williams, Martha E., ed. Annual Review of Information Science and Technology: Volume 25. Amsterdam, The Netherlands: Elsevier Science Publishers for the American Society for Information Science; 1990. 209-260. ISSN: 0066-4200; ISBN: 0-444-88531-5; CODEN: ARISBC.

EASTMAN, C.M.; WEISS, S.F. 1982. Tree Structures for High Dimensionality Nearest Neighbor Searching. Information Systems. 1982; 7: 115-122. ISSN: 0306-4379.

FALOUTSOS, CHRISTOS. 1985. Access Methods for Text. Computing Surveys. 1985 March; 17(1): 49-74. ISSN: 0360-0300.

FENG, T.Y. 1972. Some Characteristics of Associative/Parallel Processing. In: Proceedings of the 1972 Sagamore Computer Conference; 1972; Raquette Lake, NY. Syracuse, NY: Syracuse University; 1972. 5-16. OCLC: 1522157.

FLYNN, MICHAEL J. 1966. Very High-Speed Computing Systems. IEEE Proceedings. 1966; 54(12): 1901-1909. ISSN: 0018-9219.

FLYNN, MICHAEL J. 1972. Some Computer Organizations and Their Effectiveness. IEEE Transactions on Computers. 1972; C-21: 948-960. ISSN: 0018-9340.

FRIEDER, OPHIR; SIEGELMANN, HAVA TOVA. 1991. On the Allocation of Documents in Multiprocessor Information Retrieval Systems. In: Bookstein, A.; Chiaramella, Y.; Salton, G.; Raghavan, V.V., eds. SIGIR '91: Proceedings of the Association for Computing Machinery Special Interest Group on Information Retrieval (ACMSIGIR) 14th Annual International Conference on Research and Development in Information Retrieval; 1991 October 13-16; Chicago, IL. New York, NY: ACM; 1991. 230-239. (Special issue of the SIGIR Forum). ISBN: 0-89791-448-1.

GILDER, GEORGE. 1992. Hillis Versus the Law of the Microcosm. Upside. 1992; 24-42. ISSN: 1052-0341.

GUSTAFSON, JOHN L. 1988. Reevaluating Amdahl's Law. Communications of the ACM. 1988 May; 31(5): 532-533. ISSN: 0001-0782.

HANDLER, WOLFGANG. 1977. The Impact of Classification Schemes on Computer Architecture. In: Baer, Jean-Loup, ed. Proceedings of the 1977 International Conference on Parallel Processing; 1977 August 23-26; Wayne State University, Detroit, MI. New York, NY: IEEE; 1977. 7-15. LC: 78-105159.

HARDWICKE, JAMES J.; CONNOLLY, JOHN H.; EDWARDS, JANET. 1991. Parallel Access to an English Dictionary. Microprocessors and Microsystems. 1991 July/August; 15(6): 291-298. ISSN: 0141-9331.

HILLIS, W.D.; STEELE, G.L., JR. 1986. Data Parallel Algorithms. Communications of the ACM. 1986; 29: 1170-1183. ISSN: 0001-0782.

HOCKNEY, R.W.; JESSHOPE, C.R. 1988. Parallel Computers 2: Architecture, Programming and Algorithms. Bristol, England: Adam Hilger; 1988. 625p. ISBN: 0-85274-811-6.

HOLLAAR, LEE A. 1979. Unconventional Computer Architectures for Information Retrieval. In: Williams, Martha E., ed. Annual Review of

Information Science and Technology: Volume 14. White Plains, NY: Knowledge Industry Publications, Inc. for the American Society for Information Science; 1979. 129-151. ISSN: 0066-4200; ISBN: 0-91423-644-X; CODEN: ARISBC.

HOLLAAR, LEE A. 1985. A Testbed for Information Retrieval Research: The Utah Retrieval System Architecture. In: Proceedings of the Association for Computing Machinery Special Interest Group on Information Retrieval (ACMSIGIR) 8th Annual International Conference on Research and Development in Information Retrieval; 1985 June 5-7; Montreal, Quebec. New York, NY: ACM; 1985. 227-232. LC: 86-144096.

HOLLAAR, LEE A. 1991. Special-Purpose Hardware for Text Searching: Past Experience, Future Potential. Information Processing & Management. 1991; 27(4): 371-378. ISSN: 0306-4573; CODEN: IPMADK.

HOLLAAR, LEE A. 1992. Special-Purpose Hardware for Information Retrieval. In: Frakes, William B.; Baeza-Yates, Ricardo, eds. Information Retrieval: Data Structures and Algorithms. Englewood Cliffs, NJ: Prentice-Hall; 1992. 443-458. ISBN: 0-13-463837-9.

HOLLAAR, LEE A.; SMITH, KENT F.; CHOW, WING HONG; EMRATH, PERRY A.; HASKIN, ROGER L. 1983. Architecture and Operation of a Large, Full-Text Information Retrieval System. In: Hsaio, David K., ed. Advanced Database Machine Architecture. Englewood Cliffs, NJ: Prentice-Hall; 1983. 256-299. ISBN: 0-13-011262-3.

HOUSE, STEVEN R. 1984. Symbol Processing on the Distributed Array Processor. In: Feilmeier, M.; Joubert, G.; Schendel, U., eds. Parallel Computing 83: Proceedings of the International Conference on Parallel Computing; 1983 September 26-28; Berlin, Germany. Amsterdam, The Netherlands: North-Holland; 1984. 419-424. ISBN: 0-444-87528-X; LC: 84-6093.

HSAIO, DAVID K. 1983. Advanced Database Machine Architecture. Englewood Cliffs, NJ: Prentice-Hall; 1983. 394p. ISBN: 0-13-011262-3.

HURSON, A.R.; MILLER, L.L.; PAKZAD, S.H.; CHENG, JIA-BING. 1990. Specialized Parallel Architectures for Textual Databases. Advances in Computers. 1990; 30: 1-37. ISSN: 0065-2458; ISBN: 0-12-012130-1.

HURSON, A.R.; MILLER, L.L.; PAKZAD, S.H.; EICH, M.H.; SHIRAZI, B. 1989. Parallel Architectures for Database Systems. Advances in Computers. 1989; 28: 107-151. ISSN: 0065-2458; ISBN: 0-12-012128-X.

HWANG, KAI; BRIGGS, FAYE E. 1984. Computer Architecture and Parallel Processing. New York, NY: McGraw-Hill; 1984. 846p. ISBN: 0-07-031556-6.

JAMIESON, LEAH H. 1987. Characterizing Parallel Algorithms. In: Jamieson, Leah H.; Gannon, Dennis; Douglass, Robert J., eds. The Characteristics of Parallel Algorithms. Cambridge, MA: MIT Press; 1987. 65-100. (MIT Press Series in Scientific Computation). ISBN: 0-262-10036-3.

KAPALEASWARAN, T.N.; RAJARAMAN, V. 1990. Parallel Search Methods of a Document Database in a Distributed Computer System: A Case Study. Journal of Information Science. 1990; 16: 291-298. ISSN: 0165-5515.

KARP, ALAN H.; FLATT, HORACE P. 1990. Measuring Parallel Processor Performance. Communications of the ACM. 1990 May; 33(5): 539-543. ISSN: 0001-0782.

KUNG, H.T. 1980. The Structure of Parallel Algorithms. Advances in Computers. 1980; 19: 65-113. ISSN: 0065-2458; ISBN: 0-12-012119-0.

KWOK, K.L. 1989. A Neural Network for Probabilistic Information Retrieval. In: Belkin, N.J.; van Rijsbergen, C.J., eds. SIGIR '89: Proceedings of the Association for Computing Machinery Special Interest Group on Information Retrieval (ACMSIGIR) 12th Annual International Conference on Research and Development in Information Retrieval; 1989 June 25-28; Cambridge, MA. New York, NY: ACM; 1989. 21-30. (Special issue of the SIGIR Forum). ISBN: 0-89791-321-3; OCLC: 22731311.

LYALL, A.; HILL, C.; COLLINS, J.F.; COULSON, A.F.W. 1986. Implementation of Inexact String Matching Algorithms on the I.C.L. DAP. In: Feilmeier, M.; Joubert, G.; Schendel, U., eds. Parallel Computing 85: Proceedings of the 2nd International Conference on Parallel Computing; 1985 September 23-25; Berlin, Germany. Amsterdam, The Netherlands: North-Holland; 1986. 235-240. ISBN: 0-444-70009-9.

MACLEOD, IAN A.; MARTIN, T. PATRICK; NORDIN, BRENT; PHILLIPS, JOHN R. 1987. Strategies for Building Distributed Information Retrieval Systems. Information Processing & Management. 1987; 23(6): 511-528. ISSN: 0306-4573; CODEN: IPMADK.

MACLEOD, KEVIN J.; ROBERTSON, W. 1991. A Neural Algorithm for Document Clustering. Information Processing & Management. 1991; 27(4): 337-346. ISSN: 0306-4573; CODEN: IPMADK.

MARTIN, T. PATRICK; MACLEOD, IAN A.; RUSSELL, JUDY I. 1990. A Case Study of Caching Strategies for a Distributed Full Text Retrieval System. Information Processing & Management. 1990; 26(2): 227-247. ISSN: 0306-4573; CODEN: IPMADK.

MEILANDER, W.C. 1980. High-Speed Text Retrieval with MPP: A Parallel Processor. In: Benenfeld, Alan R.; Kazlauskas, Edward John, eds. Proceedings of the American Society for Information Science (ASIS) 43rd Annual Meeting: Volume 17; 1980 October 5-10; Anaheim, CA. White Plains, NY: Knowledge Industry Publications, Inc. for ASIS; 1980. 332-334. ISBN: 0-91423-673-3; LC: 64-8303.

MITKAS, PERICLES A.; BERRA, P. BRUCE; GUILFOYLE, PETER S. 1989. An Optical System for Full Text Search. In: Belkin, N.J.; van Rijsbergen, C.J., eds. SIGIR '89: Proceedings of the Association for Computing Machinery Special Interest Group on Information Retrieval (ACMSIGIR) 12th Annual International Conference on Research and Development in Information Retrieval; 1989 June 25-28; Cambridge, MA. New York, NY: ACM; 1989. 98-107. (Special issue of the SIGIR Forum). ISBN: 0-89791-321-3; OCLC: 22731311.

MOITRA, ABHA; IYENGAR, S. SITHARAMA. 1987. Parallel Algorithms for Some Computational Problems. Advances in Computers. 1987; 26: 93-153. ISSN: 0065-2458; ISBN: 0-12-012126-3.

ODDY, ROBERT N.; BALAKRISHNAN, BHASKARAN. 1991. PThomas: An Adaptive Information Retrieval System on the Connection Machine. Information Processing & Management. 1991; 27(4): 317-335. ISSN: 0306-4573; CODEN: IPMADK.

OLDFIELD, D.E. 1984. Document Abstracting on the Distributed Array Processor. In: Paddon, D.J., ed. Supercomputers and Parallel Computation. Oxford, England: Clarendon Press; 1984. 135-146. (The Institute of Mathematics and Its Applications Conference Series, New Series: v. 1). ISBN: 0-19-853601-1.

OZKARAHAN, ESEN. 1985. Evolution and Implementations of the RAP Database Machine. New Generation Computing. 1985; 3: 237-271. ISSN: 0288-3635.

OZKARAHAN, ESEN. 1986. Database Machines and Database Management. Englewood Cliffs, NJ: Prentice-Hall; 1986. 636p. ISBN: 0-13-196031-8.

OZKARAHAN, ESEN. 1991. System Architectures for Information Processing. Information Processing & Management. 1991; 27(4): 347-369. ISSN: 0306-4573; CODEN: IPMADK.

PAGE, R.M.R.; REDDAWAY, S.F. 1990. The DAP as a Filestore Search Engine. Parallel Computing. 1990; 13: 369-376. ISSN: 0167-8191.

PARKINSON, DENNIS. 1985. Supercomputers and Non-Numeric Processing. In: Informatics 8: Advances in Intelligent Retrieval; 1985 April 16-17; Wadham College, Oxford, England. London, England: Aslib; 1985. 28-34. ISBN: 0-85142-195-4.

PARKINSON, DENNIS. 1986. Performance Analysis in a 4096 Processor Environment. Journal of Systems and Software. 1986; 1(2): 11-15. ISSN: 0164-1212.

POGUE, CHRISTINE A.; WILLETT, PETER. 1984. An Evaluation of Document Retrieval from Serial Files Using the ICL Distributed Array Processor. Online Review. 1984; 8(6): 569-584. ISSN: 0309-314X.

POGUE, CHRISTINE A.; WILLETT, PETER. 1987. Use of Text Signatures for Document Retrieval in a Highly Parallel Environment. Parallel Computing. 1987; 4: 259-268. ISSN: 0167-8191.

QUINN, MICHAEL JAY. 1987. Designing Efficient Algorithms for Parallel Computers. New York, NY: McGraw-Hill; 1987. 288p. ISBN: 0-07-051071-7.

RASMUSSEN, EDIE M. 1991. Introduction: Parallel Processing and Information Retrieval. Information Processing & Management. 1991; 27(4): 255-263. ISSN: 0306-4573; CODEN: IPMADK.

RASMUSSEN, EDIE M.; DOWNS, GEOFFREY M.; WILLETT, PETER. 1988. Automatic Classification of Chemical Structure Databases Using a Highly Parallel Array Processor. Journal of Computational Chemistry. 1988; 9(4): 378-386. ISSN: 0192-8651.

RASMUSSEN, EDIE M.; WILLETT, PETER. 1987. Non-Hierarchic Document Clustering Using the Distributed Array Processor. In: Yu, C.T.; van Rijsbergen, C.J., eds. Proceedings of the Association for Computing Machinery Special Interest Group on Information Retrieval (ACMSIGIR) 10th Annual International Conference on Research and Development in Information Retrieval; 1987 June 3-5; New Orleans, LA. New York, NY: ACM; 1987. 132-139. ISBN: 0-89791-232-2.

RASMUSSEN, EDIE M.; WILLETT, PETER. 1989. Efficiency of Hierarchic Agglomerative Clustering Using the ICL Distributed Array Processor. Journal of Documentation. 1989 March; 45(1): 1-24. ISSN: 0022-0418.

REDDAWAY, S.F. 1991. High Speed Text Retrieval from Large Databases on a Massively Parallel Processor. Information Processing & Management. 1991; 27(4): 311-316. ISSN: 0306-4573; CODEN: IPMADK.

SALTON, GERARD; BERGMARK, DONNA. 1981. Parallel Computations in Information Retrieval. Lecture Notes in Computer Science. 1981; 111: 328-342. ISSN: 0302-9743.

SALTON, GERARD; BUCKLEY, CHRIS. 1988a. On the Use of Spreading Activation Methods in Automatic Information Retrieval. In: Chiaramella, Yves, ed. Proceedings of the 11th International Conference on Research and Development in Information Retrieval; 1988 June 13-15; Grenoble, France. New York, NY: Association for Computing Machinery; 1988. 147-160. ISBN: 0-89791-274-8.

SALTON, GERARD; BUCKLEY, CHRIS. 1988b. Parallel Text Search Methods. Communications of the ACM. 1988 February; 31(2): 202-215. ISSN: 0001-0782.

SHARMA, RAVI. 1989. A Generic Machine for Parallel Information Retrieval. Information Processing & Management. 1989; 25(3): 223-235. ISSN: 0306-4573; CODEN: IPMADK.

SHARP, JOHN A. 1987. An Introduction to Distributed and Parallel Processing. Oxford, England: Blackwell Scientific; 1987. 174p. ISBN: 0-632-01462-8.

SINGER, ALEXANDER. 1990. Implementations of Artificial Neural Networks on the Connection Machine. Parallel Computing. 1990; 14: 305-315. ISSN: 0167-8191.

SKILLICORN, DAVID B. 1988. A Taxonomy for Computer Architectures. Computer. 1988 November; 21(11): 46-57. ISSN: 0018-9162.

STANFILL, CRAIG. 1988. Parallel Computing for Information Retrieval: Recent Developments. Cambridge, MA: Thinking Machines Corp.; 1988. 14p. (Technical Report Series DR88-1). Available from: Thinking Machines Corporation, 245 First Street, Cambridge, MA 02142-1264.

STANFILL, CRAIG. 1990. Partitioned Posting Files: A Parallel Inverted File Structure for Information Retrieval. In: Vidick, Jean-Luc, ed. SIGIR '90: Proceedings of the 13th International Conference on Research and Development in Information Retrieval; 1990 September 5-7; Brussels, Belgium. New York, NY: Association for Computing Machinery; 1990. 413-428. ISBN: 0-89791-408-2.

STANFILL, CRAIG. 1992. Parallel Information Retrieval Algorithms. In: Frakes, William B.; Baeza-Yates, Ricardo, eds. Information Retrieval: Data Structures and Algorithms. Englewood Cliffs, NJ: Prentice-Hall; 1992. 459-496. ISBN: 0-13-463837-9.

STANFILL, CRAIG; KAHLE, BREWSTER. 1986. Parallel Free-Text Search on the Connection Machine System. Communications of the ACM. 1986 December; 29(12): 1229-1239. ISSN: 0001-0782.

STANFILL, CRAIG; THAU, ROBERT. 1991. Information Retrieval on the Connection Machine: 1 to 8192 Gigabytes. Information Processing & Management. 1991; 27(4): 285-310. ISSN: 0306-4573; CODEN: IPMADK.

STANFILL, CRAIG; THAU, ROBERT; WALTZ, DAVID. 1989. A Parallel Indexed Algorithm for Information Retrieval. In: Belkin, N.J.; van

Rijsbergen, C.J., eds. SIGIR '89: Proceedings of the Association for Computing Machinery Special Interest Group on Information Retrieval (ACMSIGIR) 12th Annual International Conference on Research and Development in Information Retrieval; 1989 June 25-28; Cambridge, MA. New York, NY: ACM; 1989. 88-97. (Special issue of the SIGIR Forum). ISBN: 0-89791-321-3; OCLC: 22731311.

STELLHORN, WILLIAM H. 1977. An Inverted File Processor for Information Retrieval. IEEE Transactions on Computers. 1977 December; C-26(12): 1258-1267. ISSN: 0018-9340.

STEWART, MARK; WILLETT, PETER. 1987. Nearest Neighbour Searching in Binary Search Trees: Simulation of a Multiprocessor System. Journal of Documentation. 1987 June; 43(2): 93-111. ISSN: 0022-0418.

STONE, HAROLD S. 1987. Parallel Querying of Large Databases: A Case Study. Computer. 1987 October; 20(10): 11-21. ISSN: 0018-9162.

SU, STANLEY Y.W. 1988. Database Computers: Principles, Architectures, and Techniques. New York, NY: McGraw-Hill; 1988. 497p. ISBN: 0-07-062295-7.

THINKING MACHINES CORPORATION. 1991. The Connection Machine CM-200 Series Technical Summary. Cambridge, MA: Thinking Machines Corp.; 1991 June. 124p. Available from: Thinking Machines Corporation, 245 First Street, Cambridge, MA 02142-1264.

TREW, ARTHUR. 1991. SIMD: Specialisation Equals Success. In: Trew, Arthur; Wilson, Greg, eds. Past, Present, Parallel: A Survey of Available Parallel Computing Systems. London, England: Springer-Verlag; 1991. 13-53. ISBN: 3-540-19664-1.

TREW, ARTHUR; WILSON, GREG, eds. 1991. Past, Present, Parallel: A Survey of Available Parallel Computing Systems. London, England: Springer-Verlag; 1991. 392p. ISBN: 3-540-19664-1.

WALDEN, MARINA; SERE, KAISA. 1989. Free Text Retrieval on Transputer Networks. Microprocessors and Microsystems. 1989 April; 13(3): 179-187. ISSN: 0141-9331.

WALTZ, DAVID L. 1987. Applications of the Connection Machine. Computer. 1987 January; 20(1): 85-97. ISSN: 0018-9162.

WEYER, STEPHEN A. 1989. Questing for the "Dao": DowQuest and Intelligent Text Retrieval. Online. 1989 September; 13(5): 39-48. ISSN: 0146-5422.

WILKINSON, ROSS; HINGSTON, PHILIP. 1991. Using the Cosine Measure in a Neural Network for Document Retrieval. In: Bookstein, A.; Chiaramella, Y.; Salton, G.; Raghavan, V.V., eds. SIGIR '91: Proceedings of the Association for Computing Machinery Special Interest Group on Information Retrieval (ACMSIGIR) 14th Annual International Conference on Research and Development in Information Retrieval; 1991 October 13-16; Chicago, IL. New York, NY: ACM; 1991. 202-210. (Special issue of the SIGIR Forum). ISBN: 0-89791-448-1.

WILLETT, PETER; RASMUSSEN, EDIE M. 1990. Parallel Database Processing: Text Retrieval and Cluster Analysis Using the DAP. London, England: Pitman; 1990. 173p. (Research Monographs in Parallel and Distributed Computing). ISSN: 0953-7767; ISBN: 0-273-08828-9.

WILSON, GREG. 1991. An Introduction to Parallel Processing. In: Trew, Arthur; Wilson, Greg, eds. Past, Present, Parallel: A Survey of Available Parallel Computing Systems. London, England: Springer-Verlag; 1991. 1-12. ISBN: 3-540-19664-1.

YOUNT, RUSSELL J.; VRIES, JOHN K.; COUNCILL, CAROLYN D. 1991. The Medical ARchival System: An Information Retrieval System Based on Distributed Parallel Processing. Information Processing & Management. 1991; 27(4): 379-389. ISSN: 0306-4573; CODEN: IPMADK.

III

Applications

The section on applications includes three chapters, "Data Representations for Geographic Information Systems" by Clifford A. Shaffer of Virginia Polytechnic Institute and State University, "Environmental Research: Communication Studies and Information Sources" by Zorana Ercegovac of the University of California at Los Angeles, and "The Information Environment of Managers" by Jeffrey Katzer and Patricia T. Fletcher of Syracuse University.

Clifford Shaffer provide the first *ARIST* chapter on geographical information systems. Shaffer notes that a geographic information system (GIS) is a spatial data application that has seen both great difficulty in implementation and great promise over the past 20–30 years. Despite its inherent complexity, the enormous potential of the GIS has made it widely available and accepted by both government and commercial users. Powerful personal computers with more memory, disk capacity, and CPU power, coupled with a new generation of data structures and algorithms, promise to bring GIS technology to many new users.

Primary applications for GIS technology include forest management, property management, utilities and physical plant management, transportation planning, military planning, agriculture management, and environmental management. In his chapter Shaffer provides a guide to the literature on GIS and a general introduction to the field, concentrating on the state of the art for the representation of spatial data as related GISs.

Shaffer defines GIS terminology and explains GIS data types and operations. He discusses vector and raster representations, elevation data representations, large spatial databases, and the new spatial indexing methods. There is general agreement among the GIS research community that some form of spatial indexing is required to handle modern needs. However, there is considerable controversy as to even the general form such indexing should take. Shaffer identifies problem areas, such as time-varying data and three-dimensional databases, and notes that artificial intelligence (AI) will play a greater role in GIS analysis in the future.

Zorana Ercegovac reviews the literature on international environmental information since 1986 with special emphasis on U.S.-produced machine-readable sources. Two areas selected for particular attention are: (1) environmental communication research, which is subdivided into artifact, user, and risk communication studies; and (2) information sources, which are organized according to pollution medium (e.g., land, water, air), pollutant (e.g., toxic substances, pesticides), and pollution concerns (e.g., risk assessment and safety).

According to Ercegovac the literature suggest the following trends. (1) Research interest in risk communication issues, including experimental laboratory research and field research, has received growing attention in the communication and sociological literature. (2) Published activity in environmental information, unevenly distributed under the three headings of media, pollutants, and pollution concerns, focuses primarily on the descriptive aspects rather than analytical, evaluative, or policy-related questions. (3) A growing number of EPA-produced electronic information resources have become more accessible to the public. She notes that while information sources in various formats, channels, and structures have become more plentiful and accessible, we have not seen much progress in understanding the working habits of various groups of environmentalists and their information-seeking patterns, nor have we significantly advanced our techniques of organizing environmental bibliographic data to help the user move through the information effectively and smoothly. Much research remains to be done in these areas and in the related areas of analysis, modeling, and performance evaluation.

Jeffrey Katzer and Patricia T. Fletcher analyze the information behaviors of managers in terms of a model of their information environment. The model is composed of those factors that view managers as people who work in a specific setting (the organization), take on various roles, and carry out various activities. The model posits that the problematic situations managers face are influenced by these factors and the perceived importance of different problem dimensions that affect how information is valued. The components of the model are used as the framework for reviewing the literature, with the intent of showing how these factors affect information seeking and use by managers. The review also identifies the special challenges that managers pose for the information professional.

Katzer and Fletcher argue that "the information environment of managers is defined by those factors that are related to managers as people who work in a setting, taking on various roles and carrying out various activities." "The goal of the information professional is to provide information services that treat the manager as a 'clinician' who deals with the unique circumstances in a time-compressed complex setting." As noted previously, the manager needs his information screened, synthesized, highlighted, and presented in a useful manner.

4 Data Representations for Geographic Information Systems

CLIFFORD A. SHAFFER
Virginia Polytechnic Institute and State University

INTRODUCTION

A geographic[1] information system (GIS) integrates spatial data with object-attribute data such as are found in traditional database systems. GISs have proven difficult to implement yet have shown great promise over the past 10-20 years. Despite its inherent complexity, the enormous potential of GIS technology has made it widely available and accepted by both government and commercial users. Powerful personal computers with increased memory, more disk space, and more central processing unit power, coupled with a new generation of data structures and algorithms, promise to bring GIS technology to many new users. Primary applications for GISs include forest management, property management, utilities and physical plant management, transportation planning, military planning, and agricultural and environmental management. Notice the key words "planning" and "management" in these descriptions. Both TOMLINSON (1987) and MAGUIRE ET AL. give further details on application areas for GISs.

A GIS lies at the intersection of such fields as architecture, computer science, engineering, forestry, geography, geology, remote sensing, surveying, and government planning. Given such wide application and divergent constituencies, there is no widely accepted definition of a GIS. Its primary purpose is as a tool for decision making and resource

---

[1]In North America, the term geographic is most often used, while in Europe the term is geographical.

Annual Review of Information Science and Technology (ARIST), Volume 27, 1992
Martha E. Williams, Editor
Published for the American Society for Information Science (ASIS)
By Learned Information, Inc., Medford, N.J.

management, most often by government entities (COWEN). According to STAR & ESTES, a true GIS integrates:

- Data collection (acquiring data about the earth either automatically or manually);
- Data processing (organizing the collected data);
- Data organization (using various data structures);
- Data analysis (manipulation of the data for the user's desired result); and
- Data output (e.g., graphical displays and statistical analyses).

MAGUIRE gives a long discussion of the definition and properties of a GIS.

A GIS is notable for its use of graphical display and its ability to do spatial analysis—a primary distinction from computer-aided design (CAD), image processing, or map systems that simply display geographic data by attribute. The canonical example of such spatial analytic capability is polygon overlay, which computes the intersections between two sets of disjoint polygons.

A GIS database is typically very large, in some cases containing data equivalent to tens of thousands of map sheets, with thousands of unique feature types, and requiring gigabytes of storage space. For example, the U.S. Bureau of the Census's TIGER files, used to process the 1990 census and now available to the public, are distributed as a series of 44 CD-ROMs (compact disc–read only memory).

The amount of spatial data becoming available now and in the near future is staggering. NASA's Earth Observing System is expected to produce about 100 GB of new data every day (SIMONETT). Storing these data, while a major undertaking, is possible given recent and expected advances in storage technology. The biggest problem will be to organize the data so that users can find what they need. Thus, techniques for managing large spatial databases (large in amount of data and in total surface area covered) are increasing in importance.

A new way of thinking about spatial data organization has occurred in the past decade with the advent of spatial data indexing methods. Just as any large disk-based collection of records must be indexed for fast access (traditionally by a B-tree or inverted file), so must spatial data. There is now general agreement among the GIS research community that some form of spatial indexing is required to handle modern needs. However, there is considerable controversy as to even the general form such indexing should take. Commercial GIS products have been surprisingly slow to adopt the new data structures technology despite an obvious need for greater processing speed, but there are signs of change. In defense of industry, it should be made clear that the bulk of expense, both in terms of money and labor, still lies in data collection, which masks the need for better data processing performance.

Scope

Since GIS is such a wide field, with many divergent points of view, no survey can hope to cover more than a small part. In particular, the background of the author is sure to influence such work; thus, this review represents one computer scientist's view. This survey attempts to: (1) serve as a general introduction to the field and guide to the GIS literature; and (2) survey the history and state of the art for spatial data representation as it relates to GIS. Whenever possible, I reference works that are likely to be accessible in a good research library. The time period covered is from the mid-1960s to the present.

A GIS database is composed of both spatial data (where objects are, metrical data about their position and shape, and spatial relationships among objects) and attribute data (nonspatial properties of the objects). A typical GIS database might contain 90% attribute data vs. 10% spatial data. However, I concentrate here on representations of spatial data for several reasons. First, attribute data are often represented with standard database technology, such as a relational database management system (RDBMS) (for information about attribute representation methods, see ARONSON and also HEALEY). Second, the spatial data, while a small fraction of the total, are the more expensive to process and the less understood as to their best representation. Third, it has been many years since a survey of spatial data representation techniques for GIS has been done (NAGY & WAGLE; PEUQUET, 1984), with none since the arrival on the research scene of spatial indexing methods. Finally, while there has been a recent explosion in the number of GIS textbooks, recent advances in data representation techniques usually get little attention. Probably the last up-to-date text is the 1986 book by BURROUGH, but that is now becoming outdated. Reasonably good (but short) overviews of spatial data representation can be found in the texts by STAR & ESTES and CLARKE.

Many GISs have a relational database component to store attribute data and a separate spatial data organization. A primary example is ARC/INFO (MOREHOUSE), a widely used commercial GIS. Work has also been done to extend SQL (Standard Query Language) to GIS application by including specifications for graphical display (EGENHOFER). Some researchers have advocated that spatial and attribute data be unified within a single relational database, perhaps augmented by indexing support for spatial keys within the relational table(s) to speed searching of sorted lists (LAURINI & MILLERET;

WAUGH & HEALEY). This approach is based on the idea that it is easier to rely on the theory and existing software of such DBMSs, combined with the expectation that computers will become fast enough to compensate the loss of efficiency resulting from unification. RDBMS advocates note that efficiency may be regained by taking advantage of spatial indexing techniques in the form of sorting objects by their position along a one-dimensional space-filling curve (a key technique from spatial indexing methods). I believe that efficiency is still a major practical issue (which in part motivates this review of spatial data representations) and that current state-of-the-art GIS technology is too slow to handle future needs.

Brief Guide to GIS Literature and Data Sources

GIS use and research constitute a truly international enterprise. Many countries use GISs to organize information about their own resources. British Commonwealth and European countries in particular have long traditions of geographical study, which has translated into world class GIS research. Thus, the journals for the cartographical societies of Germany, France, Sweden, England, Canada, Australia, and the United States all commonly publish articles related to GIS. However, this survey is limited to English-language sources. Further information on GIS literature is given by MAGUIRE ET AL. and by PERKINS & PARRY. The reader should also see various educational and technical publications from the National Science Foundation's National Center for Geographic Information and Analysis (NCGIA)(ABLER).

The following are major archival journals of the respective cartographic societies: *CARTOGRAPHICA*, published by the Canadian Cartographic Society; *THE CARTOGRAPHIC JOURNAL*, published by the British Cartographic Society; *CARTOGRAPHY*, published by the Australian Institute of Cartographers; *CARTOGRAPHY AND GEOGRAPHIC INFORMATION SYSTEMS*, published by the American Congress on Surveying and Mapping. *INTERNATIONAL JOURNAL OF GEOGRAPHICAL INFORMATION SYSTEMS* is a commercial publication devoted entirely to GIS in contrast to the society journals that serve both GIS and traditional cartography communities. *GEO-PROCESSING*, also devoted to GIS, is no longer published. *PHOTOGRAMMETRIC ENGINEERING & REMOTE SENSING* has many GIS and GIS related articles. *GEO INFO SYSTEMS* and *GIS WORLD* are aimed primarily at users, particularly of governmental GIS. Articles relating to GIS also appear in journals from a wide range of fields such as computer science, geology, and surveying.

The following are some major annual or regular conferences. AUTO-CARTO, co-sponsored by the American Society for Photogrammetry and Remote Sensing and the American Congress on Surveying and Mapping, meets every two years in Baltimore, Md. The International Symposium on Spatial Data Handling meets in AUTO-CARTO's off years and is co-sponsored by a number of geographic, information, and computer science societies. Its fifth symposium is scheduled for August 1992. GIS/LIS (Geographic Information Systems/Land Information Systems), URISA (Urban and Regional Information Systems Association), and AM/FM (automated mapping/facilities management) conferences meet annually in the United States. ERIS meets annually in Europe.

The following are some notable special-topic conferences whose proceedings have been published as books. *Building Databases for Global Science* (MOUNSEY & TOMLINSON) covers world-scale databases. *Accuracy of Spatial Databases* (GOODCHILD & GOPAL) treats such issues as improving, certifying, and registering the accuracy of spatial databases. DIAZ & BELL edited the proceedings of a conference on tesseral addressing methods for spatial data. The proceedings of two conferences on large-scale databases were edited by BUCHMANN ET AL. and GÜNTHER & SCHECK. The third conference in this series is scheduled for 1993.

GIS textbooks have been rare until the past couple of years. The one by BURROUGH, published in 1986, had been considered the leader in the field. Other recent GIS textbooks include those by ARONOFF, CLARKE, DALE & MCLAUGHLIN, MONMONIER, and STAR & ESTES. HUXHOLD concentrates on specific applications of GIS to urban planning. PEUQUET & MARBLE provide a good selection of introductory readings on GIS from the published literature; however, most of these papers date from the mid-1980s and thus antedate the recent explosion in personal computing power and GIS data structures technology, which, in combination, promise to alter radically the patterns of GIS use. The two-volume set edited by MAGUIRE ET AL. contains up-to-date articles by many practitioners in the field.

The following are some major literature surveys related to material covered here. PEUCKER & CHRISMAN and PEUQUET (1984) provide early surveys on data structures for GIS. In two journal articles PEUQUET (1981) surveys methods for converting between raster and vector data representations. NIEVERGELT discusses issues related to selecting the proper data representation for a geographic application. NAGY & WAGLE provide a comprehensive and excellent survey of the literature on GIS design and development up to 1979. Although the present survey concentrates on work done since then, much of the work covered by Nagy and Wagle is still relevant. DOYLE surveys traditional representations and operations for digital elevation data. SAMET (1990a; 1990b) provides an extensive survey of and introduction to the use of hierarchical spatial data structures and related methods for various applications including GIS.

In the United States numerous government agencies sell geographic data to the public. A principal source of such data is the TIGER file series (MARX; SOBEL), created by the U.S. Bureau of the Census for the 1990 census and available from the United States Geological Survey (USGS). TIGER databases are widely distributed on CD-ROM; many archival libraries, for example, have these data available for their patrons (although the libraries may not have adequate equipment to deliver the information). Also available from USGS are Digital Line Graph (DLG) data and GBF/DIME data; however, TIGER has largely replaced these. USGS distributes elevation data at scales of 1:250,000 and 1:24,000. Another widely distributed data set is the World Data Bank II, developed by the U.S. CENTRAL INTELLIGENCE AGENCY (CIA) and available from the National Technical Information Service of the Department of Commerce. World Data Bank II is also widely available through public computer network archives. Requiring 12 MB of space in compressed form, it provides coastlines, country and state boundaries, rivers, and other features to resolutions of one second.

Brief History of GIS[2]

The term "geographic information system" dates from the 1970s. The first true GIS was the Canadian Geographic Information System (CGIS) (TOMLINSON ET AL.), created for the Canada Lands Inventory in the mid-1960s. Approved by the Canadian government in 1964, it was initially implemented on what now appears to be impossibly primitive equipment. CGIS was intended to help manage rural agricultural land that was facing urban encroachment. It was operational by 1971 and is still used today. CGIS includes many innovative GIS concepts; Tomlinson goes so far as to say that most GIS capability today is little different from what was developed for CGIS in the 1960s. CGIS was the first vector-based GIS.

The state of Minnesota built a GIS shortly after CGIS was initiated, while the state of New York initiated GIS work that eventually failed because of poor system design (MARBLE). The history of GIS has seen numerous failed attempts, illustrating the unexpected difficulties involved. Note that in the 1960s, nearly all GIS were designed and used by large government entities due to the cost of hardware (and, as was quickly discovered, the costs of software development, data collection,

---

[2]The material in this section is based loosely on information from TOMLINSON (1990) (see also COPPOCK & RHIND).

and training). One notable exception was the Harvard Laboratory for Computer Graphics, which produced the popular raster-based system SYMAP, a cartographic package that was widely distributed to other universities, government agencies, and industry.

The 1970s saw increased governmental interest in GIS since limited natural resources required greater monitoring. Manual processing of geographic data was proving to be too difficult or costly; automation seemed required. The advent of interactive graphics and cheaper memory combined to boost the possibilities for automation at the same time that they widened the field of users who could afford a GIS. Note that this new hardware improved the user's ability to interact (leading to qualitative change in how a GIS was used) without changing the analytic capability of the GIS. The U.S. Bureau of the Census began automating its geographic processing for the 1970 census and used the GBF/DIME topological vector database to support the 1980 census (U.S. BUREAU OF THE CENSUS). Universities could acquire the necessary equipment and, with help from their students, were able to develop experimental systems or acquire systems for research purposes. The Harvard lab created the vector-based ODYSSEY system. The CIA created and made publicly available the World Data Banks I and II, bringing relatively high-quality data to a wide audience.

The first GIS conference was held by the International Geographical Union (IGU) in 1970. The AUTO-CARTO conference series began shortly thereafter. By the late 1970s, an IGU survey listed over 80 GIS. The 1970s also saw the beginnings of commercial participation in GIS. Environmental Systems Research Institute (ESRI), now a leader in commercial GIS, started as a nonprofit environmental consulting firm in the early 1970s. The successful grid-based MAGI (Maryland Automated Geographic Information) system (MARYLAND) was developed for the state of Maryland in 1974 by ESRI.

The 1980s marked the widespread use of ESRI's vector-based ARC/INFO system (MOREHOUSE). This was due in part to its capabilities and in part to its availability on a wide range of computers. By the end of the 1980s, however, a number of commercial competitors arrived, including TIGRIS (Topologically Integrated Geographic Information System) (HERRING) from Intergraph Corporation. During the late 1980s, Tydac introduced the SPANS system.

More recently, the TIGER database (Topologically Integrated Geographic Encoding and Referencing) was developed by the U.S. Bureau of the Census in conjunction with USGS to support the 1990 census (MARX; SOBEL). Covering the entire United States, it was built from the 1:100,000 scale map sheet series from USGS and the GBF/DIME database built in the 1970s by the U.S. Bureau of the Census (MARX). It is claimed to be the largest integrated, automated geographic database in the world. It is likely to be the primary source of geographic data available in the United States and is already widely available. TIGER provides data on the position, topology, address range, and various other attributes for every street block in the United States.

The Digital Chart of the World (DCW) (DANKO) from the U.S. Defense Mapping Agency will digitize the 1:1,000,000 scale Operational Navigational Charts (ONC). This project is a multinational effort by the United States, Canada, Australia, and the United Kingdom (joint producers of ONC). Like TIGER, DCW will be a topological vector database. The exchange standard was designed and the maps were digitized by ESRI. DCW will consist of 2 GB of data distributed on a series of four CD-ROMs and is aimed for use on personal computers.

As will become apparent in what follows, there are many ways to represent spatial data. Standards for exchanging spatial data have been attempted for at least a decade but are still not well accepted. A new attempt to standardize geographic data exchange has recently been introduced (NATIONAL COMMITTEE FOR DIGITAL CARTOGRAPHIC DATA STANDARDS).

GIS TERMS, DATA TYPES, AND OPERATIONS

The GIS field is young enough that its activities are largely computerized extensions of traditional manual cartography. A number of terms used in GIS technology are either borrowed from manual cartography or newly coined. There are also several operations (some also borrowed from cartography) that are expected to be included in any modern GIS. This section defines various terms and operations discussed in this chapter.

A GIS is often designed for a particular management or planning application. For example, a land information system supports management of land use. A cadastral database maintains information on land ownership. AM/FM stands for automated mapping/facilities management. Geocoding is the conversion of spatial information into computer-readable form. The U.S. Bureau of the Census builds geographic databases that support efficient address geocoding, which is the assignment of a range of street addresses to a stretch of road.

Typical spatial features stored in a GIS include: elevation; parcel boundaries; political boundaries; soil and/or vegetation type boundaries; roads and railways (perhaps with addresses associated); census track boundaries; zip code boundaries; sea and lake coasts; and rivers and other hydrographic features. Attributes may be associated with any or all spatial features.

Symbolization is the system of graphical symbols that appear on a map to indicate geographic features. In general, all marks are the product of symbolization; in particular, symbolization may refer to the specific iconographic figures that indicate the general position of (point) objects whose logical importance requires their presentation even though their physical size may not. Symbolization also includes place names.

A layer is a group of thematically similar features, such as roads, soil type boundaries, or house locations. A GIS database for some physical region is typically composed of several layers; GIS analysis often involves the determination of spatial correlations between two or more layers. For example, the polygons making up suitable soil types in one layer and parcel ownership in another layer may be combined when a farm is sited. The operation is thus often called polygon overlay and will produce new polygons that have both properties (correct soil type and ownership); this is the intersection of the two sets of polygons. Other applications may require the union or set difference for two sets of polygons.

Registration is the process of determining the relative positions of spatial data. In particular, registration refers to the correct relative positioning of two map layers or the integration of update information with the existing map contents.

Any region of space contains more detail than can be represented in a database. Cartographic generalization (BRASSEL & WEIBEL; MCMASTER; MULLER) is the selection of detail appropriate for presentation at a particular scale or level of detail. Generalization has always concerned manual cartographers. Within the context of GIS, generalization often refers to the process of selecting a subset of "most important" data when creating a new database at lower resolution (i.e., change of scale). Brassel and Weibel survey many aspects of generalization, while McMaster concentrates on line-generalization algorithms (i.e., the elimination of unnecessary points that define a curve or line on a map). Many line-generalization algorithms have been suggested over the years. This operation is particularly important in the context of raster-to-vector conversion since the output of this process may produce an unreasonable number of data points to describe each curve. Simple but effective line-generalization techniques include the elimination of a point when the distance from that point to a line connecting its neighbors along the original line is less than some threshold value, or the elimination of a point when the angle formed with its two neighbors is within some tolerance.

The most popular line-generalization algorithm is that of DOUGLAS & PEUCKER. While it is slightly more complicated and takes longer to run than other algorithms, it gives high-quality results. For example, consider the two end points on a curve, A and Z. If all intervening points along the curve are within a specified distance of line segment $\overline{AZ}$, they can all be removed. Otherwise, the point that is furthest from $\overline{AZ}$ is used to split the curve into two sections. The algorithm is then recursively called on the two sections.

Following PEUQUET (1984), we distinguish between a data model and its implementation as a data structure. For two-dimensional maps, there are four principal data types: (1) points, (2) lines, (3) homogeneous regions (such as a country), and (4) two-dimensional fields (such as a grid of elevation data). GIS data model implementations can generally be classified into one of two categories: (1) raster (using a grid of cells, each with some value), or (2) vector (where line segments are used to define linear features or polygon boundaries). Many variations on each of these types are described. For example, grid cells may or may not be square or even regular; curves may be used instead of line segments. The organization for the cells or line segments may vary widely, and there may or may not be an explicit index. However, nearly all implementations of spatial data can be classified as one of these two types.

During cartography's long precomputer history, efficient manual techniques for manipulating geographic data were developed. The first computer algorithms were, naturally, attempts to automate these manual procedures. Vector methods were implemented first, as the automation of manual procedures based on the drawing of lines. As computer memory became cheaper and raster technology became prevalent in both input and output devices, the relative ease of raster-based algorithms caused a movement toward raster representations and algorithms. However, their high costs in terms of storage space (and resultant disk accesses) quickly resulted in a balance between vector and raster technology that has persisted to the present.

During the past decade, increasing attention has focused on spatial indexing. Although it is not yet widely used in commercial GIS, the research community generally recognizes the necessity for spatial indexing as an integral part of GIS spatial data organization. Intergraph and Tydac appear to be the current industry leaders in spatial indexing.

Based on DANGERMOND (1990a), the following are some typical GIS operations:

- Conversion between data representations, traditionally between raster and vector representations;
- Polygon overlay;
- Data input (digitization) and data output (hard copy and interactive display);
- Generalization;
- Rubbersheeting operations that stretch or compress specified areas, usually to rectify distorted input data;

GEOGRAPHIC INFORMATION SYSTEMS 145

- Generation of buffer zones around cartographic objects;
- Attribute matching and Boolean queries (similar to traditional relational database queries);
- Location of nearest neighbors;
- Scale and projection changes;
- Edge matching to join adjacent map sheets into a single database;
- Windowing to select a subset of the database (windows may be arbitrary in shape but are typically rectangular);
- Map editing;
- Reclassification of polygons (which may merge polygons, also called "dropline");
- Distance, area, and volume calculations;
- Point-in-polygon determination (i.e., determine which polygon contains a specified query point);
- Region search (find objects in a generalized region, most commonly within some radius of a given point);
- Search radius aggregation (for each of a collection of objects or grid cells, calculate some property, such as the number of objects within a given distance); and
- Corridor selection (compute the least cost path/corridor between two points).

For operations on digital terrain models, see the section on Elevation Data Representations.

VECTOR AND RASTER REPRESENTATIONS

To store a collection of polygons, vector representations are used more commonly than raster representations. For each polygon the simplest vector representation stores the list of line segments that form its boundary. This is often called a "spaghetti file" since the representation contains no information about line interrelationships, such as intersections or connections between line segments at "T" junctions. Thus, it can be difficult to find all line segments that intersect at a given vertex or to find the polygons adjacent to a specified line segment. Spaghetti files are adequate only for display and for operations in which the interrelationships among lines are irrelevant.

An organizational improvement over the spaghetti file is the topological model, which stores polygon adjacencies explicitly; an example of a topological vector model is the GBF/DIME file representation (U.S. BUREAU OF THE CENSUS). DIME files contain a list of points, a list of line segments, and a list of regions (city blocks). The points indicate positions along roads, rivers, political boundaries, and so forth. Thus, they represent vertices along polygon boundaries and along linear features. Line segments are straight lines that connect a pair of points. Regions are a closed connected series of line segments. The heart of the DIME file is the segment list. Each segment contains pointers to its two endpoints and pointers to the two regions for which it is the boundary. This provides sufficient information to perform "topological edits," which ensure that the database is internally consistent in its topology.

For a more complicated example of topological vector representation, consider the organization of the TIGER file (MARX). There are 0-cells (intersections of linear features and ends of linear features), 1-cells (linear features with 0-cells at the ends), and 2-cells (a region defined by a linked set of 1-cells). There are three lists, one list for each cell type. Spatial data, such as curvature of 1-cells, are kept in other lists (note that the 0-cell, 1-cell, and 2-cell lists indicate only the topological structure, not the metric structure of the data). Directories are created for the 0-cells and 2-cells, organized as B-trees (1-cells are only referenced as parts of 2-cells or connected to 0-cells). The 1-cells contain pointers to the 2-cells on each side—that's what makes TIGER "topological." The 0-cell directory is entry only. You can search for data given a 0-cell address, but no pointers from the other lists allow access into the 0-cell directory. The 0-cell directory supports nearest-neighbor searching through use of a Morton code—a space-filling curve that imposes a one-dimensional ordering on the two-dimensional point coordinates (described in the section on Spatial Indexing). The 0-cell records contain a pointer to one of the 1-cells attached to that 0-cell. This 1-cell in turn points to the next 1-cell attached to that 0-cell, and so on in a linked list. This organization is called "threading." The 0-cell record also points to a 0-cell attribute list, allowing access to the attribute data for that point. The 2-cell records point to a 1-cell on its boundary; the 1-cell record then points to the next 1-cell along the boundary; this is another example of threading. The TIGER organization makes it easy to recover all segments that meet at a particular 0-cell and to recover all segments that form the boundary of a particular 2-cell.

Chaincodes (FREEMAN) are a second type of boundary representation. The chaincode is a series of unit steps comprising a curve, each step being typically one pixel-width in length. Given the start coordinate for the chain, the next step can only be in one of a fixed number of directions (for example, the allowed directions could be the four cardinal directions and the four diagonals). Thus, each successive step can be coded with only a few bits (3 bits in this case for eight possible directions). More sophisticated implementations augment the scheme with codes to indicate such things as runs of steps in a given direction. Since no spatial relationships are stored, chaincodes are in effect a compact spaghetti line representation (PEUQUET, 1984).

Raster or grid representations require less time to complete many analytic tasks than vector representations and certainly are easier to implement. In particular, polygon overlay is quite simple to implement and often faster in execution for rasters than for vectors. Another major incentive for the use of raster representations is the wealth of satellite data now being generated. Scanner output is also typically in raster format. However, in practice a vector representation requires much less storage than does the equivalent raster representation for a given data resolution. The space requirements for each type can easily differ by an order of magnitude (SHAFFER, 1988).

Raster grid methods can be generalized to other regular tesselations of the plane, such as triangles or hexagons. Each has advantages and disadvantages. For example, on a hexagon grid, all neighbors of a cell are equally distant, unlike square grids with one distance to side neighbors and another distance to corner neighbors. BELL ET AL. give details on the pros and cons of various tesselations.

Discussions of vector representations in this survey primarily consider vectors as boundaries of polygons. Although a significant aspect of spatial data representation and analysis, this discussion ignores their use in network models. Many significant problems in resource allocation are well modeled and solved with networks. ARC/INFO (MOREHOUSE), for example, has a strong network analysis component. MORELAND & LUPIEN give examples of network analysis problems.

Data Input and Conversion

Data entry has always been the biggest cost in building a GIS due to the extensive manual labor involved. Many GIS map databases have been built by human operators using manual digitizing equipment. A manual digitizer classically consists of a flat table to hold the map and a pointing device, such as a mouse equipped with a cross hair to allow precise positioning of the mouse on the map. The operator moves the mouse over the map, tracing out linear features by clicking at bends or vertices along the linear feature.

The traditional alternative to direct manual entry is to "scan" paper maps, producing raster output, followed by automatic processing to convert to vector representation (DANKO; PEUQUET & BOYLE). While most data entry now comes from scanners, most GISs still operate on vector data. Thus, conversion from raster to vector is required. This process requires input from extremely high quality scanners. Lines on the map must be thick compared with the resolution of the scanner to ensure that there are no breaks. The scanned line must then be "thinned" to a single pixel width before conversion to vector representation. It should then be generalized, both to reflect the original precision in the data (much lower than scanner resolution) and to save space.

Improvements in scanner technology and algorithms have made scanning more attractive then hand digitizing, but it is still a labor-intensive process. Substantial manual editing and automated consistency checking are required, particularly when generating topological vector representations. In recent years, service bureaus have emerged to scan and subsequently edit map data.

Scanning is usually done on the color separations of a map rather than the final composite image that the public sees. Color separations, while technically depicting all features of a single color, often correspond to cartographic features. For example, the hydrographic features are usually found on the blue (cyan) separation. However, DANGERMOND (1990b) notes that putting several features together on the same separation integrates these data, thus avoiding the registration problems encountered in aligning separations.

Manual map creation is slowly adapting to the expectation that hard copy maps will be scanned for online use. Separation sheets are now more likely to be unsymbolized and nongeneralized. Cartographic data types are being assigned to color separations so as to ease scanning (in particular, symbolization is more likely to be found on its own separate overlay). Maps may be rescribed by hand to produce clean line work before scanning (see PEUQUET, 1981); CGIS is a system that takes this approach.

Another method of data entry is through coordinates and bearings from, for example, surveying data. These data are then used to construct the map (DANGERMOND, 1990b).

Eventually data collection will consist of automatic direct entry of online data into the GIS. One approach is to create maps automatically from aerial photographs and satellite images. EHLERS ET AL. and SIMONETT survey the progress in this area and provide suggestions for future advances based on the integration of remote sensing and GIS research. The major technical issue is to determine for each point or object on the photograph its proper position on the map and its relationship to existing objects on the map. Previous map errors combined with distortions in the photographs make this a difficult proposition. However, as automatic entry techniques progress, there will be less need for digitization of data from paper maps. This will lead to more focus on data update rather than data collection. However, although this sentiment has been expressed for many years, there is a long way to go before totally automatic updating of GIS data is feasible.

Virtually all modern computer terminals are bit-mapped raster displays. Film recorders also produce raster output. Hard copy output may be either vector or raster based. These various output devices motivate the need for vector-to-raster conversion.

The need for conversion between raster and vector data has yielded many algorithms (see PEUQUET, 1981). The primary operations in raster-to-vector conversion are line thinning (skeletonization), line generalization or vectorization (extract the vector from a series of adjacent pixels), and topology reconstruction (store relationships between vectors comprising polygons and networks). An example of skeletonization is to peel away layers from a multipixel wide line until only a single chain of pixels remains. Line smoothing and removal of spikes and gaps may then be required.

Once the rasterized lines have been thinned and cleaned, vectors are generated typically by one of two methods:

- Follow along each line in turn, which requires random access to the entire raster data set. This makes topology determination easy but requires some form of bookkeeping to handle intersections. Its cost is linear on the total line length if the entire raster is in memory.

- Process the raster row by row while maintaining information about each line segment currently being processed. This method requires the merging of line segments forming a "U" into a single chain. Its memory requirements are based on the number of active line segments. This method may use a table of line junctions for topological postprocessing.

Vector-to-raster processing involves digitizing vectors (perhaps followed by line thickening), followed by a polygon-fill operation using standard graphics techniques (FOLEY ET AL.). Even vector output devices may require polygon-fill operations to, for example, crosshatch a polygon.

The simplest approach for vector-to-raster conversion is to move along each vector and, for each pixel crossed, turn on the corresponding cell in the raster. The computer graphics community has developed efficient methods for digitizing vectors. Here the primary complication is insufficient memory to store the entire raster in main memory. In this case, a scan-line approach can be used. The collection of vectors is sorted according to minimum y value, and then the sorted list is processed by scan lines, maintaining in memory a list of currently "active" vectors. FRANKLIN (1979) recommends bucket sorting the vectors to strips of rasters that fit in memory, followed by the simple in-memory digitization technique described above for each bucket. Vector-to-raster conversion has become so common that high-end graphics processors now support algorithms to convert a polygon to raster in hardware.

SPATIAL INDEXING

A spatial index is an arrangement of spatial data for fast search and retrieval by location. Spatial indexing takes many forms, but nearly all require space in addition to that used to store the actual data set. The various methods typically provide a tradeoff between the amount of space overhead required by the index vs. speedup of search and retrieval. The general survey for this material is provided by SAMET (1990a; 1990b). In the following discussion, all representations are assumed to store two-dimensional data unless otherwise noted.

NIEVERGELT provides an excellent discussion of the problems unique to spatial data processing that separate it from other types of database processing. He points out that the main task of a spatial data structure is to represent space. According to this view, such data structures have two main components: (1) a scheme for partitioning space into cells, and (2) a two-way mapping that relates regions of space to the cells that inhabit them; note that the cells will contain the actual data.

Spatial indexing methods can be generally categorized as either tree based (hierarchical) or dictionary based (incorporating a grid and/or address computation). A second basis for categorization is the method of space partitioning used: split on actual data values (called object space partitioning) or split space at predetermined positions (image space partitioning). The best known of the hierarchical indexing methods is the quadtree (SAMET, 1990b). An example of image space decomposition, the quadtree organizes a collection of data objects by recursively subdividing the unit square containing the objects into four equal quadrants, associating with each subtree the data objects falling within the corresponding quadrant. Subdivision for each quadrant halts when each leaf node meets some decomposition criterion. For example, the region quadtree decomposes a grid into homogeneous regions.

Just as space may be tiled by triangular or hexagonal grids, regular hierarchical decompositions may decompose space into triangular or hexagonal regions. GIBSON & LUCAS describe a hexagon-based decomposition called the septree.

Several well-known hierarchical methods exist for indexing point data. The point quadtree was originally presented by FINKEL & BENTLEY. The first data point is stored in the root, and the (two-dimensional) data space is split horizontally and vertically at that point into four disjoint regions. Thus the point quadtree is an example of object space decomposition. All points that fall northwest of the root are stored in the first subtree, those to the northeast are stored in the second, and so on. These subtrees are recursively subdivided as necessary until each node of the tree contains no more than one data point.

The k-d tree was originally presented in BENTLEY. It is an augmentation of the binary search tree to support multiple dimensions. It is similar to the point quadtree in that it forms an object decomposition; however, each point splits search space in one dimension. The root splits search space in the first dimension (e.g., x), the child splits in the second dimension (e.g., y), the grandchild splits again in the first dimension, and so on.

The PR quadtree is described in SAMET (1990b). Like the point quadtree, it decomposes space into quadrants. However, where the point quadtree and k-d tree split space at the data points, the PR quadtree splits the unit square into equal-sized quadrants, regardless of the actual positions of the data points. The space may need to be subdivided several times for two points that are close together, but this is not typically a problem. A close variant is the PR bintree (SAMET, 1990b), which splits space into two equal parts, with the direction of split (parallel to the x or y axes) alternating with level in the tree, as does the k-d tree. All of these point indexing methods allow for efficient search by point or region query.

Line data are indexed hierarchically by the PM quadtree and its variants (IBBS & STEVENS; NELSON & SAMET; SAMET & WEBBER). Several variants of the PM quadtree have been suggested, but once again they are all based on the concept of subdividing nodes that do not meet some decomposition criteria. One such decomposition criterion is to split any node containing more than one vertex or intersection point. MARTIN proposed simply to decompose any quadtree block with more than N line segments (he suggests $N = 3$). This works well except when more than N lines meet at a vertex. PM quadtrees in principle support arbitrary vertex degree, but implementing variable-sized nodes is more complex (one such implementation is described by SHAFFER ET AL.). Martin's approach is superior when the degree of all vertices is guaranteed to be small.

The field tree (FRANK & BARRERA) can be viewed as a variant of the quadtree in which many of the rules have been relaxed. The field "tree" can actually be a directed acyclic graph (i.e., a node can have multiple parents). Each node contains objects within a rectangular region, but a node's children can represent rectangles that need not be disjoint; nor must their union be the space covered by the parent. Objects are stored in the smallest node that completely contains them (i.e., unlike disjoint decompositions such as the quadtree, objects are never fragmented among multiple nodes).

The R-tree (GUTTMAN) is similar to the field tree in that it stores each object in a single node of the tree. All objects are stored at the leaves of the R-tree, each object contained within the smallest possible bounding rectangle. A group of leaf rectangles is collected into the smallest rectangle that contains them; this new rectangle will be stored in the parent node. Several parents are in turn collected into a rectangle, stored at their parent, and so on until finally the root stores the bounding rectangle containing all of the objects represented by the R-tree. As with a B-tree, all leaf nodes are at the same level, and each node corresponds physically to one page in memory. A major disadvantage of the R-tree is that the decomposition method does not uniquely specify how rectangles must be grouped. Thus, parent nodes may represent rectangles that overlap or poorly fit the region covered by the actual objects. This increases retrieval time since searching is done by traversing the tree from the root, visiting those children whose rectangles cover the search region or point. The R^+ tree (SELLIS ET AL.) eliminates the overlapping parent rectangles but at the cost of allowing objects to appear at multiple nodes.

Holey-brick (HB)-trees (LOMET & SALZBERG) are designed to provide good worst-case space utilization and search times. HB-trees are based on an index for pages of data very much in the style of B^+-trees. Each page contains the objects that fall within a rectangular region, possibly with rectangular holes; thus the name, "holey brick." Objects within each page are indexed by a variant of the k-d tree.

Binary Space Partitioning (BSP)-trees, originally suggested for use in hidden surface removal algorithms for computer graphics applications, have been adapted by VAN OOSTEROM to GIS. BSP-trees can be viewed as an extension to the k-d tree to support line data. The BSP-tree selects one vector (typically not parallel to the x or y axes) to be used as the central binary division. All vectors to the left of this line form a BSP-tree that comprises the left subtree, and similarly for the right. Vectors that cross the dividing line are fragmented and treated as two vectors. Thus the choice of vector stored in the root will determine whether the BSP-tree is balanced and will also affect how many vectors are fragmented (thus requiring more nodes in the BSP-tree). Note that BSP-tree leaves represent empty space—they don't store lines as do PM quadtrees. The lines are stored at internal nodes. A region may be all or partly bounded by vectors of the database. Thus it is a region representation for shapes but much more flexible than the region quadtree.

We now describe an important technique for generating a one-dimensional sort key from two- or three-dimensional coordinates; it has been used directly or indirectly by many spatial indexing methods. In general, the technique creates an index value for each object according to its position along a space-filling curve. This index value is variously called a "Peano key," "Morton code," or "Z-order code." We will use Morton code, named for the first person to use this method in GIS (TOMLINSON ET AL.). Various space-filling curves can be applied, but the most common is that derived by bit-interleaving the x and y (and, in three dimensions, z) coordinates. This yields a single key that can be used to sort the objects uniquely. In the case of nonpoint objects, a representative point may be used to construct the key. For example, binning methods typically sort the bins by the upper-left corner coordinate of the bin.

Quadtree implementations are closely tied to Morton codes since sorting the squares corresponding to the leaf nodes of a quadtree will yield the same order as would be encountered during a traversal of the tree. Alternatively, if the branches of the quadtree are assigned 2-bit codes based on their direction (NW, NE, SW, SE), the path from the root to the leaf will yield the Morton code.

CGIS was the first to apply this method, using it as an indexing scheme for separate map sheet files. This key tends to place objects that are nearby in space also nearby in the key ordering. Morton codes are also used to sort objects for indexing relational database tables by proponents of unification of spatial and attribute data in a relational database (LAURINI & MILLERET; WAUGH & HEALEY). For more details on Morton code implementations, see SAMET (1990a; 1990b).

As with any data representation, there are various ways to implement hierarchical tree structures. An alternative to storing the complete quadtree structure is the linear quadtree (GARGANTINI). The linear quadtree replaces the pointer-based tree structure with a sorted linear list of nodes consisting of the leaf values from the original quadtree, each associated with its Morton code. The linear quadtree representation, since it yields a sorted list, easily lends itself to storage in pages on a disk. B-trees have been used for efficient search (ABEL, 1984; SHAFFER ET AL.). LAUZON ET AL. further compress the node list by run length encoding of adjacent quadtree blocks of the same value.

Some GISs are based on hierarchical structures. For example, QUILT (SHAFFER ET AL.) was an early attempt to demonstrate the applicability of hierarchical data structures (in particular, the quadtree) to GIS. It is based on the linear quadtree representation. Its primary contributions were a demonstration of the efficiency of quadtrees for GIS applications and hierarchical representations for linear feature (vector) data (NELSON & SAMET; SAMET & WEBBER). KBGIS (knowledge-based GIS) (SMITH ET AL.) was built to test the use of artificial intelligence (AI) in GIS, but it also was an early system using quadtrees to index spatial data. A third system based on the linear quadtree is IGIS (Integrated Geo-information System) (JACKSON & MASON). IGIS was created to support data structures research as well as to study the integration of spatial data with knowledge-based systems. JACKSON & MASON survey the various experimental GISs based on hierarchical data structures in existence in 1986.

Perhaps the most sophisticated use of spatial indexing in a commercial system is TIGRIS (HERRING) from Intergraph Corporation (not to be confused with TIGER files created by the U.S. Bureau of the Census). TIGRIS uses R-trees to index spatial data and also integrates attribute and spatial data in an object-oriented database. Intergraph's "Geographic Data Manager" product uses the field tree. Tydac's SPANS system uses the region quadtree representation as an optional alternative to its raster representation.

In contrast to hierarchical indexing methods, dictionary methods use an array (possibly adaptable) to organize a set of buckets that store the actual spatial data. Given a search location, a simple computation provides the correct cell in the dictionary, which in turn specifies the location of its contents on disk. The dictionary array should be kept in main memory if possible to speed the searching. For truly large databases this will not be possible and will lead to either a two-tier disk-based system or to a hierarchy of dictionaries.

The simplest dictionary method is the uniform (or adaptive) grid (FRANKLIN, 1984). This is simply an array of a prespecified resolution, where the resolution is selected according to certain statistics of the data set. For line segments, a grid cell size of $1/L$, where L is the average length of a line segment, is suggested. All data objects are then inserted into all grid cells that contain them—in effect, the uniform grid is a bucket sort. The grid may be represented as a series of (grid address, value) pairs sorted by grid address. Operations such as location search, intersection determination, and polygon overlays may then be performed on the sorted grid cells. This method assumes that the data are "reasonably" uniformly distributed. This grid is only adaptive in the sense that a grid size may be selected for the data at hand, so clustering can lead to too much data in some bins for efficient operation.

I know of no empirical statistics to determine the amount of clustering of real geographical data in general, although FRANKLIN ET AL. present empirical results for uniform grid algorithms on real map data. These tests demonstrate that the uniform grid will perform well on real geographic data, but they don't track the rate at which uniform grids degrade with increased clustering, nor do they compare the uniform grid with hierarchical methods. However, they do show that the uniform grid holds promise. TAMMINEN (1985) presents theoretical results to suggest that neither the uniform grid nor the hierarchical method will always be superior. Little work has been done to extend uniform grid approaches to operations on multicell objects or dynamic operations; however, the literature on dynamic hashing may yield applicable ideas. Neither the proponents of hierarchical methods nor the proponents of uniform grids has demonstrated how to index a topological vector database in contrast to a simple collection of vectors. In general, little empirical work has been done to compare the various spatial indexing methods. SHAFFER (1988) compares grids, vectors, and region quadtrees for operations such as overlay.

GAHEGAN essentially extends the uniform grid method to index region data stored as the leaves of a region quadtree. The linear quadtree requires overhead in the form of an address value for each leaf node. If the list were read in sequence from the beginning, all that is required in order to know the location of any block B is the size and location of the block preceding B and the size of B. Thus, when processed sequentially, all that need be stored is the size for each block. Typically 4 bits is sufficient to specify some power of 2 for the block size, as opposed to 32 bits or more required to specify the interleaved coordinates of a Morton code. To gain fast access, a dictionary grid of some predetermined size is used. Each directory cell indicates a byte offset in the node list where the data for the corresponding square region on the map are stored. The directory cells may also store a précis of the thematic contents of the corresponding region in order to speed search by allowing the contents of many cells to be skipped.

Adaptive directory-based methods include EXCELL (for Extendible Cell) (TAMMINEN, 1984) and grid files (NIEVERGELT ET AL.). EXCELL was derived from extendible hashing methods. EXCELL divides the data space into an adaptive grid. EXCELL buckets may never contain more than a fixed number of elements. Initially the dictionary consists of a 1 x 1 array. When more data elements are inserted than can fit in the single bucket, one axis is selected along which the bucket is split in half. The dictionary is expanded by doubling the number of index cells in that dimension (typically this splitting alternates among dimensions). Multiple dictionary entries may point to the same bucket in order to save space (i.e., a bucket becoming full forces a dictionary split, with most dictionary cells continuing to point to their original bucket).

The grid file is a directory method that splits space into buckets like EXCELL. However, the grid file is more flexible than EXCELL due to the addition of linear scales, which define the split positions along each axis. Thus, they allow a split at any position, unlike EXCELL, which requires that a split be an increase in resolution along the entire axis. These linear scales are small enough to fit into main memory. Both grid files and EXCELL require some method for storing the (dynamic) grid directory on disk. In particular, both require the ability to insert a $d-1$ dimension hyperplane into the directory when it is split.

ELEVATION DATA REPRESENTATIONS

The representation of elevation data, also referred to as a digital terrain model (DTM), has been of concern since the first GIS. Elevation data are qualitatively different from the GIS data types previously discussed since they are best thought of as a field rather than as a collection of objects. Thus, their representation will be different from that of a collection of points, lines, or regions, which can be indexed as a set of distinct objects. The most commonly used representation is the raster, often referred to as a digital elevation model (DEM) (DOYLE).

Although they are simple to understand and manipulate, DEMs require a lot of space. They also do not store explicit slope information—a property typically manipulated in GIS analysis. Thus, other approaches have been suggested with the goal of saving space and/or storing slope information explicitly.

One alternative to the raster is the triangulated irregular network (TIN) (DE FLORIANI; PEUCKER & CHRISMAN), which represents the surface as a collection of planar triangles in three dimensions. Given a set of data points, many triangulations are possible. Dulaunay triangulation (the dual of the Voronoi diagram) is often used since it minimizes thin triangles. De Floriani surveys methods of constructing and storing triangulations for DTM. A related method is the finite element mesh (EBNER & REISS). Their implementation provides the ability to represent crease lines in terrain.

Several hierarchical methods have been suggested, most of them based on quadtrees. CHEN & TOBLER decompose the DEM using a quadtree until each node can be modeled by a polynomial within some tolerance. Their results showed no clear space advantage for the quadtree over the DEM. Similar approaches are proposed by LEIFER & MARK and by MARTIN. Leifer and Mark were consistently able to improve space requirements, with the total space saved depending on the accuracy required. Root mean square errors of 3.5 meters for a data set in the Pennsylvania mountains typically required about one-fourth to one-third of the space required by a DEM for a range of terrain types. Martin uses a plane whose least-squares value for the set of data points within the quadtree node is below some threshold. At issue in these three approaches is the specific set of polynomials supported (which affects the amount of storage required for each quadtree node and the accuracy of the representation). CEBRIAN ET AL. propose that the grid representation be maintained but that the DEM grid cells be reordered to Morton order if the DEM is to be used in conjunction with a GIS whose other spatial components are indexed by quadtrees.

DUTTON (1984; 1989) and SHAFFER (1990) all aggregate adjacent pixel values to compress the DEM using hierarchical methods. Since adjacent pixels typically have similar values, shared similarity can be stored once, with the differences stored at the pixels. Dutton's view is that lower resolution requires lower precision. Typically space is reduced by factors of 3 or 5 with some loss of accuracy.

When millions of line segments are stored on disk, fast retrieval will require some form of spatial index. In contrast, it is quite difficult to improve on the basic DEM since the grid already provides a highly efficient spatial index. The primary objection to DEM is its space requirement. Most of the methods described above attempt to reduce these space requirements, but it is done at the cost of lowered accuracy, increased processing time, or greater algorithmic complexity. In some cases the alternatives may not even save much space. Only further experience and comparative testing will show which methods are the most effective overall.

Hill shading is a technique for shading pixels according to their slope and orientation with respect to a specified position for the sun. This visualization technique provides the viewer with some understanding of the terrain's qualitative shape. A more sophisticated visualization technique is to render the three-dimensional data set as though the viewer were actually looking at the scene from the viewing position of choice. This approach is much more computationally expensive than hill shading.

WEIBEL & HELLER survey the use, history, and literature of DTM. DTM analysis operations include (DOYLE):

- Display cross sections and three-dimensional views;
- Interpolate elevation values and generate contour maps;
- Compute slope;
- Compute sun intensities (for terrain simulation, hill shading, and display);
- Compute best highway or corridor positioning (based on slopes and construction costs);
- Compute the amount of earth to be moved to create a specified contour;
- Compute the extent of watersheds;
- Determine the visibility between two points; and
- Compute a viewshed (i.e., show all regions visible from a specified point).

LARGE SPATIAL DATABASES

Large GISs are becoming increasingly important. As an illustration of the amount of spatial data that will soon be available, NASA predicts that the Earth Observing System will provide roughly 100 GB of information per day (SIMONETT). There have been two conferences on large spatial databases (BUCHMANN ET AL.; GÜNTHER & SCHECK) and another that focused on world-scale databases (MOUNSEY & TOMLINSON). The history of large-scale GIS goes back to CGIS, where the problems of creating a "continental scale" GIS for all of Canada resulted in the development of Morton codes. ABEL (1989) discusses how to organize a collection of data sets to allow users to select the most appropriate one for their needs.

A typical operation on a large GIS is browsing, which allows users to look at any part of the database at any scale. This requires two interrelated capabilities: (1) tiling methods that support fast retrieval of areas of interest during horizontal motion, and (2) multiscale representations.

Tiling is the process of splitting a large spatial database into pieces for storage on (possibly many) secondary storage devices. Tiling is analogous to separate paper map sheets. This is a significant practical problem for large databases such as DCW (DANKO) because secondary devices may have high throughput but slow seek time. As an example of tiling, CGIS originated bit interleaving tile coordinates to generate the tile sort order (Morton coding). The idea was that tiles sorted in this way would place tiles that were nearby in space also nearby in the ordering and thus reduce seek time. GOODCHILD provides a methodology for comparing tiling methods when the goal is to place tile B as close as possible to tile A when the expectation is high that examination of A will be followed by examination of B. Goodchild's analysis finds that for the case of counting the number of times that a rook's move neighbor is adjacent to a given tile, row order and bit interleaved order are equal. Note, however, that Morton order allows the aggregation of tiles into larger blocks, with the tiles within an aggregate being contiguous. Certainly, block-shaped aggregates are more reasonable units of analysis than rows. Also, a multicell object will likely fall within fewer blocks than rows, thus being spread over fewer extents on disk.

Ad hoc implementations that store and display data at two or more predetermined scales are common. For large databases, presentation at arbitrary scale requires many levels of stored resolution. Cartographic generalization procedures are needed to generate the lower resolution versions of the data. Note that the cost of storing a series of resolutions need not be much more than the cost of storing the base level. For example, if the full resolution database requires N bytes of storage, then a half-scale version of the database should require approximately $\frac{1}{4} N$ bytes of storage after suitable generalization of the data. Repeated halving of the data will result in a hierarchical set of databases requiring a total size of approximately $\frac{1}{3} N$ bytes.

To avoid redundancy, a hierarchical method that integrates the points at the various resolution levels is desirable. JONES & ABRAHAM describe such a method, presenting a version of the PR quadtree with space at each node for several points. Points are marked according to their level in the generalization hierarchy, and each level is stored in its own quadtree.

VAN OOSTEROM uses a binary space partitioning tree to support multiscale in a similar manner. "Global" or low-resolution data are inserted first so that they will be at the top levels of the BSP-tree. Then higher-resolution data are inserted and fall to lower levels of the tree. The user's selected resolution determines how deeply one needs to search in the tree. Van Oosterom recognizes an important issue in multiscale databases: the amount of data displayed (or stored) per resolution unit should be consistent regardless of resolution. The major problem with his method is that its hierarchy classifies curves (i.e., country vs. state boundaries) and not points along curves; thus, important curves are stored at high resolution. This eliminates redundancy but does not support generalization.

Multiscale representations are relevant not just for world databases. City planners, for example, typically work at 1:1000 scale for parcel boundary maps and at 1:50,000 scale for transportation and emergency planning (TOMLINSON, 1987).

MULLER discusses an additional pitfall of automated multiscale generalization. As objects are generalized, they may reach a "catastrophic" breakpoint. For example, a city might properly be represented as a polygon over a range of resolutions, but beyond some resolution it should be represented as a point object. TOBLER also discusses resampling issues relating to map projection.

Representations for the surface of a sphere have received some attention in recent years. One approach to storing global-scale databases is to project the surface of the sphere onto the plane and then use one of the many representations for planar data. MARK & LAUZON propose decomposition based on widely used Universal Transverse Mercator (UTM) projection coordinates, while TOBLER & CHEN favor a projection based on authalic coordinates (which have the property that each tile of the index corresponds to an equal surface area on the sphere). Other researchers have tried approximating the sphere with regular polyhedra and then decomposing the planar surfaces of the selected polyhedron for representing high-resolution data. The cube, the icosahedron (DUTTON, 1984; FEKETE), and the octahedron (DUTTON, 1989; GOODCHILD & YANG) have all been proposed as the basis for a planetary database. In each case, mappings from the representation's coordinate system to the user's coordinate system (typically latitude and longitude) are required as well as techniques for search and retrieval of locations and regions within the database. The octahedron appears to yield more efficient mappings than the icosahedron, although the differences are probably minor.

PROBLEM AREAS AND FUTURE TRENDS

At this time GISs are not all that different from the CGIS that was pioneered in the 1960s. Data are still converted from map sheets largely by manual processes (although scanning techniques have improved). The data structures used in commercial offerings are still mostly simple raster and topological vector representations but with growing attention to spatial indexing techniques. User interface still has received relatively little attention, although there are signs of change. Probably the greatest change since the 1960s is the use of interactive computer graphics, made feasible by advances in display technology and computer processing speed.

However, in the near future GISs will probably undergo major changes. The new spatial indexing methods, automated map updates from satellite data, new user interfaces, and large-scale systems based on multiresolution databases all seem to be on the horizon. How long before they arrive is anybody's guess.

Vehicle navigation systems are of growing interest for city planners and have great potential for bringing GIS to the public through in-vehicle navigation aids (WHITE). Annual transportation conferences now often include sessions on in-vehicle navigation systems, and a recent conference was devoted exclusively to such systems (REEKIE ET AL.). There is extensive research going on in the United States, Japan, and Germany on these aids. Currently, most operational systems rely on dead reckoning, but this method is limited by the accuracy of the sensors that determine direction and distance traveled. Thus, dead reckoning systems are augmented by some method for correcting position. For example, the ETAK system uses map matching to keep the dead reckoning result in line with the roads in the map database. In the future, the Global Positioning System (GPS), a set of satellites designed to provide very accurate positioning, will be used by in-vehicle navigation aids. Major problems facing the designers include where to locate the display and how to provide data without distracting the driver. Map data for in-vehicle use can already be found on CD-ROM, typically stored as a topological vector database.

Current GISs are not adept at handling time-varying data. Consider for example a lake that changes shape over the course of a year or several years. Both the shape and the nonspatial attributes of an object can change over time (DANGERMOND, 1990a; see also LANGRAN and VRANA). As another example, a parcel map for a town should store information about fluctuating property lines and ownership over time. Simply time stamping all database elements is inadequate since prior history is omitted. A transaction log file can give the history, but organizing the historical data (particularly the spatial component) is an unsolved problem. One promising approach is to break the polygons into pieces with a homogeneous history. This means that a single plot with complicated history could be stored as many polygons. LANGRAN discusses methods for integrating time into relational databases.

Three-dimensional database needs bring additional complexity to spatial data representation. True three-dimensional data are more complex than, for example, elevation data. The elevation for any position is a single value. Elevation data are thus sometimes referred to as being two-and-a-half-dimensional. True three-dimensional representations treat the z dimension equally with x and y dimensions in order to map an arbitrary amount of data at various z values for each x, y pair. Grid methods require excessive amounts of storage in three dimensions. Consider that a grid of size 256^2 is typical for images stored today. However, a single grid of size 256^3 contains 16 million cells, now considered an exceptionally large data set. The field of solid modeling offers several three-dimensional data structures potentially useful to GIS (JONES).

Artificial intelligence (AI) will play a greater role in GIS analysis in the future. SMITH discusses AI as applied to geographical research in the following areas: (1) studying the decision-making behavior stemming from an individual's spatial knowledge would aid in understanding GIS users and thus improve GIS; (2) AI research may lead to improved (spatial) knowledge representations; (3) AI decision-making capability may reduce the amount of explicit spatial knowledge required (reducing the amount of labor-intensive data collection); (4) intelligent image analysis may improve the ability to perform automatic database update; and (5) expert systems may improve spatial statistical analysis and resource management (see DAVIS ET AL. for an expert system to assist natural resource managers in applications such as estimating the fire danger in national parks in Australia). Expert systems may also prove useful for map-data presentation. One such example is map-name placement. DOERSCHLER & FREEMAN and ZORASTER present different approaches to the map-name placement problem.

SMITH ET AL. present KBGIS, a system that attempts to apply AI techniques within a true GIS. A unique feature of KBGIS is its ability to learn about new spatial objects. Thus, the user can define temporary subclasses for existing object types and new functions that operate on these subclasses. KBGIS also attempts to integrate a wide range of spatial data representations.

Human–computer interaction (HCI) issues have historically been a weak point for GIS but have recently become the subject of intensive research (EGENHOFER & FRANK; MARK & GOULD; MCGRANAGHAN & VOLTA). Mark and Gould survey relevant HCI work and conclude that HCI should concentrate on letting users interact with or manipulate geographical information. To these authors the term "human–computer interaction" puts too much focus on devices, and they observe that the HCI discipline focuses too much on the interface rather than the application. They also note that currently most geographic information systems are aimed at GIS experts (in particular, geographically knowledgeable individuals willing to learn the system), and not general end users.

GIS query languages are also of growing concern. FRANK & MARK state that a GIS query language must fulfill two functions: (1) select the subset of data that the user needs, and (2) render those data in a form that is meaningful to the user. FRANK presents an early attempt to address the issue as opposed to creating an ad hoc language for a particular system. EGENHOFER discusses extensions to SQL for use in GIS queries. The requirements include: (1) the ability to specify windows of interest; (2) topological relationships, such as "A within B"; (3) support for multiple object types displayed on the screen; and (4) the specification of display parameters.

The quality of GIS output has risen steadily over the years, largely due to hardware improvements, such as high-resolution raster-based displays. However, software techniques are also important. In particular, many visualization techniques from the field of computer graphics are readily applicable to geographic data (MCLAREN). These include hidden surface removal, anti-aliasing (the technical term for removing display artifacts, such as the jagged stairstep appearing on digitized lines, caused by limited display resolution), shading, and texture. Each of these contributes to more realistic and/or clearer presentations. Techniques for visualization of (typically nonvisual) data are also crucial because of the increasing mass of data available for analysis. Many display techniques were pioneered by cartographers since viewing thematic data in the context of a map has always been a key component of cartography. Good visualization techniques allow the viewer to detect patterns but only if correctly presented. For example, homogeneous shading density for states based on per-capita statistics can lead to a false sense of importance for the overall contribution of large regions with low population. BUTTENFIELD & MACKANESS provide a survey of visualization in GIS, and TUFTE gives an excellent introduction to graphical data presentation techniques and their misuse.

The accuracy of spatial databases has always been of concern, but now the concern is increasing. Loss of accuracy can stem from numeric instability of algorithms (a relatively minor source of error), errors in source data (both positional and classification error), and errors in conversion of hard-copy analog maps (a major source of error). As a canonical example of accuracy problems, consider the result of taking the polygon overlay for two data sets derived from different sources.

Many of the polygon boundaries in the two sets are intended to be identical (for example, the coastline on a soil map and on a parcel map). Although the coastlines on the two maps are similar, they are often not identical. When overlaid, the coastlines form a number of very small, spurious "sliver" polygons.

The issue of accuracy becomes more important in the face of liability on the part of organizations that use GIS to make decisions (EPSTEIN & ROITMAN). Liability can result from inaccurate data or a misuse of data. The data producer, the GIS implementor, the GIS user, and the clients of commercial information providers can all make poor decisions for either of these reasons. Additional legal issues involve confidentiality, ownership, and control of information. EPSTEIN discusses these issues in the context of global databases, which include concerns relating to national political and economic security, along with nondisclosure of commercial trade secrets.

ACKNOWLEDGMENTS

Several people aided me in compiling reference material for this survey. Thanks to David Mark and Max Egenhofer for supplying online bibliographic material and to Bill Carstensen for access to his library. Special thanks to Kim Tran for secretarial assistance. I apologize for the inevitable gaps and missed references in the final result.

BIBLIOGRAPHY

ABEL, DAVID J. 1984. A B$^+$-Tree Structure for Large Quadtrees. Computer Vision, Graphics and Image Processing. 1984 July; 27(1): 19-31. ISSN: 0734-189X.

ABEL, DAVID J. 1989. A Model for Data Set Management in Large Spatial Information Systems. International Journal of Geographical Information Systems. 1989 October-December; 3(4): 291-301. ISSN: 0269-3798.

ABLER, R. 1987. The National Science Foundation National Center for Geographic Information and Analysis. International Journal of Geographical Information Systems. 1987 October-December; 1(4): 303-326. ISSN: 0269-3798.

ANDERSON, K. ERIC, ed. 1989. AUTO-CARTO 9: 9th International Symposium on Computer-Assisted Cartography; 1989 April 2-7; Baltimore, MD. Falls Church, VA: American Society for Photogrammetry and Remote Sensing and American Congress on Surveying and Mapping; 1989. 879p. ISBN: 0-944426-55-7.

ARONOFF, STANLEY. 1989. Geographic Information Systems: A Management Perspective. Ottawa, Canada: WDL Publications; 1989. 294p. ISBN: 0-921804-00-8.

ARONSON, PETER. 1987. Attribute Handling for Geographic Information Systems. See reference: CHRISMAN, NICHOLAS R., ed. 346-355.

BELL, S.B.M.; DIAZ, B.M.; HOLROYD, F.; JACKSON, M.J. 1983. Spatially Referenced Methods of Processing Raster and Vector Data. Image and Vision Computing. 1983 November; 1(4): 211-220. ISSN: 0262-8856.

BENTLEY, JON L. 1975. Multidimensional Binary Search Trees Used for Associative Searching. Communications of the ACM. 1975 September; 18(9): 509-517. ISSN: 0001-0782.

BRASSEL, KURT E.; WEIBEL, ROBERT. 1988. A Review and Conceptual Framework of Automated Map Generalization. International Journal of Geographical Information Systems. 1988 July-September; 2(3): 229-244. ISSN: 0269-3798.

BUCHMANN, A.; GÜNTHER, O.; SMITH, T.R.; WANG, Y.-F., eds. 1990. Design and Implementation of Large Spatial Databases: Proceedings of the 1st Symposium SSD '89; 1989 July 17-18; Santa Barbara, CA. Berlin, Germany: Springer-Verlag; 1990. 364p. (Lecture Notes in Computer Science: Volume 409). ISBN: 3-540-52208-5.

BURROUGH, P. 1986. Principles of Geographical Information Systems for Land Resources Assessment. Oxford, England: Oxford University Press; 1986. 193p. ISBN: 0-19-854592-4.

BUTTENFIELD, B.P.; MACKANESS, W.A. 1991. Visualization. See reference: MAGUIRE, DAVID J.; GOODCHILD, MICHAEL F.; RHIND, DAVID W., eds. Volume 1: 427-443.

CARTOGRAPHIC JOURNAL, THE. 1964-. Fairbairn, David J., ed. London, England: The British Cartographic Society. ISSN: 0008-7041.

CARTOGRAPHICA. 1968-. Gutsell, B.V., ed. Toronto, Canada: University of Toronto Press. ISSN: 0317-7173.

CARTOGRAPHY. 1954-. Clarke, Andrew, ed. Canberra, Australia: Australian Institute of Cartographers. ISSN: 0069-0805.

CARTOGRAPHY AND GEOGRAPHIC INFORMATION SYSTEMS. 1974-. McMaster, Robert B., ed. Bethesda, MD: American Congress on Surveying and Mapping. ISSN: 1050-9844.

CEBRIAN, JUAN A.; MOWER, JAMES E.; MARK, DAVID M. 1985. Analysis and Display of Digital Elevation Models within a Quadtree-Based Geographic Information System. In: Vogel, Steven J., ed. AUTO-CARTO 7: 7th International Symposium on Computer-Assisted Cartography; 1985 March 11-14; Baltimore, MD. Falls Church, VA: American Society for Photogrammetry and Remote Sensing and American Congress on Surveying and Mapping; 1985. 55-65. ISBN: 0-937294-65-9.

CHEN, ZI-TAN; TOBLER, WALDO R. 1986. Quadtree Representations of Digital Terrain. In: Blakemore, Michael, ed. Proceedings of Auto-Carto London: Volume 1; 1986 September 14-19; London, England. London, England: Auto-Carto London, Ltd.; 1986. 475-484. ISBN: 0-85406-312-9.

CHRISMAN, NICHOLAS R., ed. 1987. AUTO-CARTO 8: 8th International Symposium on Computer-Assisted Cartography; 1987 March 29–April 3; Baltimore, MD. Falls Church, VA: American Society for Photogrammetry and Remote Sensing and American Congress on Surveying and Mapping; 1987. 763p. ISBN: 0-937294-88-8.

CLARKE, K.C. 1990. Analytical and Computer Cartography. Englewood Cliffs, NJ: Prentice-Hall; 1990. 290p. ISBN: 0-13-033481-2.

COPPOCK, J.T.; RHIND, D.W. 1991. The History of GIS. See reference: MAGUIRE, DAVID J.; GOODCHILD, MICHAEL F.; RHIND, DAVID W., eds. Volume 1: 21-43.

COWEN, DAVID J. 1988. GIS versus CAD versus DBMS: What Are the Differences? Photogrammetric Engineering & Remote Sensing. 1988 November; 54(11): 1551-1555. ISSN: 0099-1112.

DALE, P.F.; MCLAUGHLIN, J.D. 1988. Land Information Systems. Oxford, England: Clarendon Press; 1988. 280p. ISBN: 0-19-858405-9.

DANGERMOND, JACK. 1990a. A Classification of Software Components Commonly Used in Geographic Information Systems. See reference: PEUQUET, DONNA J.; MARBLE, DUANE F., eds. 30-51.

DANGERMOND, JACK. 1990b. A Review of Digital Data Commonly Available and Some of the Practical Problems of Entering Them into a GIS. See reference: PEUQUET, DONNA J.; MARBLE, DUANE F., eds. 222-232.

DANKO, DAVID M. 1992. Global Data: The Digital Chart of the World. Geo Info Systems. 1992 January; 2(1): 29-36. ISSN: 1051-9858.

DAVIS, J.R.; WHIGHAM, P.; GRANT, I.W. 1990. Representing and Applying Knowledge about Spatial Processes in Environmental Management. See reference: PEUQUET, DONNA J.; MARBLE, DUANE F., eds. 195-205.

DE FLORIANI, LEILA. 1987. Surface Representations Based on Triangular Grids. The Visual Computer. 1987; 3: 27-50. ISSN: 0178-2789.

DIAZ, B.M.; BELL, S.B.M., eds. 1986. Spatial Data Processing Using Tesseral Methods; 1984 September; Swindon, Great Britain. Swindon, Great Britain: NERC Unit for Thematic Information, Natural Environmental Research Council; 1986. 425p. OCLC: 20541794.

DOERSCHLER, JEFFREY S.; FREEMAN, HERBERT. 1992. A Rule-Based System for Dense-Map Name Placement. Communications of the ACM. 1992 January; 35(1): 68-79. ISSN: 0001-0782.

DOUGLAS, DAVID H.; PEUCKER, THOMAS K. 1973. Algorithms for the Reduction of the Number of Points Required to Represent a Digitized Line or Its Caricature. Canadian Cartographer. 1973 December; 10(2): 112-122. ISSN: 0008-3127.

DOYLE, FREDERICK J. 1978. Digital Terrain Models: An Overview. Photogrammetric Engineering & Remote Sensing. 1978 December; 44(12): 1481-1485. ISSN: 0099-1112.

DUTTON, GEOFFREY. 1984. Geodesic Modelling of Planetary Relief. Cartographica. 1984; 21: 188-207. ISSN: 0317-7173.

DUTTON, GEOFFREY. 1989. Planetary Modeling via Hierarchical Tessellation. See reference: ANDERSON, K. ERIC, ed. 462-471.

EBNER, H.; REISS, P. 1984. Experience with Height Interpolation by Finite Elements. Photogrammetric Engineering & Remote Sensing. 1984 February; 50(2): 177-182. ISSN: 0099-1112.

EGENHOFER, MAX J. 1991. Extending SQL for Cartographic Display. Cartography and Geographic Information Systems. 1991 October; 18(4): 230-245. ISSN: 1050-9844.

EGENHOFER, MAX J.; FRANK, ANDREW U. 1988. Towards a Spatial Query Language: User Interface Considerations. In: DeWitt, D.; Bancilhon, F., eds. Proceedings of the 14th International Conference on Very Large Data

Bases; 1988 August 29–September 1; Los Angeles, CA. Los Altos, CA: Morgan Kaufmann Publishers; 1988. 124-133. ISBN: 0-934613-75-3.

EHLERS, MANFRED; EDWARDS, GEOFFREY; BÉDARD, YVAN. 1989. Integration of Remote Sensing with Geographic Information Systems: A Necessary Evolution. Photogrammetric Engineering & Remote Sensing. 1989 November; 55(1): 1619-1627. ISSN: 0099-1112.

EPSTEIN, EARL F. 1988. Legal and Institutional Aspects of Global Databases. See reference: MOUNSEY, HELEN; TOMLINSON, ROGER F., eds. 10-30.

EPSTEIN, EARL F.; ROITMAN, HOWARD. 1990. Liability for Information. See reference: PEUQUET, DONNA J.; MARBLE, DUANE F., eds. 364-371.

FEKETE, GYÖRGY. 1990. Rendering and Managing Spherical Data with Sphere Quadtrees. In: Kaufman, Arie, ed. Visualization '90: Proceedings of the 1st IEEE Conference on Visualization; 1990 October 23-26; San Francisco, CA. Los Alamitos, CA: IEEE Computer Society Press; 1990. 176-186. ISBN: 0-8186-2083-8; 0-8186-9083-6.

FINKEL, R.A.; BENTLEY, JON L. 1974. Quad Trees: A Data Structure for Retrieval on Composite Keys. Acta Informatica. 1974; 4(1): 1-9. ISSN: 0001-5903.

FOLEY, JAMES D.; VAN DAM, ANDRIES; FEINER, STEVEN K.; HUGHES, JOHN F. 1990. Computer Graphics: Principles and Practice. 2nd edition. Reading, MA: Addison-Wesley; 1990. 1174p. ISBN: 0-201-12110-7.

FRANK, ANDREW U. 1982. Mapquery—Database Query Language for Retrieval of Geometric Data and Its Graphical Representation. Computer Graphics. 1982 July; 16(3): 199-207. ISBN: 0-89791-076-1.

FRANK, ANDREW U.; BARRERA, RENATO. 1990. The Fieldtree: A Data Structure for Geographic Information Systems. See reference: BUCHMANN, A.; GÜNTHER, O.; SMITH, T.R.; WANG, Y.-F., eds. 29-44.

FRANK, ANDREW U.; MARK, DAVID M. 1991. Language Issues for GIS. See reference: MAGUIRE, DAVID J.; GOODCHILD, MICHAEL F.; RHIND, DAVID W., eds. Volume 1: 147-163.

FRANKLIN, WILLIAM RANDOLPH. 1979. Evaluation of Algorithms to Display Vector Plots on Raster Devices. Computer Graphics and Image Processing. 1979 December; 11(4): 377-397. ISSN: 0146-664X.

FRANKLIN, WILLIAM RANDOLPH. 1984. Adaptive Grids for Geometric Operations. Cartographica. 1984; 21(2 & 3): 160-167. ISSN: 0317-7173.

FRANKLIN, WILLIAM RANDOLPH; CHANDRASEKHAR, N.; KANKANHALLI, M.; SESHAN, M.; AKMAN, V. 1988. Efficiency of Uniform Grids for Intersection Detection on Serial and Parallel Machines. In: Magnenat-Thalmann, Nadia; Thalmann, Daniel, eds. New Trends in Computer Graphics: Proceedings of CG International '88; 1988; Geneva, Switzerland. Berlin, Germany: Springer-Verlag; 1988. 288-297. ISBN: 0-387-19328-6.

FREEMAN, HERBERT. 1974. Computer Processing of Line-Drawing Images. Computing Surveys. 1974 March; 6(1): 57-97. ISSN: 0306-0300.

GAHEGAN, MARK N. 1989. An Efficient Use of Quadtrees in a Geographical Information System. International Journal of Geographical Information Systems. 1989 July-September; 3(3): 201-214. ISSN: 0269-3798.

GARGANTINI, IRENE. 1982. An Effective Way to Represent Quadtrees. Communications of the ACM. 1982 December; 25(12): 905-910. ISSN: 0001-0782.
GEO INFO SYSTEMS. 1991-. Maynard, Guy, ed. Eugene, OR: Aster Publishing Corp. ISSN: 1051-9858.
GEO-PROCESSING. 1979-1985. Poiker, T.K., ed. Amsterdam, The Netherlands: Elsevier Scientific Publishing Co. ISSN: 0165-2273.
GIBSON, L.; LUCAS, D. 1982. Vectorization of Raster Images Using Hierarchical Methods. Computer Graphics and Image Processing. 1982 September; 20(1): 82-89. ISSN: 0146-664X.
GIS WORLD. 1988-. Eynon, Derry, ed. Fort Collins, CO: GIS World, Inc. ISSN: 0897-5507.
GOODCHILD, MICHAEL F. 1989. Optimal Tiling for Large Cartographic Databases. See reference: ANDERSON, K. ERIC, ed. 444-451.
GOODCHILD, MICHAEL F.; GOPAL, SUCHARITA, eds. 1990. Accuracy of Spatial Databases. London, England: Taylor & Francis; 1990. 290p. ISBN: 0-19-858405-9.
GOODCHILD, MICHAEL F.; YANG, SHIREN. 1992. A Hierarchical Spatial Data Structure for Global Geographic Information Systems. Computer Vision, Graphics and Image Processing: Graphical Models and Image Processing. 1992 January; 54(1): 31-44. ISSN: 1049-9652.
GÜNTHER, OLIVER; SCHECK, HANS J., eds. 1991. Proceedings of the 2nd Symposium on the Design and Implementation of Large Spatial Databases; 1991 August 28-30; Zurich, Switzerland. Berlin, Germany: Springer-Verlag; 1991. 471p. (Lecture Notes in Computer Science: Volume 525). ISBN: 0-387-54414-3.
GUTTMAN, A. 1984. R-Trees: A Dynamic Index Structure for Spatial Searching. In: Yorkmark, B., ed. Proceedings of the Annual Meeting of ACM SIGMOD; 1984 June; Boston, MA. New York, NY: Association for Computing Machinery; 1984. 47-57.
HEALEY, R.G. 1991. Database Management Systems. See reference: MAGUIRE, DAVID J.; GOODCHILD, MICHAEL F.; RHIND, DAVID W., eds. Volume 1: 251-267.
HERRING, JOHN R. 1987. TIGRIS: Topologically Integrated Geographic Information System. See reference: CHRISMAN, NICHOLAS R., ed. 282-291.
HUXHOLD, WILLIAM E. 1991. An Introduction to Urban Geographic Information Systems. Oxford, England: Oxford University Press; 1991. 337p. ISBN: 0-19-506535-2.
IBBS, T.J.; STEVENS, A. 1988. Quadtree Storage of Vector Data. International Journal of Geographical Information Systems. 1988 January-March; 2(1): 43-56. ISSN: 0269-3798.
INTERNATIONAL JOURNAL OF GEOGRAPHICAL INFORMATION SYSTEMS. 1987-. Coppock, J.T.; Anderson, K. Eric, eds. London, England: Taylor & Francis. ISSN: 0269-3798.
JACKSON, M.J.; MASON, D.C. 1986. The Development of Integrated Geo-Information Systems. International Journal of Remote Sensing. 1986 May; 7(6): 723-740. ISSN: 0143-1161.

JONES, CHRISTOPHER B. 1989. Data Structures for Three-Dimensional Spatial Information Systems in Geology. International Journal of Geographical Information Systems. 1989 January-March; 3(1): 15-31. ISSN: 0317-7173.

JONES, CHRISTOPHER B.; ABRAHAM, I.M. 1987. Line Generalization in a Global Cartographic Database. Cartographica. 1987 Autumn; 24(3): 32-45. ISSN: 0317-7173.

LANGRAN, GAIL. 1989. A Review of Temporal Database Research and Its Use in GIS Applications. International Journal of Geographical Information Systems. 1989 July-September; 3(3): 215-232. ISSN: 0269-3798.

LAURINI, ROBERT; MILLERET, FRANCOISE. 1989. Solving Spatial Queries by Relational Algebra. See reference: ANDERSON, K. ERIC, ed. 426-435.

LAUZON, JEAN PAUL; MARK, DAVID M.; KIKUCHI, LAWRENCE; GUEVARA, J. ARMANDO. 1985. Two-Dimensional Run-Encoding for Quadtree Representation. Computer Vision, Graphics, and Image Processing. 1985 April; 30(1): 56-69. ISSN: 0734-189X.

LEIFER, LLOYD A.; MARK, DAVID M. 1987. Recursive Approximation of Topographic Data Using Quadtrees and Orthogonal Polynomials. See reference: CHRISMAN, NICHOLAS R., ed. 650-659.

LOMET, DAVID B.; SALZBERG, BETTY. 1990. The Hb-Tree: A Robust Multiattribute Indexing Method with Good Guaranteed Performance. ACM Transactions on Database Systems. 1990 December; 15(4): 625-658. ISSN: 0362-5915.

MAGUIRE, DAVID J. 1991. An Overview and Definition of GIS. See reference: MAGUIRE, DAVID J.; GOODCHILD, MICHAEL F.; RHIND, DAVID W., eds. Volume 1: 9-20.

MAGUIRE, DAVID J.; GOODCHILD, MICHAEL F.; RHIND, DAVID W., eds. 1991. Geographical Information Systems: Principles and Applications. Harlow, England: Longman Scientific and Technical; 1991. 2 volumes. (Volume 1: Principles; Volume 2: Applications). ISBN: 0-470-21789-8.

MARBLE, DUANE F. 1990. Geographic Information Systems: An Overview. See reference: PEUQUET, DONNA J.; MARBLE, DUANE F., eds. 8-17.

MARK, DAVID M.; GOULD, MICHAEL D. 1991. Interacting with Geographic Information: A Commentary. Photogrammetric Engineering & Remote Sensing. 1991 November; 57(11): 1427-1430. ISSN: 0099-1112.

MARK, DAVID M.; LAUZON, JEAN PAUL. 1985. Approaches for Quadtree-Based Geographic Information Systems at Continental or Global Scales. In: Vogel, Steven J., ed. AUTO-CARTO 7: 7th International Symposium on Computer-Assisted Cartography; 1985 March 11-14; Baltimore, MD. Falls Church, VA: American Society for Photogrammetry and Remote Sensing and American Congress on Surveying and Mapping; 1985. 355-365. ISBN: 0-937294-65-9.

MARTIN, JOHANNES J. 1982. Organization of Geographic Data with Quad Trees and Least Squares Approximation. In: Hall, Ernie, ed. Proceedings of IEEE Conference on Pattern Recognition and Image Processing; 1982 June 14-17; Las Vegas, NV. Silver Spring, MD: IEEE Computer Society Press; 1982. 458-463. LC: 82-80366.

MARX, ROBERT W. 1990. The TIGER System: Automating the Geographic Structure of the United States Census. See reference: PEUQUET, DONNA J.; MARBLE, DUANE F., eds. 120-141.

MARYLAND. 1990. MAGI: Maryland Automated Geographic Information System. See reference: PEUQUET, DONNA J.; MARBLE, DUANE F., eds. 65-89.

MCGRANAGHAN, M.; VOLTA, G. 1991. An Annotated Bibliography on Human Computer Interaction for GIS. Santa Barbara, CA: National Center for Geographic Information and Analysis; 1991. 88p. (Technical Report 91-15). Available from: National Center for Geographic Information and Analysis, Geography Department, 3510 Phelps Hall, University of California, Santa Barbara, CA 93106.

MCLAREN, ROBIN A. 1989. Visualization Techniques and Applications within GIS. See reference: ANDERSON, K. ERIC, ed. 5-14.

MCMASTER, ROBERT B. 1987. Automated Line Generalization. Cartographica. 1987 Summer; 24(2): 74-111. ISSN: 0317-7173.

MONMONIER, MARK S. 1982. Computer-Assisted Cartography: Principles and Prospects. Englewood Cliffs, NJ: Prentice-Hall; 1982. 214p. ISBN: 0-13-165308-3.

MOREHOUSE, SCOTT. 1989. The Architecture of ARC/INFO. See reference: ANDERSON, K. ERIC, ed. 266-277.

MORELAND, WILLIAM H.; LUPIEN, ANTHONY E. 1987. Realistic Flow Analysis Using a Simple Network Model. See reference: CHRISMAN, NICHOLAS R., ed. 122-128.

MOUNSEY, HELEN; TOMLINSON, ROGER F., eds. 1988. Building Databases for Global Science. London, England: Taylor & Francis; 1988. 419p. ISBN: 0-85066-485-3.

MULLER, J.C. 1991. Generalization of Spatial Databases. See reference: MAGUIRE, DAVID J.; GOODCHILD, MICHAEL F.; RHIND, DAVID W., eds. Volume 1: 457-475.

NAGY, GEORGE; WAGLE, SHARAD. 1979. Geographic Data Processing. Computing Surveys. 1979 June; 11(2): 139-181. ISSN: 0360-0300.

NATIONAL COMMITTEE FOR DIGITAL CARTOGRAPHIC DATA STANDARDS. 1988. The Proposed Standard for Digital Cartographic Data. The American Cartographer. 1988 January; 15(1): 21-140. ISSN: 0094-1689.

NELSON, RANDAL C.; SAMET, HANAN. 1986. A Consistent Hierarchical Representation for Vector Data. Computer Graphics. 1986 August; 20(4): 197-206. ISBN: 0-89791-196-2.

NIEVERGELT, JURG. 1990. 7 ± 2 Criteria for Assessing and Comparing Spatial Data Structures. See reference: BUCHMANN, A.; GÜNTHER, O.; SMITH, T.R.; WANG, Y.-F., eds. 3-27.

NIEVERGELT, JURG; HINTERBERGER, H.; SEVCIK, K.C. 1984. The Grid File: An Adaptable, Symmetric Multi-Key File Structure. ACM Transactions on Database Systems. 1984 March; 9(1): 38-71. ISSN: 0362-5915.

PERKINS, C.R.; PARRY, R.B. 1990. Information Sources in Cartography. London, England: Bowker-Saur; 1990. 540p. ISBN: 0-408-02458-5.

PEUCKER, THOMAS K.; CHRISMAN, NICHOLAS. 1975. Cartographic Data Structures. American Cartographer. 1975 October; 2(2): 55-69. ISSN: 0094-1689.

PEUQUET, DONNA J. 1981. An Examination of Techniques for Reformatting Digital Cartographic Data. Part 1: The Raster-to-Vector Process. Cartographica. 1981 January; 18(1): 34-48. Part 2: The Vector-to-Raster Process. Cartographica. 1981 March; 18(3): 21-33. ISSN: 0317-7173.

PEUQUET, DONNA J. 1984. A Conceptual Framework and Comparison of Spatial Data Models. Cartographica. 1984 Winter; 21(4): 66-113. ISSN: 0317-7173.

PEUQUET, DONNA J.; BOYLE, A. RAYMOND. 1990. Interactions between the Cartographic Document and the Digitizing Process. See reference: PEUQUET, DONNA J.; MARBLE, DUANE F., eds. 215-221.

PEUQUET, DONNA J.; MARBLE, DUANE F., eds. 1990. Introductory Readings in Geographic Information Systems. London, England: Taylor & Francis; 1990. 371p. ISBN: 0-85066-857-3.

PHOTOGRAMMETRIC ENGINEERING & REMOTE SENSING. 1975-. Case, James B., ed. Bethesda, MD: American Society for Photogrammetry and Remote Sensing. ISSN: 0099-1112.

REEKIE, D.H.M.; CASE, E.R.; TSAI, J., eds. 1989. Proceedings of the 1st Vehicle Navigation & Information Systems Conference (VNIS '89); 1989 September 11-13; Toronto, Ontario. New York, NY: IEEE Vehicular Technology Section; 1989. 156p. ISBN: 0-969231-62-8.

SAMET, HANAN. 1990a. Applications of Spatial Data Structures: Computer Graphics, Image Processing, and GIS. Reading, MA: Addison-Wesley Publishing Co.; 1990. 507p. ISBN: 0-201-50300-X.

SAMET, HANAN. 1990b. The Design and Analysis of Spatial Data Structures. Reading, MA: Addison-Wesley Publishing Co.; 1990. 493p. ISBN: 0-201-50255-0.

SAMET, HANAN; WEBBER, ROBERT E. 1985. Storing a Collection of Polygons Using Quadtrees. ACM Transactions on Graphics. 1985 July; 4(3): 182-222. ISSN: 0730-0301.

SELLIS, T.; ROUSSOPOULOS, N.; FALOUTSOS, C. 1987. The R$^+$-Tree: A Dynamic Index for Multi-Dimensional Objects. In: Stocker, P.; Kent, W., eds. Proceedings of the 13th International Conference on Very Large Data Bases; 1987 September 1-4; Brighton, England. Los Altos, CA: Morgan Kaufmann Publishers; 1987. 507-518. ISBN: 0-934613-46-3.

SHAFFER, CLIFFORD A. 1988. An Empirical Comparison of Vectors, Rasters, and Quadtrees for Representing Geographic Data. Geologisches Jahrbuch. 1988; A(104): 99-115. ISSN: 0341-6399.

SHAFFER, CLIFFORD A. 1990. A Full Resolution Elevation Representation Requiring Three Bits Per Pixel. See reference: BUCHMANN, A.; GÜNTHER, O.; SMITH, T.R.; WANG, Y.-F., eds. 45-64.

SHAFFER, CLIFFORD A.; SAMET, HANAN; NELSON, RANDAL C. 1990. QUILT: A Geographic Information System Based on Quadtrees. International Journal of Geographic Information Systems. 1990 August; 4(2): 103-131. ISSN: 0269-3798.

SIMONETT, DAVID S. 1988. Considerations on Integrating Remote Sensing and Geographic Information Systems. See reference: MOUNSEY, HELEN; TOMLINSON, ROGER F., eds. 105-128.
SMITH, TERENCE R. 1984. Artificial Intelligence and Its Applicability to Geographic Problem Solving. Professional Geographer. 1984 May; 36(2): 147-158. ISSN: 0033-0124.
SMITH, TERENCE R.; PEUQUET, DONNA J.; MENON, SUDHAKAR; AGARWAL, PANKAJ. 1987. KBGIS-II: A Knowledge-Based Geographical Information System. International Journal of Geographical Information Systems. 1987 April; 1(2): 149-172. ISSN: 0269-3798.
SOBEL, JOEL. 1990. Principal Components of the Census Bureau's TIGER File. See reference: PEUQUET, DONNA J.; MARBLE, DUANE F., eds. 112-119.
STAR, J.; ESTES, J. 1990. Geographic Information Systems: An Introduction. Englewood Cliffs, NJ: Prentice-Hall; 1990. 303p. ISBN: 0-13-351123-5.
TAMMINEN, MARKKU. 1984. Efficient Geometric Access to a Multirepresentation Geo-Database. Geo-Processing. 1984 March; 2(2): 177-196. ISSN: 0165-2273.
TAMMINEN, MARKKU. 1985. On Search by Address Computation. BIT. 1985; 25(1): 135-147. ISSN: 0006-3835.
TOBLER, WALDO R. 1988. Resolution, Resampling, and All That. See reference: MOUNSEY, HELEN; TOMLINSON, ROGER F., eds. 129-137.
TOBLER, WALDO R.; CHEN, ZI-TAN. 1986. A Quadtree for Global Information Storage. Geographical Analysis. 1986 October; 18(4): 360-371. ISSN: 0016-7363.
TOMLINSON, ROGER F. 1987. Current and Potential Uses of Geographic Information Systems: The North American Experience. International Journal of Geographical Information Systems. 1987 July-September; 1(3): 203-218. ISSN: 0269-3798.
TOMLINSON, ROGER F. 1990. Geographic Information Systems—A New Frontier. See reference: PEUQUET, DONNA J.; MARBLE, DUANE F., eds. 18-29.
TOMLINSON, ROGER F.; CALKINS, H.W.; MARBLE, DUANE F. 1976. The Canada Geographic Information System (CGIS). In: Computer Handling of Geographical Data. Paris, France: The UNESCO Press; 1976. 27-73. (Natural Resources Research Series XIII). ISBN: 92-3-101340-8.
TUFTE, EDWARD R. 1983. The Visual Display of Quantitative Information. Cheshire, CT: Graphics Press; 1983. 197p. OCLC: 9480885.
U.S. BUREAU OF THE CENSUS. 1990. Technical Description of the DIME System. See reference: PEUQUET, DONNA J.; MARBLE, DUANE F., eds. 100-111.
U.S. CENTRAL INTELLIGENCE AGENCY. 1977. World Data Bank II. General Users Guide. Washington, DC: Office of Geographic and Cartographic Research; 1977 July. 11p. NTIS: PB-271869.
VAN OOSTEROM, PETER. 1990. A Modified Binary Space Partitioning Tree for Geographic Information Systems. International Journal of Geographic Information Systems. 1990 April-June; 4(2): 133-146. ISSN: 0269-3798.

VRANA, RIC. 1989. Historical Data as an Explicit Component of Land Information Systems. International Journal of Geographic Information Systems. 1989 January-March; 3(1): 33-49. ISSN: 0269-3798.

WAUGH, T.C.; HEALEY, R. 1987. The GEOVIEW Design: A Relational Database Approach to Geographical Data Handling. International Journal of Geographical Information Systems. 1987 April-June; 1(2): 101-118. ISSN: 0269-3798.

WEIBEL, ROBERT; HELLER, M. 1991. Digital Terrain Modelling. See reference: MAGUIRE, DAVID J.; GOODCHILD, MICHAEL F.; RHIND, DAVID W., eds. Volume 1: 269-297.

WHITE, MARK. 1991. Car Navigation Systems. See reference: MAGUIRE, DAVID J.; GOODCHILD, MICHAEL F.; RHIND, DAVID W., eds. Volume 2: 115-125.

ZORASTER, STEVEN. 1986. Integer Programming Applied to the Map Label Placement Problem. Cartographica. 1986 Autumn; 22(3): 16-27. ISSN: 0317-7173.

5

Environmental Research: Communication Studies and Information Sources

ZORANA ERCEGOVAC
University of California, Los Angeles

INTRODUCTION

For some time society has been concerned with the effects of its production and consumption on the environment. A more recent concern is with the implications of growing rates of hazardous substances, a concern that has become even more acute with increased disposal costs.

The 1978 incident at Love Canal, where long-buried chemicals were seeping into homes, triggered the public discovery of thousands of other dump sites around the United States, alarming the public and mobilizing the administration and the Congress. In 1980 Congress responded to the public's demand for hazardous waste cleanup with the passage of legislation to create a "superfund," the Comprehensive Environmental Response, Compensation, and Liability Act (CERCLA) (U.S. CONGRESS, 1980). In 1986, the Superfund Amendments and Reauthorization Act (SARA) (U.S. CONGRESS, 1986b) became law. Title III of SARA establishes requirements regarding emergency planning and "community right-to-know." Since then, Congress has defined a new era of environmental stewardship by emphasizing the importance of environmental technology transfer (Federal Technology Transfer Act, 1986) (U.S. CONGRESS, 1986a), education and training (National Environmental Education Act, 1990) (U.S. CONGRESS, 1990), and the commitment for conducting fundamental research. HOWE ET AL., of the Committee for the National Institutes for the Environment (NIE), have noted that currently no federal agency is charged with developing a scientific basis for understanding the environment and compiling knowledge relevant to public policy. As a result, they argue, we don't have the information we need, and we don't have adequate channels to apply such information to public problems. Modeled after the National Institutes of Health (NIH), the proposed NIE would, through its five extramural research institutes (Changing Human Environments; Biotic Resources; Ecosystem Protection and Management; Sustainable Resource Use; Climate Change) and three support centers (National Library for the Environment; Office of Environmental Education; Office of Fellowships and Grants), promote education and research and facilitate the evaluation of various policies for dealing with environmental concerns. Clearly such evaluations should depend critically on informed decision making and their benefits and risks to society. The NIE research efforts would complement rather than replace those covered by existing federal agencies (National Aeronautics and Space Administration (NASA), National Science Foundation (NSF), National Oceanic and Atmospheric Administration (NOAA), Department of the Interior (DOI), Department of Agriculture (DOA), Environmental Protection Agency (EPA), and Department of Energy (DOE)).

All this suggests that the information professions have special responsibilities and opportunities to define environmental information policy. There is a clear need to design, implement, and evaluate access to information systems that relate to complex environmental concerns and to deal with the emerging paradigms described below.

New Paradigm for Studying Environmental Issues

Only recently have we become concerned with global climate effects associated with increased levels of carbon dioxide and other greenhouse gases. The concern with global warming has prompted scientists to admit that to protect the environment, they must take a more comprehensive view of the environment, particularly the interplay of all ecological variables. Recently the Science Advisory Board of the Environmental Protection Agency (EPA) released a landmark document, *Reducing Risk: Setting Priorities and Strategies for Environmental Protection* (U.S. ENVIRONMENTAL PROTECTION AGENCY. SCIENCE ADVISORY BOARD). Of the ten recommendations of the advisory board, two are key: (1) EPA should improve public understanding of environmental risks and train a professional work force to help reduce them; (2) EPA—and the nation as a whole—should make greater use of all the tools available to reduce risk. The recommendations suggest a new paradigm shift away from piecemeal legislative mandates to one that will address environmental problems comprehensively throughout all media: land, water, and air. Traditionally, as Figure 1 illustrates (U.S.

LIBRARY OF CONGRESS. CONGRESSIONAL RESEARCH SERVICE), each of the laws prescribed specific cleanup standards, control technologies, and provisions to command and control pollution in the land, water, and air in order to protect human, animal, and plant health. Equally important, a new paradigm looks beyond its traditional end-of-pipe approach and seeks to prevent pollution before it is created. The report also expects that education, technology transfer, and information dissemination will each play a significant part in preventing pollution.

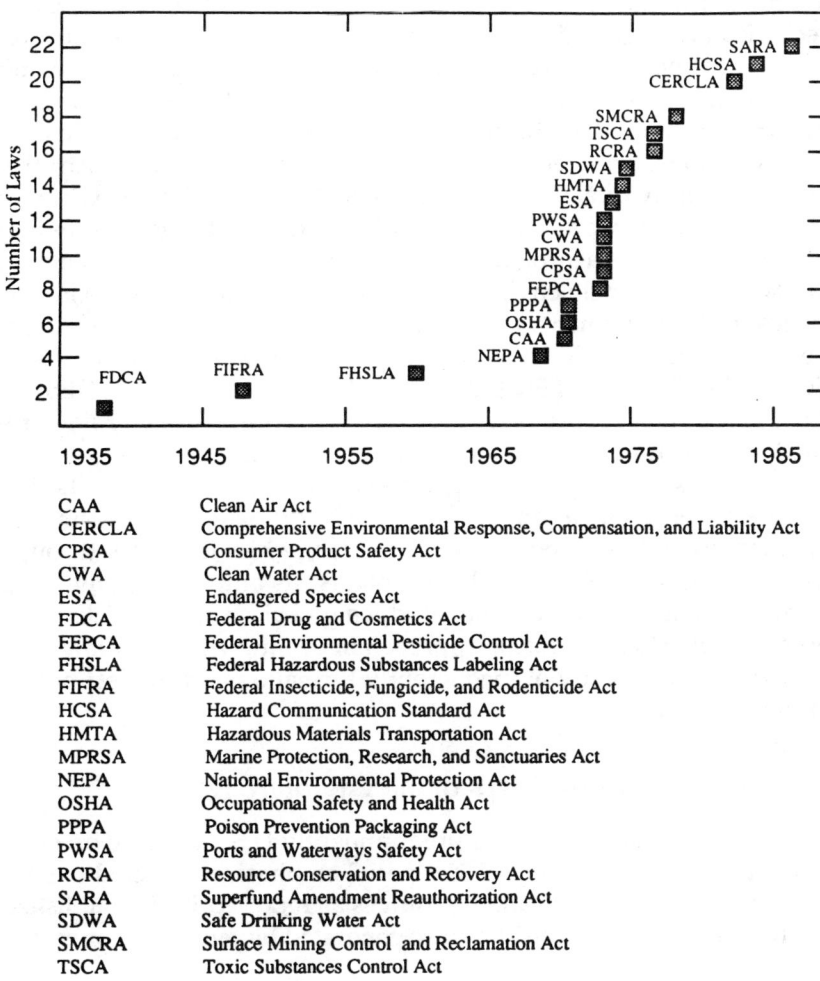

CAA	Clean Air Act
CERCLA	Comprehensive Environmental Response, Compensation, and Liability Act
CPSA	Consumer Product Safety Act
CWA	Clean Water Act
ESA	Endangered Species Act
FDCA	Federal Drug and Cosmetics Act
FEPCA	Federal Environmental Pesticide Control Act
FHSLA	Federal Hazardous Substances Labeling Act
FIFRA	Federal Insecticide, Fungicide, and Rodenticide Act
HCSA	Hazard Communication Standard Act
HMTA	Hazardous Materials Transportation Act
MPRSA	Marine Protection, Research, and Sanctuaries Act
NEPA	National Environmental Protection Act
OSHA	Occupational Safety and Health Act
PPPA	Poison Prevention Packaging Act
PWSA	Ports and Waterways Safety Act
RCRA	Resource Conservation and Recovery Act
SARA	Superfund Amendment Reauthorization Act
SDWA	Safe Drinking Water Act
SMCRA	Surface Mining Control and Reclamation Act
TSCA	Toxic Substances Control Act

Figure 1. Environmental Legislation

In this chapter, terms such as hazardous substances, solid waste, toxic substances, hazardous material, and pollutants are used interchangeably. In general, the term hazardous material includes toxic substances together with explosive, flammable, and corrosive agents. Specific definitions for each of the above terms and the corresponding properties are published in the *Federal Register*. Hazardous substances are identified under various regulations, depending upon the nature of their use, degree and type of hazard, and final disposal requirements. When discarded, hazardous substances become regulatable waste if ignitable, reactive, corrosive, toxic, or listed in the *Federal Register*.

As FREEMAN & SMITH have noted, the still-evolving environmental field is interdisciplinary, the terminology is varied, and research specialties are highly dynamic. Some of these characteristics are reflected in the patterning of environmental information production and dissemination—i.e., information sources are often fragmented and redundant. In particular, the fragmented nature of EPA's information sources may be attributed to the agency's decentralized administrative structure of individual units (e.g., Office of Air and Radiation, Office of Water, of Solid Waste and Emergency Response, and of Pesticides and Toxic Substances), each of which is intended to control emissions of pollutants into a single environmental medium. Accordingly, EPA organizes and disseminates its information sources and services separately, under each of its main offices (U.S. ENVIRONMENTAL PROTECTION AGENCY. OFFICE OF INTERNATIONAL ACTIVITIES).

The redundant nature of environmental information may have resulted from a number of overlapping disciplinary perspectives and specific issues relating to the intermedia transport of pollutants. For example, when a single source, such as sulfur dioxide, travels through air, it leaves sulfate deposits on structures; when it travels through water, it affects people, animals and plants. Its emissions pollute our air, contaminate our water, and produce global ecological risks from acid rain. Yet, EPA's atomistic approach in dealing with pollutants has resulted in a large body of incoherent information and modest bibliographic control.

Defining Parameters of the Literature Reviewed

Scope. This chapter reviews predominantly U.S. literature on environmental information since 1986. Special emphasis is directed toward U.S.-produced machine-readable sources as reported in the published literature rather than in the literature generated by publishers or manufacturers.

This is the second *ARIST* chapter devoted to environmental information; the first was the review by FREEMAN & SMITH in 1986. Other, excellent *ARIST* reviews have covered the related information on energy (COYNE ET AL.), toxicology (KISSMAN & WEXLER), agriculture (FRANK), and medical and health-related issues (TILLEY).

Domain. To define boundaries for this review, we used the broad guidelines set forth in *Unfinished Business: A Comparative Assessment of Environmental Problems* (U.S. ENVIRONMENTAL PROTECTION AGENCY. OFFICE OF POLICY ANALYSIS, PLANNING AND EVALUATION, 1987a; 1987b).

In early 1986 EPA commissioned a special task force of experts and policy makers to examine the risks associated with a series of major environmental concerns that could offer a broad guideline on which EPA could set priorities. The study resulted in a matrix that intersects 31 environmental problems along the variables of: (1) cancer risks (e.g., cardiovascular, immunological, reproductive, respiratory), (2) noncancer health effects (e.g., mercury, pesticides), (3) ecological effects (e.g., crops, forests, fisheries, recreation), and (4) welfare effects. The study ranked environmental problems against the four types of risk.

The study found that EPA's current statutory program priorities do not correspond closely with rankings by risk. For example, EPA's high-priority efforts with respect to RCRA sites, Superfund, underground storage tanks, and municipal nonhazardous waste sites got low-risk ratings. On the other hand, high-risk pollutants, including radon, carbon dioxide, stratospheric ozone, and toxic releases in different media, got low EPA's statutory priorities. The report notes that "EPA's priorities appear more closely aligned with public opinion than with our estimated risks" (U.S. ENVIRONMENTAL PROTECTION AGENCY. OFFICE OF POLICY ANALYSIS, PLANNING AND EVALUATION, 1987a, p. xv).

The divergence that exists between EPA's relatively low effort and the perceived risks suggests: that scientific knowledge may not be communicated properly to the public and policy makers; that information, when available, is often voluminous, complex, redundant, and produced by many sources (MARCUS & FOX); and that scientific data are often severely flawed (MALONE; U.S. GENERAL ACCOUNTING OFFICE, 1990d; 1991). The result is that decision makers are often unable to perceive, understand, or use the existing information effectively.

The 31 problems identified in *Unfinished Business* (U.S. ENVIRONMENTAL PROTECTION AGENCY. OFFICE OF POLICY ANALYSIS, PLANNING AND EVALUATION, 1987a; 1987b) are related to the following broad groups: (1) air pollutants (e.g., acid precipitation, chlorofluorocarbons (CFCs), carbon dioxide, global warming, hazardous and toxic substances); (2) water pollutants (e.g., industrial discharges to surface water, sludge, coastal waters and oceans, wetlands, drinking water); (3) land pollutants (e.g., active and inactive hazardous waste sites, mining waste, accidental releases of toxics in all media, oil spills, and storage tanks); (4) pesticide residues on food; and (5) consumer product exposure, and worker exposure to chemicals.

These environmental problems and related communication issues listed in *Unfinished Business* provided the following basic headings under which we searched the literature for this chapter: (1) scholarly communication (e.g., risk communication, disaster research, bibliometrics, user studies, innovation, and technology transfer); (2) pollutants across the three environmental media; and (3) exposure emissions affecting people, animals, and plants. These headings delimited the environmental territory considerably. We searched two main sources: (1) all appropriate DIALOG databases with corresponding controlled vocabularies; and (2) UCLA's online public access catalog, ORION, under the following Library of Congress Subject Headings (LCSH): "Air—Pollution," all headings containing the term "Environment," "Extraterrestrial Environment," "Man—Influence of Environment" along with form and geographical subdivisions, "Pesticides and the Environment," and "Water—Pollution." We also solicited information from selected national and international environmental agencies. Finally, this reviewer used material collected through formal and informal channels while heading the Information Center of the National Science Foundation's Engineering Research Center for Hazardous Substances Control at the University of California, Los Angeles, between 1987 and 1990.

Since the above sources produced over 500 references, we focused primarily on the selected material from the first two sources. In addition, a literature search on the topic of innovation and technology transfer alone produced enough literature to warrant a separate chapter. Therefore, we exclude the literature on information transfer and on the information sources in the areas of energy, toxicology, agriculture, and the biomedical, atmospheric, and geosciences.

The literature here is reviewed under the broad headings of environmental communication studies and information sources. The issues identified under these headings underpin both ecological and societal concerns.

ENVIRONMENTAL COMMUNICATION STUDIES

Environmental communication examines how scholars use and disseminate information through formal and informal channels (BORGMAN). The reviewed literature suggests the following three interrelated approaches to studying scholarly communication:

- Artifact studies, where artifact refers to a unit of analysis ranging from individual journal and conference papers to books, patents, and citations;

- User studies, including R&D laboratory studies; and
- Risk communication studies, where risk communication means "any purposeful exchange of information and interaction between interested parties regarding health, safety, or environmental threats" (COVELLO ET AL., 1986a, p. 112).

Artifact Studies

Artifact studies have used nonreactive methods of bibliometrics to study research fronts, scientific specialties, publication growth curves, and bibliographic core and scatter and to understand the concept of interdisciplinarity in environmental research. Bibliometrics is a body of research techniques for expressing the written products of scientific communication in a quantitative way (SMALL).

Prompted by earlier studies, which had shown that the articles in the field-oriented ecology cited literature in other disciplines more frequently and a greater variety of bibliographic types than did the articles in the laboratory-oriented biochemistry, KELLAND (1990) compared citation patterns in the literatures of ecology and biochemistry. Using *Science Citation Index*'s *Journal Citation Reports*, published by the Institute for Scientific Information (ISI), Kelland randomly selected 35 of 8,630 articles in biochemistry and 78 of 19,199 in ecology. In contrast to the claims made in earlier studies, the investigator found a significant similarity between ecology and biochemistry on the variables of citation age and publication type diversity. With regard to subject diversity, ecologists, as expected, cite a greater number of disciplines than do the biochemists.

LAW ET AL. applied co-word analysis to detect and show general themes or contexts of research in the literature of environmental acidification. Using the Pascal database, the investigators discovered strong links among forest science, atmospheric and water pollution, and forest management and conservation. These research fronts also serve as crossroads for seven peripheral yet relevant topics on acidification research (LAW ET AL., p. 255).

ROTHMAN & LESTER studied publication growth curves for insecticide research. They examined references in textbooks and the annual publication of ISI's *Journal Citation Reports* (*JCR*) between 1916 and 1970 to test citation-based measures of interdisciplinarity based on the percentage of citations made by selected journals to others outside their *JCR* subject categories. The authors found a much higher level of interdisciplinarity for toxicology journals than for demography and operations research.

AMIR contends that science policy makers are responsible for defining and quantifying the notion of interdisciplinarity in order to justify funding and to measure the scientific contribution of interdisciplinary projects. Using 155 research studies under Israel's Environmental Protection Service, Amir operationalized the concept of interdisciplinarity by defining its indicators as functions of the number of scientists per study and of the number of their scientific fields. Accordingly, a study may be considered interdisciplinary if its scientific team is multidisciplinary and its team members interact with each other. Although "multidisciplinarity" is taken to mean a sum of preexisting independent disciplines, "interdisciplinarity" implies its own identity and represents an intensive union of parts of well-defined disciplines.

User Studies

The early era of scientific and technical communication has been well represented in the U.S. information science literature in the 1960s and early 1970s (ALONI). The studies used surveys and studied questions related to characteristics that differentiate scientists from technologists, the time that each group spends on browsing, scanning, and reading journal articles over a year, and the usage patterns of primary vs. secondary literature in a given discipline (ALLEN; CHUBIN; CRANE; GARVEY ET AL.).

Since the 1970s, scientific findings about stratospheric ozone depletion, greenhouse warming, acid deposition, and other environmental concerns have taken on increasingly economic and political overtones in public debates. It is not surprising, therefore, that nearly one-third of the first *ARIST* chapter on environmental information (FREEMAN & SMITH) was devoted to the concepts of environmental economics as embodied in the economic literature.

DERVIN & NILAN have noted that most of the user studies observe users in terms of systems rather than in terms of users. They identified and described the following six approaches to "information needs assessment" that underlie the system-oriented studies: (1) the demand on system/resources approach, (2) the awareness approach, (3) the likes–dislikes approach, (4) the priorities approach, (5) the community profile approach, and (6) the interests, activities, and group memberships approach. This section reviews four user studies. The first three studies use the system-oriented approach, while the fourth takes the user-oriented approach.

Toxic Release Inventory (TRI) study. One of the most effective ways to reduce toxic air emissions has been the Community Right-to-Know Law (SARA—P.L. 99-499). Title III of SARA has four major sections: (1) emergency planning (§301-§303), (2) emergency notification (§304), (3) community right-to-know reporting requirements (§311, 312), and (4) toxic chemical release reporting—emissions inventory (§313). Section

313 of Title III requires EPA to create an inventory of toxic chemical emissions from certain facilities and inform the government and the public about releases of toxic chemicals in the environment. Using EPA's Toxic Release Inventory (TRI) electronically through NLM's Toxicology Data Network (TOXNET) system, the public can determine amounts of toxic emissions into specific environmental media by facility name, chemical name, and other searchable data elements. TRI data are also available on microfiche as well as on compact disc–read only memory (CD-ROM).

The U.S. GENERAL ACCOUNTING OFFICE (1990e) used an 11-page, self-stamped paper-and-pencil questionnaire to collect affective measures and determine users' level of satisfaction with different aspects of TRI service. Thus, the study takes the "likes–dislikes approach" (DERVIN & NILAN). The 1990 questionnaire attempted to examine the extent of using the database and for which purposes, the frequency of using the database, and the ease of using two different interface styles (e.g., menus vs. command) to perform simple and complex searches. Questions relating to the extent of training and documentation were also included. The study concluded that the TRI online database, currently searchable on NLM's TOXNET, is not user friendly during log-on and searching. The word "user" refers to public interest groups who may have different computer skills, little or no domain knowledge, or even an awareness of the TRI database. More research is needed to evaluate a growing number of EPA-produced databases that are becoming increasingly available to the public in different packages (e.g., online, microform, stand-alone, CD-ROM). In the context of the classic model of information transfer (LANDAU ET AL.), it would be useful to establish which formats would be suitable to which specific environmental user groups.

Online Access to Knowledge (OAK) study. The prospect that interactive systems are potentially more successful by adjusting the systems' design features to meet the specific characteristics of the main user population rather than by adapting the user to match the systems' characteristics holds for the Online Access to Knowledge (OAK) intermediary system (BORGMAN ET AL.; MEADOW ET AL.). This study takes the "community profile approach" (DERVIN & NILAN) by acknowledging differences among energy searchers according to academic discipline, job title, subject experience, computer experience, and cognitive style. Users' background characteristics were gathered by two questionnaires, observations of the experimental subjects ($n = 7$), and interviews. The researchers concluded that it was possible to construct a 10- to 15-minute instructional program that would allow most of the experimental users to conduct a reasonable search. However, various term-selection problems in the more complicated searches remain.

Engineering Research Center (ERC) study. A combination of two approaches—"the priority" and "the interests, activities, and group memberships"—characterizes the UCLA Engineering Research Center's information needs assessment study.[1] The study considered design criteria of ERC's Information Center (IC) to support specific information needs and information-seeking behavior of the interdisciplinary group of users. Data gathered on environmental professionals from industrial, governmental, and academic organizations from California would serve as a testbed in developing a larger data set for the subsequent study. During a one-day National Science Foundation (NSF)-sponsored workshop, data were collected through personal interviews, a questionnaire ($n = 37$), several close-group discussions on preselected topics, and formal presentations. The data revealed that although people spend an enormous amount of time on various information-gathering activities, they are often disappointed with their results and "current retrieval methods." About 70% of the respondents find technical report literature, professional conferences, and informal direct contact the most useful information channel in their work. Industry newsletters and regulatory updates are described as highly useful sources. Secondary and tertiary information sources seem to be desirable but less useful sources of information.

Finally, respondents emphasized the importance of the following sources: (1) reports from national laboratories, work in progress, and case studies; (2) research questions; (3) networks of environmental experts; (4) research requests for proposals and workshops at other ERC centers; (5) prepublished or in-press articles; and (6) training programs to teach end users how to use information services and systems.

In an ethnographic study of a molecular biology laboratory, AMMAN & KNORR-CETINA described four patterns of interactions that scientists use in their problem-solving activities: (1) the procedural pattern of scientific exchange, which reconstructs fine details of scientists' research; (2) the opposite pattern, which is adversarial and describes scientists' arguments and alternative proposals; (3) optical induction, which draws on visual materials, and is used by the scientists to prompt or to control the conclusion; and (4) thinking-aloud patterns, which are argumentative and episodic exchanges of scientific communication between and among laboratory participants. It would be useful to apply Amman and Knorr-Cetina's model of "shop talk" from a molecular biology to an environmental laboratory to discover and examine various roles of scientific communication in solving environmental problems.

---

[1]Ercegovac, Zorana. 1988. Variables Considered in the Design of an Environmental Information Center. Paper presented at the Workshop on Information Assessment of Environmentalists in the State of California, April 1988, Los Angeles, Calif.

Risk Communication Studies

Most recently the divergence among scientific knowledge, policy, and public opinion on matters of risk has suddenly made the concept of risk communication a widely discussed framework for public policy in the environmental and health areas (DISASTER RESEARCH CENTER). Much of this divergence has been attributed to inadequate communication channels used to inform the public about natural hazards (e.g., earthquakes, volcanic eruptions, fires, hurricanes) and technological hazards and hazardous agents (e.g., contamination involving the Love Canal, Three Mile Island, Chernobyl, Rhine River, acid rain, and radon). In 1988, EPA sponsored the three-day Symposium on Science Communication: Environmental and Health Research[2] and presented a number of important papers on how to communicate scientific information to the media, the practitioners, and the public.

According to TRI data, 19,762 manufacturing facilities reported 6.2 billion pounds of environmental releases and off-site transfers of chemical wastes for 1988 (U.S. ENVIRONMENTAL PROTECTION AGENCY. OFFICE OF TOXIC SUBSTANCES). Translating this kind of information to different interest groups often goes beyond communicating technical information. As NELKIN points out, risk communication is a social process. She addresses the social dynamics of risk communication in a cross-cultural context and asks: (1) How are people informed about the risks and benefits of particular technologies and products; (2) Why is risk communication controversial; and (3) What is the influence of communication on perceptions, behavior, and public policy? The answers suggest that concerns about risk may depend more on political, economic, and cultural biases than on the actual risk threats.

Relatively new interest in risk communication may be attributed to a requirement for or desire by government to inform the people and a desire to share power between government and public groups (U.S. NATIONAL ACADEMY OF SCIENCES. NATIONAL RESEARCH COUNCIL. COMMITTEE ON RISK PERCEPTION AND COMMUNICATION).

Scientists have suggested that risk-communication problems generally fall within the classical communication paradigm defined by SHANNON & WEAVER. Accordingly, COVELLO ET AL. (1986a) have proposed that four basic sources of risk communication problems are due to: (1) message problems resulting from uncertainties in scientific understanding, modeling, methodologies, and data; (2) source problems resulting from expert disagreements and deficiencies of risk

---

[2] I thank Marcia Bates of UCLA for bringing to my attention the unpublished proceedings of this symposium.

communicators to explain complex issues to the public; (3) channel problems resulting from selective, biased, and inaccurate reporting by the media as well as from premature disclosure of scientific information; and (4) receiver problems, including inaccurate perceptions of risk levels and the overall lack of interest in risk problems.

QUARANTELLI first gives a broad historical perspective of disasters in the social and behavioral literature since 1920 and examines the human response to natural disasters, nuclear disasters, toxic and chemical spills and other ecological risks. Next, the author discusses ten empirical studies in a 4 x 3 matrix of intersecting behaviors from the perspectives of an individual, an organization, a community, and society, in the pre-impact phase, the emergency phase, and the post-impact phase.

This approach has also been used by DRABEK (1986), who developed one of the most comprehensive typologies of system responses to disaster. His study uses a 4 x 6 matrix, defined by four disaster phases (e.g., preparedness, response, recovery, and mitigation) across six different systemic levels, beginning with the individual system level responses and then moving to other systems of increased structural complexity (e.g., group, organizational, societal, international).

ENVIRONMENTAL INFORMATION SOURCES

While a comprehensive approach for research in global biology (e.g., oceans, atmosphere, biota, and geographic areas) has been proposed, information systems have not yet supported this approach adequately. Most of the individual online databases, for instance, are designed to sift data at different levels of granularity by a single environmental medium—land, water, air (e.g., CERCLA Information System (CERCLIS); Aquatic Information Retrieval (AQUIRE); Chemical Evaluation Search and Retrieval System (CESARS); Aquaculture; Aquatic Sciences and Fisheries Abstracts; Information System for Hazardous Organics in Water (ISHOW); Oceanic Abstracts; Water Resources Abstracts; Waternet; APTIC; and Acid Rain; these are available from DIALOG Information Services, Chemical Information Systems (CIS), and Bowker A & I Abstracts); by a single receptor—human, plants (e.g., Integrated Risk Information System (IRIS); and PHYTOTOX; these are available from CIS and NLM's[3] TOXNET); and by a single exposure route—skin, gastrointestinal absorption (e.g., Dermal Absorption (DERMAL); Gastrointestinal Absorption Database (GIABS); GENE-TOX; Developmental and Reproductive Toxicology (DART); these are available from CIS and NLM's TOXNET). Further, most of the current environ-

---

[3]U.S. National Library of Medicine, 8600 Rockville Pike, Bethesda, MD 20894.

mental information supports the traditional "command-and-control" or "end-of-pipe" approach rather than the pollution-prevention approach. That is, most of the existing databases offer information to assist an emergency response team (e.g., ANSWER; Oil and Hazardous Materials/Technical Assistance Data System (OHM/TADS); Hazardous Chemicals Information and Disposal (HAZINF); and Chemical Hazard Response Information System (CHRIS); these are available from NLM's TOXNET and CIS) rather than to prevent pollution in the first place.

As noted earlier, EPA's recent report, *Reducing Risk* (U.S. ENVIRONMENTAL PROTECTION AGENCY. SCIENCE ADVISORY BOARD), recommends the new paradigm shift from the compartmentalized "command-and-control" approach. The new approach fosters pollution prevention and collaboration between and among EPA's policy makers, regulators, and engineers as well as with other governmental agencies. It has become clear that linking the national agricultural policy, which influences the quality of wetlands and groundwater resources, with the national transportation policy, which affects air quality, and the policies of the Department of Housing and Urban Development may have a greater potential for reducing the health risks posed by lead than anything EPA's programs could do alone.

The review is divided into two sections and uses a model proposed by LANDAU ET AL., which is defined in terms of three broad parameters: (1) the user parameter, (2) the subject content parameter, and (3) the package parameter. The subject content is here subdivided into the following two areas: (1) pollution element, which in this chapter is called environmental medium and includes land, water, and air, and (2) pollutants, which include toxic substances, pesticides, industrial effluents, and municipal and hazardous wastes. Pollution concerns, such as risk assessment and occupational and safety concerns, are treated as attributes of pollutants. Table 1 shows the publication activity in the two main areas. Examples of subareas that have been explored better include those relating to water, pesticides, and toxic substances. Examples of areas studied relatively little include those relating to land and to the air. In the past several years a growing number of EPA's information sources have become accessible to the public. Risk assessment and safety have become particularly active research areas.

The literature reviewed focuses on descriptive rather than on analytical, methodological, and evaluative issues; the "descriptive" papers range from those covering a wide spectrum of multidisciplinary environmental sources and services (ALSTON; *ASLIB PROCEEDINGS*; STOSS) to a brief description of commercially accessible environmental online databases on a single retrieval system (HUDDART) to those focusing on a specific medium such as water (HAAS; MOULDER; NIEUWENHUYSEN ET AL.) and further looking into special problems

Table 1
Publication Activity as Reflected in the Reviewed Literature

Pollution Medium	Publication Activity
☐ Land	☐ Mainly EPA documents
☐ Water	☐ Relatively well explored
☐ Air	☐ Little explored
Pollutants and Pollution Concerns	
☐ Toxic substances	☐ Relatively well explored
☐ Pesticides	☐ Relatively well explored
☐ Risk assessment	☐ Becoming well explored
☐ Safety information	☐ Becoming well explored

of, for instance, the fugitive literature of acid rain (LOVENBURG & STOSS). Papers with a thorough treatment of a few selected sources along a chosen variable have just started to appear (BRONSON; HOWARD ET AL.; SANTODONATO ET AL.; SNOW). In particular, any cluster of publications designed to address a specific research question is surprisingly small (CASSIDY & KOSTREWSKI; HELLER ET AL.; TAPASWI; U.S. GENERAL ACCOUNTING OFFICE, 1990e). In contrast, there is a growing body of information focusing on system implementation features (BRUEGGEMAN, 1988, 1992; FREEMAN & HANFMAN; HARRINGTON; SCHNEIDER).

This brief overview of the surveyed literature is based primarily on formally published studies; it does not include material that is produced and disseminated through printed or electronic channels by producers and vendors of environmental sources (e.g., NLM's *Fact Sheets*, DIALOG's[4] *Chronolog* publications, and EPA's documents or manuals listing and briefly describing its databases, clearinghouses, networks, and electronic bulletin boards).

We identified over 150 machine-readable environmental databases from several directories (CUADRA/ELSEVIER; KNOWLEDGE INDUSTRY PUBLICATIONS; MARCACCIO ET AL.; WILLIAMS). Only a few

---

[4]DIALOG Information Services, Inc., 3460 Hillview Ave., Palo Alto, CA 94304.

sources fit the taxonomy that separates databases into reference and source databases and further subdivides them into bibliographic and referral, and full-text and numeric. WILLIAMS has recently suggested an updated taxonomy that classes databases into word-oriented, number-oriented, image, audio, electronic service and software databases. Since most of the characteristics of these basic groups of databases are beginning to converge, adding new data structures, capabilities, and implementation media, this literature review does not differentiate databases by their type or implementation medium.

Pollution Media

We found little published information describing EPA's mission with regard to its collection and dissemination activities as well as its relationship to other governmental agencies including the Government Printing Office (GPO) and the National Technical Information Service[5] (NTIS). The 1989 article by KADEC attempts to discuss various EPA responsibilities and functions under the agency's offices and specific environmental media. Kadec summarizes EPA's dissemination mechanisms, which range from informal channels (e.g., press conferences, releases, and advisories) to more formal publications (e.g., policy documents, project summaries, and technical reports that are included in the *EPA Publications Bibliography* and are published quarterly by NTIS). From the perspective of EPA's piecemeal legislative mandate, the article surveys various other publications and programs, both printed and electronic. EPA's network of regional libraries and information centers is also described. Little is said, however, about EPA's user groups, their information-seeking patterns, and EPA's overall vision for future information design efforts.

A similar approach, organized by pollution medium, is offered in numerous EPA directories and referral guides (U.S. ENVIRONMENTAL PROTECTION AGENCY. OFFICE OF INFORMATION RESOURCES MANAGEMENT; U.S. ENVIRONMENTAL PROTECTION AGENCY. OFFICE OF INTERNATIONAL ACTIVITIES). The document, *Directory of Information Resources Related to Health, Exposure, and Risk Assessment of Air Toxics,* takes a slightly different approach (U.S. ENVIRONMENTAL PROTECTION AGENCY. AIR RISK INFORMATION SUPPORT CENTER). It first divides the entire territory into EPA primary and secondary information sources and non-EPA information sources regardless of the environmental medium. Next it provides information sources by 14 EPA offices (e.g., Atmospheric and Indoor

---

[5]U.S. Department of Commerce, National Technical Information Service (NTIS), 5285 Port Royal Rd., Springfield, VA 22161.

Air, Pesticides and Toxic Substances, and Solid Waste and Emergency Response). The last section lists "several key reference materials" (p. 59), with special emphasis on health, exposure, and risk assessment relating to air toxics.

On the international scene, DESCHAMPS samples an impressive amount of environmental sources and services produced by the United Nations Environment Program (UNEP), the Organization for Economic Cooperation and Development (OECD) and the Commission of the European Communities (CEC). The article focuses on UNEP's production, paying particular attention to online sources such as the International Register of Potentially Toxic Chemicals (IRPTC), which is searchable on the ECDIN system. INFOTERRA, the International Environmental Information network, has established over 130 national focal points worldwide. Among its varied sources, its *International Directory* contains about 7,000 information sources, organizations, main information centers, and databases. Although we have collected vast amounts of primary literature on INFOTERRA and other organizations' activities and information products covering Europe, Australia, Canada, Africa, and Japan, we have found very few descriptions of international efforts in environmental information sources (GALCZYNSKA & WITOWSKI; HARUYAMA & HOSOYAMA).

Environmental sources limited to the polar region have been well covered in two complementary literature reviews by ANDREWS (1988; 1990), by GOMEZ, and by WALTON & PHILLIPS. ANDREWS (1988) surveys international literature covering the organization, storage, and retrieval of polar information from 1945 through 1978 when the first online database of the *Bibliography of Cold Regions Science and Technology*, COLD, became available. The article is important because very few of the reviewed sources are indexed and abstracted in the *Library and Information Science Abstracts* online database. In addition, the article includes important references on classification systems and cooperative efforts to provide systematic storage and retrieval of polar multidisciplinary information.

Computerized polar information (ANDREWS, 1990), international in scope, complements the information in Andrews's first review article. Here the author discusses 81 references under the headings of online services, bibliographic utilities, CD-ROM databases, and computer networks. Again, much of the important literature surveyed is poorly represented in commercial online databases. Besides the COLD database, available exclusively on ORBIT or searchable in its CD-ROM version, special attention is directed to the core polar-related databases, including those accessible through QL Systems, Ltd., a relatively small Canadian database vendor. These sources, also described by GOMEZ, include: Arctic Science and Technology Information System (ASTIS), produced by the Arctic Institute of North America of the University of Calgary; the Boreal database, produced by the Boreal Institute for Northern Studies (BINS); and sources produced by the Scott Polar Research Institute (SPRI) at the University of Cambridge in England.

Land. A large body of information provides detailed analyses and descriptions of various federal hazardous waste regulatory programs, but surprisingly little has been published in the library and information science literature beyond EPA-produced material. This is unfortunate for two reasons. First, by understanding the mission of certain regulatory programs established by Congress (e.g., Resource Conservation and Recovery Act (RCRA) (U.S. CONGRESS, 1976b), Comprehensive Environmental Response, Compensation, and Liability Act (CERCLA) (U.S. CONGRESS, 1980), and the Superfund Amendments and Reauthorization Act (SARA) (U.S. CONGRESS, 1986b)), information providers might become more effective users and interpreters of environmental sources. Second, by making its sources more accessible to the public, EPA could fulfill its mission with regard to technology transfer, education, and protection of human health and the environment more effectively than it has in the past.

In the EPA-produced domain of materials there is an overwhelming number of sources transmitted through different channels and packaged in varied formats. Until recently, EPA's many unique sources were accessible mainly to EPA staff, affiliated contractors, and a few other governmental agencies and firms. Recently, however, EPA has made a number of its sources available to the public. These sources are increasingly becoming accessible through NTIS as computerized datafiles and software programs. The material, as well as new releases, are listed in the *U.S. Government Environmental Datafiles & Software* (U.S. DEPARTMENT OF COMMERCE. NATIONAL TECHNICAL INFORMATION SERVICE, 1992). For instance, by using the EPA's Comprehensive Environmental Response, Compensation, and Liability Information System (CERCLIS), which is available through the commercial vendor Chemical Information Systems or by NTIS annual subscription, the public can now access information on over 34,000 hazardous waste disposal sites or spills that are listed on EPA's National Priority List for cleanup under the Superfund Program. CERCLIS, updated quarterly, offers various searchable fields, including geographic locators, codes and names for locating cleanup sites, and other data useful in identifying potentially responsible parties for cleanup costs. For those who wish to obtain more detailed information, EPA's Superfund Docket and Information Center (SDIC) maintains CERCLA-related documents for EPA's Office of Emergency and Remedial Response within the Office of Solid Waste and Emergency Response (OSWER). The dockets are the official, legal files of rule-making documents, which are organized around eight major regulatory statutes (U.S. ENVIRONMENTAL PROTECTION AGENCY. INFORMATION MANAGEMENT AND SERVICES DIVISION). SDIC's other information sources include the OSWER Directives System, which contains policy, strategy, and guidance documents, and Records of Decision, which describe EPA's course of action to clean up proposed or listed NPL Superfund sites. These documents, together with transcripts of congressional hearings and other fact sheets, hotlines, and referral lists, in printed or machine-readable form, are becoming increasingly available through NTIS subscription.

Further, Section 313 of the Emergency Planning and Community Right-to-Know Act of 1986 provides access to annual toxic chemicals released to the land, water, and air from over 20,000 U.S. manufacturing facilities. EPA's Toxic Release Inventory (TRI) is based on the premise that the public has a right to know about toxics that may affect health or the environment. It offers extensive data on the estimated quantities of releases for more than 300 listed toxic chemicals into land, water, and air by specific manufacturers located in particular geographic locations (WEXLER & STROUP). While the TRI database, like CERCLIS, is a valuable indicator of growing environmental concerns, its usefulness for effluent guidelines planning is limited because: (1) the data do not indicate the extent to which humans or the environment are exposed or at risk, and (2) the accuracy and comprehensiveness of the data are seriously hampered by the estimated emissions of the individual facility and by the various thresholds that exempt some facilities.

In addition, EPA's Offices of Solid Waste, of Emergency and Remedial Response, and of Waste Programs Enforcement have designed together more than 30 independent software programs to support various EPA's waste management practices, projects, methods, data collections, referrals, and documents. With rapid technological advances, we have seen a growing number of networks designed to foster informal communication between and among EPA scientists, engineers, and policy makers. Most of these products are menu-driven electronic bulletin boards (EPA's Solid and Hazardous Waste Technology Transfer Electronic Bulletin Board; Hazardous Materials Information Exchange (HMIX), which is sponsored jointly by the Federal Emergency Management Agency and the Research and Special Programs Administration of the Department of Transportation), clearinghouses (EPA's Alternative Treatment Technology Data Base and Information Center (ATTIC)), and hotlines. Most recently, network-based systems have incorporated some or all of the above features. For instance, ATTIC's database contains abstracts and executive summaries from more than 1,200 technical documents obtained from various governmental agencies (DORRIS; SPROAT ET AL.). The database contains: information on RCRA delisting actions on hazardous waste facilities that treat, store, incinerate, or dispose of solid waste; Records of Decision; the Superfund Innovative Technology Evaluation (SITE) Program (also available from NTIS); OSWER bulletin boards; and EPA's Hazardous Waste Collection Database (U.S. ENVIRONMENTAL PROTECTION AGENCY. OFFICE OF INFORMATION RESOURCES MANAGEMENT. INFORMATION SERVICES AND LIBRARY, 1988b).

Since its inception, EPA has experimented with various applications of geographic information system (GIS) technology (PARENT & CHURCH). (For an overview of GIS technology and its applications, see the chapter by SHAFFER in this volume.) Currently EPA uses GIS to develop emergency response management plans for hazardous spills and to monitor remedial actions at Superfund sites (U.S. GENERAL ACCOUNTING OFFICE, 1990a). The Agency for Toxic Substances and Disease Registry (ATSDR), created to implement the health-related measures mandated by the Superfund law, uses GIS technology to evaluate a randomly selected set of 30 hazardous waste sites on EPA's National Priority List (NPL) (HARRIS & WILLIAMS). Developed by the U.S. Army Construction Engineering Research Laboratory (U.S. ARMY CORPS OF ENGINEERS) and the U.S. Department of Agriculture, the SOIL database contains access to 32,000 soil series records and 210,000 soil mapping units along with environmental information, legislation, economics, and demographics. In the context of the U.S. approach for global environmental stewardship, some GIS, initially designed to deal with storm occurrences affecting coastal zones, are extending their data variables to include broader coverage of global climatic phenomena (BIRDWELL & DANIELS). With the advances in the data structures that can manipulate complex overlays of spatial data (SAMET), in the near future, we can expect to see much more sophisticated uses of GIS in modeling and creating centralized multilayered real-time information systems that can integrate spatial data with demographic and statistical data.

Water. As Table 1 illustrates, we found more published information on water-related sources than on land-related sources. The literature can be divided into general surveys ranging from comprehensive coverage of water-related databases (DE MES; LEWIS & FITZGERALD; MOULDER; NIEUWENHUYSEN ET AL.) to only a few selected databases (BROWNLOW; HAAS; KELLAND, 1989; MARKHAM, 1990c; TAPASWI), system-oriented product reviews of specific databases and systems (BALDRIDGE; BRUEGGEMAN, 1988, 1992; FREEMAN & HANFMAN; HARRINGTON), special issues relating to indexing languages and classification systems (MARKHAM, 1990a, 1990b; MINGJU; SEARS, 1988a), and producer-generated documentation that typically focuses on mechanical aspects of their products.

The international Unesco study first presents computerized water-related information and then suggests possible improvements in high, medium, and low priorities (NIEUWENHUYSEN ET AL.). The study summarizes some of the recent developments in the area of water information by noting the increased number of intelligent user interfaces to facilitate searching by end users, the gradual shift from bibliographic to full-text databases, and a growing number of online databases available on optical storage media, including CD-ROM technology. The second part of the study recommends the following high-priority actions: (1) support a network of water-related information centers; (2) train end users as well as information intermediaries in the effective uses of water-related sources; (3) cooperate with various sections of Unesco's International Hydrological Program on education and information transfer; (4) create a directory of water-related information products for intermediaries; (5) create guidance material on database building for water-related information intermediaries; and (6) foster cooperation between nationally and internationally available water-related databases. The appendix contains much of the valuable information and lists 52 international online databases, ranging from the comprehensive (AGRICOLA, COMPENDEX, GEOREF, and NTIS) to the specific (Acid Rain, Banque des Donnees du Sous-Sol Francais, ENREP, SIGLE (System for Information on Grey Literature in Europe, also available on CD-ROM on SilverPlatter), and ULIT (Umweltliteratur-Datenbank). Finally, the study carefully defines the intellectual territory searched as well as the criteria used to compile these 52 publicly accessible water-related databases.

DE MES presents a "global, but incomplete" map of the ocean covering "mega-databases" (BIOSIS, Chemical Abstracts, COMPENDEX, NTIS, Pascal), "water-related" databases (Aquaculture, Asian Geotechnology, Oceanic Abstracts), and "water" databases (Aquatic Sciences and Fisheries Abstracts, Hydroline, Yugoslav Water-Related Information System (YUWAT)) accessible on eight commercial information retrieval systems. To compare the results of nine different online databases operating on different computer hosts, De Mes runs a relatively simple search on the topic of irrigation in Senegal published by a given author. Drawing on literature findings and his own experiment, De Mes speculates that water-related information is spread over a number of computer hosts and over a large number of databases, with a considerable overlap between and among databases. De Mes has noticed, however, that access to water-related "grey" literature is somewhat wanting as is the access to spatial information.

One of the most comprehensive studies of water-related online databases concerns the Great Lakes–St. Lawrence Winter Navigation Program. It was conducted jointly by the U.S. Army Corps of Engineers and the U.S. Fish and Wildlife Service (LEWIS & FITZGERALD) and used 11 directories of water-related databases in addition to an eight-page questionnaire. The questionnaire was used by the survey staff during the interviews "to ensure completeness and consistency in the survey process" (p. 4). The investigators located 187 databases potentially useful to the U.S. Fish and Wildlife Service environmental study program. The databases, of all types, were classified under 11 nonmutually exclusive topics and were produced by both public and private sectors. Each database is described in about 30 different categories, including hardware and software-related characteristics, geographic and subject coverage, types of searching data elements, frequency rate, and types of possible outputs. A random check on the databases, classified under the subject categories of hydrology/limnology ($n = 21$), water quality ($n = 42$), environmental chemistry ($n = 21$), and wildlife including fish, birds, and plants ($n = 52$), has shown that since the investigation in the late 1970s, most of the databases evolved into their more sophisticated versions; some are closed and could not be traced, and some have continued to operate under different names.

MOULDER divides information on marine pollution into bibliographic, data, and referral sources and discusses both printed and machine-readable material. However, those subdivisions are not exhaustive. For example, bibliographic primary sources include journals, reports, books, and conferences but exclude dissertations, guidelines and hearings, fact sheets, and other technical material.

To quantify just how much overlap exists between certain water-related databases, HAAS examined and compared CD-ROM versions of Aquatic Sciences & Fisheries Abstracts (ASFA), Wildlife & Fisheries Worldwide (WFW), and Selected Water Resources Abstracts (SWRA). Haas selected core subject listings from the *Science Citation Index* (*SCI*) *Journal Citation Reports*, published in 1987 by the Institute for Scientific Information (ISI). From the five core subjects of fisheries, marine and freshwater biology, limnology and oceanography, Haas randomly sampled up to ten articles from each of the 69 unique journal titles, and obtained 663 articles or 11% of the total number of articles published in 69 journals in 1987. Of the 663 articles searched in the three databases, the study's findings indicate that the ASFA CD-ROM is the most complete database, containing 61% unique titles, that the WFW and SWRA databases together contribute 17% unique titles, and that there is an overlap of 22% of commonly indexed titles. For the five core subject listing, the results show that when the three databases are searched together, coverage ranged from 95% in fisheries to 64% in oceanography. These preliminary findings suggest that more rigorous research is needed in the areas of reliability, validity, and ease of searching CD-ROM databases, particularly in view of the growing number of end users as searchers.

Motivated by a similar question, MARKHAM (1990c) examined optimal search strategies, indexing conventions, and retrieval across BIOSIS Previews, Aquatic Sciences & Fisheries Abstracts (ASFA), and Oceanic Abstracts for literature on marine and freshwater macroalgae. Using eight different search statements with a total of 30 search terms, Markham found little overlap among the records from the three databases but with a greater precision in ASFA and Oceanic Abstracts than in BIOSIS Previews.

KELLAND (1989) did an exploratory study that compared six online nonmarine databases (BIOSIS Previews, Chemical Abstracts, International Pharmaceutical Abstracts, Life Sciences Collection, MEDLINE, and Zoological Record) to determine how much and what kind of marine science literature can be obtained in these databases. The author lists concept codes, subject headings, and descriptors used to index the biological aspects of marine science from the databases, provides the corresponding number of citations per year for each of the databases, and concludes that there is a considerable amount of marine literature covering a wide variety of topics in databases that are not exclusively marine databases (p. 137).

TAPASWI asks: (1) How good is ASFA, and (2) How reliable is ASFA? The concepts of "goodness" and of "reliability" are not operationalized, but the reader infers that a number of system difficulties relating to downloading and saving complex search strategies, as well as difficulties relating to indexing policy, pertain to the first question. The question of reliability is discussed with regard to ASFA's journal coverage. Tapaswi found that, for the three-year period covered, ASFA did not index articles from one of the Indian leading journals (*Indian Journal of Marine Science*) and only partially covered some other major marine journal titles. The finding would have been less surprising if the producer had precisely defined the scope and the domain of the database, explained the principles of journal inclusion and indexing policy, and listed the journal titles covered by the database.

BRUEGGEMAN[6] (1988) takes a systems approach in his discussion of the Aquatic Sciences & Fisheries Abstracts (ASFA) on CD-ROM at the University of California's San Diego Library. The emphasis is on hardware, software, and interface style characteristics of ASFA, but attention is also directed to some cognitive aspects of database searching. Brueggeman contrasts the menu-based interface to the command-language interface in terms of ease of learning and enjoyment of use by 190 graduate students and 270 academics.

---

[6] I thank Peter Brueggeman of the Scripps Library for reading the entire manuscript, suggesting additional marine pollution references, and supplying the articles.

HARRINGTON takes a similar approach in his overview of ASFA on CD-ROM. He starts off by describing ASFA's sources of information and indexed journals; then he examines hardware, software, and documentation features; finally he suggests improvements.

Of special interest is the recent article by BRUEGGEMAN (1992) that describes the use of AskSam software at the Scripps Institution of Oceanography Library to maintain a separate database on the San Diego marine environment. While the software itself has hypertext capability through its HyperSift and HyPeruse search-only interfaces, the Scripps Library currently uses the InfoSift search-only interface, which does not have the hypertext capability but allows keyword searching and the mechanics of Boolean logic. It promises to become a truly centralized local databank with possibilities of modular extension and real-time processing.

FREEMAN & HANFMAN discuss the development of a prototype Regional Information System for African Aquaculture (REGIS), which uses hypermedia and expert system software technology to provide information on various aspects of aquaculture of the Sub-Saharan Africa region. Drawing on earlier work (HANFMAN), the authors set an ambitious goal to demonstrate new methods for providing rapid access to the broad range of information on aquaculture needed by the Food and Agriculture Organization of the United Nations (FAO), researchers, field project managers, and administrators. New methods seem to refer to a combination of hypermedia and expert systems features that would offer comprehensiveness and ease of use for very different user requirements. It is not clear, however, which features would be selected from which technologies and how the features would be combined into the REGIS system design. To make a system powerful, the REGIS knowledge base should have integrated a body of published material, beyond a single document, with private knowledge from specific areas of aquaculture expertise. To make REGIS easy to learn, use, and relearn, groundwork is needed to answer questions pertaining to understanding various characteristics of potential user groups, their information-seeking behavior and related user-computer interface issues and to aiding the user at the heart of the search process—i.e., in selecting the appropriate search terms, laying out the most effective search strategy, and in helping the user understand the complexity and diversity of aquaculture. With regard to providing rapid access to what promises to become a very large database, different sets of hardware configuration would seem more suitable than the ones described in the article. The article, however, proposes a number of innovative approaches to make water-related searching more fluid and transparent.

Some new, useful software programs are appearing. Typically they are designed to help the staffs of wastewater treatment plants manage information about Clean Water Act regulations, offer animated training aid and simulation programs for operators, support real-time monitoring, and facilitate water-related modeling (CHEREMISINOFF).

In the domain of indexing languages and classification systems, which are used to index and search the marine pollution literature, the articles reviewed address the questions of: (1) compatibility of two different indexing languages (MARKHAM, 1990b); (2) an in-depth analysis of a single thesaurus (SEARS, 1988a); (3) guiding principles in the construction of a thesaurus (MINGJU); and (4) comparing classification systems with respect to the degree of synthesis and hierarchy for classifying some 20,000 species of algae (MARKHAM, 1990a).

MARKHAM (1990b) compares the Aquatic Sciences & Fisheries Information System (ASFIS) Thesaurus and Library of Congress Subject Headings (LCSH) and finds that fewer than half the terms are common to both indexing languages. This finding has important retrieval implications because monographic collections, including books, reports, dissertations, and monographic series, which are cataloged by libraries, will have a different set of subject headings assigned to them (LCSH) than the nonmonographic collection. These documents, including journal articles, reviews, and chapters in books, are typically not cataloged by libraries and are assigned a set of descriptors from thesauri (e.g., the ASFIS Thesaurus) designed for an in-depth indexing of mainly nonmonographic collections.

Markham examines the compatibility between and among two sets of index terms with respect to their equivalence, similarity (e.g., variations in form, spelling, and order), and hierarchy (e.g., broader and narrower term relationships). The overall match rate between a set of subject headings from LCSH and descriptors from the Thesaurus is less than 50%, with the highest rate in the Science and Technology facet (56%) and the lowest rate in the Residual Concepts facet (12%). The article also discusses the two indexing languages with regard to the changing roles of descriptors and subject headings and the decreasing differences between them in the online environment.

In spite of being conceived in different technological eras, for different purposes, and with different philosophical underpinnings, lists of subject headings and descriptors are both members of alphabetically arranged indexing languages that share common properties of, for instance, entry vocabulary, semantic relationships (e.g., hierarchical and the syndetic relations), and specificity of index terms. Examining indexing languages on many of these variables remains open for further investigation. For instance, the question currently under study by this reviewer is: of the index terms obtained from two or more different indexing languages, which is superior with respect to other documents in a given collection and with respect to its users.

SEARS (1988a) first provides an in-depth analysis of the ASFA Thesaurus with respect to its rules and conventions, terminology, facet classification, and semantic relationships. Then he suggests a few examples of how the thesaurus might be effectively applied when searching the ASFA database.

Some progress in designing a detailed, comprehensive, and multilingual agricultural thesaurus, which would provide unified access to the creation of agricultural core databases, is reported by THOMAS (1991). She lists a number of important display and conversion attributes that are proposed for the agricultural thesaurus. Perhaps it is time that similar efforts be made in the creation of an integrated and cooperative environmental thesaurus. Meanwhile, questions of compatibility, switchability between and among terms, linkages, and specificity remain open for investigation.

Finally, MARKHAM (1990a) compares and contrasts the Library of Congress Classification (LCC) and the Dewey Decimal Classification (DDC) schedules for classifying algal library collections, which cover, at varying degrees of comprehensiveness and specificity, some 20,000 species of algae with particular interest to ecology. Markham compares LCC and DDC with respect to the degree of synthesis and hierarchy and finds DDC superior to LCC. DDC uses a natural taxonomic arrangement, which separates divisions and allows the linking of discipline with type of algae at all levels (e.g., linking specific aspects of ecology with specific groups of algae).

Future analyses might consider a comparison of the two schedules with respect to their amenability to electronic browsing since one of the main uses for classification has been, at least in the U.S. tradition, to facilitate browsing of documents on shelves.

Numerous water-related sources have not received attention in the published literature. These include EPA's Drinking Water Docket (U.S. ENVIRONMENTAL PROTECTION AGENCY. INFORMATION MANAGEMENT AND SERVICES DIVISION), Ground Water (NATIONAL GROUND WATER INFORMATION CENTER), Clearinghouse on Clean Lakes (TERRENE INSTITUTE), and the Aquatic Effects Research Program (AERP) *status* (U.S. ENVIRONMENTAL PROTECTION AGENCY. OFFICE OF ACID DEPOSITION, ENVIRONMENTAL MONITORING AND QUALITY ASSURANCE). The Clean Lakes Clearinghouse offers selected information concerning in-lake treatment, watershed management, water quality assessment, and modeling. The National Ground Water Information Center offers access to the Ground Water Network, which maintains 13 online and three CD-ROM databases on groundwater and water-well technology. While AERP closed in 1991, its databases for the Eastern Lake Survey, Western Lake Survey, and the National Stream Survey remain available from NTIS.

Air. During the past two decades, atmospheric levels of sulfur dioxide, total suspended particles, and lead have all dropped 27%, 63%, and 90%, respectively. However, the problems of stratospheric ozone depletion and global warming, also known as greenhouse effect, have proved particularly serious, and health standards for ozone and carbon monoxide emissions are being violated in 41 metropolitan areas. Atmospheric carbon dioxide, which is produced by fossil fuel combustion, deforestation, cement manufacture, and respiration by living organisms, has increased by about 25% since the beginning of the industrial revolution (JOHNSON; U.S. GENERAL ACCOUNTING OFFICE, 1990b, 1990c). So have the concentrations of other greenhouse gases including methane, chlorofluorocarbons (CFCs), and nitrous oxide. Rapid advances in information technologies, coupled with international concerns about acidic precipitation, with its serious impacts on the aquatic and terrestrial ecosystem, have increased air-related research activity here and abroad. However, when we turn to the published literature on air-related information sources, the situation is disappointing.

EPA's *Directory of OAQPS Information Services* (U.S. ENVIRONMENTAL PROTECTION AGENCY. OFFICE OF AIR QUALITY PLANNING AND STANDARDS) first organizes numerous information sources and services under four broad headings (pollutants, technical support, administrative support, and compliance) and then subdivides, for instance, pollutants into air toxics, ozone, and sulfur dioxide. Information services include various outreach activities, such as short courses, workshops, educational videotapes and self-study programs on air quality-related topics. The *Directory* also identifies major clearinghouses, such as National Air Toxics Information Clearinghouse (NATIC) and the Emission Measurement Technical Information Center (EMTIC). The NATIC database, also available to the public through NTIS, contains acceptable ambient concentrations, ambient air monitoring information, source test data, emissions inventory data, permitting, and research and development information. The database divides research information into a factual file, with descriptions of ongoing research and regulatory projects, and a bibliographic file, with citations to published documents. NATIC's information is collected annually from forms submitted to EPA by U.S. and international agencies. Information is distributed both through a computer database and through hard-copy reports.

Under a grant from the U.S. Department of Education, the University of Vermont (UV) has been responsible for identifying, acquiring, cataloging, preserving, and disseminating Canadian and selected U.S. government documents on acid rain not widely held or fully described and identified in conventional U.S. online sources, such as OCLC,[7] BRS,[8] DIALOG, or ORBIT[9] (JOY ET AL.). The UV project used several online database directories as well as several printed bibliographies to pinpoint the most fruitful acid rain databases to be reviewed. The project identified and processed thousands of pages of acid rain literature to be cataloged on the OCLC system and made available for interlibrary loan. Furthermore, subsets of the UV collection are to be scanned, digitized, and produced on CD-ROM as a part of the National Agricultural Text Digitizing Project (NATDP). We await the results with enthusiasm.

LOVENBURG & STOSS argue that a well-developed and well-accessed vertical file can be an important mechanism for collecting, storing, and disseminating "fugitive" or nonconventional information sources on acid rain. They offer an annotated checklist of 113 acid-rain-related entries produced by nearly 50 different U.S. and Canadian organizations.

From an international perspective, the information sources on radioactivity offered by GAINES give a brief yet informative overview of some of the major roles of the International Commission on Radiological Protection (ICRP) and the International Atomic Energy Agency (IAEA). Gaines's last section lists publications produced by major international organizations including ICRP, UN agencies, OECD, and CEC as well as those produced in the United Kingdom.

Pollutants and Safety Concerns

Toxic substances. Most of the papers reviewed below describe individual databases or groups of databases that are designed to respond to a specific regulatory program or law.

The Toxic Substances Control Act (TSCA) (U.S. CONGRESS, 1976a) and the Federal Insecticide, Fungicide, and Rodenticide Act (FIFRA) regulate how commercial chemicals are used. Under the major provisions of TSCA, industry submits to EPA's Office of Toxic Substances the health and safety studies on certain chemicals that are known to be hazardous or are potentially hazardous to human health and the environment. This information was initially available to the public from EPA only by request under the Freedom of Information Act (FOIA). The TSCA Test Submission (TSCATS) database online is now commercially accessible via CIS and NTIS tape. Indexing terms and codes at different

---

[7]Online Computer Library Center, Inc. (OCLC), 6565 Frantz Rd., Dublin, OH 43017-0702.
[8]BRS Information Technologies, 8000 Westpark Dr., McLean, VA 22102.
[9]ORBIT Search Service, 8000 Westpark Dr., McLean, VA 22102.

levels of specificity enable users to access over 36,000 citations on more than 4,200 chemical substances. Details about the contents of the main TSCATS files (i.e., reference file and pointer file) and an additional set of six index files, which facilitate rapid searching of the data, are well documented by SANTODONATO ET AL.

HOWARD ET AL. discuss and contrast seven interrelated files in the environmental fate and exposure databases. The files are DATALOG, CASLST, XREF, BIOLOG, BIODEG, CHEMFATE, FATE/EXPOS and are described according to content, data elements, basic file organization, access time, and size. DATALOG indicates types of fate and exposure available on a particular chemical with corresponding references initially obtained from *Chemical Abstracts*, NTIS, and *Current Contents*. In contrast, BIOLOG obtained biodegradation data and sources of the microorganisms from the Syracuse Research Corp. studies and Cornell University's "Alexander's" files. The FATE/EXPOS database contains values as well as bibliographic data linked to DATALOG, XREF, and CASLST. It combines in one file chemical marketing data, chemical and physical properties, chemical fate data, and monitoring data and allows the sorting of chemicals based on exposure. Equally important, the article describes different levels of quality control of fate exposure files during different phases of their development.

KIM ET AL., in an excellent review on conventional hazardous waste remediation treatment technologies, have organized the primary literature under biological treatment, chemical and physical treatment, and thermal treatment. However, the authors do not define their domain and scope of the literature discussed, which can be inferred only by examining some 167 citations.

Risk assessment, a relatively recent discipline, aims to quantify risk. No longer satisfied with determining, for example, whether DDT is carcinogenic and mutagenic, risk assessment studies increasingly account for socioeconomic measures and examine not only the effects of smaller amounts of substances on different segments of people in different age and health groups but also their different levels of activity. HATTIS & KENNEDY suggest that risk analysts should try to disclose biases in their thinking. Instead of trying to answer, "exactly how much risk does some hazard pose," the scientists ought to ask, "How much do we know about a particular hazard, and what are the important uncertainties in that picture?" (p. 66). EPA's approach to assessing the risk associated with chronic exposures to carcinogens has followed the general format recommended by the National Academy of Sciences (U.S. NATIONAL ACADEMY OF SCIENCES. NATIONAL RESEARCH COUNCIL. COMMITTEE ON THE INSTITUTIONAL MEANS FOR ASSESSMENT OF RISKS TO PUBLIC HEALTH): (1) hazard identification, to determine whether human exposure to the substance in question can increase the incidence of cancer; (2) dose-response assessment, to derive a quantitative relationship between the dose and the probability of a carcinogenic effect; (3) exposure assessment, to identify the exposed population, describe its composition and size, and present the type, magnitude, frequency, and duration of exposure; and (4) risk characteristics, which combine the exposure and dose–response assessments to produce a quantitative risk estimate in which the strengths and weaknesses, major assumptions, and estimates of uncertainties are discussed.

With the Integrated Risk Information System (IRIS, now available on CIS, the TOXNET system (BRONSON; WEXLER, 1990), and NTIS), users can obtain information for the first two elements of the risk-assessment process—i.e., the hazard identification and dose–response assessment. The IRIS database contains health risk and regulatory information on the carcinogenic and noncarcinogenic data for oral and inhalation exposures. Regulatory information includes Health Advisories developed by EPA's Office of Drinking Water along with regulatory strategies under the Clean Air Act (U.S. CONGRESS, 1963), Clean Water Act (U.S. CONGRESS, 1977), Federal Insecticide, Fungicide, and Rodenticide Act, TSCA (U.S. CONGRESS, 1976a), RCRA (U.S. CONGRESS, 1976b), and CERCLA (U.S. CONGRESS, 1980). While IRIS is an important tool in risk-assessment decision making, it needs to incorporate the last two elements to support a full four-step process.

The IBM personal computer-based version of the IRIS database, Risk Assistant, has been recently supported jointly by EPA, the New Jersey Department of Environmental Protection, and the Toxic Substance Control Program of the California Department of Health Services. The program supports interface styles for both novice and experienced users. In addition to a text editor, spreadsheets, and "canned" explanations, the software contains an exposure calculation submodule that enables the user to calculate exposures and doses from chemical concentrations in air, surface water, groundwater, soil, sediment, and biota (THISTLE PUBLISHING).

Teratogenic effects of drugs and other environmental agents account for a small yet preventable proportion of all congenital anomalies among some 150,000 children born in the U.S. each year (FRIEDMAN ET AL., 1986; 1990). The TERatogen Information System (TERIS), developed by Friedman and his colleagues of The University of Texas Health Science Center at Dallas, supplements three other databases that are maintained and accessible on NLM's TOXNET. These are the Developmental and Reproductive Toxicology Database (DART), the Environmental Teratology Information Center Backfile (ETIBACK), and the EPA's GENE-TOX database, which contains mutagenicity data on over 4,000 chemicals. TERIS supplies published information on the teratogenicity of chemicals along with the online version of Shepard's Catalog of Teratogenic Agents. For example, on cocaine, TERIS first presents the agent's magnitude of teratogenic risk to children born after exposure during gestation, followed by quality and quantity of data on which risk estimate is based. The system provides extensive comments supplemented with information for environmental and occupational exposures and a list of key references. The CD-ROM version of TERIS is also distributed by Micromedex, Inc.,[10] as a part of their Computerized Clinical Information System (CCIS) CD-ROM version. CCIS databases that cover information on emergency medicine (Emergindex, Material Safety Data Sheets) and hazardous effects on the fetus and reproductive system (Reprotext, TERIS, Shepard's Catalog, Reprorisk) have just started to receive some attention in the literature (FISHMAN).

CASSIDY & KOSTREWSKI designed a study to evaluate the relative performance of 11 sources in providing information to answer a preselected set of 30 questions on household product poisoning. The investigators used both bibliographic and factual sources across different implementation media (e.g., two commercial online databases, Toxline and Excerpta Medica; Registry of Toxic Effects of Chemical Substances (RTECS) on microfilm; six textbooks; and two internally developed sources). The study used the performance measures of completeness of information (not operationalized in the article) and search time, defined as time needed to retrieve documents. The two in-house databases performed better (not operationalized) than the other nine sources with regard to both performance measures. The study's findings would have been stronger if the terminology had been carefully defined and if the researchers' prior experience in the use of 11 sources had been described. It would be useful to examine which individual independent variables influenced the relatively higher performance of the two internally produced sources.

Pesticides. Pesticides account for a relatively small fraction of the 100,000 chemicals in common use, but their high toxicity levels through various pathways (residues in food crops and contaminated drinking water) may cause considerable ecological damage (POSTEL). Postel reviews some new and promising strategies, which include integrated pest management, biological control, pollution prevention, and an overall commitment to education and R&D.

A random check of several pesticide reference sources, all of which are widely used and highly regarded, has revealed inconsistent reporting of the solubility of Alachlor. Motivated by this initial finding, and in order to make environmental modeling and risk assessment more reliable and rigorous, the Agricultural Research Service (ARS) Pesticide

---

[10]Mead Corp. announced that it has sold Micromedex Inc., to a U.S. subsidiary of the Thomson Corp., which will operate the company under its Medical Economics Data company.

Properties Database (PPD) has assumed the responsibility for creating and validating the physical and chemical values of pesticides (HELLER ET AL.). The investigators briefly report on the decision tree of an expert system called SOL, which through a series of questions, finds a more accurate pesticide property source. The authors expect to use the ARS PPD as a centralized and accurate reference for chemical and physical properties of pesticides, which then can be used in groundwater modeling and regulatory assessments of pesticides. KADEC describes major information sources produced by the EPA's Office of Pesticides and Toxic Substances, including the National Pesticide Information Retrieval System (NPIRS), the Pesticide Data Management System (PDMS), and the docket file. That office also produces a PC-based menu-driven Pesticide Information Network (PIN), which contains the following three files: (1) the Pesticides Monitoring Inventory, which compiles governmental and private pesticide monitoring projects; (2) the Restricted Use Products File, which lists pesticide products together with canceled products; and (3) the Chemical Index, which serves as a dictionary for the chemicals included in the above two files (U.S. ENVIRONMENTAL PROTECTION AGENCY. OFFICE OF PESTICIDES AND TOXIC SUBSTANCES).

With the growing interest in and concerns with various aspects of pesticide information, the marketplace has seen many electronic sources with pesticide information competing with their printed counterparts. SCHNEIDER describes and compares The Pesticide Disk with similar products (e.g., SilverPlatter's Pest-Bank, DIALOG's databases, *AgroChemical Handbook* and the *European Directory of Agrochemical Products*) with regard to cost, content, and frequency of update. The article emphasizes hardware, software, and user interface components rather than conceptual or cognitive elements of learning and searching.

Safety concerns. The Registry of Toxic Effects of Chemical Substances (RTECS) database, built by the National Institute for Occupational Safety and Health (NIOSH), includes data on over 100,000 known toxic substances, including drugs, food additives, preservatives, ores, pesticides, dyes, detergents, lubricants, soaps, plastics, plant and animal extracts, toxic plants and animals, industrial intermediates, and waste products. While several safety-related databases are publicly available on commercial systems (e.g., RTECS on NLM's TOXNET; NIOSH and Chemical Exposure on DIALOG; Hazardline on the Occupational Health Services (OHS)[11] and BRS; and HAZINF, Clinical Toxicology of Commercial Products (CTCP), Federal Register Search System (FRSS), RTECS, and Material Safety Data Sheets (MSDS) available in the Baker & Mallin

---

[11]Occupational Health Services (OHS), Inc., 450 7th Ave., Suite 2407, New York, NY 10123.

files on CIS, through OHS, and on the MSDS Engine[12]), little has been reported in the literature about these and similar safety-related sources (ALSTON; BERNAL; ROBERTS).

From the U.K. perspective, the case study by ROBERTS first describes some of the major safety information sources in printed, online, and CD-ROM formats and then reports on a project that is designed to create an in-house hazardous information database. The article also discusses strengths of the safety information sources with regard to substance identification, chemical and physical properties, hazardous characteristics, and data relating to precautions, emergencies, and transport.

As Table 2 suggests, a subset of only 13 safety-related databases available through as many as eight commercial vendors raises questions about the conceptual and mechanical aspects of searching and the cost-effectiveness and ease of learning and searching of the available databases. In addition, many safety-related databases have become available on CD-ROM families of health, safety, and the environmental data banks accessible on SilverPlatter (CHEM-BANK with its RTECS, Hazardous Substances Data Bank (HSDB), OHM/TADS, and CHRIS; the OCLC Environment Library, with over 300,000 abstracts drawn from the OCLC Online Union Catalog; OSH-ROM with its four databases covering international occupational health and safety information; OSH-UK full-text database covering occupational safety and health legislation, and guidance notes from the United Kingdom; and the European Inventory of Existing Commercial Chemical Substances (EINECS) covering over 100,000 chemical substances).

Although written with the biomedical searcher in mind, the article by SNOW illustrates command entries to DIALOG's Federal Register full-text database on a sample of eight environmental queries. The article notes that information collected in many government-produced databases is underutilized by biomedical information professionals.

With the increasing diversity of available online databases, the need to use search tools to evaluate the most relevant sources seems apparent. The method of search hedges, which groups search terms together according to a given concept and makes them accessible to users, has been explored to show how database technology can be used to enhance information retrieval (CURNUTT & CURNUTT). The procedure has been used with reactive chemicals and to develop and illustrate the potential utility of the reactive chemical value index.

---

[12] MSDS Engine is available from Genium Publishing Corp., 1145 Catalyn St., Schenectady, NY 12303-1836.

Table 2
Some Safety-Related Databases

Databases	BRS	CCIS	CIS	DIALOG	Genium Publishing	NLM	OHS	Silver-Platter
Baker & Mallin			x					
CHEM-BANK								x
Chemical Exposure				x				
CTCP			x					
FRSS			x					
Hazardline	x						x	
MSDS		x						
MSDS Engine					x			
NIOSH				x				x
OCLC Environment Library								x
OHM/TADS			x					x
OSH-ROM								x
RTECS				x		x		x

New Winds of Change

Most recently, we have seen early efforts to link various information systems with the underlying research concerns and regulatory programs. For instance, EPA's Health Effects Research Laboratory (HERL) has recently proposed a research strategy model as a three-dimensional matrix with seven research topics that link the corresponding regulatory program concerns with HERL's scientific disciplines (U.S. ENVIRONMENTAL PROTECTION AGENCY. OFFICE OF RESEARCH AND DEVELOPMENT).

CHURGIN describes the Oceanic Network Information Center (OCEANIC) as a collaborative effort at the University of Delaware using the National Aeronautics and Space Administration (NASA) Space Physics Analysis Network (SPAN). The project is also supported by NSF and NOAA. NASA's SPAN links oceanographic centers by high-speed computer networks and facilitates retrieval and dissemination of a unified marine information by integrating bibliographic records, inventories, directories, and scientific data with pictorial and graphic representations. Systems such as OCEANIC will play an increasingly important role in reducing key environmental uncertainties, as addressed by the

U.S. Global Change Research Program (USGCRP), and in developing more reliable predictions on which national and international policies to global change can be based (U.S. DEPARTMENT OF THE INTERIOR. GEOLOGICAL SURVEY. OFFICE OF SCIENCE AND TECHNOLOGY POLICY).

One such effort has been made by the Interagency Working Group on Data Management for Global Change (IAWGDMGC). Specifically, the U.S. Department of Commerce, the Department of Energy, NASA, NLM, and the Department of Defense have started to establish cooperation among the members of the research, policy, and information communities in order to effectively use existing information technologies and make the existing resources more coherent and easier to use (CARROLL ET AL.).

In its response to new environmental paradigms, mentioned earlier, EPA has created two comprehensive information sources: the Alternative Treatment Technology Information Center (ATTIC) and the Pollution Prevention Information Clearinghouse (PPIC) (U.S. ENVIRONMENTAL PROTECTION AGENCY. OFFICE OF ENVIRONMENTAL ENGINEERING AND TECHNOLOGY DEMONSTRATION). ATTIC has received some attention in the literature (DORRIS; SPROAT ET AL.); information about PPIC is available only internally. ATTIC integrates hazardous waste data into a centralized searchable source and offers information on innovative treatment processes that destroy, decontaminate, or transform wastes by thermal treatments that use flame combustion, infrared incineration, and plasma heat systems or by biological treatments that use fungi and bacteria to transform waste compounds into solids, liquids, and sludges. Some of ATTIC's programs, including the Superfund Innovative Technology Evaluation (SITE) and Records of Decision, are available on tape through NTIS. The PPIC network contains technical and legislative information dedicated to reducing industrial multimedia pollutants and preventing pollution in the first place.

The Earth Science Data Directory (ESDD), developed and produced by the U.S. Geological Survey (USGS) (U.S. DEPARTMENT OF THE INTERIOR. GEOLOGICAL SURVEY) is another example of early attempts to deal with environmental issues globally. Databases referenced in ESDD are both textual and graphic, produced by public and private sectors, and concerned with the geologic, topographic, hydrologic, cartographic, and biological sciences as well as with demography. ESDD, online or on a compact disc (Earth Sciences Disc) (available from SilverPlatter[13]), is the USGS repository of information on databases relating to interagency global-change activities offering information "overlays" for GIS applications.

---

[13]SilverPlatter Information, Inc., 100 River Ridge Dr., Norwood, MA 02062-5026.

CONCLUSIONS

The literature on environmental machine-readable sources since 1986 shows that although the production of information sources has increased in pace and sophistication, the growth rate of the literature that describes and evaluates these products is somewhat wanting. The pollution-prevention paradigm has just begun to influence information delivery mechanisms that are specifically designed to respond to pollution prevention, replacing the traditional end-of-pipe command and control approach. Similarly, the new emphasis on total quality management suggests that interrelated databases can be linked to form a coherent environmental universe. While a literature search on the information perspective of global change has produced several hundreds of bibliographic citations, most of the papers enumerate various existing technologies and toolkits and speculate on how to use most of what is currently available. Little progress, however, has been made in the areas of understanding the diversity of current and potential users of information resources and in advancing our knowledge, through laboratory studies and precisely defined questions, as to which technologies would be the most productive in organizing, searching, disseminating, and synthesizing environmental data. Much of the analytical and evaluative work awaits the mobilization of the information community first before the technological community can address and solve some of the investigative and basic information questions. That a growing number of communications researchers have started to consider the tasks of informing and educating the public of the highest priority, has special implications for the information profession in shaping information policy and applying communication research findings into designing new classes of information systems. More research is needed on user modeling and the searching effectiveness of both information specialists and end users in the way they handle interactive information technologies. As more information sources become available to the public, we need to evaluate how different groups use and should use the same database across different implementation media (e.g., CD-ROM vs. online, print version, or network). A rigorous quantification of the spread of, for instance, water-related databases might shed light on the way we use these resources cost effectively. Equally important would be a study designed to explore preferences among environmentalists to use information sources in certain media over others. LANDAU ET AL. have proposed the following seven variables for their package parameter: media (channel), format, extent, technical sophistication, temporal qualities, editorial qualities, and information accuracy. A study that examined and compared various EPA sources along some or all of these variables would extend the public's effectiveness in using the existing sources. For instance, by knowing that we can move through the sources along the variables of extent (e.g., from general information to more specific), and time (e.g., from current and typically not peer-reviewed literature to more mature and reviewed literature), searchers can incorporate some of these options into their search strategies. Finally, we need to find ways to integrate textual, spatial, and temporal data to create a comprehensive ecological system warranted by demands of the new environmental era.

BIBLIOGRAPHY

ALLEN, THOMAS J. 1977. Managing the Flow of Technology: Technology Transfer and the Dissemination of Technological Information within the R & D Organization. Cambridge, MA: MIT Press; 1977. 320p. ISBN: 0-262-01048-8.

ALONI, MICHAELA. 1985. Patterns of Information Transfer among Engineers and Applied Scientists in Complex Organizations: A Partial Review. Scientometrics. 1985 November; 8(5-6): 279-300. ISSN: 0138-9130.

ALSTON, PATRICIA GAYLE. 1991. Environment Online: The Greening of Databases. Part 2. Scientific and Technical Databases. Database. 1991 October; 14(5): 34-52. ISSN: 0162-4105.

AMERICAN PETROLEUM INSTITUTE (API). 1986. API Thesaurus. New York, NY: API Central Abstracting and Indexing Service (CAIS); 1986 January. 355p. Available from: API Central Abstracting and Indexing Service, 156 William St., New York, NY 10038.

AMIR, S. 1985. On the Degree of Interdisciplinarity of Research Programs: A Quantitative Assessment. Scientometrics. 1985 July; 8(1-2): 117-136. ISSN: 0138-9130.

AMMAN, CLAUS; KNORR-CETINA, KARIN. 1988. Thinking through Talk: An Ethnographic Study of a Molecular Biology Laboratory. Paper presented at: 1988 Symposium on Science Communication: Environmental and Health Research; 1988 December 15-17; Los Angeles, CA. 41p. Available from: the second author, Faculty of Sociology, University of Bielefeld, P.O. Box 8640, 4800 Bielefeld 1, Germany.

ANDREWS, MARTHA. 1988. The Organization of Polar Information before the Advent of Online Databases. Geography and Map Division Bulletin. 1988 December; 154: 5-22. ISSN: 0036-1607.

ANDREWS, MARTHA. 1990. Computerized Information Retrieval and Bibliographic Control of the Polar and/or Cold Regions Literature: A Review. Geography and Map Division Bulletin. 1990 March; 159: 21-42. ISSN: 0036-1607.

ASLIB PROCEEDINGS. 1988. Sources of Environmental Pollution Information. Aslib Proceedings. 1988 May; 40(5): 139-162. (Entire issue on title topic). ISSN: 0001-253X.

BALDRIDGE, SHEILA. 1988. Creating an Online Monterey Bay Bibliography. In: Swim, Frances F.; Brownlow, Judith, eds. Marine Science Library Network: Proceedings of the International Association of Aquatic and Marine

Science Libraries and Information Centers (IAMSLIC) 12th Annual Conference; 1986 October 7-11; Newport, OR. Port Aransas, TX: IAMSLIC; 1988. 77-82. ISSN: 8755-6332; ISBN: 0-932939-04-X.

BAWDEN, DAVID. 1988. Chemical Toxicology Databanks. Aslib Proceedings. 1988 March; 40(3): 79-85. ISSN: 0001-253X.

BERNAL, NANCY E. 1992. Hazard Awareness Health and Safety Library: Multimedia Interactive Learning on CD-ROM. CD-ROM Professional. 1992 January; 5(1): 92-97. ISSN: 1049-0833.

BIRDWELL, K. R.; DANIELS, R. C. 1991. Global Geographic Information System Data Base of Storm Occurrences and Other Climatic Phenomena Affecting Coastal Zones. Washington, DC: Department of Energy; 1991 May. 304p. NTIS: DE91014949/XAB.

BORGMAN, CHRISTINE L., ed. 1990. Scholarly Communication and Bibliometrics. Newbury Park, CA: Sage Publications; 1990. 363p. ISBN: 0-8039-3879-9.

BORGMAN, CHRISTINE L.; CASE, DONALD O.; MEADOW, CHARLES T. 1990. The Design and Evaluation of a Front-End User Interface for Energy Researchers. Journal of the American Society for Information Science. 1990 March; 40(2): 99-109. ISSN: 0002-8231.

BRONSON, ROBERTA J. 1991. IRIS: Integrated Risk Information System Database. Medical Reference Services Quarterly. 1991 Summer; 10(2): 73-85. ISSN: 0276-3869.

BROWN, LESTER R., ed. 1988. State of the World 1988: A Worldwatch Institute Report on Progress toward a Sustainable Society. 1st edition. New York, NY: W. W. Norton & Company; 1988. 237p. ISBN: 0-393-02515-2.

BROWNLOW, JUDITH. 1986. Sources for Aquaculture Information in the United States. In: Grundy, R. L.; Ford, R. T.; Beardsley, Mary Jane, eds. Marine Science Information: An International Commodity: Proceedings of the International Association of Aquatic and Marine Science Libraries and Information Centers (IAMSLIC) 11th Annual Conference; 1985 October 14-18; Gloucester Point, VA. Port Aransas, TX: IAMSLIC; 1986. 55-70. ISSN: 8755-6332; ISBN: 0-932939-02-3.

BRUEGGEMAN, PETER. 1988. ASFA on CD-ROM at Scripps Institution. Laserdisk Professional. 1988 July; 1(2): 39-47. ISSN: 0896-4149.

BRUEGGEMAN, PETER. 1992. Managing a Local Aquatic Science Database with AskSam. In: McDowell, Elizabeth Fuseler; Wilst, Stephen, eds. The Aquatic Environment: Description, Management, Conservation: Proceedings of the International Association of Aquatic and Marine Science Libraries and Information Centers (IAMSLIC) 17th Annual Conference; 1991 October 7-11; Galveston, TX. Fort Collins, CO: IAMSLIC; 1992. 151-159. ISSN: 8755-6332.

BRUENING, JOHN C. 1990. Risk Communication: A Two-Way Connection. Occupational Hazards. 1990 October; 52(10): 76-80. ISSN: 0029-7909.

CALIFORNIA. DEPARTMENT OF HEALTH SERVICES. CALIFORNIA OCCUPATIONAL HEALTH PROGRAM. 1991. Hazard Evaluation Systems & Information Services (HESIS). Berkeley, CA: HESIS Publications; 1991 June. Available from: California Occupational Health Program, 2151 Berkeley Way, Annex 11, 3rd Floor, Berkeley, CA 94704.

CARLE, SUSAN D. 1988. A Hazardous Mix: Discretion to Disclose and Incentives to Suppress under OSHA's Hazard Communication Standard. The Yale Law Journal. 1988 March; 97(4): 581-601. ISSN: 0044-0094.

CARROLL, B. C.; JACK, R. F.; COTTER, G. A. 1990. Data Policy and Availability Supporting Global Change Research, Development, and Decision-Making: An Information Perspective. Washington, DC: National Aeronautics and Space Administration; 1990 October. 15p. NTIS: N91-30592/0/ZAB.

CASSIDY, S. L.; KOSTREWSKI, B. J. 1986. An Evaluation of Information Sources in Household Product Poisoning. Journal of Information Science. 1986; 12(4): 143-151. ISSN: 0165-5515.

CHEREMISINOFF, NICHOLAS P. 1987. Environmental Software Review—1987. Pollution Engineering. 1987 January; 19(1): 30-43. ISSN: 0032-3640.

CHUBIN, DARYL E. 1985. Beyond Invisible Colleges: Inspirations and Aspirations of Post-1972 Social Studies of Science. Scientometrics. 1985 March; 7(3-6): 221-254. ISSN: 0138-9130.

CHURGIN, JAMES. 1989. Ocean Network Information Center (OCEANIC)—Developing an Online Ocean Information Center. In: Winn, Carolyn P.; Burkhart, Robert W.; Burkhart, Joyce C., eds. Marine Science Information throughout the World: Sharing the Resources: Proceedings of the International Association of Aquatic and Marine Science Libraries and Information Centers (IAMSLIC) 14th Annual Conference; 1988 October 3-7; Miami, FL. St. Petersburg, FL: IAMSLIC; 1989. 207-215. ISSN: 8755-6332; ISBN: 0-932939-06-6.

CIS NEWS. 1985-. Baltimore, MD: Chemical Information Systems, Inc. Available from: Chemical Information Systems, Inc., 7215 York Rd., Baltimore, MD 21212.

COVELLO, VINCENT T.; VON WINTERFELDT, DETLOF; SLOVIC, PAUL. 1986a. Communicating Scientific Information about Health and Environmental Risks: Problems and Opportunities from a Social and Behavioral Perspective. In: Davies, Clarence J.; Covello, Vincent T.; Allen, Frederick W., eds. Risk Communication: Proceedings of the National Conference on Risk Communication; 1986 January 29-31; Washington, DC. Washington, DC: The Conservation Foundation; 1986. Appendix: 109-134. ISBN: 0-89164-103-3.

COVELLO, VINCENT T.; VON WINTERFELDT, DETLOF; SLOVIC, PAUL. 1986b. Risk Communication: A Review of the Literature. Risk Abstracts. 1986; 3(4): 171-182. ISSN: 0824-3336.

COYNE, JOSEPH G.; CARROLL, BONNIE C.; REDFORD, JULIA S. 1983. Energy Information Systems and Services. In: Williams, Martha E., ed. Annual Review of Information Science and Technology: Volume 18. White Plains, NY: Knowledge Industry Publications, Inc. for the American Society for Information Science; 1983. 231-274. ISSN: 0066-4200; ISBN: 0-86729-050-1.

CRANE, DIANA. 1971. Information Needs and Uses. In: Cuadra, Carlos A.; Luke, Ann W., eds. Annual Review of Information Science and Technology: Volume 6. Chicago, IL: Encyclopaedia Britannica, Inc. for the American Society for Information Science; 1971. 1-39. ISBN: 0-85229-166-3.

CUADRA/ELSEVIER. 1989. Directory of Online Databases. 1989 July; 10(3): 753p. ISSN: 0193-6840.

CURNUTT, GERALD L.; CURNUTT, KIRK L. 1991. Reactive Chemical Hedges: A Search Tool for Comprehensive Retrieval of Chemical Safety Data. Journal of Chemical Information and Computer Sciences. 1991 February; 31(1): 116-119. ISSN: 0095-2338.

DE MES, W. W. 1990. Oceans of Information ..... But Where Is the Water? Paper presented at the Seminar on Water-Related Information Retrieval; 1990 June 28-29; Dubrovnik, Yugoslavia. Available from: the author, International Hydrological Programme, 7 Place de Fontenoy, 75700 Paris, France.

DECK, KATHRYN S.; BONZO, SANDRA E. 1990a. Environmental Health and Toxicology: A Selected Bibliography of Printed Information Sources. Atlanta, GA: U. S. Department of Health and Human Services, Public Health Service, Centers for Disease Control, Center for Environmental Health and Injury Control, Information Resources Management Group; 1990. 105p. Available from: Centers for Disease Control, Center for Environmental Health and Injury Control, Information Resources Management Group, Atlanta, GA 30333.

DECK, KATHRYN S.; BONZO, SANDRA E. 1990b. Some Publicly Available Sources of Computerized Information on Environmental Health and Toxicology. Atlanta, GA: U.S. Department of Health and Human Services, Public Health Service, Centers for Disease Control, Center for Environmental Health and Injury Control, Information Resources Management Group; 1990. 50p. (Unpublished typescript). Available from: Centers for Disease Control, Center for Environmental Health and Injury Control, Information Resources Management Group, Atlanta, GA 30333.

DERVIN, BRENDA; NILAN, MICHAEL. 1986. Information Needs and Uses. In: Williams, Martha E., ed. Annual Review of Information Science and Technology: Volume 21. White Plains, NY: Knowledge Industry Publications, Inc. for the American Society for Information Science; 1986. 3-33. ISSN: 0066-4200; ISBN: 0-86729-209-1.

DESCHAMPS, JUDITH. 1988. International Sources. Aslib Proceedings. 1988 May; 40(5): 157-162. ISSN: 0001-253X.

DISASTER RESEARCH CENTER. 1991. Publications List. Newark, DE: University of Delaware; 1991 February. 23p. Available from: Disaster Research Center—Publications, University of Delaware, Newark, DE 19716.

DORRIS, VIRGINIA KENT. 1989. Data on Cleanup Technology Is in the ATTIC. Engineering News Record. 1989 August 3; 223(5): 37. ISSN: 0013-807X.

DRABEK, THOMAS E. 1986. Human System Responses to Disaster: An Inventory of Sociological Findings. New York, NY: Springer-Verlag; 1986. 509p. (Springer Series on Environmental Management). ISBN: 3-540-96323-5; LC: 86-15622.

DRABEK, THOMAS E. 1990. Emergency Management: Strategies for Maintaining Organizational Integrity. New York, NY: Springer-Verlag; 1990. 281p. ISBN: 3-540-97114-9; LC: 89-37042.

ENVIRONMENTAL SCIENCE & TECHNOLOGY. 1991. 25th Anniversary Issue. Environmental Science & Technology. 1991 April; 25(4). (Entire issue on title topic). ISSN: 0013-936X.

EPA JOURNAL. 1990. The First Twenty Years. EPA Journal. 1990 September/October; 16(5): 64p. (Entire issue on title topic). Single issues are available from: U.S. Environmental Protection Agency, Public Information Center, 401 M Street S.W., P.M.-211B, Washington, DC 20460. Subscription is available from: Government Printing Office, Washington, DC 20402.

FENWICK, WENDY STERN. 1990. How the Numerical System Can Help Information Specialists, Chemists and Environmental Scientists. In: Williams, Martha E., ed. Proceedings of the 11th National Online Meeting; 1990 May 1-3; New York, NY. Medford, NJ: Learned Information, Inc.; 1990. 385-388. ISBN: 0-938734-44-X.

FISHMAN, DIANE L. 1992. Computerized Clinical Information System—CCIS from Micromedex. Database. 1992 April; 15(2): 58-62. ISSN: 0162-4105.

FORTUNA, RICHARD C.; LENNET, DAVID J. 1987. Hazardous Waste Regulation, The New Era: An Analysis and Guide to RCRA and the 1984 Amendments. New York, NY: McGraw-Hill; 1987. 393p. ISBN: 0-07-021634-7.

FRANK, ROBYN. 1987. Agricultural Information Systems and Services. In: Williams, Martha E., ed. Annual Review of Information Science and Technology: Volume 22. Amsterdam, The Netherlands: Elsevier Science Publishers for the American Society for Information Science; 1987. 293-334. ISSN: 0066-4200; ISBN: 0-444-70302-0.

FREEMAN, ROBERT R.; HANFMAN, DEBORAH T. 1990. REGIS: A Prototype Regional Information System for African Aquaculture. In: Burkhart, Robert W.; Burkhart, Joyce C., eds. IAMSLIC at a Crossroads: Proceedings of the International Association of Aquatic and Marine Science Libraries and Information Centers (IAMSLIC) 15th Annual Conference; 1989 October 7-11; St. George's, Bermuda. St. Petersburg, FL: IAMSLIC; 1990. 55-64. ISSN: 8755-6332; ISBN: 0-932939-07-4.

FREEMAN, ROBERT R.; SMITH, MONA F. 1986. Environmental Information. In: Williams, Martha E., ed. Annual Review of Information Science and Technology: Volume 21. White Plains, NY: Knowledge Industry Publications, Inc. for the American Society for Information Science; 1986. 241-305. ISSN: 0066-4200; ISBN: 0-86729-209-1.

FRICK, WILLIAM G.; SULLIVAN, THOMAS F. P., eds. 1990. Environmental Regulatory Glossary. 5th edition. Rockville, MD: Government Institutes, Inc.; 1990. 449p. ISBN: 0-86587-798-X; LC: 89-82642.

FRIEDMAN, J. M.; LITTLE, B.; BOST, R.; GERRITY, L. W.; MIZE, S. G.; SINGLETON, W. L. 1986. The Teratogen Information System. In: Salamon, Roger; Blum, Bruce; Jorgensen, Mogens, eds. MEDINFO 86: Proceedings of the 5th Conference on Medical Informatics: Part 1; 1986 October 26-30; Washington, DC. Participants edition. New York, NY: North-Holland; 1986. 462-464. ISBN: 0-444-70108-7.

FRIEDMAN, J. M.; LITTLE, B. B.; BRENT, R. L.; CORDERO, J. F.; HANSON, J. W.; SHEPARD, T. H. 1990. Potential Human Teratogenicity of Frequently Prescribed Drugs. Teratogenicity of Common Drugs. 1990 April; 75(4): 596-599. ISSN: 0029-7844.

GAINES, MATTHEW J. 1988. Sources of Environmental Pollution Information Radioactivity. Aslib Proceedings. 1988 May; 40(5): 147-156. ISSN: 0001-253X.

GALCZYNSKA, T.; WITOWSKI, A. 1989. The Environmental Information System—INFOTERRA. Zagadnienia Informacji Naukowej. 1989; 2(55): 177-186. ISSN: 0030-6282.

GARVEY, WILLIAM D.; TOMITA, KAZUO; WOOLF, PATRICIA. 1979. The Dynamic Scientific-Information User. In: Garvey, William D., ed. Communication: The Essence of Science. Elmsford, NY: Pergamon Press; 1979. 256-279. ISBN: 0-08-022254-4.

GOMEZ, MICHAEL J. 1990. Polar Science Information Resources. In: Burkhart, Robert W.; Burkhart, Joyce C., eds. IAMSLIC at a Crossroads: Proceedings of the International Association of Aquatic and Marine Science Libraries and Information Centers (IAMSLIC) 15th Annual Conference; 1989 October 7-11; St. George's, Bermuda. St. Petersburg, FL: IAMSLIC; 1990. 9-22. ISSN: 8755-6332; ISBN: 0-932939-07-4.

GORDON, JUDY A. 1991. Meeting the Challenge of Risk Communication. Public Relations Journal. 1991 January; 47(1): 28-29. ISSN: 0033-3670.

GOVERNMENT INSTITUTES, INCORPORATED. 1990. Environmental Statutes. Rockville, MD: Government Institutes, Inc.; 1990. 1,169p. ISBN: 0-86587-796-3 (softcover); ISBN: 0-86587-797-1 (hardcover).

GROSSER, KERRY. 1991. Human Networks in Organizational Information Processing. In: Williams, Martha E., ed. Annual Review of Information Science and Technology: Volume 26. Medford, NJ: Learned Information, Inc. for the American Society for Information Science; 1991. 349-404. ISSN: 0066-4200; ISBN: 0-938734-55-5.

HAAS, STEPHANIE. 1991. Gaps and Overlaps: A Comparison of CD-ROM Coverage of Selected Water Resources Abstracts, Wildlife Review/Fisheries Review, and Aquatic Sciences and Fisheries Abstracts. In: McDowell, Elizabeth Fuseler; Wilst, Stephen, eds. Breaking the Barriers to the Free Flow of Information: Proceedings of the International Association of Aquatic and Marine Science Libraries and Information Centers (IAMSLIC) 16th Annual Conference; 1990 October 2-5; Seattle, WA. Fort Collins, CO: IAMSLIC; 1991. 129-136. ISSN: 8755-6332.

HALPIN, PETER. 1978. Standard Air Pollution Classification Network: A Thesaurus of Terms (As Used in the APTIC Data Base). 2nd edition. Research Triangle Park, NC: U.S. Environmental Protection Agency; 1978 March. 185p. (EPA/450/1-78/002). NTIS: PB-292038.

HANFMAN, DEBORAH. 1989. AquaRef: An Expert Advisory System for Reference Support. Reference Librarian. 1989; (23): 113-133. ISSN: 0276-3877.

HARRINGTON, JAMES. 1990. Aquatic Sciences and Fisheries Abstracts. CD-ROM Librarian. 1990 November; 5(10): 41-45. ISSN: 0893-9934.

HARRIS, CYNTHIA; WILLIAMS, ROBERT C. 1992. Research Directions: The Public Health Service Looks at Hazards to Minorities. EPA Journal. 1992 March/April; 18(1): 40-41. Single issues are available from: U.S. Environmental Protection Agency, Public Information Center, 401 M Street S.W., P.M.-211B, Washington, DC 20460. Subscription is available from: Government Printing Office, Washington, DC 20402.

HARUYAMA, AKEMI; HOSOYAMA, MIKI. 1987. INFOTERRA File on Sources of Environmental Information Provided through JOIS in Japanese. Information Processing and Management. 1987 July; 30(4): 335-344. ISSN: 0306-4573.

HATTIS, DALE; KENNEDY, DAVID. 1986. Assessing Risk from Health Hazards: An Imperfect Science. Technology Review. 1986 May/June; 89(4): 60-71. ISSN: 0040-1692.

HELLER, STEPHEN R.; SCOTT, KAREN; BIGWOOD, DOUGLAS W. 1989. The Need for Data Evaluation of Physical and Chemical Properties of Pesticides: The ARS Pesticide Properties Database. Journal of Chemical Information and Computer Sciences. 1989 August; 29(3): 159-162. ISSN: 0095-2338; CODEN: JCISD8.

HOWARD, PHILIP H.; HUEBER, AMY E.; MULESKY, BARBARA C.; CRISMAN, JENNY S.; MEYLAN, WILLIAM; CROSBIE, ERIN; GRAY, ANTHONY D.; SAGE, GLORIA W.; HOWARD, KAREN P.; LAMACCHIA, ANTHONY; BOETHLING, ROBERT; TROAST, RICHARD. 1986. Biolog, Biodeg, and Fate/Expos: New Toxicity As Well As Environmental Fate/ Exposure of Chemicals. Environmental Toxicology and Chemistry. 1986; 5(11): 977-988. ISSN: 0730-7268.

HOWE, HENRY F.; HUBBELL, STEPHEN P.; BLOCKSTEIN, DAVID E. 1990. Rationale for the National Institutes for the Environment. The Environmental Professional. 1990; 12(4): 360-363. ISSN: 0191-5398.

HUDDART, DAVID. 1988. Environmental Databanks on the Chemical Information System. Aslib Proceedings. 1988 May; 40(5): 133-137. ISSN: 0001-253X.

JOHNSON, ARTHUR H. 1986. Acid Deposition: Trends, Relationships, and Effects—Academy of Sciences Report. Environment. 1986 May; 28(4): 6-11, 34-39. ISSN: 0013-9157.

JOY, ALBERT H.; EATON, NANCY L.; GOINS, RODNEY K. 1989. Access to the Canadian Government Publications on Acid Rain: The University of Vermont's HEA Title II-C Grant. Government Publications Review. 1989 January/February; 16(1): 31-39. ISSN: 0277-9390.

KADEC, SARAH T. 1989. The Environmental Protection Agency: A Profile of Its Information Collection and Dissemination. Government Information Quarterly. 1989; 6(3): 295-309. ISSN: 0740-624X.

KELLAND, JOHN LAURENCE. 1989. Marine Science Information in Non-Marine Databases. In: Winn, Carolyn P.; Burkhart, Robert W.; Burkhart, Joyce C., eds. Marine Science Information throughout the World: Sharing the Resources: Proceedings of the International Association of Aquatic and Marine Science Libraries and Information Centers (IAMSLIC) 14th Annual Conference; 1988 October 3-7; Miami, FL. St. Petersburg, FL: IAMSLIC; 1989. 133-137. ISSN: 8755-6332; ISBN: 0-932939-06-6.

KELLAND, JOHN LAURENCE. 1990. Biochemistry and Environmental Biology: A Comparative Citation Analysis. Library & Information Science Research. 1990 January-March; 12(1): 103-115. ISSN: 0740-8188.

KIM, BYUNG J.; GEE, CHAI SUNG; BANDY, JOHN T.; HUANG, CHING-SAN; GUZEWICH, DAVID C. 1991. Hazardous Waste Treatment Technologies. Journal of the Water Pollution Control Federation. 1991 June; 63(4): 501-509. ISSN: 0043-1303.

KISSMAN, HENRY M.; WEXLER, PHILIP. 1983. Toxicological Information. In: Williams, Martha E., ed. Annual Review of Information Science and Technology: Volume 18. White Plains, NY: Knowledge Industry Publications, Inc. for the American Society for Information Science; 1983. 185-230. ISSN: 0066-4200; ISBN: 0-86729-050-1.

KNOWLEDGE INDUSTRY PUBLICATIONS. 1989. Database Directory. White Plains, NY: Knowledge Industry Publications, Inc.; 1989. 629p. ISSN: 0749-6680; ISBN: 0-86729-236-9.

KRAWCZAK, D.; SMITH, P. J.; SHUTE, S. J. 1987. EP-X: A Demonstration of Semantically-Based Search of Bibliographic Databases. In: Yu, C. T.; van Rijsbergen, C. J., eds. Proceedings of the Association for Computing Machinery Special Interest Group on Information Retrieval (ACM SIGIR)10th Annual International Conference on Research and Development in Information Retrieval; 1987 June 3-5; New Orleans, LA. New York, NY: ACM Press; 1987. 263-271. ISBN: 0-89791-232-2.

LANDAU, HERBERT B.; MADDOCK, JEROME T.; SHOEMAKER, FLOYD F.; COSTELLO, JOSEPH G. 1983. An Information Transfer Model to Define Information Users and Outputs with Specific Application to Environmental Technology. Journal of the American Society for Information Science. 1983 March; 33(2): 82-96. ISSN: 0002-8231.

LAW, J.; BAUIN, S.; COURTIAL, J.-P.; WHITTAKER, J. 1988. Policy and the Mapping of Scientific Change: A Co-Word Analysis of Research into Environmental Acidification. Scientometrics. 1988 September; 14(3-4): 251-264. ISSN: 0138-9130.

LEWIS, DON A.; FITZGERALD, CATHY M. 1979. Environmental Data Base Survey: Great Lakes–St. Lawrence Seaway Navigation Season Extension Program. (Prepared for Office of Biological Services, Fish and Wildlife Service. U. S. Department of the Interior.) Los Angeles, CA: The Aerospace Corporation; 1979 September. 220p. (Unpublished typescript). (Contract No. 14-16-0009-78-094). Available from: The Aerospace Corporation, P.O. Box 92957, Los Angeles, CA 90009.

LOVENBURG, SUSAN L.; STOSS, FREDERICK W. 1988. The Fugitive Literature of Acid Rain: Making Use of Nonconventional Information Sources in a Vertical File. Reference Services Review. 1988; 16(1-2): 95-104. ISSN: 0090-7324.

MAILLOUX, ELIZABETH N. 1989. Engineering Information Systems. In: Williams, Martha E., ed. Annual Review of Information Science and Technology: Volume 24. Amsterdam, The Netherlands: Elsevier Science Publishers for the American Society for Information Science; 1989. 239-266. ISSN: 0066-4200; ISBN: 0-444-87418-6.

MALONE, THOMAS F. 1986. Mission to Planet Earth: Integrating Studies of Global Change. Environment. 1986 October; 28(8): 6-11, 39-42. ISSN: 0013-9157.

MARCACCIO, KATHLEEN YOUNG, ed.; HILLSTROM, KEVIN; TOMASSINI, CHRISTINE; TURECKI, GWEN E., assoc. eds.; WILLIAMS, MARTHA E., founding ed. 1992. Computer-Readable Databases: A Directory and Data Sourcebook. 8th edition. Detroit, MI: Gale Research Inc.; 1992. 1,691p. ISSN: 0271-4477; ISBN: 0-8103-2946-8.

MARCUS, ALFRED; FOX, ISAAC. 1988. Lessons Learned about Communicating Safety-Related Concerns to Industry: The Nuclear Regulatory Commission after Three Mile Island. Paper presented at: 1988 Symposium on Science Communication: Environmental and Health Research; 1988 December 15-17; Los Angeles, CA. 39p. Available from: the first author, Carlson School of Management, University of Minnesota, 271 19th Avenue, South Minneapolis, MN 55455.

MARKHAM, JAMES W. 1990a. LCC, DDC, and Algae. Library Resources & Technical Services. 1990 January; 34(1): 54-61. ISSN: 0024-2527.

MARKHAM, JAMES W. 1990b. Library of Congress Subject Headings and the ASFIS Thesaurus. In: Winn, Carolyn P., ed. Oceans from a Global Perspective: International Cooperation in Marine Science Information Transfer: Proceedings of the International Association of Aquatic and Marine Science Libraries and Information Centers (IAMSLIC) 13th Annual Conference; 1987 October 5-9; Halifax, N.S., Canada. Woods Hole, MA: IAMSLIC; 1990. 89-95. ISSN: 8755-6332; ISBN: 0-93293-05-8.

MARKHAM, JAMES W. 1990c. Online Retrieval Strategies and Database Comparison for Literature on Macroalgae. In: Burkhart, Robert W.; Burkhart, Joyce C., eds. IAMSLIC at a Crossroads: Proceedings of the International Association of Aquatic and Marine Science Libraries and Information Centers (IAMSLIC) 15th Annual Conference; 1989 October 7-11; St. George's, Bermuda. St. Petersburg, FL: IAMSLIC; 1990. 157-162. ISSN: 8755-6332; ISBN: 0-932939-07-4.

MEADOW, CHARLES T.; CERNY, BARBARA A.; BORGMAN, CHRISTINE L.; CASE, DONALD O. 1989. Online Access to Knowledge: System Design. Journal of the American Society for Information Science. 1989 March; 40(2): 86-98. ISSN: 0002-8231.

MESSENGER, MANETTE M. 1983. The Hazardous Materials Management System (HMMS). Champaign, IL: U.S. Army Corps of Engineers Construction Engineering Research Laboratory (CERL); 1983 June. 14p. Available from: U.S. Army Corps of Engineers, CERL, P.O. Box 4005, Champaign, IL 61820.

MINGJU, GAI. 1992. The Chinese Marine Thesaurus and Its Compiling Techniques. In: McDowell, Elizabeth Fuseler; Wilst, Stephen, eds. The Aquatic Environment: Description, Management, Conservation: Proceedings of the International Association of Aquatic and Marine Science Libraries and Information Centers (IAMSLIC) 17th Annual Conference; 1991 October 7-11; Galveston, TX. Fort Collins, CO: IAMSLIC; 1992. 129-136. ISSN: 8755-6332.

MONARCH, IRA; CARBONELL, JAIME. 1987. CoalSORT: A Knowledge-Based Interface. IEEE Expert. 1987 Spring; 2(1): 39-53. ISSN: 0885-9000.

MOULDER, DAVID S. 1988. Sources of Environmental Pollution Information: The Marine Environment. Aslib Proceedings. 1988 May; 40(5): 139-146. ISSN: 0001-253X.

NATIONAL GROUND WATER INFORMATION CENTER. Ground Water. Dublin, OH: National Ground Water Information Center. Available in online or CD-ROM form from: National Ground Water Information Center, 6375 Riverside Dr., Dublin, OH 43017.

NELKIN, DOROTHY. 1988. Communicating the Risks and Benefits of Technology. Paper presented at: 1988 Symposium on Science Communication: Environmental and Health Research; 1988 December 15-17; Los Angeles, CA. 25p. Available from: the author, Department of Sociology, New York University, New York, NY 10011.

NIEUWENHUYSEN, PAUL; PROVOST, FRANK; DE MES, W. W.; SICEVIC, MIRJANA. 1989. Scientific and Technical Water-Related Documentary Information in the International Hydrological Programme (UNESCO-IHP III, Project 17.1). Paris, France: Unesco; 1989. 51p. (Technical Documents in Hydrology. SC-89/WS-49). Available from: the authors, Unesco International Hydrological Programme, 7 Place de Fontenoy, 75700 Paris, France.

OAK RIDGE NATIONAL LABORATORY. 1988. Bibliography on Tropical Rain Forests and the Global Carbon Cycle. Volume 1: An Introduction to the Literature. Volume 2: South Asia. Oak Ridge, TN: Oak Ridge National Laboratory; 1988 May. Volume 1: 161p.; Volume 2: 343p. (DOE: ORNL/CDIAC-24/V1; DOE: ORNL/CDIAC-24/V2). Available from: Oak Ridge National Laboratory, P.O. Box 2008, Oak Ridge, TN 37831.

OCCUPATIONAL HEALTH SERVICES INCORPORATED. 1991. HAZARDLINE. Information about HAZARDLINE and OHS MSDS ON DISC is available from: Occupational Health Services, Inc., 450 7th Ave., Suite 2407, New York, NY 10123.

ORBIT SEARCH SERVICE SEARCHLIGHT. 1992a. Check on the Environment with ERTH. ORBIT Search Service Searchlight. 1992 January; 20(1): 5. Available from: ORBIT Search Service, 8000 Westpark Drive, McLean, VA 22102.

ORBIT SEARCH SERVICE SEARCHLIGHT. 1992b. Search CISD for Occupational Hazards. ORBIT Search Service Searchlight. 1992 January; 20(1): 4. Available from: ORBIT Search Service, 8000 Westpark Drive, McLean, VA 22102.

PACKER, DAVID J. 1989. Bowker A & I Environment Database: Major Features and Editorial Policies. Science and Technology Libraries. 1989 Winter; 10(2): 57-65. ISSN: 0194-262X.

PALMER, CRYSTAL S., ed. 1989. GeoRef Thesaurus and Guide to Indexing. 5th edition. Alexandria, VA: American Geological Institute; 1989. 731p. ISBN: 0-913312-98-3.

PANTRY, SHEILA. 1989. Health and Safety Information on CD-ROM. Program. 1989 October; 23(4): 447-451. ISSN: 0033-0337.

PARENT, PHILLIP; CHURCH, RICHARD. 1989. Evolution of Geographic Information Systems as Decision Making Tools. In: Ripple, William J., ed. Fundamentals of Geographic Information Systems: A Compendium. Washington, DC: American Congress on Surveying and Mapping and American Society for Photogrammetry and Remote Sensing; 1989. 9-18. ISBN: 0-944426-60-3.

PORTER, ALAN L.; CHUBIN, DARYL E. 1985. An Indicator of Cross-Disciplinary Research. Scientometrics. 1985 September; 8(3-4): 161-176. ISSN: 0138-9130.

PORTER, NANCY L.; HULLINGER, CHRIS. 1989. Asbestos Information Sources. Science and Technology Libraries. 1989 Summer; 9(4): 107-122. ISSN: 0194-262X.

POSTEL, SANDRA. 1988. Controlling Toxic Chemicals. See reference: BROWN, LESTER R., ed. 118-136.

QUARANTELLI, E. L. 1988. Disaster Crisis Management: A Summary of Research Findings. Journal of Management Studies. 1988 July; 25(4): 373-385. ISSN: 0022-2380.

RENNIE, JANET; HANTON, FABIENNE; ROSE, KEITH. 1990. "Green" Business Information Resources. Business Information Review. 1990 January; 6(3): 3-16. ISSN: 0266-3821.

ROBERTS, HALINA. 1990. The Use of Health and Safety Information Sources to Create an In-house Substance Information Database. Aslib Proceedings. 1990 November/December; 42(11/12): 293-301. ISSN: 0001-253X.

ROTHMAN, H.; LESTER, G. 1985. The Use of Bibliometric Indicators in the Study of Insecticide Research. Scientometrics. 1985 September; 8(3-4): 247-262. ISSN: 0138-9130.

ROYCE, CHRISTOPHER L.; FLETCHER, JOHN S.; RISSER, PAUL G.; MCFARLANE, JAMES C.; BENENATI, FRANK E. 1984. PHYTOTOX: A Database Dealing with the Effect of Organic Chemicals on Terrestrial Vascular Plants. Journal of Chemical Information and Computer Sciences. 1984 February; 24(1): 7-10. ISSN: 0095-2338.

SAMET, HANAN. 1990. Applications of Spatial Data Structures: Computer Graphics, Image Processing, and GIS. Reading, MA: Addison-Wesley; 1990. 507p. (Addison-Wesley Series in Computer Science). ISBN: 0-201-50300-X.

SANDMAN, PETER M.; SACHSMAN, DAVID B.; GREENBERG, MICHAEL R.; GOCHFELD, MICHAEL, eds. 1987. Environmental Risk and the Press: An Exploratory Assessment. New Brunswick, NJ: Transaction Books; 1987. 149p. ISBN: 0-88738-172-3; LC: 87-10849.

SANTODONATO, JOSEPH; BUSH, CHRISTOPHER; HOWARD, PHILIP; HOWARD, KAREN; DELFAVERO, STEVEN; MILES, PAULA C.; MERRICK, T.; SMITH, LINDA K. 1987. TSCATS: A Database for Chemical and Subject Indexing of Health and Environmental Studies Submitted under the Toxic Substances Control Act. Environmental Toxicology and Chemistry. 1987; 6(12): 921-927. ISSN: 0730-7268.

SCHNEIDER, KARL R. 1991. The PESTICIDES Disk. Journal of Chemical Information and Computer Sciences. 1991 May; 31(2): 355-357. ISSN: 0095-2338.

SEARS, JONATHAN R. L. 1988a. The Aquatic Sciences and Fisheries Thesaurus. In: Swim, Frances F.; Brownlow, Judith, eds. Marine Science Library Network: Proceedings of the International Association of Aquatic and Marine Science Libraries and Information Centers (IAMSLIC) 12th Annual Conference; 1986 October 7-11; Newport, OR. Port Aransas, TX: IAMSLIC; 1988. 143-156. ISSN: 8755-6332; ISBN: 0-932939-04-X.

SEARS, JONATHAN R. L. 1988b. Coverage of Conference Documents in Scientific Databases: Viewpoint of Cambridge Scientific Abstracts. Science and Technology Libraries. 1988 Winter; 9(2): 35-45. ISSN: 0194-262X.

SHAFFER, CLIFFORD A. 1992. Data Representations for Geographic Information Systems. In: Williams, Martha E., ed. Annual Review of Information Science and Technology: Volume 27. Medford, NJ: Learned Information, Inc. for the American Society for Information Science; 1992. 135-172. ISSN: 0066-4200.

SHANNON, CLAUDE E.; WEAVER, WARREN. 1949. The Mathematical Theory of Communication. Urbana, IL: University of Illinois Press; 1949. 125p. LC: 49-11922.

SMALL, HENRY. 1988. Contributions of Citation Analysis to Understanding Scientific Communication. Paper presented at: 1988 Symposium on Science Communication: Environmental and Health Research; 1988 December 15-17; Los Angeles, CA. 21p. Available from: the author, Institute for Scientific Information, 3501 Market Street, Philadelphia, PA 19104.

SNOW, BONNIE. 1991. Searching the Federal Register. Online. 1991 May; 15(3): 94-99. ISSN: 0146-5422.

SOKOLOVA, T. A. 1987. Comparative Analysis of Secondary Information Sources on Environmental Issues. Nauchno-Tekhnicheskaya Informatsiya. Seriia 1 (USSR). 1987; (12): 28-29. (In Russian; English abstract). ISSN: 0028-1131.

SPROAT, WILLIAM; PENNINGTON, JAMES; MASRACCI, MICHAEL; MORSE, MYLES. 1990. Development of an Alternative Treatment Technology Data Base and Information Center. Proceedings of the 7th National Conference on Hazardous Wastes and Hazardous Materials; 1990 May 2-4; St. Louis, MO. Greenbelt, MD: Hazardous Materials Control Resource Institute; 1990. 410-412. ISBN: 0-944989-91-8.

STERN, RICHARD M.; TARKOWSKI, STANISLAW. 1990. The Need for a Unified European Environmental Health Data Base. Information Services & Use. 1990; 10(1/2): 5-14. ISSN: 0167-5265; CODEN: ISUDX8.

STOSS, FREDERICK W. 1991. Environment Online: The Greening of Databases. Part 1. General Interest Databases. Database. 1991 August; 14(4): 13-27. ISSN: 0162-4105.

TAPASWI, M. P. 1990. How Good Is Compact Cambridge ASFA? (Aquatic Science Bibliographic Data Base on CD-ROM). In: Burkhart, Robert W.; Burkhart, Joyce C., eds. IAMSLIC at a Crossroads: Proceedings of the International Association of Aquatic and Marine Science Libraries and Information Centers (IAMSLIC) 15th Annual Conference; 1989 October 7-11; St. George's, Bermuda. St. Petersburg, FL: IAMSLIC; 1990. 151-156. ISSN: 8755-6332; ISBN: 0-932939-07-4.

TERRENE INSTITUTE. 1992. Clean Lakes Clearinghouse. Washington, DC: Terrene Institute; 1992 November. Available from: Terrene Institute, 1000 Connecticut Avenue, N.W., Suite 802, Washington, DC 20036.

THISTLE PUBLISHING. Risk Assistant. Alexandria, VA: Thistle Publishing. (Software). Available from: Thistle Publishing, P.O. Box 1327, Alexandria, VA 22313-1327.

THOMAS, SARAH E. 1990. Bibliographic Control and Agriculture. Library Trends. 1990 Winter; 38(3): 542-561. ISSN: 0024-2594.

THOMAS, SARAH E. 1991. Improved Access to Agricultural Literature through a Comprehensive, Detailed Agricultural Thesaurus. Quarterly Bulletin of the International Association of Agricultural Librarians and Documentalists. 1991; 36(1-2): 80-82. ISSN: 0020-5966.

TILLEY, CAROLYN B. 1990. Medical Databases and Health Information Systems. In: Williams, Martha E., ed. Annual Review of Information Science and Technology: Volume 25. Amsterdam, The Netherlands: Elsevier Science Publishers for the American Society for Information Science; 1990. 313-382. ISSN: 0066-4200; ISBN: 0-444-88531-5.

TOMLIN, DANA C. 1990. Geographic Information Systems and Cartographic Modeling. Englewood Cliffs, NJ: Prentice-Hall; 1990. 249p. ISBN: 0-13-350927-3.

U.S. ARMY CORPS OF ENGINEERS. 1985. Introduction to the Environmental Technical Information System (ETIS) and Its Subsystems. Urbana, IL: University of Illinois at Urbana-Champaign, Bureau of Urban and Regional Planning Research; 1985 February. 129p. Available from: ETIS Support Center, University of Illinois, 909 West Nevada, Urbana, IL 61801.

U.S. CONGRESS. 88TH CONGRESS, 1ST SESSION. 1963. An Act to Improve, Strengthen and Accelerate Programs for the Prevention and Abatement of Air Pollution: Public Law 88-206, 88th Congress, 1st Session. United States Statutes at Large. 1963; 77: 392-401. Washington, DC: Government Printing Office; 1964. (Clean Air Act).

U.S. CONGRESS. 91ST CONGRESS, 2ND SESSION. 1970. To Assure Safe and Healthful Working Conditions for Working Men and Women;... and for Other Purposes: Public Law 91-596, 91st Congress, 2nd Session. United States Statutes at Large. 1970; 84: 1590-1620. Washington, DC: Government Printing Office; 1971. (Occupational Safety and Health Act).

U.S. CONGRESS. 92ND CONGRESS, 2ND SESSION. 1972a. To Amend the Federal Insecticide, Fungicide and Rodenticide Act, and for Other Purposes: Public Law 92-516, 92nd Congress, 2nd Session. United States Statutes at Large. 1972; 86: 973-999. Washington, DC: Government Printing Office; 1973. (Federal Environmental Pesticide Control Act).

U.S. CONGRESS. 92ND CONGRESS, 2ND SESSION. 1972b. To Protect Consumers against Unreasonable Risk of Injury from Hazardous Products, and for Other Purposes: Public Law 92-573, 92nd Congress, 2nd Session. United States Statutes at Large. 1972; 86: 1207-1233. Washington, DC: Government Printing Office; 1973. (Consumer Product Safety Act).

U.S. CONGRESS. 94TH CONGRESS, 2ND SESSION. 1976a. To Regulate Commerce and Protect Human Health and the Environment by Requiring Testing and Necessary Use Restrictions on Certain Chemical Substances, and for Other Purposes: Public Law 94-469, 94th Congress, 2nd Session. United States Statutes at Large. 1976; 90: 2003-2051. Washington, DC: Government Printing Office; 1978. (Toxic Substances Control Act).

U.S. CONGRESS. 94TH CONGRESS, 2ND SESSION. 1976b. To Provide Technical and Financial Assistance for the Development of Arrangement Plans and Facilities for the Recovery of Energy and Other Resources from Discarded Materials, 94th Congress, 2nd Session. United States Statutes at Large. 1976; 90: 2795-2841. Washington, DC: Government Printing Office; 1978. (Resource Conservation and Recovery Act).

U.S. CONGRESS. 95TH CONGRESS, 1ST SESSION. 1977. To Amend the Federal Water Pollution Control Act to Provide for Additional Authorizations, and for Other Purposes: Public Law 95-217, 95th Congress, 1st Session. United States Statutes at Large. 1977; 91: 1566-1611. Washington, DC: Government Printing Office; 1980. (Clean Water Act of 1977).

U.S. CONGRESS. 96TH CONGRESS, 2ND SESSION. 1980. An Act to Provide for Liability, Compensation, Cleanup and Emergency Response for Hazardous Substances Released into the Environment and the Cleanup of Inactive Hazardous Waste Disposal Sites: Public Law 96-510, 96th Congress, 2nd Session. United States Statutes at Large. 1980; 94: 2767-2811. Washington, DC: Government Printing Office; 1981. (Comprehensive Environmental Response, Compensation, and Liability Act of 1980—commonly referred to as "Superfund" Act).

U.S. CONGRESS. 99TH CONGRESS, 2ND SESSION. 1986a. An Act to Permit Government Laboratories to Enter into Cooperative R&D Agreements with Nonfederal Entities;... and for Other Purposes: Public Law 99-502, 99th Congress, 2nd Session. United States Statutes at Large. Washington, DC: Government Printing Office; 1986. (Federal Technology Transfer Act).

U.S. CONGRESS. 99TH CONGRESS, 2ND SESSION. 1986b. Superfund Amendments and Reauthorization Act of 1986, to Amend the Comprehensive Environmental Response, Compensation, and Liability Act of 1980: Public Law 99-499, 99th Congress, 2nd Session. United States Statutes at Large. Washington, DC: Government Printing Office; 1986. (SARA).

U.S. CONGRESS. 101ST CONGRESS, 2ND SESSION. 1990. To Promote Environmental Education, and for Other Purposes: Public Law 101-619, 101st Congress, 2nd Session. United States Statutes at Large. 1990 January 23. 15p.Washington, DC: Government Printing Office; 1990. (National Environmental Education Act).

U.S. CONGRESS. SENATE. COMMITTEE ON ENVIRONMENT AND PUBLIC WORKS. 102ND CONGRESS, 1ST SESSION. 1991. Report of the Environmental Protection Agency's Science Advisory Board: Hearing before the Committee on Environment and Public Works. Washington, DC: Government Printing Office; 1991 January 25. 82p. (S. hrg. 102-29). GPO: 91073550.

U.S. DEPARTMENT OF COMMERCE. NATIONAL TECHNICAL INFORMATION SERVICE. 1984-. Environmental Pollution & Control: An Abstract Newsletter. Springfield, VA: National Technical Information Service. ISSN: 0364-4936; NTIS: PB90-906821.

U.S. DEPARTMENT OF COMMERCE. NATIONAL TECHNICAL INFORMATION SERVICE. 1992. U.S. Government Environmental Datafiles & Software. Springfield, VA: National Technical Information Service; 1992 March. NTIS: PR758.

U.S. DEPARTMENT OF THE INTERIOR. GEOLOGICAL SURVEY. Earth Science Data Directory. Available in CD-ROM from: SilverPlatter Information Inc., 100 River Ridge Drive, Norwood, MA 02062-5026.

U.S. DEPARTMENT OF THE INTERIOR. GEOLOGICAL SURVEY. OFFICE OF SCIENCE AND TECHNOLOGY POLICY. FEDERAL COORDINAT-

ING COUNCIL FOR SCIENCE, ENGINEERING, AND TECHNOLOGY. COMMITTEE ON EARTH AND ENVIRONMENTAL SCIENCES. 1990. Our Changing Planet: The FY 1991 Research Plan of the U.S. Global Change Research Program. Washington, DC: Office of Science and Technology Policy; 1990 October. 266p. NTIS: PB91-145813/XAB.

U.S. ENVIRONMENTAL PROTECTION AGENCY (EPA). AIR RISK INFORMATION SUPPORT CENTER (Air RISC). 1989. Directory of Information Resources Related to Health, Exposure, and Risk Assessment of Air Toxics. Research Triangle Park, NC: U.S. Environmental Protection Agency; 1989 August. 92p. (EPA 450/3-88-015). NTIS: PB90-119785/XAB.

U.S. ENVIRONMENTAL PROTECTION AGENCY (EPA). INFORMATION MANAGEMENT AND SERVICES DIVISION. 1991. Access EPA: Major EPA Dockets. 1991 edition. Washington, DC: U.S. Environmental Protection Agency; 1991 July. 28p. (EPA/IMSD-91/102). NTIS: PB91-151589/XAB.

U.S. ENVIRONMENTAL PROTECTION AGENCY (EPA). OFFICE OF ACID DEPOSITION, ENVIRONMENTAL MONITORING AND QUALITY ASSURANCE. 1990. Aquatic Effects Research Program (AERP) status. 1990 September. (EPA/600/M-90/018). Available from: U.S. Environmental Protection Agency, 26 West Martin Luther King Drive, Cincinnati, OH 45268.

U.S. ENVIRONMENTAL PROTECTION AGENCY (EPA). OFFICE OF AIR QUALITY PLANNING AND STANDARDS. 1990. Directory of OAQPS Information Services. Washington, DC: U.S. Environmental Protection Agency; 1990 November. 10p. (EPA-450/2-91-001). NTIS: PB91-191049.

U.S. ENVIRONMENTAL PROTECTION AGENCY (EPA). OFFICE OF ENVIRONMENTAL ENGINEERING AND TECHNOLOGY DEMONSTRATION. POLLUTION PREVENTION OFFICE. 1989. Pollution Prevention Information Clearinghouse (PPIC): Electronic Information Exchange System (EIES) — User Guide, Version 1.1. Washington, DC: U.S. Environmental Protection Agency; 1989 September. 64p. (EPA/600/9-89/086). Available from: U.S. Environmental Protection Agency, 401 M Street, S.W., Washington, DC 20460.

U.S. ENVIRONMENTAL PROTECTION AGENCY (EPA). OFFICE OF INFORMATION RESOURCES MANAGEMENT. 1990. Access EPA: Libraries and Information Services. Washington, DC: U.S. Environmental Protection Agency; 1990 July. 106p. (EPA/IMSD/90-008). NTIS: PB90-237074/XAB.

U. S. ENVIRONMENTAL PROTECTION AGENCY (EPA). OFFICE OF INFORMATION RESOURCES MANAGEMENT. INFORMATION SERVICES AND LIBRARY. 1988a. Hazardous Waste Collection Database Thesaurus. Washington, DC: Government Printing Office; 1988 December. 69p. (EPA/IMSD/87-010). GPO: 1988-516-002/80127.

U.S. ENVIRONMENTAL PROTECTION AGENCY (EPA). OFFICE OF INFORMATION RESOURCES MANAGEMENT. INFORMATION SERVICES AND LIBRARY. 1988b. Searching the Hazardous Waste Collection Database: Using the Menu. Revised edition. Washington, DC: U.S. Environmental Protection Agency; 1988 October. 42p. (EPA/IMSD/88-001). NTIS: PB87-945000CBT.

U.S. ENVIRONMENTAL PROTECTION AGENCY (EPA). OFFICE OF INTERNATIONAL ACTIVITIES. 1991. Environmental Technology Sources: Matching Solutions to Problems. Washington, DC: U.S. Environmental Protection Agency; 1991 August. 19p. (EPA/600/9-91/011). Available from: U.S.Environmental Protection Agency, 401 M Street, S.W., Washington, DC 20460.

U.S. ENVIRONMENTAL PROTECTION AGENCY (EPA). OFFICE OF PESTICIDES AND TOXIC SUBSTANCES. 1992. Pesticide Information Network. Washington, DC: U.S. Environmental Protection Agency; 1992 June. Available from: U.S. Environmental Protection Agency, Office of Pesticide Program, 401 M Street, H 7507 C, S.W., Washington, DC 20460.

U.S. ENVIRONMENTAL PROTECTION AGENCY (EPA). OFFICE OF POLICY ANALYSIS, PLANNING AND EVALUATION. 1987a. Unfinished Business: A Comparative Assessment of Environmental Problems: Overview Report. Volume I: Overview. Washington, DC: Government Printing Office; 1987 February. 100p. NTIS: PB88-127048/XAB.

U.S. ENVIRONMENTAL PROTECTION AGENCY (EPA). OFFICE OF POLICY ANALYSIS, PLANNING AND EVALUATION. 1987b. Unfinished Business: A Comparative Assessment of Environmental Problems: 5 Volumes. Washington, DC: U.S. Environmental Protection Agency. Office of Policy, Planning and Evaluation; 1987 February. 856p. (Report no. EPA-SAB-EC-90-021). NTIS: PB88-127089.

U.S. ENVIRONMENTAL PROTECTION AGENCY (EPA). OFFICE OF RESEARCH AND DEVELOPMENT. 1990. Strategy for Environmental Health Research at EPA. Washington, DC: U.S. Environmental Protection Agency; 1990 December. 98p. (EPA/600/9-90/053). Available from: U.S. Environmental Protection Agency, 401 M Street, S.W., Washington, DC 20460.

U.S. ENVIRONMENTAL PROTECTION AGENCY (EPA). OFFICE OF SOLID WASTE. WASTE MINIMIZATION TECHNICAL INFORMATION CLEARINGHOUSE. 1988. Electronic Bulletin Board (E-Board): Draft User Guide, Version 1.0. Washington, DC: U.S. Environmental Protection Agency; 1988 November. 46p. Available from: U.S. Environmental Protection Agency, 401 M Street, S.W., Washington, DC 20460.

U.S. ENVIRONMENTAL PROTECTION AGENCY (EPA). OFFICE OF TOXIC SUBSTANCES. ECONOMICS AND TECHNOLOGY DIVISION. 1990. Toxics in the Community: National and Local Perspectives: A Report on Data Collected under Section 313 of the Emergency Planning and Community Right-to-Know Act of 1986. Washington, DC: U.S. Environmental Protection Agency; 1990 September. 364p. (EPA 560/4-90-017). NTIS: PB91-167577/XAB.

U.S. ENVIRONMENTAL PROTECTION AGENCY (EPA). SCIENCE ADVISORY BOARD. 1990. Reducing Risk: Setting Priorities and Strategies for Environmental Protection: 4 Volumes. Washington, DC: U.S. Environmental Protection Agency;1990 September. 361p. NTIS: PB91-155234/XAB.

U.S. GENERAL ACCOUNTING OFFICE (GAO). 1990a. Geographic Information Systems: Status at Selected Agencies. Washington, DC: Government Printing Office; 1990 August. 30p. (GAO/IMTEC-90-74FS). GPO: 91084558.

U.S. GENERAL ACCOUNTING OFFICE (GAO). 1990b. Global Warming: Emission Reductions Possible as Scientific Uncertainties Are Resolved. Washington, DC: Government Printing Office; 1990 September. 72p. (GAO/RCED-90-58). Available from: U.S. General Accounting Office, P.O. Box 6015, Gaithersburg, MD 20877.

U.S. GENERAL ACCOUNTING OFFICE (GAO). 1990c. Greenhouse Effect: DOE's Programs and Activities Relevant to the Global Warming Phenomenon. Washington, DC: Government Printing Office; 1990 March. 49p. (GAO/RCED-90-74BR). GPO: 91072824.

U.S. GENERAL ACCOUNTING OFFICE (GAO). 1990d. Information Resources: Management Commitment Needed to Meet Information Challenges. Washington, DC: Government Printing Office; 1990 April. 17p. (GAO/IMTEC-90-27). GPO: 92052601.

U.S. GENERAL ACCOUNTING OFFICE (GAO). 1990e. Public Access: Two Case Studies of Federal Electronic Dissemination. Washington, DC: Government Printing Office; 1990 May. 12p. (GAO/IMTEC-90-44BR). Available from: U.S. General Accounting Office, P.O. Box 6015, Gaithersburg, MD 20877.

U.S. GENERAL ACCOUNTING OFFICE (GAO). 1991. Waste Minimization: EPA Data Are Severely Flawed. Washington, DC: Government Printing Office; 1991 August. 9p. (GAO/PEMD-91-21). Available from: U.S. General Accounting Office, P.O. Box 6015, Gaithersburg, MD 20877.

U.S. LIBRARY OF CONGRESS. CONGRESSIONAL RESEARCH SERVICE. ENVIRONMENTAL PROTECTION SECTION. ENVIRONMENT AND NATURAL RESOURCES POLICY DIVISION. 1991. CRS Report for Congress: Summaries of Environmental Laws Administered by the Environmental Protection Agency. Washington, DC: Congressional Research Service; 1991 March 14. 101p. (91-251 ENR). Available from: Library of Congress, Congressional Research Service, Washington, DC 20540.

U.S. NATIONAL ACADEMY OF SCIENCES. NATIONAL RESEARCH COUNCIL. COMMITTEE ON THE INSTITUTIONAL MEANS FOR ASSESSMENT OF RISKS TO PUBLIC HEALTH. 1983. Risk Assessment in the Federal Government: Managing the Process. Washington, DC: National Academy Press; 1983. 191p. ISBN: 0-309-03349-7.

U.S. NATIONAL ACADEMY OF SCIENCES. NATIONAL RESEARCH COUNCIL. COMMITTEE ON RISK PERCEPTION AND COMMUNICATION. 1989. Improving Risk Communication. Washington, DC: National Academy Press; 1989. 332p. ISBN: 0-309-03946-0.

VAN HOOK, R. I. 1990. Agenda and Abstracts for the Annual Information Meeting of the Environmental Sciences Division. Washington, DC: U.S. Department of Energy; 1990 May 2-3. 19p. (DOE/OR/21400-T422). Available from: Oak Ridge National Laboratory, P.O. Box 2008, Oak Ridge, TN 37831.

VEGA-SANCHEZ, FERNANDO E. 1987. Pesticides and Food: The Need for an International Information Source for Developing Countries. Quarterly Bul-

letin of the International Association of Agricultural Librarians and Documentalists. 1987; 32(2): 69-78. ISSN: 0020-5966.
VIGDEN, GRANT A.; MADGE, BRUCE. 1989. Computerized Information Sources in Toxicology and Their Use in a Poisons Centre. Health Libraries Review. 1989 September; 6(3): 150-167. ISSN: 0265-6647.
WAGNER, TRAVIS P. 1989. Where Do You Turn for Regulatory Information? Pollution Engineering. 1989 February; 21(2): 72-75. ISSN: 0032-3640.
WALTON, D.W.H.; PHILLIPS, CHRISTINE M. 1988. Green Information for a White Continent—Environmental Information for Antarctica. Aslib Proceedings. 1988 June; 40(6): 187-194. ISSN: 0001-253X.
WATSON, TOM. 1991. Finding the Trees in the Forest: Environmental Information Sources. Wilson Library Bulletin. 1991 February; 65(6): 34-39. ISSN: 0043-5651.
WELLS, BARBARA B. 1990. The Potential for Linking Environmental and Health Data. Washington, DC: National Governors' Association; 1990. 26p. ISBN: 1-55877-104-2.
WEXLER, PHILIP. 1988. Information Resources in Toxicology. 2nd edition. New York, NY: Elsevier Science Publishing; 1988. 510p. ISBN: 0-444-01214-1.
WEXLER, PHILIP. 1990. IRIS: File Structure and Searching. The NLM Technical Bulletin. 1990 March; (251): 1, 7-14. ISSN: 0146-3055.
WEXLER, PHILIP; STROUP, DOROTHY. 1989. TRI [Toxic Release Inventory]: File Structure and Searching. The NLM Technical Bulletin. 1989 May; (241): 1, 6-16. ISSN: 0146-3055.
WHITE, HOWARD D.; MCCAIN, KATHERINE W. 1989. Bibliometrics. In: Williams, Martha E., ed. Annual Review of Information Science and Technology: Volume 24. Amsterdam, The Netherlands: Elsevier Science Publishers for the American Society for Information Science; 1989. 119-186. ISSN: 0066-4200; ISBN: 0-444-87418-6.
WIGGINS, GARY. 1991. Chemical Information Sources. New York, NY: McGraw-Hill; 1991. 352p. ISBN: 0-07-909939-4.
WILLIAMS, MARTHA E. 1992. The State of Databases Today: 1992. In: Marcaccio, Kathleen Young, ed.; Hillstrom, Kevin; Tomassini, Christine; Turecki, Gwen E., assoc. eds.; Williams, Martha E.,. founding ed. Computer-Readable Databases: A Directory and Data Sourcebook. 8th edition. Detroit, MI: Gale Research Inc.; 1992. xi-xxi. ISSN: 0271-4477; ISBN: 0-8103-2946-8.
WOOD, FRANCES E.; BERRIE, ANDREW T.; PLAMPIN, HELEN R.; WILKINSON-TOUGH, MARGARET L. 1989. Evaluations Using Test Queries of Chemical Hazards Databases and Databanks. Journal of Information Science. 1989; 15(4/5): 269-276. ISSN: 0165-5515.

6 The Information Environment of Managers

**JEFFREY KATZER and
PATRICIA T. FLETCHER
Syracuse University**

INTRODUCTION

By virtue of their position, managers receive more information from more sources through more channels than almost anyone else in an organization. Whether one describes a manager's job in terms of overt behaviors (e.g., talking on the phone, reading a report, attending a meeting), functional responsibilities (e.g., planning, staffing, budgeting), or cognitive activities (e.g., decision making, problem solving, path finding), it is clear that management is an information-intensive profession (HUBER, 1980; MCCALL & KAPLAN; WHITTEMORE & YOVITS). Organizations provide the setting in which managers act, and are being viewed more and more as information processing entities (TUSHMAN & NADLER).

In a world of diminishing resources, the key managerial resource—information—abounds. Unfortunately, managers find themselves bombarded with information—too much, too fast, too late. Interestingly, even with an oversupply of information, managers believe that they do not get all the information they need to do their jobs. The dilemma is clear: on the one hand, managers receive too much information, while, on the other hand, they don't get enough of the right information. A recent editorial in *Harvard Business Review* reinforces this point:

The authors thank William Murray for his assistance in preparing the bibliography and checking the citations in the text.

> Reports and data pile up faster and higher, but information is harder to get—and harder still to get meaning out of, even though colleagues and staff constantly suggest lots of meaning. From the outside, explosive quantities of communications constantly bombard managers, promising big payoffs for their time and attention—heaps of magazines (trade, professional, technical, general, specialized), books, newspapers, TV and cable programs, radio reports, syndicated studies, newsletters, special mailings, special pleadings. Experts, consultants, speakers, tapes, seminars, and cassettes insist on and compete for attention. . . .With less and less time for managers to catch their breaths, to read, study and think, things submitted to them for attention are shrunk by others into skimpy summaries and threadbare conversations. Information and interpretations are delivered quickly via technicolor slides, easel presentations, and abbreviated conversations on the go. (LEVITT, p. 4)

However, this problem cannot be easily solved by applying information systems and services as we commonly know them. One difficulty is that managers and organizations seem to use information in a way that appears illogical and unlike the way that many information professionals would expect them to act. March's description of organizational information behaviors reflects some of what is alluded to by "illogical." He says that organizations "gather information and don't use it. Ask for more and ignore it. Make decisions first and look for the relevant information afterwards. In fact, organizations seem to gather a great deal of information that has little or no decision relevance... "(MARCH, 1982, p. 38). Nevertheless, the professional life of a manager is at least as information intensive as that of other user-community members, and the organization and the manager represent an increasingly important user population for *ARIST* readers. Thus, we believe that the ability of information professionals to function effectively in this environment requires some preliminary understanding of that environment. That belief forms the premise of this chapter.

We describe the information environment of managers by presenting a model of that environment and by reviewing selected writings that bear on the components of that model. The literature reviewed is bound by neither discipline nor time; it encompasses work from information and library science, business, management, public administration, psychology, organizational behavior, and related fields to provide a strong baseline for understanding the information behaviors of managers.

Because this is the first *ARIST* chapter on this topic and because the body of relevant literature is immense, we restrict our review to those writings—classical and contemporary—that support the model's structure or its components. The chapter also includes general studies that encompass the entire range of managers' information behaviors as well as those studies that focus primarily on the individual aspects of managerial information seeking and use. Toward the end of the chapter, we analyze what we think this literature means for information professionals. These implications focus on the challenges managers pose and the potential resolutions of these challenges in an applied setting.

To provide a focus that serves the aim of this chapter, the information behaviors of the individual manager are used as the thread to unite the literature review. It is at the level of the individual that we can begin to understand the information needs and uses of this group. To focus on the individual manager, the notion of problematic situations is developed and explicated to provide a basis for describing, understanding, and predicting the information behaviors.

To save space and to avoid unnecessary duplication, we do not include several related topics. Literature with an organizational perspective on information processing is included only if it directly sheds light on the information behaviors of the individual manager; for a broader review of the organizational perspective, see CHOO. Although environmental analysis and scanning as well as organizational climate and culture are all important to managers, they are ancillary to this review. Communication behaviors and information networks in organizations are also excluded because organizational communication is regularly covered in the field of communication and organizational behavior. A recent *ARIST* chapter (GROSSER) provides a broad and interdisciplinary review of the literature in this area.

This review is also limited to those problematic situations in which managers immerse themselves as individuals. When studied in the context of group activities, problematic situations interact with the manager differently from the way they would if they were dealt with by that same manager alone. Thus, group decision making, teamwork, and the like are not covered. Nor is there any systematic review of the relationship between managers and information systems, whether formal or informal. Although the literature reviewed here obviously has implications for system design, it would muddy the waters to review specific applications, such as decision-support systems (DSS), management information systems (MIS), executive information systems (EIS), and expert systems. Finally, unlike previous *ARIST* chapters on information behaviors, we do not include a separate consideration of methodology.

Even though there have been no previous *ARIST* chapters entitled "The Information Environment of Managers," this one is related to earlier *ARIST* writings. The most obvious connection is with the 11 chapters that covered information needs and uses. Of these, the two most recent (DERVIN & NILAN; HEWINS) also make a case for revising how one should think about the information behaviors of users; the model presented here is consonant with those revisions. As noted above, the chapter by GROSSER includes many studies of organizational communication and informal networks that are directly connected with this one. In the same *ARIST* volume, ALLEN reviews a related area of cognitive research. Interested readers will find discussion of the present topic regularly included in the annual reviews of related fields, such as sociology (e.g., HICKSON), organizational communication (e.g., O'REILLY ET AL.), and psychology (e.g., HOUSE & SINGH). Interestingly, the title of one such review (HUBER & DAFT) is similar to ours, but the authors focus on the organization rather than the manager.

TOWARD A MODEL OF THE INFORMATION ENVIRONMENT OF MANAGERS

The model of the manager's information environment has its basis in the writings of Taylor. He defines "information use environments" as: "the set of those elements (a) that affect the flow of information messages into, within, and out of any definable entity or group of clients; and (b) that determine the criteria by which the value of information messages will be judged in these contexts" (TAYLOR, 1986, pp. 34-35). The major components of these environments are characteristics of people, the settings they are in, the problems they have, and the range of resolutions that are desirable or acceptable (TAYLOR, 1990). These components, in a very real sense, provide clues about the information needs of any user group, and they provide the parameters that constrain how that group will seek and use information.

The structural components of the proposed model are also based on various descriptions of managerial behavior. The major variables in the model are related to the context in which the person functions, positing that context effectively constrains a person's information behaviors. As such, the model is part of a developing field of thought that argues that cognitive behaviors should be analyzed within the framework of the person's real-time situation. This approach has been advanced in several fields. In information science, NEWBY ET AL. argue this position for studying users' information behaviors in general, SCHAMBER ET AL. apply it to the concept of relevance, NELSON uses it to study how people adjust to information technology, and SUCHMAN advocates it in her examination of human–computer interaction (HCI). The same sort of viewpoint is evident in the presentation of managerial decision making by MCCALL & KAPLAN, in the analysis of organizational information use by O'REILLY (1983), and in the study of the behaviors of professionals in several fields by SCHON.

The model, as shown in Figure 1, portrays the components of a person's information environment as that person interacts over time. The dynamics of the model focus on the factors (including contextual ones) and processes that: (1) affect a person's subjective understanding of the situation he or she is facing and, (2) stimulate different information behaviors. Although the model as described here contains one-directional causal relationships, that is an oversimplification; most likely some of the links are bidirectional. The model's dynamics arise most immediately from the writings of Dervin, Nilan, Fletcher, their predecessors, colleagues, and students (see, e.g., DERVIN, DERVIN & NILAN, and FLETCHER).

Components of the Model

The starting points for the model are two fairly fixed components: the context and the person. They exist in an objective, tangible sense, and they directly generate and significantly affect the other components. In the managerial realm, the person is instantiated most straightforwardly as the manager, and the setting as the organization.

A problematic situation is a personally defined subset of the endless and murky stream of events and meanings that continuously "flow through" a person's life. By identifying selected parts of that stream, by putting a fuzzy boundary around those parts, and by labeling those parts as a single entity that requires attention and possible action, the person creates a problematic situation. A problematic situation can be thought of as an "agenda item" that will require cognitive and perhaps behavioral action in order for it to be taken off that person's agenda and be considered resolved. Although a problematic situation is created and defined by a single individual, it is also shaped by features of the setting. Common problematic situations in the life of a manager include hiring new personnel, developing a marketing plan, and preparing the annual budget.

Settings differ in terms of their typical activities and roles. In the organizational setting, typical managerial activities include problem solving, decision making, and report writing while typical managerial roles include leader, negotiator, and communicator. In the laboratory setting, activities might include data collection and data analysis; typical roles might include statistician, interviewer, and communicator. Activities and roles are often defined or constrained by the legal requirements of a society, the standards of a profession, or the normative practices of a work group.

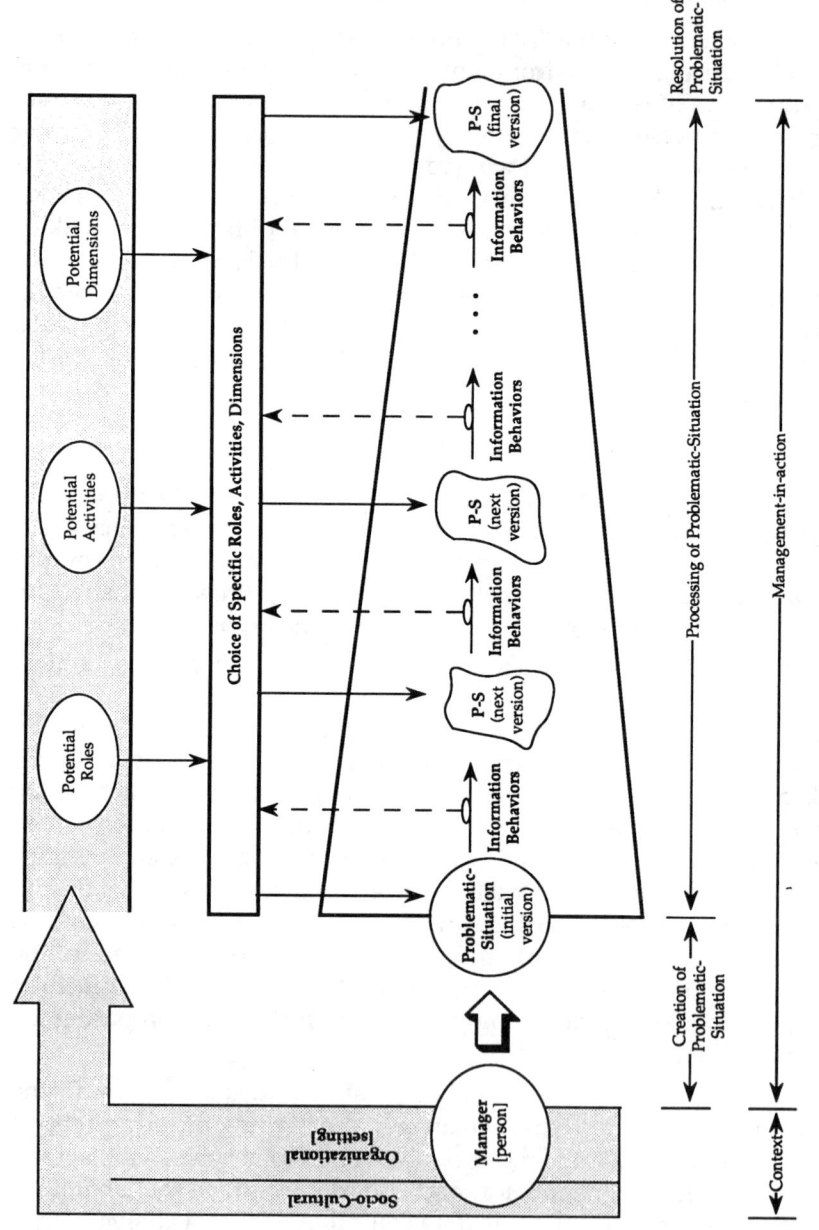

Figure 1. Model of the information environment of managers

The model is concerned with how the activities and roles are related to the person's understanding of his or her current problematic situation and the person's information behaviors: managers who operate as leaders needing to make a decision are likely to have different information behaviors than managers who act as cost savers doing budgeting.

Problem dimensions are perceived characteristics of problematic situations and can, therefore, serve as criteria for determining the value of information. There are many potential dimensions, and they exist relatively independently of any particular user population or setting. In use with a given problematic situation, however, only a few dimensions would be treated as important. For example, among the many ways to think about a proposed merger, a manager might view it primarily as new, scary, and involving others. The salience of these dimensions (novelty, risk, interpersonalness) is affected by who the person is and what setting he or she is in. The dimensions perceived as important will also affect what information is sought and how it is valued. Information, in turn, may also change the relative importance of different dimensions.

When acted on by the person, problematic situations generate information behaviors—i.e., the actions that contribute to the usefulness of information (TAYLOR, 1990). The person needs to determine whether or not to seek information, what information to seek, where to seek it, how to seek it, how much to seek, how to interpret it, how to assess it, and how to use it. The person's responses to questions such as these produce information behaviors.

The Model in Action

The model is based on the belief that these problematic situations are the cognitive basis for the manager's uncertainties and concerns, which, in turn, may manifest themselves in overt information-seeking and -use behaviors. In making the problematic situation his or her own, the manager will determine (perhaps subconsciously) what type of managerial activity and role are called for and what dimensions of the situation are most salient. Over time, as the manager reflects and acts on the problematic situation, it changes; new uncertainties and concerns may emerge, different activities or roles become dominant, and other dimensions increase in importance. As long as the (revised) problematic situation remains unresolved, additional information behaviors will emerge. These, in turn, are influenced by the manager's current definition of the situation and current "choice" of activities, roles, and dimensions. This process continues until the problematic situation becomes resolved (but not necessarily "solved" in an objective sense) in the mind of the manager.

CONCLUSION

This model, like all models, provides a framework for identifying the variables that affect the information behaviors of any user population, although our focus is on managers. For *ARIST* readers, the model argues that it is not enough to study overt information behaviors. Instead, we believe that information scholars and professionals will gain a more useful understanding of these behaviors through knowledge of the information environment. In addition, we believe that this model can lead to practical applications. Dervin, Nilan, and their coworkers (e.g., HERT & NILAN; NILAN ET AL.) have shown that contextual factors limit the range of how problematic situations are perceived, the patterns of dimensions that are relevant for judging the usefulness of information, and the variety of information behaviors likely to occur. Results such as these can guide those who wish to develop information systems or provide services that better "understand" users as they work through their context-based, problematic situations.

STRUCTURAL COMPONENTS OF THE MODEL

Over the past 300 years, the United States has changed from a family-based social and work unit to one that is organizationally based (ZAND). We have become a society of organizations, with our main social tasks being carried out by large, managed organizations; in addition, for all organizations, management is the emerging function, task, and work that facilitates effectiveness (DRUCKER, 1967). Drucker clearly defines this new and key role as follows:

> The emergence of management may be the pivotal event of our time, far more important than all the events that make the headlines. Rarely, if ever, has a new basic institution, a new leading group, a new central function, emerged as fast as has management since the turn of the century. Rarely in human history has a new institution proven so indispensable so quickly. Even less often has a new institution arrived with so little opposition, so little disturbance, so little controversy.... Today's developed society, sans aristocracy, sans large landowners, even sans capitalists and tycoons, depends for leadership on the managers of its major institutions. It depends on their knowledge, on their vision, and on their responsibility. (DRUCKER, 1974, p. 10)

The attention given to managers in the literature has been considerable, too much to be thoroughly reviewed here. The early writings can be mostly ignored. The exception is not a specific body of writing as much as it is the flavor of that writing. Much of the early literature in this field (especially in the first half of this century) portrays management as a scientifically based profession whose members can and should act efficiently to maximize organizational objectives. Within this framework, managers are careful and deliberate planners, problem solvers, decision makers, and leaders who precisely assess the situation before them, acquire the relevant information, weigh it carefully, and reach the best solution.

Far fewer people today believe in this characterization of the manager than did so in the past. Nevertheless, it is a view that may be difficult to erase among information researchers and professionals because it is consonant with their view of how information ought to be sought and used (KATZER; ROBERTS). Thus, it affects how they design information systems for, and provide information services to, this population. In the current view of management, information also plays a crucial role (e.g., DRUCKER, 1988; ETZIONI, 1989; MCCALL & KAPLAN), but it is a role based on a more realistic understanding of what managers actually do, in contrast with what they ought to do.

General Managerial Behaviors

A surprisingly consistent description of what managers do has emerged from a series of studies beginning in the 1960s that used structured observations and other methods to observe the manager in action. Of these, the results of Mintzberg's 1968 doctoral dissertation (MINTZBERG, 1973; 1975; 1980) and Kotter's study of the general manager (KOTTER, 1982a; 1982b) are the most significant. Other works (e.g., ALLAN; BREWER & TOMLINSON; KANTER; LAU ET AL.; LUTHANS & LARSEN; LUTHANS ET AL.; STEWART, 1976) also contribute to the overall description.

From these studies we see that in terms of overt information behaviors there is much similarity among managers in different organizations. First, managers work long hours. KOTTER (1982b), for example, found that the average general manager he studied worked nearby 60 hours per week, and BREWER & TOMLINSON report that the managers in their study had to take home some 4-5 hours of reading per week. Managers spend most of this time with others or communicating with others about a wide variety of topics. In their communication, it is clear that managers favor oral channels, preferably face-to-face conversation (ACHLEITNER & GROVER; BREWER & TOMLINSON; GROVER & GLAZIER; HALE; KOTTER, 1982a; LUTHANS & LARSEN; MINTZBERG, 1973). Also managers show a strong preference for quickly finding out what is or may be happening. If they had to choose, it seems that managers prefer speed of information over accuracy of information

(MINTZBERG, 1973; O'REILLY, 1982). BREWER & TOMLINSON suggest that the greatest fear a manager has is being caught without information; consequently, managers spend most of their time accumulating information.

The literature also shows some important differences in the information behaviors of senior-level managers vs. lower-level managers. Because of their level, senior-level managers are expected to deal with strategic and ill-structured problems (GORRY & SCOTT MORTON). Thus, they have different needs for and sources of information (e.g., external vs. internal; soft vs. hard), and they exert more effort to make sense of that information (MINTZBERG ET AL.; O'REILLY & PONDY; PERKINS & RAO).

Broad studies of managerial behavior also suggest that the manager-in-practice appears to be far less rational than generally believed. In a study of successful senior-level managers in the public and private sector, ISENBERG (1984) found that managers' decision making didn't seem to follow any standard model (although their decisions could later be justified by data and logic). In terms of planning, these managers had no precise goals or objectives but rather a few "overriding concerns." Similarly, MCCASKEY noted that "managers do face ambiguous situations and are sometimes forced to take action before goals or technology are clarified" (p. 31). SCHON argues that managers cannot follow standard models of rationality because these models do not deal well with the situations that practitioners face: "uncertainty, instability, uniqueness, and conflict" (p. 50).

From these general studies, it would be easy to conclude that managerial behavior is characterized by chaos, overload, and superficiality—i.e., too much to do about too many items involving too many people with too little time to resolve any of these items on any one occasion. However, there is a logic to these apparently frenetic managerial behaviors, and an understanding of that logic is a prerequisite for providing value-added information services to managers. We suggest that the logic has as its basis the structural components in the model of the manager's information environment. Our review of two of these components (the organization and the person) is somewhat abbreviated because these areas are vast and are reasonably well documented elsewhere (CHOO; LEAVITT; PAISLEY; PUGH ET AL.). Instead, our emphasis here is on managerial roles, managerial activities, and problem dimensions.

Managerial Roles

The landmark study by MINTZBERG (1973) provides a framework for understanding managerial roles. Based on week-long structured observations and interviews of five upper-level managers, Mintzberg concludes that all managers' jobs are basically alike and can be described most usefully in terms of ten roles. Differences in managers are primarily differences in the relative importance of each of these roles. The ten roles were separated into three groups: interpersonal, informational, and decisional. All three rely on information as a key resource for the successful enactment of the roles. The interpersonal group includes the roles of the figurehead, leader, and liaison. The informational roles include monitor, disseminator, and spokesperson. The decisional roles are the entrepreneur, disturbance handler, resource allocator, and the negotiator. The specific information behaviors of managers are generally determined by the roles they "play." Although these ten roles are plausible, later studies have questioned whether other roles need to be included or whether these roles interact with managerial level and responsibility (see, e.g., LUTHANS & LARSEN).

Managerial Activities

Traditionally the manager's job is described in terms of functional responsibilities—i.e., planning, staffing, budgeting, coordinating. These responsibilities can be translated into managerial activities, which in turn may be linked to information behaviors. For example, planning may require different information from different sources than staffing would; budgeting may require more current and accurate information than coordinating. The problem with these traditional functional activities is that they rarely appear as discrete entities in observational studies of managerial behavior. Thus, MINTZBERG (1989) concludes that they "tell us little about what managers actually do. At best, they indicate some vague objectives managers have when they work" (p. 9). However, it must be remembered that the observational studies focused primarily on overt behaviors rather than the mental activities of their respondents. So while it is true that most managers had few occasions that could be labeled "planning" or "staffing," they do engage in these activities but probably in short bursts, spread out over long time periods, with frequent interruptions.

The in-depth study of 15 general managers by KOTTER (1982a; 1982b) provides another class of managerial activities. According to Kotter, general managers have to find ways to resolve two job-related dilemmas: (1) to figure out what to do despite uncertainty, diversity, and an enormous quantity of potentially relevant information; and (2) to get it done through a large and diverse group of people over whom they have little or no direct control (KOTTER, 1982a, p. 76).

As with Mintzberg, Kotter described a set of behaviors that managers had in common and that relied heavily on information. The first set of behaviors come under the rubric of agenda setting. Agenda setting consists of information behaviors that are based on a loosely defined set of goals, strategies, and priorities. The managers develop, refine, and set their agendas through a vigorous search for information, gathered on a continuous basis, from a wide variety of sources. Kotter claims that better managers had longer time frames for their agendas and included more issues in their agendas. They also were more aggressive in seeking information.

The second set of behaviors is defined as network building. Here the managers "grow and feed" an interrelated network of cooperative relationships that could help further their agendas. These networks are created and maintained through various interactions, often oral and face to face, in which both business and nonbusiness topics are discussed. The people in the networks can include individuals from inside and outside the organization in all relevant functional areas and at all levels, both formal and informal. Kotter reports that the better general managers were more successful at building these networks; they had broader networks containing more useful people.

More recent studies (KANTER; LUTHANS) reinforce the centrality of networks to successful management. KANTER states that "the ability of managers to get things done depends more on the number of networks in which they're centrally involved than on their height in a hierarchy" (p. 89). As managers increase their involvement in networks, they increase the number of channels available to them for strategic contacts. They then have more information available to them and greater opportunities to initiate action.

The description of managerial work has been developed further by Luthans and his colleagues (LUTHANS; LUTHANS ET AL.). These authors argue that the major activities of "real managers" come under the headings of communications, traditional management, networking, and human resource management. The exchange of information—i.e., communicating—by and large made the greatest contribution to managerial effectiveness. However, communicating may be too general a managerial activity to be helpful in constraining the range of the manager's information behaviors.

Decision Making

Although managerial activities can be analyzed in terms of communicating, agenda setting, network building, and various functional responsibilities, the largest body of "activity" literature focuses on decision making. In fact, an entire school of management thought proposes decision making as the defining element of management (see, e.g., DRUCKER, 1974; SIMON, 1976, 1977). Of the many hundreds of studies in this area, which ones should be reported here? To answer this question we first expand the scope of what is included under decision making; then we focus on a few useful examples that illustrate how these activities affect the information behaviors of managers.

In the classical definition of decision making, a person must select from among several known alternatives; that is, decision making is concerned with choice. In contrast, problem solving involves only one alternative and some obstacle. That is, the task is to prevent, remove, or minimize a barrier. Decision making and problem solving can be thought of separately and have been studied separately, but "in the managerial world, these activities are so entangled that distinctions among them are only of semantic interest" (MCCALL & KAPLAN, p. 122). A third and related activity is "problem finding." Although this has been written about less frequently, the challenge of determining which events and situations deserve managerial attention should not be minimized. As commonly viewed, problem finding is a logical antecedent of problem solving, but, as ACKOFF (1974) points out, problems don't always stay solved and problem finding can emerge from problem solving rather than vice versa. There are other intriguing variations on how these activities are defined, what roles they play, and what information they require and produce (see, e.g., DRUCKER, 1974; HUBER, 1980; MINTZBERG ET AL.; SIMON, 1978). However, in terms of this chapter, the only distinctions that matter are those that affect managerial information behaviors.

A good example of the relationship between problem finding and managerial information behaviors is the work of POUNDS. He studied 50 executives in a large, technically based organization to determine how they knew when they had a problem. Pounds defined a problem in terms of a difference, perceived by the manager, between what exists and what is desired. When a difference existed, managers tended to question only one side of the gap. For example, if sales for the quarter failed to reach the goals for that quarter, managers would focus on what was wrong with the sales efforts; they never questioned whether the goal was realistic.

According to Pounds's argument, many problems in organizations may be a function of the information that is used to define the goal. If the information is out of date, irrelevant, or otherwise limited, the organization creates a needless "problem," which in turn will lead to information-intensive, problem-solving activities. Another intriguing information-related consequence of managerial problem finding was reported by LYLES & MITROFF. In their study of 33 upper-level managers they found that almost 90% of their subjects learned of significant problems in their organizations through "informal sensing techniques"—that is, outside official reporting channels.

The fact that decision making is an information-intensive activity can be asserted without fear of challenge. The question of what information is related to decision making is far less certain. The classic model of decision making is based on a long history of Western rationalism. It assumes that the decision maker can and will engage in a thorough search for all relevant information (see JANIS & MANN (p. 11) for an example of what is meant by "thorough"). HUBER (1980) identifies seven types of information that must be searched for: (1) possible alternatives, (2) criteria to evaluate the alternatives, (3) the relative importance of these criteria, (4) possible future conditions, (5) the probability that those futures will occur, (6) the possible payoffs, and (7) the constraints involved. Taken together, the totality of the information needed and the thoroughness of the search process make the classic model of decision making impossible in most realistic circumstances.

One method for coping within this impossible world is to restrict the information search. SIMON (1976) suggests that people don't optimize their decisions but search for alternatives until they find the first one that meets their minimum requirements; they "satisfice." A related method is through what TVERSKY calls "elimination-by-aspect." Under this approach all the (remaining) alternatives are compared against one criterion or aspect. The number of alternatives are quickly reduced because only those that remain from a previous step are compared with the next criterion.

Another approach is to recognize the limits that exist in the classical model of decision making: limits of information, time, and the human decision maker. These limits define realistic bounds on an individual's rationality, and the task then is to determine what it means to work "optimally" within those bounds. In their classic work on "bounded rationality" MARCH & SIMON identified only the most basic limits on rationality. FORESTER (1984) extended this idea to include situations in which there are social (more than one person), oppositional (they are in conflict), and political (with unequal amounts of power) bounds as well.

To see how these different levels of boundedness can lead to different kinds of information behaviors, consider how organizational decision making would change according to which sets of bounds are explicitly recognized. Huber's analysis of organizational decision making and the design of decision-support systems offers some insight here (HUBER, 1981). He notes that under the classical model of decision making (relatively unbounded), organizational databases would need to include the seven kinds of information noted above. However, if the organization recognized that it made decisions in a competitive area (a higher level of boundedness), then the databases ought to include information that would be useful for bargaining, threatening, compromising, and so forth. Huber's suggestions are attempts to incorporate alternative models of decision making in the design of decision-support systems. Each model postulates a different view of how organizations work, and each has different implications for information behaviors.

In addition to the standard (fully rational) model, other approaches to decision making deserve mention. For example, LINDBLOM (1959; 1979) describes organizational decision making as a series of successive, limited comparisons, commonly called "muddling through." He argues that in many organizations there usually is no ideal objective to maximize in decision making, but even if one did exist, it would be difficult if not impossible for key stakeholders to agree on. Thus, the organization moves incrementally through sub-objectives toward a goal that remains unclear or is continually redefined as the process evolves. Muddling through is noncomprehensive in the sense that many outcomes are never examined, alternative courses of action are neglected, and many of the values affected by the decision are ignored—all of which decreases the information requirements of the decision maker.

Muddling through assumes that long-term objectives cannot and should not be identified prematurely; instead they emerge as a result of limited approximations. In those situations in which they can be specified early ETZIONI (1967; 1989) suggests that "mixed scanning" will enable the manager to work toward that goal without needing a complete information search. This model of decision making combines aspects of the fully rational model with some of the incrementalism found in muddling through. In information terms, the model begins with a broad (but perhaps shallow) scanning for agenda setting or problem finding, followed by a narrower but deeper analysis of those items or areas that are identified as important.

A completely different approach to organizational decision making is proposed by COHEN ET AL. Recognizing that few organizations make decisions in a fully rational and unbounded way, they suggest that organizations be viewed as "organized anarchies," and accordingly, a large component of chance should be imposed on their decision processes. In their model, a set of decision opportunities can be looked at as a garbage can that contains a mix of problems, participants, solutions, and choice opportunities. The problems that get addressed and "solved" depend on the chance encounter of a particular problem with a workable solution and the availability of the right people to see it through. "The central idea of garbage can models is the substitution of a temporal order for a consequential one" (MARCH & OLSEN, p. 17). A related model is proposed by MCCALL & KAPLAN, who argue that organizations decide to act on problems when three conditions co-occur: (1) recognition of the problem, (2) resources needed to solve the problem, and (3) external pressure to motivate action. ISENBERG (1984) adds to this perspective by noting that in his study, successful senior-level managers tended not to accept problems for consideration unless they thought they could be solved. Because these models of organizational choice contain a significant element of chance, managers in these environments must have the information needed to capitalize on that chance. For example, in Huber's models of decision-support systems, the database (or the manager's memory) for the garbage can model might include a list of problems and a list of unused resources (HUBER, 1981).

Problem Dimensions

The conceptual and actual study of situational dimensions has a considerable history, but it is fragmented. In a seminal article by MACMULLIN & TAYLOR, the notion of what they label problem dimensions is presented in terms of possible enhancements to the more traditional information system design criteria. Dimensions serve as supplements in that they offer criteria for assessing the usefulness of information to a user's situation. As defined by the authors, "problem dimensions are those characteristics that, beyond specific subject matter, establish the criteria for judging the relevance of information to a problem or to a class of problems" (MACMULLIN & TAYLOR, p. 103). As such, problem dimensions can indicate what information would be useful to a manager working through a problematic situation. Because for MacMullin and Taylor these situations have multiple dimensions, they cannot always be categorized easily.

The problem dimensions proposed by MacMullin and Taylor are manifest in the subject and nonsubject components of the person's situation. Problem dimensions take into account characteristics of the information need that are idiosyncratic to the user group, to the individual in that group, and to that person's problematic situation. Acknowledging that problems are dynamic—i.e., they change as the information changes and as the person changes—TAYLOR (1986) suggests that the perceived salience of particular dimensions may also change.

MacMullin and Taylor proposed 22 dimensions, portrayed as 11 dichotomous categories (e.g., familiar–new, complex–simple) although they suggest that they are more likely to be continua. Their enumeration of dimensions was based on a conceptual analysis, not empirical data. The authors did not claim that their list was complete, that the dimensions were independent of each other, or that all dimensions would apply in all situations.

A review of the literature in information studies, management science, and public administration reveals that while many others have suggested similar approaches to problems, no one has defined such a range of dimensions or clarified the connection between dimensions and information behaviors as have MacMullin and Taylor. While given many other labels—e.g., "problem typologies" (KOCHEN; LYLES & MITROFF), "routines" (MINTZBERG ET AL.), "variables" (THOMPSON & TUDEN), and the like, the literature supports the fact that the concept of problem dimensions is well represented. There is considerable overlap between the dimensions noted by MacMullin and Taylor and those described by others (CYERT ET AL.; DAFT & MACINTOSH; EINHORN & HOGARTH; MARCH, 1959; MCCALL & KAPLAN; MINTZBERG ET AL.; RADFORD; THOMPSON & TUDEN; ZAND).

Empirical work by FLETCHER further substantiates the existence of problem dimensions. In a study of 26 managers in the public and private sectors, Fletcher found support for 18 broad categories of problem dimensions. The managers related 52 problematic situations in which they were integrally involved and described the salient features of each event in these situations that could be interpreted as problem dimensions. Further analysis of the data indicated that ten of the 11 problem dimension categories proposed by MacMullin and Taylor existed for managers.

Whether viewed as dimensions of the problem or criteria for assessing relevance, it is clear that many attributes of a situation may be salient at any one time and that these attributes may affect how information is valued and used as the person moves through his or her problematic situation.

The Person

Characteristics of the person are central to the description of the manager's information environment. These characteristics function separately and together to affect the other components of the model, including the manager's overt information behaviors. For the manager, the key factors include those cognitive, psychological, and physical attributes—whether innate or learned—that affect information-seeking and -use behaviors.

Much of the literature in previous *ARIST* chapters on information needs and uses might apply, including perhaps the survey of cognitive research in information science by ALLEN. An early but more applicable review of how managers process information can be found in UNGSON ET AL. Rather than repeat some of the same topics reported, we limit ourselves to introducing two research areas as examples of topics that link individual variables more directly with the information behaviors of managers.

The first research area focuses on how managers think. In a series of studies, AGOR (1984; 1986) found that in comparison with other managers, those who were more senior were more intuitive and claimed that intuition helped them with their most important decisions. ISENBERG (1984) also found support for the use of intuition among senior-level managers. Related to these studies are those that try to categorize managers according to how they think. A common tool here is the Myers-Briggs Type Indicator (MBTI). This personality test classifies individuals along four dimensions, two of which are directly related to information behaviors: the sensing–intuition dimension measures how information is acquired; the thinking–feeling dimension measures how that information is used. The working premise is that managers with different cognitive styles will prefer different kinds of information and will process information differently. Using the MBTI, DAVIS & ELNICKI found that MBA students with different cognitive types differed significantly in their performance on certain tasks. Similar findings were reported by MCKENNEY & KEEN, who studied about 200 MBA students and classified them (without using the MBTI) according to their cognitive styles for acquiring and using information. As predicted, they found that students who differed in their cognitive styles had different approaches to solving problems. There is some controversy about whether cognitive style should be a factor in implementing computerized information systems for managers (HUBER, 1983), but there is much less disagreement that these variables affect information behaviors of managers.

The other research area of interest is the application of cognitive biases to managerial information processing. Managers spend a lot of their time acting as what NISBETT & ROSS call "intuitive scientists"—i.e., they engage in observation, categorization, prediction, inference, and so forth. These mental activities are difficult enough to do well in the scientist's laboratory; in a manager's daily life, the difficulties increase considerably. Because of the pressures of time, overload, complexity, or uncertainty, managers frequently use shortcuts in their information processing, which can lead to suboptimal decisions or judgments. Over the past decade or two, cognitive psychologists have learned a lot about how and when people tend to simplify their judgment processes (for general surveys see HOGARTH, KAHNEMAN ET AL., and NISBETT & ROSS). More recently, researchers have tried to apply these learnings to the manager.

HOGARTH & MAKRIDAKIS listed about 30 potential biases, identified by cognitive scientists, that can affect judgment and choice behaviors. They analyzed these biases in the context of two important managerial activities—forecasting and planning—that require that information be accumulated to make useful predictions. Of particular relevance to forecasting and planning are the potential biases of "illusion of control" and "overconfidence in judgment." They also noted that the information-search component of planning and forecasting may be weakened through the manager's preference for redundancy in confirming information and avoiding disconfirming information. Similar results were found by SCHWENK (1984; 1985; 1988) who studied strategic decision making in organizations. Schwenk classified potentially biasing heuristics according to the standard stages of decision making, such as goal formulation, problem identification, evaluation, and selection. With respect to seeking and use behaviors, a body of research shows that managers don't revise their judgments appropriately according to existing or new information (see, e.g., MOSKOWITZ ET AL.).

Many of the potential biases are related to inference. Managers live in an uncertain world and need to make plans for an even more uncertain future. They frequently need to incorporate information about probabilities and uncertainties in their decision making. A reasonable body of evidence indicates that as lay statisticians, managers may not be using this information appropriately. For example, the success of a plan is often based on conjunctive assumptions (A, B, and C must occur for the plans to succeed), whereas risk assessment often requires disjunctive assumptions (if A or B or C fails, then. . .). The basic rules of probability theory state that under plausible conditions, the conjunction of events ought to be smaller than the disjunction of the same events. In practice, however, when people make these calculations mentally, they seem to produce something like an average that falls between the conjunctive and disjunctive results. This average estimate is too high for success and too low for failure and leads the decision maker to be more confident of the future than the data justify (TVERSKY & KAHNEMAN, 1974).

Another bias related to uncertainty is the tendency to act as if conclusions based on small samples were as reliable as those based on larger samples. This so-called "law of small numbers" is another source of unjustified overconfidence (TVERSKY & KAHNEMAN, 1971) and is a problem of concern to most practicing professionals, including managers, who don't have access to large sample sizes or who may have to act before sufficient information can be obtained.

The Setting

Characteristics of the organization also play an important role in describing the manager's information environment. If we include: (1) the size of the organization, (2) its goals, product/service line, culture, and procedures, and (3) the external environment in which it functions, there would be too many organizational variables to be included in this chapter. Two interesting research areas are reviewed here to illustrate the relevance of setting variables to the information behavior of the individual manager: (1) the "rationality" of organizations, and (2) the structure of the organization.

As with managers, organizations often fail to follow completely the tenets of rationality (e.g., unboundedness, optimization) in terms of their information behaviors. Organizations also use shortcuts to escape or minimize the problems of overload, complexity, and ambiguity (DAFT & WEICK; O'REILLY, 1983; SIMS & GIOIA).

One key to understanding the rationality of organizations is to view them differently—i.e., to recognize that they are social and political systems as well as technical and financial ones. TICHY identifies three dimensions of the organization: (1) the technical dimension, which is concerned with those factors related to the production of goods and services; (2) the cultural dimension, which includes the norms, expectations, and values of the organization; and (3) the political dimension, which addresses matters related to power. DIESING identifies five dimensions: (1) technical, (2) economic, (3) social, (4) legal, and (5) political. Multiple dimensions, combined with what FORESTER (1984) calls the social, political, and structural aspects of boundedness, contribute to a more complex but more realistic understanding of the organization. It is from this perspective that we can better appreciate the logic of alternative models of decision making such as the "muddling through" of LINDBLOM (1959) and the "garbage can" process of COHEN ET AL.

Organizational information behaviors also seem more reasonable when seen in the broader view of multiple dimensions and levels of boundedness. Organizations that gather information after the decision is made, that gather more information before processing what they already have, and that insist on having information regardless of its relevance do not conform to a traditional view of rationality. In an insightful analysis of these sorts of information behaviors, FELDMAN & MARCH posit four reasons why organizations might behave like this. First, there are organizational incentives for acquiring too much information. Units that are responsible for gathering information are not always administratively linked to or evaluated by the users of that information. There is no punishment for those who acquire more and more information; in fact, they may be rewarded. Second, in order to anticipate opportunities and threats in their environment, organizations need to operate partly in a surveillance mode, which requires information across a broad range of sources and topics. Third, because decision making in organizations is political as well as technical, managers request additional information to protect themselves from others who may try to use that same information to advance their own objectives.

The fourth cause of "irrational" information use in organizations is related to the symbolic value of information. Organizations and the managers who work in them want to let others know that they are following a model of action (e.g., decision making, planning, problem solving) that conforms to society's beliefs about rationality. From this point of view, managers request information but don't necessarily use it because by merely requesting it or having it on their desks, they are letting others know that they are engaged in a thorough information search that will be used as part of a rational decision-making process. The symbolic role of information can be extended to information technology and may explain why some people have computers on their desks that they never use. The need to signal to others that the organization is acting rationally can also be used to understand the true role of many meetings, task forces, and the like that occupy so much of the manager's time and contribute so much to the manager's information load. O'REILLY (1983) suggests that "in order to achieve a semblance of rationality, if only to satisfy constituencies outside the organization, procedures may be established that give the appearance of comprehensive rationality but which, in fact, may be more symbolic than real" (O'REILLY, 1983, p. 132).

The structure of the organization—whether it is tall or short, centralized or decentralized, flexible or rigid—ought to affect the kinds of information the manager needs or receives. Differences in structure are often associated with differences in processes and differences in culture, which also affect information flow and use.

MINTZBERG (1981; 1983) presents one of the most intriguing analyses of organizational structure. He categorizes organizations in terms of how they effect coordination and control, which are information-intensive managerial activities. Mintzberg's "simple structure" usually describes a small, new organization; it has a manager and workers but no technocrats or staff. Communication and coordination are usually straightforward because there is little or no hierarchy or bureaucracy. Two other types of organizational form are: (1) the "machine bureaucracy," which fits the stereotypic view of the large, procedure-driven, formalized organization, and (2) the "divisionalized form," which covers organizations with separate operating divisions. Mintzberg's other two structures, the "adhocracy" and the "professional bureaucracy," are younger and consequently are still determining what information managers need and how that information should be obtained.

The organization of the future is expected to be leaner, have fewer levels, and be "boundaryless" (DRUCKER, 1988; HIRSCHHORN & GILMORE; NAISBITT & ABURDENE); the key managerial functions of coordination and control will be carried out to a greater degree through information technology. Responding to increased competition on a global scale, more organizations are moving toward Mintzberg's adhocracies, workteams, and "skunkworks" to obtain the flexibility and fast response time needed. Managers are urged to get out of their offices and "walk around," coach their subordinates, and be close to their customers (PETERS & WATERMAN). In these kinds of organizations, information needs to be shared widely, and more people from more areas both inside and outside the organization will participate in decision making. Clearly, managers in these organizations will need different kinds of information from different sources and may need to use that information in a different way (SCHEIN; STRASSMANN; ZAND).

DYNAMICS OF THE MODEL

Although this chapter uses a model of the information environment of managers, the emphasis is not on the validity of that model. Rather the model's structural components have been used as a framework for organizing our review of the literature on managerial information behaviors. This short section contains some of the literature that relates to the dynamics of the model. Readers interested in the validity of this model or in other, perhaps related, models in information science can start with the recent *ARIST* review by BURT & KINNUCAN and the review of organizational information processing models by CHOO.

The dynamic nature of the model—i.e., problematic situations change over time—is an important concept in understanding information behaviors. As managers move through their problem situations, new information can shift their focus to a subproblem or to a different problematic situation, and in many instances it can redefine the problematic situation (DILL; MCCALL & KAPLAN; TAYLOR, 1986; VICKERY; WHITTEMORE & YOVITS).

WERSIG & WINDEL present a model for problematic situations that reflects this essential dynamism: a continuous redefining of the problem and the desired solution. The manager progresses through a number of phases and uses information in all the phases. The authors further propose that the information that may be useful will change from one phase to another, with each new iteration requiring very different information.

Probably the most comprehensive articulation of this dynamism is presented by DERVIN. She asserts that constantly changing situational conditions evoke the information behaviors. People go through their daily lives confronted by a wide array of problem situations that create uncertainties or "gaps." For some reason they become "stopped" and cannot move. They perceive this condition as troublesome and attempt, via information behaviors, to move either physically or cognitively. The notion of a journey down a road with detours is offered as a metaphor.

The important thing to remember is that problematic situations are not static. This fact has implications for the information provider in that information that is relevant at one point in the process may not be useful later on even though the problematic situation may have the same title or may be about the same topic.

SUMMARY AND IMPLICATIONS

What does this review of the literature tell us about managerial information behaviors? At a general level, the structure of the review argues for understanding the information behaviors of managers in terms of context-based dynamic cognitions. Specifically, we argue that the information environment of managers is defined by those factors that are related to managers as people who work in a setting, taking on various roles and carrying out various activities. Further, the model posits that the problematic situations that managers face are affected by these factors and the relative importance of different problem dimensions.

Since managers are people, the advice that information scientists give to those who deliver information services to other user populations applies to managers as well. Specifically, library and information science (LIS) professionals know that they must understand the user's information need in the context of the user's situation. For managers this means that information professionals need to refocus the query-negotiation process from that of answering questions to that of helping to resolve problematic situations (e.g., DERVIN & DEWDNEY; TAYLOR, 1968), and they need to add value by filtering information to reduce overload. This view is not new. The literature in information science abounds with excoriations of technology-driven information systems and calls to develop user-driven models of these systems (DERVIN & NILAN; MICK ET AL.; NILAN & FLETCHER; ROUSE & ROUSE; TAYLOR, 1986).

While such recommendations are known and are sensible, the information behaviors of managers present special challenges to information professionals. The literature review suggests that the following characteristics of managers are important and relevant:

- The activities that command their attention are dynamic, uncertain, complex, fast-paced, unstable, and unique;
- The situations they face are what ACKOFF (1974) calls "messes"; they are not well defined, well articulated, unchanging, or independent;
- The environment in which these activities occur is informationally overloaded, socially constrained, and politically laden;
- The preferred mode of communication is oral, especially, face-to-face, and there is little time to read long documents;

- The gathering of information is often external, occurring outside their offices, to learn what ought to be on their agendas and who can help them; and
- The basis for decision making includes the use of intuition (especially for those at more senior levels), perhaps relegating formally requested information to legitimize those decisions after they are made.

We don't have an easy solution for meeting the unique and challenging demands of managers as users, but we can make a few suggestions. First, managers, as a population, can become an increasingly significant proportion of the users we serve. If we gain proficiency with managers, we can increase our value to other professionals (e.g., lawyers, politicians) because many user communities work in environments with similar characteristics.

Managers are becoming keenly aware that they need help in dealing with information overload. As key decision makers in organizations, they get most of their information (both formal and informal) from others. These people are instrumental to the manager and to the organization that enacts the manager's decisions. While information professionals with training in dealing with unstructured natural-language materials ought to have a competitive advantage over other information providers (e.g., system designers) when it comes to serving senior-level managers, it is necessary that they augment this skill with an understanding of how managers and organizations function. The immediate challenge, therefore, is for information scientists and information professionals to enhance their knowledge of this user environment.

The relationship between LIS professionals and managers-in-action is analogous to that between the manager and the management scientist, as described by Churchman and his colleagues (CHURCHMAN; CHURCHMAN & SCHAINBLATT). They noted that these two different communities often acted as if they were two different cultures. They did not communicate, and there were differences in the values and norms of each community, which probably contributed to that lack of interaction. To surmount these differences, Churchman and Schainblatt argued for "mutual understanding," with both communities considered equally responsible for moving in that direction.

We also believe that information professionals would benefit by gaining more of an understanding of the multidimensional nature of organizations. LIS professionals have historically focused on information related to the technical dimension. However, in the world of the manager, the cultural, social, and political dimensions also matter—perhaps quite a bit. Within the framework of multiple dimensions, the information professional can gain a better appreciation of the alternative notions of "rationality," such as the advice of FORESTER (1989) that to be rational, one must be political.

Given an understanding of these broader, fundamental concerns, the LIS professional can specifically contribute in a useful way to the information activities of managers by:

- Supplying the manager with the information in the format appropriate to the problematic situation—i.e., not always relying on lengthy printed materials as solutions;
- Insulating the manager from the raw and often superfluous data that contribute to information overload;
- Acting as a filter by analyzing, grouping, and formatting the information for the manager;
- Generating a common organizational database for use in group-decision situations;
- Scanning the external environment to keep managers supplied with relevant information for their problematic situations;
- Generating an audit trail of information that can be linked to specific problematic situations;
- Alerting the manager to the existence of conflicting or contradictory data to provide a broader base for the solution; and
- Working with the manager to develop an organizational resource center that is timely, reliable, and relevant to the needs of both the manager and the organization.

The goal of the information professional is to provide information services that treat the manager as a "clinician" who deals with unique circumstances in a time-compressed, complex setting. What the manager needs are the value-added services of screening, summarizing, synthesizing, highlighting, and presenting information in a useful and timely manner (TAYLOR, 1986). Only then will the information professional be able to ameliorate the manager's dilemma, which is too much information, but not enough of the right information in the right format through the right channel at the right time.

BIBLIOGRAPHY

ACHLEITNER, HERBERT K.; GROVER, ROBERT. 1988. Managing in an Information-Rich Environment: Applying Information Transfer Theory to Information Systems Management. Special Libraries. 1988 Spring; 79(2): 92-100. ISSN: 0038-6723.

ACKOFF, RUSSELL L. 1967. Management Misinformation Systems. Management Science. 1967 December; 14(4): B-147–B-156. ISSN: 0025-1909.

ACKOFF, RUSSELL L. 1974. Beyond Problem Solving. General Systems. 1974; 19: 237-239. ISSN: 0072-0798.

AGNEW, N.M.; BROWN, J.L. 1982. From Skyhooks to Walking Sticks: On the Road to Nonrational Decision Making. Organizational Dynamics. 1982 Autumn; 11: 40-58. ISSN: 0090-2616.

AGOR, WESTON H. 1984. Intuitive Management: Integrating Left and Right Brain Management Skills. Englewood Cliffs, NJ: Prentice-Hall, Inc.; 1984. 143p. ISBN: 0-13-502733-0; ISBN: 0-13-502725-X.

AGOR, WESTON H. 1986. How Top Executives Use Their Intuition to Make Important Decisions. Business Horizons. 1986 January/February; 29: 49-53. ISSN: 0007-6813.

ALLAN, P. 1981. Managers at Work: A Large-Scale Study of the Managerial Job in New York City Government. Academy of Management Journal. 1981 September; 24(3): 613-619. ISSN: 0001-4273.

ALLEN, BRYCE L. 1991. Cognitive Research in Information Science: Implications for Design. In: Williams, Martha E., ed. Annual Review of Information Science and Technology: Volume 26. Medford, NJ: Learned Information, Inc. for the American Society for Information Science; 1991. 3-37. ISSN: 0066-4200; ISBN: 0-938734-55-5.

ALTER, S.L. 1976. How Effective Managers Use Information Systems. Harvard Business Review. 1976 November/December; 54(6): 97-104. ISSN: 0017-8012.

ARGYRIS, C. 1971. Management Information Systems: The Challenge to Rationality and Emotionality. Management Science. 1971 February; 17(6): B-275-B-292. ISSN: 0025-1909.

BEHLING, O.; ECKEL, N.I. 1991. Making Sense Out of Intuition. Academy of Management Executive. 1991; 5(1): 46-54. ISSN: 0896-3789.

BELKIN, NICHOLAS J. 1984. Cognitive Models and Information Transfer. Social Science Information Studies (England). 1984; 4: 111-129. ISSN: 0143-6236.

BENBASAT, IZAK; TAYLOR, RONALD N. 1978. The Impact of Cognitive Styles on Information System Design. Management Information Systems Quarterly. 1978 July; 2(2): 43-54. ISSN: 0276-7783.

BENBASAT, IZAK; TAYLOR, RONALD N. 1982. Behavioral Aspects of Information Processing for the Design of Management Information Systems. IEEE Transactions on Systems, Man and Cybernetics. 1982 July/August; SMC 12(4): 439-450. ISSN: 0018-9472.

BLAYLOCK, G.K.; REES, L.P. 1984. Cognitive Style and Usefulness of Information. Decision Sciences. 1984; 15(6): 74-91. ISSN: 0011-7315.

BOYNTON, A.C.; ZMUD, ROBERT W. 1984. An Assessment of Critical Success Factors. Sloan Management Review. 1984 Summer; 25: 17-24. ISSN: 0019-848X.

BREWER, E.; TOMLINSON, J.W.C. 1964. The Manager's Working Day. Journal of Industrial Economics (England). 1964 June; 12(3): 191-197. ISSN: 0022-1821.

BRITTAIN, J. MICHAEL. 1975. Information Needs and Application of the Results of User Studies. In: Debons, A.; Cameron, W.J., eds. Perspectives in Information Science: Proceedings of the NATO Advanced Study Institute on Perspectives in Information Science; 1973 August 13-24; Aberystwyth, Wales. Leyden, The Netherlands: Noordhoff International Publishing; 1975. 425-447. ISBN: 90-286-0583-5.

BRUNSSON, NILS. 1985. The Irrational Organization: Irrationality as a Basis for Organizational Action and Change. New York, NY: Wiley; 1985. 193p. ISBN: 0-471-90795-2; LC: 85-6527.

BURT, PATRICIA V.; KINNUCAN, MARK T. 1990. Information Models and Modeling Techniques for Information Systems. In: Williams, Martha E., ed. Annual Review of Information Science and Technology: Volume 25. Amsterdam, The Netherlands: Elsevier Science Publishers for the American Society for Information Science; 1990. 175-208. ISSN: 0066-4200; ISBN: 0-444-88531-5.

CARROLL, S.J.; GILLEN, D.J. 1987. Are the Classical Management Functions Useful in Describing Managerial Work? Academy of Management Review. 1987; 12: 38-51. ISSN: 0363-7425.

CHEN, CHING-CHIH; HERNON, PETER. 1982. Information Seeking: Assessing and Anticipating User Needs. New York, NY: Neal-Schuman; 1982. 205p. ISBN: 0-918212-50-2; LC: 82-6320.

CHOO, CHUN WEI. 1991. Towards an Information Model of Organizations. Canadian Journal of Information Science (Canada). 1991 September; 16(3): 32-62. ISSN: 0380-9218.

CHURCHMAN, C.W. 1964. Managerial Acceptance of Scientific Recommendations. California Management Review. 1964 Fall; 7(1): 31-38. ISSN: 0008-1256.

CHURCHMAN, C.W.; SCHAINBLATT, A.H. 1965. The Researcher and the Manager: A Dialectic of Implementation. Management Science. 1965 February; 11(4): B-69-B-87. ISSN: 0025-1909.

CLEVELAND, HARLAN. 1985. The Knowledge Executive: Leadership in an Information Society. New York, NY: Truman Talley Books; 1985. 261p. ISBN: 0-525-24307-0.

COHEN, MICHAEL D.; MARCH, JAMES G.; OLSEN, JOHAN P. 1972. A Garbage Can Model of Organizational Choice. Administrative Science Quarterly. 1972 March; 17: 1-25. ISSN: 0001-8392.

COMPAINE, BENJAMIN M.; MCLAUGHLIN, JOHN F. 1987. Management Information: Back to Basics. Information Management Review. 1987 Winter; 2(3): 15-24. ISSN: 8756-1557.

CONNOLLY, TERRY. 1977. Information Processing and Decision-Making in Organizations. In: Staw, B.M.; Salancik, G.R., eds. New Directions in Organizational Behavior. Chicago, IL: St. Clair Press; 1977. 205-234. ISBN: 0-914292-06-4; LC: 76-47795.

COTTON, J.L. 1984. Why Getting Additional Data Often Slows Decision-Making and What to Do about It. Management Review. 1984 May; 73(5): 56-61. ISSN: 0025-1895.

CRAIG, R. 1979. Information Systems Theory and Research: An Overview of Individual Information Processing. Communication Yearbook. 1979; 3: 99-121. ISBN: 0-87855-341-X.

CRAVENS, D.W. 1970. An Exploratory Analysis of Individual Information Processing. Management Science. 1970 June; 16(10): B-656-B-670. ISSN: 0025-1909.

CURCURU, E.H.; HEALEY, J.H. 1972. The Multiple Roles of the Manager. Business Horizons. 1972 August; 15(4): 15-24. ISSN: 0007-6813.

CYERT, RICHARD M.; SIMON, HERBERT A.; TROW, D.B. 1956. Observations of a Business Decision. The Journal of Business. 1956; 29(4): 237-248. ISSN: 0021-9398.

DAFT, RICHARD L.; LENGEL, ROBERT H. 1984. Information Richness: A New Approach to Managerial Information Processing and Organization Design. In: Staw, B.M.; Cummings, L.L., eds. Research in Organizational Behavior. 1984; 6: 191-233. ISSN: 0191-3085.

DAFT, RICHARD L.; LENGEL, ROBERT H. 1986. Organizational Information Requirements, Media Richness and Structural Design. Management Science. 1986 May; 32(5): 554-571. ISSN: 0025-1909.

DAFT, RICHARD L.; MACINTOSH, NORMAN B. 1978. A New Approach to Design and Use of Management Information. California Management Review. 1978; 21(1): 820-892. ISSN: 0008-1256.

DAFT, RICHARD L.; WEICK, KARL E. 1984. Toward a Model of Organizations as Interpretation Systems. Academy of Management Review. 1984; 9(2): 284-295. ISSN: 0363-7425.

DANIELS, P.J. 1986. Cognitive Models in Information Retrieval—An Evaluative Review. Journal of Documentation. 1986; 42(4): 272-304. ISSN: 0022-0418.

DAVIS, DONALD L.; ELNICKI, RICHARD A. 1984. User Cognitive Types for Decision Support Systems. Omega (England). 1984; 12(6): 601-614. ISSN: 0305-0483.

DERVIN, BRENDA. 1983. An Overview of Sense-Making Research: Concepts, Methods, and Results to Date. Paper presented at: The International Communication Association Annual Meeting; 1983 May 26-30; Dallas, TX. 68p. Available from: the author, Department of Communication, Ohio State University, Columbus, Ohio 43210.

DERVIN, BRENDA; DEWDNEY, P. 1986. Neutral Questioning: A New Approach to the Reference Interview. RQ. 1986; 25(4): 506-512. ISSN: 0033-7072..

DERVIN, BRENDA; NILAN, MICHAEL S. 1986. Information Needs and Uses. In: Williams, Martha E., ed. Annual Review of Information Science and Technology: Volume 21. White Plains, NY: Knowledge Industry Publications, Inc. for the American Society for Information Science; 1986. 3-33. ISSN: 0066-4200; ISBN: 0-86729-209-1.

DEWHIRST, H.D. 1971. Influence of Perceived Information Sharing Norms in Communication Channel Utilization. Academy of Management Journal. 1971 September; 14(3): 305-315. ISSN: 0001-4273.

DICKSON, GARY W.; SENN, JAMES A.; CHERVANY, NORMAN L. 1977. Research in Management Information Systems: The Minnesota Experiments. Management Science. 1977 May; 23(9): 913-923. ISSN: 0025-1909.

DIESING, PAUL. 1973. Reason in Society; Five Types of Decisions and Their Social Conditions. Westport, CT: Greenwood Press; 1973. 262p. ISBN: 0-8371-6660-8; LC: 72-11328.

DILL, WILLIAM R. 1964. Varieties of Administrative Decision. In: Leavitt, Harold J.; Pondy, L.R., eds. Readings in Managerial Psychology. Chicago, IL: University of Chicago Press; 1964. 457-473. LC: 64-15811.

DOKTOR, ROBERT H.; HAMILTON, WILLIAM F. 1973. Cognitive Style and the Acceptance of Management Science Recommendations. Management Science. 1973 April; 19(8): 884-894. ISSN: 0025-1909.

DOWNS, ANTHONY. 1965. Nonmarket Decision Making: A Theory of Bureaucracy. American Economic Review. 1965 May; 55: 439-446. ISSN: 0002-8282.

DOWNS, ANTHONY. 1967. Search Problems in Bureaus. In: Inside Bureaucracy. Boston, MA: Little Brown; 1967. 175-190. LC: 67-18259. Also in: Horton, Forest W.; Marchand, Donald A., eds. Information Management in Public Administration. Arlington, VA: Information Resources Press; 1982. 103-119. ISBN: 0-87815-038-2.

DREYFUS, S.E. 1983. How Expert Managers Tend to Let the Gut Lead the Brain. Management Review. 1983 September; 72(9): 56-61. ISSN: 0025-1895.

DRUCKER, PETER F. 1967. The Effective Executive. New York, NY: Harper and Row; 1967. 178p. LC: 67-11341.

DRUCKER, PETER F. 1974. Management: Tasks, Responsibilities, Practices. New York, NY: Harper and Row; 1974. 839p. ISBN: 0-06-011092-9.

DRUCKER, PETER F. 1988. The Coming of the New Organization. Harvard Business Review. 1988 January/February; 66(1): 45-53. ISSN: 0017-8012.

EINHORN, H.J.; HOGARTH, ROBIN M. 1987. Decision Making: Going Forward in Reverse. Harvard Business Review. 1987 January/February; 65(1): 66-70. ISSN: 0017-8012.

ETZIONI, A. 1967. Mixed-Scanning: A "Third" Approach to Decision Making. Public Administration Review. 1967 December; 27: 385-392. ISSN: 0033-3352.

ETZIONI, A. 1989. Humble Decision Making. Harvard Business Review. 1989 July/August; 67: 122-126. ISSN: 0017-8012.

FELDMAN, MARTHA S.; MARCH, JAMES G. 1981. Information in Organizations as Signal and Symbol. Administrative Science Quarterly. 1981 June; 26(2): 171-186. ISSN: 0001-8392.

FERENCE, T.P. 1970. Organizational Communications Systems and the Decision Process. Management Science. 1970 October; 17(2): B-83-B-96. ISSN: 0025-1909.

FLEISCHER, M.; MORRELL, J.A. 1988. The Use of Office Automation by Managers: A Survey. Information Management Review. 1988 Summer; 4(1): 29-40. ISSN: 8756-1557; ISBN: 0-87189-137-9.

FLETCHER, PATRICIA T. 1991. An Examination of Situational Dimensions in the Information Behaviors of General Managers. Syracuse, NY: Syracuse University; 1991. 380p. (Ph.D. dissertation). Available from: University Microfilms, Ann Arbor, MI. (UMI order no. DA9204503).

FORESTER, JOHN. 1984. Bounded Rationality and the Politics of Muddling Through. Public Administration Review. 1984 January/February; 44: 23-31. ISSN: 0033-3352.

FORESTER, JOHN. 1989. Planning in the Face of Power. Berkeley, CA: University of California Press; 1989. 283p. ISBN: 0-520-06413-5.

GORRY, G.A.; SCOTT MORTON, MICHAEL S. 1971. A Framework for Management Information Systems. Sloan Management Review. 1971; 13: 55-70. ISSN: 0019-848X.

GROSSER, KERRY. 1991. Human Networks in Organizational Information Processing. In: Williams, Martha E., ed. Annual Review of Information Science and Technology: Volume 26. Medford, NJ: Learned Information, Inc. for the American Society for Information Science; 1991. 349-402. ISSN: 0066-4200; ISBN: 0-938734-55-5; LC: 66-25096.

GROVER, ROBERT; GLAZIER, J. 1984. Information Transfer in City Government. Public Library Quarterly. 1984 Winter; 5(4): 9-27. ISSN: 0161-6846.

HALE, MARTHA LARSON. 1983. A Structured Observation Study of the Nature of City Managers' Work. Los Angeles, CA: University of Southern California; 1983. (Ph.D. dissertation). (Copies available from Micrographics Department, Doheny Library, University of Southern California, Los Angeles, CA 90089).

HALES, COLIN P. 1986. What Do Managers Do? A Critical Review of the Evidence. Journal of Management Studies (England). 1986; 23: 88-115. ISSN: 0022-2380.

HELLRIEGEL, D.; SLOCUM, J.W., JR. 1975. Managerial Problem Solving Styles. Business Horizons. 1975 December; 18: 29-37. ISSN: 0007-6813.

HENDERSON, JOHN G.; NUTT, PAUL C. 1980. The Influence of Decision Style on Decision Making Behavior. Management Science. 1980 April; 26(4): 371-385. ISSN: 0025-1909.

HERNSTEIN, R.J. 1990. Rational Choice Theory: Necessary But Not Sufficient. American Psychologist. 1990 March; 45(3): 356-367. ISSN: 0003-066X.

HERT, CAROL A.; NILAN, MICHAEL S. 1992. Incorporating the User in System Evaluation and Design. In: Proceedings of the National Online Meeting; 1992 May 5-7; New York, NY. Medford, NJ: Learned Information, Inc.; 1992. 217-234. ISBN: 0-938734-63-6.

HEWINS, ELIZABETH T. 1990. Information Need and Use Studies. In: Williams, Martha E., ed. Annual Review of Information Science and Technology: Volume 25. Amsterdam, The Netherlands: Elsevier Science Publishers for the American Society for Information Science; 1990. 145-172. ISSN: 0066-4200; ISBN: 0-444-88531-5.

HICKSON, DAVID J. 1987. Decision-Making at the Top of Organizations. Annual Review of Sociology. 1987; 13: 165-192. ISSN: 0360-0572; ISBN: 0-8243-2213-4.

HIRSCHHORN, LARRY; GILMORE, THOMAS. 1992. The New Boundaries of the "Boundaryless" Company. Harvard Business Review. 1992 May/June; 70(3): 104-115. ISSN: 0017-8012.

HOGARTH, ROBIN. 1980. Judgment and Choice. New York, NY: Wiley & Sons; 1980. 250p. ISBN: 0-471-27744-4.

HOGARTH, ROBIN; MAKRIDAKIS, SPYROS. 1981. Forecasting and Planning: An Evaluation. Management Science. 1981 February; 27(2): 115-138. ISSN: 0025-1909.

HOUSE, ROBERT J.; SINGH, JITENDRA V. 1987. Organizational Behavior: Some New Directions for I/O Psychology. Annual Review of Psychology. 1987; 38: 669-718. ISSN: 0066-4308.

HUBER, GEORGE P. 1980. Managerial Decision Making. Glenview, IL: Scott, Foresman & Co.; 1980. 781p. ISBN: 0-8039-2387-2.
HUBER, GEORGE P. 1981. The Nature of Organizational Decision Making and the Design of Decision Support Systems. Management Information Systems Quarterly. 1981 June; 5(3): 1-10. ISSN: 0276-7783.
HUBER, GEORGE P. 1983. Cognitive Style as a Basis for MIS and DSS Designs: Much Ado about Nothing? Management Science. 1983 May; 29(5): 567-578. ISSN: 0025-1909.
HUBER, GEORGE P.; DAFT, RICHARD L. 1987. The Information Environments of Organizations. In: Jablin, Fredric M.; Putnam, Linda L.; Roberts, Karlene H.; Porter, Lyman W., eds. Handbook of Organizational Communication: An Interdisciplinary Perspective. Newbury Park, CA: Sage; 1987. 130-164. ISBN: 0-8039-2387-2.
ISABELLA, L. 1990. Evolving Interpretations as a Change Unfolds: How Managers Construe Key Organizational Events. Academy of Management Journal. 1990; 33(1): 7-41. ISSN: 0001-4273.
ISENBERG, DANIEL J. 1984. How Senior Managers Think. Harvard Business Review. 1984 November/December; 62(6): 81-90. ISSN: 0017-8012.
ISENBERG, DANIEL J. 1986. Thinking and Managing: A Verbal Protocol Analysis of Managerial Problem Solving. Academy of Management Journal. 1986; 29(4): 775-788. ISSN: 0001-4273.
JANIS, IRVING L.; MANN, LEON. 1977. Decision Making: A Psychological Analysis of Conflict, Choice, and Commitment. New York, NY: The Free Press; 1977. 488p. ISBN: 0-02-916160-6.
KAHNEMAN, DANIEL; SLOVIC, P.; TVERSKY, AMOS, eds. 1982. Judgment under Uncertainty: Heuristics and Biases. New York, NY: Cambridge University Press; 1982. 555p. ISBN: 0-521-28414-7.
KAHNEMAN, DANIEL; TVERSKY, AMOS. 1979. Intuitive Prediction: Biases and Corrective Procedures. TIMS: Studies in the Management Sciences (The Netherlands). 1979; 12: 313-327. ISSN: 0378-3766.
KANTER, ROSABETH MOSS. 1989. The New Managerial Work. Harvard Business Review. 1989 November/December; 67(6): 85-92. ISSN: 0017-8012.
KATZER, JEFFREY. 1991. Understanding How Information "Works" in Organizations: Plausible Assumptions and Confounding Realities. Paper presented at: American Society for Information Science (ASIS) 54th Annual Meeting; 1991 October 27-31; Washington, DC. Available from: the author, Syracuse University, School of Information Studies, Syracuse, NY 13244.
KIESLER, S.; SPROULL, L. 1982. Managerial Response to Changing Environments: Perspectives on Problem Sensing from Social Cognition. Administrative Science Quarterly. 1982 December; 27(4): 548-570. ISSN: 0001-8392.
KOCHEN, MANFRED. 1980. Coping with Complexity. Omega (England). 1980; 8(1): 11-19. ISSN: 0305-0483.
KOTTER, JOHN P. 1982a. The General Managers. New York, NY: The Free Press; 1982. 232p. ISBN: 0-02-918230-1.
KOTTER, JOHN P. 1982b. What Effective General Managers Really Do. Harvard Business Review. 1982 November/December; 60: 156-167. ISSN: 0017-8012.

LAU, ALAN W.; NEWMAN, ARTHUR R.; BROEDLING, LAURIE A. 1980. The Nature of Managerial Work in the Public Sector. Public Administration Review. 1980 September/October; 40: 513-520. ISSN: 0033-3352.

LAU, ALAN W.; PAVETT, C.M. 1983. Managerial Work: The Influence of Hierarchical Level and Functional Speciality. Academy of Management Journal. 1983 March; 26(1): 170-177. ISSN: 0001-4273.

LEAVITT, HAROLD J. 1978. Managerial Psychology. 4th edition. Chicago, IL: University of Chicago Press; 1978. 385p. ISBN: 0-226-46947-3.

LENGEL, ROBERT H.; DAFT, RICHARD L. 1988. The Selection of Communication Media as an Executive Skill. Academy of Management Executive. 1988 August; 2(3): 225-233. ISSN: 0896-3789.

LEVITT, T. 1987. From the Editor. Harvard Business Review. 1987 January-February; 87(1): 4-5. ISSN: 0017-8012.

LINDBLOM, CHARLES G. 1959. The Science of Muddling Through. Public Administration Review. 1959 Spring; 19: 79-88. ISSN: 0033-3352.

LINDBLOM, CHARLES G. 1979. Still Muddling, Not Yet, Through. Public Administration Review. 1979 November/December; 39: 40-45. ISSN: 0033-3352.

LUTHANS, FRED. 1988. Successful vs. Effective Real Managers. Academy of Management Executive. 1988; 2(2): 127-132. ISSN: 0896-3789.

LUTHANS, FRED; LARSEN, JANET K. 1986. How Managers Really Communicate. Human Relations. 1986; 39(2): 161-178. ISSN: 0018-7267.

LUTHANS, FRED; ROSENKRANTZ, STUART A.; HENNESSEY, HARRY W. 1985. What Do Successful Managers Really Do? An Observation Study of Managerial Activities. Journal of Applied Behavioral Science. 1985; 21(3): 255-270. ISSN: 0021-8863.

LYLES, M.A.; MITROFF, I.I. 1980. Organizational Problem Formulation: An Empirical Study. Administrative Science Quarterly. 1980 March; 25: 102-119. ISSN: 0001-8392.

MACMULLIN, SUSAN E.; TAYLOR, ROBERT S. 1984. Problem Dimensions and Information Traits. Information Society. 1984; 3(1): 91-111. ISSN: 0197-2243.

MARCH, JAMES G. 1959. Business Decision Making. Industrial Research. 1959 Spring; 1: 64-70. ISSN: 0019-8722.

MARCH, JAMES G. 1978. Bounded Rationality, Ambiguity and the Engineering of Choice. Bell Journal of Economics. 1978; 9: 587-608. ISSN: 0741-6261.

MARCH, JAMES G. 1982. Theories of Choice and Making Decisions. Society. 1982; 20: 29-39. ISSN: 0147-2011.

MARCH, JAMES G.; OLSEN, J.P. 1986. Garbage Can Models of Decision Making in Organizations. In: March, James G.; Weissenger-Baylon, Roger W., eds. Ambiguity and Command: Organizational Perspectives on Military Decision Making. Boston, MA: Pitman; 1986. 11-35. ISBN: 0-582-98831-4.

MARCH, JAMES G.; SIMON, HERBERT A. 1958. Organizations. New York, NY: Wiley & Sons; 1958. 262p. LC: 58-13464.

MCCALL, MORGAN W., JR.; KAPLAN, R.E. 1990. Whatever It Takes: The Realities of Managerial Decision Making. 2nd edition. Englewood Cliffs, NJ: Prentice-Hall, Inc.; 1990. 150p. ISBN: 0-13-952136-4.

MCCASKEY, MICHAEL B. 1979. The Management of Ambiguity. Organizational Dynamics. 1979 Spring; 7(4): 31-48. ISSN: 0090-2616.

MCGOWAN, R.P. 1984. Organizational Decision Making and Information Systems. In: Nigro, L.G., ed. Decision Making in the Public Sector. New York, NY: Marcel Dekker, Inc.; 1984. 261-288. ISBN: 0-8247-7155-9.

MCKENNEY, JAMES L.; KEEN, PETER G.W. 1974. How Managers' Minds Work. Harvard Business Review. 1974 May/June; 52(3): 79-90. ISSN: 0017-8012.

MICK, COLIN K.; LINDSEY, GEORGE N.; CALLAHAN, DANIEL. 1980. Toward Usable User Studies. Journal of the American Society for Information Science. 1980 September; 31: 347-356. ISSN: 0002-8231.

MINTZBERG, HENRY. 1973. The Nature of Managerial Work. New York, NY: Harper and Row; 1973. 298p. ISBN: 0-06-044555-6; LC: 72-9400.

MINTZBERG, HENRY. 1975. The Manager's Job: Folklore and Fact. Harvard Business Review. 1975 July/August; 53: 49-61. ISSN: 0017-8012.

MINTZBERG, HENRY. 1976. Planning on the Left Side and Managing on the Right. Harvard Business Review. 1976 July/August; 54(4): 49-58. ISSN: 0017-8012.

MINTZBERG, HENRY. 1980. The Nature of Managerial Work. Englewood Cliffs, NJ: Prentice Hall; 1980. 217p. ISBN: 0-13-610402-9.

MINTZBERG, HENRY. 1981. Organization Design: Fashion or Fit? Harvard Business Review. 1981 January/February; 59(1): 103-116. ISSN: 0017-8012.

MINTZBERG, HENRY. 1983. Structure in Fives; Designing Effective Organizations. Englewood Cliffs, NJ: Prentice-Hall, Inc.; 1983. 312p. ISBN: 0-13-854349-6.

MINTZBERG, HENRY. 1989. Mintzberg on Management: Inside Our Strange World of Organizations. New York, NY: The Free Press; 1989. 418p. ISBN: 0-02-921371-1; LC: 89-1241.

MINTZBERG, HENRY; RAISINGHANI, DURU; THEORET, ANDRE. 1976. The Structure of "Unstructured" Decision Processes. Administrative Science Quarterly. 1976 June; 21(2): 246-275. ISSN: 0001-8392.

MOSKOWITZ, HERBERT; SCHAEFER, RALF E.; BORCHERDING, KATRIN. 1976. "Irrationality" of Managerial Judgments: Implications for Information Systems. Omega (England). 1976 June; 4(2): 125-140. ISSN: 0305-0483.

MUNRO, MALCOLM C. 1978. Determining the Manager's Information Needs. Journal of Systems Management. 1978 June; 29: 34-39. ISSN: 0022-4839.

MUNRO, MALCOLM C.; WHEELER, BASIL R. 1980. Planning, Critical Success Factors and Management's Information Requirements. Management Information Systems Quarterly. 1980 December; 4: 27-38. ISSN: 0276-7783.

NAISBITT, JOHN; ABURDENE, PATRICIA. 1985. Re-inventing the Corporation: Transforming Your Job and Your Company for the New Information Society. New York, NY: Warner Books; 1985. 308p. ISBN: 0-446-51284-2.

NELSON, DEBRA L. 1990. Individual Adjustment to Information-Driven Technologies: A Critical Review. MIS Quarterly. 1990 March; 14(1): 79-98. ISSN: 0276-7783.

NEWBY, GREGORY B.; NILAN, MICHAEL S.; DUVALL, LORRAINE M. 1991. Toward a Reassessment of Individual Differences for Information Systems: The Power of User-Based Situational Predictors. In: Griffiths, José-

Marie; Belkin, Nicholas J., eds. Proceedings of the American Society for Information Science (ASIS) 54th Annual Meeting: Volume 28; 1991 October 27-31; Washington, DC. Medford, NJ: Learned Information, Inc. for ASIS; 1991. 73-81. ISSN: 0044-7870; ISBN: 0-938734-56-3.

NEWMAN, M. 1985. Managerial Access to Information: Strategies for Prevention and Promotion. Journal of Management Studies (England). 1985; 22(2): 193-221. ISSN: 0022-2380.

NILAN, MICHAEL S.; FLETCHER, PATRICIA T. 1987. Information Behaviors in the Preparation of Research Proposals: A User Study. In: Chen, Ching-Chih, ed. ASIS '87: Proceedings of the American Society for Information Science (ASIS) 50th Annual Meeting: Volume 24; 1987 October 4-8: Boston, MA. Medford, NJ: Learned Information, Inc. for ASIS; 1987. 186-192. ISBN: 0-938743-19-9.

NILAN, MICHAEL S.; NEWBY, GREGORY B.; PAIK, WOOJIN; LOPATIN, KEVIN. 1989. User-Oriented Interfaces for Computer Systems: A User-Defined On-Line Help System for Desktop Publishing. In: ASIS '89: Proceedings of the American Society for Information Science (ASIS) 52nd Annual Meeting: Volume 26; 30 October–2 November 1989; Washington, DC. Medford, NJ: Learned Information, Inc. for ASIS; 1989. 104-110. ISSN: 0044-7870; ISBN: 0-938734-40-7.

NISBETT, RICHARD; ROSS, LEE. 1980. Human Inference: Strategies and Shortcomings of Social Judgment. Englewood Cliffs, NJ: Prentice-Hall; 1980. 334p. ISBN: 0-13-445130-9.

NUTT, PAUL C. 1990. Strategic Decisions Made by Top Executives and Middle Managers with Data and Process Dominant Styles. Journal of Management Studies (England). 1990 March; 27: 173-194. ISSN: 0022-2380.

O'REILLY, CHARLES A., III. 1982. Variations in Decision Makers' Use of Information Sources: The Impact of Quality and Accessibility of Information. Academy of Management Journal. 1982 December; 25(4): 756-771. ISSN: 0001-4273.

O'REILLY, CHARLES A., III. 1983. The Use of Information in Organizational Decision Making: A Model and Some Propositions. In: Cummings, L.L.; Staw, B.M., eds. Research in Organizational Behavior: Volume 5. Greenwich, CT: JAI; 1983. 103-140. ISSN: 0191-3085.

O'REILLY, CHARLES A., III. 1991. Organizational Behavior: Where We've Been, Where We're Going. Annual Review of Psychology. 1991; 42: 427-458. ISSN: 0066-4308.

O'REILLY, CHARLES A., III; CHATMAN, JENNIFER A.; ANDERSON, JOHN C. 1987. Message Flow and Decision Making. In: Jablin, Fredric M.; Putnam, Linda L.; Roberts, Karlene H.; Porter, Lyman W., eds. Handbook of Organizational Communication: An Interdisciplinary Perspective. Newbury Park, CA: Sage; 1987. 600-623. ISBN: 0-8039-2387-2.

O'REILLY, CHARLES A., III; PONDY, L.R. 1979. Organizational Communication. In: Kerr, Steven, ed. Organizational Behavior. Columbus, OH: Grid Publishing; 1979. 119-150. ISBN: 0-88244-182-5; LC: 78-26718.

PAISLEY, WILLIAM J. 1980. Information and Work. In: Dervin, B.; Voigt, M.J., eds. Progress in Communication Sciences: Volume 2. Norwood, NJ: Ablex Publishing Corp.; 1980. 113-165. ISSN: 0163-5689; ISBN: 0-89391-060-0.

PERKINS, W. STEVEN; RAO, RAM C. 1990. The Role of Experience in Information Use and Decision Making by Marketing Managers. Journal of Marketing Research. 1990 February; 27 (1): 1-10. ISSN: 0022-2437.
PETERS, THOMAS J.; WATERMAN, ROBERT H., JR. 1982. In Search of Excellence: Lessons from America's Best-Run Companies. New York, NY: Harper and Row; 1982. 360p. ISBN: 0-06-015042-4.
POUNDS, W.F. 1969. The Process of Problem Finding. Industrial Management Review. 1969; 11(1): 1-20. ISSN: 0019-848X.
PUGH, D.S.; HICKSON, D.J.; HININGS, C.R. 1985. Writers on Organizations. Beverly Hills, CA: Sage Publications; 1985. 234p. ISBN: 0-8039-2419-4.
RADFORD, K.J. 1981. Modern Managerial Decision Making. Reston, VA: Reston Publishing Company, Inc.; 1981. 258p. ISBN: 0-8359-4571-5.
ROBERTS, NORMAN. 1982. A Search for Information Man. Social Science Information Studies (England). 1982; 2: 93-104. ISSN: 0143-6236.
ROBEY, DANIEL; TAGGART, WILLIAM. 1981. Measuring Managers' Minds: The Assessment of Style in Human Information Processing. Academy of Management Review. 1981 July; 6(3): 375-383. ISSN: 0363-7425.
ROBEY, DANIEL; TAGGART, WILLIAM. 1982. Human Information Processing in Information and Decision Support Systems. MIS Quarterly. 1982 June; 6(2): 61-73. ISSN: 0276-7783.
ROCKART, JOHN F. 1979. Chief Executives Define Their Own Data Needs. Harvard Business Review. 1979 March/April; 57: 81-93. ISSN: 0017-8012.
ROUSE, WILLIAM B.; ROUSE, SANDRA H. 1984. Human Information Seeking and Design of Information Systems. Information Processing and Management. 1984; 20(1): 129-138. ISSN: 0306-4573.
ROWAN, ROY. 1986. The Intuitive Manager. Boston, MA: Little, Brown; 1986. 188p. ISBN: 0-316-75974-0.
SCHAMBER, LINDA; EISENBERG, MICHAEL; NILAN, MICHAEL S. 1990. A Re-examination of Relevance: Toward a Dynamic, Situational Definition. Information Processing and Management. 1990; 26(6): 755-776. ISSN: 0306-4573.
SCHEIN, EDGAR H. 1989. Reassessing the Divine Rights of Managers. Sloan Management Review. 1989 Winter; 30: 63-68. ISSN: 0019-848X.
SCHON, DONALD A. 1983. The Reflective Practitioner: How Professionals Think in Action. New York, NY: Basic Books; 1983. 374p. ISBN: 0-465-06878-2; LC: 82-70855.
SCHWEIGER, D.M. 1983. Measuring Managers' Minds: A Critical Reply to Robey and Taggart. Academy of Management Review. 1983 January; 8(1): 143-150. ISSN: 0363-7425.
SCHWENK, C.R. 1984. Cognitive Simplification Processes in Strategic Decision-Making. Strategic Management Journal. 1984 April/June; 5(2): 111-128. ISSN: 0143-2095.
SCHWENK, C.R. 1985. Management Illusions and Biases: Their Impact on Strategic Decisions. Long Range Planning. 1985 October; 18(5): 74-80. ISSN: 0024-6301.
SCHWENK, C.R. 1988. The Cognitive Perspective on Strategic Decision Making. Journal of Management Studies (England). 1988 January; 25(1): 41-55. ISSN: 0022-2380.

SIMON, HERBERT A. 1976. Administrative Behavior: A Study of Decision-Making Processes in Administrative Organization. 3rd edition. New York, NY: Free Press; 1976. 364p. ISBN: 0-02-928970-X.

SIMON, HERBERT A. 1977. The New Science of Management Decision. Englewood Cliffs, NJ: Prentice-Hall; 1977. 175p. ISBN: 0-13-616144-8; LC: 76-40414.

SIMON, HERBERT A. 1978. Rationality as a Process and as a Product of Thought. American Economic Review. 1978; 68: 1-16. ISSN: 0002-8282.

SIMON, HERBERT A. 1981. Information-Processing Models of Cognition. Journal of the American Society for Information Science. 1981 September; 32(5): 364-377. ISSN: 0002-8231.

SIMS, HENRY P., JR.; GIOIA, DENNIS A. 1986. The Thinking Organization: Dynamics of Organizational Social Cognition. San Francisco, CA: Jossey-Bass; 1986. 375p. ISBN: 0-87589-690-1; LC: 85-45913.

SOELBERG, P.O. 1967. Unprogrammed Decision Making. Industrial Management Review. 1967 Spring; 8(2): 19-29. ISSN: 0019-848X.

STEWART, R. 1976. To Understand the Manager's Job: Consider Demands, Constraints, Choices. Organizational Dynamics. 1976 Spring; 4(4): 22-32. ISSN: 0090-2616.

STEWART, R. 1982. A Model for Understanding Managerial Jobs and Behavior. Academy of Management Review. 1982; 7(1): 7-13. ISSN: 0363-7425.

STRASSMANN, PAUL A. 1982. Overview of Strategic Aspects of Information Management. Office: Technology and People (England). 1982; 1: 71-89. ISSN: 0167-5710.

SUCHMAN, LUCY A. 1987. Plans and Situated Actions: The Problems of Human/Machine Communication. Cambridge, England: Cambridge University Press; 1987. 203p. ISBN: 0-521-33137-4; LC: 87-8013.

TAGGART, WILLIAM; ROBEY, DANIEL. 1981. Minds and Managers: On the Dual Nature of Human Information Processing and Management. Academy of Management Review. 1981 April; 6(2): 187-195. ISSN: 0363-7425.

TAGGART, WILLIAM; ROBEY, DANIEL; KROECK, K. GALEN. 1985. Managerial Decision Styles and Cerebral Dominance: An Empirical Study. Journal of Management Studies (England). 1985; 22(2): 175-192. ISSN: 0022-2380.

TAYLOR, ROBERT S. 1968. Question Negotiation and Information Seeking in Libraries. College and Research Libraries. 1968; 29: 178-194. ISSN: 0010-0870.

TAYLOR, ROBERT S. 1985. Information Values in Decision Contexts. Information Management Review. 1985; 1(1): 47-55. ISSN: 8756-1557; ISBN: 0-87189-125-5.

TAYLOR, ROBERT S. 1986. Value-Added Processes in Information Systems. Norwood, NJ: Ablex Publishing Corp.; 1986. 257p. ISBN: 0-89391-273-5.

TAYLOR, ROBERT S. 1991. Information Use Environments. In: Dervin, B.; Voigt, M.J., eds. Progress in Communication Sciences: Volume 10. Norwood, NJ: Ablex Publishing Corp.; 1991. 217-255. ISSN: 0163-5689; ISBN: 0-89391-645-5.

THOMPSON, JAMES D.; TUDEN, ARTHUR. 1964. Strategies, Structures, and Processes of Organizational Decision. In: Leavitt, Harold J.; Pondy, L.R., eds. Readings in Managerial Psychology. Chicago, IL: University of Chicago Press; 1964. 496-515. LC: 64-15811.

TICHY, NOEL M. 1983. Managing Strategic Change: Technical, Political, and Cultural Dynamics. New York, NY: Wiley; 1983. 434p. (A Wiley Interscience Publication). ISBN: 0-471-86559-1; LC: 82-15941.

TUSHMAN, M.; NADLER, D. 1978. Information Processing as an Integrating Concept in Organizational Design. Academy of Management Review. 1978 July; 3: 613-624. ISSN: 0363-7425.

TVERSKY, AMOS. 1972. Elimination by Aspects: A Theory of Choice. Psychological Review. 1972; 79: 281-299. ISSN: 0033-295X.

TVERSKY, AMOS; KAHNEMAN, DANIEL. 1971. Belief in the Law of Small Numbers. Psychological Bulletin. 1971; 76(2): 105-110. ISSN: 0033-2909.

TVERSKY, AMOS; KAHNEMAN, DANIEL. 1974. Judgment under Uncertainty: Heuristics and Biases. Science. 1974; 185: 1124-1131. ISSN: 0036-8075.

UNGSON, G.R.; BRAUNSTEIN, D.N.; HALL, P.D. 1981. Managerial Information Processing: A Research Review. Administrative Science Quarterly. 1981 March; 26: 116-130. ISSN: 0001-8392.

VICKERY, BRIAN CAMPBELL. 1965. On Retrieval System Theory. 2nd edition. London, England: Butterworths; 1965. 191p. LC: 65-7589.

WEICK, KARL E. 1979. Cognitive Processes in Organizations. In: Staw, Barry M., ed. Research in Organizational Behavior: Volume 1. Greenwich, CT: JAI Press; 1979. 41-74. ISSN: 0191-3085.

WEICK, KARL E. 1983. Managerial Thought in the Context of Action. In: Srivastva, Suresh, ed. The Executive Mind. San Francisco, CA: Jossey-Bass; 1983. 221-242. (Based on a symposium held at Case Western Reserve University in 1982). ISBN: 0-87589-584-0.

WERSIG, G.; WINDEL, G. 1985. Information Science Needs a Theory of "Information Actions." Social Science Information Studies (England). 1985; 5: 11-23. ISSN: 0143-6236.

WETHERBE, J.C. 1991. Executive Information Requirements: Getting It Right. MIS Quarterly. 1991 March; 15(1): 51-65. ISSN: 0276-7783.

WHITTEMORE, B.J.; YOVITS, M.C. 1973. A Generalized Conceptual Development for the Analysis and Flow of Information. Journal of the American Society for Information Science. 1973; 24(3): 221-231. ISSN: 0002-8231.

WILDAVSKY, AARON. 1983. Information as an Organizational Problem. Journal of Management Studies (England). 1983 January; 20(1): 29-40. ISSN: 0022-2380.

WILSON, T.D. 1984. The Cognitive Approach to Information-Seeking Behavior and Information Use. Social Science Information Studies (England). 1984; 4: 197-204. ISSN: 0143-6236.

WRIGHT, WILLIAM F. 1980. Cognitive Information Processing Biases: Implications for Producers and Users of Financial Information. Decision Sciences. 1980; 11: 284-298. ISSN: 0011-7315.

ZAND, DALE E. 1981. Information, Organization and Power: Effective Management in the Knowledge Society. New York, NY: McGraw-Hill; 1981. 209p. ISBN: 0-07-072743-0.

IV

The Profession

The section on the profession includes two chapters: "Education and Training for Information Science in the Soviet Union" by Pamela Spence Richards of Rutgers University, and "Ethical Considerations of Information Professionals" by Thomas J. Froehlich of Kent State University. Pamela Spence Richards contributes the first *ARIST* chapter on information science in the Soviet Union. She has limited the scope to training for information science. Her travels to the Soviet Union and her facility with the language have made this unique chapter possible. Pamela Richards first explains the ideological foundations of Soviet science policy, discussing dialectical materialism as it relates to the various branches of science. Citing Graham of MIT, she refers to the dilemma faced by Soviet philosophers in wrestling with the problem of information ("According to dialectical materialism, objective reality consists of matter and energy; if information is neither, what is it?").

During its 74 years of existence the Soviet central government planned a variety of programs to train workers in the processing of scientific and technical information. Such work was seen as fostering both increased industrial productivity and a higher standard of living. After 1952, the growth of information science education was stimulated by the founding of the Institute of Scientific Information in the Academy of Sciences of the USSR (retitled after 1955 as the All-Union Institute of Scientific and Technical Information, or VINITI). VINITI became the locus of information science research in the USSR, and after the establishment of a graduate program leading to the Ph.D., it was the nation's center for advanced information science education. Responsibility for planning and implementing postsecondary and distance education in information science was given to the Institute for the Raising of the Qualifications of Information Workers (IPKIR), founded in 1971. IPKIR established branches nationwide and supervised postsecondary programs in engineering and information technology at polytechnic institutes and some universities. In the late 1960s and 1970s, information science courses were introduced into the more than 20 departments of library science that existed in the Soviet Union's postsecondary institutes of culture. Richards traces the information science institution through the 1960s and 1970s up to the days of glasnost and perestroika and their impact on information science instruction in the USSR. She concludes with a discussion of the strengths and weaknesses of information science education in the Soviet Union. The main strength was the government's encouragement of scientific communication as a means of fostering industrial productivity; the primary weakness was the fact that library schools in universities were cut off from contact with information science research that was carried out at VINITI. Efforts at curricular reform since 1985 have been slowed by the nation's economic crisis.

Thomas J. Froehlich is also concerned with the information profession, specifically the ethics within the profession. He restricts his consideration of ethical issues to information science and discusses resources in such related areas as libraries, computer-based systems, and business. He divides ethical considerations into those of the practitioners and those of the theoreticians and researchers. To address practitioner concerns he uses a model to integrate the ethical problems reflected in the literature. His model provides a framework for elucidating the tensions that arise among the self, the organization, the profession, and other factors emerging from the environment, and the model illustrates such problem areas as organizational–professional conflicts, information malpractice, and legal liability.

Froehlich discusses these problems or tensions in the light of moral principles. He examines the concerns of theoreticians and researchers, including global imbalances between the information rich and poor, the erosion of democratic processes, tacit ideologies related to information systems, and moral principles implicit in the creation and use of information systems, products, and services. Currently the American Society for Information Science (ASIS) is developing a policy on ethics in the form of a code of ethics. This effort makes Froehlich's chapter particularly relevant. Issues under consideration include: downloading, privacy of files, copyright, pricing, computer crime, security, intellectual freedom, career paths, transborder data flow, public/private sectors, client relationships, and concealment/falsification of information.

7

Education and Training for Information Science in the Soviet Union

PAMELA SPENCE RICHARDS
Rutgers University

INTRODUCTION

From the founding of the Soviet Union in 1917 until its dissolution in 1991, its leaders stressed the importance of science and scientific information in developing their planned utopian socialist society. Lenin regarded the diffusion of scientific and technical information to intellectual workers as a key both to increased industrial productivity and to a higher standard of living for the manual laborer. He and his successors approved a massive transfer of Western technical information to the Soviet Union as a means of defending the country against the supposed inevitable encroachments of capitalism. Given the sociopolitical context in which it developed, it was inevitable that Soviet documentation and information science would have philosophical goals, institutional forms, and educational foundations that were different from this discipline in the West. The purpose of this chapter is to present the literature that can most clearly explain the status of Soviet information science education at the beginning of the 1990s. A better understanding of this status will not only make Western cooperative and assistance projects more efficient, it will also allow information scientists to assess the extent to

---

The author is indebted to the Association for Library and Information Science Education, the Ministry of Culture of the USSR, and Rutgers University for funding the trips to the Soviet Union which made the research for this chapter possible. She also thanks R.S. Giliarevskii for his assistance in providing Russian materials.

Annual Review of Information Science and Technology (ARIST), Volume 27, 1992
Martha E. Williams, Editor
Published for the American Society for Information Science (ASIS)
By Learned Information, Inc., Medford, N.J.

which centralized government information control can subvert the legitimate educational goals of their field—even when those goals are applauded by the government which subverts them.

Where possible, works that are available in English are cited, but the Soviets' own interest in the "science of science" (naukovedenie) has produced a wealth of untranslated material to which this chapter attempts to provide partial access. Coverage of Soviet material is limited to works that could be obtained during two trips to the Soviet Union in 1991, to publications made available by Russian colleagues, and to Soviet periodicals available in American libraries. Materials that are not available in English are reviewed in greater detail than English-language materials.

Because of the link between the Communist party's official science policies and government support for scientific information and training, the chapter begins with a review of the literature on the philosophical foundations of Soviet science policy. This is followed by a section on Soviet documentation activities in the 1920s and 1930s, when the groundwork was laid for formal instruction in information work. A more detailed look at curricula follows in the section on centralized information science instruction. This section focuses particularly on VINITI, the All-Union Institute for Scientific and Technical Information,[1] the site of important developments in graduate and continuing information science education from the 1960s on. Also reviewed in this section are works describing the cold war's impact on party science policy and the preconditions that made possible the unprecedented government support for information science during the height of the arms race with the West. A penultimate section addresses the spread of information science instruction after 1970 to the vast audience comprising the Soviet Union's library school students. The last section is a review of literature dealing with developments in information science instruction since 1985, when Mikhail Gorbachev introduced glasnost and perestroika.

IDEOLOGICAL FOUNDATIONS

Of the many studies of the ideological foundations of Soviet science policy, none are more authoritative and thorough than those by Graham of MIT's Program in Science, Technology and Society (GRAHAM, 1972; 1975). For our purposes, the most useful is his book on science and philosophy in the Soviet Union. In almost 600 pages Graham explains dialectical materialism as it applies to the different branches of science.

---

[1]All-Union institutions of the former Soviet Union are either being restructured along republican lines or have been abolished at the time of this writing (January 1992).

According to Graham, dialectical materialism's core consists of: (1) the assumption of the independent and sole existence of matter-energy, and (2) the assumption of a continuing process in nature in accordance with dialectical laws. The major question he poses is whether government-supported dialectical materialism had a real effect on Soviet science or was, on the contrary, mere meaningless window dressing. He concludes that dialectical materialism cannot be written off—as it so often is in the West—as a pseudophilosophy. Graham reports that dialectical materialism has been taken seriously by a number of distinguished Soviet scientists and that "in certain cases these influences helped them arrive at views that won them international recognition among their foreign colleagues" (GRAHAM, 1972, p.6).

Graham's greatest contribution for information scientists comes in his chapter on cybernetics, which he tells us enjoyed more prestige in the Soviet Union in the 1960s than in any other country in the world. Its appeal lay in the Russian revolution's promise of a rational direction for society, a promise that seemed hopelessly out of reach by the time of Stalin's death in 1953. Although there seemed to be empirical evidence then that centralized direction of an industrial society could not be achieved, the new science of cybernetics seemed to offer the solutions necessary to salvage central control.

Graham explains how cybernetics studies organisms that are arranged so efficaciously that through certain dynamic processes they can resist the tendency toward the disorder present in all complex organisms. One of the most interesting common features of such organisms is their use of information to counter disorder. In his 10-page subchapter, "What is 'Information,'" Graham gives an overview of how various Soviet philosophers have wrestled with the problem of "information." (According to dialectical materialism, objective reality consists of matter and energy; if information is neither, what is it?) Graham cites at length the arguments of mathematician URSUL, whose 1968 book, *Priroda informatsii* [*The Nature of Information*], defends the belief that information is a characteristic of all matter, from the simplest inorganic forms to human society. Ursul argues that this concept of the unity of nature is closely tied to dialectical materialism, and he claims that dialectical laws help one to understand information processes.

Consideration of the proper role of information in a socialist state predates the debates on cybernetics by many years. A straightforward chronological discussion of the background is provided by VUCINICH in his 1984 history of the Academy of Sciences of the USSR from 1917 to 1970. From Vucinich we learn that the four pillars of Marxist science are ideological unity, group effort, utilitarian orientation, and centralized planning—all information-intense phenomena. Vucinich reports that the origins of support for information in Soviet socialism lay in Lenin's insistence that socialism could not be built without "a successful blending of the victorious proletarian revolution and bourgeois culture—bourgeois science and technology" (VUCINICH, p.120). As we will see, Lenin's insistence on importing Western scientific information was the foundation of the earliest Soviet documentation activities.

Raymond's biography of Lenin's wife, the literacy pioneer Nadezhda Krupskaia, offers useful information about the centralized library infrastructure that Lenin inherited from the czarist regime (RAYMOND, 1979). In 1914 it consisted of 14,000 public libraries and three huge research libraries—the Imperial Public Library at St. Petersburg, the Rumiantsev Museum in Moscow, and the Academy of Sciences Library at St. Petersburg. Raymond also describes the beginnings of library education at Sheniavskii University in Moscow in 1913 and how Western traditions of librarianship gave way in the 1920s to the revolutionary idea of librarians as propagandists for the state. (This trend partly explains the divergent courses followed by library and information science education in the Soviet Union.) In a recent survey of Soviet library development from 1917 to 1980, RAYMOND (1991a) offers a decade-by-decade description of how evolving political conditions in the Soviet Union affected the growth of the public, scholarly, and scientific library network.

EARLY SOVIET DOCUMENTATION ACTIVITIES

The best available English-language account of early Soviet documentation activities is the 1984 English translation of the 1976 Russian text, *Scientific Communications and Informatics,* by MIKHAILOV ET AL. The authors point to the long Russian abstracting tradition stemming from the work of the great 18th-century scientist, M.V. Lomonosov, who laid down the principles of systematic abstracting for the Russian Academy. MIKHAILOV ET AL. give the details of the original Soviet scientific information system as established by Lenin during the Russian civil war. This system had two branches. The first, established in Berlin in 1920, was the Bureau of Foreign Science and Technology, known as BINT. Among BINT's tasks were the survey of Western science and technology and the large-scale translation and publication into Russian of current Western works (i.e., by establishing a Soviet publishing program in Germany, where paper and presses were more readily available than in civil-war ravaged Russia). BINT existed until 1928. From its presses came Russian translations of works in chemistry, optics, and physics, including an account of Einstein's special and general theories of relativity.

The second branch of the early Soviet information system was an agency concerned with distributing foreign information within the Soviet Union. Established by Lenin in 1921, Kominolit was planned as a clearinghouse for all Russian orders for foreign literature and was directed by Lenin to publish indexes of the most important foreign scientific and technical journals and to cite their location in Russia. Although Kominolit ceased to exist after six months, it was an extraordinary project to be launched personally by a head of state.

The prodigious amount of documentation connected with importing technical information from the West required new training programs, as detailed by KEDROVSKAIA in her 1979 history of Soviet information activity. In 1931 a four-year program (later reduced to two years) was begun to prepare students for the new profession of "engineer-information specialist" (inzhener-informator) at the Moscow Institute for Foreign Languages. The site of the course indicated the high proportion of information work that was concerned with gathering, translating, and disseminating foreign information to Russians. The technical information faculty consisted of chemists, electrotechnologists and metallurgists. Graduates were employed in information centers of heavy industry. A year later a two-year correspondence program for technical librarianship was organized at the new State Scientific Library, founded in 1927 as a merger of several of the capital's scientific and technical libraries. Practical skills in classification, annotation, and abstracting were taught as well as what Kedrovskaia calls the "principles of industrial information work." Graduates worked in the reference sections of technical libraries. Kedrovskaia also describes the importance of the 1929 publication of A.G. Fomin's textbook on annotation; it helped to spread the skills on which the dissemination of scientific knowledge in the impoverished country depended.

These were the preconditions necessary for the establishment in the 1930s of the abstracting journals in science and technology that were published by the government's new information centers. These centers for technical-economic information (TSITEIN) were set up in 1932 to serve different branches of industry. In addition to their abstracting, editing, and publishing responsibilities, many of the centers also provided courses in their fields' documentation. The most important center, one that served heavy industry (TSITEIN-CO), laid the foundation of what would become in 1961 the national Soviet technical information network GOSINTI.

Of particular value in Kedrovskaia's publication are her references to the importance of foreign special libraries to Russian library development in the 1930s and her coverage of wartime documentation activities; she provides information not available anywhere in English.

CENTRALIZED INSTITUTIONS FOR INFORMATION SCIENCE INSTRUCTION

Socioeconomic Preconditions: The Lag in Soviet Science

The confrontations of the cold war and the grip of Stalinism from 1945 until the dictator's death in 1953 brought about a period of scientific isolation for the Soviet Union. MEDVEDEV (1971) reports on the refusal of Soviet scientists to take part in international conventions and discussions on patents and licenses. He claims that with the formation of a socialist bloc in Europe and Asia in the immediate postwar period, the policy of isolation at first grew stronger since the technological and scientific potential of the scientific sector increased and made autonomous socialist science look possible. Medvedev's central thesis is that Soviet scientific productivity required: (1) freedom to travel and communicate with foreign scientists; (2) open exchange of information and criticism; and (3) freedom to work with non-Soviet scientists. According to Medvedev, none of these requirements was ever met.

VUCINICH reports that despite obvious Soviet accomplishments like the detonation of an atomic bomb (1949) and a hydrogen bomb (1953), and the launching of Sputnik (1957), Soviet scientists became anxious about their own lack of productivity by the late 1950s. Both VUCINICH and KNEEN note that by 1965 anxiety was so high in top scientific circles that Nobel laureate P. Kapitsa made a formal report to the USSR Academy of Sciences claiming that the productivity of Soviet scientists, as measured by the number of publications per individual engaged in research, was only half that of their American counterparts.

KNEEN and LUBRANO are the richest sources for material demonstrating how the anxiety about the science lag translated into support for Soviet information science. The patterns of support were much influenced by the work of BERNAL, British author of *The Social Function of Science* (1939). Lubrano cites Bernal as critical to the work of Soviet scientific planners, who called him the "pioneer" and "founder" of the "science of science." Bernal is praised by Soviet sociologists for his suggestion that science be planned and placed at the service of all society. He was an enthusiastic advocate of centralized scientific information distribution by means of photoduplication, and he was an admirer of the American documentation pioneer Watson Davis, whose plans for a scientific information institute he included in toto in the appendix of his book.

Lubrano reports that for the development of indigenous Soviet information science, the appearance in 1966 of *Nauka o nauke* [*Science of Science*] by DOBROV was a "landmark." Dobrov tried to measure the interrelationships between the scientific fields and the evolution of scientific knowledge in terms of the exchange, publication, and growth of scientific information. He developed formulas to describe the relationship between the existing quantity of published scientific information and the rate of increase in new knowledge. Dobrov found that, on the average, out of every 1,000 claims for inventions made in the Soviet Union only 240–280 did not duplicate former solutions. He calculated the "density" of such repeated claims and showed that there was a peak of repetitions in the years 1936–1938 and 1950–1955. MEDVEDEV (1971) points out that exactly in those periods in which Dobrov found a density of repeated claims, "the terror of contacts with foreign countries also reached a maximum" (p. 126). Dobrov was convinced that an understanding of the complex network of information exchange would permit the organization and management of the future development of science.

KNEEN describes the Soviet adoption of Derek de Solla Price's techniques of citation analysis as a way to study their perceived science lag in the 1960s. In their 1969 book *Naukometriia* [*Scienceometrics*], V.V. NALIMOV & MUL'CHENKO set out to compare the impact on world science made by scientists publishing in different disciplines in the principal scientific nations (e.g., the United States, Germany, Great Britain, etc.). Nalimov and Mul'chenko found that Soviet scientists were not being cited at a rate consistent with their published output. They contributed around 20% of articles published but received only around 3–4% of the citations in non-Soviet publications. Further, Soviet scientists were citing British and American articles six or seven times more frequently than their own articles were being cited by scientists publishing in the United States or Great Britain (presumably because of the language barrier).

Foundation and Early Years of VINITI

In 1952 the Soviet Academy of Sciences founded the Institute of Technical Information, which was transformed in 1955 into the All-Union Institute of Scientific and Technical Information (VINITI). As the institute's director, MIKHAILOV gives a concise overview of the first years. The institute was to be responsible for: (1) abstracting the world's scientific and technical literature; (2) publishing comprehensive abstracting journals; and (3) conducting research for improving scientific information work. The phenomenal growth of this institute, which by the 1970s employed over 25,000 workers and published more than 70 abstracting journal series, was a result both of the anxiety over the science lag described above and of the desire to improve Soviet productivity by better information flow.

Another factor in VINITI's growth was the inclusion of science in the state's central planning activities, notoriously information-dependent processes. FORTESCUE describes the relatively late adoption of science into central economic planning and reports that in 1949 Gostekhnika—predecessor of the GKNT (State Committee for Science and Technology), which operated until 1991 as a sort of science ministry—prepared a list of special science and technology projects; this became a regular practice after 1953.

The most thorough English-language account of the information-processing goals and activities of VINITI from 1952 through the 1970s is given by VLADUTZ; it is especially valuable because the author was formerly a member of the VINITI staff who emigrated to the United States. Unlike Mikhailov, Vladutz mentions the introduction of information science instruction at VINITI. He reports that VINITI got into this area because so many of the workers in their scientific and technical information system lacked either the experience or background for the work. The lectures and courses initiated for VINITI's own staff later became the basis for the Institut povysheniia kvalifikatsii informatsionykh rabotnikov (Institute for the Raising of Information Workers' Qualifications, or IPKIR), an independent organization under the State Committee for Science and Technology (GKNT). In 1963 VINITI set up a program for doctoral studies in information science, and in 1966 it was authorized to confer academic degrees.

Another VINITI activity covered by Vladutz and not by Mikhailov concerns the work of VINITI's KGB unit, the "First Department." This unit opened all incoming mail and scanned the foreign journals received for all articles containing political notes or facts unfavorable to the Soviet Union. Such material was physically removed from the journals and the deletion masked. Vladutz reports that the standards for such deletions were stricter at VINITI than at some of the large libraries, probably because the VINITI journals were destined for photoreproduction and dissemination all over the country (at least before the USSR signed the Universal Copyright Convention in 1973). Vladutz also describes the classified work done at VINITI in abstracting and indexing foreign articles of strategic military importance.

MEDVEDEV (1978), who is generally scathingly critical of the whole Soviet scientific information infrastructure, comments that when the massive duplicating of foreign journals was first introduced (in 1953–1955) and developed (in 1956–1958), it was a significant stimulus to science after years of postwar isolation. VINITI's translation services were important in a country where in the 1950s few of its scientists could read a foreign language. He finds inexcusable the slowness of VINITI's service, however, which he attributes to the failure of VINITI throughout the 1970s to computerize its indexing operations. Medvedev is also contemptuous of the "First Department" censorship, which produced the VINITI "surrogate" of Western journals. What he calls the "castration department" at VINITI usually replaced the lead editorials and the letters to the editors of the important Western journals with advertisements. He claims that "something is cut out by the [VINITI] censorship in the reproduction of almost every issue of *Science*" (MEDVEDEV, 1971, p. 360).

This writer has not yet been able to find any description either of the training received by the VINITI First Department members engaged in these activities or of where that training took place. It is possible that the post-coup histories of the KGB that are being written will shed some light here.

Information Instruction Initiatives at VINITI and IPKIR after 1963

Before looking at the details of what has been written about recent information science curricula initiated at VINITI, we must pause to consider the philosophical plight of Soviet information science educators. Convinced like their Western colleagues that the targeted distribution of current knowledge serves mankind by stimulating scientific creativity and initiative, they planned study programs along lines similar to those designed by their European and American counterparts. However, Soviet information science educators existed in a society crafted to discourage the very initiatives that their profession sought to stimulate. POPOVSKY, writing from inside the Soviet Union at the same time as Medvedev, points out the results of the party's prizing of control above all: while praising the importance of scientific creativity, the party and the state bureaucracy so organized Soviet society that they could at any moment stop any initiatives they did not approve. Popovsky calls this a "normal defensive reaction of the totalitarian state to surprises of any kind" (p. 49). He reports that although the party paid much lip service to the idea of efficiency, it did not really mind that Soviet science was totally inefficient. The party's sole concern was that science should not escape its control for an instant. Popovsky claims that the party officials who monitored science and kept scientists from working properly knew exactly what they were doing: "There is nothing unsystematic or thoughtless about the control they exercise" (p. 49). This, then, is the environment in which Soviet information science educators devised their curricula and trained more than a generation of young people.

KEDROVSKAIA offers a chronology of information science education developments at VINITI after the introduction of the courses designed for information workers in 1963. For details of the various curricula, however, one must use the exhaustive survey published by the International Center for Scientific and Technical Information on training and raising the qualifications of information workers in the USSR (MEZHDUNARODNYI TSENTR NAUCHNOI I TEKHNICHESKOI INFORMATSII). The center was set up in Moscow in 1969 to disseminate information science techniques, research, and education for the member countries of the Council for Mutual Economic Assistance (COMECON). In cooperation with VINITI, it has been the hub from which Soviet information science research radiated to the USSR's client countries as well as an important organizing and funding source for the developing information infrastructures of these countries. (The center was also the host of the First East-West Conference on Scientific, Technical and Online Information in Moscow in October 1989.)

The report offers a short history of Soviet information science instruction similar to that given by Kedrovskaia but with more clearly indicated trends. It describes the search for educational directions for information scientists in the 1960s and gives the curriculum of the first VINITI courses. Post-secondary instruction at VINITI was taken over in 1971 by the Institute for the Raising of Information Workers' Qualifications (IPKIR), founded in that year. IPKIR, like VINITI, was under the authority of the State Committee for Science and Technology (GKNT). IPKIR assumed the role of a national information science education planning center and helped organize all-Soviet and international conferences for Soviet and Communist-bloc information science educators in 1974 and 1975, respectively.

Most valuable is the overview in the report of the various foci of Soviet information science education in 1977: (1) automation, machine processing, and dissemination of information; (2) library science and bibliography; (3) structural and applied linguistics; (4) archival science for scientific and technical archives; (5) information science for scientific and technical archives and for the national scientific and technical information system; and (6) scientific and technical editing. The report also indicates exactly where most of the various types of instruction were available and the number of students involved: education in automation was done mainly at polytechnical institutes, with 285 students registered in 1976; information science courses for future librarians were offered at 22 institutions of higher education, including a number of state cultural institutes (the most important being in Moscow, Leningrad, Kiev, and Khar'kov), and at some universities and teacher's colleges. Structural and applied linguistics specialties resided at the larger state universities, and the archival programs were located at the Moscow State Historical-Archival Institute and at the historical faculty of the Ural State University. Graduate study (aspirantura) in information science was available at VINITI, which enrolled about 100 such students in 1976. At the time of the report, VINITI had awarded 13 candidates either the degree of kandidat tekhnicheskikh nauk (Ph.D. in technical sciences) or doktor nauk (doctor of sciences), equivalent to the German Habilitation and awarded only to the most advanced scholars.

An interesting feature of the report is the space it devotes to user education, which has been obligatory for students in many of the natural sciences since 1975. By 1977 a course entitled Fundamentals of Information, Library and Bibliographic Science, comprising 12–30 credit hours, had been instituted for natural science students at the Moscow and Latvian state universities, at the polytechnical institutes at Riga and Kiev, and at 50 agricultural and other institutes. In 1963 a separate information science faculty had been organized at Moscow State University to serve students in the natural sciences.

Education to raise the qualifications of those already involved in information work was centered at IPKIR in Moscow; in 1977 IPKIR offered a full-time two-month program, a six-month evening program, and a 12-month distance education course. By 1977 the different IPKIR educational programs for information workers averaged 320 instructional hours. By the beginning of that year more than 12,000 students had been through the IPKIR program. Courses were available in: (1) fundamental theories of information science; (2) organization of information activities; (3) origins of information; (4) information sources and services; (5) classification; (6) information processing; (7) automation; and (8) scientific and technical propaganda. BORISOVA ET AL. describe this last area as focusing on the dissemination of scientific and technical information through mass media, publishing, and exhibits. This dissemination is seen as playing a key role in science popularization and is important to scientific communication because it helps break down the jargon barriers between the scientific specialties.

Innovation and planning in information science education were centralized at IPKIR in Moscow, and IPKIR's decisions on curricula were influential in the national network of information science education. Tables on pages 27 and 29 of the International Center's report show the distribution of courses by credit hour and demonstrate changing curricular emphases during the 1970s. For example, after a curriculum review in 1973, courses in automation were increased from 5.7% of the overall curriculum to 18–20% and became the second most important component of the IPKIR program; the organization of information activities held first place.

The chapter in the International Center's report on "Tendencies in Education" cites the push in the 1970s toward more possibilities for specialization and differentiation in information science education. It bemoans the fact that at that time there was no mechanism or any criteria for the professional selection of information workers, and it called for the drawing up of "professiongrams," which would show which courses were required for each kind of information work.

Of special interest to Western information science educators is the report's chapter that describes the research on teaching conducted at IPKIR. In order to devise the national curricular plan for 1976–1980, the staff analyzed the contents of *Informatika*, VINITI's review journal for information science. They also surveyed American information science articles to determine the direction of the field in the United States. All these data were fed into a Minsk-32 computer, which indicated the relative importance of the different information science subspecialities. Course units addressing the various components were designed and then incorporated into the new curriculum. The 1976–1980 curriculum also included such proactive teaching methods as role playing and games. What is striking to a Western observer is that despite all the research that went into devising the new curriculum, it contained no components on the administration or management of information. Perhaps in Soviet eyes, perfection in organization and planning made management science unnecessary.

As a document that reflects Soviet educational plans at the country's high point—i.e., before the war in Afghanistan and the economic crises of the 1980s—the report is of more than passing interest. First, it lets us see how education in a legitimate field of scholarly inquiry was poured into the orthodox Marxist mold. In its appendices the report gives sample study plans for the different areas in information science available in the USSR. For example, the undergraduate courses concentrating on the automation of information processes offered at the Polytechnical Institute at Kuibyshev required foundation courses in the history of the Communist party of the USSR, Marxist-Leninist philosophy, political economics, and "scientific communism." The program given for archivists at the Moscow State Historical-Archival Institute required, in addition, a course in the fundamentals of "scientific atheism." One may assume that such requirements were fairly typical of all undergraduate information science programs in the USSR until very recently.

The second general insight into Soviet education philosophy offered by the report is the emphasis on the Soviet role in international educational development. The document's publication by the International Center for Scientific and Technical Information rather than by VINITI or IPKIR indicates, first, that the document was seen as a model of pedagogic planning to serve the COMECON countries. Moreover, the report's final chapter is a useful overview of the support given by the USSR until 1977 to information science education in the East-bloc nations. This support is considerable, beginning with courses given at VINITI between 1963 and 1973 for more than 300 socialist-block students and extending to the approval of a long-term plan in 1976 for the advanced education at IPKIR and VINITI of COMECON managers of national scientific and technical information centers. Further, from 1970 to 1976 VINITI hosted UNIDO- and UNESCO-sponsored courses for information workers from Asian, African, and Latin American countries which lay outside the traditional Soviet service area. In alternate years these courses were offered in English, French, and German. Given the scope of Soviet contributions to international information science education over the past 25 years, it is not an exaggeration to speak of a vacuum created when the USSR left the scene.

Dissertations. In 1980 VINITI published an annotated index of the 1,046 dissertations in information science defended in the Soviet Union between 1934 and 1975. The index (VINITI) is arranged under the following subject fields: Lenin and the Communist party on books, library, bibliography, and scientific information; information science; archival science and documentation; bibliography; library science; and book studies. Within the subject groupings the dissertations are listed chronologically by date of defense, starting with the oldest. The category "information science" is further broken down into these subsections: general questions; processing of document sources of information; information retrieval, languages, systems, and services; information technology; scientific and technical information organization in the USSR; the history of scientific and technical information; and scientific and technical information abroad. There are indexes of authors, dissertation directors, and institutions. Each entry gives the dissertation's author and title, pagination, degree obtained, institution, date of defense, and research director, followed by a summary of the dissertation's main chapter headings.

There were 302 dissertations written on information science subjects during the period surveyed. Of these, 11 were on general questions; 85 on the processing of document sources; 97 on information retrieval, languages, systems, and services; 22 on information technology; 57 on the organization of scientific and technical information in the USSR; six on the history of scientific and technical information; and five on scientific and technical information abroad.

The VINITI dissertation index reveals some patterns of research similar to those in the West. Authors of information retrieval dissertations, for example, tended to write about retrieval patterns in their own fields (e.g., electronics, physical geography, chemistry). However, there is also much valuable new material listed here. A dissertation on Cuba's use of scientific periodicals, for example, by O.I. Globachev, and a study of the use of international information systems in nuclear science by Zh. I. Turkov, would be interesting additions to any Western library.

THE SPREAD OF INFORMATION SCIENCE INSTRUCTION TO LIBRARY SCHOOLS AFTER 1965

The most thorough treatment of the relationship of information science to library science in the Soviet Union is the book by GILIAREVKSII, which is clearly intended to explain to less-than-enthusiastic instructors in undergraduate library schools why information science was being mandated in their curricula. Writing almost 20 years ago, Giliarevskii reports much that is still of practical and philosophical utility. We learn that by 1974 there were 24 post-secondary library school faculties in the USSR with 3,000 students (many of these library education faculties were located in institutes of culture with other departments, such as museum or theater education). All came under the authority of the Ministry of Culture. Some of the library schools offered the possibility of graduate study leading to the degree of kandidat pedagogicheskikh nauk po spetsial'nosti "bibliotekovedenie i bibliographiia" (Ph.D. in education specializing in library science and bibliography).

Giliarevskii reports that by 1974 post-secondary tracks in library-related information studies in the Soviet Union followed two branches, addressed by different faculties: (1) a diploma in electrical engineering in information technology, which could be obtained at the polytechnical institutes at Kuibyshev, Penza, and Karaganda, at the Tomsk electrotechnical institute, and at the engineering institute at Sevastopol'; and (2) the diploma of "librarian–bibliographer for technical libraries," which could be obtained at the library faculties of the Moscow, Leningrad, and Khar'kov institutes of culture.

By the time that this integration of information science into library education was attempted, half a century had been spent in devising curricula to educate librarians to be pillars of the socialist state. Giliarevskii describes the fundamental components of instruction of the library faculties as consisting of Lenin's views on librarianship, party decrees on librarianship, the tasks of Soviet librarianship, library organization in the USSR, and types of Soviet libraries. He points out that Lenin saw the libraries as playing a fundamental role in raising the political consciousness of the masses and stressed the importance of the socialist partisanship (partiinost') of the librarian. To insert the study of information science into such a context, Giliarevskii suggests, in a subchapter entitled "Course Integration," that a systems approach be adopted so that library and information sciences might be regarded simply as two components of scientific communication. The fundamental philosophical contradiction inherent in adopting a political orthodoxy into a scientific communication system is not addressed. It is the orthodoxy [right teaching] of the ideology that makes it inconsistent with science.

Another dilemma described but not satisfactorily resolved by Giliarevskii is the problem of an international scientific language—a problem wrestled with by Russians for over a century because of their difficult language. (Esperanto, invented by Lazarus Zamenhof of Bialystok in 1887, was one of the more interesting solutions proposed.) Presumably it was not politically acceptable in 1974 for a Soviet scholar of information science to applaud the growing use of English as the world's scientific language; in any case Giliarevskii criticizes the prevalent use of English and comments that the development of a nation's science is only possible on the basis of its own culture and language. He goes on to suggest as a possible solution the intensification of research into scientific translation, specifically machine translation. To lessen internal language barriers *among* the scientific specialities he suggests that: (1) more attention be paid to popularizing science, which breaks down jargon barriers; (2) more use be made of artificial language in searching; and (3) a general thesaurus of scientific terms be created, a project he calls "one of the most important tasks of information science."

The textbook by TARAKANOV for beginning students of information science at library schools and universities appeared in 1986 and is still widely used today. It is divided into two main sections: Information and Information Processes, and Information Services and Information Science. The first section, which explains the fundamental concepts of information and the automation of information processes, draws heavily on Western sources but also on the Soviet science of science (naukovedenie). Except for the predictable philosophical citations from Lenin, little of the content of the first part would surprise a Western student (although that student might be irritated that S.C. Bradford's nationality is never given even though Bradford's law is described at length). Although the editor lists among the tasks of Soviet information science "the study of the influence of information processes on the nature of social communication," there is no further elaboration of the relationship of communication theory to information theory. In addition a high level of mathematics is expected of the textbook's (undergraduate) users; theories of document selection, organization, and circulation prognosis are explained almost exclusively in algebraic terms.

The second section of the text, which covers information services, their automation and the effectiveness of automation, gives the impression that automated services were widespread in the Soviet Union in 1986 (as shown below, this was not the case and occasioned sharp criticism of the textbook later). The second section also lists recommended titles for additional reading, an indication of those Western information science sources that had been translated into Russian. Books by F.W. Lancaster, G. Salton, and C. Meadow are among the Western sources listed, although there is no indication that they are translations.

The textbook by TARAKANOV received five pages of review in the November 1987 issue of *Nauchno-tekhnicheskaia Informatsiia*. The consensus was that the book, although useful, had not given enough attention to programming languages or to the use of microcomputers in libraries (although, as one reviewer admits, computers were not available when the textbook was being prepared). Other inadequacies identified were insufficient attention to machine abstracting, machine translation, and artificial intelligence (AI).

THE IMPACT OF GLASNOST AND PERESTROIKA ON INFORMATION SCIENCE INSTRUCTION IN THE USSR

The past six years have seen the introduction of free speech into Soviet classrooms and publications and the beginnings of the reorganization of educational planning. Under Mikhail Gorbachev, hopes were raised that the freedom of expression and scholarly inquiry that had become a reality by 1989 would hasten the restructuring of Soviet society so that changing needs could be remedied more swiftly. As long as central planning remained at the core of organizational thinking, this could not happen. The separation of the Communist party from the governmental process and the splitting of the Soviet Union into the Commonwealth of Independent States (CIS) in late 1991 will hasten decentralization. However, for the period we are now considering, Soviet information science educators were able to speak freely for the first time about a cumbersome and inefficient system that was intractable.

RAYMOND (1991b) gives the only recent account available in English on current issues in Russian library and information science education. Most of his focus is on such education as it occurs within the library institutes. In his view the major problems in 1991 were the students and the personnel in the institutes. The students are admitted too young (generally at 16 or 17 years of age) and with too little educational background. He reports that library institutes are the easiest of the post-secondary programs to get into; consequently many students are there only to acquire an easy diploma and leave the field soon after graduation. What education they do manage to get at the institutes orients them primarily to children's and public libraries, as they have not sufficient background to work in special or research information centers. According to Raymond, the quality of the instructional personnel at the institutes is not consistent; in some of the library and information science programs the instructors themselves have no graduate degrees. While his section on "Current problems in library education" is curiously devoid of any mention of the political maelstrom in which these issues were being discussed in 1991, Raymond's article is useful as a brief overview of curricular and personnel matters in the library institutes.

A perusal of recent Russian-language literature on information science education reveals that written protests about the system were becoming much more candid by the late 1980s. Even ABRAMOV (1990), for decades a ranking member of the educational establishment, attacked the Ministry of Culture for failing to deliver the resources needed for modern information education. He claimed that because the faculties could not afford the equipment needed for proper training, more and more education had to take place after graduation in the special libraries. In principle he believed that the library faculties in the cultural institutes were assuming tasks they could not perform. He pointed out that they were now educating people not just for information work in libraries but for information agencies, for publishing, for television, and for other mass media.

Abramov suggested that a consensus be reached about what kind of education could really be provided by what environment so that informed decisions could be made about how to coordinate general library education with special knowledge tracks. He implied that library faculties in the cultural institutes were really equipped only for training workers for public, school and children's libraries, and research libraries with general humanities collections.

Resentment about the lack of equipment also triggered the 1990 article by GVOZDEV, "New Textbook Needed"; the author complained that Tarakanov's information science textbook was useless for Soviet circumstances because it assumes a level of automation for information delivery that has never existed in the Soviet Union, where "in the absolute majority of Russian libraries there are no computers at all" (p. 26). Gvozdev questions the utility of Tarakanov's theoretical complexity and technical language for a student audience that may never see a computer. Expressing clear distrust for the bureaucratic perils embedded in the creation of Soviet textbooks, Gvozdev suggests that information scientists and library educators use the new publishing possibilities offered by cooperatives to create a textbook that would reflect reality more clearly than Tarakanov's book.

At least one practical attempt has been made to confront the critical lack of computers for Soviet information education. In 1990 KOLKOVA described "automation schools" for librarians, which were set up in Kemerovo, Tomsk, and Alma Ata. The purpose of these schools (which presumably offer hands-on computer training) is to prepare library managers who have no automation experience to make individual decisions on how to prepare their own libraries for automation. Instruction is given in systems design and database construction, with lectures on how automation can be applied to library services.

Solutions are also being offered to the personnel problems endemic in Soviet library and information work. In 1985 SHUMOV &

NOVITSKAIA described how the Institute for the Raising of Information Workers' Qualifications (IPKIR) was attempting to respond to the changing needs of trainees. They reported that IPKIR was initiating more regional programs to cater to female workers with families who could not relocate for prolonged training. They also reported that retention rates in these programs improved when the students had personal contact with instructors and peers at the beginning rather than at the end of their program of instruction. However, four years later, SHEKHURIN criticized what he called the disorganization of the IPKIR network, noting that the centers are too widely dispersed to be generally accessible. Clearly, the problems imposed by geography have not been solved.

KARATYGINA describes efforts being made to deal with the inadequate educational background of library and information science teachers. She reports that the Moscow Institute of Culture (MGIK) has for ten years run a program of continuing education for instructors at the Soviet Union's cultural institutes. Instruction is divided into four areas: (1) problems of socialist instruction; (2) fundamentals of pedagogy and psychology in higher education; (3) information science and computers in instruction; and (4) current problems in library science and bibliography. Certain areas are stressed with different groups, depending on their desires and needs. In addition to teachers, the almost 4,000 graduates of this program include deans and associate deans of institutes of culture, department chairmen, library directors, and compilers of textbooks and workbooks. Part of the curriculum consists of acquainting participants—who come from all reaches of the Soviet Union—with the central authorities responsible for the cultural (including curricular) decisions handed down from Moscow. Thus, student excursions include visits to the Ministry of Culture, the Lenin State Library, and the editorial offices of leading scholarly journals. Participants are encouraged to join round-table discussions on current topics that are not included in the formal curriculum. Karatygina describes one recent series of discussions that addressed such questions as: (1) the national and regional peculiarities of teaching the history of libraries; (2) searching and discovery: sources of scientific investigation; (3) the role of books in international relations; and (4) the use of archives during glasnost and perestroika.

GUDAUSKAS makes an eloquent defense of locating library and information science education at universities. A member of the faculty of the University of Vilnius (capital of the now-independent republic of Lithuania), Gudauskas maintains that the stimulation of a university atmosphere is critical for students in the information professions. He cites both the early 20th-century writings of Russian library pedagog K.I. Rubinskii and the post-World War I Williamson Report (U.S.A.) for support. Gudauskas claims that experience at his own university verifies the importance of the propinquity of researchers in varied fields to the library and information science students' understanding of the unity of knowledge and of their own potential professional role. This exposure can also help avoid what the author calls "the isolation of library science, bibliography and information science from the other sciences" (p. 25). Gudauskas points out that in the smaller republics of the Soviet Union, library and information science faculties have been located at the national universities for historical and economic reasons; he cites specifically the universities of Lithuania, Azerbaijan, Dagestan, Latvia, Moldavia, and Turkmenistan. (By early 1992, the ties of these universities with the central planning authority in Moscow had been weakened, if not severed, by the new sovereign status of their republics.)

The question of professionalism and ethics for information professionals under the changing political conditions is the subject of several recent articles. In the recent Russian-language literature on information science education, VOROB'EV defines the information professional as someone who possesses a knowledge base and who puts that knowledge at the disposal of those who need it. He counts librarians, archivists, and museum workers as members of this profession *only* if they believe that they are part of a global system of communication and are carriers of higher information culture. Using the results of a wide-ranging series of questionnaires administered to managers of different information institutions (libraries, archives, museums), Vorob'ev creates a "professiongram," a matrix that shows which professional qualities are most in demand in which types of work. One of Vorob'ev's conclusions is that there is simply no agreement on the educational goals for certified information workers and that existing education for employment in the traditional arenas—libraries, archives, and museums—is out of touch with other information specialties and does not provide "information literacy."

AZAROVA describes a course on professional ethics that was recently included in the curriculum of the library faculty of the Kuibyshev Institute of Culture. The course focuses on: (1) moral attitudes appropriate to library work, such as the interest of the librarian in his or her work; (2) staff morale; (3) the librarian–user relationship; and (4) personal qualities of the librarians. Other components address the implications of Marxism–Leninism for professional ethics, the substance and function of ethics, outstanding members of the profession, the image of the librarian in literature, status of librarians in society, and the culture of service and the ethics of library administration. The course uses a combination of role playing, mock interviews with patrons, and mock searches to simulate ethically complex situations.

Azarova concedes that one of the greatest problems facing students who complete the course will be the discrepancy they will encounter between the actual conditions in Soviet libraries and information centers and the professional norms taught in the course as proper to the "culture of service." She acknowledges that it is impossible to change the situation into which the young librarians graduate. She hopes nonetheless that perestroika, which encourages individuals to develop a more responsible and creative attitude toward their work, will stimulate information workers to start fulfilling their professional obligations. Azarova concludes, in an oblique reference to prerevolutionary morality, that the course's outcomes have demonstrated the possibility of satisfying the demands that ethics make of all professions: the coordination of the interests of society and individuals within the context of one professional group and the guarantee of the succession of the principal ethical norms worked out by members of the profession through the centuries.

CONCLUSION

Information science education in the Soviet Union had great strengths and great weaknesses, as the literature reveals. The strengths lay in the central government's encouragement of scientific communication as a method of fostering industrial productivity. From this encouragement grew the power and creativity of the Academy of Science's information science institute, VINITI, the locus of the highest level of information science education in the USSR. However, the very centralization that gave VINITI its strength diminished its impact as an educational institution for a nation as vast as the USSR. With its world-class full-time researchers, VINITI was separated from the diffusion of information science education nationwide, which was largely in the hands of IPKIR and was directed mainly at an audience with little or no higher education. Similarly, information science students who were taught in Soviet library schools were cut off from direct contact with the information science research pursued at VINITI, as were post-secondary students in information science in polytechnical institutes and provincial universities.

The severance of the teaching function from the research function is a phenomenon widely documented in the Soviet Union. Western historians of Soviet science, such as Graham (1972); and Vucinich, have both noted it, pointing out that it was safer for a totalitarian state not to have its students exposed to the state's most inquiring minds. In practice this meant that Soviet students of information science were doubly disadvantaged: most of their teachers, even those of the few university courses, were remote from the research being done in their own fields, and most of the information science students themselves were educated in an atmosphere where there were no general activities of a scholarly or scientific nature.

Gudauskas's argument for locating information science education at universities rather than at institutes holds up even in conditions like those in the USSR, where the university was more a locus of teaching than of research. Gudauskas rightly believes that the intercourse between generational peers in different fields with different modes of inquiry is fundamental to higher education and particularly to education in information science. This intercourse can be provided only in a university atmosphere. It will be interesting to see whether the now-independent republics will follow the course on which Gudauskas reports they were embarked and continue the integration of the discipline into the university curriculum. In many ways this would mirror the trend, now evident at some leading Western universities, to include information science, as a modern branch of epistemology, in the central core of the liberal arts.

For the many hundreds of information science educators who will, for the immediate future, continue to function in independent institutes in the larger emerging states of the former Soviet Union, a number of philosophical issues remain. It is possible that the sheer weight of the country's organizational difficulties over the past five years has kept the attention of educators riveted on practical issues. Nonetheless, it is remarkable to a Westerner that in the recent Soviet articles dealing with such matters as information ethics and professionalism, there is little reference to the information professional's individual commitment to the user's maximal information access (Azarova's plea for a commitment to a "culture of service," admirable in itself, is not the same thing). Educators at the institutes must be willing to get involved in discussions about the dedication of information scientists to the growth of knowledge in general, not just to the service to the state and its industrial productivity. The logical outcome of such a discussion at the highest levels will be the location of information research and education at universities.

BIBLIOGRAPHY

ABRAMOV, K.I. 1987. Zadachi bibliotechnogo obrazovaniia v svete reformy vysshei shkoly [The Aims of Library Education in the Light of the Reform of Higher Education]. Sovetskoe Bibliotekovedenie (USSR). 1987; (6): 3-8. Available from: Columbia University Libraries. ISSN: 0134-6695.

ABRAMOV, K.I. 1990. Perekhodit' ot obsuzhdeniia k prakticheskim resheniiam [Switching from Discussion to Practical Resolutions]. Sovetskoe Bibiotekovedenie (USSR). 1990; (2): 49-53. Available from: Columbia University Libraries. ISSN: 0134-6695.

AZAROVA, V.A. 1989. Budushchim bibliotekariam o professional'noi etike [To Future Librarians, on Professional Ethics]. Sovetskoe Bibliotekovedenie (USSR). 1989; (4): 50-52. Available from: Columbia University Libraries. ISSN: 0134-6695.

BERNAL, J.D. 1939. The Social Function of Science. London, United Kingdom: Routledge; 1939. 482p. LC: 39-6795.

BIBLIOTEKAR'. 1988. Bibliotechnyi vuz: otvechal zaprosam vremeni [The Library School Answers the Demands of the Times]. Bibliotekar' (USSR). 1988; (9): 8. (Editorial). Available from: Columbia University Libraries. ISSN: 0006-1808.

BORISOVA, N.V.; DERA, V.G.; KRASNOV, B.I.; SOLOV'EVA, A.A. 1987. Razvitie spetsializatsii i aktivizatsiia uchebnogo protsessa po nauchno-tekhnicheskoi propagande [Development of the Specialty and Activation of the Educational Process for Scientific and Technical Propaganda]. Nauchno-tekhnicheskaia informatsiia. Seriia 1 (USSR). 1987; (12): 21-23. Available from: Columbia University Libraries. ISSN: 0547-0019.

DOBROV, G.M. 1966. Nauka o nauke. [Science of Science]. Kiev, USSR: Naukova Dumka; 1966. 269p. LC: 75-559775.

FORTESCUE, STEPHEN. 1990. Science Policy in the Soviet Union. London, United Kingdom: Routledge; 1990. 230p. ISBN: 0-415-02379-3.

GILIAREVSKII, R.S. 1974. Informatika i bibliotekovedenie: obshchie tendentsii razvitii i prepodavanii [Information Science and Library Science: General Trends in Their Development and Teaching]. Moscow, USSR: Nauka; 1974. 201p. LC: 75-563962.

GRAHAM, LOREN S. 1972. Science and Philosophy in the Soviet Union. New York, NY: Knopf; 1972. 584p. ISBN: 0-394-44387-X.

GRAHAM, LOREN S. 1975. The Development of Science Policy in the Soviet Union. In: Long, T. Dixon; Wright, Christopher, eds. Science Policies of Industrialized Nations. New York, NY: Praeger; 1975. 12-58. ISBN: 0-275-05600-7.

GUDAUSKAS, R.IU. 1989. Rol' i mesto universitetov v sisteme vysshego bibliotechno-bibliograficheskogo obrazovaniia USSR [Role and Place of Universities in the System of Higher Education for Librarianship and Bibliography in the USSR]. Nauchnye i Tekhnicheskie Biblioteki v SSSR (USSR). 1989; (4): 24-26. Available from: Columbia University Libraries. ISSN: 0130-9765.

GVOZDEV, IU. A. 1990. Nuzhen novyi uchebnik [New Textbook Needed]. Nauchnye i Tekhnicheskie Bilioteki v SSSR (USSR). 1990; (1): 25-26. Available from: Columbia University Libraries. ISSN: 0130-9765.

KARATYGINA, T.F. 1990. Ucheba prepodavatelei: opyt i perspektivy [Instruction of Teachers: Experience and Outlook]. Sovetskoe Bibliotekovedenie (USSR). 1990; (2): 53-58. Available from: Columbia University Libraries. ISSN: 0134-6695.

KEDROVSKAIA, L.G. 1979. Osnovnye etapy razvitiia nauchno-informatsionnoi deiatel'nosti v SSSR [Major Steps in the Development of Scientific-Technical Information in the USSR]. Moscow, USSR: Institut povysheniia kvalifikatsii informatsionnykh rabotnikov; 1979. 48p. Available from: the author, Rutgers SCILS, 4 Huntington Street, New Brunswick, NJ 08903.

KEDROVSKAIA, L.G.; NEMIROVSKAIA, V.S. 1986. Opyt i zadachi obucheniia po spetsial'nosti "organizatsiia metodicheskoi raboti v GSNTI" v IPKIRe [Experience and Aims of the Study for the Specialty "Organization of Methodological Work at GSNTI" at IPKIR]. Nauchno-tekhnicheskaia Informatsiia. Seriia 1. (USSR). 1986; (1): 9-12. Available from: Columbia University Libraries. ISSN: 0547-0019.

KNEEN, PETER. 1985. Soviet Scientists and the State. Albany, NY: State University of New York Press; 1985. 138p. ISBN: 0-87395-895-0.

KOLKOVA, N.I. 1990. Shkoly po avtomatizatsii dlia bibliotekarei [Automation Schools for Librarians]. Sovetskoe Bibliotekovedenie (USSR). 1990; (1): 56-59. Available from: Columbia University Libraries. ISSN: 0134-6695.

LUBRANO, LINDA L. 1976. Soviet Sociology of Science. Columbus, OH: American Association for the Advancement of Slavic Studies; 1976. 102p. LC: 77-155982.

MEDVEDEV, ZHORES A. 1971. The Medvedev Papers. London, United Kingdom: Macmillan; 1971. 470p. ISBN: 0-333-12520-7.

MEDVEDEV, ZHORES A. 1978. Soviet Science. New York, NY: Norton; 1978. 262p. ISBN: 0-393-06435-2.

MEZHDUNARODNYI TSENTR NAUCHNOI I TEKHNICHESKOI INFORMATSII. 1977. Podgotovka i povyshenie kvalifikatsii informatsionnykh rabotnikov v SSSR [The Training and Raising of Qualifications of Information Workers in the USSR]. Moscow, USSR: Mezhdunarodnyi tsentr nauchnoi i tekhnicheskoi informatsii; 1977. 99p. Available from: the author, Rutgers SCILS, 4 Huntington Street, New Brunswick, NJ 08903.

MIKHAILOV, A.I. 1968. All Union Institute of Scientific and Technical Information. In: Kent, Allen; Lancour, Harold; Nasri, William Z., eds. Encyclopedia of Library and Information Science: Volume 1. New York, NY: Marcel Dekker; 1968. 161-166. ISBN: 0-8247-2034-2.

MIKHAILOV, A.I.; CHERNYI, A.I.; GILIAREVSKII, R.S. 1984. Scientific Communications and Informatics. (Translated by Robert H. Burger). Arlington, VA: Information Resources Press; 1984. 402p. ISBN: 0-87815-046-3.

NALIMOV, V.V.; MUL'CHENKO, Z.M. 1969. Naukometriia [Scienceometrics]. Moscow, USSR: Nauka; 1969. 192p. LC: 79-497075.

NAVROTSKAIA, V. 1988. Knizhnyi vuz i zhizn' [Library School and Life]. Bibliotekar' (USSR). 1988; (10): 12-16. Available from: Columbia University Libraries. ISSN: 0006-1808.

POPOVSKY, MARK. 1980. Science in Chains: The Crisis of Science and Scientists in the Soviet Union Today. London, United Kingdom: Collins and Harvill; 1980. 244p. ISBN: 0-00-262761-2.

RAYMOND, BORIS. 1979. Krupskaia and Soviet Russian Librarianship 1917-1939. Metuchen, NJ: Scarecrow; 1979. 222p. ISBN: 0-8108-1209-6.

RAYMOND, BORIS. 1991a. Libraries in the Soviet Union. In: Remnek, Miranda Beaven, ed. Books in Russia and the Soviet Union: Past and Present. Wiesbaden, Germany: Harrassowitz; 1991. 117-258. ISBN: 3-447-03124-7.

RAYMOND, BORIS. 1991b. Russian Education for Library and Information Service. Canadian Library Journal (Canada). 1991; 47(12): 399-404. ISSN: 0008-4352.

SHEKHURIN, E.E. 1989. O povyshenii informatsionnymi rabotnikami svoei kvalifikatsii [On the Raising of Their Own Qualifications by Information Workers]. Nauchno-tekhnicheskaia informatsiia. Seriia 1 (USSR). 1989(3): 27-29. Available from: Columbia University Libraries. ISSN: 0548-0019.

SHUMOV, IU.A.; NOVITSKAIA, L.I. 1985. Sovershenstvovanie zaochnogo obucheniia informatsionnykh rabotnikov v IPKIRe [Perfection of the Correspondence Instruction of Information Workers at IPKIR]. Nauchno-tekhnicheskaia informatsiia. Seriia 1 (USSR). 1985; (7): 24-25. Available from: Columbia University Libraries. ISSN: 0547-0019.

TARAKANOV, K.V., ed. 1986. Informatika [Information Science]. Moscow, USSR: Kniga; 1986. 304p. Available from: the author, Rutgers SCILS, 4 Huntington Street, New Brunswick, NJ 08903.

URSUL, A.D. 1968. Priroda Informatsii [The Nature of Information]. Moscow, USSR: Politizdat; 1968. 285p. LC: 76-428963.

VINITI [VSESOIUZNYI INSTITUT NAUCHNOI I TEKHNICHESKOI INFORMATSII]. 1980. Nauchno-tekhnicheskaia Informatsiia: Ukazatel' dissertatsii 1934-1975 [Scientific and Technical Information: Index of Dissertations 1934-1975]. Moscow, USSR: VINITI; 1980. 262p. Available from: the author, Rutgers SCILS, 4 Huntington Street, New Brunswick, NJ 08903.

VLADUTZ, GEORGE. 1981. The All-Union Institute for Scientific and Technical Information (VINITI). Cambridge, MA: Program on Science, Technology and Society, Massachusetts Institute of Technology; Russian Research Center, Harvard University; 1981. 27p. Available from: Russian Research Center, Harvard University, 1737 Cambridge Street, Cambridge, MA 02138.

VOROB'EV, G.G. 1989. Professional'nyi kharakter informatsionnogo rabotnika [Professional Character of the Information Worker]. Nauchno-tekhnicheskaia informatsiia. Seriia 1 (USSR). 1989; (11): 38-44. Available from: Columbia University Libraries. ISSN: 0548-0019.

VUCINICH, ALEXANDER. 1984. Empire of Knowledge: The Academy of Sciences of the USSR 1917-1970. Berkeley, CA: University of California Press; 1984. 484p. ISBN: 0-520-04871-7.

8 Ethical Considerations of Information Professionals

THOMAS J. FROEHLICH
Kent State University

INTRODUCTION

With the current concern of the American Society for Information Science (ASIS) for formalizing a policy on ethics in the form of a code of ethics, it seems fitting for *ARIST* to include a chapter on ethical considerations of information professionals, focusing on those who do work or conduct research in this field. However, it is no easy task to develop an essay on applied ethics in the information professions because one is grappling with two variable or shifting areas: (1) ethical principles and theories, and (2) the plurality of ethical applications that emerge in the varied contexts of information work.

On the one hand, we already have many ethical theories and principles, and they often compete—e.g., deontological ethics and consequentialism. Deontological ethics are those theories that maintain that an action may be held as right, regardless of considerations of goodness, including the actual consequences of an action or even the motive of the moral agent. One example is Kant's view, which contends that the goodness of a person's moral action is traceable to a good will and that the action's moral worth flows from the actor's performance for the sake of duty and not merely in accord with duty (KANT).

On the other hand, consequentialist theories of ethics hold that the rightness or obligatoriness of an act depends on its consequences, either actual or intended. One version of consequentialism is Mill's utilitarianism, which asserts that the value of a moral action is determined by its results—i.e., whether an action promotes the greatest amount of happiness for the most people (MILL).

However, the ethical environment of information work occurs in broader organizational contexts; that is, ethical issues in the information professions often cannot be isolated from ethical issues in business, in the library community, in computer-based systems, and in specialized subject matters, such as medicine or law.

To complicate matters, KOSTREWSKI & OPPENHEIM claimed in 1980 that "Information science is not a profession, and may never be. In no country in the world is it necessary to belong to a given professional society to practice information science" (p. 282). Their point is overstated. For example, membership in the American Library Association (ALA) or attainment of a degree from an ALA-accredited institution is not a requirement for belonging to the profession of librarianship. These characteristics are common signs of librarianship, but the absence of those signs, including a code of ethics in the professional society (sometimes appealed to as a hallmark of a professional society), does not disqualify one from the profession. The same can be said of information science. The profession of information science is defined by shared activities (e.g., work in information retrieval systems, particularly bibliographic and computerized systems) and common beliefs and practices (e.g., defining a user and/or usage base) of those who call themselves information scientists. Professions can be defined by their prototypical activities rather than by clear boundaries and exact definitions.

For the most part, this review is confined to the domain of information science and appeals only to related areas when they elucidate matters of concern to information professionals in this domain. For those interested in these related areas, the following starting points are suggested.

For ethical issues in the library professions, there are several good initial sources. In *Ethical Challenges in Librarianship*, HAUPTMAN (1988) provides an overview of issues in library work with a fairly substantial bibliography. Papers given at the 31st Allerton Park Institute are devoted to *Ethics and the Librarian* (LANCASTER). Some ethical aspects of librarianship have been treated in special journal editions: *The Acquisitions Librarian* (STRAUCH & STRAUCH) on "Legal and Ethical Issues in Acquisitions"; *The Reference Librarian* (KATZ & FRALEY) on "Ethics and Reference Services"; *Library Trends* (WOODWARD, 1990b) on "Intellectual Freedom/Parts I & II"; *Library Trends* (BURGER) on "Privacy, Secrecy, and National Information Policy"; and *Library Trends* (HAUPTMAN, 1991b) on "Ethics and the Dissemination of Information." SWAN & PEATTIE offer a rich debate on intellectual freedom and social responsibility in *The Freedom to Lie: A Debate about Democracy*. Other articles that deal with related areas or that are particularly important are in the bibliography.

There are some good resources for issues that pertain to the computer area. Many of the texts are edited compilations (ERMANN ET AL.; JOHNSON & SNAPPER). *Computer Ethics* (JOHNSON) was one of the first cohesive treatments of ethical issues in computer-based systems. A more recent treatment is *Ethical Conflicts in Information and Computer Science, Technology and Business* (PARKER ET AL.), a book of scenarios about piracy, professional standards, accountability, confidentiality, business practices, and employer/personnel relationships. Discussions of particular issues, such as data security and the teaching of computer ethics, emerge in the publication entitled *COMPUTERS AND SOCIETY* (especially the October 1991 issue), a publication of the Special Interest Group (SIG) on Computers and Society of the Association for Computing Machinery (ACM). Computer Professionals for Social Responsibility (CPSR) is another society that often addresses ethical issues in the use of computers through its conferences, proceedings, and publications, such as the *CPSR NEWSLETTER*. There is also a corresponding electronic discussion group, CPSR@GWUVM.

A major resource on business ethics is the *JOURNAL OF BUSINESS ETHICS*. There are also textbooks, such as *Business Ethics* (DE GEORGE). Within this broad-based area there are treatments of information systems, particularly management information systems (MIS).

Aside from these related areas, there is no large body of articles on ethical issues in information science contexts. GARRETT provides resources on practical ethical problems, but her article covers various professions, not just information science. KAPLAN offers 38 references in "Information Ethics" (MINTZ, 1990) as a supplement to those given by HAUPTMAN (1988). There have been many discussion sessions at the annual ASIS meetings, notably involving Manfred Kochen, Julia Blixrud, Edmond Sawyer, Homer Hall, Robert Barnes, Anthony Debons, and Diana Woodward, but many of these have not been published, although some have been abstracted.

When issues do emerge, they can often be separated into concerns of information professionals who are working in organizations and concerns of academics, researchers, and theoreticians. This review follows this division. Within the discussion of practitioner-related concerns, a model for ethical issues, a list of factors that commonly enter ethical deliberations, and a set of ethical principles are developed. Within the discussion of research/theoretician-related concerns, moral principles related to systems are developed together with an analysis of the moral context of information work.

CONCERNS OF PRACTITIONERS/INDUSTRY

To address the concerns of practitioners and the information industry as reflected through the work of information scientists, one can develop a prototype model for ethical contexts. This model provides a structure for integrating the literature and establishing a framework for discussion of ethical issues. It is derived from a series of the author's previous articles (FROEHLICH, 1990; 1991a; 1991b; 1992a; 1992b) and from extensive and ongoing discussions with a colleague at Kent State University, Richard Rubin. It adapts and integrates some of the latter's work on ethical issues in library personnel administration (RUBIN) and other ethical issues in libraries. It shares similarities with a behavioral model developed by BOMMER ET AL. for ethical decision making in a business environment.

Prototype for Ethical Contexts in Information Work

A prototype is a general framework that may not be suitable for all contexts but that can be adapted if it is sufficiently robust. In other words, one should be able to see "family resemblances" between the prototype and a particular problem so that the prototype helps to clarify whatever ethical dimensions or dilemmas occur.

In the prototypical context, practitioners are primarily involved in publicly available reference or source databases, whether bibliographic, referral or full-text. In this environment, there are seven stakeholders: (1) authors, (2) primary publishers, (3) database producers, (4) database vendors or networks, (5) information professionals, whether as intermediaries or brokers, (6) the organization and its managers for whom the professionals work, and (7) the end users or consumers of information products/services (adapted in part from WILLIAMS). Each stakeholder, whether individual, institutional, or organizational, has moral claims and demands in any moral deliberation. Not all stakeholders appear in all situations. For information professionals, the stakeholder interests of the original authors (1) and the primary publishers (2) are often indirect because they are mediated by or consequent to the interests of the secondary publishers (3), the providers (4), or employer demands (6).

To simplify matters, a triangular model can be used that represents the three facets of most ethical situations: self, organization, and environment. The lines between the points indicate a dynamic relationship, often in conflict. The self is the active moral agent in whom an ethical issue resides; the organization is the institution for which the information professional works; the environment represents all those forces that surround and affect ethical decision making, including corporate and community standards that shape ethical conduct in a general way or the specific demands of an end user for special treatment.

Self. Looking at the model, the self is the unique and autonomous moral agent, typically the actor facing the moral problem. The self is the subject and/or object of moral choice who has to accept the consequences of moral action. One force that motivates the self is survival, although survival, while always a factor in moral deliberation, is not a sufficient ground for establishing the morality of an action.

Organization. The organization is the institution that makes demands on persons in the role that they undertake on the institution's behalf. The organization is a moral agent as a whole, whether it be a large corporate structure or an individual (e.g., a freelance information broker). Just as with the person, the organization operates under principles of survival and social utility, striving to perpetuate itself and to produce goods or services for society (RUBIN). It has a relative autonomy because it can establish a will for the whole organization that may not be the sum of the wills of its employees or managers or its chief executive officer or governing board (although the latter two often dominate). Wherever or however this autonomous will arises, it can provoke tension between the self as autonomous moral agent and self as organizational agent (e.g., online searcher).

The tension between self and organization emerges in such areas as the extent to which an employee can criticize (from within or outside) the institution for which he works. If we assume that an institution has a right to survive if it promotes socially useful ends and that most information organizations have socially useful ends, employee criticism can either enhance or impair that survival. Criticism can be constructive if it aims to better the institution, or it can challenge an organization's survival if it is inappropriate, inaccurate, or too severe. In some cases, the situation appears to be a matter of constructive or destructive criticism, but often these categories are a matter of personal perspective (e.g., the CEO might view criticism as threatening, but employees view criticism as one way to initiate essential change). Thus, tension between the individual and the organization can exist in two directions in terms of how the employee can best manifest his role. One problem of moral deliberation is that even though actors sometimes agree on a moral objective (such as organizational survival), men of equally good faith can disagree about the way to ensure that objective.

Paradoxically, an individual can hold opposing professional and personal opinions on the same issue. For example, as a professional consultant, a person may advocate one brand of computerized equipment (for example, the system fits the company's objectives, cost constraints, and information requirements), but as an individual that same person could favor a different company because of personal preference.

Conflicting moral objectives will also exist in an organization, such as whether making a profit is more important than employee morale and what the relative priorities should be.

Environment. The third aspect of the triangle is called "environment" and encompasses those broad features of the surroundings that come into play in the context of a particular moral problem. The context remains latent if the ethical problem does not involve specific aspects of the environment. This horizon can appear in two forms: (1) as imperatives or standards without any specific moral agency and (2) as an institution, community, or individual that makes specific demands.

With regard to nonspecific imperatives or moral influences, for example, JONAS in *The Imperative of Responsibility: In Search of an Ethics for the Technological Age* points out that the earthly environment itself has become a global issue and proposes a new moral imperative, along the model of Kant's categorical imperative, to avert ecological disaster (KANT). Whereas Kant's categorical imperative commands, "Act so as to treat human beings as ends and never merely as means," Jonas's version asserts: "Act so that the effects of your action are compatible with the permanence of genuine human life" (p. 11). An information professional, in complicity with or as an employee of an agricultural chemical company that discloses only the benefits of a pesticide while ignoring or omitting its long-range environmental effects would violate this imperative. FROEHLICH (1991b) discusses how this imperative operates in terms of technological transfer in the case of information packages for economic development.

Along with the planetary environment there are other nonspecific environments. For example, information professionals who promote information products that advocate pedophilia would likely provoke some individuals to invoke generic "community standards," which are latent until a disturbance is created. Sometimes the standards relate to the moral standards of the community (e.g., against pornography), but these standards may also relate to the reasonable standards of the profession in serving that community (e.g., reasonable care in the health professions).

Another nonspecific environment relates to ethical decision making: the imperative of social responsibility. A utilitarian concept of social responsibility requires that the status of society as a whole be improved, that the distribution of goods be just, and that people be given, if not the right to survive, at least equal opportunity for access (physical access to facilities), shelter, food, education, and employment. This imperative exerts influence and takes form in political, social, and legal actions (e.g., legislation for social security, equal employment opportunity, desegregated schooling, wheelchair access to buildings, and free access to libraries).

With regard to specific demands by moral agents, certain defined groups, communities, and institutions are moral agencies and may influence moral deliberation in the information professions. Several kinds of institutions commonly occur: other organizations, such as producers, vendors, or competing organizations, professional societies, and legislative or law enforcement agencies. Depending on the nature of the problem, one or more of these agencies may affect moral deliberation. For example, vendors, producers, mediators, users, and legal and judicial agencies may be involved in a case of database copyright infringement.

The environment includes individuals, such as end users whom the organization serves, or other members of the organization who are not acting as institutional representatives (e.g., managers acting apart from their managerial role). It may seem odd to include such individuals as part of the environment, but their role as active agents only emerges in the context of an organizational process in which they may make a demand. They only make claims when their demands exceed their proper roles (e.g., an employee's asking another employee to cover for his absence). An employee patron to an information center who demands formal respect may be making demands about her personhood, not about her role as organizational employee.

Another case occurs when information professionals are asked by managers, using their personal judgment, to pad the accounts of clients with searches for the employing institution. While organizational survival may be enhanced (or threatened if the manager is found out), professional standards and individual rights are certainly violated, and the manager is exceeding his assigned role.

Concerns and Conflicts Represented in the Literature

Factors for ethical consideration. The proposed model acknowledges that there are always three definite elements present in an ethical situation: self, organization, and environment. However, whereas the self and the organization always have clear presence and influence, the ethical factors that emerge from the environment depend on the specific moral problem. Sometimes the focus entails end users or consumers, sometimes other organizations, sometimes community standards or professional standards. The environmental factors that will come into play are present a priori the specific context.

In his article, "Ethical Issues in Library Personnel Management," RUBIN outlines some forces that affect ethical decisions in the organization: survival, social utility, social responsibility, and individuality. As noted earlier, the first deals with the organization's right to survive and to perpetuate itself. Social utility deals with the organization's contributions to society in performing its defined function. Factors associated with social responsibility are concerned with advancing broader goals of society (e.g., affirmative action). The factors associated with individuality concern respect for the individual's moral worth as an individual so that he is treated fairly and with due process.

FROEHLICH (1991a; 1991b; 1992a) generalized and expanded this taxonomy and established the following set of factors that affect decision making in a broader context: organizational survival, social utility, social responsibility, respect for self, respect for other individuals and institutions, professional survival, legal standards, and community standards. The problem with this taxonomy is that it is unwieldy and confuses moral imperatives and factors that sometimes affect moral deliberation. The moral imperatives, as we shall see, are moral principles that are commonly invoked in ethical contexts. Respect for persons as individuals (inherent in the factor of individuality) and promotion of the greater good (inherent in the factor of social responsibility) are examples. The other factors emerge from the environment according to the ethical problem: professional survival (the right of the profession to survive and perpetuate itself), legal standards, and community standards.

Tensions between professional and organizational demands. Environmental demands can cause tension between the self-as-professional and the organization, as when an employee believes that pay scales are not commensurate with professional standards but the organization will not follow professional guidelines.

There are differences among the roles of the self-as-person, the self-as-employee, and the self-as-professional, the latter two roles taken on in response to the organization or environment. One would hope that the tension among these roles is not frequent. In general, one pursues a particular career because one's personal values are harmonious with the values held by those in the profession. Thus, persons might become librarians because they believe in free and open access to information, in providing reading for leisure, and in tolerance for a wide variety of viewpoints. However, the relationship of self-as-person to self-as-employee may be more ambiguous. One might join an organization for reasons that are more than merely economic, but compromises in values may occur more readily because of economic motivation. Nonetheless, there are occasions for conflict when one's personal values (e.g., a personal belief that an unborn child has the right to exist as soon as it is conceived) might be at odds with organizational and professional demands (e.g., both the organization and the profession enjoin the employee-professional to supply abortion-on-demand information for a client or end user) (WHITE, 1991b). This point is ambiguously and cryptically expressed in the current Code of Ethics of the American Library Association: "Librarians must distinguish clearly in their actions and statements between their personal philosophies and attitudes and those of an institution or professional body." This statement is ambiguous because it is not clear what one should do after making this distinction. Is one to suppress personal beliefs? The statement is cryptic because it "seems" to suggest that professional practice (in the form of the code) should promote a dichotomy between one's personal beliefs and one's professional *and* organizational practice. Put another way, self-as-professional (role engendered by code allegiance) should mediate the roles of the self-as-person, self-as-professional, and self-as-employee. Does this mean that professional practice should endorse organizational practice? Even though one would hope that the values of an organization are generally in harmony with the values of its professional employees, what if some or many professional beliefs oppose organizational beliefs? It is unclear in this code what the relationship is between professional demands and organizational demands because although the code acknowledges the potential conflict among personal, professional, or organizational values, it emphasizes a separation of personal beliefs from the other two. Yet professionals often do feel a conflict in loyalty between the organization and the profession. RAELIN describes this difference as one between "locals" and "cosmopolitans": "The cosmopolitan pledges first loyalty to the profession and is interested in being recognized and evaluated by his or her peers in the profession. The local, on the other hand, extends loyalty to the organization and is interested in being recognized and evaluated by the organization's official agents, its managers" (p. 40). For doctors and lawyers the loyalty tends perhaps to be cosmopolitan, but it is not clear that this is true for information professionals. WHITE (1991a) urges that librarians take a more cosmopolitan view. Obviously one cannot say that a cosmopolitan allegiance is necessarily more ethical than a local one; it depends on the context and the problem. Actually the waters are even muddier if one considers that loyalty may entail allegiance to local unions or other national associations (e.g., the American Civil Liberties Union or the American Association of University Professors).

Because we are trying to develop a prototype, the self-as-union member and the self-as-association member are deferred to the three major roles: self-as-person vs. the self-as-employee and the self-as-professional. Strictly speaking the self-as-person is not a role but the source of the decision to embrace or acquiesce to the other roles. Further complications occur because the role as perceived by the self—whether personal, professional, or organizational—is not necessarily the role as seen by the organization (particularly by managers) or by the profession (through peers, codes, and professional literature). To have the assurance that one's perception of his role agrees with the organization's perception, honest communication is in order.

Information malpractice. MINTZ (1984; 1985; 1991) provides some illustrations for this prototypical model in the form of "information malpractice," conceived in the context of information brokers, but most of these illustrations can be generalized to other settings: "misrepresenting oneself in obtaining information; industrial espionage; misrepresenting the work one can perform; presenting 'half-baked' products; breaches of client or source confidentiality; doing something illegal; purposely giving false information; and incomplete or sloppy research" (MINTZ, 1985, p. 38).

All these cases represent tension between the person-as-organization member and the environment. The environment in the cases above can be other organizations, such as a source for competitive information or consumers of information products or services. It could also be professional or organizational standards. For example, in cases of industrial espionage, the environment is an organization from which information is being obtained in a deceitful manner. While one must grant that there may be a thin line between competitive information gathering and industrial espionage, in some cases the rights of information providers are conceivably being violated if they are unaware of the use to which their supplied information is put. Such concerns have been aired by BELTRAMINI in his article on competitive information acquisition. If one accepts the belief that the self and organizations demand moral respect, then honesty in information transactions is imperative, including the provision of adequate information about the background of the request by information seekers, especially if the request rendered the information provider vulnerable (e.g., to an unfair competitive disadvantage) or at an economic disadvantage (e.g., when the provider would otherwise be paid for the information). In the cases of providing false information, the environment is the unwitting organization or persons for whom information is being provided. In both cases there are elements of deceit that erode trust.

In another case of misrepresentation—e.g., of the work that one can perform—there is a discontinuity between the information professional's abilities and the expectations of the client and/or profession if the former fails to disclose his or her degree of expertise, particularly the ability to handle an information request in a timely and competent manner. This kind of misrepresentation may also result in instances of "half-baked" products and incomplete or sloppy research. Competence concerns the individual and the profession and its standards and/or the organization and its standards. The organization can be either the firm in which the employee works or for which the professional works. In either case one can fall short of the organization's standards. The profession also sets standards, sometimes implicit, which may or may not be in accord with the organization's standards. The dilemma is that a person may be viewed as competent as far as the organization is concerned but be incompetent in terms of the profession's standards, particularly if the person has not kept up with the field and has neglected continuing education.

While competence, whether in terms of organizational or professional standards, is an important criterion for evaluating professionals, it is often difficult to assess. On the one hand, for some search and research questions, there may be no one right answer, or else a satisfactory set of results requires an inordinate amount of effort, time, or expense. On the other hand, the information technology in an online environment can obscure a satisfactory answer from both the searcher and client. SHAVER ET AL. make several important points about assessing competence in an online environment. One cannot be expected to master all the diverse systems and databases, especially when it would be prohibitively expensive to acquire all the search tools and aids. Again, it is difficult for clients to evaluate the quality of service they receive because the invisibility and lack of browsability protect the incompetent or mediocre searcher and/or his or her biases in choosing search systems or search techniques. Online searchers play a stronger gatekeeper role, and if they do not open the gate or if they open it onto the wrong pasture, end users can not be expected to know unless they are trained in the literature of the search subject. Even with the growth of CD–ROM products available to the end user, the same issue shifts from searcher-as-searcher to searcher-as-educator because most end users are not as knowledgeable or well trained as intermediaries.

Related to this issue is searcher bias, the inclinations of a searcher to favor certain search techniques, databases, and vendors. Searcher bias may compromise competence to the extent that inappropriate choices are based on these biases; yet if one knows certain databases and vendors well, one is more likely to exploit them effectively. Obviously these same problems can exist to a degree in manual searches.

Any list of information malpractices can be misleading and wrongly used or invoked. Mintz admits that this may be the case when one attempts to do something illegal; for example, the publication of "The Pentagon Papers" by the *New York Times* may have been illegal but ultimately moral. The truth is that any of the above behaviors may be engaged in if some higher moral principle is at stake—e.g., the prevention of war or serious bodily injury or harm. WOODWARD (1984), appealing in effect to a nonspecific environment of social responsibility, points out that issues in client or source confidentiality are not simple, and violations may be permissible. In general, she argues that the information professional will obey the wishes of the client or the information source or its representatives if such wishes can be determined. However, the information professional may disclose confidential information: (1) in his own interest if such disclosure is required to collect a just fee and/or to provide a defense against alleged misconduct; (2) in the interest of other clients if such disclosure is required to provide contracted services to the client and if confidentiality is not protected by a nondisclosure oath; and (3) in the public interest if serious harm is to be avoided, if attempts to resolve the problem have been exhausted, if the practice or defect can be documented, and if there is good reason to believe that disclosure will avert the harm.

Legal liability for information malpractice. NASRI defines malpractice as "any professional misconduct or unreasonable lack of skill in the performance of professional duties through intentional carelessness or simple ignorance" (p. 3). Insofar as it is a matter of competence or care, malpractice would fall into the ethical domain. Whether it is a matter for litigation is another issue.

As an extension to Anne Mintz's concern for information malpractice, the literature is concerned with the possibility of legal liability for information malpractice. Strictly speaking, legal liability and moral responsibility are not identical, but they are related. They are not identical because one may be legally liable for an event without being morally responsible. Such is the case of the *T.J. Hooper* and the *Montrose*, which set the following legal precedent.

In March 1928, two tugboats (the *T.J. Hooper* and the *Montrose*) hauling three barges of coal each were on the high seas on a course to New York and New England ports. Two of the barges foundered in a storm off New Jersey. In subsequent litigation, Judge Learned Hand ruled that while there was no custom for supplying radios to tugboat captains so that they could have heard weather reports and avoided an oncoming storm, the tugboat owner was still legally liable for the accident because some professions may avoid or adopt too slowly the available technologies that would provide a measure of safety. This case (*EASTERN TRANSPORTATION CO. V. NORTHERN BARGE CORP. ET AL.*) established the doctrine of "reasonable prudence" and has become the basis for litigation in failure to use information technology, particularly in the health sciences.

For example, BERNSTEIN & WATSON believe that the failure to use information technologies, such as the use of computers to gather data or to provide medical information from medical databases, will eventually result in findings of negligence in certain areas of medical practice. Since information technologies are readily available, accurate, and inexpensive, the doctrine of "reasonable prudence" increases the likelihood that doctors and hospitals may be held liable for their failure to use such technologies. In a case involving a pharmacist, *DOOLEY V. EVERETT*, the courts ruled that the pharmacist had the duty to warn the patient about possible drug interactions because of the availability of computer technology to identify such interactions. If doctors, hospitals, and pharmacists are increasingly liable, will medical information professionals also be held liable for faulty, incomplete, or inaccurate information?

MINTZ (1985) raised the issue of information malpractice and potential litigation in citing the case of *DUN AND BRADSTREET, INC. V. GREENMOSS BUILDERS*. Dun & Bradstreet (D&B) hired a 16-year old high-school girl to report on the proceedings of the U.S. Federal Bankruptcy Court. When she heard that a former carpenter for Greenmoss Builders had filed for bankruptcy, she mistakenly told D&B that Greenmoss Builders had filed for bankruptcy, and D&B listed this information in their Business Information Report database. Greenmoss Builders's credit rating plunged, and they lost considerable business. In subsequent action, they sued D&B and the jury awarded $50,000 in compensatory damages and $300,000 in punitive damages. D&B did not appeal the verdict (because they knew that the information was erroneous) but did appeal the punitive damages, arguing that Greenmoss Builders had to prove "actual malice." Dun & Bradstreet ultimately lost its appeal. For Mintz, this case raises questions for information publishers and database producers, in that some mechanisms might have to be developed to ensure the veracity of information contained in their information products.

BARNES (1990a) discusses this issue of whether information producers can be held liable for their products, and BARSUMYAN and DRAGICH extend it to the question of whether or not information providers are legally bound to provide accurate information. Dragich notes the legal requirements for professional negligence: "that there be a duty to the client that was breached, causing actual damage to the client" (p. 266). Her discussion focuses on what constitutes elements and breaches of duty as they might apply to information professionals. There are no clear standards for reasonable care in the information professions; perhaps such standards will only emerge when client discontent leads to litigation. EVERETT believes that a society such as the Association of Independent Information Professionals (AIIP) can develop standards for "reasonable care" in fulfilling one's professional duties through such mechanisms as a code of ethics, so that these unclear standards can take definite shape. PUCKETT ET AL. concur that reasonable standards need to be developed for information provision in the health professions, and they suggest some possibilities: disclaimer statements (e.g., about the incompleteness of online searches), insistence on minimum educational credentials for entry-level positions, liability insurance, collection development policies to guarantee the currency of an information collection, continuing education, referrals to subject experts, and thorough reference interviews for elucidation of search problems.

Principles for Ethical Action

Principles defined and enumerated. Principles are maxims that are invoked in ethical situations; they are general rules by which conduct is governed and by which situational factors may be weighed, prioritized, or evaluated. Some caveats are in order. Several authors (BAKER; FROEHLICH, 1992a; RUBIN) have suggested principles for dealing with ethical problems in everyday contexts. No author believes that his or her list of principles is exhaustive or that the principles are mutually exclusive; neither do the authors believe that their principles are moral absolutes that can replace moral deliberation. BAKER generated such a list in her article "Needed: An Ethical Code for Library Administrators," following the work of KITCHENER. Froehlich and Rubin arrived at the following similar list, which adapted two of Baker's principles: (1) act in such a way that the amount of harm is minimized; (2) respect the autonomy of self and others; (3) seek justice or fairness; (4) seek social harmony; and (5) be faithful to organizational, professional, and public trust. Their list is based on major ethical thinkers in the Western tradition, such as Aristotle, KANT, and MILL.

The first principle argues that in a given situation the amount of harm be minimized; in some sense, this idea articulates the negative side of the utilitarian principle to maximize the happiness for the most number of people. In many ethical situations, harm does and must occur—e.g., organizational downsizing leads to layoffs, and a recession can lead to lack of bonuses and no or minimal pay raises.

One may argue that although the first principle has utilitarian foundations, it also endorses a feminist ethic according to the following reasoning. GILLIGAN, partly following the work of CHODOROW, argues that women, because of a different process of ego development, are committed to an "ethic of care" and of nurturing relationships. In her effort to correct and enlarge the notion of moral development in children (KOHLBERG) so as to include women's distinctive voices, Gilligan uses the responses of two children to an ethical situation. A man named Heinz tries to decide whether to steal an expensive drug, which he cannot afford to buy, to save his wife's life. Jake, who represents the male perspective in an "ethic of rights," views the situation as a logical problem in which the wife's life has a higher priority, so that if there is no way to obtain the money, stealing is the obvious solution. Amy, on the other hand, reasons that Heinz would be thrown into jail, would no longer be able to take care of his wife, and would be unable to negotiate any alternative with the druggist. She does not want Heinz to steal the drug but rather to appeal to the druggist's sympathy, to take out a loan, or to appeal to others for help. If this example typifies feminist thought, then an ethic of care would be more contextual. This attention to contextuality would entail minimizing the amount of harm to all parties by trying to retain and sustain relationships. Feminists are generally not interested in overthrowing an "ethic of rights," as male-dominated ethical theory has been characterized; rather they are concerned that women's distinctive voice be heard, acknowledged, and negotiated (HELD).

The second principle of respecting the autonomy of self and others finds its origin in Kant's categorical imperative mentioned earlier: act so as to treat human beings as ends and never merely as means. Each person and organization is a moral agent worthy of respect, from the problem patron in the library to the problem employee who gossips to the governmental agency that seeks information about clients. Respecting these agents does not mean to accede to their wishes, only to recognize that each has a voice worthy of being heard and acknowledged. A derivative of this principle is truthfulness in representing oneself, one's capabilities and limitations, one's company, or the information system in which one works or which one represents. To respect others usually means to tell them the truth when it is appropriate and when it does not compromise proprietary interests.

The third principle of seeking justice and fairness is simple to state but difficult to achieve. Being fair means treating each stakeholder in a given context in an equitable but not necessarily equal manner. For example, although each client is treated equally as a client, the provision of information appropriate to different clients will vary according to their respective needs, cognitive styles, and economic constraints. An important aspect of being fair is the supply of adequate information, either by the information providers or the information consumers. Information seekers must be informed of the information provider's limitations and abilities to perform a service. Information providers should be informed of all constraints and parameters that may affect the provision of a proper product or service. Fairness may also mean consistency in setting forth job requirements or job changes over time. Seeking justice may mean seeking a balance among stakeholders, but it usually does not mean an equal weighing of factors; it means an impartial or appropriate weighing of factors according to conditions, circumstances, and objectives that come into play.

The fourth principle of seeking social harmony is derived from a positive articulation of the utilitarian principle: maximizing the social good. It is tied to achieving goals of social utility and for harmonizing the interests of all stakeholders: clients, staff, managers, boards of trustees, representatives of legal or community standards, and whoever else belongs to the specific context.

The fifth principle—being faithful to organizational, professional, and public trust—acknowledges that ethical action requires a spirit of faithfulness to one's organizational, professional, and public trusts. One should work for the best interests of all of these as far as possible. Although conflicts may arise, none of these trusts can be disavowed; their interests must be balanced or compromised if higher values come into play.

Principles applied. Some of these principles clearly deal with some common problems in the information professions. KOSTREWSKI & OPPENHEIM, in their article, "Ethics in Information Science," provide some illustrations that violate one or more of these principles: (1) misuse of employer's resources and facilities (e.g., betrayal of organizational trust); (2) avoidance of giving advice on health or pharmaceutical questions (betrayal of the trust of two professions: the information sciences and the health sciences); and (3) avoidance of producing biased information products. (In these illustrations all or many principles are violated: failure to minimize harm, failure to respect others and to be truthful, failure to be just or fair, failure to create social harmony, and betrayal of trust.)

Conflicts among principles. Other ethical situations are less clear. Consider the case of information brokers who must compete with subsidized public services either by providing extensive expertise or by providing free or lower-cost online searches. In a free market, this practice does not seem fair to the brokers who have fewer resources and facilities and must pass online costs onto the client. However, businesses pay taxes to support such facilities as libraries, and their tax dollars are just as valuable as those of ordinary citizens. As long as the ordinary services of the library are not jeopardized (and often they are enhanced because the library may earn additional income from underutilized resources), why should not a business benefit, as long as all information-providing companies have an equal chance in bidding for information products or services? However, the fourth principle suggests that social harmony be sought, such as striving to fulfill the utilitarian goal of providing the greatest amount of happiness for the most people. Such a goal seems to imply that some sort of calculation is involved, in which one could add, subtract, and sum the happinesses and unhappinesses of the various stakeholders. Yet, how could one determine the ultimate sum of happiness, even if one restricts his focus to three stakeholders in this problem: (1) the happiness realized by a business's enhanced success through economically priced information; (2) the happiness of the library in increased revenues and services; and

(3) the unhappiness of information businesses that may have been deprived of an adequate living? This problem of a calculation of happiness is not restricted to utilitarian principles but is an ongoing problem for political and social planners.

Just as conflicts can occur among individuals, they can occur within individuals—e.g., trying to negotiate a conflict among personal values (principle 2), professional values (principle 5), and societal values (principles 1, 3, and 4). CROWE & ANTHES, using the context of academic libraries and information technology, illustrate such conflicts and ethical dilemmas and the dubious value of invoking simple rules or simplistic conformity to them. PREER, in the context of delineating ethical conflicts of special librarians with the ALA Code of Ethics and the Library Bill of Rights, sees the tensions falling into three categories: (1) public/private, (2) universal/particular, and (3) principle/practice. The first tension is between a general duty owed to society (social responsibility) or to the profession and private duty, characterized as that duty owed to a particular library. This is ambiguous since "private" generally refers to personal rather than to organizational allegiance; further, conflict can occur among all three, as noted above.

The second tension is a common conflict within individuals and among individuals in trying to apply a principle to a particular situation. The third tension often highlights the discrepancy between ideal behavior and actual practice—e.g., the conflict between advocating free and equal access while charging fees for access or discriminating among patrons. To address such ethical issues as conflict of interest, confidentiality, and access to information, Preer devises a test in which the principles advocated by the ALA code might be balanced with various other interests, such as the special library, its parent organization, its patrons, or society in general in a manner similar to the principles suggested above.

However, analyses of this sort cannot substitute for moral deliberation. Analysis does not help one to arrive at some clear, unambiguous answer to one's moral dilemmas, nor does all malaise in moral judgment disappear. The most that analysis can do is discover the forces behind the competing demands, provide a framework to ensure that all relevant factors are considered, and establish some ideals for which to strive. When deliberation leads to ambiguous solutions or decisions, success can be measured by discovering the source of ethical malaise or conflict, not in removing it.

WOODWARD (1990a), in her article, "A Framework for Deciding Issues in Ethics," postulates that one might examine such ethical concerns as intellectual freedom (which she sees as the right to have access to the intellectual work of others and the right to distribute one's own work), under both deontological ethical and consequentialist grounds in a sort of dialectical process. Whatever principles one is examining, such as intellectual freedom, they must have grounds in each theory; for example, out of a duty to respect one's fellow human beings, one can argue that one has a duty to share and to provide access to information (deontological grounds); in order to promote the general welfare and the growth of society, one should also share and provide access to information (consequentialist grounds). However, what would happen if two duties came into conflict? First, one would establish the duties that everyone has, using a deontological approach. Then one would employ consequentialist reasoning to resolve the conflict. For example, an information manager may have to balance one person's right to privacy against another person's right to information. To do this, he might use consequentialist reasoning to develop rules that would apply to certain types of cases. For example, intellectual freedom would be upheld, except in those cases where the right is withheld for economic reasons, such as payment for work done or in the proprietary interests of the company for which the work was done. The information manager would reject all claims to free access when economic or proprietary interests intervened.

Although this method may not be successful for all cases, it is useful for some. It acknowledges the value conflicts in moral deliberation arising from different ethical orientations and suggests an approach to deal with the tension. A similar tension is seen in the principles above, although priority is not placed on any principles. Principles 1 and 4 have strong consequentialist foundations because they are grounded in utilitarian principles; principles 2 and 5 have strong deontological or Kantian roots because they focus on such duties as respecting the rights of persons and promoting the public, professional, or organizational trust. Principle 3, on seeking justice, can be argued on either ground. Woodward's approach seems to suggest that in some cases, principles 1 and 4 might resolve conflicts created by 2 and 5 or vice versa.

CONCERNS OF THEORETICIANS/RESEARCHERS

The ethical concerns of theoreticians and researchers are often broader than those of the practitioners; they focus on research and system issues, global imbalances, and democratic processes. One set of concerns pertains to the area of research, its production, dissemination, and use. Writing in the context of scientific research, but with an eye to research in information science, ADAM raises ethical concerns in the following areas: (1) how the availability of funding biases the research agenda of a field; (2) the nonlogical aspects of science that permit scientists to be driven by their egos; (3) the improper use of human subjects and data held about them; (4) the misuse of statistics; and (5) publishing and citation irregularities.

OPPENHEIM raises some skepticism about the quality of scientific research and its corresponding publications. Cheating seems to have increased in science, and the peer review system is capricious and unreliable. Oppenheim cites several studies indicating that typically referees have agreed only on very poor papers; with regard to the other papers, they had different views on evaluation criteria and what constituted topics of importance. Referees often recommend publication if the conclusions of a paper correspond to the referees' views. Again, many papers that muddled through the referee process got high citation counts, whereas those that were uniformly commended did not.

KOSTREWSKI & OPPENHEIM, while articulating some of the concerns of practitioners mentioned earlier, turn specifically to information science research. Although cheating in research has increased, they maintain that it is less likely to occur in information science than in hard science because the demand for publication and the research base are smaller. Questions about who should publish research results and take the credit are more critical—i.e., should the supervisor or the junior author take credit, especially if the latter did most of the work? SEREBNICK identifies some of the unethical practices in journal publishing, following a study by SEREBNICK & HARTER on ethical practices of library and information science journals. The latter study consisted of a questionnaire sent to editors to identify unethical actions. This careful study, too detailed to fully represent here, used a 60% decision rule: if 60% of the editors considered the action unethical, it was so classified. Plagiarism, falsification or fabrication of data, dual submissions of manuscripts, and duplicate publication of identical or largely identical manuscripts without telling the editors were actions regarded as unethical by the editors. However, the editors regarded the submission of identical or largely identical manuscripts to different publishers as ethical if the authors informed them of this fact. Serebnick calls for attention to the ethical responsibilities of editors and to the peer review process.

BELKIN & ROBERTSON (1976b) are concerned that the results of information science research, particularly in a possible shift from recipient-controlled (user requesting information) systems to sender-oriented (publisher automatically distributing information) systems, as in electronic publishing, should not be manipulated for the enhanced use of propaganda.

To enhance awareness of ethical issues, KOSTREWSKI & OPPENHEIM turn to issues in teaching information science. Although the teaching of all subjects entails bias on the professor's part, information science is particularly vulnerable because it does not have a generally recognized theoretical foundation against which dishonest representation might be checked. Further, because the field is so all-encompassing, professors should present as broad a picture as possible. Another avenue for developing ethical awareness is through courses; WOODWARD (1989) and WHITE (1991b) have developed suggestions for ethics courses in the information professions.

System Principles

One of the most thoughtful and systematic thinkers in the ethics in information science is Rafael Capurro. Taking a broad-based philosophical approach to various dimensions of information systems, products, and services, including related ethical issues, he is developing a comprehensive theory (CAPURRO, 1981; 1985; 1986; 1988; 1992). In an early essay, "Moral Issues in Information Science," he generates a series of ethical principles in information production, dissemination, and use (CAPURRO, 1985). Principles, as he uses the term, are not the same as the moral principles elucidated above, although they are related. The principles of which he speaks are not moral maxims by which practitioners can address daily ethical questions; rather, they are guidelines derived from a global sense of social responsibility. With regard to information production, particularly in scientific research, Capurro argues that authors are responsible for the truthfulness and objectivity of their assertions. Truthfulness involves integrity in searching for the truth and openness to criticism and evaluation. Objectivity is related to the degree of informativeness, which, as designating an evaluative measure of the research product, generally should be more qualitative than quantitative.

Three principles emerge for information dissemination: (1) the principle of accessibility, (2) the principle of confidentiality, and (3) the principle of completeness. The principle of accessibility means that specialized information should be made available to all who need it without violating proprietary constraints or other restrictions. This ideal entails the pursuit of intellectual freedom and an information democracy. The principle of confidentiality ensures the proper handling and security of proprietary interests of information producers as well as personal data about producers and consumers (and their search histories and results).

The principle of completeness is not altogether clear. CAPURRO (1985, p. 115) says:

> In the case of a database producer, for instance, this principle points to the possibility of information discrimination or of biased selectivity, through which users would be misled. The question concerns also the process of abstracting and indexing. At the same time, it should be remembered that a database producer is not responsible for the truth content but only for the correctness (or correct reproduction) of data.

His explication seems to confuse several issues, and perhaps a different title for the principle or another set of principles should be generated. On the one hand, end users have mistaken notions about the completeness of databases, but few databases claim to be complete; virtually all have selection policies. Information professionals are obligated to explain the limits and constraints of the system they are using. Thus, this principle might be better called the principle of proper or adequate representation, whereby database producers strive to record descriptive information accurately and attempt to assign descriptors and construct abstracts that truly represent adequately the contents of the article. In addition, a principle of validity and/or authority might be generated for information brokers or other professionals who claim to have insight into the value or authority of the information resources. In this principle the means for ethically grounding the authority or value of the work might be established.

In Capurro's view, it is difficult to generate ethical principles about information use because information seekers have many different goals. If scientific and technological information is desired, the principles of truthfulness and objectivity come into play. However, if the goals are abstract (as in philosophy) or practical (as in art), these notions must be broadened for what constitutes truth in these areas is less exact and more diversified.

Ideological, Political, and Social Frameworks

Several authors view ethical dimensions as outgrowths of tacit or explicit ideologies and large-scale social, political, and economic frameworks. For KOSTREWSKI & OPPENHEIM recent trends will continue: the information rich will get richer because corporations and those who are familiar with information sources and technology will continue to have the easiest and cheapest access. With the advent of computer technology, there exist the possibilities of more control of information flows and quick invasion of privacy. While developing countries need information, they may be more easily disenfranchised from the technological means to obtain it, and some do not have as much use for computerized information. Nevertheless, few developing countries want to return to the old technologies (e.g., the printed book) to satisfy their needs. KUMAR calls for a Gandhian solution, in which the technology adopted in a given setting would suit the local talents. This is preferable to a top-down approach, in which developed technologies would be imposed on local problems, often only to fail.

FROHMANN claims that some theoreticians in library and information science have subscribed to a "cognitive viewpoint," which treats information essentially as a commodity and human beings as surveyable information consumers within a capitalist market economy model. While it may be the case that the cognitive viewpoint is more diversified than Frohmann realizes, in a "discourse analysis" of this viewpoint, he examines the models, metaphors, and language that theoreticians in library and information science with a cognitive viewpoint adopt. Using Nicholas J. Belkin and Stephen E. Robertson's "Information Science and the Phenomenon of Information" (BELKIN & ROBERTSON, 1976a) as a paradigmatic text, he argues that information-seeking behavior in this viewpoint is a process of image-modification in which there is the interaction of two fundamental "structures": (1) the user's "images" or mental representations, and (2) "knowledge stores" conceived as repositories of corresponding images in the form of graphic records. From this model, Frohmann extrapolates the view that information seekers become pawns of a technology of surveillance and that information professionals become "experts in image interpretation and delivery" and perform "ideological labour for modern capitalist image markets" (p. 135). What is wrong with the ideology for which they labor is that it discounts the social, intersubjective aspects of information production, seeking, and use because in this model whatever is social has to be reduced to subjective mental representations or images. However, communication of information occurs within a social and political framework that mediates the process. It has dimensions that are both conscious and unconscious in the sense that agendas, attitudes, and tacit understandings are produced at the same time as conscious information. According to Frohmann, the cognitive viewpoint misrepresents the social agency of the communication of information and distorts creative and interpretive processes. Further, since it is to a large extent motivated by power, control, and economic interests, it promotes an ideology that subverts notions of free access and information democracy.

In a similar vein CAPURRO (1992) argues that information databases are designed for the universal consumer and thereby betray the particularity that characterizes information production and consumption. Again, FROEHLICH (1990), following the work of MOWSHOWITZ (1984) and KLING (1990) who have discussed the value-laden social framework of computer technologies, contends that contrary to the common belief that all technologies are morally neutral, information technologies such as classifying, abstracting, and indexing are not morally or value neutral. Classification schemes often reflect the biases of the general population. Further, most databases are based on a selection policy that colors their contents and predisposes them to certain problems—e.g., the use to which they are put. And since most databases are oriented to science, technology, and business, they establish a tacit ideology that is seen, in part, as an agenda about what constitutes the important problems in society and how they might be solved. The problem is that while databases and technologies can be useful if they are properly understood and used, their underlying agendas may remain unquestioned, and they can be promoted irrespective of proper ends or as substitutes for original work. For example, information literacy could be a euphemism for consumer training, and literature searching can become a substitute for creative or critical thought or for the hard choices about value decisions required to promote national cohesion, international harmony, and planetary survival.

SLACK sees the declaration of an information age as an ideology: "descriptions of the information age are ideological, and ideology permeates what the information age is, how it is lived, how it is experienced and what it will become" (p. 2). To deal with this ideology, a critique is required, especially when the prevailing ideology promotes exploitation rather than the facilitation of human freedom. Essays in SLACK & FEJES define aspects of this ideology and provide challenges to its domination.

In agreement with ELLUL and FROEHLICH (1990), CHRISTIANS also acknowledges the non-neutrality of technologies but with JONAS discovers that the technological order simultaneously faces a conundrum and a paradox. The conundrum is this: on the one hand, we cannot predict the effects of large-scale technologies because we lack sufficient knowledge or experience of them; on the other hand, such knowledge is needed for us to be assured that the consequences of using these technologies will not be ultimately harmful (e.g., to predict accurately the consequences of holes in the ozone layer). The paradox is that whatever norms are used, they must function universally since exceptions could destroy the desired equilibrium or promote an unjust distribution of burdens; for example, if the United States were exempt from a ban on the use of fluorocarbons, the planet would still suffer and other countries would have to compensate disproportionately. In terms of the information professions, we lack experience in understanding how the long-range effects of networked computerized systems will affect the privacy of individuals or the control of information.

Although the gap between the information-rich and -poor has not been measured in various contexts, many authors believe that it is increasing and that there is diminishing free and public access to information. Some have argued that information is a right, not a privilege (DOWLIN), and is a fundamental right of developing countries to secure economic development (DOSA; TSEBE). Developing countries must also acquiesce to English imperialism (the dominant language of access to information retrieval systems) because most non-English materials are either excluded from commercial databases or are effectively denied access. HAYWOOD is concerned about the supposed trend toward centralized control whereby the owners of information systems also own the means of transmission. In an effort to curb infringement of privacy and to maintain confidentiality, HORTON proposes that every organization establish an "Information Bill of Rights," which would make clear to its constituencies and its publics how it deals with such issues as the collection of information (particularly personal), data security, access to information, and accuracy of data.

All these trends are seen as part of a disturbing agenda whereby information technologies possibly intensify such traditional issues as privacy, freedom of information, and intellectual property rights. Some of these concerns, as well as the concerns of practitioners, are reflected in the proposed code of ethics being considered by ASIS.

CODE OF ETHICS

Background

One way to address ethical issues in a profession is to provide a code of ethics, such as the one ASIS has been developing. BLIXRUD & SAWYER sounded the call for such a code in 1984, listing the following issues to be addressed: "Downloading, privacy (deliberate or inadvertent disclosure of files/data), copyright, pricing (competition), computer crime (felonious actions), security (protection of passwords, IDs, etc.), intellectual/academic freedom, career paths/job security/tenure, transborder data flow, public/private sector (fee paid, free good, subsidy, etc.), client relationships, employer/employee relationships, concealing or falsifying information" (p. 9). This list is a provocative agenda, and the ASIS Professionalism Committee has developed a draft that addresses many but not all of these concerns. Academic freedom, tenure, career paths, job security, and pricing are thus far not confronted. Similarly, downloading and computer crime are not directly addressed; they fall under proprietary concerns in the final draft.

The ASIS code of ethics has been eight years in the making, partly as a result of the time it took to determine whether such a code could be useful, what form it should take, and what its objectives should be.

BARNES (1986b) suggests that there have been two typical objections to a code. Reflecting doubt about the real power of a code, the first type of objection argues that a code is either unnecessary or unworkable. If the code reflects generally accepted standards and professional practices, it is not required; if it does not, it will have little or no effect because if professional practice is corrupt, a code is unlikely to correct it. Along the same line, others have argued that people who are ethical are likely to be ethical without a code; those who are not will at best only pay lip service to it. The second type of objection questions the appropriateness of a professional society to set standards for the entire field. Further, a code's provisions tend to be general because if they are too detailed, few people will be able to deal with their intricacies; but if they are too general, the code will be useless because of its lack of detail (BARNES, 1990b). In a related view, KOCHEN argues that ethical deliberation is too dynamic and unpredictable to make a fixed code useful. Although these arguments have some merit, Barnes reasons that they are not definitive objections if the code is not imperative or regulatory.

According to FRANKEL there are three types of codes: (1) aspirational, (2) educational, and (3) regulatory. Aspirational codes establish ideal practices to be followed; educational codes elaborate the initial statements about standards with commentary and interpretation; and regulatory codes establish detailed rules and mechanisms for adjudicating grievances and sanctions. BARNES (1986b; 1990b) has consistently argued against the development of a regulatory code, partly because the major sanction—rejection of membership in a professional society such as ASIS—is unlikely to create the desired effect. Even if sanctions exist, the code should not be grounded on them. Consequently, the code should be aspirational and educational, and these dimensions are reflected in the current ASIS draft. It sets ideals for the information science profession, raises consciousness about important issues, and educates the public and potential members by bearing witness to ASIS's collective beliefs, by enhancing the profession's reputation, and by offering a basis for public evaluation of professional performance.

ASIS Code of Ethics

The code begins with a brief introduction, acknowledging the diversity of uses and users of information systems, services, products, and technologies and the diversity of goals and objectives of various stakeholders in information systems: producers, vendors, mediators, and users. It divides the obligations of information professionals into three areas: (1) responsibility to employers/clients/system users; (2) responsibility to the profession; and (3) responsibility to society. The first section deals with professionals' faithfulness to organizational, employer, or client trust; respect for confidentiality and proprietary rights of information users and providers; and equal treatment of all persons. The second section divides the professional's responsibility into two parts: (1) truthfulness of representations of individuals about themselves, their credentials, and the systems they use or represent and about potential conflicts of interest, and (2) aspirations to be and to remain competent and to encourage the same among fellow professionals. This includes conscientiousness in research, undertaking assignments for which they are qualified and which they can complete in reasonable time, seeking and providing honest criticism, and adhering to principles of due process and equality of opportunity. The section on fiduciary responsibility to society focuses on improving information systems and services, including making errors and biases known, striving to correct them, providing reliable and accurate information, ensuring the credibility of sources, resisting censorship, avoiding or correcting inappropriate selection and acquisition policies, and promoting free and equal access to information within the scope of organizational or professional trust.

CONCLUSION

The literature on ethics in information science is limited and dispersed. However, as this review demonstrates, reflection has occurred on two fronts: among the practitioners and the theoreticians. The practitioners have been concerned with such issues as privacy, confidentiality, proprietary interests, information malpractice, the possibility of legal liability, and conflicts in roles they assume, often stemming from tensions between professional and organizational demands. The theoreticians have been concerned with many issues related to social responsibility: principles to guide proper system creation, development, and use and the tacit or explicit ideologies that underlie information systems and the information society. As the roles of information professionals grow and diversify in response to the information explosion, to the increasing demand for quality information, and to the increased forms of electronic communication, more thought will be required to disentangle and evaluate ethical issues. With the development of codes, models, and principles and an understanding of the often conflicting factors that confront moral deliberation, the moral universe can be clarified. No maxims or ideals can substitute for moral deliberation or ethical judgment about difficult choices, but such devices may illuminate the competing ethical demands in information work and/or establish a framework of shared values and ideals.

BIBLIOGRAPHY

ADAM, RALPH. 1989. Ethical Issues in Research and Publication. Library and Information Science Research News. 1989 Summer; 12(45): 12-24. ISSN: 0141-6561.

AMERICAN LIBRARY ASSOCIATION. OFFICE FOR INTELLECTUAL FREEDOM. 1989. Intellectual Freedom Manual. 3rd edition. Chicago, IL: American Library Association; 1989. 230p. ISBN: 0-8389-3368-8; OCLC: 9556592.

BAKER, SHARON L. 1992. Needed: An Ethical Code for Library Administrators. Journal of Library Administration. 1992. (In press). ISSN: 0193-0826.

BARNES, ROBERT F. 1986a. Professional Ethics for Information Science. Bulletin of the American Society for Information Science. 1986 August/September; 12(6): 23. ISSN: 0095-4403.

BARNES, ROBERT F. 1986b. Some Thoughts on Professional Ethics Codes. Bulletin of the American Society for Information Science. 1986 April/May; 12(4): 19-20. ISSN: 0095-4403.

BARNES, ROBERT F. 1990a. Ethical and Legal Issues Raised by Information Technology: The Professional-Producer-Product Mix. See reference: MINTZ, ANNE P., ed. 1990. 24-31.

BARNES, ROBERT F. 1990b. The Making of an Ethics Code. Bulletin of the American Society for Information Science. 1990 August/September; 16(6): 24-25. ISSN: 0095-4403.

BARSUMYAN, SILVA E. 1990. Can Your Client Sue You for Misinformation? See reference: MINTZ, ANNE P., ed. 1990. 32-52.

BELKIN, NICHOLAS J.; ROBERTSON, STEPHEN E. 1976a. Information Science and the Phenomenon of Information. Journal of the American Society for Information Science. 1976 July/August; 26(4): 197-204. ISSN: 0002-8231; CODEN: AISJB6.

BELKIN, NICHOLAS J.; ROBERTSON, STEPHEN E. 1976b. Some Ethical and Political Implications of Theoretical Research in Information Science. In: Martin, Susan K., comp. Information Politics: Proceedings of the American Society for Information Science (ASIS) 39th Annual Meeting: Volume 13; 1976 October 4-9; San Francisco, CA. Washington, DC: ASIS; 1976. Part II: Microfiche, fiche 7, frame B14-C8. OCLC: 2957698.

BELTRAMINI, RICHARD F. 1986. Ethics and the Use of Competitive Information Acquisition Strategies. Journal of Business Ethics (The Netherlands). 1986 August; 5(4): 307-311. ISSN: 0167-4544; CODEN: JBEUDJ.

BERNSTEIN, JODI M.; WATSON, BRUCE L. 1991. Will the Use of Grateful Med Reduce Physician Liability? Gratefully Yours. 1991 September/October; 1-3. ISSN: 1049-6653.

BLIXRUD, JULIA C.; SAWYER, EDMOND J. 1984. A Code of Ethics for ASIS: The Challenge before Us. Bulletin of the American Society for Information Science. 1984 October; 11(1): 8-10. ISSN: 0095-4403.

BLUM, ELEANOR; CHRISTIANS, CLIFFORD. 1981. Ethical Problems in Book Publishing. Library Quarterly. 1981 April; 51(2): 155-169. ISSN: 0024-2519.

BOMMER, MICHAEL; GRATTO, CLARENCE; GRAVANDER, JERRY; TUTTLE, MARK. 1987. A Behavioral Model of Ethical and Unethical Decision Making. Journal of Business Ethics (The Netherlands). 1987 May; 6(4): 265-280. ISSN: 0167-4544; CODEN: JBEUDJ.

BURGER, ROBERT H., ed. 1986. Privacy, Secrecy, and National Information Policy. Library Trends. 1986 Summer; 35(1): 185p. (Entire issue; Guest editor). ISSN: 0024-2594.

CAMPBELL, ANN MORGAN, ed. 1980. The Society of American Archivists. American Archivist. 1980 Summer; 43(3): 411-423. (Includes a Code of Ethics for Archivists). ISSN: 0360-9081.

CAPURRO, RAFAEL. 1981. Zur Frage der Ethik in Fachinformation und -kommunikation [Ethics in Scientific and Technical Information and

Communication]. Nachrichten für Dokumentation (Germany). 1981 February; 32(1): 9-12. (In German; English abstract). ISSN: 0027-7436.

CAPURRO, RAFAEL. 1985. Moral Issues in Information Science. Journal of Information Science. 1985; 11(2): 113-123. ISSN: 0165-5515.

CAPURRO, RAFAEL. 1986. Hermeneutik der Fachinformation. Freiburg, Germany: Karl Alber; 1986. 239p. ISBN: 3-495-47593-1.

CAPURRO, RAFAEL. 1988. Informationsethos und Informationsethik— Gedanken zum Verantwortungsvollen Handeln im Bereich der Fachinformation [Information Ethos and Information Ethics—Ideas to Take Responsible Action in the Field of Information]. Nachrichten für Dokumentation (Germany). 1988 February; 39(1): 1-4. (In German; English abstract). ISSN: 0027-7436.

CAPURRO, RAFAEL. 1992. Pour une "Poli-Ethique" de l'Information. Concordia. 1992. (In press; In French).

CHODOROW, NANCY. 1978. The Reproduction of Mothering: Psychoanalysis and the Sociology of Gender. Berkeley, CA: University of California Press; 1978. 263p. ISBN: 0-520-03133-4.

CHRISTIANS, CLIFFORD G. 1991. Information Ethics in a Complicated Age. See reference: LANCASTER, F.W., ed. 3-17.

COMPUTERS AND SOCIETY. 1968- . Rosenberg, Richard S., ed. New York, NY: Association for Computing Machinery, Special Interest Group on Computers and Society. ISSN: 0095-2737.

COOKE, ANNE. 1987. A Code of Ethics for Archivists: Some Points for Discussion. Archives and Manuscripts (Australia). 1987 November; 15(2): 95-104. ISSN: 0003-9551.

CPSR Newsletter (Computer Professionals for Social Responsibility). Available from: Computer Professionals for Social Responsibility, P.O. Box 717, Palo Alto, CA 94301.

CRAWFORD, HELEN. 1978. In Search of an Ethic of Medical Librarianship. Bulletin of the Medical Library Association. 1978 July; 66(3): 331-337. ISSN: 0025-7338.

CROWE, LAWSON; ANTHES, SUSAN H. 1988. The Academic Librarian and Information Technology: Ethical Issues. College & Research Libraries. 1988 March; 49(2): 123-130. ISSN: 0010-0870.

DE GEORGE, RICHARD T. 1986. Business Ethics. 2nd edition. New York, NY: Macmillan; 1986. 431p. ISBN: 0-02-328010-7.

DOOLEY V. EVERETT. 1990. 805 SW2d 380 (1990).

DOSA, MARTA L. 1985. Information Transfer as Technical Assistance for Development. Journal of the American Society for Information Science. 1985; 36(3): 146-152. ISSN: 0002-8231; CODEN: AISJB6.

DOWLIN, KENNETH E. 1987. Access to Information: A Human Right? In: Simora, Filomena, comp., ed. The Bowker Annual of Library and Book Trade Information. 32nd edition. New York, NY: R.R. Bowker Co.; 1987. 64-68. ISSN: 0068-0540; ISBN: 0-8352-2333-7; OCLC: 15869836.

DRABENSTOTT, JON, ed. 1986. Ethics in the Library Automation Process. Library Hi Tech. 1986 Winter; 4(4): 107-119. ISSN: 0737-8831.

DRAGICH, MARTHA J. 1989. Information Malpractice: Some Thoughts on the Potential Liability of Information Professionals. Information Technology and Libraries. 1989 September; 8(3): 265-272. ISSN: 0730-9295.

DUN AND BRADSTREET, INC. V. GREENMOSS BUILDERS. 1984. 472 U.S. 749 (1984).
DURRANCE, JOAN C. 1983. The Generic Librarian: Anonymity versus Accountability. RQ. 1983 Spring; 22(3): 278-283. ISSN: 0033-7072.
EASTERN TRANSPORTATION CO. V. NORTHERN BARGE CORP. ET AL. 1932. 287 U.S. 662 (1932). (Cert. denied).
ELLUL, JACQUES. 1980. The Power of Technique and the Ethics of Non-Power. In: Woodward, Kathleen, ed. The Myths of Information: Technology and Postindustrial Culture. Madison, WI: Coda Press; 1980. 243-247. ISBN: 0-930956-12-5.
EPSTEIN, SUSAN BAERG. 1990. Ethical Considerations in an Automated Environment. Library Journal. 1990; 115(15): 59-60. ISSN: 0023-9283.
ERMANN, M. DAVID; WILLIAMS, MARY B.; GUTIERREZ, CLAUDIO, eds. 1990. Computer Ethics and Society. New York, NY: Oxford University Press, Inc.; 1990. 376p. ISBN: 0-19-505850-X.
EVERETT, JOHN H. 1989. Independent Information Professionals and the Question of Malpractice. Online. 1989 May; 13(3): 65-70. ISSN: 0146-5422.
FOSKETT, D.J. 1962. The Creed of a Librarian—No Politics, No Religion, No Morals. London, England: The Library Association; 1962. 13p. OCLC: 204611.
FRANKEL, MARK. 1989. Professional Codes: Why, How and with What Impact? Journal of Business Ethics. 1989; 8: 109-115. ISSN: 0167-4544.
FROEHLICH, THOMAS J. 1990. Ethics, Ideology and the Practices of Information Systems. In: Henderson, Diane, ed. ASIS '90: Information in the Year 2000: From Research to Applications: Proceedings of the American Society for Information Science (ASIS) 53rd Annual Meeting: Volume 27; 1990 November 4-8; Toronto, Canada. Medford, NJ: Learned Information, Inc. for ASIS; 1990. 245-255. ISSN: 0044-7870; ISBN: 0-938734-48-2; CODEN: PAISDQ.
FROEHLICH, THOMAS J. 1991a. Ethical Considerations in End-User Searching and Training End-Users to Be Self Searchers of CD-ROM and Online Databases. In: Williams, Martha E., ed. Proceedings of the 12th National Online Meeting; 1991 May 7-9; New York, NY. Medford, NJ: Learned Information, Inc.; 1991. 93-98. ISBN: 0-938734-51-2.
FROEHLICH, THOMAS J. 1991b. Ethical Considerations in Technology Transfer. Library Trends. 1991 Fall; 40(2): 274-302. ISSN: 0024-2594.
FROEHLICH, THOMAS J. 1992a. Ethical Issues in the Consultant-Library Relationship. In: Garten, Edward, ed. Using Consultants in Libraries and Information Centers: A Management Handbook. Westport, CT: Greenwood Press; 1992. (In press). ISBN: 0-313-27878-4.
FROEHLICH, THOMAS J. 1992b. Library and Information Professions. In: Becker, Lawrence C., ed. The Encyclopedia of Ethics. New York, NY: Garland Publishing; 1992. 711-716. ISBN: 0-8153-0403-X; OCLC: 24065366.
FROHMANN, BERND. 1992. Knowledge and Power in Library and Information Science: Toward a Discourse Analysis of the Cognitive Viewpoint. In: Vakkari, Pertti; Cronin, Blaise, eds. Conceptions of Library and Information Science: Historical, Empirical and Theoretical Perspectives. London, England: Taylor Graham; 1992. 135-148. ISBN: 0-947568-52-2.

GARRETT, MARIE. 1990. Applied and Professional Ethics: Resources for Research. RQ. 1990 Summer; 29(4): 497-503. ISSN: 0033-7072.

GILLIGAN, CAROL. 1982. In a Different Voice: Psychological Theory and Women's Development. Cambridge, MA: Harvard University Press; 1982. 184p. ISBN: 0-674-44543-0.

GOEHNER, DONNA M. 1991. Ethical Aspects of the Librarian/Vendor Relationship. See reference: LANCASTER, F.W., ed. 73-82.

GRAY, JOHN A. 1989. The Health Sciences Librarian's Exposure to Malpractice Liability Because of Negligent Provision of Information. Bulletin of the Medical Library Association. 1989 January; 77(1): 33-37. ISSN: 0025-7338.

GREMMELS, GILLIAN S. 1991. Reference in the Public Interest: An Examination of Conscience. RQ. 1991 Spring; 30(3): 362-369. ISSN: 0033-7072.

GROEN, FRANCES. 1983. Provision of Health Information Has Legal and Ethical Aspects. Canadian Library Journal. 1983 December; 40(6): 359-362. ISSN: 0008-4352.

HAUPTMAN, ROBERT. 1976. Overdue: Professionalism or Culpability? An Experiment in Ethics. Wilson Library Bulletin. 1976 April; 50(8): 626-627. ISSN: 0043-5651.

HAUPTMAN, ROBERT. 1979. Ethical Commitment and the Professions. Catholic Library World. 1979 December; 51(5): 196-199. ISSN: 0008-820X.

HAUPTMAN, ROBERT. 1982. Computers, Reference, and Revolution. The Reference Librarian. 1982 Fall/Winter; (5/6): 71-75. ISSN: 0276-3877; CODEN: RELBD6.

HAUPTMAN, ROBERT. 1988. Ethical Challenges in Librarianship. Phoenix, AZ: Oryx Press; 1988. 110p. ISBN: 0-89774-271-0.

HAUPTMAN, ROBERT. 1990a. A Brief Note on Confidentiality. Wilson Library Bulletin. 1990 November; 65(3): 70-71. ISSN: 0043-5651.

HAUPTMAN, ROBERT. 1990b. Ethical Concerns in Librarianship: An Overview. See reference: MINTZ, ANNE P., ed. 1990. 14-23.

HAUPTMAN, ROBERT. 1991a. Ethics and Law Librarianship: A Panel Discussion. Law Library Journal. 1991 Winter; 83(1): 1-19. ISSN: 0023-9283.

HAUPTMAN, ROBERT, ed. 1991b. Ethics and the Dissemination of Information. Library Trends. 1991 Fall; 40(2): 375p. (Entire issue; Guest editor). ISSN: 0024-2594.

HAUPTMAN, ROBERT. 1991c. Five Assaults on Our Integrity. See reference: LANCASTER, F.W., ed. 83-91.

HAYWOOD, TREVOR. 1988. Electronic Information: The Withering of Public Access. In: Dyer, Hilary; Tseng, Gwyneth, eds. New Horizons for the Information Profession: Meeting of the Challenge of Change: Proceedings of the Institute of Information Scientists Annual Conference; 1987; Warwick, England. London, England: Taylor Graham; c1988. 195-206. ISBN: 0-947568-32-8; OCLC: 19267983.

HELD, VIRGINIA. 1988. Report on Feminist Moral Theory. American Philosophical Association. Newsletter on Feminism and Philosophy. 1988 April; 11-13. ISSN: 1049-7870.

HORTON, FOREST WOODY, JR. 1984. An Information Bill of Rights. Information Management. 1984; 18(10): 24. ISSN: 0739-9049.

HOUK, JUDITH. 1983. Freelancing: Keeping It Ethical. Wilson Library Bulletin. 1983 June; 57(10): 854-855, 895. ISSN: 0043-5651.
HURYCH, JITKA M.; GLENN, ANN C. 1987. Ethics in Health Sciences Librarianship. Bulletin of the Medical Library Association. 1987 October; 75(4): 342-348. ISSN: 0025-7338.
JOHNSON, DEBORAH G. 1985. Computer Ethics. Englewood Cliffs, NJ: Prentice-Hall, Inc.; 1985. 110p. ISBN: 0-13-164005-4.
JOHNSON, DEBORAH G.; SNAPPER, JOHN W. 1985. Ethical Issues in the Use of Computers. Belmont, CA: Wadsworth Publishing; 1985. 363p. (Out of print). ISBN: 0-543-04257-0.
JONAS, HANS. 1984. The Imperative of Responsibility: In Search of an Ethics for the Technological Age. Chicago, IL: University of Chicago Press; 1984. 256p. ISBN: 0-226-40596-6.
JOURNAL OF BUSINESS ETHICS. 1982- . Michalos, Alex C., ed. Dordrecht, The Netherlands: Kluwer Academic Publishers. ISSN: 016,7-4544; CODEN: JBEUDJ.
KANT, IMMANUEL. 1959. Foundations of the Metaphysics of Morals, and What Is Enlightenment? Indianapolis, IN: Bobbs-Merrill; 1959. 92p. LC: 59-11679; OCLC: 1484601.
KAPLAN, SUSAN JANE. 1990. Information Ethics: An Annotated Bibliography. See reference: MINTZ, ANNE P., ed. 1990. 53-61.
KATZ, BILL; FRALEY, RUTH, eds. 1982. Ethics and Reference Services. The Reference Librarian. 1982; (4): 185p. (Entire issue). ISSN: 0276-3877; CODEN: RELBD6.
KIRKWOOD, C.C.; WATTS, TIM J. 1983. Legal Reference Service: Duties and Liabilities. Legal Reference Services Quarterly. 1983 Summer; 3(2): 67-82. ISSN: 0270-319X; CODEN: LRSQD9.
KITCHENER, K.S. 1985. Ethical Principles and Ethical Decisions in Student Affairs. In: Canon, Harry J.; Brown, Robert D., eds. Applied Ethics in Student Services. San Francisco, CA: Jossey-Boss; 1985. 17-29. ISBN: 0-87589-768-1; OCLC: 12166752.
KLING, ROB. 1984. Value Conflicts in the Deployment of Computing Applications. In: Cassel, Lillian N.; Little, Joyce Currie, eds. Special Interest Group on Computer Science Education (SIGCSE) Bulletin: Papers of the 15th SIGCSE Technical Symposium on Computer Science Education; 1984 February 16-17; Philadelphia, PA. New York, NY: Association for Computing Machinery, Inc.; 1984. Appendix C (unpaged). ISBN: 0-89791-126-1.
KLING, ROB. 1990. Information Systems, Social Transformations, and Quality of Life. Computers and Society. 1990 October; 20(3): 76-85. (Special issue: Proceedings of the Conference on Computers and the Quality of Life: CQL '90; 1990 September 13-16; Washington, DC). ISBN: 0-89791-403-1.
KNIGHT, LYDIA F. 1985. Professional or Personal Ethics? Library Journal. 1985 July; 10(12): 9. (Letter to the editor). ISSN: 0363-0277.
KOCHEN, MANFRED. 1987. Ethics and Information Science. Journal of the American Society for Information Science. 1987 May; 38(3): 206-210. ISSN: 0002-8231; CODEN: AISJB6.
KOHLBERG, LAWRENCE. 1976. Moral Stages and Moralization: The Cognitive-Developmental Approach. In: Lickona, Thomas, ed. Moral Develop-

ment and Behavior: Theory, Research, and Social Issues. New York, NY: Holt, Rinehart and Winston; 1976. 31-53. ISBN: 0-03-002811-6; OCLC: 1982281.
KOSTREWSKI, B.J.; OPPENHEIM, CHARLES. 1980. Ethics in Information Science. Journal of Information Science: Principles and Practice. 1980 January; 1(5): 277-283. ISSN: 0165-5515.
KUMAR, GIRJA. 1976. Computer Technology, the Book and Human Freedom. Journal of Library and Information Science (Delhi). 1976 December; 1(2): 243-261. ISSN: 0970-714X.
LANCASTER, F.W., ed. 1991. Ethics and the Librarian: Proceedings of the Allerton Park Institute: Volume 31; 1989 October 29-31; Monticello, IL. Urbana-Champaign, IL: University of Illinois, Graduate School of Library and Information Science; 1991. 126p. ISBN: 0-87845-085-8.
MIKA, JOSEPH J.; SHUMAN, BRUCE A. 1988. Legal Issues Affecting Libraries and Librarians. American Libraries. 1988 April; 19(4): 314-317. ISSN: 0002-9769.
MILL, JOHN STUART. 1957. Utilitarianism. 2nd revised edition. New York, NY: The Liberal Arts Press, Inc.; 1957. 79p. OCLC: 171390.
MINTZ, ANNE P. 1984. Information Practice and Malpractice... Do We Need Malpractice Insurance? Online. 1984 July; 8(4): 20-26. ISSN: 0146-5422.
MINTZ, ANNE P. 1985. Information Practice and Malpractice. Library Journal. 1985 September; 110(15): 38-43. ISSN: 0363-0277.
MINTZ, ANNE P., ed. 1990. Information Ethics: Concerns for Librarianship and the Information Industry: Proceedings of the 27th Annual Symposium of the Graduate Alumni and Faculty of the Rutgers School of Communication, Information, and Library Studies; 1989 April 14; New Brunswick, NJ. Jefferson, NC: McFarland & Co.; 1990. 86p. ISBN: 0-89959-514-7.
MINTZ, ANNE P. 1991. Ethics and the News Librarian. Special Libraries. 1991 Winter; 82(1): 7-11. ISSN: 0038-6723.
MOBLEY, KATHLEEN S. 1985. Ethical Issues and New Technology: The Downloading Dilemma. Show-Me Libraries. 1985 May; 36(8): 5-8. ISSN: 0037-4326.
MOOR, JAMES H. 1990. The Ethics of Privacy Protection. Library Trends. 1990 Summer/Fall; 39(1/2): 69-82. ISSN: 0024-2594.
MOWSHOWITZ, ABBE. 1976. The Conquest of Will: Information Processing in Human Affairs. Reading, MA: Addison-Wesley; 1976. 365p. ISBN: 0-201-04930-9; OCLC: 1995627.
MOWSHOWITZ, ABBE. 1984. Computers and the Myth of Neutrality. In: Cassel, Lillian N.; Little, Joyce Currie, eds. Special Interest Group on Computer Science Education (SIGCSE) Bulletin: Papers of the 15th SIGCSE Technical Symposium on Computer Science Education; 1984 February 16-17; Philadelphia, PA. New York, NY: Association for Computing Machinery, Inc.; 1984. Appendix C (unpaged). ISBN: 0-89791-126-1.
NASRI, WILLIAM. 1981. Malpractice Liability: Myth or Reality? Journal of Library Administration. 1981 Winter; 1(4): 3-6. ISSN: 0193-0826.
OPPENHEIM, CHARLES. 1981. Ethics of Information Supply. In: The Library Association. The Nationwide Provision and Use of Information: Proceedings of the Aslib/Institute of Information Scientists/Library Association

(Aslib/IIS/LA) Joint Conference; 1980 September 15-19; Sheffield, England. London, England: The Library Association; 1981. 105-111. ISBN: 0-85365-563-4.

PARKER, DONN B.; SWOPE, SUSAN; BAKER, BRICE N. 1990. Ethical Conflicts in Information and Computer Science, Technology and Business. Wellesley, MA: Q.E.D. Information Sciences, Inc.; 1990. 214p. ISBN: 0-89435-313-6.

PREER, JEAN. 1991. Special Ethics for Special Librarians? Special Libraries. 1991 Winter; 18(1): 12-18. ISSN: 0038-6723; CODEN: SPLBAN.

PUCKETT, MARIANNE; ASHLEY, PAMELA; CRAIG, J. PAT. 1991. Issues in Information Malpractice. Medical Reference Services Quarterly. 1991 Summer; 10(2): 33-46. ISSN: 0276-3869.

RAELIN, JOSEPH. 1989. Professional and Business Ethics: Bridging the Gap. Management Review. 1989 November; 78(11): 39-42. ISSN: 0025-1895.

ROTHSTEIN, SAMUEL. 1989. Where Does It Hurt? Identifying the Real Concerns of the Ethics of Reference Service. The Reference Librarian. 1989; (25-26): 307-320. ISSN: 0276-3877; CODEN: RELBD6.

RUBIN, RICHARD. 1991. Ethical Issues in Library Personnel Management. Journal of Library Administration. 1991; 14(4): 1-16. ISSN: 0193-0826.

SCHMIDMAIER, DIETER. 1989. Ethik in der Nutzerschulung [Ethics in User Training]. Zentralblatt für Bibliothekswesen (Germany). 1989 July; 103(7): 297-301. (In German; English abstract). ISSN: 0044-4081.

SCHUMAN, PATRICIA. 1976. Social Responsibility: An Agenda for the Future. Library Journal. 1976 January 1; 101(1): 251-254. ISSN: 0363-0277.

SEREBNICK, JUDITH. 1991. Identifying Unethical Practices in Journal Publishing. See reference: HAUPTMAN, ROBERT, ed. 1991b. 357-372.

SEREBNICK, JUDITH; HARTER, STEPHEN P. 1990. Ethical Practices in Journal Publishing: A Study of Library and Information Science Periodicals. Library Quarterly. 1990 April; 60(2): 91-119. ISSN: 0024-2519.

SHAVER, DONNA B.; HEWISON, NANCY S.; WYKOFF, LESLIE W. 1985. Ethics for Online Intermediaries. Special Libraries. 1985 Fall; 76(4): 238-245. ISSN: 0038-6723; CODEN: SPLBAN.

SHIELDS, GERALD R. 1991. The FBI Creates an Awareness of Librarian Ethics: An Opinionated Historical Review. See reference: LANCASTER, F.W., ed. 19-30.

SLACK, JENNIFER D. 1987. The Information Age as Ideology: An Introduction. See reference: SLACK, JENNIFER D.; FEJES, FRED, eds. 1-11.

SLACK, JENNIFER D.; FEJES, FRED, eds. 1987. The Ideology of the Information Age. Norwood, NJ: Ablex Publishing Corp.; 1987. 278p. ISBN: 0-89391-139-9.

STAHL, WILSON M. 1986. Automation and Ethics: A View from the Trenches. Library Hi Tech. 1986 Winter; 4(4): 53-57. ISSN: 0737-8831.

STIEG, MARGARET F. 1985. Fee vs. Free in Historical Perspective. The Reference Librarian. 1985 Spring/Summer; (12): 93-103. ISSN: 0276-3877; CODEN: RELBD6.

STRAUCH, KATINA; STRAUCH, BRUCE, eds. 1990. Legal and Ethical Issues in Acquisitions. The Acquisitions Librarian. 1990; (3): 146p. (Entire issue; Guest editors). ISSN: 0896-3576.

SUGNET, C., ed. 1986. Ethics in the Marketplace. Library Hi Tech. 1986 Winter; 4(4): 93-105. ISSN: 0737-8831.

SWAN, JOHN C.; PEATTIE, NOEL. 1989. The Freedom to Lie: A Debate about Democracy. Jefferson, NC: McFarland & Co.; 1989. 182p. ISBN: 0-89950-409-4.

SWEETLAND, JAMES H. 1989. Errors in Bibliographic Citations: A Continuing Problem. Library Quarterly. 1989 October; 59(4): 291-304. ISSN: 0024-2519.

TJOUMAS, RENEE; HAUPTMAN, ROBERT. 1982. Education for Librarianship in the Developing Countries: A Radical Departure. Libri. 1982 June; 32(2): 91-108. ISSN: 0024-2667.

TSEBE, JOHN KGWALE. 1984. Ethical Issues in Information Work. In: El-Hadidy, Bahaa; Horne, Esther E., eds. The Infrastructure of an Information Society: Proceedings of the 1st International Information Conference; 1982 December 13-15; Cairo, Egypt. Amsterdam, Holland: Elsevier Science Publishers; 1984. 511-519. ISBN: 0-444-87549-2; OCLC: 19840503.

WHITE, HERBERT S. 1991a. The Conflict between Professional and Organizational Loyalty. Library Journal. 1991 May 15; 116(9): 59-60. ISSN: 0363-0277.

WHITE, HERBERT S. 1991b. Teaching Professional Ethics to Students of Library and Information Science. See reference: LANCASTER, F.W., ed. 31-43.

WILLIAMS, MARTHA E. 1984. Policy Issues for Electronic Databases and Database Systems. The Information Society. 1984; 2(3/4): 381-417. ISSN: 0197-2243.

WOODWARD, DIANA. 1984. Standards of Confidentiality for Information Professionals. In: Flood, Barbara; Witiak, Joanne; Hogan, Thomas H., eds. 1984: Challenges to an Information Society: Proceedings of the American Society for Information Science (ASIS) 47th Annual Meeting: Volume 21; 1984 October 21-25; Philadelphia, PA. White Plains, NY: Knowledge Industry Publications, Inc. for ASIS; 1984. 44-47. ISSN: 0044-7870; ISBN: 0-86729-115-X; CODEN: PAISDQ.

WOODWARD, DIANA. 1987. Commentary on F.W. Horton's "An Information Bill of Rights". Journal of the American Society for Information Science. 1987 March; 38(2): 130-132. ISSN: 0002-8231; CODEN: AISJB6.

WOODWARD, DIANA. 1989. Teaching Ethics for Information Professionals. Journal of Education for Library and Information Science. 1989 Fall; 30(2): 132-135. ISSN: 0748-5786.

WOODWARD, DIANA. 1990a. A Framework for Deciding Issues in Ethics. See reference: MINTZ, ANNE P., ed. 1991. 4-13.

WOODWARD, DIANA, ed. 1990b. Intellectual Freedom/Parts I & II. Library Trends. 1990 Summer-Fall; 39(1&2): 185p. (Entire issue; Guest editor). ISSN: 0024-2594.

Introduction to the Index

Index entries have been made for names of individuals, corporate bodies, subjects, geographic locations, and author names included in the text pages and for author and conference names from the bibliography pages. The page numbers referring to the bibliography pages are set in italics and are listed after the page numbers relating to the text pages. This format allows one to distinguish references to bibliographic materials from references to text.

Acronyms are listed either under the acronym or under the fully spelled-out form, depending on which form is more commonly used and known. In either case a cross reference from the alternate form is provided. Postings associated with PRECIS, for example, would be listed under PRECIS as readers are generally less familiar with the full name, "Preserved Context Index System." In a few cases, such as names of programs, systems, and programming languages, there is no spelled-out form either because there is none or because the meaning has been changed or is no longer used.

The index is arranged on a word-by-word basis. The sort sequence employed follows the University of Chicago Press and British Standards BS3700 and BS1749. In general, special characters are listed first, followed by numbers, then alpha characters. Thus, 3M Company would file before the "A"s, and O'Neill would precede Oakman. Government organizations are generally listed under country name, with *see* references provided from names of departments, agencies, and other subdivisions. While index entries do correspond precisely in spelling and format, they do not follow the typographical conventions used in the text. Author names, which are all upper case in the text, and programming languages, which are in small caps in the text, are in upper and lower case or normal upper case in the index.

Subject indexing is by concepts rather than by words. When authors have used different words or different forms of the same word to express the same or overlapping concepts, the terminology has been standardized. An effort was made to use the form of index entries for concepts that had previously appeared in *ARIST* indexes. Cross references have been used freely to provide access to subject concepts. *See also* references are used for overlapping or related (but not synonymous) concepts; *see* references are used to send the reader to the accepted form of a term used in the index.

The index was prepared by Debora Shaw, using the MACREX Plus Indexing Program, version 4.01 developed by Hilary and Drusilla Calvert and distributed in the United States by Bayside Indexing. The overall direction and coordination of the index were provided by Martha E. Williams. Comments and suggestions should be addressed to the Editor.

Index*

A&I services (abstracting and indexing)
 ethics, 294, 297, 311, 313
 liability, 303
Aalbersberg, Ijsbrand, 117, *122*
AAUP, *see* American Association of University Professors
Abbott, Andrew, 19, 20, *33*
Abel, David J., 153, 158, *163*
Abler, R., 138, *163*
Abortion, ethics, 298-299
Abraham, I.M., 158, *168*
Abramov, K.I., 283, *287*
Abramson, Jeffrey B., 29, 31, *33*
Abstracting
 Soviet Union, 270, 271, 282
Abstracting journals, Soviet Union, 271, 273-274
Abstractors, telecommuting, 23
Aburdene, Patricia, 3, 247, *39*, *259*
Academy of Sciences Library, St. Petersburg (Soviet Union), 270
Academy One, National Public Telecomputing Network, 69
Accessibility, information, 310
Accountability, information professionals, 293
Accountants, telecommuting, 23
Accuracy, geographic information systems, 162
Accuracy vs. speed, management information, 235
Achleitner, Herbert K., 235, *251*
Acid rain, 177, 180, 198
 bibliometrics, 179
 government publications, 198-199

Acid rain, (cont.)
 risk communication, 183
Acid Rain database, 184, 192
Ackoff, Russell L., 239, 249, *251*
ACLU, *see* American Civil Liberties Union
ACM (Association for Computing Machinery)
 SIGCSE (Special Interest Group on Computer Science Education), Technical Symposium on Computer Science Education, 1984, *321*, *322*
 SIGIR (Special Interest Group on Information Retrieval)
  International Conference on Research and Development in Information Retrieval
  1985, *125*
  1987, *127*, *215*
  1988, *128*
  1989, *123*, *126*, *129*
  1990, *123*, *128*
  1991, *123*, *124*, *129*
 SIGMOD (Special Interest Group on Management of Data), Annual Meeting, 1984, *167*
 SIGUCCS (Special Interest Group on University and College Computing Services), User Services Conference, 1989, *85*
 Special Interest Group on Computers and Society, 293
The Acquisitions Librarian, 292
Active Memory Technology, 103
Adam, Ralph, 308, *316*

---

*Italicized page numbers refer to bibliography pages.

Adams, John, 44, *81*
Adelman, Mara B., 9, *33*
Adhocracy, organizational structure, 247
Administrators, use of electronic mail, 15
Advanced Research Projects Agency, *see* U.S., Department of Defense, Advanced Research Projects Agency
Advertisers, telecommuting, 23
Advertising, Prodigy videotex, 75
Advocacy
  and information services, 59
  information and referral systems, 66
Aerial photographs, geographic information systems, 148
AERP, *see* Aquatic Effects Research Program
Affirmative action, ethics, 298
Africa, information science education, Soviet Union, 279
Agarwal, Pankaj, *171*
Age, and risk from toxic substances, 200
Age of access, 46
Agency for Toxic Substances and Disease Registry (ATSDR), 191
Agenda setting, management information, 231, 238, 241
Agor, Weston H., 243, *252*
Agosti, Maristella, 108, *122*
AGRICOLA database, 192
Agricultural chemicals, ethics of use, 296
Agricultural industry, impact of information technology, 28
Agricultural Research Service (ARS), 202
Agriculture, pollution, 185, 202-203
Agrochemical Handbook database, 203
Ahn, Jongsuk, *123*
Aho-Corasick Algorithm, 111
Ahuvia, Aaron C., 9, *33*
AI, *see* Artificial intelligence
AIIP, *see* Association of Independent Information Professionals

Air pollution, 177
  information sources, 198-199
Air RISC, *see* U.S., Environmental Protection Agency, Air Risk Information Support Center
Air toxics, 198
  risk assessment, 187-188
Air travel, innovation, 7
Airline reservations, impact of information technology, 19-20
AIRS, *see* Alliance of Information and Referral Systems
Akman, V., *166*
ALA, *see* American Library Association
Alabama, telephone service, 57
Alachlor, 202
Alaska, legislative teleconferencing, 29, 32
ALEX information gateway, 77, 78
Alexander, Christopher A., 59, *81*
Algorithms
  line generalization, 143-144
  parallel computing, 104-106
Alic, John A., 20, *33*
Alienation, workers, information technology, 19
Allan, P., 235, *252*
Allen, Bryce L., 230, 243, *252*
Allen, Thomas J., 180, *208*
Alliance for Public Technology, 64, *81*
Alliance for Public Technology Quarterly Newsletter, 44, 71, *81*
Alliance of Information and Referral Systems (AIRS), 65, *81*
Aloni, Michaela, 180, *208*
Alston, Patricia Gayle, 185, 204, *208*
Alter, S.L., *252*
Alternative Treatment Technology Database and Information Center, *see* ATTIC
Alternatives, decision making, 240
AM/FM (automated mapping/facilities management), 139, 142
Ambiguity, information seeking, 246
Ambiguity reduction, communication media, 15
Amdahl's Law, parallel computing, 107-108

INDEX 329

America Online, 64
American Association of University
  Professors (AAUP), 299
American Civil Liberties Union
  (ACLU), 299
American Congress on Surveying
  and Mapping, 138
  AUTO-CARTO, 139
American Libraries, 70, *81*
American Library Association (ALA),
  70, 292, *81*
  Code of Ethics, 299, 307
  Library Administration Division,
    57, *81*
  Office for Intellectual Freedom, *316*
American Newspaper Publishers
  Association, 77
American Petroleum Institute (API),
  208
American Society for Information
  Science, *see* ASIS
American Society for Photogramme-
  try and Remote Sensing, AUTO-
  CARTO, 138
American Telephone and Telegraph,
  see AT&T
Americans, desire for change, 7
Ameritech telephone company, 76
Amir, S., 179, *208*
Amman, Claus, 182, *208*
Analytical engine, 99
Andersen, Robin, *34*
Anderson, Jacqueline, *88*
Anderson, John C., *260*
Anderson, K. Eric, *163*
Anderson, R.C., 59, *92*
Andrews, Martha, 188, *208*
Animal extracts, safety, 203
ANN, *see* Artificial neural networks
Annotation, Soviet Union, 271
ANSWER database, 185
Answering machines, social impact, 7
Antarctic, information sources, 189
Anthes, Susan H., 307, *318*
Anti-aliasing, geographic informa-
  tion systems, 162
APAL programming language,
  parallel computing, 103

API, *see* American Petroleum
  Institute
Appalachian State University,
  campus-wide information system,
  73
Appelbaum, Eileen, *33*
Apple Computer Inc., 10, 11
APTIC database, 184
Aquaculture database, 184, 192
Aquatic Effects Research Program
  (AERP), 197-198
Aquatic Information Retrieval
  (AQUIRE) database, 184
Aquatic Sciences & Fisheries Ab-
  stracts (ASFA) database, 184, 192-
  195
Aquatic Sciences & Fisheries Infor-
  mation System (ASFIS) Thesaurus,
  196-197
AQUIRE, *see* Aquatic Information
  Retrieval
ARC/INFO geographic information
  system, 137, 141, 147
Archives, Soviet Union, 276, 277, 284
Arctic Science and Technology
  Information System (ASTIS), 188-
  189
Argyris, C., *252*
Aristotle, 44, 304, *81*
Aronoff, Stanley, 139, *163*
Aronowitz, Stanley, *34*
Aronson, Peter, 137, *163*
ARPA, *see* U.S., Department of
  Defense, Advanced Research
  Projects Agency
ARPANET computer network, 61, 62
ARS, *see* Agricultural Research
  Service
Arterton, F. Christopher, 29, *33*
Artifact studies, environmental
  communication, 179-180
Artificial intelligence (AI)
  geographic information systems,
    153, 161-162
  parallel computing, 107
  Soviet Union, 282
Artificial neural networks (ANN),
  information retrieval, 120

ASFA, see Aquatic Sciences & Fisheries Abstracts
ASFIS, see Aquatic Sciences & Fisheries Information System
Ashley, Pamela, 323
Asia, information science education, Soviet Union, 279
ASIS (American Society for Information Science)
  Annual Meeting
    1976, *317*
    1980, *126*
    1984, *325*
    1987, *260*
    1989, *260*
    1990, *319-320*
    1991, *34*, *257*, *260*
    1992, *92*
  draft code of ethics, 291, 314-316
  Professionalism Committee, 314
AskSam software, 195
Aslib (Association of Special Libraries and Information Bureaux)/Institute of Information Scientists/Library Association, Joint Conference, 1980, 322-323
Aslib Proceedings, 187, *208*
Asokan, N., 114, *122*
Aspirational codes of ethics, 315
Assembly language, parallel computing, 103
Association for Computing Machinery, see ACM
Association of Independent Information Professionals (AIIP), 303
Association of Special Libraries and Information Bureaux, see Aslib
Associative memories
  information retrieval, 108
  parallel computing, 119
ASTIS, see Arctic Science and Technology Information System
Astrid, E. Merget, 57, *82*
AT&T (American Telephone and Telegraph), divestiture, 75-76
Atomic bomb, and Soviet science, 272
ATSDR, see Agency for Toxic Substances and Disease Registry

Attention span, impact of information technology, 8
Attewell, Paul, 18, *33*
ATTIC (Alternative Treatment Technology Database and Information Center), 190-191, 206
Attorneys
  ethics, 299
  telecommuting, 23
Audiotex, 61
Audit trails, management information, 251
Australia
  geographic information systems, 138
  Operational Navigational Charts project, 142
Australian Institute of Cartographers, 138
Authors, ethics, 294, 309
AUTO-CARTO, see also International Symposium on Computer-Assisted Cartography, 138, 141
AUTO-CARTO London, 1986, *164*
Automated mapping/facilities management, see AM/FM
Automatic classification, see Classification, automatic
Automatic indexing, see Indexing, automatic
Autonomy, ethical principles, 304, 305
Aydin, Carolyn E., 14, *33*, *40*
Azarov, V.A., 285, 286, 287, *288*
Azerbaijan, 285

B-trees, spatial indexing, 153
Babbage, Charles, 99
Back-end processors, information retrieval, parallel computing, 119-120
Bacon, Francis, 43, *82*
Bacteria, hazardous waste treatment, 206
Baker & Mallin databases, 203-204, 205
Baker, Brice N., *323*
Baker, Sharon L., 304, *316*

Balakrishnan, Bhaskaran, 120, *126*
Baldridge, Sheila, 191, *208*
Bandler, Jean, *87*
Bandy, John T., *214*
Banister, Michael, *84*
Bankes, Steve, 29, *33*
Banking information, Teletel system, 74
Banque des Donnees du Sous-Sol Francais, 192
Barnes, Robert F., 293, 303, 314, *317*
Barrera, Renato, 151, *166*
Barron, Iann M., 104, *122*
Barsumyan, Silva E., 303, *317*
Basch, Reva, *33*
Bates, Marcia, 183
Battberg, Robert C., 26, *34*
Bauin, S., *215*
Bawden, David, *209*
Beck, Donald M., 28, *35*
Becker, Carol A., 70, *82*
Becker, Samuel L., *35*
Becker, Theodore L., 31, *33*
Bédard, Yvan, *166*
Behavior
see also Communication behaviors; Information behaviors
management information, 230
Behling, O., *252*
Belew, Rick, 120, *122*
Belkin, Nicholas J., 309, 312, *252, 317*
Bell Atlantic telephone company, 76
Bell Canada telephone company, 76, 77, 78
Bell, S.B.M., 139, 147, *164, 165*
BellSouth telephone company, 76
Beltramini, Richard F., 300, *317*
Benbasat, Izak, *252*
Benchmarks, parallel computing, 107
Benenati, Frank E., *218*
Beniger, James R., 7, 46, *33, 82*
Benson, Charles S., 57, 60, *82*
Bentley, Jon L., 150, 151, *164, 166*
Bergmark, Donna, 115, *128*
Bernal, J.D., 272, *288*
Bernal, Nancy E., 204, *209*
Bernard, S.E., 59, *82*
Bernstein, Jodi M., 302, *317*

Berra, P. Bruce, 120, *122, 126*
Berrie, Andrew T., *225*
Biases
information services, 306
online searching, 301
risk assessment, 200
Bibliographic utilities, environmental information, 188
Bibliography, information science education, Soviet Union, 276
Bibliography of Cold Regions Science and Technology, 188
Bibliometrics
environmental communication, 179
Soviet science, 273
Bibliotekar', *288*
Bigwood, Douglas W., *214*
Bimber, Bruce, 30, *33*
Binary search trees, parallel computing, 115
Binary space partitioning (BSP) trees, spatial indexing, 152-153, 159
BINS, *see* Boreal Institute for Northern Studies
BINT, *see* U.S.S.R., BINT (Bureau of Foreign Science and Technology)
Biochemistry, bibliometrics, 179
BIODEG file, environmental fate and exposure databases, 200
BIOLOG file, environmental fate and exposure databases, 200
Biomedicine, databases, 204
BIOSIS database, 192
BIOSIS Previews, 194
Biotic Resources Research Institute, National Institutes for the Environment (proposed), 174
Birdwell, K.R., 191, *209*
Bishop, Ann P., 60, *90*
BITNET (Because It's Time Network), 23
Black, D.V., 57, *82*
Blake, Virgil L., 23, *33*
Blank, Blanche D., 59, *82*
Blaylock, G.K., *252*
Blixrud, Julia C., 293, 314, *317*
Block, E., 60, *82*
Blockstein, David E., *214*

BLS, *see* U.S., Bureau of Labor Statistics
Blue collar workers, impact of information technology, 13
Blum, Eleanor, *317*
Boehm, Barry, 46, 79, *92*
Boethling, Robert, *214*
Bommer, Michael, 294, *317*
Bonzo, Sandra E., *211*
Bookkeepers, telecommuting, 23
Books, management information, 228
Boolean queries
  geographic information systems, 145
  parallel computing, 117
Borcherding, Katrin, *260*
Boreal database, 189
Boreal Institute for Northern Studies (BINS), 189
Boredom, impact of information technology, 8
Borgman, Christine L., 178, 181, *209*, *216*
Borisova, N.V., 277, *288*
Bost, R., *212*
Bottlenecks, parallel computing, 106, 108
Boundedness, organizations, 240-241, 246
Bowker A&I Abstracts, environmental databases, 184
Boyer-Moore algorithm, 111
Boyle, A. Raymond, 147, *170*
Boynton, A.C., *252*
Bradford, S.C., 281
Bradford's law of literature scatter, 281
Brainard, Robert, 17, *34*
Brand, Stewart, 51, 52, 74, *82*
Brassel, Kurt E., 143, *164*
Braunstein, D.N., *263*
Brent, R.L., *212*
Brewer, E., 235, 236, *252*
Briggs, Faye E., 101, 107, *125*
Brimmer, Karl W., 75, *82*
British Cartographic Society, 138
Brittain, J. Michael, *252*
Broadbent, Marianne, 4, *34*
Broedling, Laurie A., *258*

Brokers, *see* Information brokers
Bronson, Roberta J., 191, 201, *209*
Brown, Eleanor Frances, 60, *82*
Brown, Lester R., *209*
Brownlow, Judith, 191, *209*
Browsing
  classification support, 197
  geographic information systems, 158
  parallel computing, 117
BRS Information Technologies, 61, 64, 199, 204, 205
Brueggeman, Peter, 186, 191, 194, 195, *209*
Bruening, John C., *209*
Brunsson, Nils, *253*
Bryant, Jennings, 8, 64, 34, *82*
BSP, *see* Binary space partitioning (BSP) trees
Buchmann, A., 139, 157, *164*
Buckley, Chris, 112, 113, 120, *128*
Budgeting
  information managers, 237
  management information, 231
Builder, Carl, 29, *33*
Building Databases for Global Science, 139
Bulletin boards, *see* Electronic bulletin boards
Bundy, M.L., *82*
Burd, Reginald, *88*
Bureau of Labor Statistics, *see* U.S., Bureau of Labor Statistics
Bureaucracy, organizational structure, 247
Burger, Robert H., 292, *317*
Burrough, P., 137, 139, *164*
Burrows, Lodema, 70, *96*
Burt, Patricia V., 248, *253*
Bush, Christopher, *218*
Bush, William R., 22, *34*
Business Ethics, 293
Buttenfield, B.P., 162, *164*

C programming language, parallel computing, 103
C-SPAN (Cable Satellite Public Affairs Network), 31

INDEX

CAA, see Clean Air Act
CAB, see National Association of Citizens' Advice Bureaux
Cable Satellite Public Affairs Network, see C-SPAN
Cable television, 29, 77
  see also Television
Caching, distributed information retrieval systems, 117
CAD, see Computer-aided design
Cadastral databases, 142
CAFS (Content-Addressable Filestore) search engine, 119
CAI, see Computer-assisted instruction
California
  Department of Health Services
    California Occupational Health Program, 209
    Toxic Substance Control Program, 201
Calkins, H.W., 171
Callahan, Daniel, 259
Campbell, Ann Morgan, 317
Campus-wide information systems (CWIS), 61, 73-74
Canada
  geographic information systems, 138
  Operational Navigational Charts project, 142
Canadian Cartographic Society, 138
Canadian Geographic Information System (CGIS), 140, 148, 157, 160
  indexing, 153
Cancer risks, environmental pollution, 177
Capurro, Rafael, 310, 311, 312, *317, 318*
Carbon dioxide, air pollution, 177
Carbon monoxide, air pollution, 198
Carbonell, Jaime, *216*
Carcinogens, risk assessment, 200-201
Career paths, 314
CARL (Colorado Alliance of Research Libraries), 71, 72
Carle, Susan D., *210*
Carmichael, J.W.S., 119, *122*

Carnevale, Mary Lu, 77, *82*
Carpignano, Paolo, 9, *34*
Carroll, Bonnie C., 206, *210*
Carroll, David M., 111, *122*
Carroll, S.J., *253*
Carstensen, Bill, 163
Cartographic generalization, 143
The Cartographic Journal, 138, *164*
Cartographica, 138, *164*
Cartography, 138, *164*
Cartography & Geographic Information Systems, 138, *164*
CAS, see Chemical Abstracts Service
Case, Donald Owen, 30, *34*, 209, 216
Case, E.R., *170*
Case Western Reserve University
  Cleveland Free-Net, 68, 74
  FreePort, campus-wide information system, 73
Casey, Genevieve M., 70, *82*
CASLST file, environmental fate and exposure databases, 200
Cassidy, S.L., 186, 202, *210*
Castells, Manuel, 28, *34*
Catalog of Teratogenic Agents, 201
Categorical imperative, 296, 305
Caudle, Sharon L., 31, *34*
CAUSE, 73
CCIS, see Computerized Clinical Information System
CD-ROM (compact disc-read only memory)
  census data, 136
  credit histories, 27
  end-user searching, 301
  environmental databases, 188, 192
  geographic information systems, 140, 142
  in-vehicle navigation systems, 160
  safety information databases, 204
  Teratogenic Information System, 202
  Toxic Release Inventory (TRI), 181
  water pollution databases, 193-195
Cebrian, Juan A., 156, *164*
CEC, see Commission for the European Communities
Cellular telephones, 78
  social impact, 7

Censorship, 316
  scientific and technical information, Soviet Union, 274-275
Census, 1990, 44
Census Bureau, *see* U.S., Bureau of the Census
Census data
  information retrieval, parallel computing, 116
  privacy, 27
Central Intelligence Agency, *see* U.S., Central Intelligence Agency
Central planning, scientific and technical information, Soviet Union, 273-274
CERCLA, *see* Comprehensive Environmental Response, Compensation, and Liability Act
CERCLA Information System (CERCLIS), 184, 189, 190
CERCLIS, *see* CERCLA Information System
Cerny, Barbara A., *216*
Cerulo, Karen A., 9, *34*
CESARS (Chemical Evaluation Search and Retrieval System), 184
CFCs, *see* Chlorofluorocarbons
CG (Computer Graphics) International, 1988, *166*
CGIS, *see* Canadian Geographic Information System
Chaincodes, geographic information systems, 146-147
Chance, decision making, 242
Chandrasekhar, N., *166*
Changing Human Environments Research Institute, National Institutes for the Environment (proposed), 174
Charan, Ram, *34*
Charities, information and referral systems, 65
Chartrand, Robert Lee, *34*
Chat services, Teletel system, 74
Chatham, Jennifer A., *260*
Chatman, Elfreda A., 12, 58, 59, *35, 83*
Chayko, Mary, *34*
CHEM-BANK database, 204, 205

CHEMFATE file, environmental fate and exposure databases, 200
Chemical Abstracts, 200
Chemical Abstracts database, 192, 194
Chemical Abstracts Service (CAS), information retrieval, parallel computing, 118
Chemical Evaluation Search and Retrieval System, *see* CESARS
Chemical Exposure database, 203, 205
Chemical Hazard Response Information System, *see* CHRIS
Chemical Information Systems, *see* CIS
Chemical marketing data, 200
Chemical spills, risk communication, 184
Chemical structures, information retrieval, parallel computing, 116
Chemistry publications, translation to Russian, 270-271
Chen, Ching-chih, 58, *83*, 253
Chen, Zi-Tan, 156, 159, *164*, 171
Cheney, Paul H., 18, *35*
Cheng, Jia-Bing, *125*
Cheremisinoff, Nicholas P., 196, *210*
Chernobyl nuclear accident, 183
Chernyi, A.I., *289*
Cherry, Colin, 45, 46, 47, 48, 50, 51, 80, *83*
Chervany, Norman L., *254*
Child care, 13
Childers, Thomas, 44, 58, 59, 70, *83*
Children
  computer use, 11
  exposure to adult situations, 6
  library services, Soviet Union, 282
China, Tiananmen Square crisis, 27
Chlorofluorocarbons (CFCs), 177, 198
Chodorow, Nancy, 304, *318*
Choo, Chun Wei, 229, 236, 248, *253*
Chow, Wing Hong, *125*
CHRIS (Chemical Hazard Response Information System), 185, 204, 205
Chrisman, Nicholas R., 139, 156, *164*, 170

INDEX   335

Christians, Clifford G., 313, *317*
Chronolog, 186
Chubin, Daryl E., 180, *210*, *217*
Church, Richard, 191, *217*
Churcher, P.R., *35*
Churchman, C.W., 250, *253*
Churgin, James, 205, *210*
CIA, *see* U.S., Central Intelligence Agency
Circuit Court, National Public Telecomputing Network, 70
CIS, *see* Commonwealth of Independent States
CIS (Chemical Information Systems), 204, 205
 environmental databases, 184, 185, 189
 IRIS (Integrated Risk Information System), 201
 TSCA Test Submission database, 199
CIS News, *210*
Citation practices, 308
Citations, Soviet scientists, 273
Cities, impact of information technology, 28
Citizens' Advice Bureaux, *see* National Association of Citizens' Advice Bureaux
Citizenship, impact of information technology, 8, 24-31
City council, community information systems, 72
City planning, geographic information systems, 159
Clark, Felicia, *87*
Clarke, K.C., 137, 139, *164*
Class conflict, impact of information technology, 6
Classification
 automatic, parallel computing, 116-117
 management problems, 242-243
 Soviet Union, 271
Classification schemes
 algal ecology, 197
 biases, 312
 environmental information, 188

Classification schemes, (cont.)
 information needs, 58
 water pollution, 196
Classified ads, Teletel system, 74
Clean Air Act (CAA), 175, 201
Clean Water Act (CWA), 175, 196, 201
Clearinghouse on Clean Lakes, 197
Clearinghouses, environmental information, 190-191, 197
Clerical workers, impact of information technology, 19-20
Cleveland, community information system, 68-71, 74
Cleveland Free-Net, 68-69, 74, *83*
Cleveland, Harlan, 25, 26, 28, 29, 50, 51, *35*, *83*, *253*
Climate Change Research Institute, National Institutes for the Environment (proposed), 174
Clinical Toxicology of Commercial Products (CTCP) database, 203, 205
Clinics, information and referral systems, 65
Clustering
 information retrieval, parallel computing, 108, 115-116, 118
 spatial indexing, 154-155
CM, *see* Connection Machine
CMC, *see* Computer-mediated communication
Coates, Joseph F., *35*
Cockshott, Paul, 109, *122*
Codes of ethics
 American Library Association, 299, 307
 American Society for Information Science, 291, 314-316
Cognitive maps, information needs, 58, 65
Cognitive perspective, ethics, 311-312
Cognitive science, management information, 230
Cognitive styles, 305
 impact of information technology, 8, 11
Cohen, Michael D., 241, 246, *253*

Cohen, Paul R., 120, *122*
COLD (Cold Regions Science and Technology) database, 188
Cold War, and Soviet science, 272
Collection development policies, 303
Collins English Dictionary, information retrieval, parallel computing, 114
Collins, H.M., *35*
Collins, J.F., *123, 126*
Colorado Alliance of Research Libraries, *see* CARL
Colorado Springs, community information system, 70-71
Combustion, hazardous waste treatment, 206
COMECON (Council for Mutual Economic Assistance), information science education, 276, 278
Command-mode interfaces, Aquatic Sciences & Fisheries Abstracts, 194
Commission for the European Communities (CEC), 5, 199
 environmental information sources, 188
Committee for the National Institutes for the Environment (proposed), 173
Commonwealth of Independent States (CIS), 282
Communication, managers, 235
Communication behaviors
 see also Behavior; Information behaviors
 management information, 229, 230
Communication Conference, 1992, *86*
Communication patterns, hospitals, 14
Communication theory, information science education, Soviet Union, 281
Communications Act, 1934, 63, 76
Communications age, 46
Communications research, 8
Communist Party, Soviet Union, 268
Community, impact of information technology, 11-13
Community education, information and referral systems, 66

Community events, information services, 66
Community information systems, 70-73
Community Memory messaging system, 68
Community profile, online searching, 181
Community right to know, environmental hazards, 173, 180-181, 190
Community standards, ethics, 296, 298
Compact disc-read only memory, *see* CD-ROM
Compaine, Benjamin, *253*
COMPENDEX database, 192
Competence, information professionals, 300-301
Competitive advantage, information technology, 4
Competitor information, 300
Completeness, information services, 310-311
Complexity, information seeking, 246
Complexity analysis, parallel computing, 107
Comprehensive Environmental Response, Compensation, and Liability Act (CERCLA), 173, 175, 189, 201
CompuServe, 61, 64, 75
Computer architectures, 99, 100
 parallel processing, 104, 105
 taxonomy, 102
Computer competence, ethnic differences, 56
Computer crime, 314
Computer Ethics, 293
Computer graphics
 see also Graphics
 geographic information system applications, 162
Computer industry, 51
Computer Professionals for Social Responsibility (CPSR), 293
Computer use, cognitive effects, 11
Computer-aided design (CAD), geographic information systems, 136

Computer-assisted instruction (CAI), 11
Computer-mediated communication (CMC), 4, 15-16
  see also Electronic mail
Computerized Clinical Information System (CCIS), 202
Computers
  see also Information technology
  and schools, 56
  information science education, Soviet Union, 282, 283
  manufacturing, 21
Computers and Society, 293, *318*
Computers and the Quality of Life Conference, 1990, *86*, *321*
Conference on Medical Informatics (MEDINFO), 1986, *212*
Confidentiality, 293, 300, 302, 310, 314, 315
Congressional Memory Project, National Public Telecomputing Network, 69
Congressional Research Service, *see* Library of Congress, Congressional Research Service
Conhaim, Wallys W., 74, 75, 77, 78, *83*
Connection Machine (CM), 100, 102, 103, 105, 108, 112, 113, 114, 117, 120
  see also Massively parallel processors
Connolly, John, *124*
Connolly, Terry, *253*
Consequentialism, 291-292, 307
Constraints, decision making, 240
Consumer marketing, Prodigy videotex service, 75
Consumer Product Safety Act (CPSA), 175
Consumer-based information systems, 61, 68-79
Consumers, information needs, 58, 59, 68
Content-Addressable Filestore, *see* CAFS
Context, management information, 230
Contextuality, ethics, 305

Continuing education, information professionals, 301, 303
Contour maps, geographic information systems, 157
Cook, Annabel Kirschner, 28, *35*
Cooke, Anne, *318*
Coordinating, information managers, 237
Coppock, J.T., 140, *165*
Copyright, ethics, 297, 314
Cordero, J.F., *212*
Cornell University, 200
Cornfield, Daniel B., 13, *35*
Corporate public records, 27
Corridor selection, geographic information systems, 145
Cosmopolitans, ethics, 299
Costello, Joseph G., *215*
Costs
  information and referral systems, 65
  parallel computing, 106
  information retrieval, 108, 117
Cotter, C.A., *210*
Cotton, J.L., *253*
Coulson, A.F.W., 111, *123*, *126*
Council, Carolyn D., *130*
Council for Mutual Economic Assistance, *see* COMECON
Counseling, information and referral systems, 65, 66
Courtial, J.-P., *215*
Covello, Vincent T., 179, 183, *210*
Cowen, David J., 136, *165*
Coyne, Joseph G., 177, *210*
CPSA, *see* Consumer Product Safety Act
CPSR, *see* Computer Professionals for Social Responsibility
CPSR Newsletter (Computer Professionals for Social Responsibility), 293, *318*
Craig, J. Pat, *323*
Craig, R., *253*
Crane, Diana, 180, *210*
Cravens, D.W., *253*
Crawford, Helen, *318*
CRAY Y-MP supercomputer, 102
CRAY-1 supercomputer, 111

Credentials, information professionals, 303
Credit cards, and privacy, 25-26
Cringean, Janey K., 104, 111, 113, *123*
Crisis intervention, information and referral systems, 65
Crisman, Jenny S., *214*
Criteria, decision making, 240
Criticism, ethics, 295
Croft, W. Bruce, 120, *123*
Cronin, Blaise, 18, *35*
Crosbie, Erin, *214*
Crowe, Lawson, 307, *318*
Crowley, Terrence, 59, *83*
CRS, *see* Library of Congress, Congressional Research Service
CTCP, *see* Clinical Toxicology of Commercial Products
Cuadra/Elsevier, 186, *211*
Cuba, scientific periodicals, 279
Cultural biases, risk communication, 183
Cultural lag, information age, 46
Culture
  impact of information technology, 5-7
  management information, 245, 251
Cunningham, J. Barton, 20, 21, *35*
Curcuru, E.H., *253*
Curnutt, Gerald L., 204, *211*
Curnutt, Kirk L., 204, *211*
Current Contents, 200
Current Population Surveys, 28, 53
Curricula
  information science education, Soviet Union, 276, 278
  library science, Soviet Union, 280-281
Customer service, impact of information technology, 20
CWA, *see* Clean Water Act
CWIS, *see* Campus-wide information systems
CWIS-L (Campus-Wide Information Systems Listserv), 74
Cybercasting, National Public Telecomputing Network, 69
Cybernetics, Soviet Union, 269

Cyberpunk, 10
Cyert, Richard M., 243, *254*

Daft, Richard L., 230, 243, 246, *254, 257, 258*
Dagestan, 285
Dahl, Robert A., 48, 49, 50, *83*
Dale, P.F., 139, *165*
Dangermond, Jack, 144, 148, 160, *165*
Daniels, P.J., *254*
Daniels, R.C., 191, *209*
Danko, David M., 142, 147, 158, *165*
Danzig, Peter B., 118, *123*
Danziger, James N., 13, 19, 21, 46, *38, 84*
DAP, *see* Distributed Array Processor
DART (Developmental and Reproductive Technology) database, 184, 201
Data analysis, management information, 231
Data collection, geographic information systems, 161
Data compression, parallel computing, 114
Data dependencies, parallel computing, 105
Data entry, geographic information systems, 147-150
Data representation, geographic information systems, 135-163
Data security, 314
Data structures
  geographic information systems, 191
  parallel computing, 104
Data Vault, Connection Machine, 103
Database and Expert System Applications International Conference (DEXA), 1990, *122*
Database construction, Soviet Union, 283
Database machines (DBM), 100, 119
Database management systems (DBMS), and spatial indexing, 150
Database producers
  ethics, 294, 297, 310, 313

INDEX

Database producers, (cont.)
  liability, 303
Database vendors
  ethics, 294, 297
  information democracy, 61, 64
  safety databases, 204-205
  water pollution files, 192
Databases
  air pollution, 198
  biases, 312
  environmental studies, 184-206
  full text, 117, 192
    legislative information, 31
    occupational safety and health, 204
  indexing, parallel computing, 109, 113, 114
  management information, 251
  overlap, 192
  parallel computing, evaluation, 107
  quality, 311, 314
  spatial, 157-159
  taxonomy, 187, 193
DATALOG file, environmental fate and exposure databases, 200
Dating services, 9-10
Davenport, Elisabeth, 18, *35*
Davidson, William H., 75, *87*
Davis, Donald L., 244, 254
Davis, J.R., 161, *165*
Davis, Watson, 272
DBM, *see* Database machines
DBMS, *see* Database management systems
DCW, *see* Digital Chart of the World
DDC, *see* Dewey Decimal Classification
DDT (dichlorodiphenyltrichloroethane), risk assessment, 200
De Floriani, Leila, 156, *165*
De George, Richard T., 293, *318*
De Lury, N.A., 70, *84*
De Mes, W.W., 191, 192, *211, 217*
De Santis, Maggie, 66, 70, *89*
De-skilling, labor force, 17-18
Dead reckoning, in-vehicle navigation, 160-161
Deahl, Thomas F., 60, *84*

Debons, Anthony, 293
DEC (Digital Equipment Corp.) workstations, 118
Decegama, Angel L., 99, *123*
Decision making, 230, 231, 235
  definition, 239
  democracies, 48
  geographic information system users, 161
  impact of information technology, 14, 16-17
  information managers, 238-242
  models, 294
  risk assessment, 201
Decision support systems (DSS), 229, 240-241, 242
Decisional roles, managers, 237
Deck, Kathryn S., *211*
Deforestation, air pollution, 198
Delacy, Justine, 9, *35*
Delfavero, Steven, *218*
DEM, *see* Digital elevation model
Deming, Caren J., *35*
Democracy
  and wealth, 44
  decision making, 48
  impact of information technology, 19, 28-31, 32
  information resources, 48-52
Demographics, impact of information technology, 8-9, 12, 28
Demography, bibliometrics, 179
Denver, information gateway, 77, 78
Denzin, N.K., 59, *94*
Deontological ethics, 291, 307
Department of Education, *see* U.S., Department of Education
Department of Energy, *see* U.S., Department of Energy
Department of Housing and Urban Development, *see* U.S., Department of Housing and Urban Development
Department of the Interior, *see* U.S., Department of the Interior
Department of Transportation, *see* U.S., Department of Transportation
Dera, V.G., *288*

DERMAL (Dermal Absorption) database, 184
Dervin, Brenda, 50, 58, 59, 66, 180, 181, 230, 231, 234, 248, *84, 211, 254*
Deschamps, Judith, 188, *211*
Descriptors, compared with subject headings, 196-197
Desegregation, ethics, 296
Deshpande, Rohit, *35*
Detergents, safety, 203
Detroit Public Library, The Information Place (TIP), 66, 70
Developing countries, information access, 311-312, 313
Developmental and Reproductive Technology database, *see* DART
Dewdney, P., 249, *254*
Dewey Decimal Classification (DDC), ecology, 197
Dewhirst, H.D., *254*
Di-graphs, spatial indexing, 151-152
Dialectical materialism, and science policy, 268-269
Dialectics, ethics, 308
DIALOG Information Services, 61, 64, 178, 186, 199, 204, 205
 environmental databases, 184
 pesticides databases, 203
 safety databases, 203
Diaz, B.M., 139, *164, 165*
Dickinson, Timothy, *38*
Dickson, Gary W., *254*
Diesing, Paul, 246, *254*
Difazio, William, *34*
Differentiating norms, distribution of wealth, 54-56
Digital Chart of the World (DCW), 142, 158
Digital elevation model (DEM), geographic information systems, 156-157
Digital Equipment Corp., *see* DEC
Digital line graph (DLG), geographic information systems, 140
Digital terrain model (DTM), geographic information systems, 155-157
Dill, William R., 248, *254*

Dillman, Don A., 28, 56, *35, 84*
DIME (Dual Independent Map Encoding), *see* GBF/DIME
Directed acyclic graphs, *see* Di-graphs
Directories, Environmental Protection Agency, 187
Directory of Information Resources Related to Health, Exposure, and Risk Assessment of Air Toxics, 187
Directory of OAQPS Information Services, 198
Disaster Research Center, 183, *211*
Disconfirming information, managers, 245
Discourse analysis, information science, 312
Disseminator role, managers, 237
Dissertations, information science, Soviet Union, 279
Distance education, Soviet Union, 277
Distributed Array Processor (DAP), 100, 102, 103, 108, 111, 114, 116, 117, 121
Distributed processing, parallel computing, 101-102
Disturbance handler role, managers, 237
Dittmar, P.G., 118, *123*
Diversity, management information, 237
Divorce rates, impact of information technology, 9
DNA structure, Human Genome Project, 12
Dobrov, G.M., 272, 273, *288*
Doctor, Ronald D., 30, 50, 52, 56, 60, 62, 63, 79, *35, 84*
Doctoral studies, information science, Soviet Union, 274, 277
Doctors
 ethics, 299
 malpractice, 303
 telecommuting, 23
Document ranking, parallel computing, 113

INDEX 341

Documentation, Soviet Union, 270-271
DOD, see U.S., Department of Defense
DOE, see U.S., Department of Energy
Doerschler, Jeffrey S., 161, *165*
DOI, see U.S., Department of the Interior
Doktor, Robert H., *255*
Dominy, G.R., 28, *37*
Donohue, George A., 8, 60, *36, 94*
Donohue, Joseph C., 58, 60, 64, 65, *84, 87*
Dooley v. Everett, 302, *318*
Dordick, Herbert S., 64, *84*
Dorr, Aimee, 11, *36*
Dorris, Virginia Kent, 190, 206, *211*
Dosa, Marta L., 313, *318*
Doszkocs, Tamas E., 120, *124*
Doty, Philip, *90*
Douglas, David H., 143, *165*
Dow Jones News/Retrieval Service, DowQuest, 117
Dowlin, Kenneth E., 71, 313, *84, 318*
Downloading
  Aquatic Sciences & Fisheries Abstracts, 194
  ethics, 314
Downs, Anthony, *255*
Downs, Geoffrey M., *127*
DowQuest information retrieval system, 117
Doyle, Frederick J., 139, 156, 157, *165*
Drabek, Thomas E., 184, *211*
Drabenstott, Jon, *318*
Dragich, Martha J., 303, *318*
Dreyfus, S.E., *255*
Drinking water, pollution, 177-178
Drinking Water Docket, 197
Drucker, Peter F., 13, 17, 19, 24, 234, 235, 238, 239, 247, *36, 255*
Drug testing, and privacy, 26
Drugs
  risk assessment, 201-202
  safety, 203
DSS, see Decision support systems
DTM, see Digital terrain model
Dual submissions, 309

Dumais, Susan, *38*
Dun & Bradstreet, Business Information Report database, 303
Dun and Bradstreet, Inc. v. Greenmoss Builders, 303, *319*
Duncan, George T., 26, *35*
Durrance, Joan C., 60, *85, 319*
Dutton, Geoffrey, 156, 159, *165*
Dutton, William H., 46, 56, 72, *85, 86*
Duvall, Lorraine M., *259*
Dyes, safety, 203
Dynamics, management information, 248-249

Early adopters, information technology, 11
Early, Steven, *36*
Earth Observing System (EOS), 136, 157
Earth Science Data Directory (ESDD), 206
Earth Sciences Disc (CD-ROM), 206
Earthquake safety, community information systems, 72
Earthquakes, risk communication, 183
East-West Conference on Scientific, Technical and Online Information, 1989, 276
Eastern Lake Survey, 198
Eastern Transportation Co. v. Northern Barge Corp. et al., 302, *319*
Eastman, C.M., 115, *124*
Eaton, Nancy L., *214*
Ebner, H., 156, *165*
ECDIN search system, 188
Eckel, N.I., *252*
Ecology
  bibliometrics, 179
  environmental pollution, 177
  ethics, 296
EcoNet computer network, 68
Economic development, ethics, 296, 311-312, 314
Economic planning, scientific and technical information, Soviet Union, 274

Economics
  democracy, 49-50
  environmental studies, 180
  ethics, 298, 308
  information, 51, 311-312, 314
  information technology, 5, 6, 12
  social equity, 52-57
Ecosystem Protection and Management Research Institute, National Institutes for the Environment (proposed), 174
Edelman, Hendrik, 71, *85*
Edge matching, geographic information systems, 145
Editing, scientific and technical information, Soviet Union, 276
Editors, ethics, 309
Education
  acceptance of social change, 6
  impact of information technology, 8
  information and referral systems, 65
  information needs, 58, 59, 66
  information professionals, Soviet Union, 267-287
  information science educators, Soviet Union, 284-285
  labor force, 13
  National Public Telecomputing Network, 69
Educational Testing Service (ETS), 56
Educational codes of ethics, 315
Edwards, Geoffrey, *166*
Edwards, Janet, *124*
Efficiency
  government officials, 31
  parallel computing, 106
Egalitarian distribution of wealth, 54-56
Egenhofer, Max J., 137, 161, 163, *165*
Ehlers, Manfred, 148, *166*
Eich, M.H., *125*
EINECS, *see* European Inventory of Existing Chemical Substances
Einhorn, H.J., 243, *255*
Einstein, Albert, 270

EIS, *see* Executive information systems
Eisenberg, Michael, *261*
Elderly, use of information technology, 12
Electrical engineering, Soviet Union, 280
Electronic bulletin boards, 4, 11, 15
  community information systems, 71
  environmental information, 190
Electronic city, Free-Nets, 69
Electronic cottage, 21-22
Electronic discussion groups, ethics, 293
Electronic immigrants, 23
Electronic mail, 4, 7, 11, 14-16, 27
  see also Computer-mediated communication
  community information systems, 72
  National Public Telecomputing Network, 69
  Prodigy videotex, 75
Electronic publishing, 309-310
  gateway information systems, 77
Electronic texts, 7
Electronic Yellow Pages, 77, 78
Elevation data representations, geographic information systems, 155-157
Elimination by aspect, decision making, 240
Ellul, Jacques, 313, *319*
Elnicki, Richard A., 244, *254*
Emergency assistance, information needs, 66
Emergency medicine, databases, 202
Emergency planning, geographic information systems, 159
Emergindex database, 202
Emission Measurement Technical Information Center (EMTIC), 198
Employment, information needs, 58, 59, 66, 68
Emrath, Perry A., *125*
EMTIC, *see* Emission Measurement Technical Information Center

INDEX 343

End users, 311
  education, Soviet Union, 277
  ethics, 294
End-user searching, 181, 193, 301
  environmental databases, 181, 192
Endangered Species Act (ESA), 175
Engineer-information specialist,
  Soviet Union, 271
Engineers, telecommuting, 23
England, Roger, *123*
English language, scientific and
  technical information, 281
ENIAC (Electronic Numerical
  Integrator and Calculator), 99
ENREP database, 192
Entertainment, impact of information
  technology, 8, 11, 13
Entrepreneur role, managers, 237
Environment, ethics, 294, 296-297
Environmental chemistry, databases,
  193
Environmental communication, 178-
  184
Environmental fate and exposure
  databases, 200
Environmental Protection Agency,
  see U.S., Environmental Protection
  Agency
Environmental research, information
  sources, 173-208
Environmental scanning, management
  information, 229, 251
Environmental Science & Technology,
  211
Environmental Systems Research
  Institute (ESRI), 141, 142
EOS, *see* Earth Observing System
EPA, *see* U.S., Environmental
  Protection Agency
EPA Journal, 212
EPA Publications Bibliography, 187
Epstein, Earl F., 163, *166*
Epstein, Susan Baerg, *319*
Equal employment opportunities,
  296-297
Equality, and justice, 55
Equality of opportunity, 316

Equifax credit reporting bureau, 25,
  27
Ercegovac, Zorana, 182
ERIS, 139
Ermann, M. David, 293, *319*
Errors, geographic information
  systems, 163
ESA, *see* Endangered Species Act
ESDD, *see* Earth Science Data
  Directory
Esperanto, 281
ESRI, *see* Environmental Systems
  Research Institute
Estabrook, Leigh, 71, *85*
Estes, J., 136, 137, 139, *171*
ETAK navigation system, 160-161
Ethical Challenges in Librarianship, 292
*Ethical Conflicts in Information and
  Computer Science, Technology and
  Business*, 293
Ethics
  information professionals, 291-317
  information science education,
    Soviet Union, 285, 287
  online searching, 306
  principles, 304-308
Ethics and the Librarian, 292
ETIBACK (Environmental Teratology
  Information Center Backfile), 201
ETS, *see* Educational Testing Service
Etzioni, A., 230, 241, *255*
Euro-Barometers, 5
Europe
  geographic information systems,
    138
  labor force, 17
European Directory of Agrochemical
  Products database, 203
European Inventory of Existing
  Chemical Substances (EINECS),
  204
European Value System Study
  Group, 5
Evans, Fred, 19, *36*
Everett, John H., 303, *319*
EXCELL (Extendible Cell), spatial
  indexing, 155

Excerpta Medica database, 202
Executive information systems (EIS), 229
Executive officers, ethics, 295
Experimental Mass Information Utilities, 79
Expert systems
  aquaculture, 195
  community information, 11
  management information, 229
  pesticides, 203
Extendible Cell, *see* EXCELL
Ezrahi, Yaron, 31, *36*

Facsimile transmission, social impact, 4, 7, 14, 27
Fairness, 304, 305-306
Faloutsos, Christos, *124*, *170*
Falsification of data, 309
Families, information needs, 58, 66, 68
Family, impact of information technology, 9
FAO, *see* U.N., Food and Agriculture Organization
Farm policy, impact of information technology, 24
Farmer, N.A., *123*
Farquharson, John, *35*
Fast Input Output facility, parallel computing, 111
FATE/EXPOS file, environmental fate and exposure databases, 200
Fax, *see* Facsimile transmission
FCC, *see* Federal Communications Commission
FDCA, *see* Federal Drug and Cosmetics Act
Fear of change, information technology, 20-21
Federal Communications Commission (FCC), 76
Federal Drug and Cosmetics Act (FDCA), 175
Federal Emergency Management Agency, *see* U.S., Federal Emergency Management Agency
Federal Environmental Pesticide Control Act (FEPCLA), 175

Federal funding, information delivery, 60
Federal Hazardous Substances Labeling Act (FHSLA), 175
Federal Insecticide, Fungicide, and Rodenticide Act (FIFRA), 175, 199, 201
Federal Register, 176
Federal Register database, 204
Federal Register Search System (FRSS), 203, 205
Federal Technology Transfer Act, 173
Fees
  gateway services, 78
  NREN access, 63
Fees for services, ethics, 297, 307, 314
Feiner, Steven K., *166*
Fejes, Fred, 313, *323*
Fekete, György, 159, *166*
Feldman, Martha S., 246, *255*
FEMA, *see* U.S., Federal Emergency Management Agency
Feminist ethics, 304-305
Feng, T.Y., 102, *124*
Fenwick, Wendy Stern, *212*
FEPCLA, *see* Federal Environmental Pesticide Control Act
Ference, T.P., *255*
FHSLA, *see* Federal Hazardous Substances Labeling Act
Fiduciary responsibility, information professionals, 316
Field trees, spatial indexing, 151-152
FIFRA, *see* Federal Insecticide, Fungicide, and Rodenticide Act
Figurehead role, managers, 237
Financial news
  Prodigy videotex, 75
  Teletel system, 74
Finholt, Tom, 16, *36*
Finite-state computers, parallel computing, 119
Finkel, R.A., 150, *166*
Fire safety, community information systems, 72
Fires, risk communication, 183
Fisanick, W., *123*
Fisher, Janice, *93*
Fishman, Diane L., 202, *212*

Fitzgerald, Cathy M., 191, 193, *215*
Flaherty, David H., 25, *36*
Flatt, Horace P., 106, 107, *125*
Fleischer, M., *255*
Fletcher, John S., *218*
Fletcher, Patricia T., 231, 243, 249, *255*, *260*
Flexibility, organizational structure, 247
Floating point operations per second, *see* FLOPS
FLOPS (floating point operations per second), parallel computing, 107
Flynn, Michael J., 102, *124*
FOIA, *see* Freedom of Information Act
Foley, James D., 149, *166*
Foley, Timothy J., 73, *85*
Follow-up, information and referral systems, 66
Fomin, A.G., 271
Food additives, safety, 203
Food and Agriculture Organization, *see* U.N., Food and Agriculture Organization
Forecasting, managers, 244
Forest science, bibliometrics, 179
Forester, John, 240, 246, 250, *255*
Forester, Tom, 21, *36*
Forsman, Carolyn, 60, 65, *85*
Fortescue, Stephen, 274, *288*
FORTRAN PLUS programming language, parallel computing, 103
FORTRAN programming language, parallel computing, 103
Fortuna, Richard C., *212*
Fortune 500 companies, computer-mediated communication, 15-16
Foskett, D.J., *319*
Fossier, Marc, 74, 75, *85*
Fossil fuels, air pollution, 198
Fox, Isaac, 177, *216*
FPS 190-L computer, 115
Fraley, Ruth, 292, *321*
France
 geographic information systems, 138
 privacy protection, 25
France Telcom, 73, 74, 75, *85*

France Telcom, (cont.)
 Teletel System, 74-75
Frank, Andrew U., 151, 161, *165*, *166*
Frank, Robyn, 177, *212*
Frankel, Mark, 315, *319*
Franklin, William Randolph, 149, 154, *166*
Fraser, Benson, 58, *84*
Free market, *see* Market economics
Free-Nets, 68-69
Freedom of information, 314
Freedom of Information Act (FOIA), 199
Freedom to Lie: A Debate about Democracy, 293
Freeman, Herbert, 146, 161, *165*, *166*
Freeman, Robert R., 176, 180, 186, 191, 195, *212*
Frenkel, Karen A., 12, *36*
Frick, William G., *212*
Frieder, Ophir, 116, 118, *122*, *124*
Friedman, J.M., 201, *212*
Friedman, Jonathan, *38*
Froehlich, Thomas J., 294, 296, 298, 304, 312, 313, *319*
Frohmann, Bernd, 311, *320*
FRSS, *see* Federal Register Search System
Fugitive literature, acid rain, 186, 199
Fulk, Janet, 14, *41*
Full text databases, *see* Databases, full text
Fullgate, Kym, 17, *34*
Funding
 community information systems, 71
 information delivery, 60
 research, 308
Fungi, hazardous waste treatment, 206
Funkhouser, G. Ray, 8, *36*
Furlong, Mary S., 12, *36*
Futurists, 3

Gabriel, Michael, *84*
Gahegan, Mark N., 155, *166*
Gaines, Matthew J., 199, *212*
Galczynska, T., 188, *213*
Galkin, Florence, *87*

Games, Teletel system, 74
Gandhi, Mohandas Karamchand, 311
Gandy, Oscar H., Jr., 26, 51, *36*, *85*
GAO, *see* U.S., General Accounting Office
Garbage can models, decision making, 241-242
Gardening, expert systems, 11
Gargantini, Irene, 153, *167*
Garrett, Marie, 293, *320*
Garson, Barbara, 19, 20, *36*
Garvey, William D., 180, *213*
Gastrointestinal Absorption Database (GIABS), 184
Gateways, technology and society, 47
GBF/DIME (Geographic Base File/Dual Independent Map Encoding), 140, 141, 145
GDSS, *see* Group Decision Support Systems
Gee, Chai Sung, *214*
GENE-TOX database, 184, 201
General Accounting Office, *see* U.S., General Accounting Office
Generalization, geographic information systems, 143, 159
Genetic algorithms, parallel computing, 109, 116
Genie information service, 64
Genium Publishing Corp., 204, 205
Geo Info Systems, 138, *167*
Geo-Processing, 138, *167*
Geocoding, 142
Geographic dispersion, impact of information technology, 21-24, 27-28
Geographic information systems (GIS)
  accuracy, 163
  applications, 135-136
  data representations, 135-163
  definitions, 135-137
  Earth Science Data Directory, 206
  environmental information, 191
  terminology, 142-143
  textbooks, 137, 139
Geographic Information Systems/Land Information Systems (GIS/LIS), 139

Geological Survey, *see* U.S., Geological Survey
GEOREF database, 192
Gerbner, George, *93*
Gergen, Kenneth J., 6, 7, 9, *36*
Germany
  geographic information systems, 138
  in-vehicle navigation research, 160
  privacy protection, 25
Gerrity, L.W., *212*
GESCAN 2, 119
GIABS, *see* Gastrointestinal Absorption Database
Gibson, L., 150, *167*
Gilder, George, 100, 102, 103, *124*
Giliarevskii, R.S., 267, 280-281, *288*, *289*
Gillen, D.J., *253*
Gillespie, Andrew, *37*
Gilligan, Carol, 304, *320*
Gilmore, Thomas, 247, *256*
Gioia, Dennis A., 246, *262*
GIS, *see* Geographic information systems
GIS World, 138, *167*
GIS/LIS, *see* Geographic Information Systems/Land Information Systems
Glasnost, impact on information science education, 282-286
Glazier, J., 235, *256*
Glendale, Calif., community information system, 72
Glenn, Ann C., *321*
Globachev, O.I., 279
Global environment, 174, 177, 180, 184, 191, 198, 207
Global movement of workers, 13
Global Positioning System (GPS), 160
Global projections, geographic information systems, 159-160
Goals
  management information, 239
  managers, 236, 238, 245
Gochfield, Michael, *218*
Goehner, Donna M., *320*
Goins, Rodney K., *214*
Golding, Peter, *39*

INDEX

Goldman, Alvin L., *85*
Goldstein, Morris, 23
Gomez, Michael J., 188, *213*
Goodchild, Michael F., 139, 158, 159, *167*, *168*
Goodman, S.E., 27, *37*
Goodyear Aerospace Corporation, Massively Parallel Processor (MPP), 102
Gopal, Sucharita, 139, *167*
Gorbachev, Mikhail S., 268, 282
Gordon, Judy A., *213*
Gorry, G.A., 236, *256*
Gossip, information needs, 65
Gould, Michael D., 161, *168*
Government, impact of information technology, 28-31
Government agencies, pollution prevention, 185
Government Institutes, Inc., *213*
Government officials, National Public Telecomputing Network, 70
Government planning, geographic information systems, 135, 136
Government Printing Office, *see* U.S., Government Printing Office
Government publications, acid rain, 198-199
Governmental control, scientific and technical information, Soviet Union, 275
GPO, *see* U.S., Government Printing Office
GPS, *see* Global Positioning System
Graham, Loren S., 268, 269, 286, *288*
Graham, S.D.N., 28, *37*
Grant, I.W., *165*
Granularity, parallel computing, 105, 106
Graphics
see also Computer graphics
geographic information systems, 160
Gratto, Clarence, *317*
Gravander, Jerry, *317*
Gray, Anthony D., *214*
Gray, John A., *320*

Great Lakes-St. Lawrence Winter Navigation Program, 192
Greenawalt, Kent, *87*
Greenberg, Michael R., *218*
Greenberger, Martin, 12, *37*
Greene, Harold, 76, 77
Greenhouse effect, *see* Global environment
Greenmoss Builders, 303
Gremmels, Gillian S., *320*
Grey literature, *see* Fugitive literature
Grids, spatial indexing, 154-155
Grievances, codes of ethics, 315
Groen, Frances, *320*
Grosser, Kerry, 229, 230, *213*, *256*
Grossman, Lawrence, *87*
Grothe, Roger, 21, *38*
Ground Water Network, 197
Groundwater
pesticides, 203
pollution prevention, 185
Group decision making, 229
Group Decision Support Systems (GDSS), 14, 16-17
Group work, impact of information technology, 16-17
Grover, Robert, 235, *251*, *256*
Grundner, Thomas M., 68, 69, *85*
Gudauskas, R.Iu., 284, 285, 287, *288*
Guevara, J. Armando, *168*
Guilfoyle, Peter S., 126
Günther, Oliver, 139, 157, *164*, *167*
Gustafson, John L., 107, *124*
Guthrie, K. Kendall, 70, 72, *86*
Gutierrez, Claudio, *319*
Guttman, A., 151, *167*
Guzewich, David C., *214*
Gvozdev, Iu.A., 283, *288*

Haas, Stephanie, 185, 191, 193, *213*
Hackers (computer users), 10
Haefner, Katie, 10, *37*
Haines, R.C., *123*
Hale, David P., *35*
Hale, Martha Larson, 235, *256*
Hales, Colin P., *256*
Hall, Edward P., *84*
Hall, Homer, 293

Hall, P.D., *263*
Hallman, Judy, 73, *86*
Halpin, Peter, *213*
Hamilton, William F., *255*
Hand, Learned, 302
Handler, Wolfgang, 102, *124*
HandsNet citizens' network, 68
Haneman, Deborah T., 186, 191, 195, *212*
Hanfman, Deborah, *213*
Hanson, J.W., *212*
Hanton, Fabienne, *218*
Hardware, parallel computing, 118-120
Hardwicke, James J., 114, *124*
Harm, ethical principles, 304-305
Harrington, James, 186, 191, 195, *213*
Harris, Cynthia, 191, *213*
Harris, John, *86*
Harris, Louis, 25
Harter, Stephen P., 309, *323*
Hartley, R.J., 11, *37*
Hartwick, Jon, 18, *39*
Haruyama, Akemi, 188, *213*
Harvard Business Review, 227
Harvard Laboratory for Computer Graphics, 141
Hashing
  parallel computing, 114
  spatial indexing, 154
Haskin, Roger L., *125*
Hathi-2 computer, 113
Hattis, Dale, 200, *214*
Hauptman, Robert, 292, 293, *320, 324*
Hawaii, 72, *86*
Hawaii FYI information system, 72-73
Hawaii, Inc., 72, *86*
Hawaii Information Network Corp., 72
Hawaii Telecommunications and Information Industries Act, 1988, 72
Haynes, Karen S., 66, *88*
Haywood, Trevor, 313, *320*
Hazard Communication Standard Act (HCSA), 175

Hazardline database, 203, 205
Hazardous Chemicals Information and Disposal, *see* HAZINF
Hazardous materials, definition, 176
Hazardous Materials Information Exchange (HMIX), 190
Hazardous Materials Transportation Act (HMTA), 175
Hazardous Substances Data Bank (HSDB), 204, 205
Hazardous waste, 173, 178
  databases, 206
  information sources, 189
  remediation, 200
HAZINF (Hazardous Chemicals Information and Disposal) database, 185, 203
HB, *see* Holey-brick (HB) trees
HCI, *see* Human-computer interaction
HCSA, *see* Hazard Communication Standard Act
Healey, J.H., *253*
Healey, R.G., 137, 138, 153, *167, 172*
Health, information needs, 58, 59, 66
Health Advisories, Environmental Protection Agency, 201
Health care
  see also Medicine
  ethics, 296
  information technology, 12
Health risks
  environmental pollution, 177
  toxic substances, 200
Health sciences, information malpractice, 302-303
Hedges, online searching, 204
Held, Virginia, 305, *320*
Heller, M., 157, *172*
Heller, Stephen R., 186, 203, *214*
Hellriegel, D., *256*
Henderson, John G., *256*
Hennessey, Harry W., *258*
Hernon, Peter, *253*
Hernstein, R.J., *256*
Herring, John R., 141, 154, *167*
Hert, Carol A., 234, *256*

INDEX 349

Hess, Karl, 60, *86*
Heuristics, decision making, 245
Hewins, Elizabeth T., 230, *256*
Hewison, Nancy S., *323*
Heydebrand, Wolf V., *37*
Hickson, David J., 230, *256*, *261*
Hidden surface removal, geographic information systems, 162
Hierarchical agglomerative methods, parallel computing, 115
Hierarchical decomposition, spatial indexing, 150
Hierarchy, organizational structure, 247
High Performance Computing Act, 1991, 62
High-performance computing, *see* Supercomputers
Highway construction, geographic information systems, 157
Highway metaphor, NREN, 62-63
Hill, C., *126*
Hill shading, geographic information systems, 157
Hillis, W.D., 106, *124*
Hillstrom, Kevin, *215*
Hiltz, S.R., 59, *86*
Himmelfarb, Gertrude, 64, *86*
Hingston, Philip, 120, *129*
Hinings, C.R., *261*
Hinterberger, H., *169*
Hiring, management information, 231
Hirschhorn, Larry, 247, *256*
Historical data, geographic information systems, 160
Hjortdal, Helge, 31, *37*
HMIX, *see* Hazardous Materials Information Exchange
HMTA, *see* Hazardous Materials Transportation Act
Hochschild, Jennifer L., 44, 53, 54, 55, 57, 72, *86*
Hockney, R.W., 99, 102, *124*
Hogarth, Robin M., 243, 244, *255*, *256*
Hoge, Rose Mary, 291
Holey-brick (HB) trees, spatial indexing, 152

Hollaar, Lee A., 100, 118, 119, 121, *124*, *125*
Holroyd, F., *164*
Holt, Glen E., 70, 71, *87*
Home life, impact of information technology, 10-11
Horspool, R.N., 111
Horton, Forest Woody, Jr., 314, *320*
Hosoyama, Miki, 188, *213*
Hospital information systems, 14
Hospitals, malpractice, 303
Hotlines, information and referral systems, 65
Houk, Judith, *321*
House, Robert J., 230, *256*
House, Steven R., 111, *125*
Housel, Thomas J., 75, *87*
Housing, information needs, 58, 66, 68
Howard, Karen P., *214*, *218*
Howard, Philip H., 186, 200, *214*, *218*
Howe, Henry F., 173, *214*
Hsaio, David K., 100, *125*
HSDB, *see* Hazardous Substances Data Bank
Huang, Chingsan, *214*
Hubbell, Stephen P., *214*
Huber, George P., 227, 230, 239, 240, 241, 242, 244, *257*
HUD, *see* U.S., Department of Housing and Urban Development
Huddart, David, 185, *214*
Hueber, Amy E., *214*
Hughes, John F., *166*
Hull, Denis, *35*
Hullinger, Chris, *218*
Human Genome Project, 12
Human resource management, 238
Human subjects, 308
Human-computer interaction
  Aquatic Sciences & Fisheries Abstracts, 194
  cognitive behaviors, 230
  environmental databases, 181, 192, 194, 195, 201
  geographic information systems, 160, 161-162
  mass information systems, 61

Human-computer interaction, (cont.)
  NREN, 63
  Regional Information System for African Aquaculture, 195
  Risk Assistant database, 201
  videotex, 10
Hungary, Teletel access, 75
Hurricanes, risk communication, 183
Hurson, A.R., 100, 119, *125*
Hurych, Jitka M., *321*
Hutchens, Susan, *40*
Huxhold, William E., 139, *167*
Hwang, Kai, 101, 107, *125*
Hydrogen bomb, and Soviet science, 272
Hydroline database, 192
Hydrology, databases, 193
Hypercube configuration, parallel computing, 103, 104, 116
Hypermedia, water pollution databases, 195
HyperSift interface, 195
Hypertext
  as mentor, 18
  water pollution databases, 195
HyPeruse interface, 195

I&R, *see* Information and referral
I/O (input/output)
  parallel computing, 107, 111
  information retrieval, 113
IAEA, *see* International Atomic Energy Agency
IAMSLIC, *see* International Association of Aquatic and Marine Science Libraries and Information Centers
Ibbs, T.J., 151, *167*
IBM, Prodigy videotex service, 75
IBM Informa '92, *85, 91*
ICL, *see* International Computers Ltd.
ICRP, *see* International Commission on Radiological Protection
Ideology
  and information science, Soviet Union, 280
  ethics, 311-314
IEEE, *see* Institute of Electrical and Electronics Engineers

IFIP (International Federation for Information Processing), World Computer Congress, 1986, *122*
IGIS (Integrated Geo-information System), 153
Ignorance, impact of information technology, 8
IGU, *see* International Geographical Union
Illusion of control, managers, 244
Image processing
  geographic information systems, 136, 161
  parallel computing, 105, 107
Image space partitioning, spatial indexing, 150, 154-156
Images, information seeking, 312
Immerman, Rita J., *82*
The Imperative of Responsibility: In Search of an Ethics for the Technological Age, 296
Imperial Public Library, St. Petersburg (Soviet Union), 270
IMS T800 transputers, 113
Incineration, hazardous waste treatment, 206
Income, and computer competence, 56
Income maintenance, information needs, 66
Indexed files, parallel computing, 109, 113, 114-115
Indexers, telecommuting, 23
Indexing
  see also A&I services
  Aquatic Sciences & Fisheries Abstracts, 194
  automatic, Soviet Union, 274
  toxic substances databases, 199-200
  water pollution, 196
Indian Journal of Marine Science, 194
Indiana, legislative information use, 30
Individuality, ethics, 298
Individuals
  impact of information technology, 3-33
  isolation, 7, 8-10, 22, 32
Industrial espionage, 300

INDEX   351

Industrial productivity, scientific and technical information, Soviet Union, 286
Industrial revolution, 7
Industrialized countries, labor force, 13
Inference, decision making, 245
InfoGuide information retrieval system, 117
Infoma, *see* IBM Informa '92
Informal sensing, managers, 239
Informatics 8: Advances in Intelligent Retrieval, 1985, 127
Informatika, 278
Information
  characteristics, 26, 27-28
  definitions, Soviet Union, 269
  value, 233
Information access, 312
  Soviet Union, 287
Information Access Co., 23
Information age, 46-48, 313
Information and referral (I&R), 60, 61, 64-68
  history, 64
Information behaviors, 229-230, 248
  see also Behavior; Communication behaviors
  decision making, 239, 240, 241
  managers, 233-234, 235-236, 243-245
  organizations, 246
  symbolism, 247
Information Bill of Rights, 314
Information brokers, ethics, 294, 295, 300-304, 306
Information control, 50-52
Information democracy, 43-81
  definition, 44
Information environments
  managers, 227-252
  models, 230-249
Information evaluation, 234
Information flow, 230
  Soviet Union, 273
Information gap, 53-54
Information literacy, 313
  Soviet Union, 285

Information management, information science education, 278
Information needs, 57-60
  management information, 230
Information overload, 246-247, 250, 251
Information poor, 30, 44, 52, 53-54
Information processing
  computer-mediated entertainment, 11
  managers, 244-245
Information professionals
  education, Soviet Union, 285-286
  ethics, 291-317
  impact of information technology, 18
  information and referral systems, 64
  limitations, 305
  management information, 249-252
  managers' information needs, 228, 229, 235
Information resources
  access, 52
  democracy, 48-52
  distribution, 55-57
Information retrieval
  artificial languages, 281
  dissertations, Soviet Union, 279-280
  neural networks, 120-121
  parallel computing, 106, 108-121
Information retrieval systems, comparison, 117-119, 202
Information revolution, 46
Information science
  dissertations, Soviet Union, 279
  education, ethics, 310
  interdisciplinarity, 4
  management information, 228
  research, 308-310
  Soviet Union, 286
Information seeking, 60, 311, 312
  environmental researchers, 182
  managers, 233, 236, 238, 243
  retirees, 12
Information sources, environmental studies, 173-208
Information System for Hazardous Organics in Water, *see* ISHOW

Information systems
  design, 242
  environmental studies, 184, 186
  user-driven models, 249
Information technology
  see also Computers
  cognitive behaviors, 230
  dissertations, Soviet Union, 279
  ethics, 311-313
  global change, 206
  impact on individuals, 3-33
  malpractice, 302-303
  managerial functions, 247
  social equity, 43-81
  symbolic value, 247
Information transfer, environmental information, 181
Information use, legislators, 30
Information Utility and Social Choice, 1969, 93
Informational roles, managers, 237
InfoSift interface, 195
INFOTERRA (International Environmental Information network), 188
Inglehart, Ronald, 5, 6, 8, 37
Innovation, transportation, 7
Insecticide research, bibliometrics, 179
INSPEC database, parallel computing, 111
Institute for Scientific Information, *see* ISI
Institute of Electrical and Electronics Engineers (IEEE)
  Conference on Pattern Recognition and Image Processing, 1982, *168*
  Conference on Visualization, 1990, *166*
Institute of Global Communications, 68
Institute of Information Scientists
  see also Aslib/Institute of Information Scientists/Library Association, Joint Conference
  Annual Conference, 1987, *320*
Insurance, information professionals, 303
Insurance industry, impact of information technology, 18, 21

Integrated Geo-information System, *see* IGIS
Integrated pest management, 202
Integrated Risk Information System, *see* IRIS
Integrated Services Digital Network, *see* ISDN
Intellectual freedom, 292-293, 307, 314
Intellectual property rights, 314
Interagency Working Group on Data Management for Global Change (IAWGDMGC), 206
Interdependence, impact of information technology, 16
Interdisciplinarity
  environmental studies, 176, 179-180
  information science, 4
Interface, *see* Human-computer interaction
Intergraph Corporation, 141, 154
Interlibrary loan, *see* Libraries, resource sharing
Intermediaries, *see* Information professionals
International Association of Aquatic and Marine Science Libraries and Information Centers (IAMSLIC) Annual Conference
  1985, *209*
  1986, *208-209, 218*
  1987, *216*
  1988, *210, 214*
  1989, *212, 213, 216, 219*
  1990, *213*
  1991, *209, 216*
International Atomic Energy Agency (IAEA), 199
International Commission on Radiological Protection (ICRP), 199
International Communications Association, Annual Meeting, 1983, *254*
International Computers Ltd. (ICL), 103
  CAFS (Content-Addressable Filestore) search engine, 120

INDEX
353

International Conference on Parallel Computing
1983, *125*
1985, *126*
International Conference on Parallel Processing, 1977, *124*
International Conference on Text Processing Systems, 1984, *122*
International Conference on Very Large Data Bases
1987, *170*
1989, *166*
International education, Soviet Union, 278
International Environmental Information network, *see* INFOTERRA
International Federation for Information Processing, *see* IFIP
International Geographical Union (IGU), 141
International Information Conference, 1982, *324*
International Journal of Geographical Information Systems, 138, *167*
International Pharmaceutical Abstracts, 194
International Register of Potentially Toxic Chemicals (IRPTC), 188
International relations, Soviet Union, 284
International Research Associates, 57, 87
International Symposium on Computer-Assisted Cartography (AUTO-CARTO)
see also AUTO-CARTO London
1985, *164, 168*
1987, *164*
1989, *163*
International Symposium on Spatial Data Handling, 139
Internet, 23, 71
  campus-wide information systems, 73
  history, 62
  information democracy, 61-62
Interpersonal roles, managers, 237
Intuition, managers, 244, 250
Inventions, Soviet Union, 273

Inverted indexes, parallel computing, 113, 114, 117, 119
IRIS (Integrated Risk Information System), 184, 201
IRPTC, *see* International Register of Potentially Toxic Chemicals
Isabella, L., 257
ISDN (integrated services digital network), France, 75
Isenberg, Daniel J., 236, 241, 244, *257*
Ishikawa, Sara, *81*
ISHOW (Information System for Hazardous Organics in Water), 184
ISI (Institute for Scientific Information), *Journal Citation Reports*, 179, 193
Isolation, individuals, 7, 8-10, 22, 32
Israel, Environmental Protection Service, 180
Italy, Teletel access, 75
Iyengar, S. Sitharama, 105, *126*

Jack, R.F., *210*
Jackson, M.J., 153, *164, 167*
Jamieson, Leah H., 105, *125*
Janis, Irving L., 240, *257*
Japan
  in-vehicle navigation research, 160
  labor force, 17
  Teletel access, 75
Jarvis-Patrick clustering algorithm, 116
JCR, *see Journal Citation Reports*
Jesshope, C.R., 99, 103, *124*
Job announcements, community information systems, 72
Job enhancement, impact of information technology, 17-19, 32
Job requirements, ethics, 305
Job satisfaction, impact of information technology, 20-21, 22
Job security, 314
Jobs, Steven, 10
Johansen, Robert, *91*
Johnson, Arthur H., 198, *214*
Johnson, Deborah G., 293, *321*
Johnson, Haynes B., 37
Johnson, H.R., *82*

Johnson, Lyndon B., 65
Johnston, William B., 13, 37
Joint Statistical Meetings, 1989, 36
Jonas, Hans, 296, 313, *321*
Jones, Christopher B., 158, 161, *168*
Jones, Clara Stanton, 70, *87*
Jones, Ernest, 73
Journal Citation Reports (JCR), 179, 193
Journal of Business Ethics, 293, *321*
Journals, censorship, Soviet Union, 274-275
Joy, Albert H., 199, *214*
Judgments, managers, 244-245
Jun, Suk-Ho, *85*
Justice, 304, 305-306
  and social equity, 49, 52-57
Justice system, information needs, 68

K-d trees, spatial indexing, 151
Kadec, Sarah T., 187, 203, *214*
Kahle, Brewster, 112, 117, *128*
Kahn, Alfred J., 60, 65, 67, 68, *87*
Kahneman, Daniel, 244, 245, *257, 263*
Kankanhalli, M., *166*
Kant, Immanuel, 291, 296, 304, 305, 308, *321*
Kanter, Rosabeth Moss, 235, 238, *37, 257*
Kapaleaswaran, T.N., 118, *125*
Kapitsa, P., 272
Kaplan, J.E., 227, 230, 235, 239, 241, 243, 248, *258*
Kaplan, Susan Jane, 293, *321*
Karaganda Polytechnical Institute, 280
Karatygina, T.F., 284, *288*
Karp, Alan H., 106, 107, *125*
Karraker, Roger, 61, 62, *87*
Kasper, George M., *35*
Katz, Bill, 292, *321*
Katzer, Jeffrey, 235, *257*
KBGIS, *see* Knowledge-Based GIS
Kedrovskaia, L.G., 271, 275, *288, 289*
Keen, Peter G.W., 13, 244, *37, 259*
Kelland, John Laurence, 179, 191, 194, *214*
Kennedy, David, 200, *214*
Kent State University, 294
Kerr, James M., 13, *37*

Kidd, Jerry S., 60, *87*
Kiesler, Sara, 15, 16, *41, 257*
Kikuchi, Lawrence, *168*
Kim, Byung J., 200, *214*
King, Alan, 27, *37*
King, John Leslie, 17, *38*
Kinnucan, Mark T., 248, *253*
Kirkwood, C.C., *321*
Kissman, Henry M., 177, *215*
Kitchen, Karen, *38*
Kitchen, Will, *38*
Kitchener, K.S., 304, *321*
Kjeldsen, Rick, 120, *122*
Kling, Rob, 312, *321*
Kneen, Peter, 272, 273, *289*
Knight, Lydia F., *321*
Knorr-Cetina, Karin, 182, *208*
Knowledge, and democracy, 50
Knowledge Industry Publications, 186, *215*
Knowledge representation, geographic information systems, 161
Knowledge-Based GIS (KBGIS), 153, 161
Koch, Susan, *38*
Kochen, Manfred, 4, 60, 64, 65, 243, 293, 315, *37, 87, 257, 321*
Koenig, Michael E.D., 4, *34*
Kohlberg, Lawrence, 304, *321*
Kohli, Ajay K., *35*
Kolkova, N.I., 283, *289*
Kominolit, 271
Kominski, Robert, 56, *87*
Kostrewski, B.J., 186, 202, 292, 306, 309, 311, *210, 322*
Kotter, John P., 235, 237, *257*
Kraemer, Kenneth L., 13, 17, 19, 21, *38*
Kranzberg, Melvin, 45, 46, 47, *87*
Krasnov, B.I., *288*
Kraut, Robert E., 18, 20, 21, 23, *38*
Krawczak, D., *215*
Kroeck, K. Galen, *262*
Krueger, Rick, 31, *38*
Krupskaia, Nadezha K., 270
Kuibyshev Institute of Culture, 285
Kuibyshev Polytechnical Institute, 278, 280
Kumar, Girja, 311, *322*

Kung, H.T., 105, *126*
Kunkel, Dale, 11, *36*
Kurtagh, E., *82*
Kwan, Colleen, *84*
Kwok, K.L., 120, *126*

Labor force, impact of information technology, 13, 21
Labor unions, impact of information technology, 21
Lakes, modeling, 197
Lamacchia, Anthony, *214*
LAN, *see* Local area networks
Lancaster, F. Wilfrid, 281, 292, *322*
Land pollution, information sources, 189-191
Landau, Herbert B., 181, 185, 207, *215*
Lane, Nancy D., 74, *88*
Lane, Robert E., 49, *88*
Langran, Gail, 160, *168*
Language, scientific and technical information, 281
Larose, Robert, 56, *88*
Larsen, Gitte, 70, *88*
Larsen, Janet K., 235, 237, *258*
Larsen, Ron, 61, *94*
Larson, Charles U., 9, *38*
Lash, Scott, *38*
Laskowski, Linda J., 77, 78, *88*
Lasswell, Harold, 51, *88*
Latin America, information science education, Soviet Union, 279
Latvia, 285
Lau, Alan W., 235, *258*
Laurini, Robert, 137, 153, *168*
Lautenberg, F.R., 56, *88*
Lauzon, Jean Paul, 153, 159, *168*
Laver, Murray, 26, *38*
Law, information needs, 58, 66
Law enforcement, ethics, 297
Law, J., 179, *215*
Law of small numbers, 245
Lawyers, *see* Attorneys
LC, *see* Library of Congress
LCC, *see* Library of Congress Classification
LCSH, *see* Library of Congress Subject Headings
Leadership, managers, 231, 234-235

Least effort, information seeking, 60
Leavitt, Harold J., 236, *258*
Leebart, Derek, *38*
Legal standards, ethics, 297, 298
Legal texts, information retrieval, parallel computing, 111
Legislators, information use, 30
Legislatures
  ethics, 297
  use of information technology, 29, 31
Leifer, Lloyd A., 156, *168*
Leisure time, impact of information technology, 10-11
Lengel, Robert H., 254, *258*
Lenin State Library, 284
Lenin, V.I., 269, 271
  views on libraries, 280
Lennet, David J., *212*
Less developed countries, labor force, 13
Lester, G., 179, *218*
Levin, Marc A., 31, *38*
Levine, E.J., 59, *88*
Levinson, Risha W., 66, *88*
Levitt, T., 228, *258*
Levy, Frank S., 57, 60, *88*
Lewis, Don A., 191, 193, *215*
Liability
  geographic information systems, 163
  information professionals, 302-304, 316
Liaison role, managers, 237
Librarians, ethics, 298, 306, 307
Libraries
  see also Public libraries; Special libraries
  community information systems, 70-71
  equal access to information, 30
  NREN use, 62, 63
  resource sharing, 199
  Soviet Union, 270, 280, 285
    automation, 276, 281, 283
    history, 284
  user needs, 57-60
Library and Information Science Abstracts, 188

Library Association (U.K.), *see* Aslib/Institute of Information Scientists/Library Association, Joint Conference
Library Bill of Rights, 307
Library of Congress Classification (LCC), ecology, 197
Library of Congress (LC), Congressional Research Service (CRS), Environmental Protection Section, Environment and Natural Resources Policy Division, 174-175, 224
Library of Congress Subject Headings (LCSH), 178, 196
Library science
  and information science, Soviet Union, 280
  management information, 228
Library services, distribution, 57
Library Trends, 292
Liden, Robert C., 39
Life Sciences Collection, 194
Lifestyles, impact of information technology, 6
Lin, Xia, *124*
Lindblom, Charles G., 241, 246, *258*
Linden, Fabian, 54, *88*
Lindsey, George N., *259*
Line thinning, geographic information systems, 149
Linear quadtrees, spatial indexing, 153
Linguistics, information science education, Soviet Union, 276, 277
Lipsman, Claire K., 60, *88*
LISP programming language, parallel computing, 103
Lithuania, 284
Little, B.B., *212*
Load sharing, supercomputers, 101
Local area networks (LANs), information retrieval, parallel computing, 118-119
Lomet, David B., 152, *168*
Lomonosov, M.V., 270
Long distance services, 76
Long, Nicholas, 60, 64, 66, *88*, *89*

Lopatin, Kevin, *260*
Lotus Technology Corp., 27
Louis Harris & Associates, 56, *88*
Love Canal, 173, 183
Lovenburg, Susan L., 186, 199, *215*
Lubrano, Linda L., 272, *289*
Lubricants, safety, 203
Lucas, D., 150, *167*
Lucia, Joe, *85*
Lucia, T.J., *123*
Lucy, William H., 57, *89*
Luke, A.W., 60, *82*, *89*
Lukes, Steven, *89*
Lund, Peter B., 57, 60, *82*
Lupien, Anthony E., 147, *169*
Luthans, Fred, 235, 237, 238, *258*
Lyall, A., 111, *123*, *126*
Lyles, M.A., 239, 243, *258*

Maas, Norman, 66, 70, *89*
Macaulay, Lord T.B., 44, *89*
Machine translation (MT), Soviet Union, 281, 282
Machlup, Fritz, 46, *89*
MacIntosh, Norman B., 243, *254*
Maciuszko, Kathleen, 70, *89*
Mackaness, W.A., 162, *164*
MacLeod, Ian A., 117, *126*
MacLeod, Kevin J., 120, *126*
MacMullin, Susan E., 242, 243, *258*
Macroalgae, databases, 194
Maddock, Jerome T., *215*
Madge, Bruce, *225*
Madison, James, 43
Magazines, management information, 228
Maggie's Place III community information system, 70-71
MAGI, *see* Maryland Automated Geographic Information
Magrath, Lynn L., 70, *89*
Maguire, David J., 135, 136, 138, 139, *168*
Mail
  censorship, Soviet Union, 274
  compared with computer-mediated communication, 15

Mailbox algorithm, parallel computing, 113
Mailloux, Elizabeth N., *215*
Makridakis, Spyros, 244, *256*
Malone, Thomas F., 174, *215*
Malpractice, information professionals, 300-304
Malyshev, Nina Alexis, 70, *89*
Management
  impact of information technology, 4, 19-20
  role in society, 234-235
Management analysts, telecommuting, 23
Management information systems (MIS), 229, 293
Managers
  behaviors, 235-236
  cognitive styles, 243-245
  illogical use of information, 228
  information environment, 227-252
  information models, 230-249
  leadership, 234-235
Mann, Leon, 240, *257*
Mann, Patricia S., *38*
Manson, Gordon A., *123*
Manufacturing, impact of information technology, 17
Manz, Charles C., 21, *38*
Manzi, Jim, 27
Map creation, geographic information systems, 148
Map editing, geographic information systems, 145
Map-name placement, 161
Mapping, information retrieval, parallel computing, 116
Marble, Duane F., 137, 150, *168, 170, 171*
Marcaccio, Kathleen Young, 186, *215*
March, James G., 49, 228, 240, 241, 243, 246, *89, 253, 255, 258*
Marchand, Donald A., 31, *34*
Marcus, Alfred, 177, *216*
Marine Protection, Research, and Sanctuaries Act (MPRSA), 175
Marine science, databases, 194
Mark, David M., 156, 159, 161, 163, *164, 166, 168*

Market economics
  information democracy, 79
  social equity, 53
Marketing
  and privacy, 26
  gateway systems, 78
  management information, 231
MarketPlace CD-ROM, 26-27
Markham, James W., 191, 194, 196, 197, *216*
Markoff, John, 10, *37*
Markuson, Barbara Evans, 62, *89*
Marriage, impact of information technology, 9
Martin, Johannes J., 151, 156, *168*
Martin, Lowell, 57, *89*
Martin, T. Patrick, 117, *126*
Martin, Thomas H., 4, *38*
Martin, William, 60, 70, *89*
Martin, William J., *38*
Martinez, Michael E., 56, *90*
Marx, Karl, 49
Marx, Robert W., 140, 141, 146, *169*
Marxism, 31
Marxist critique, information technology, 19
Marxist science, 269-270
Maryland, 141, *169*
Maryland Automated Geographic Information (MAGI), 141
Masking techniques, privacy protection, 26
Mason, D.C., 153, *167*
MasPar Computer Corporation, 103
Masracci, Michael, *219*
Mass information systems, 60-79
Mass media
  Soviet Union
    information professionals, 283
    scientific and technical information, 277
Massachusetts, legislative information use, 30
Massachusetts Institute of Technology, *see* MIT
Massively Parallel Processor (MPP), 102
  text processing, 110

Massively parallel processors
  see also Connection Machine
  text processing, 105
Material Safety Data Sheets (MSDS), 202, 203, 205
Mathematicians, telecommuting, 23
Mathematics, information science education, Soviet Union, 281
Matheson, Kimberly, 15, *38*
Mathis, Mary Elizabeth, *88*
Mayo, John S., 47, *90*
MBA students, cognitive styles, 244
MBTI, see Myers-Briggs Type Indicator
McCain, Katherine W., *225*
McCall, Morgan W., Jr., 227, 230, 235, 239, 241, 243, 248, *258*
McCaskey, Michael B., 236, *259*
McClure, Charles R., 62, *90*
McFarlane, James C., *218*
McGowan, R.P., *259*
McGranaghan, M., 161, *169*
MCI telecommunications company, 76
McKeen, J.D., *41*
McKenney, James L., 244, *259*
McLaren, Robin A., 162, *169*
McLaughlin, J.D., 139, *165*
McLaughlin, John F., *253*
McLuhan, Marshall, *39*
McMaster, Robert B., 143, *169*
Mead Corp., Micromedex, Inc., 202
Mead, Nancy A., 56, *90*
Meadow, Charles T., 181, 281, *209*, *216*
Meadows, Arthur Jack, *39*
Media Lab, see MIT, Media Lab
Medical Economics Data Co., 202
Medical services, information and referral systems, Hotlines, 65
Medicine
  see also Health care
  malpractice, 303
MEDINFO, see Conference on Medical Informatics
MEDLINE database, 194
  parallel computing, 118
Mednick, Ruth W., 60, 66, *90*

Medvedev, Zhores A., 272, 273, 274, 275, *289*
Meetings, symbolic value, 247
Meiko computing surface, 104
Meilander, W.C., 110, *126*
Meltsner, Arnold J., *88*
Memory, parallel computing, 104
Menon, Sudhakar, *171*
Mentors, hypertext, 18
Menu-based interfaces, Aquatic Sciences & Fisheries Abstracts, 194
Merrick, T., *218*
Messages, information environment, 230
Messenger, Manette M., *216*
Metaphor, information seeking, 248
Methane, air pollution, 198
Metropolitan areas, impact of information technology, 28
Mettler, Jennifer, 56, *88*
Meylan, William, *214*
Meyrowitz, Joshua, 6, 7, *39*
Mezhdunarodnyi Tsentr Nauchnoi i Tekhnicheskoi Informatsii, 276, *289*
Mick, Colin K., 249, *259*
Microcomputers
  community information systems, 71, 73
  geographic information systems, 139
  impact on society, 12
  information access, 60
  information science education, Soviet Union, 282
  pesticide information sources, 203
  toxic substances information sources, 201
Microfilm, 202
Micromedex, Inc., 202
Microprocessors, parallel computing, 104
Microvax workstations, 118
Middle class, information gap, 54
Mika, Joseph J., 322
Mikhailov, A.I., 270, 273, 274, *289*
Miles, Ian, 10, *39*
Miles, Paula C., *218*

INDEX

Military information, abstracting and indexing, Soviet Union, 274
Milkman, Ruth, 39
Mill, John Stuart, 292, 304, 322
Miller, L.L., 125
Milleret, Francoise, 137, 153, *168*
Millions of instructions per second, *see* MIPS
Millman, Zeeva, 18, 39
MIMD (multiple instruction stream, multiple data stream) computers, 102-106
  see also Transputers
  information retrieval, 109, 111-116, 118
Mingju, Gai, 191, 196, *216*
Minicomputers, information retrieval, parallel computing, 118
Mining, pollution, 178
Minitel, 74-75
Minitel telecommunications system, 9, 30
Minitel USA, 75, 78
Minneapolis, information gateway, 77, 78
Minnesota, geographic information systems, 140
Minsk-32 computer, 278
Mintz, Anne P., 293, 300, 302, 303, *322*
Mintzberg, Henry, 235, 236, 237, 239, 243, 247, *259*
MIPS (millions of instructions per second), parallel computing, evaluation, 106, 107
MIS, *see* Management information systems
MISD (multiple instruction stream, single data stream) computers, 102
Misrepresentation, information professionals, 300-301
MIT (Massachusetts Institute of Technology)
  Media Lab, 51
  Program in Science, Technology and Society, 268
Mitkas, Pericles A., 120, *126*
Mitroff, I.I., 239, 243, *258*

Mixed scanning, decision making, 241
Mize, S.G., *212*
Mladenka, Kenneth R., 57, *89*
Mobley, Kathleen S., *322*
Mock interviews, information science education, 285
Mockus, J., *123*
Modeling
  geographic information systems, 161, 191
Models
  communication, 183
  decision making, 240-242
  ethical behavior, 294
  information environments, 230-249
  lakes, 197
Moitra, Abha, 105, *126*
Moldavia, 285
Molecular biology, information sources, 182
Monarch, Ira, *216*
Monitor role, managers, 237
Monitoring, wastewater treatment, 196
Monmonier, Mark S., 139, *169*
Montreal
  insurance industry, 18
  videotex service, 78
Montrose (tugboat), 302
Mooney, Christopher Z., 30, *39*
Moor, James H., *322*
Moral agents, ethics, 294-296
Moral imperative, 296, 298
Moran, Julio, 71, *90*
Morehouse, Scott, 137, 141, 147, *169*
Moreland, William H., 147, *169*
Morrell, J.A., *255*
Morse, Myles, *219*
Morton Code, spatial indexing, 158, 323
Mosco, Vincent, 51, *90*
Moscow Institute for Foreign Languages, 271
Moscow Institute of Culture (MGIK), 276, 284, 285
Moscow State Historical-Archival Institute, 276, 278

Moscow State University, 277
Moskowitz, Herbert, 245, *259*
Motion picture industry, 51
Moulder, David S., 185, 191, 193, *216*
Mounsey, Helen, 139, 157, *169*
Mountains, geographic information systems, 156-157
Mower, James E., *164*
Mowshowitz, Abbe, 312, *322*
MP-1 computer, 103
MPP, *see* Massively Parallel Processor
MPRSA, *see* Marine Protection, Research, and Sanctuaries Act
MSDS, *see* Material Safety Data Sheets
MSDS Engine, 204, 205
MT, *see* Machine translation
Muddling through, decision making, 241, 246
Mul'chenko, Z.M., 273, *289*
Mulesky, Barbara C., *214*
Muller, J.C., 143, 159, *169*
Multidisciplinarity, *see* Interdisciplinarity
Multimedia, 4, 10-11
Multinational corporations, telecommuting, 23
Multiple instruction stream, multiple data stream, *see* MIMD
Multiple instruction stream, single data stream, *see* MISD
Multiresolution databases, geographic information systems, 160
Multiscale representations, geographic information systems, 159-160
Municipal waste, pollution, 177
Munro, Malcolm C., *259*
Murdock, Graham, *39*
Murray, William, 227
Museums, Soviet Union, 285
Mutagenicity, risk assessment, 201
Myers-Briggs Type Indicator (MBTI), managers, 244

NACAB, *see* National Citizens' Advice Bureaux

Nadler, D., 227, *263*
Nagel, Jack H., 49, *90*
Nagy, George, 137, 139, *169*
Naisbitt, John, 3, 247, *39*, *259*
Nalimov, V.V., 273, *289*
NASA, *see* U.S., National Aeronautics and Space Administration
Nasar, Sylvia, 53, *90*
Nasri, William, 302, *322*
NATDP, *see* National Agricultural Text Digitizing Project
NATIC, *see* National Air Toxics Information Clearinghouse
National Academy of Sciences, *see* U.S., National Academy of Sciences
National Aeronautics and Space Administration, *see* U.S., National Aeronautics and Space Administration
National Agricultural Text Digitizing Project (NATDP), 199
National Air Toxics Information Clearinghouse (NATIC), 198
National Association of Citizens' Advice Bureaux (NACAB), 64, 67-68
National Book Committee, 60, *90*
National CAB Council, 67-68
National Center for Geographic Information and Analysis (NCGIA), 138
National Citizens' Advice Bureaux (NACAB), 67-68, *90*
National Citizens' Advice Bureaux Committee, 59, *90*
National Commission on Libraries and Information Science (NCLIS), 43, *91*
National Committee for Digital Cartographic Data Standards, 151, 154, *169*
National Communications Forum, 1990, *87*
National Conference on Hazardous Wastes and Hazardous Materials, 1990, *219*

National Conference on Risk
  Communication, 1986, *210*
National Environmental Protection
  Act (NEPA), 175
National Ground Water Information
  Center, 195, *216*
National Institute for Occupational
  Safety and Health (NIOSH),
  Registry of Toxic Effects of
  Chemical Substances (RTECS)
  database, *see* Registry of Toxic
  Effects of Chemical Substances
National Institute of Occupational
  Safety and Health database, 203,
  205
National Institutes for Information
  Democracy, 79
National Institutes for the Environ-
  ment, *see* U.S., National Institutes
  for the Environment
National Institutes of Health, *see* U.S.,
  National Institutes of Health
National laboratories, environmental
  researchers, 182
National Library for the Environ-
  ment, National Institutes for the
  Environment (proposed), 174
National Library of Medicine (NLM),
  184, 206
  Fact Sheets, 186
  Toxicology Data Network
    (TOXNET), *see* TOXNET
National Oceanic and Atmospheric
  Administration, *see* U.S., National
  Oceanic and Atmospheric
  Administration
National Online Meeting
  1986, *89*
  1990, 212
  1991, *319*
  1992, 257
National Pesticide Information
  Retrieval System (NPIRS), 203
National Public Radio (NPR)
  model for National Public
    Telecomputing Network, 69
  A Prairie Home Companion, 9

National Public Telecomputing
  Network (NPTN), 61, 68, *69-70*
National Research and Education
  Network, *see* NREN
National Research Council, *see* U.S.,
  National Academy of Sciences,
  National Research Council
National Science Foundation (NSF),
  174, 182
  Engineering Research Center for
    Hazardous Substances Control,
    178
  geographic information systems,
    138
  Internet, 62
  Network Service Center, 61, *91*
  Space Physics Analysis Network
    (SPAN), 205
National security, information
  technology, 4
National Security Agency, *see* U.S.,
  National Security Agency
National Stream Survey, 198
National Technical Information
  Service, *see* NTIS
NATO (North Atlantic Treaty
  Organization), Advanced Study
  Institute on Perspectives in
  Information Science, 1973, 252
Natural disasters, risk communica-
  tion, 183-184
Natural language interfaces,
  DowQuest, 117
Natural law, 52
Natural resources management,
  geographic information systems,
  141
The Nature of Information [Priroda
  informatsii], 269
Nauchno-tekhnicheskaia Informatsiia,
  282
Navrotskaia, V., *289*
NCGIA, *see* National Center for
  Geographic Information and
  Analysis
NCLIS, *see* National Commission on
  Libraries and Information Science

Nearest-neighbor searching, parallel computing, 109, 114
Neff, Raymond K., 73
Negligence, information professionals, 303
Negotiating, management information, 231
Neighborhoods, information needs, 58, 59
Nelkin, Dorothy, 183, *217*
Nelson, Debra L., 230, *259*
Nelson, Nancy Melin, 70, 71, *91*
Nelson, Randal C., 151, 153, *169*, *170*
Nemirovskaia, V.S., *289*
NEPA, *see* National Environmental Protection Act
Network models, information retrieval, 109, 120-121
Networks
 consequences, 313
 environmental information, 190, 205
 management information, 229, 230, 238
 social information processing, 14
Neural networks
 parallel computing, 109
 information retrieval, 120-121
New Jersey, Department of Environmental Protection, 201
New York, geographic information systems, 140
New York (City), library services, 57
New York Times, 301
New York University, 60, *91*
Newby, Gregory B., 230, *259*, *260*
Newman, Arthur R., *258*
Newman, M., *260*
News services
 National Public Telecomputing Network, 69
 Prodigy videotex, 75
Newsletters, environmental researchers, 182
Newspapers, 59
 information technology, 8
Newstead, Anthony, 28, *39*
Newtonian physics, compared with politics, 31

Nie, Norman, 46, 79, *92*
Nielsen, Brian, 73, *39*, *91*
Nieuwenhuysen, Paul, 185, 191, 192, *217*
Nievergelt, Jurg, 139, 150, 155, *169*
NIH, *see* U.S., National Institutes of Health
Nilan, Michael S., 58, 180, 181, 230, 231, 234, 249, *84*, *211*, *254*, *256*, *260*, *261*
Nisbett, Richard, 244, *260*
Nitrous oxide, air pollution, 198
NLM, *see* National Library of Medicine
NOAA, *see* U.S., National Oceanic and Atmospheric Administration
Noll, John, *123*
Nonprofit organizations, impact of information technology, 11
 NREN access, 63
Nordhaus, William D., 53, 79, *93*
Nordin, Brent, *126*
Normative practices, management information, 231
North Atlantic Treaty Organization, *see* NATO
Novitskaia, L.I., 284, *290*
NPIRS, *see* National Pesticide Information Retrieval System
NPR, *see* National Public Radio
NPTN, *see* National Public Telecomputing Network
NREN (National Research and Education Network)
 highway metaphor, 62-63
 information democracy, 61, 62-64
 policy issues, 62
NSA, *see* U.S., National Security Agency
NSF, *see* National Science Foundation
NSF Network News, 62, *91*
NSFNET, 62
NTIS (National Technical Information Service), 187, 189, 190, 191, 198, 206, *221*
 database, 192 200

INDEX 363

NTIS, (cont.)
  IRIS (Integrated Risk Information System), 201
  TSCA Test Submission database, 199
  World Data Bank, 140, 141
Nucleic acid databases, parallel computing, 111
Nutt, Paul C., *256, 260*
Nyhan, Michael, 74, *91*
Nynex telephone company, 76

O'Connor, Edward J., *39*
O'Reilly, Charles A., III, 230, 231, 236, 246, *247, 260*
OAK (Online Access to Knowledge), 181
Oak Ridge National Laboratory, *217*
Object space, spatial indexing, 150, 151-154
Object-oriented computing, parallel computing, 117
Objectives, managers, 236
Objectivity, 310
Obraczka, Katia, *123*
OCCAM programming language, 104
Occupational Health Services, Inc., *217*
Occupational Health Services (OHS) search service, 203, 204, 205
Occupational Safety and Health Act (OSHA), 175
Occupations, impact of information technology, 19
Oceanic Abstracts database, 184, 194
Oceanic Network Information Center, *see* OCEANIC
OCEANIC (Oceanic Network Information Center), 205
OCLC (Online Computer Library Center), 199
  Environmental Library, 204, 205
Oddy, Robert N., 120, *126*
ODYSSEY geographic information system, 141
OECD, *see* Organization for Economic Cooperation and Development

Oettinger, Anthony, 79, *91*
Office automation, 4
  insurance industry, 18
Office of Environmental Education, National Institutes for the Environment (proposed), 174
Office of Fellowships and Grants, National Institutes for the Environment (proposed), 174
Office of Technology Assessment, *see* U.S., Congress, Office of Technology Assessment
Ogburn, William F., 47, *91*
Ogg, Elizabeth, 59, *92*
Ogozalek, Virginia Z., 12, *39*
Ohio, Supreme Court, National Public Telecomputing Network, 70
OHM/TADS (Oil and Hazardous Materials/Technical Assistance Data System), 185, 204, 205
OHS, *see* Occupational Health Services
Oil and Hazardous Materials/Technical Assistance Data System, *see* OHM/TADS
Oil spills, 178
Oldfield, D.E., 111, *127*
Olien, Clarice N., *36, 94*
Olsen, Johan P., 241, *253, 258*
Olson, Margrethe H., 22, *39*
Omaha, Neb., information gateway, 77
ONC, *see* Operational Navigational Charts project
Online Access to Knowledge, *see* OAK
Online Computer Library Center, *see* OCLC
Online industry, history, 30
Online public access catalogs (OPAC), community information systems, 72
Online searching
  disclaimers, 303
  end users, 181
  ethics, 297, 301, 306
  poisons, 202

Online searching, (cont.)
  safety information, 204
Operational Navigational Charts
  project (ONC), 142
Operations research, bibliometrics,
  179
Opinion leaders, information
  sources, 58-59
Oppenheim, Charles, 292, 306, 309,
  311, 322
Optical induction, scientists, 182
Optical technology, parallel computing, 120
Optics publications, translation to
  Russian, 270-271
Optimization, organizations, 246
Oral communication, managers, 235,
  249
Oravec, Christine, 9, *38*
ORBIT Search Service, 199
  environmental information, 188
ORBIT Search Service Searchlight, 217
Oregon, legislative information use,
  30
Organization for Economic Cooperation and Development (OECD),
  17, 199
  environmental information
    sources, 188
Organizational structure, 247-248
  impact of information technology,
    15-16, 19
Organizations
  ethics, 294-296
  management information, 228, 229,
    230-231, 234
Organized anarchy, decision making,
  241-242
ORION online catalog, 178
Orren, Gary R., *33*
OSH-ROM (CD-ROM), 204, 205
OSH-UK (CD-ROM), 204
OSHA, *see* Occupational Safety and
  Health Act
OSWER, *see* U.S., Environmental
  Protection Agency (EPA), Office
  of Solid Waste and Emergency
  Response

OTA, *see* U.S., Congress, Office of
  Technology Assessment
Outreach, information and referral
  systems, 66
Overconfidence in judgment,
  managers, 244
Overlap, databases, 192-194
Ozkarahan, Esen, 100, 119, *127*
Ozone, environmental pollution, 177
Ozone depletion, 180, 198

Pacific Telesis telephone company, 76
Packer, David J., *217*
PACS-L (Public Access Computer
  Services Listserv), 27
Padover, Saul K., 44, *92*
Page, R.M.R., 111, *127*
Paik, Woojin, *260*
Paisley, William J., 59, 236, *92*, *260*
Pakzad, S.H., *125*
Palmer, Crystal S., *217*
Pantry, Sheila, *217*
Paradigms, environmental studies,
  174-176
Parallel distributed processing, 120
Parallel information processing, 99-
  122
Parallel processing, 101-104
Parbase-90: International Conference
  on Databases, Parallel Architectures, and Their Applications, *122*
Parent, Philip, 191, *217*
Parker, Donn B., 293, *323*
Parker, Edwin B., 59, *92*
Parkinson, Dennis, 99, 106, *127*
Parks, community information
  systems, 72
Parry, D.B., 138, *169*
Parsons, Charles K., *39*
Participatory democracy, 51
Partitioned finite-state automata
  (PFSA), 119
Pasadena, Calif., community
  information systems, 72
Pascal database, 179, 192
Patents, Soviet Union, 272
Pattern matching, parallel computing, 105, 110-112, 118

INDEX

Paul, Nora, 27, *39*
Pavett, C.M., *258*
Pay scales, ethics, 298
Payoffs, decision making, 240
PDMS, *see* Pesticide Data Management System
PeaceNet computer network, 68
Peano key, spatial indexing, 323
Pearson, Robert W., 26, *35*
Peattie, Noel, 292, *324*
Peer review, ethics, 309
Pemberton, Jeffery K., 24, *39*
Pennington, James, *219*
Pennsylvania, cable television, 29
Pentagon Papers, 301
Penza Polytechnical Institute, 280
Peppi, Carole E., 60, 67, *92*
Perestroika, impact on information science education, 282-286
Performance evaluation, parallel computing, 106-108, 111-112
Perkins, C.R., 138, *169*
Perkins, W. Steven, 236, *261*
Perrolle, Judith A., 4, *40*
Personal computers, *see* Microcomputers
Personal experience, impact of information technology, 8
Personnel, management information, 231
Personnel administration, ethics, 293, 294
Personnel issues, information science education, Soviet Union, 283
The Pest Disk, 203
Pesticide Data Management System (PDMS), 203
Pesticide Information Network (PIN), 203
Pesticides
  ethics of use, 296
  pollution, 178
  safety, 202-203
Peters, Thomas J., 248, *261*
Petrie, Howard, 10, *40*
Peucker, Thomas K., 139, 143, 156, 165, *170*
Peuquet, Donna J., 137, 139, 144, 146, 148, 149, *170, 171*

Pfaffenberger, Bryan, 30, *40*
PFSA, *see* Partitioned finite-state automata
Pharmacists, malpractice, 303
Phillips, Christine M., 188, *225*
Phillips, John R., *126*
Photoduplication, scientific and technical information, 272
Photogrammetric Engineering & Remote Sensing, 138, *170*
Physicians, *see* Doctors
Physics publications, translation to Russian, 270
PHYTOTOX database, 184
Pikes Peak Public Library District (Colorado Springs), 70-71
PIN, *see* Pesticide Information Network
Piracy, information, 293
Plagiarism, 309
Plampin, Helen R., *225*
Planning, management information, 235, 237, 244
Plant extracts, safety, 203
Plasma heat systems, hazardous waste treatment, 206
Plastics, safety, 203
PLEXUS expert system, 11
Plummer, Robert, *91*
PM quadtrees, spatial indexing, 151
Pogue, Christine A., 107, 112, 114, *122, 127*
Poison Prevention Packaging Act (PPPA), 175
Poisons, information sources, 202
Polar regions, environmental information sources, 188
Police, community information systems, 72
Policy issues, NREN, 62
Politeness, computer-mediated communication, 15
Political candidates, National Public Telecomputing Network, 70
Politics
  ethics, 311-314
  impact of information technology, 5, 8, 24-31

Politics, (cont.)
  information needs, 58
  information resources, 48-52
  organizations, 246
Pollution, remote sensing, 27
Pollution media, information sources, 187-199
Pollution prevention, 174-175, 185, 207
Pollution Prevention Information Clearinghouse (PPIC), 206
Polygon overlay, geographic information systems, 143, 147
Polytechnical institutes, information science education, Soviet Union, 276
Pondy, L.R., 236, *260*
POOMA computer, 108
Poor, *see* Information poor
Popovsky, Mark, 275, *289*
Popularization of science, Soviet Union, 277, 281
Porat, Marc Uri, 46, *92*
Pornography, 296
Porter, Alan L., *217*
Porter, Nancy L., *218*
Ports and Waterways Safety Act (PWSA), 175
Post, Joyce A., 44, 58, *83*
Post-industrial era, 46
Postal information, privacy, 27
Postel, Sandra, 202, *218*
Postman, Neil, 5, 7, 8, *40*
Pounds, W.F., 239, *261*
Powers, Bruce R., *39*
PPPA, *see* Poison Prevention Packaging Act
PR bintrees, spatial indexing, 151
PR quadtrees, spatial indexing, 151, 158
A Prairie Home Companion radio program, 9
Preer, Jean, 307, *323*
Preservatives, safety, 203
Pressman, Steven, 26, *40*
Prestel videotex system, 30
Preston, E., 59, *88*
Price, Derek de Solla, 273

Princeton University, PNN campus-wide information system, 73
Priorities, managers, 238
Pritchard, Teresa, 25, 26, 27, *40*
Privacy, 51, 308, 311, 313, 314, 316
  impact of information technology, 25-27
Probability theory, decision making, 245
Problem dimensions, management information, 242-243
Problem finding, 231-234, 239, 241
Problem solving
  definition, 239
  management information, 231
  scientists, 182
Processing elements, parallel computing, 103, 116
Prodigy videotex service, 61, 75
Productivity, impact of information technology, 19-20, 22
Professional issues, information workers, Soviet Union, 285, 287
Professional societies, ethics, 297
Professional standards
  ethics, 298
  management information, 231
Professionals
  ethics, 298-300
  impact of information technology, 17, 19
  information behavior, 231
PROFS electronic communication system, 14-15
Programming languages, information science education, Soviet Union, 282
Project Hermes, National Public Telecomputing Network, 69
Propaganda, 309
Propagandists, librarians, Soviet Union, 270
Proprietary interests, ethics, 305, 308, 315
Protein databases, parallel computing, 111
Provost, Frank, *217*
Proximity, social information processing, 14

INDEX 367

Psychology, management information, 228, 230, 243
PThomas information retrieval system, 121
Public Access Computer Services Listserv, *see* PACS-L
Public administration, management information, 228
Public Electronic Network (PEN), 70, 71-72
Public libraries, 57
  see also Libraries
  NREN access, 63
  Soviet Union, 270, 282
Public opinion, environmental pollution risks, 177
Public policy
  environmental studies, 205-206
  risk communication, 183
Public trust, 304, 306
Public utilities information, Teletel system, 74
Publication activity, environmental studies, 186
Publication growth curves, 179
Publishing
  ethics, 294, 308
  information professionals, Soviet Union, 283
Publishing industry, 51
Puckett, Marianne, 303, *323*
Puffer, James C., 12, *37*
Pugh, D.S., 236, *261*
Pullman, Cydney, *39*
Pursell, Carroll W., Jr., 45, *87*
PWSA, *see* Ports and Waterways Safety Act

QL Systems, Ltd. database vendor, 188
Quadtrees, spatial indexing, 150-156, 158
Quality of work life (QWL), impact of information technology, 5, 19-20, 21, 32
Quantum physics, compared with politics, 31

Quarantelli, E.L., 184, *218*
Query languages, geographic information systems, 162
Query resolver, information retrieval, parallel computing, 119
Question negotiation, 249
Quilling, Joan, 8, 9, *40*
QUILT (geographic information system), 153
Quinn, Cathy J., 57, *94*
Quinn, Michael J., 102, 104, 105, 106, 107, *127*
QWL, *see* Quality of work life

R+ trees, spatial indexing, 152
R-trees, spatial indexing, 151-152, 154
Radford, K.J., 243, *261*
Radio, 59
  management information, 228
  social impact, 4, 9, 32
Radioactivity, pollution, 199
Radon, environmental pollution, 177, 183
Rae, Douglas W., 49, 50, 51, *92*
Raelin, Joseph, 294, *323*
Raisinghani, Duru, *259*
Rajaraman, V., 118, *125*
Rakow, Lana F., *40*
Rand Corp., 24
Ranka, Sanjay, *122*
Ranked output
  DowQuest, 117
  parallel computing, information retrieval, 108, 111, 113-116
Rao, Ram C., 236, *261*
RAP.3 database machine, 119
Rasmussen, Edie M., 100, 107, 109, 110, 112, 115, 116, *127*, *131*
Raster data representations, geographic information systems, 144, 145-150
Raster-to-vector conversion, geographic information systems, 143-144
Rationality
  managers, 236, 240, 241, 250
  organizations, 246-248
Raymond, Boris, 270, 282, *289*, *290*

RBOCs, *see* Regional Bell operating companies
RCRA, *see* Resource Conservation and Recovery Act
Reading, managers, 235
Reasonable care, information professionals, 302-303
Recall, environmental databases, 193
Records management, insurance industry, 18
Recreation
   community information systems, 72
   impact of information technology, 6
   information needs, 58
Recycling, community information systems, 72
Reddaway, S.F., 111, 114, *127, 128*
Redford, Julia S., *210*
Redistribution of wealth, 53-56
Reduced instruction set computers, *see* RISC
Reducing Risk: Setting Priorities and Strategies for Environmental Protection, 174, 185
Redundancy
   geographic information systems, 159
   management information, 245
Reeher, Grant, 49, *93*
Reekie, D.H.M., 160, *170*
Rees, L.P., 252
Reference interviews, 304
The Reference Librarian, 292
Reggia, James, *124*
Regional Bell operating companies (RBOCs)
   gateway systems, 75-79, 94-103
   Teletel access, 75
Regional Information System for African Aquaculture, *see* REGIS
REGIS (Regional Information System for African Aquaculture), 195
Registry of Toxic Effects of Chemical Substances (RTECS) database, 202, 203, 205
Regulations, pesticides, 203

Regulatory codes of ethics, 315
Regulatory updates, environmental researchers, 182
Reiner, Steven, *88*
Reiss, P., 156, *165*
Relational databases, geographic information systems, 137, 153
Relativity theories, translations to Russian, 270
Relevance, management information, 230, 242
Relevance feedback
   DowQuest, 117
   information retrieval, parallel computing, 112, 121
Religion, impact of information technology, 6, 9
Remediation, hazardous waste, 200
Remote operations, distributed information retrieval systems, 117
Remote sensing, geographic information systems, 148
Remote sensing technology, 27
Rennie, Janet, *218*
Report writing, management information, 231
Reproductive health, databases, 202
Reprorisk database, 202
Reprotext database, 202
Requests for proposals, environmental researchers, 182
Researchers, ethics, 308-314
Resource allocator role, managers, 237
Resource Conservation and Recovery Act (RCRA), 175, 177, 189, 191, 201
Resource files, information and referral systems, 66
Resource management, geographic information systems, 161
Response time, parallel computing, 106, 108
Retail trade, innovation, 7
Retirees, information seeking, 12
Reuters news releases, information retrieval, parallel computing, 112
Reynolds, T.S., *92*
Rhind, David W., 140, *165, 168*

Rhine River, pollution, 183
Rice, Ronald E., 14, *40*
Rich, Richard C., 57, *92*
Rieger, J.H., 59, *92*
Right to access, 52
Right to benefit from access, 52
RISC (reduced instruction set computers), 104
Risk assessment
 air toxics, 187-188
 environmental research, 185
 toxic substances, 200
Risk Assistant database, 201
Risk communication, 183-184
Risser, Paul G., *218*
Roberts, Halina, 204, *218*
Roberts, Norman, 235, *261*
Robertson, Douglas S., 7, *40*
Robertson, Stephen E., 309, 312, *317*
Robertson, W., 120, *126*
Robey, Daniel, *261, 262*
Robins, Kevin, 46, 51, *37, 92, 95*
Rockart, John F., 16, *40, 261*
Rogers, Everett M., *85, 86*
Roitman, Howard, 163, *166*
Role playing, information science education, 278, 285
Roles
 information environment, 236-237
 information professionals, 298-300
Roper polls, 26
Rose, Keith, *218*
Rosenbaum, Howard, *90*
Rosenkrantz, Stuart A., *258*
Ross, Lee, 244, *260*
Rothman, H., 179, *218*
Rothschild, Joan, *40*
Rothstein, Samuel, *323*
Rouse, Sandra H., 249, *261*
Rouse, William B., 249, *261*
Roussopoulos, N., *170*
Rowan, Roy, *261*
Royce, Christopher L., *218*
RTECS, *see* Registry of Toxic Effects of Chemical Substances
Ruane, Janet M., *34*
Rubbersheeting, geographic information systems, 144

Rubin, Michael Rogers, 46, *92*
Rubin, Richard, 294, 295, 297, 304, *323*
Rubinskii, K.I., 284
Rubinyi, Robert M., 11, *41*
Rumiantsev Museum, 270
Rural areas
 computer competence, 56
 impact of information technology, 28
 NREN access, 63
 telephone service, 56-57
Russell, Bertrand, 31
Russell, Judy I., *126*
Russia, information science education, 282
Russian Academy, abstracting principles, 270
Rutgers University, School of Communication, Information, and Library Studies, Annual Symposium of the Graduate Alumni and Faculty, 1991, 322
Rydell, C. Peter, *82*
Ryu, Daehee, *86*

Sachsman, David B., *218*
Sackman, Harold, 46, 79, *92*
Safe Drinking Water Act (SDWA), 175
Safety
 environmental research, 185
 pollutants, 199-205
Sagamore Computer Conference, 1972, 124
Sage, Gloria W., *214*
Saghafi, Massoud, 78
Sales supervisors, telecommuting, 23
Salomon, Gavriel, 11, *41*
Salton, Gerard, 112, 113, 115, 120, 281, *128*
Salzberg, Betty, 152, *168*
Samet, Hanan, 139, 150, 151, 153, 191, *169, 170, 218*
Samuelson, Paul A., 53, 79, *93*
Sanctions, codes of ethics, 315
Sandman, Peter M., *218*
Santa Monica, Calif., 71, *93*

Santa Monica, Calif., (cont.)
  Public Electronic Network (PEN), 70, 71-72
Santodonato, Joseph, 186, 200, *218*
SARA, *see* Superfund Amendments and Reauthorization Act
Satellite data, geographic information systems, 147, 148, 160, 161
  NREN transmission, 62
Satisficing, decision making, 240
Sawyer, Edmond J., 293, 314, *317*
Scan rate, parallel computing, 106
Scanning
  decision making, 241
  geographic information systems, 147-148
Schaefer, Ralf E., *259*
Schainblatt, A.H., 250, *253*
Schamber, Linda, 230, *261*
Scheck, Hans J., 139, 157, *167*
Schein, Edgar H., 248, *261*
Schettkat, Ronald, 33
Schiffman, Leon G., 12, *41*
Schiller, Anita R., 51, *93*
Schiller, Dan, 51, *93*
Schiller, Herbert I., 51, *93*
Schmidmaier, Dieter, *323*
Schmitz, Joseph, 14, *41*, *86*
Schneider, Karl R., 195, 203, *218*
Schon, Donald A., 231, 236, *261*
School libraries, *see* Libraries
Schools, computers, 56
  NREN access, 63
Schroeder, Eunice M., 3
Schuman, Patricia, *323*
Schwartz, Nancy L., 49, *94*
Schweiger, D.M., *261*
Schwenk, C.R., 245, *261*
SCI, *see Science Citation Index*
Science, and democracy, 31
Science Citation Index (SCI), 179, 193
Science fiction, 10
Science of science, Soviet Union, 281
Science of Science [Nauka o nauke], 272
Science policy, Soviet Union, 268-275
Scientific and technical information (STI)

Scientific and technical information (cont.)
  Soviet Union, 267
  abstracting, 273-274
  censorship, 274-275
  dissertations, 279-280
  governmental control, 275
  inventions, 273
  translation to Russian, 270-271
Scientific communication, 177, 182
Scientific Communications and Informatics, 270
Scientific productivity, Soviet Union, 272-273
Scientists, computer-mediated communication, 23
Scientometrics [Naukometriia], 273
Scott, Karen, *214*
Scott Morton, Michael S., 236, *256*
Scott Polar Research Institute, *see* University of Kent, Scott Polar Research Institute
Scripps Institution of Oceanography, Library, 195
SDI (selective dissemination of information), parallel computing, 118-119
SDIC, *see* Superfund Docket Information Center
SDWA, *see* Safe Drinking Water Act
Search services, *see* Database vendors
Searching, effectiveness, 207
Sears, Prodigy videotex service, 75
Sears, Jonathan R.L., 191, 196, 197, *218*
Seattle, information gateway, 77, 78
Second industrial revolution, 46
Secretaries, telecommuting, 23
Security, *see* Data security
Seiden, H., *82*
Selected Water Resources Abstracts (SWRA), 193
Selective dissemination of information, *see* SDI
Self concept, impact of information technology, 6, 7, 15
Sellis, T., 147, *170*
Seminar on Water-Related Information Retrieval, 1990, *211*

INDEX

SeniorNet computer network, 68
Senn, James A., *254*
Sense making, information needs, 58, 60
Septrees, spatial indexing, 150
Sere, Kaisa, 104, 113, *129*
Serebnick, Judith, 309, *323*
Service sector, 46
  impact of information technology, 17
Seshan, M., *166*
Sevastopol Engineering Institute, 280
Sevcik, K.C., *169*
Sexual norms, impact of information technology, 6, 9
Shaffer, Clifford A., 147, 151, 153, 155, 156, 191, *170, 219*
Shaiken, Harley, 20, *41*
Shannon, Claude E., 183, *219*
Shannon-Weaver communication model, 183
Shapiro, Ian, 49, *94*
Sharma, Ravi, 116, 118, *128*
Sharp, John A., 101, *128*
Shattuck, John, *41*
Shaver, Donna B., 301, *323*
Shavit, David, 57, *93*
Shaw, Eugene F., 8, *36*
Shekhurin, E.E., 284, *290*
Sheniavskii University, 270
Shepard, Thomas H., 201, *212*
Sherman, Elaine, 12, *41*
Sherrill, Laurence L., 70, *93*
Shields, Gerald R., *323*
Shirazi, B., *125*
Shoemaker, Floyd F., *215*
Shopping services
  Prodigy videotex, 75
  Teletel system, 74
Short, James E., 16, *40*
Shuman, Bruce A., *322*
Shumov, Iu.A., 283, *290*
Shute, S.J., *215*
Sicevic, Mirjana, *217*
Siefert, Marsha, 51, *93*
Siegelmann, Hava Tova, 116, 118, *124*
SIGLE, *see* System for Information on Grey Literature in Europe database

Sijstermans, Frans, 117, *122*
SilverPlatter, 192, 204, 205, 206
  Earth Sciences Disc, 206
  Pest-Bank, 203
Silverstein, Murray, *81*
SIMD (single instruction stream, multiple data stream) computers, 102-103
  information retrieval, 109-116
Simon, Herbert A., 238, 239, 240, *254, 258, 262*
Simonds, A.P., *41*
Simonett, David S., 136, 148, 157, 161, *171*
Sims, Henry P., Jr., 246, *262*
Singer, Alexander, 120, *128*
Singh, Jitendra V., 230, *256*
Single instruction stream, multiple data stream, *see* SIMD
Single instruction stream, single data stream, *see* SISD
Singleton, Loy A., 57, *94*
Singleton, W.L., *212*
SISD (single instruction stream, single data stream) computers, 102
SITE, *see* Superfund Innovative Technology Evaluation
Skeletonization, geographic information systems, 149
Skillicorn, David B., 102, *128*
Slack, Jennifer Daryl, 313, *41, 323*
Slocum, J.W., Jr., *256*
Slovic, Paul, 210, *257*
Sludge, pollution, 177
Small, Henry, 179, *219*
Smart homes, 10
SMCRA, *see* Surface Mining Control and Reclamation Act
Smith, H.A., *41*
Smith, Kent F., *125*
Smith, Linda K., *218*
Smith, Mona F., 176, 180, *212*
Smith, P.J., *215*
Smith, Randolph B., 77, 78, *94*
Smith, Terence R., 153, 161, *164, 171*
Snapper, John W., 293, *321*
Snizek, William E., 23, *41*
Snow, Bonnie, 186, 204, *219*
Soaps, safety, 203

Sobel, Joel, 140, 141, *171*
Social equity
 and information technology, 43-81
 and justice, 49, 52-57
 NREN, 63
The Social Function of Science, 272
Social gate, technology and society, 47
Social harmony, 304, 306, 307
Social information processing, 14
Social interactions
 impact of information technology, 11
 work environment, 14-16
Social responsibility
 ethics, 296, 298, 302, 310
 information professionals, 293
Social security, 296
 information needs, 68
Socialism, information science, 269-270
Socialist societies, scientific and technical information, 267
Society, impact of information technology, 3-33
Sociology, management information, 230
Soelberg, P.O., *262*
Software development, impact of information technology, 22
SOIL database, 191
Sokolova, T.A., *219*
Solid and Hazardous Waste Technology Transfer Electronic Bulletin Board, 190
Solid modeling, geographic information system applications, 161
Solov'eva, A.A., *288*
Southwestern Bell telephone company, 76, 78
Soviet Union, *see* U.S.S.R.
Space Physics Analysis Network, *see* U.S., National Aeronautics and Space Administration (NASA), Space Physics Analysis Network
Spaghetti file, geographic information systems, 145

SPAN, *see* U.S., National Aeronautics and Space Administration (NASA), Space Physics Analysis Network
SPANS (geographic information system), 141, 154
Spatial data, geographic information systems, 136, 137, 142
Spatial databases, *see* Databases, spatial
Spatial indexing, geographic information systems, 144, 150-156
Spatial information, water pollution databases, 192
Special librarians, ethics, 307
Special libraries, support for Soviet Union, 271-272
 see also Libraries
Speed, parallel computing, 106-108, 113
Speed vs. accuracy, management information, 235
Spence, Muriel Morisey, *41*
Spinning jenny, 7
Spitzer, S.F., 59, *94*
Spokesperson role, managers, 237
Sports information, Teletel system, 74
Spreading activation models, parallel computing, 109
 information retrieval, 120-121
SPRI, *see* University of Kent, Scott Polar Research Institute
Sprint telecommunications company, 76
Sproat, William, 190, 206, *219*
Sproull, Lee S., 15, 16, *36*, *41*, *257*
Sputnik, and Soviet science, 272
SQL (Structured Query Language), geographic information systems, 137, 162
St. George, Art, 61, *94*
St. Louis, community information system, 70, 71
St. Paul, Minn., information gateway, 77, 78
St. Petersburg (Soviet Union) Academy of Sciences Library, 270

St. Petersburg, (cont.)
  Imperial Public Library, 270
Staff morale, information science education, 285
Staffing, information managers, 237
Stahl, Wilson M., *323*
Stalinism, and Soviet science, 272
Standards
  geographic information systems, 142
  information professionals, 301
Stanfill, Craig, 100, 107, 108, 110, 112, 113, 114, 117, 121, *128*
Star, J., 136, 137, 139, *171*
Statistical Abstract of the United States, 12
Statistical analysis, geographic information systems, 161
Statistics, 308
  decision making, 245
Steckel, Marie-Monique, 74, 75, *85*
Steele, G.L., Jr., 106, *124*
Steinfield, Charles W., 4, *41*
Stellhorn, William H., 119, *129*
Stern, Richard M., *219*
Stevens, A., 151, *167*
Stewart, Mark, 115, *129*
Stewart, R., 235, *262*
STI, *see* Scientific and technical information
Stieg, Margaret F., *323*
Stone, Harold S., 113, *129*
Storage, parallel computing, 107
Storage technology, geographic information systems, 136
Stoss, Frederick W., 185, 186, 199, *215, 219*
Strassmann, Paul A., 5, 248, *41, 262*
Strategic problems, management information, 236, 245
Strategies, managers, 238
Strauch, Bruce, 292, *323*
Strauch, Katina, 292, *323*
String searching, parallel computing, 105, 110
Stroup, Dorothy, 190, *225*
Structured Query Language, *see* SQL

Stueart, Robert D., 60, *94*
Su, Stanley Y.W., 100, *129*
Subject headings, compared with descriptors, 196-197
Suchman, Lucy A., 230, *262*
Sugnet, C., *324*
Sulfur dioxide, air pollution, 198
Sullivan, Thomas F.P., 212
Sun network, parallel computing, 117
Sun workstations, parallel computing, 103, 112, 114, 118
Suominen, Elina, 59, *94*
Supercomputers, 101
  history, 99
Superfund, 177
  national priority list, 189-190, 191
Superfund Amendments and Reauthorization Act (SARA), 173, 175, 180-181, 189
Superfund Docket Information Center (SDIC), 189-190
Superfund Innovative Technology Evaluation (SITE), 191, 206
Superlinear speed-up, parallel computing, 106
Surface Mining Control and Reclamation Act (SMCRA), 175
Surprenant, Thomas T., 23, *33*
Surveillance, 51
  information gathering, 246
  information technology, 19-20
Survey data, geographic information systems, 148
Survival, ethics, 296, 298
Sustainable Resource Use Research Institute, National Institutes for the Environment (proposed), 174
Swan, John C., 292, *324*
Sweden
  geographic information systems, 138
  privacy protection, 25
Swetland, James H., *324*
Switchboards, information and referral systems, 65
Swope, Susan, *323*
SWRA, *see* Selected Water Resources Abstracts

SYMAP (Synargraphic Map) cartographic software, 141
Symbolic information, 247
Symbolization, geographic information systems, 143
Symposium on Science Communication: Environmental and Health Research, 1988, 183, *208*, *216*, *219*
Symposium on the Design and Implementation of Large Spatial Databases, 1991, *167*
Synthetic experience, information technology, 8
Syracuse Research Corp., 200
System for Information on Grey Literature in Europe (SIGLE) database, 192
Systems design, Soviet Union, 283
Systems development, ethics, 316

Taggart, William, *261*, *262*
Tailby, Stephanie, *41*
Talk shows, 9
Tamminen, Markku, 154, *171*
Tapaswi, M.P., 186, 191, 194, *219*
Tarakanov, K.V., 281, 282, 283, *290*
Tarkowski, Stanislaw, *219*
Task forces, symbolic value, 247
Tawney, Richard Henry, *94*
Tax evasion, use of information technology, 25
Taxes, information needs, 68
Taxonomy, databases, 187, 193
Taylor, Robert S., 230, 233, 242, 243, 248, 249, 252, *258*, *262*
Taylor, Ronald N., 252
TBDF, *see* Trans-border data flow
Teacher's colleges, information science education, Soviet Union, 276
Teamwork, management information, 229
Technology, and society, 45-48
Technology transfer, ethics, 296
Telecommunications, political power, 52
Telecommunications industry, 51
Telecommunications technology, 45
Telecommunications workers, impact of information technology, 20-21
Telecommuting, 22
Teleconferencing, 14
Teledemocracy, 28-31, 32
Teledemocracy Project, National Public Telecomputing Network, 69-70
Telefacsimile, *see* Facsimile transmission
Telemedicine, 12
Telephone companies, gateway systems, 61, 75-79, 94-103
Telephone metaphor, NREN, 64
Telephone referrals, information and referral systems, 66, 67
Telephone service, 56-57
Telephone system, universal access, 63-64
Telephones
  compared with computer-mediated communication, 15
  social impact, 7
Teleshopping, *see* Shopping services
Teletel System, 74-75
Teletext, 10
Television, 59
  see also Cable television
  information professionals, Soviet Union, 283
  management information, 228
  social impact, 4, 6, 8, 9, 11, 12, 32
Tenure, ethics, 314
Teratogen Information System, *see* TERIS
Teratogenic effects, risk assessment, 201-202
TERIS (Teratogen Information System), 201-202
Term comparator, information retrieval, parallel computing, 119-120
Term-frequency, inverse document frequency weights (TFXIDF), 112
Terrene Institute, 197, *219*
Text processing, parallel computing, 99-122

INDEX 375

Text signatures, information retrieval, parallel computing, 111-113, 118
Textbooks, 202
Texts, electronic, see Electronic texts
TFXIDF, see Term-frequency, inverse document frequency weights
Thau, Robert, 107, 114, 121, *128*
Theoret, Andre, *259*
Theoreticians, ethics, 308-314
Thermostats, information technology, 10
Thesauri
  agriculture, 196-197
  scientific and technical information, 281
  water pollution, 196
Think-aloud patterns, scientists, 182
Thinking Machines Corporation, 103, *129*
Thistle Publishing, 201, *219*
Thomas, Robert J., *42*
Thomas, Sarah E., 197, *219*
Thompson, James D., 243, *262*
Thomson Corp., Medical Economics Data Co., 202
Three Mile Island, 183
Three-dimensional data, geographic information systems, 161
Thurow, Lester C., 54, *94*
Tiananmen Square crisis, 27
Tichenor, Phillip J., 56, 59, *36, 94*
Tichy, Noel M., 246, *263*
TIGER (Topically Integrated Geographic Encoding and Referencing) database, 136, 140, 142, 146
TIGRIS (Topically Integrated Geographic Information System), 141, 154
Tiling, geographic information systems, 158-159
Tilley, Carolyn B., 177, *220*
Time data, geographic information systems, 160
Timing
  parallel computing
    evaluation, 107
    information retrieval, 116

TIN, see Triangulated irregular network
TIP, see Detroit Public Library, The Information Place
T.J. Hooper (tugboat), 302
Tjoumas, Renee, *324*
Tobler, Waldo R., 156, 159, *164, 171*
Todd, Seldon P., *88*
Toffler, Alvin, 3, 19, *42, 94*
Tomassini, Christine, *215*
Tomita, Kazuo, *213*
Tomlin, Dana C., *220*
Tomlinson, J.W.C., 235, 236, *252*
Tomlinson, Roger F., 135, 139, 140, 152, 157, 159, *169, 171*
Tomsk Electrotechnical Institute, 280
Topically Integrated Geographic Encoding and Referencing, see TIGER
Topological models, geographic information systems, 145
Topology, parallel computers, 104
Topology reconstruction, geographic information systems, 149
Toronto, videotex service, 78
Total quality management, 207
Toxic Release Inventory (TRI), 180-181, 190
Toxic substances, safety, 199-202
Toxic Substances Control Act (TSCA), 175, 199, 201
Toxicology, bibliometrics, 179
Toxicology Data Network, see TOXNET
Toxline database, 202
TOXNET (Toxicology Data Network), 181, 184, 185, 201
  IRIS (Integrated Risk Information System), 201
  Registry of Toxic Effects of Chemical Substances (RTECS) database, 203
Training, NREN use, 63
Tran, Kim, 163
Trans-border data flow (TBDF), 23, 314
Translations, scientific and technical information, Soviet Union, 271, 275

Transportation
  geographic information systems, 159
  information needs, 58
  innovation, 7
Transportation policy, pollution prevention, 185
Transputers, 104
  see also MIMD (multiple instruction stream, multiple data stream) computers
  information retrieval, 111, 113, 114
Trew, Arthur, 103, 104, *129*
TRI, see Toxic Release Inventory
Triangulated irregular network (TIN), geographic information systems, 156
Troast, Richard, *214*
Troullinos, Nikos B., 120, *122*
Trow, D.B., *254*
Truncation, information retrieval, parallel computing, 110
Truthfulness, 305, 310, 315
TRW text processor, 119
Tsai, J., *170*
TSCA, see Toxic Substances Control Act
TSCA Test Submission (TSCAT) database, 199
Tsebe, John Kgwale, 313, *324*
TSITEIN (technical-economic information centers), Soviet Union, 271
Tuden, Arthur, 243, *262*
Tufte, Edward R., 162, *171*
Tugboats, use of radios, 302
Turkey, labor force, 17
Turkle, Sherry, 3, 10, 15, *42*
Turkmenistan, 285
Turkov, Zh.I., 279
Turner, Philip M., 62, 63, *84*
Tushman, M., 227, *263*
Tuttle, Mark, *317*
Tversky, Amos, 240, 245, *257, 263*
Tydac, 141, 154

U.K.
  Department of Trade and Industry, 67
  geographic information systems, 138
  National Association of Citizens' Advice Bureaux (NACAB), 64, 67-68
  National Council of Social Service, 67-68
  Operational Navigational Charts project, 142
  radioactivity pollution, 199
  safety information, 204
  videotex, 10
U.N.
  Educational, Scientific and Cultural Organization, see Unesco
  Environmental Program (UNEP), 188
  Food and Agriculture Organization (FAO), 195
  Industrial Development Organization, see UNIDO
U.S.
  Army
    Construction Engineering Research Laboratory (CERL), 191
    Corps of Engineers, 191, 192, *220*
  Bureau of Labor Statistics (BLS), 18
  Bureau of the Census, 53, 56, 140, 141-142, 145, 154, *94, 171*
    TIGER files, see TIGER
  Central Intelligence Agency (CIA), 140, *171*
    World Data Bank, 141
  Congress, 62, 173, 189, 199, 201, *94, 210*
    C-SPAN, 31
  Congressional Budget Office, 53, *94*
  House
    Committee on Energy and Commerce, 24

U.S., (cont.)
  Congress, (cont.)
    House, (cont.)
      Committee on the Budget, 53, *95*
      information use, 30
      Member Information Network (MIN), 31
      Office of Technology Assessment (OTA), 24, 26, 43, *42, 95*
    Senate, Committee on Environment and Public Works, *221*
  Defense Mapping Agency, 142
  Department of Agriculture, 191
  Department of Commerce, 206
    economic data, National Public Telecomputing Network, 70
    National Technical Information Service, *see* NTIS
  Department of Defense (DOD), 206
    Advanced Research Projects Agency (ARPA), 62
  Department of Education, 198
    Office of Educational Research and Improvement, 71, *95*
  Department of Energy (DOE), 174, 206
  Department of Housing and Urban Development (HUD), 185
  Department of Justice, 76
  Department of Labor, Retraining and Reemployment Administration, 65, *95*
  Department of the Interior (DOI), 174
    Geological Survey, *see* U.S., Geological Survey
  Department of Transportation, Research and Special Programs Administration, 190
  Environmental Protection Agency (EPA)
    Air Risk Information Support Center (Air RISC), 187, 222
    databases, 181
    decentralization, 176

U.S., (cont.)
  Environmental Protection Agency, (cont.)
    Health Effects Research Laboratory, 205
    information dissemination, 187-188, 189
    Information Management and Services Division, 190, 197, 222
    Office of Acid Deposition, Environmental Monitoring and Quality Assurance, 197, 222
    Office of Air Quality Planning and Standards, 198, 222
    Office of Drinking Water, 201
    Office of Environmental Engineering and Technology Demonstration, Pollution Prevention Office, 206, 222
    Office of Information Resources Management, 222
    Information Services and Library, 187, 191, 222
    Office of International Activities, 176, 187, 223
    Office of Pesticides and Toxic Substances, 203, 223
    Office of Policy Analysis, Planning and Evaluation, 177, 223
    Office of Research and Development, 205, 223
    Office of Science Advisory Board, 174, 185, 223
    Office of Solid Waste, Waste Minimization Technical Information Clearinghouse, 223
    Office of Solid Waste and Emergency Response (OSWER), Office of Emergency and Remedial Response, 189-190
    Office of Toxic Substances, 199
      Economics and Technology Division, 183, 223

U.S., (cont.)
  Environmental Protection Agency (cont.)
    Office of Waste Programs Enforcement, 190
    regional libraries and information centers, 187
    Superfund Docket Information Center (SDIC), 189-190
    Toxic Release Inventory, see Toxic Release Inventory
  Federal Communications Commission, see Federal Communications Commission
  Federal Emergency Management Agency (FEMA), 190
  Fish and Wildlife Service, 193
  General Accounting Office (GAO), 57, 177, 181, 186, 191, 198, 95, 224
  Geological Survey, (USGS), 140, 141, 206, 221
    Office of Science and Technology Policy, Federal Coordinating Council for Science, Engineering, and Technology, Committee on Earth and Environment, 206, 221-222
  Government Printing Office (GPO), 187
  information science education, model for Soviet Union, 278
  Library of Congress, see Library of Congress
  National Academy of Sciences
   National Research Council
    Committee on Risk Perception and Communication, 183, 224
    Committee on the Institutional Means for Assessment of Risks to Public Health, 200, 224
  National Aeronautics and Space Administration (NASA), 157, 174, 206
    Earth Observing System, see Earth Observing System
    Space Physics Analysis Network (SPAN), 205

U.S., (cont.)
  National Institutes for the Environment (proposed), 173-174
  National Institutes of Health, 174
  National Library of Medicine, see National Library of Medicine
  National Oceanic and Atmospheric Administration (NOAA), 174
    Space Physics Analysis Network (SPAN), 205
  National Science Foundation, see National Science Foundation
  National Security Agency (NSA), 25
  National Technical Information Service, see NTIS
  privacy protection, 25
  Supreme Court, National Public Telecomputing Network, 69
  U.S. Global Change Research Program (USGCRP), 206
  U.S. Government Environmental Datafiles & Software, 189
U.S.S.R.
  Academy of Sciences, 269, 272, 273
    Institute of Technical Information, 273
  BINT (Bureau of Foreign Science and Technology), 270-271
  electronic mail, 27
  GKNT (State Committee for Science and Technology), 274, 276
  GOSINTI (technical information network), 271
  Gostekhnika, 274
  information science education, 267-287
  International Center for Scientific and Technical Information, 275, 278
  IPKIR (Institute for the Raising of Information Workers' Qualifications), 274, 276-277, 284, 286
  libraries, 270
  Ministry of Culture, 280
    information science education, 284
  science policy, 268-275

INDEX 379

U.S.S.R., (cont.)
  State Scientific Library, 271
  technical information network, 271
  VINITI (All-Union Institute for Scientific and Technical Information), see VINITI
UCLA, see University of California at Los Angeles
Udell, J.G., 59, 95
ULIT, see Umweltliteratur Datenbank
Umweltliteratur Datenbank (ULIT), 192
Uncertainty, information managers, 237
Underground storage tanks, pollution, 177
UNEP, see U.N., Environmental Program
Unesco (United Nations Educational, Scientific, and Cultural Organization), information science education, 279
  International Hydrological Program, 192
Unfinished Business: A Comparative Assessment of Environmental Problems, 177, 178
Ungson, G.R., 243, 263
UNIDO (United Nations Industrial Development Organization), information science education, 279
United Kingdom, see U.K.
United Nations, see U.N.
United States, see U.S.
United Way of America, 65
Universal Copyright Convention, Soviet Union, 274
Universal service, NREN, 63
Universal Transverse Mercator projection (UTM), 159
Universities
  campus-wide information systems, 73-74
  information science education, Soviet Union, 276, 284-285, 287
University of Calgary, Arctic Institute of North America, 189

University of California at Los Angeles, 178
  Engineering Research Center, 182
University of California at San Diego, Library, 194
University of Delaware, 205
University of Hawaii, Hawaii FYI, 72
University of Illinois, Graduate School of Library and Information Science, Allerton Park Institute, 1991, 292, 322
University of Kent, Scott Polar Research Institute (SPRI), 189
University of London, 11
University of Texas, Dallas, Health Science Center, 201
University of Vermont, 198
University of Vilnius, 284
University of Wisconsin - Milwaukee, Library Conference, 1967, 93
Updating, geographic information systems, 148, 161
Ural State University, 276
Urban and Regional Information Systems Association (URISA), 139
Urban planning, geographic information systems, 139
URISA, see Urban and Regional Information Systems Association
URSA (Utah Retrieval System Architecture), 119
Ursul, A.D., 269, 290
US West telephone company, 73, 76, 77, 78
User interface, see Human-computer interaction
User studies, environmental communication, 180-182, 207
User-driven models, information systems, 249
USGCRP, see U.S. Global Change Research Program
USGS, see U.S., Geological Survey
Utah Retrieval System Architecture, see URSA
Utilitarianism, 292, 296, 304, 306, 307
UTM, see Universal Transverse Mercator projection

Value added, management information, 249
van Dam, Andries, *166*
Van Hook, R.I., *224*
Van Oosterom, Peter, 152, 159, *171*
Vax workstations, parallel computing, 103
Vector data representations, geographic information systems, 144, 145-150
Vector-based computers, 100
Vector-based information retrieval, 114-115
Vector-to-raster conversion, geographic information systems, 148-149
Vectorization, geographic information systems, 149
Vega, Sanchez, Fernando E., *224*
Vehicle navigation, geographic information systems, 160-161
Vehicle Navigation and Information Systems Conference (VNIS), 1989, *170*
Vertical files, acid rain information, 199
Very large scale integration, see VLSI
Veterans' information centers, 64
Vickery, Alina, 58, *95*
Vickery, Brian Campbell, 58, 248, *95*, *263*
Video games, 4, 11
Videotex, 9, 10, 29, 30, 74, 75
Vigden, Grant A., *225*
Vincent, David R., 13, *42*
VINITI (All-Union Institute for Scientific and Technical Information [Vsesoiuznyi Institut Nauchnoi i Tekhnicheskoi Informatsii]), 268, 273-279, 286, *290*
  First Department, 274-275
Virtual algorithms, parallel computing, 104
Visibility, geographic information systems, 157
Visualization, geographic information systems, 157, 162

Vladutz, George, 274, *290*
VLSI (very large scale integration), 99, 100
  supercomputers, 101
VNIS, see Vehicle Navigation and Information Systems Conference
Volta, G., 161, *169*
Volunteers, Free-Nets, 69
von Neumann computers, 99, 102, 118
Von Winterfeldt, Detlof, *210*
Voos, Henry, *95*
Vorob'ev, G.G., 285, *290*
Vrana, Ric, 160, *172*
Vries, John K., *130*
Vucinich, Alexander, 269, 270, 272, 286, *290*

Wagle, Sharad, 137, 139, *169*
Wagner, Travis P., *225*
Walden, Marina, 104, 113, *129*
Wall Street Journal, 74, *95*
Wallace, Michael, 13, 17, *42*
Wallich, Paul, 26, *42*
Walton, D.W.H., 188, *225*
Waltz, David, 112, *128*, *129*
Wang, Y.-F., *164*
War on Poverty, 65
Wartella, Ellen, 8, *42*
Washington Times Corporation, National Public Telecomputing Network, 69
Waste management, software, 190
Waste products, safety, 203
Wastewater treatment, software support, 195-196
Water pollution, 177
  bibliometrics, 179
  information sources, 191-198
Water quality
  assessment, 197
  databases, 193
Water Resources Abstracts, 184
Waterman, Robert H., Jr., 248, *261*
Waternet database, 184
Watershed management, 197
Watersheds, geographic information systems, 157

INDEX

Watkins, Beverly T., 73, 74, *95*
Watson, Bruce L., 302, *317*
Watson, Tom, 225
Watts, Tim J., *321*
Waugh, T.C., 138, 153, *172*
Wealth, and information gap, 53-54
Weather forecasting, supercomputers, 101
Weather information, Teletel system, 74
Weaver, Warren, 183, *219*
Webber, Robert E., 151, 153, *170*
Webster, Frank, 46, 51, 92, *95*
Weibel, Robert, 143, 157, *164*, *172*
Weick, Karl E., 246, *254*, *263*
Weighted term searching, parallel computing, 113, 117
Weinberg, Nathan, *42*
Weiner, Kevin R., *85*
Weiss, Carol H., 24, *42*
Weiss, S.F., 115, *124*
Welfare, environmental pollution, 177
Welfare fraud, use of information technology, 25
Welfare information, information technology, 11
Welfare programs, information needs, 58, 66
Wells, Barbara B., 225
Wersig, G., 248, *263*
Western Lake Survey, 198
Western scientific publications, translation to Russian, 270-271
Wetherbe, J.C., *263*
Wetlands, pollution prevention, 185
Wexler, Philip, 177, 190, 201, *215*, 225
Weyer, Stephen A., 117, *129*
WFW, *see* Wildlife & Fisheries Worldwide
Wheeler, Basil R., *259*
Whigham, P., *165*
White, Herbert S., 299, 310, *324*
White House Conference on Library and Information Services
  1979, *83*, *94*
  1991, 43, *91*
White, Howard D., 225

White, Mark, 160, *172*
Whitney, D. Charles, 8, *42*
Whitson, Colin, *41*
Whittaker, J., *215*
Whittemore, B.J., 227, 248, *263*
Wiggins, Gary, 225
Wildavsky, Aaron, 88, *263*
Wildlife, databases, 193
Wildlife & Fisheries Worldwide (WFW) database, 193
Wilkinson, Ross, 120, *129*
Wilkinson-Tough, Margaret L., 225
Willett, Peter, 100, 107, 110, 112, 114, 115, 116, *122*, *123*, *127*, *129*, *131*
Williams, Frederick, *42*
Williams, John, 11, *37*
Williams, K.I., 64, *95*
Williams, Martha E., 186, 187, 294, *215*, 225, *324*
Williams, Mary B., *319*
Williams, Robert C., 191, *213*
Williamson Report, 284
Wilson, George A., *123*
Wilson, Greg, 100, 101, 104, *129*, *130*
Wilson, Rand, *36*
Wilson, T.D., *263*
Windel, G., 248, *263*
Windowing, geographic information systems, 145
Winsor, Charlotte B., 70, *96*
Witowski, A., 188, *213*
Wolff, William M., Jr., 57, *82*
Women
  ethical development, 304
  labor force, 13
Wood, Frances E., 225
Woodward, Diana, 292, 293, 301, 307, 310, *324*
Woolf, Patricia, *213*
Work, managers, 235-236
Work, Colin, 73, *96*
Work in progress, environmental researchers, 182
Work life, impact of information technology, 6, 13-24
Workers
  exposure to chemicals, 178
  geographic dispersion, 9, 21-24
  job skills, 17

Workforce, *see* Labor force
Workplace, automation, 47
Workshop on Information Assessment of Environmentalists in the State of California, 1988, 182
World Data Bank I, 141
World Data Bank II, 140, 141
World Value Survey, 5
Wozniak, Steven, 10
Wright, William F., *263*
Wykoff, Leslie W., *323*

X-ray images, NREN transmission, 62
XREF file, environmental fate and exposure databases, 200

Yang, Shiren, 159, *167*
Yarnall, Louise, 71, *96*
Yates, Rochelle, 66, *96*

Young, Elizabeth L., *42*
Yount, Russell J., 118, *130*
Yovits, M.C., 227, 248, 263
Yugoslav Water-Related Information System (YUWAT), 192
YUWAT, *see* Yugoslav Water-Related Information System

Z-order code, spatial indexing, 323
Zamenhof, Lazarus, 281
Zand, Dale E., 234, 243, 248, *263*
Zanna, Mark P., 15, *38*
Zimmerman, Jan, *42*
Zimmerman, Shirley, *88*
Zmud, Robert W., 252
Zoological Record database, 194
Zoraster, Steven, 161, *172*
Zuboff, Shoshana, 3, 16, 19, 20, 47, *42*, *96*
Zucker, M., 59, *96*
Zweizig, Douglas, 59, *84*, *96*

Introduction to the Keyword and Author Index

The following section is an author and keyword index to *ARIST* chapters for Volumes 1 through 27. It has been produced to assist users in locating specific topics, chapters, and author names for all *ARIST* volumes to date. The index terms are sorted alphabetically and include all author names and content words from titles (a stop-word list of articles, conjunctions, and other non-content words was used). The sort word is followed by the author(s) name(s) and the *ARIST* citation.

Keyword and Author Index of *ARIST* Titles for Volumes 1-27

Abstracting
   Keenan, Stella, **4**, p273
Access
   Fox, Edward A. **23**, p85; Hildreth, Charles R. **20**, p233; Lynch, Clifford and Preston, Cecilia **25**, p. 263
Activities
   Adams, Scott and Werdel, Judith A. **10**, p303
Adams, Peter D.
   Lerner, Rita G., Metaxas, Ted, Scott, John T., Adams, Peter D., and Judd, Peggy. Primary Publication Systems and Scientific Text Processing. **18**, p127
Adams, Scott
   Adams, Scott and Werdel, Judith A. Cooperation in Information Activities through International Organizations. **10**, p303
ADI
   Cuadra, Carlos A. **1**, p1
Adkinson, Burton W.
   Berninger, Douglas E. and Adkinson, Burton W. Interaction between the Public and Private Sectors in National Information Programs. **13**, p3
Agricultural
   Frank, Robyn C. **22**, p293
Aids
   Caruso, Elaine, **16**, p317
Aines, Andrew A.
   Aines, Andrew A. and Day, Melvin S. National Planning of Information Services. **10**, p3
Allen, Bryce L.
   Allen Bryce L. Cognitive Research in Information Science: Implications for Design. **26**, p3
   Kinnucan, Mark T., Nelson, Michael J. and Allen, Bryce J. Statistical Methods in Information Science Research. **22**, p147
Allen, Thomas J.
   Allen, Thomas J. Information Needs and Uses. **4**, p3
Alper, Bruce H.
   Alper, Bruce H. Library Automation. **10**, p199
Alsberg, Peter A.
   Bunch, Steve R. and Alsberg, Peter A. Computer Communication Networks, **12**, p183

America
> Saracevic, Tefko, Braga, Gilda, and Quijano Solis, Alvaro. **14**, p249

American Institute of Physics Staff
> American Institute of Physics Staff. Techniques for Publication and Distribution of Information. **2**, p339

Amsler, Robert A.
> Amsler, Robert A. Machine-Readable Dictionaries. **19**, p161

Analysis
> Baxendale, Phyllis. **1**, p71; Carroll, Bonnie (Talmi) and Maskewitz, Betty F. **15**, p147; Fairthorne, Robert A. **4**, p73; Lancaster, F. Wilfrid, Elliker, Calvin, and Connell, Tschera Harkness. **24**, p35; Liston, David M., Jr. and Howder, Murray L. **12**, p81; Mick, Colin K. **14**, p37; Sharp, John R. **2**, p87; Schwartz, Candy and Eisenmann, Laura M. **21**, p37; Taulbee, Orrin E. **3**, p105; Travis, Irene L. and Fidel, Raya. **17**, p123

Announcements
> van Dam, Andries and Michener, James C. **2**, p187

Annual
> Cuadra, Carlos A. **1**, p1

Application
> Beard, Joseph J. **6**, p369

Applications
> Baruch, Jordan J. **1**, p255; Blumstein, Alfred. **7**, p471; Bookstein, Abraham. **20**, p117; Caceres Cesar A., Weihrer, Anna Lea, and Pulliam, Robert. **6**, p325; Levy, Richard P. and Cammarn, Maxine R. **3**, p397; Raben, Joseph and Widmann, R.L. **7**, p439; Silberman, Harry F. and Filep, Robert T. **3**, p357; Smith, Linda C. **15**, p67; Spring, William C., Jr. **2**, p311; Vinsonhaler, John F. and Moon, Robert D. **8**, p277

Architectures
> Hollaar, Lee A. **14**, p129

ARIST Staff
> *ARIST* Staff. New Hardware Developments. **1**, p191

Arnold, Stephen E.
> Arnold, Stephen E. Marketing Electronic Information: Theory, Practice, and Challenges, 1980-1990, **25**, p87

Artandi, Susan
> Artandi, Susan. Document Description and Representation. **5**, p143

Artificial
> Smith, Linda C. **15**, p67; **22**, p41

Arts
> Markey, Karen. **19**, p271; Raben, Joseph and Burton, Sarah K. **16**, p247

Aspects
> Atherton, Pauline and Greer, Roger. **3**, p329; Farradane, J. **6**, p399; Harvey, John F. **2**, p419; Shera, Jesse H. and McFarland, Anne S. **4**, p439; Taylor, Robert S. **1**, p15

Assisted
> Larson, Signe and Williams, Martha E. **15**, p251

Atherton, Pauline
  Atherton, Pauline and Greer, Roger. Professional Aspects of Information Science and Technology. 3, p329
Automated
  Becker, David. 16, p113; Bobrow, D.G., Fraser, J.B. and Quillian, M.R. 2, p161; Damerau, Fred J. 11, p107; Kay, Martin and Sparck Jones, Karen, 6, p141; Montgomery, Christine A. 4, p145; Salton, Gerard. 3, p169; Simmons, Robert F. 1, p137; Walker, Donald E. 8, p69
Automation
  Alper, Bruce H. 10, p199; Avram, Henriette, 6, p171; Bierman, Kenneth J. 9, p123; Black, Donald V. and Farley, Earl A. 1, p273; Griffin, Hillis L. 3, p241; Grosch, Audrey N. 11, p225; Kilgour, Frederick G. 4, p305; Lundeen, Gerald W. and Davis, Charles H. 17, p161; Markuson, Barbara Evans. 2, p255; Martin, Susan K. 7, p243; Martin, Thomas H. 23, p217; Parker, Ralph H. 5, p193; Reed, Mary Jane Pobst and Vrooman, Hugh T. 14, p193; Shaw, Ward and Culkin, Patricia B. 22, p265; Simmons, Peter. 8, p167; Veneziano, Velma, 15, p109
Avram, Henriette
  Avram, Henriette. Library Automation. 6, p171
Awareness
  Wente, Van A. and Young, Gifford A. 5, p259

Ballou, Hubbard W.
  Ballou, Hubbard W. Microform Technology. 8, p121
Baruch, Jordan J.
  Baruch, Jordan J. Information Systems Applications. 1, p255
Based
  Goldstein, Charles M. 19, p65
Bases
  Gechman, Marvin C. 7, p323; Luedke, James A., Jr., Kovacs, Gabor J., and Fried, John B. 12, p119; Schipma, Peter B. 10, p237; Stern, Barrie T. 12, p3; Wilde, Daniel U. 11, p267; Williams, Martha E. 9, p221
Bates, Ellen
  Ojala, Marydee and Bates, Ellen. Business Databases. 21, p87
Bates, Marcia J.
  Bates, Marcia J. Search Techniques. 16, p139
Batten, William E.
  Batten, William E. Document Description and Representation. 8, p43
Baxendale, Phyllis
  Baxendale, Phyllis. Content Analysis, Specification, and Control. 1, p71
Beard, Joseph J.
  Beard, Joseph J. Information Systems Application in Law. 6, p369; Beard, Joseph J. The Copyright Issue. 9, p381
Bearman, Toni Carbo
  Bearman, Toni Carbo. Secondary Information Systems and Services. 13, p179

Becker, David
   Becker, David. Automated Language Processing. **16**, p113
Becker, Joseph
   Becker, Joseph and Olsen, Wallace C. Information Networks. **3**, p289
Belkin; Nicholas J.
   Belkin, Nicholas J and Croft, W. Bruce. Retrieval Techniques. **22**, p109
Bennett, John L.
   Bennett, John L. The User Interface in Interactive Systems. **7**, p159
Berninger, Douglas E.
   Berninger, Douglas E. and Adkinson, Burton W. Interaction between the Public and Private Sectors in National Information Programs. **13**, p3
Berul, Lawrence H.
   Berul, Lawrence H. Document Retrieval. **4**, p203
Bibliographic
   Gechman, Marvin C. **7**, p323; Mischo, William H. and Lee, Jounghyoun. **22**, p227; Park, Margaret K. **12**, p59; Schmierer, Helen F. **10**, p105; Stern, Barrie T. **12**, p3; Tannehill, Robert S., Jr., **18**, p61
Bibliometrics
   Narin, Francis and Moll, Joy K. **12**, p35; White, Howard D. and McCain, Katherine W. **24**, p119
Bierman, Kenneth J.
   Bierman, Kenneth J. Library Automation. **9**, p123
Billingsley, Alice
   Leimkuhler, Ferdinand F. and Billingsley, Alice. Library and Information Center Management. **7**, p499
Biomedical
   Wooster, Harold. **17**, p187
Black, Donald V.
   Black, Donald V. and Farley, Earl A. Library Automation. **1**, p273;
   Black, Donald V. and Fung, Margaret C. Information Systems and Services in China and Japan. **18**, p307
Blumstein, Alfred
   Blumstein, Alfred. Information Systems Applications in the Criminal Justice System. **7**, p471
Bobrow, D.G.
   Bobrow, D.G., Fraser, J.B., and Quillian, M.R. Automated Language Processing. **2**, p161
Bookstein, Abraham
   Bookstein, Abraham. Probability and Fuzzy-Set Applications to Information Retrieval. **20**, p117
Borgman, Christine L.
   Psychological Research in Human-Computer Interaction. **19**, p33
Borko, Harold
   Borko, Harold. Design of Information Systems and Services. **2**, p35
Bourne, Charles P.
   Bourne, Charles P. Evaluation of Indexing Systems. **1**, p171

Boyce, Bert R.
   Boyce, Bert R. and Kraft, Donald H. Principles and Theories in Information Science. **20**, p153
Braga, Gilda
   Saracevic, Tefko, Braga, Gilda, and Quijano Solis, Alvaro. Information Systems in Latin America. **14,** p249
Brandhorst, Wesley T.
   Brandhorst, Wesley T. and Eckert, Philip F. Document Retrieval and Dissemination Systems. **7,** p379
Brimmer, Karl W.
   Brimmer, Karl W. U.S. Telecommunications Common Carrier Policy. **17,** p33;
   Zimmerman, Edward K. and Brimmer, Karl W. National Planning for Data Communications. **16,** p3
Broadbent, Marianne
   Broadbent Marianne and Koenig, Michael E.D. Information and Information Technology Management. **23,** p237
Brown, Patricia L.
   Brown, Patricia L. and Jones, Shirli O. Document Retrieval and Dissemination in Libraries and Information Centers. **3,** p263
Brumm, Eugenia K.
   Brumm, Eugenia K. Optical Disc Technology for Information Management. **26,** p 197
Buckland, Michael K.
   Buckland, Michael K. The Management of Libraries and Information Centers. **9,** p335
Budgeting
   Wilson, John H., Jr. **7,** p39
Bunch, Steve R.
   Bunch, Steve R. and Alsberg, Peter A. Computer Communication Networks. **12,** p183
Burt, Patricia V.
   Burt, Patricia V. and Kinnucan, Mark T. Information Models and Modeling Techniques for Information Systems. **25,** p175
Burton, Sarah K.
   Raben, Joseph and Burton, Sarah K. Information Systems and Services in the Arts and Humanities. **16,** p247
Business
   Sieck, Steven K. **19,** p311; Ojala, Marydee and Bates, Ellen. **21,** p87
Butler, Brett B.
   Spigai, Frances G. and Butler, Brett B. Micrographics. **11,** p59

Caceres, Cesar A.
   Caceres, Cesar A., Weihrer, Anna Lea, and Pulliam, Robert. Information Science Applications in Medicine. **6,** p325

Cammarn, Maxine R.
 Levy, Richard P. and Cammarn, Maxine R. Information Systems Applications in Medicine. **3**, p397
Carlson, Walter M.
 Carlson, Walter M. Privacy. **12**, p279
Carrier
 Brimmer, Karl W. **17**, p33
Carroll, Bonnie (Talmi)
 Carroll, Bonnie (Talmi) and Maskewitz, Betty F. Information Analysis Centers. **15**, p147;
 Coyne, Joseph G., Carroll, Bonnie C., and Redford, Julia S. Energy Information Systems and Services. **18**, p231
Cartridges
 Kletter, Richard C. and Hudson, Heather, **7**, p197
Caruso, Elaine
 Caruso, Elaine Computer Aids to Learning Online Retrieval. **16**, p317
Cassettes
 Kletter, Richard C. and Hudson, Heather. **7**, p197
Catalogs
 Hildreth, Charles R. **20**, p233
Cawkell, Anthony E.
 Cawkell, Anthony E. Information Technology and Communications. **15**, p37
CD-ROM
 Fox, Edward A. **23**, p85
Center
 Holm, Bart E. **5**, p353; Leimkuhler, Ferdinand F. and Billingsley, Alice. **7**, p499; Murdock, John and Sherrod, John. **11**, p381; Wasserman, Paul and Daniel, Evelyn. **4**, p405
Centers
 Brown, Patricia L. and Jones, Shirli O. **3**, p263; Buckland, Michael K. **9**, p335; Carroll, Bonnie (Talmi) and Maskewitz, Betty F. **15**, p147; Markuson, Barbara Evans. **2**, p255; Simpson, G.S., Jr. and Flanagan, Carolyn. **1**, p305
Challenges
 Arnold, Stephen E. **25**, p87
Chartrand, Robert L.
 Chartrand, Robert L. Information Science in the Legislative Process. **11**, p299
 Chartrand, Robert L. Information Technology in the Legislative Process: 1976-1985, **21**, p203
Chemical
 Lipscomb, Karen J., Lynch, Michael F., and Willett, Peter. **24**, p189; Rush, James E. **13**, p209; Tate, F.A. **2**, p285
China
 Black, Donald V. and Fung, Margaret C. **18**, p307
Clement, John
 Rath, Charla M. and Clement, John R.B. Information Policy Issues in Science and Technology. **23**, p35

Cleveland, Donald B.
  Shera, Jesse H. and Cleveland, Donald B. History and Foundations of Information Science. **12**, p249
Cleverdon, Cyril W.
  Cleverdon, Cyril W. Design and Evaluation of Information Systems. **6**, p41
Climenson, W. Douglas
  Climenson, W. Douglas. File Organization and Search Techniques. **1**, p107
Cognitive
  Allen, Bryce L. **26**, p3
Common
  Brimmer, Karl W. **17**, p33
Communication
  Bunch, Steve R. and Alsberg, Peter A. **12**, p183; Davis, Ruth M. **1**, p221; Ercegovac, Zorana **27**, p173; Hills, Philip J. **18**, p99; Licklider, J.C.R. **3**, p201; Mills, R.G. **2**, p223; Rice, Ronald E. **15**, p221; Samuelson, Kjell, **6**, p277; Steinfield, Charles W. **21**, p167
Communications
  Cawkell, Anthony E. **15**, p37; Dunn, Donald A. **10**, p165; Simms, Robert L., Jr. and Fuchs, Edward. **5**, p113; Wooster, Harold. **17**, p187; Zimmerman, Edward K. and Brimmer, Karl W. **16**, p3
Compounds
  Tate, F.A. **2**, p285
Computer
  Borgman, Christine L. **19**, p33; Bunch, Steve R. and Alsberg, Peter A. **12**, p183; Caruso, Elaine. **16**, p317; Evens, Martha. **24**, p85; Goldstein, Charles M. **19**, p65; Hollaar, Lee A. **14**, p129; Huskey, Harry D. **5**, p73; Larson, Signe and Williams, Martha E. **15**, p251; Licklider, J.C.R. **3**, p201; Long, Philip L. **11**, p211; Ramsey, H. Rudy and Grimes, Jack D. **18**, p29; Rice, Ronald E. **15**, p221; Shaw, Debora. **26**, p155; Terrant, Seldon W. **10**, p273
Computer-Mediated
  Steinfield, Charles W. **21**, p167
Computers
  Markey, Karen. **19**, p271; Terrant, Seldon W. **15**, p191
Connectionist
  Doszkocs, Tamas E., Reggia, James A. and Lin, Xia. **25**, p209
Connell, Tschera Harkness
  Lancaster, F. Wilfrid, Elliker, Calvin, and Connell, Tschera Harkness. Subject Analysis. **24**, p35
Considerations
  Froehlich, Thomas J. **27**, p291
Contemporary
  Tucker, Allen B., Jr. and Nirenburg, Sergei. **19**, p129
Content
  Baxendale, Phyllis. **1**, p71; Fairthorne, Robert A. **4**, p73; Sharp, John R. **2**, p87; Taulbee, Orrin E. **3**, p105

Control
    Baxendale, Phyllis. **1**, p71; Fairthorne, Robert A. **4**, p73; O'Neill, Edward T. and Vizine-Goetz, Diane. **23**, p125; Sharp, John R. **2**, p87; Taulbee, Orrin E. **3**, p105
Cooper, Marianne
    Cooper, Marianne and Lunin, Lois F. Education and Training of the Information Professional. **24**, p35
Cooper, Michael D.
    Cooper, Michael D. The Economics of Information. **8**, p5
Cooperation
    Adams, Scott and Werdel, Judith A. **10**, p303
Copyright
    Beard, Joseph J. **9**, p381; Keplinger, Michael S. **15**, p3; Weil, Ben H. **10**, p359
Cornog, Martha
    Neufeld, M. Lynne and Cornog, Martha. Secondary Information Systems and Services. **18**, p151
Cost
    Mick, Colin K. **14**, p37
Costs
    Wilson, John H., Jr. **7**, p39
Countries
    Keren, Carl and Harmon, Larry. **15**. p289
Coyne, Joseph G.
    Coyne, Joseph G., Carroll, Bonnie C., and Redford, Julia S. Energy Information Systems and Services. **18**, p231
Crane, Diana
    Crane, Diana. Information Needs and Uses. **6**, p3
Crawford, Susan
    Crawford, Susan. Information Needs and Uses. **13**, p61
Creps, John E., Jr.
    Grattidge, Walter and Creps, John E., Jr. Information Systems in Engineering. **13**, p297
Criminal
    Blumstein, Alfred. **7**, p471
Croft, W. Bruce
    Belkin, Nicholas J. and Croft, W. Bruce. Retrieval Techniques. **22**, p109
Cuadra, Carlos A.
    Cuadra, Carlos A. Introduction to the ADI Annual Review. **1**, p1
Culkin, Patricia B.
    Shaw, Ward and Culkin, Patricia B. Systems that Inform: Emerging Trends in Library Automation and Network Development. **22**, p265
Current
    Wente, Van A. and Young, Gifford A. **5**, p259

Damerau, Fred J.
    Damerau, Fred J. Automated Language Processing. **11**, p107

Daniel, Evelyn
> Wasserman, Paul and Daniel, Evelyn. Library and Information Center Management. 4, p405

Data
> Gechman, Marvin C. 7, p323; Luedke, James A., Jr., Kovacs, Gabor J., and Fried, John B. 12, p119; Minker, Jack and Sable, Jerome. 2, p123; Schipma, Peter B. 10, p237; Shaffer, Clifford A. 27, p135; Stern, Barrie T. 12, p3; Turtle, Howard, Penniman, W. David, and Hickey, Thomas. 16, p55; Veneziano, Velma. 15, p109; Wilde, Daniel U. 11, p267; Williams, Martha E. 9, p221; Zimmerman, Edward K. and Brimmer, Karl W. 16, p3

Database
> Eastman, Caroline M. 20, p91; Huffenberger, Michael A. and Wigington, Ronald L. 14, p153

Databases (*see also* Data and Bases for early chapters on Data Bases)
> Mischo, William H. and Lee, Jounghyoun. 22, p227; O'Neill, Edward T. and Vizine-Goetz, Diane. 23, p125; Ojala, Marydee and Bates, Ellen. 21, p87; Sieck, Steven K. 19, p311; Tenopir, Carol. 19, p215; Tilley, Carolyn B. 25, p313

Davis, Charles H.
> Lundeen, Gerald W. and Davis, Charles H. Library Automation. 17, p161

Davis, Ruth M.
> Davis, Ruth M. Man-Machine Communication. 1, p221

Day, Melvin S.
> Aines, Andrew A. and Day, Melvin S. National Planning of Information Services. 10, p3

Debons, Anthony
> Debons, Anthony and Montgomery, K. Leon. Design and Evaluation of Information Systems. 9, p25

Decentralization
> Segal, Jo An S. 20, p201

Delivery
> Raitt, David I. 20, p55

Democracy
> Doctor, Ronald D. 27, p43

Dervin, Brenda
> Dervin, Brenda and Nilan, Michael. Information Needs and Uses. 21, p3

Description
> Artandi, Susan. 5, p143; Batten, William E. 8, p43; Harris, Jessica L. 9, p81; Richmond, Phyllis A. 7, p73; Vickery, Brian C. 6, p113

Design
> Allen, Bryce L. 26, p3; Borko, Harold. 2, p35; Cleverdon, Cyril W. 6, p41; Debons, Anthony and Montgomery, K. Leon. 9, p25; Katter, Robert V. 4, p31; King, Donald W. 3, p61; Lancaster, F. Wilfrid and Gillespie, Constantine J. 5, p33; Stern, Barrie T. 12, p3; Swanson, Rowena Weiss. 10, p43; Wyllys, Ronald E. 14, p3; Yang, Chung-Shu. 13, p125

Developed
> Keren, Carl and Harmon, Larry. 15, p289

Development
    Shaw, Ward and Culkin, Patricia B. 22, p265
Developments
    ARIST Staff. 1, p191; Weil, Ben H. 10, p359; van Dam, Andries and Michener, James C. 2, p187
Devices
    Turtle, Howard, Penniman, W. David, and Hickey, Thomas. 16, p55
Dialog
    Ramsey, H. Rudy and Grimes, Jack D. 18, p29
Dictionaries
    Amsler, Robert A. 19, p161; Evens, Martha. 24, p85
Disc
    Brumm, Eugenia K. 26, p197
Disks
    Fox, Edward A. 23, p85
Display
    Turtle, Howard, Penniman, W. David, and Hickey, Thomas. 16, p55
Dissemination
    Brandhorst, Wesley T. and Eckert, Philip F. 7, p379; Brown, Patricia L. and Jones, Shirli O. 3, p263; Housman, Edward M. 8, p221; Landau, Herbert B. 4, p229; Magnino, Joseph J., Jr. 6, p219; Wente, Van A. and Young, Gifford A. 5, p259
Distribution
    American Institute of Physics Staff. 2, p339; Doebler, Paul D. 5, p223; Kuney, Joseph H. 3,.p31
Doctor, Ronald D.
    Doctor, Ronald D. Social Equity and Information Technologies: Moving toward Information Democracy. 27, p43
Document
    Artandi, Susan. 5, p143; Batten, William E. 8, p43; Berul, Lawrence H. 4, p203; Brandhorst, Wesley T. and Eckert, Philip F. 7, p379; Brown, Patricia L. and Jones, Shirli O. 3, p263; Harris, Jessica L. 9, p81; Landau, Herbert B. 4, p229; Magnino, Joseph J., Jr. 6, p219; Richmond, Phyllis A. 7, p73; Summit, Roger K. and Firschein, Oscar. 9, p285; Vickery, Brian C. 6, p113
Doebler, Paul D.
    Doebler, Paul D. Publication and Distribution of Information. 5, p223
Doszkocs, Tamas E.
    Doszkocs, Tamas E., Reggia, James A. and Lin, Xia. Connectionist Models and Information Retrieval. 25, p209
Downstream
    Koenig, Michael E.D. 25, p55
Drenth, Hilary
    Drenth, Hilary; Morris, Anne, and Tseng, Gwyneth. Expert Systems as Information Intermediaries. 26, p113
Dunn, Donald A.
    Dunn, Donald A. Communications Technology. 10, p165

KEYWORD AND AUTHOR INDEX

Eastman, Caroline M.
    Eastman, Caroline M. Database Management Systems. 20, p91
Eckert, Philip F.
    Brandhorst, Wesley T. and Eckert, Philip F. Document Retrieval and Dissemination Systems. 7, p379
Economics
    Cooper, Michael D. 8, p5; Hindle, Anthony and Raper, Diane. 11, p27; Lamberton, Donald M. 19, p3; Repo, Aaatto J. 22, p3; Wilson, John H., Jr. 7, p39
Economist's
    Spence, A. Michael. 9, p57
Education
    Cooper, Marianne and Lunin, Lois F. 24, p295; Harmon, Glynn. 11, p347; Jahoda, Gerald. 8, p321; Richards, Pamela Spence. 27, p267; Silberman, Harry F. and Filep, Robert T. 3, p357; Vinsonhaler, John F. and Moon, Robert D. 8, p277; Wanger, Judith. 14, p219
Eisenberg, Michael B.
    Eisenberg, Michael B., and Spitzer, Kathleen L. Information Technology and Services in Schools. 26, p243
Eisenmann, Laura M.
    Schwartz, Candy and Eisenmann, Laura M. Subject Analysis. 21, p37
Electronic
    Arnold, Stephen E. 25, p87; Hjerppe, Ronald. 21, p123; Lunin, Lois F. 22, p179
Elias, Arthur
    Vaupel, Nancy and Elias, Arthur. Information Systems and Services in the Life Sciences. 16, p267
Elliker, Calvin
    Lancaster, F. Wilfrid, Elliker, Calvin, and Connell, Tschera Harkness. Subject Analysis. 24, p35
Emerging
    Shaw, Ward and Culkin, Patricia B. 22, p265
Empirical
    Zunde, Pranas and Gehl, John. 14, p67
End-user
    Mischo, William H. and Lee, Jounghyoun. 22, p227
Energy
    Coyne, Joseph H., Carroll, Bonnie C., and Redford, Julia. 18, p231
Engineering
    Grattidge, Walter and Creps, John E., Jr. 13, p297; Mailloux, Elizabeth. 24, p239
Entry
    Turtle, Howard, Penniman, W. David, and Hickey, Thomas. 16, p55
Environment
    Katzer, Jeffrey and Fletcher, Patricia T. 27, p227
Environmental
    Ercegovac, Zorana. 27, p173; Freeman, Robert R. and Smith, Mona F. 21, p241

Equity
    Doctor, Ronald D. 27, p43
Ercegovac, Zorana
    Ercegovac, Zorana. Environmental Research: Communication Studies and Information Sources. 27, p173
Eres, Beth Krevitt
    Eres, Beth Krevitt. International Information Issues. 24, p3
Ethical
    Froehlich, Thomas J. 27, p291
European
    Tomberg, Alex. 12, p219
Evaluation
    Bourne, Charles P. 1, p171; Cleverdon, Cyril W. 6, p41; Debons, Anthony and Montgomery, K. Leon. 9, p25; Kantor, Paul B. 17, p99; Katter, Robert V. 4, p31; King, Donald W. 3, p61; Lancaster, F. Wilfrid and Gillespie, Constantine J. 5, p33; Rees, Alan M. 2, p63; Stern, Barrie T. 12, p3; Swanson, Rowena Weiss. 10, p43; Yang, Chung-Shu. 13, p125
Evans, Glyn T.
    Evans, Glyn T. Library Networks. 16, p211
Evens, Martha
    Evens, Martha. Computer Readable Dictionaries. 24, p85
Experimental
    McGill, Michael J. and Huitfeldt, Jennifer. 14, p93
Expert
    Drenth, Hilary, Morris, Anne, and Tseng, Gwyneth. 26, p113; Sowizral, Henry. 20, p113

Factors
    Ramsey, H. Rudy and Grimes, Jack D. 18, p29
Fairthorne, Robert A.
    Fairthorne, Robert A. Content Analysis, Specification, and Control. 4, p73
Farley, Earl A.
    Black, Donald V. and Farley, Earl A. Library Automation. 1, p273
Farradane, J.
    Farradane, J. Professional Aspects of Information Science and Technology. 6, p399
Federal
    Sy, Karen J. and Robbin, Alice. 25, p3
Feedback
    Kantor, Paul B. 17, p99
Fidel, Raya
    Travis, Irene L. and Fidel, Raya. Subject Analysis. 17, p123
Fife, Dennis
    Marron, Beatrice and Fife, Dennis. Online Systems—Techniques and Services. 11, p163

KEYWORD AND AUTHOR INDEX 397

File
    Climenson, W. Douglas. **1**, p107; Minker, Jack and Sable, Jerome. **2**, p123; Senko, Michael E. **4**, p111; Yang, Chung-Shu. **13**, p125

Filep, Robert T.
    Silberman, Harry F. and Filep, Robert T. Information Systems Applications in Education. **3**, p357

Files
    Meadow, Charles T. and Meadow, Harriet R. **5**, p169; Shoffner, Ralph M. **3**, p137

Firschein, Oscar
    Summit, Roger K. and Firschein, Oscar. Document Retrieval Systems and Techniques. **9**, p285

Flanagan, Carolyn
    Simpson, G.S., Jr. and Flanagan, Carolyn. Information Centers and Services. **1**, p305

Fletcher, Patricia T.
    Katzer, Jeffrey and Fletcher, Patricia T. **27**, p227

Foundations
    Heilprin, Laurence B. **24**, p343; Shera, Jesse H. and Cleveland, Donald B. **12**, p249; Zunde, Pranas and Gehl, John. **14**, p67

Fox, Edward A.
    Fox, Edward A. Optical Disks and CD-ROM; Publishing and Access. **23**, p85

Frank, Robyn C.
    Frank, Robyn C. Agricultural Information Systems and Services. **22**, p293

Fraser, J.B.
    Bobrow, D.G., Fraser, J.B., and Quillian, M.R. Automated Language Processing. **2**, p161

Freeman, James E.
    Freeman, James E. and Katz, Ruth M. Information Marketing. **13**, p37

Freeman, Robert R.
    Freeman, Robert R. and Smith, Mona F. Environmental Information. **21**, p241

Fried, John B.
    Luedke, James A., Jr., Kovacs, Gabor J., and Fried, John B. Numeric Data Bases and Systems. **12**, p119

Froehlich, Thomas J.
    Froehlich, Thomas J. Ethical Considerations of Information Professionals. **27**, p291

Fuchs, Edward
    Simms, Robert L., Jr. and Fuchs, Edward. Communications Technology **5**, p113

Full
    Tenopir, Carol. **19**, p215

Fung, Margaret C.
    Black, Donald V. and Fung, Margaret C. Information Systems and Services in China and Japan. **18**, p307

Fuzzy
    Bookstein, Abraham. 20, p117

Gannett, Elwood K.
    Gannett, Elwood K. Primary Publication Systems and Services. 8, p243
Garvey, William D.
    Lin, Nan and Garvey, William D. Information Needs and Uses. 7, p5
Gechman, Marvin C.
    Gechman, Marvin C. Generation and Use of Machine-Readable Bibliographic Data Bases. 7, p323
Gehl, John
    Zunde, Pranas and Gehl, John. Empirical Foundations of Information Science. 14, p67
Generation
    Gechman, Marvin C. 7, p323; Schipma, Peter B. 10, p237; Wilde, Daniel U. 11, p267
Geographic
    Shaffer, Clifford A. 27, p135
Gillespie, Constantine J.
    Lancaster, F. Wilfrid and Gillespie, Constantine J. Design and Evaluation of Information Systems. 5, p33
Global
    Surprenant, Thomas T. 20, p.3
Goldsmith, Gerry
    Williams, Philip W. and Goldsmith, Gerry. Information Retrieval on Mini- and Microcomputers. 16, p85
Goldstein, Charles M.
    Goldstein, Charles M. Computer-Based Information Storage Technologies. 19, p65
Government
    Hernon, Peter and Relyea, Harold C. 23, p3
Governments
    Hearle, Edward F. R. 5, p325
Grattidge, Walter
    Grattidge, Walter and Creps, John E., Jr. Information Systems in Engineering. 13, p297
Greer, Roger
    Atherton, Pauline and Greer, Roger. Professional Aspects of Information Science and Technology. 3, p329
Griffin, Hillis L.
    Griffin, Hillis L. Automation of Technical Processes in Libraries. 3, p241
Griffiths, José-Marie
    Griffiths, José-Marie. The Value of Information and Related Systems, Products, and Services. 17, p269

Grimes, Jack D.
   Ramsey, H. Rudy and Grimes, Jack D. Human Factors in Interactive Computer Dialog. **18**, p29
Grosch, Audrey N.
   Grosch, Audrey N. Library Automation. **11**, p225
Grosser, Kerry
   Grosser, Kerry. Human Networks in Organizational Information Processing. **26**, p349

Hammer, Donald P.
   Hammer, Donald P. National Information Issues and Trends. **2**, p395
Handling
   Rush, James E. **13**, p209; Tate, F.A. **2**, p285
Hardware
   ARIST Staff. **1**, p191; van Dam, Andries and Michener, James C. **2**, p187
Harmon, Glynn
   Harmon, Glynn. Information Science Education and Training. **11**, p347
Harmon, Larry
   Keren, Carl and Harmon, Larry. Information Services Issues in Less Developed Countries. **15**, p289
Harris, Jessica L.
   Harris, Jessica L. Document Description and Representation. **9**, p81
Harvey, John F.
   Harvey, John F. Professional Aspects of Information Science and Technology. **2**, p419
Hawkins, Donald T.
   Hawkins, Donald T. Online Information Retrieval Systems. **16**, p171
Health
   Tilley, Carolyn B. **25**, p313
Hearle, Edward F.R.
   Hearle, Edward F.R. Information Systems in State and Local Governments. **5**, p325
Heilprin, Laurence B.
   Heilprin, Laurence B. Foundations of Information Science Reexamined. **24**, p343
Herner, Mary
   Herner, Saul and Herner, Mary. Information Needs and Uses in Science and Technology. **2**, p1
Herner, Saul
   Herner, Saul and Herner, Mary. Information Needs and Uses in science and Technology. **2**, p1
Hernon, Peter
   Hernon, Peter and Relyea, Harold C. The U.S. Government as a Publisher. **23**, p3

Hersey, David F.
  Hersey, David F. Information Systems for Research in Progress. 13, p263
Hewins, Elizabeth T.
  Hewins, Elizabeth T. Information Needs and Use Studies. 25, p145
Hickey, Thomas
  Turtle, Howard, Penniman, W. David, and Hickey, Thomas. Data Entry/ Display Devices for Interactive Information Retrieval. 16, p55
Hildreth, Charles R.
  Hildreth, Charles R. Online Public Access Catalogs. 20, p233
Hills, Philip J.
  Hills, Philip J. the Scholarly Communication Process. 18, p99
Hindle, Anthony
  Hindle, Anthony and Raper, Diane. The Economics of Information. 11, p27
History
  Shera, Jesse H. and Cleveland, Donald B. 12, p249
Hjerppe, Roland
  Hjerppe, Roland. Electronic Publishing: Writing Machines and Machine Writing. 21, p123
Hollaar, Lee A.
  Hollaar, Lee A. Unconventional Computer Architectures for Information Retrieval. 14, p129
Holm, Bart E.
  Holm, Bart E. Library and Information Center Management. 5, p353;
  Holm, Bart E. National Issues and Problems. 11, p5
Housman, Edward M.
  Housman, Edward M. Selective Dissemination of Information. 8, p221
Howder, Murray L.
  Liston, David M., Jr. and Howder, Murray L. Subject Analysis. 12, p81
Hudson, Heather
  Kletter, Richard C. and Hudson, Heather. Video Cartridges and Cassettes. 7, p197
Huffenberger, Michael A.
  Huffenberger, Michael A. and Wigington, Ronald L. Database Management Systems. 14, p153
Huitfeldt, Jennifer
  McGill, Michael J.; Huitfeldt, Jennifer. Experimental Techniques of Information Retrieval. 14, p93
Human
  Borgman, Christine L. 19, p33; Grosser, Kerry. 26, p349; Ramsey, H. Rudy and Grimes, Jack D. 18, p29; Shaw, Debora. 26, p155
Humanities
  Raben, Joseph and Burton, Sarah K. 16, p247; Raben, Joseph and Widmann, R.L. 7, p439; Tibbo, Helen R. 26, p287
Huskey, Harry D.
  Huskey, Harry D. Computer Technology. 5, p73

KEYWORD AND AUTHOR INDEX

Image
   Lunin, Lois F. **22**, p179
Impact
   Palmquist, Ruth A. **27**, p3
Impacts
   Rice, Ronald E. **15**, p221
Implications
   Allen, Bryce L. **26**, p3
Indexing
   Bourne, Charles P. **1**, p171; Keenan, Stella. **4**, p273
Individual
   Palmquist, Ruth A. **27**, p3
Inform
   Shaw, Ward and Culkin, Patricia B. **22**, p265
Information
   Adams, Scott and Werdel, Judith A. **10**, p303; Aines, Andrew A. and Day, Melvin S. **10**, p3; Allen Bryce L. **26**, p3; Allen, Thomas J. **4**, p3; American Institute of Physics Staff. **2**, p339; Arnold, Stephen E. **25**, p87; Atherton, Pauline and Greer, Roger. **3**, p329; Baruch, Jordan J. **1**, p255; Beard, Joseph J. **6**, p369; Bearman, Toni Carbo. **13**, p179; Becker, Joseph and Olsen, Wallace C. **3**, p289; Berninger, Douglas E. and Adkinson, Burton W. **13**, p3; Black, Donald V. and Fung, Margaret C. **18**, p307; Blumstein, Alfred. **7**, p471; Bookstein, Abraham. **20**, p117; Borko, Harold. **2**, p35; Boyce, Bert R. and Kraft, Donald H. **20**, p153; Broadbent, Marianne and Koenig, Michael E.D. **23**, p237; Brown, Patricia L. and Jones, Shirli O. **3**, p263; Brumm, Eugenia. **26**, p197; Buckland, Michael K. **9**, p335; Burt, Patricia V. and Kinnucan, Mark T. **25**, p175; Caceres, Cesar A., Weihrer, Anna Lea, and Pulliam, Robert. **6**, p325; Carroll, Bonnie (Talmi) and Maskewitz, Betty F. **15**, p147; Cawkell, Anthony E. **15**, p37; Chartrand, Robert L. **11**, p299; Chartrand, Robert L. **21**, p203; Rath, Charla M. and Clement, John R.B. **23**, p35; Cleverdon, Cyril W. **6**, p41; Cooper, Marianne and Lunin, Lois F. **24**, p295; Cooper, Michael D. **8**, p5; Coyne, Joseph G., Carroll, Bonnie C. and Redford, Julia S. **18**, p231; Crane, Diana. **6**, p3; Crawford, Susan. **13**, p61; Debons, Anthony and Montgomery, K. Leon. **9**, p25; Dervin, Brenda and Nilan, Michael. **21** p3; Doctor, Ronald D. **27**, p43; Doebler, Paul D. **5**, p223; Doszkocs, Tamas E., Reggia, James A. and Lin, Xia. **25**, p209; Drenth, Hilary, Morris, Anne and Tseng, Gwyneth. **26**, p113; Eisenberg, Michael B. and Spitzer, Kathleen L. **26**, p243; Ercegovac, Zorana. **27**, p173; Eres, Beth Krevitt. **24**, p3; Farradane, J. **6**, p399; Frank, Robyn C. **22**, p293; Freeman, James E. and Katz, Ruth M. **13**, p37; Freeman, Robert R. and Smith, Mona F. **21**, p241; Froehlich, Thomas J. **27**, p291; Goldstein, Charles M. **19**, p65; Grattidge, Walter and Creps, John E., Jr. **13**, p297; Griffiths, José-Marie. **17**, p269; Grosser, Kerry. **26**, p349; Hammer, Donald P. **2**, p385; Harmon, Glynn. **11**, p347; Harvey, John F. **2**, p419; Hawkins, Donald T. **16**, p171; Hearle, Edward F.R. **5**, p325; Heilprin, Laurence B. **24**, p343; Herner, Saul and Herner, Mary. **2**, p1; Hersey, David F. **13**, p263; Hewins, Elizabeth T. **25**, p145; Hindle, Anthony and Raper,

Diane. 11, p27; Hollaar, Lee A. 14, p129; Holm, Bart E. 5, p353; Housman, Edward M. 8, p221; Jahoda, Gerald. 8, p321; Kantor, Paul B. 17, p99; Katter, Robert V. 4, p31; Katzer, Jeffrey and Fletcher, Patricia T. 27, p227; Keplinger, Michael S. 15, p3; Keren, Carl and Harmon, Larry. 15, p289; King, Donald W. 3, p61; Kinnucan, Mark T., Nelson, Michael J., and Allen, Bryce L. 22, p147; Kissman, Henry M. and Wexler, Philip. 18, p185; Kochen, Manfred. 18, p277; Koenig, Michael E.D. 25, p55; Kuney, Joseph H. 3, p31; Lamberton, Donald M. 19, p3; Lancaster, F. Wilfrid and Gillespie, Constantine J. 5, p33; Leimkuhler, Ferdinand F. and Billingsley, Alice. 7, p499; Levitan, Karen B. 17, p227; Levy, Richard P. and Cammarn, Maxine R. 3, p397; Lin, Nan and Garvey, William D. 7, p5; Lipetz, Ben-Ami, 5, p3; Lorenz, John G. 4, p379; Lunin, Lois F. 22, p179; Lynch, Clifford A. and Preston, Cecilia M. 25, p263; Lytle, Richard H. 21, p309; Mailloux, Elizabeth. 24, p239; Markuson, Barbara Evans. 2, p255; Martyn, John. 9, p3; McDonald, Dennis D. 17, p83; McGill, Michael J. and Huitfeldt, Jennifer. 14, p93; Menzel, Herbert. 1, p173; Murdock, John and Sherrod, John. 11, p381; Neufeld, M. Lynne and Cornog, Martha. 18, p151; Olson, Edwin E., Shank, Russell, and Olsen, Harold A. 7, p279; Overhage, Carl F.J. 4, p339; Paisley, William J. 3, p1; Palmquist, Ruth A. 27, p3; Park, Margaret K. 12, p59; Parker, Edwin B. 8, p345; Parkins, Phyllis V. and Kennedy, H.E. 6, p247; Preschel, Barbara M. and Woods, Lawrence J. 24, p267; Prywes, Noah S. and Smith, Diane Pirog. 7, p103; Raben, Joseph and Burton, Sarah K. 16, p247; Raben, Joseph and Widmann, R.L. 7, p439; Raitt, David I. 20, p55; Rasmussen, Edie M. 27, p99; Rees, Alan M. 2, p63; Repo, Aatto J. 22, p3; Richards, Pamela Spence. 27, p267; Rorvig, Mark E. 23, p157; Rosenberg, Victor. 17, p3; Rush, James E. 13, p209; Samuelson, Kjell. 6, p277; Saracevic, Tefko, Braga, Gilda, and Quijano Solis, Alvaro. 14, p249; Senko, Michael E. 4, p111; Shaffer, Clifford A. 27, p135; Shaw, Debora. 26, p155; Shera, Jesse H. and Cleveland, Donald B. 12, p249; Shera, Jesse H. and McFarland, Anne S. 4, p439; Sherrod, John. 1, p337; Sieck, Steven K. 19, p311; Silberman, Harry F. and Filep, Robert T. 3, p357; Simpson, G.S., Jr. and Flanagan, Carolyn. 1, p305; Smith, Linda C. 15, p67; 22, p41; Spence, A. Michael. 9, p57; Spigai, Fran. 26, p39; Spring, Michael B. 26, p79; Surprenant, Thomas T. 20, p3; Svenonius, Elaine and Witthus, Rutherford. 16, p291; Swanson, Rowena Weiss. 10, p43; Tannehill, Robert S., Jr. 18, p61; Tate, F.A. 2, p285; Taylor, Robert S. 1, p15; Tibbo, Helen R. 26, p287; Tilley, Carolyn B. 25, p313; Tomberg, Alex. 12, p219; Tucci, Valerie K. 23, p59; Turtle, Howard, Penniman, W. David and Hickey, Thomas. 16, p55; Vaupel, Nancy and Elias, Arthur. 16, p267; Vinsonhaler, John F. and Moon, Robert D. 8, p277; Voges, Mickie A. 23, p193; Wasserman, Paul and Daniel, Evelyn. 4, p405; Weiss, Stanley D. 5, p299; Williams, Philip W. and Goldsmith, Gerry. 16, p85; Wilson, John H., Jr. 7, p39; Zunde, Pranas and Gehl, John. 14, p67

Intelligence
    Smith, Linda C. 15, p67; 22, p41

Interaction
    Berninger, Douglas E. and Adkinson, Burton W. 13, p3; Borgman, Christine L. 19, p33; McDonald, Dennis D. 17, p83

Interactive
    Bennett, John L. 7, p159; Martin, Thomas H. 8, p203; Ramsey, H. Rudy and Grimes, Jack D. 18, p29; Turtle, Howard, Penniman, W. David, and Hickey, Thomas. 16, p55
Interface
    Bennett, John L. 7, p159; Martin, Thomas H. 8, p203; Shaw, Debora. 26, p155; Vigil, Peter. 21, p63
Intermediaries
    Drenth, Hilary, Morris, Anne, and Tseng, Gwyneth. 26, p113
International
    Adams, Scott and Werdel, Judith A. 10, p303; Lorenz, John G. 4, p379; Samuelson, Kjell. 6, p277
Internet
    Lynch, Clifford A. and Preston, Cecilia M. 25, p263
Interpersonal
    Rice, Ronald E. 15, p221
Introduction
    Cuadra, Carlos A. 1, p1
Issue
    Beard, Joseph J. 9, p381
Issues
    Eres, Beth Krevitt. 24, p3; Hammer, Donald P. 2, p385; Holm, Bart E. 11, p5; Keren, Carl and Harmon, Larry. 15, p289; Rath, Charla M. and Clement, John R.B. 23, p35; Sherrod, John. 1, p337

Jahoda, Gerald
    Jahoda, Gerald. Education for Information Science. 8, p321
Japan
    Black, Donald V. and Fung, Margaret C. 18, p307
Jones, Shirli O.
    Brown, Patricia L. and Jones, Shirli O. Document Retrieval and Dissemination in Libraries and Information Centers. 3, p263
Judd, Peggy
    Lerner, Rita G., Metaxas, Ted, Scott, John T., Adams, Peter D., and Judd, Peggy. Primary Publication Systems and Scientific Text Processing. 18, p127
Justice
    Blumstein, Alfred. 7, p471

Kantor, Paul B.
    Kantor, Paul B. Evaluation of and Feedback in Information Storage and Retrieval Systems. 17, p99
Katter, Robert V.
    Katter, Robert V. Design and Evaluation of Information Systems. 4, p31

Katz, Ruth M.
   Freeman, James E. and Katz, Ruth M. Information Marketing. 13, p37
Katzer, Jeffrey
   Katzer, Jeffrey and Fletcher, Patricia T. The Information Environment of Managers. 27, p227
Kay, Martin
   Kay, Martin and Sparck Jones, Karen. Automated Language Processing. 6, p141
Keenan, Stella
   Keenan, Stella. Abstracting and Indexing Services in Science and Technology. 4, p273
Kennedy, H.E.
   Parkins, Phyllis V. and Kennedy, H.E. Secondary Information Services. 6, p247
Keplinger, Michael S.
   Keplinger, Michael S. Copyright and Information Technology. 15, p3
Keren, Carl
   Keren, Carl and Harmon, Larry. Information Services Issues in Less Developed Countries. 15, p289
Kilgour, Frederick G.
   Kilgour, Frederick G. Library Automation. 4, p305
King, Donald W.
   King, Donald W. Design and Evaluation of Information Systems. 3, p61
Kinnucan, Mark T.
   Burt, Patricia V. and Kinnucan, Mark T. Information Models and Modeling Techniques for Information Systems. 25, p175
   Kinnucan, Mark T., Nelson, Michael J. and Allen, Bryce L. Statistical Methods in Information Science Research. 22, p147
Kissman, Henry M.
   Kissman, Henry M. and Wexler, Philip. Toxicological Information. 18, p185
Kletter, Richard C.
   Kletter, Richard C. and Hudson, Heather. Video Cartridges and Cassettes. 7, p197
Knowledge
   Lesk, Michael. Programming Languages for Text and Knowledge Processing. 19, p97
Kochen, Manfred
   Kochen, Manfred. Information and Society. 18, p277
Koenig, Michael E.D.
   Broadbent, Marianne and Koenig, Michael E.D. Information and Information Technology Management. 23, p237
   Koenig, Michael E.D. Information Services and Downstream Productivity. 25, p55
Kovacs, Gabor J.
   Luedke, James A., Jr., Kovacs, Gabor J., and Fried, John B. Numeric Data Bases and Systems. 12, p119

Kraft, Donald H.
  Boyce, Bert R. and Kraft, Donald H. Principles and Theories in Information Science. 20, p153
Kuney, Joseph H.
  Kuney, Joseph H. Publication and Distribution of Information. 3, p31

Lamberton, Donald M.
  Lamberton, Donald M. The Economics of Information and Organization. 19, p3
Lancaster, F. Wilfrid
  Lancaster, F. Wilfrid and Gillespie, Constantine J. Design and Evaluation of Information Systems. 5, p33
  Lancaster, F. Wilfrid, Elliker, Calvin, and Connell, Tschera Harkness. Subject Analysis. 24, p35
Landau, Herbert B.
  Landau, Herbert B. Document Dissemination. 4, p229
Language
  Becker, David. 16, p113; Bobrow, D.G., Fraser, J.B., and Quillian, M.R. 2, p161; Damerau, Fred J. 11, p107; Kay, Martin and Sparck Jones, Karen. 6, p141; Montgomery, Christine A. 4, p145; Salton, Gerard. 3, p169; Simmons, Robert E. 1, p137; Walker, Donald E. 8, p69; Warner, Amy J. 22, p79
Languages
  Lesk, Michael. 19, p97
Larson, Signe
  Larson, Signe and Williams, Martha E. Computer Assisted Legal Research. 15, p251
Latin
  Saracevic, Tefko, Braga, Gilda, and Quijano Solis, Alvaro. 14, p249
Law
  Beard, Joseph J. 6, p369; Voges, Mickie A. 23, p193
Learning
  Caruso, Elaine. 16, p317
Lee, Jounghyoun
  Mischo, William H. and Lee, Jounghyoun. End-User Searching of Bibliographic Databases. 22, p227
Legal
  Larson, Signe and Williams, Martha E. 15, p251
Legislative
  Chartrand, Robert L. 11, p299; Chartrand, Robert L. 21, p203
Leimkuhler, Ferdinand F.
  Leimkuhler, Ferdinand F. and Billingsley, Alice. Library and Information Center Management. 7, p499
Lerner, Rita G.
  Lerner, Rita G., Metaxas, Ted, Scott, John T., Adams, Peter D. and Judd, Peggy. Primary Publication Systems and Scientific Text Processing. 18, p127

Lesk, Michael
   Lesk, Michael. Programming Languages for Text and Knowledge Processing. **19**, p97
Less
   Keren, Carl and Harmon, Larry. **15**, p289; Levitan, Karen B. Information Resources Management. **17**, p227
Levy, Richard P.
   Levy, Richard P. and Cammarn, Maxine R. Information Systems Applications in Medicine. **3**, p397
Libraries
   Brown, Patricia L. and Jones, Shirli O. **3**, p263; Buckland, Michael K. **9**, p335; Griffin, Hillis L. **3**, p241; Markuson, Barbara Evans. **2**, p255; Pratt, Allan D. **19**, p247; Tucci, Valerie K. **23**, p59
Library
   Alper, Bruce H. **10**, p199; Avram, Henriette. **6**, p171; Bierman, Kenneth J. **9**, p123; Black, Donald V. and Farley, Earl A. **1**, p273; Evans, Glyn T. **16**, p211; Grosch, Audrey N. **11**, p225; Holm, Bart E. **5**, p353; Kilgour, Frederick G. **4**, p305; Leimkuhler, Ferdinand F. and Billingsley, Alice. **7**, p499; Lundeen, Gerald W. and Davis, Charles H. **17**, p161; Martin, Susan K. **7**, p243; Miller, Ronald F. and Tighe, Ruth L. **9**, p173; Murdock, John and Sherrod, John. **11**, p381; Olson, Edwin E., Shank, Russell, and Olsen, Harold A. **7**, p279; Palmour, Vernon E. and Roderer, Nancy K. **13**, p147; Parker, Ralph H. **5**, p193; Pearson, Karl M., Jr. **10**, p139; Reed, Mary Jane Pobst and Vrooman, Hugh T. **14**, p193; Shaw, Ward and Culkin, Patricia B. **22**, p265; Simmons, Peter. **8**, p167; Veneziano, Velma. **15**, p109; Wasserman, Paul and Daniel, Evelyn. **4**, p405
Licklider, J.C.R.
   Licklider, J.C.R. Man-Computer Communication. **3**, p201
Life
   Vaupel, Nancy and Elias, Arthur. **16**, p267
Lin, Nan
   Lin, Nan and Garvey, William D. Information Needs and Uses. **7**, p5
Lin, Xia
   Doszkocs, Tamas E., Reggia, James A. and Lin, Xia. Connectionist Models and Information Retrieval. **25**, p209
Lipetz, Ben-Ami
   Lipetz, Ben-Ami. Information Needs and Uses. **5**, p3
Lipscomb, Karen J., Lynch, Michael F., and Willett, Peter. Chemical Structure Processing. **24**, p189
Liston, David M., Jr.
   Liston, David M., Jr. and Howder, Murray L. Subject Analysis. **12**, p81
Local
   Hearle, Edward F.R. **5**, p325
Long, Philip L.
   Long, Philip L. Computer Technology—An Update. **11**, p211

Lorenz, John G.
  Lorenz, John G. International Transfer of Information. 4, p379
Luedke, James A., Jr.
  Luedke, James A., Jr., Kovacs, Gabor J., and Fried, John B. Numeric Data Bases and Systems. 12, p119
Lundeen, Gerald W.
  Lundeen, Gerald W. and Davis, Charles H. Library Automation. 17, p161
Lunin, Lois F.
  Cooper, Marianne and Lunin, Lois F. Education and Training of the Information Professional. 24, p295;
  Lunin, Lois F. Electronic Image Information. 22, p179
Lynch, Clifford
  Lynch, Clifford A. and Preston, Cecilia M. Internet Access to Information Resources. 25, p263
Lynch, Michael F.
  Lipscomb, Karen J., Lynch, Michael F., and Willett, Peter. Chemical Structure Processing. 24, p189
Lytle, Richard H.
  Lytle, Richard H. Information Resource Management: 19811986. 21, p309

Machine
  Amsler, Robert A. 19, p161; Davis, Ruth M. 1, p221; Gechman, Marvin C. 7, p323; Hjerppe, Roland, 21, p123; Meadow, Charles T. and Meadow, Harriet R. 5, p169; Mills, R.G. 2, p223; Schipma, Peter B. 10, p237; Shoffner, Ralph M. 3, p137; Tucker, Allen B., Jr. and Nirenburg, Sergei, 19, p129; Wilde, Daniel U. 11, p267; Williams, Martha E. 9, p221
Magnino, Joseph J., Jr.
  Magnino, Joseph J., Jr. Document Retrieval and Dissemination. 6, p219
Mailloux, Elizabeth
  Mailloux, Elizabeth. Engineering Information Systems. 24, p239
Maintenance
  Meadow, Charles T. and Meadow, Harriet R. 5, p169; Shoffner, Ralph M. 3, p137
Man
  Davis, Ruth M. 1, p221; Licklider, J.C.R. 3, p201; Mills, R.G. 2, p223
Management
  Broadbent, Marianne and Koenig, Michael E.D. 23,1 p237; Brumm, Eugenia. 26, p197; Buckland, Michael K. 9, p335; Eastman, Caroline M. 20, p91; Holm, Bart E. 5, p353; Huffenberger, Michael A. and Wigington, Ronald L. 14, p153; Leimkuhler, Ferdinand F. and Billingsley, Alice. 7, p499; Levitan, Karen B. 17, p227; Lytle, Richard H. 21, p309; Minker, Jack and Sable, Jerome. 2, p123; Murdock, John and Sherrod, John. 11, p381; Senko, Michael E. 4, p111; Wasserman, Paul and Daniel, Evelyn. 4, p405; Weiss, Stanley D. 5, p299
Managers
  Katzer, Jeffrey and Fletcher, Patricia T. 27, p227

Marketing
    Arnold, Stephen E. **25**, p87; Freeman, James E. and Katz, Ruth M. **13**, p37; Tucci, Valerie K. **23**, p59
Markey, Karen
    Markey, Karen. Visual Arts Resources and Computers. **19**, p271
Markuson, Barbara Evans
    Markuson, Barbara Evans. Automation in Libraries and Information Centers. **2**, p255
Marron, Beatrice
    Marron, Beatrice and Fife, Dennis. Online Systems—Techniques and Services. **11**, p163
Martin, Susan K.
    Martin, Susan K. Library Automation. **7**, p243
Martin, Thomas H.
    Martin, Thomas H. The User Interface in Interactive Systems. **8**, p203; Martin, Thomas H. Office Automation. **23**, p217
Martyn, John
    Martyn, John. Information Needs and Uses. **9**, p3
Maskewitz, Betty F.
    Carroll, Bonnie (Talmi) and Maskewitz, Betty F. Information Analysis Centers. **15**, p147
McCarn, Katherine W.
    White, Howard D. and McCain, Katherine W. Bibliometrics. **24**, p119
McCarn, Davis B.
    McCarn, Davis B. Online Systems—Techniques and Services. **13**, p85
McDonald, Dennis D.
    McDonald, Dennis D. Public Sector/Private Sector Interaction in Information Services. **17**, p83
McFarland, Anne S.
    Shera, Jesse H. and McFarland, Anne S. Professional Aspects of Information Science and Technology. **4**, p439
McGill, Michael J.
    McGill, Michael J. and Huitfeldt, Jennifer. Experimental Techniques of Information Retrieval. **14**, p93
Meadow, Charles T.
    Meadow, Charles T. and Meadow, Harriet R. Organization, Maintenance and Search of Machine Files. **5**, p169
Meadow, Harriet R.
    Meadow, Charles T. and Meadow, Harriet R. Organization, Maintenance and Search of Machine Files. **5**, p169
Measurement
    Rorvig, Mark E. **23**, p157
Mediated
    Rice, Ronald E. **15**, p221
Medical
    Tilley, Carolyn B. **25**, p313

KEYWORD AND AUTHOR INDEX 409

Medicine
    Caceres, Cesar A., Weihrer, Anna Lea, and Pulliam, Robert. 6, p325; Levy, Richard P. and Cammarn, Maxine R. 3, p397; Spring, William C., Jr. 2, p311

Menzel, Herbert
    Menzel, Herbert. Information Needs and Uses in Science and Technology. 1, p41

Metaxas, Ted
    Lerner, Rita G., Metaxas, Ted, Scott, John T., Adams, Peter D., and Judd, Peggy. Primary Publication Systems and Scientific Text Processing. 18, p127

Methods
    Kinnucan, Mark T., Nelson, Michael J., and Allen, Bryce L. 22, p147

Michener, James C.
    van Dam, Andries and Michener, James C. Hardware Developments and Product Announcements. 2, p187

Mick, Colin K.
    Mick, Colin K. Cost Analysis of Information Systems and Services. 14, p37

Microcomputers
    Pratt, Allan D. 19, p247; Williams, Philip W. and Goldsmith, Gerry. 16, p85

Microform
    Ballou, Hubbard W. 8, p121; Nelson, Carl E. 6, p77; Teplitz, Arthur. 5, p87; Veaner, Allen B. 4, p175

Micrographics
    Spigai, Frances G. and Butler, Brett B. 11, p59

Miller, Ronald F.
    Miller, Ronald F. and Tighe, Ruth L. Library and Information Networks. 9, p173

Mills, R.G.
    Mills, R.G. Man-Machine Communication and Problem Solving. 2, p223

Mini
    Williams, Philip W. and Goldsmith, Gerry. 16, p85

Minicomputers
    Pearson, Karl M., Jr. 10, p139

Minker, Jack
    Minker, Jack and Sable, Jerome. File Organization and Data Management. 2, p123

Mischo, William H.
    Mischo, William H. and Lee, Jounghyoun. End-User Searching of Bibliographic Databases. 22, p227

Modeling
    Burt, Patricia V. and Kinnucan, Mark T. 25, p175

Models
    Burt, Patricia V. and Kinnucan, Mark T. 25, p175; Doszkocs, Tamas E., Reggia, James A. and Lin, Xia. 25, p209

Moll, Joy K.
    Narin, Francis and Moll, Joy K. Bibliometrics. 12, p35

Montgomery, Christine A.
    Montgomery, Christine A. Automated Language Processing. **4**, p145
Montgomery, K. Leon
    Debons, Anthony and Montgomery, K. Leon. Design and Evaluation of Information Systems. **9**, p25
Moon, Robert D.
    Vinsonhaler, John F. and Moon, Robert D. Information Systems Applications in Education. **8**, p277
Morris, Anne
    Drenth, Hilary, Morris, Anne, and Tseng, Gwyneth. Expert Systems as Information Intermediaries. **26**, p113
Murdock, John
    Murdock, John and Sherrod, John. Library and Information Center Management. **11**, p381

Narin, Francis
    Narin, Francis and Moll, Joy K. Bibliometrics. **12**, p35
National
    Aines, Andrew A. and Day, Melvin S. **10**, p3; Berninger, Douglas E. and Adkinson, Burton W. **13**; Hammer, Donald P. **2**, p385; Holm, Bart E. **11**, p5; Rosenberg, Victor; **17**, p3; Sherrod, John. **1**, p337; Zimmerman, Edward K. and Brimmer, Karl W. **16**, p3
Natural
    Warner, Amy J. **22**, p79
Needs
    Allen, Thomas J. **4**, p3; Crane, Diana. **6**, p3; Crawford, Susan, **13**, p61; Dervin, Brenda and Nilan, Michael. **21**, p3; Herner, Saul and Herner, Mary **2**, p1; Hewins, Elizabeth T. **25**, p145; Lin, Nan and Garvey, William D. **7**, p5; Lipetz, Ben-Ami, **5**, p3; Martyn, John. **9**, p3; Menzel, Herbert. **1**, p41; Paisley, William J. **3**, p1
Nelson, Carl E.
    Nelson, Carl E. Microform Technology. **6**, p77
Nelson, Michael J.
    Kinnucan, Mark T., Nelson, Michael J., and Allen Bryce L. Statistical Methods in Information Science Research. **22**, p147
Network
    Samuelson, Kjell. **6**, p277; Shaw, Ward and Culkin, Patricia B. **22**, p265
Networking
    Segal, Jo An S. **20**, p203
Networks
    Becker, Joseph and Olsen, Wallace C. **3**, p289; Bunch, Steve R. and Alsberg, Peter A. **12**, p183; Evans, Glyn T. **16**, p211; Grosser, Kerry. **26**, p349; Miller, Ronald F. and Tighe, Ruth L. **9**, p173; Olson, Edwin E., Shank, Russell, and Olsen, Harold A. **7**, p279; Overhage, Carl F.J. **4**, p339; Palmour, Vernon E. and Roderer, Nancy K. **13**, p147; Tomberg, Alex. **12**, p219

KEYWORD AND AUTHOR INDEX 411

Neufeld, M. Lynne
    Neufeld, M. Lynne and Cornog, Martha. Secondary Information Systems and Services. **18**, p151
New
    ARIST Staff. **1**, p191
Nilan, Michael
    Dervin, Brenda and Nilan, Michael. Information Needs and Uses. **21**, p3
Nirenburg, Sergei
    Tucker, Allen B., Jr. and Nirenburg, Sergei. Machine Translation: a Contemporary View. **19**, p129
Numbers
    Sy, Karen J. and Robbin, Alice. **25**, p3
Numeric
    Luedke, James A., Jr., Kovacs, Gabor J., and Fried, John B. **12**, p119

O'Neill, Edward T.
    O'Neill, Edward T. and Vizine-Goetz, Diane. Quality Control in Online Databases. **23**, p125
Office
    Martin, Thomas H. **23**, p217
Ojala, Marydee
    Ojala, Marydee and Bates, Ellen. Business Databases. **21**, p87
Olsen, Harold A.
    Olson, Edwin E., Shank, Russell, and Olsen, Harold A. Library and Information Networks. **7**, p279
Olsen, Wallace C.
    Becker, Joseph and Olsen, Wallace C. Information Networks. **3**, p289
Olson, Edwin E.
    Olson, Edwin E., Shank, Russell, and Olsen, Harold A. Library and Information Networks. **7**, p279
Online
    Caruso, Elaine. **16**, p317; Hawkins, Donald T. **16**, p171; Hildreth, Charles R. **20**, p233; Marron, Beatrice and Fife, Dennis. **11**, p163; McCarn, Davis B. **13**, p85; O'Neill, Edward T. and Vizine-Goetz, Diane. **23**, p125; Wanger, Judith. **14**, p219
Optical
    Brumm, Eugenia. **26**, p197; Fox, Edward A. **23**, p85
Organization
    Climenson, W. Douglas. **1**, p107; Lamberton, Donald M. **19**, p3; Meadow, Charles T. and Meadow, Harriet R. **5**, p169; Minker, Jack and Sable, Jerome. **2**, p123; Prywes, Noah S. and Smith, Diane Pirog. **7**, p103; Senko, Michael E. **4**, p111; Shoffner, Ralph M. **3**, p137
Organizational
    Grosser, Kerry. **26**, p349; Rice, Ronald E. **15**, p221

Organizations
  Adams, Scott and Werdel, Judith A. **10**, p303
Overhage, Carl F.J.
  Overhage, Carl F.J. Information Networks. **4**, p339

Paisley, William J.
  Paisley, William J. Information Needs and Uses. **3**, p1
Palmour, Vernon E.
  Palmour, Vernon E. and Roderer, Nancy K. Library Resource Sharing through Networks. **13**, p147
Palmquist, Ruth A.
  Palmquist, Ruth A. Impact of Information Technology on the Individual. **27**, p3
Parallel
  Rasmussen, Edie M. **27**, p99
Park, Margaret K.
  Park, Margaret K. Bibliographic and Information Processing Standards. **12**, p59
Parker, Edwin B.
  Parker, Edwin B. Information and Society. **8**, p345
Parker, Ralph H.
  Parker, Ralph H. Library Automation. **5**, p193
Parkins, Phyllis V.
  Parkins, Phyllis V. and Kennedy, H.E. Secondary Information Services. **6**, p247
Pearson, Karl M., Jr.
  Pearson, Karl M., Jr. Minicomputers in the Library. **10**, p139
Penniman, W. David
  Turtle, Howard, Penniman, W. David and Hickey, Thomas. Data Entry/Display Devices for Interactive Information Retrieval. **16**, p55
Planning
  Aines, Andrew A. and Day, Melvin S. **10**, p3; Zimmerman, Edward K. and Brimmer, Karl W. **16**, p3
Policies
  Rosenberg, Victor. **17**, p3; Sy, Karen J. and Robbin, Alice. **25**, p3
Policy
  Brimmer, Karl W. **17**, p33; Rath, Charla M. and Clement, John R.B. **23**, p35
Practice
  Arnold, Stephen E. **25**, p87
Pratt, Allan D.
  Pratt, Allan D. Microcomputers in Libraries. **19**, p247
Preschel, Barbara M.
  Preschel, Barbara M. and Woods, Lawrence J. Social Science Information. **24**, p267

Preston, Cecilia M.
    Lynch, Clifford A. and Preston, Cecilia M. Internet Access to Information Resources. **25**, p263
Pricing
    Spigai, Fran. **26**, p39
Primary
    Gannett, Elwood K. **8**, p243; Lerner, Rita G., Metaxas, Ted, Scott, John T., Adams, Peter D., and Judd, Peggy. **18**, p127
Principles
    Boyce, Bert R. and Kraft, Donald H. **20**, p153; Wyllys, Ronald E. **14**, p3
Privacy
    Carlson, Walter M. **12**, p. 279; Turn, Rein. **20**, p27
Private
    Berninger, Douglas E. and Adkinson, Burton, W. **13**, p3; McDonald, Dennis D. **17**, p83
Probability
    Bookstein, Abraham. **20**, p117
Problem
    Mills, R.G. **2**, p223
Problems
    Holm, Bart E. **11**, p5
Process
    Chartrand, Robert L. **11**, p299; Chartrand, Robert L. **21**, p203; Hills, Philip J. **18**, p99
Processes
    Griffin, Hillis L. **3**, p241
Processing
    Becker, David. **16**, p113; Bobrow, D.G., Fraser, J.B., and Quillian, M.R. **2**, p161; Damerau, Fred J. **11**, p107; Grosser, Kerry. **26**, p349; Kay, Martin and Sparck Jones, Karen. **6**, p141; Lerner, Rita G., Lipscomb, Karen J., Lynch, Michael F., and Willett, Peter. **24**, p189; Metaxas, Ted, Scott, John T., Adams, Peter D., and Judd, Peggy. **18**, p127; Lesk, Michael. **19**, p97; Montgomery, Christine A. **4**, p145; Park, Margaret K. **12**, p59; Rasmussen, Edie M. **27**, p99; Salton, Gerard. **3**, p169; Simmons, Robert F. **1**, p137; Tannehill, Robert S., Jr. **18**, p61; Veneziano, Velma. **15**, p109; Walker, Donald E. **8**, p69; Warner, Amy J. **22**, p79; Wilson, John H., Jr. **7**, p39
Product
    van Dam, Andries and Michener, James C. **2**, p187
Productivity
    Koenig, Michael E.D. **25**, p55
Products
    Griffiths, José-Marie. **17**, p269
Profession
    Svenonius, Elaine and Witthus, Rutherford. **16**, p291

Professional
    Atherton, Pauline and Greer, Roger. 3, p329; Cooper, Marianne and Lunin, Lois F. 24, p295; Farradane, J. 6, p399; Harvey, John F. 2, p419; Shera, Jesse H. and McFarland, Anne S. 4, p439; Taylor, Robert S. 1, p15
Professionals
    Froehlich, Thomas J. 27, p291
Programming
    Lesk, Michael. 19, p97
Programs
    Berninger, Douglas E. and Adkinson, Burton W. 13, p3; Sy, Karen J. and Robbin, Alice. 25, p3
Progress
    Hersey, David F. 13, p263
Protection
    Turn, Rein. 20, p27
Prywes, Noah S.
    Prywes, Noah S. and Smith, Diane Pirog. Organization of Information. 7, p103
Psychological
    Borgman, Christine L. 19, p33
Psychometric
    Rorvig, Mark E. 23, p157
Public
    Berninger, Douglas E. and Adkinson, Burton W. 13, p3; Hildreth, Charles R. 20, p233; McDonald, Dennis D. 17, p83
Publication
    American Institute of Physics Staff. 2, p339; Doebler, Paul D. 5, p223; Gannett, Elwood K. 8, p243; Kuney, Joseph H. 3, p31; Lerner, Rita G., Metaxas, Ted, Scott, John T., Adams, Peter D., and Judd, Peggy. 18, p127
Publisher
    Hernon, Peter and Relyea, Harold C. 23, p3
Publishing
    Fox, Edward A. 23, p85; Hjerppe, Roland. 21, p123; Terrant, Seldon W. 10, p273; Terrant, Seldon W. 15, p191
Pulliam, Robert
    Caceres, Cesar A., Weihrer, Anna Lea, and Pulliam, Robert. Information Science Applications in Medicine. 6, p325

Quality
    O'Neill, Edward T. and Vizine-Goetz, Diane. 23, p125
Quijano Solis, Alvaro
    Saracevic, Tefko, Braga, Gilda, and Quijano Solis, Alvaro. Information Systems in Latin America. 14, p249
Quillian, M.R.
    Bobrow, D.G., Fraser, J.B., and Quillian, M.R. Automated Language Processing. 2, p161

Raben, Joseph
    Raben, Joseph and Burton, Sarah K. Information Systems and Services in the Arts and Humanities. 16, p247;
    Raben, Joseph and Widmann, R.L. Information Systems Applications in the Humanities. 7, p439
Raitt, David I.
    Raitt, David I. Information Delivery Systems. 20, p55
Ramsey, H. Rudy
    Ramsey, H. Rudy and Grimes, Jack D. Human Factors in Interactive Computer Dialog. 18, p29
Raper, Diane
    Hindle, Anthony and Raper, Diane. The Economics of Information. 11, p27
Rasmussen, Edie M.
    Rasmussen, Edie M. Parallel Information Processing. 27, p99
Rath, Charla M.
    Rath, Charla M. and Clement, John R.B. Information Policy Issues in Science and Technology. 23, p35
Readable
    Amsler, Robert A. 19, p161; Evens, Martha. 24, p85; Gechman, Marvin C. 7, p323; Schipma, Peter B. 10, p237; Wilde, Daniel U. 11, p267; Williams, Martha E. 9, p221
Redford, Julia S.
    Coyne, Joseph G., Carroll, Bonnie C., and Redford, Julia S. Energy Information Systems and Services. 18, p231
Reed, Mary Jane Pobst
    Reed, Mary Jane Pobst and Vrooman, Hugh T. Library Automation. 14, p193
Rees, Alan M.
    Rees, Alan M. Evaluation of Information Systems and Services. 2, p63
Reexamined
    Heilprin, Laurence B. 24, p343
Reggia, James A.
    Doszkocs, Tamas E., Reggia, James A. and Lin, Xia. Connectionist Models and Information Retrieval. 25, p209
Related
    Griffiths, José-Marie. 17, p269
Relyea, Harold C.
    Hernon, Peter and Relyea, Harold C. The U.S. Government as a Publisher. 23, p3
Repo, Aatto J.
    Repo, Aatto J. Economics of Information. 22, p3
Representation
    Artandi, Susan. 5, p143; Batten, William E. 8, p43; Harris, Jessica L. 9, p81; Richmond, Phyllis, A. 7, p73; Vickery, Brian C. 6, p113
Representations
    Shaffer, Clifford A. 27, p135

Reprography
  Teplitz, Arthur. **5**, p87; Veaner, Allen B. **4**, p175
Research
  Allen, Bryce L. **26**, p3; Borgman, Christine L. **19**, p33; Ercegovac, Zorana. **27**, p173; Hersey, David F. **13**, p263; Kinnucan, Mark T., Nelson, Michael J., and Allen, Bryce L. **22**, p147; Larson, Signe and Williams, Martha E. **15**, p251
Resource
  Lytle, Richard H. **21**, p309; Palmour, Vernon E. and Roderer, Nancy K. **13**, p147
Resources
  Levitan, Karen B. **17**, p227; Markey, Karen. **19**, p271; Lynch, Clifford A. and Preston, Cecilia M. **25**, p263
Retrieval
  Belkin, Nicholas J. and Croft, W. Bruce. **22**, p109; Berul, Lawrence H. **4**, p203; Bookstein, Abraham. **20**, p117; Brandhorst, Wesley T. and Eckert, Philip F. **7**, p379; Brown, Patricia L. and Jones, Shirli O. **3**, p263; Caruso, Elaine. **16**, p317; Doszkocs, Tamas E., Reggia, James A. and Lin, Xia. **25**, p209; Hawkins, Donald T. **16**, p171; Hollaar, Lee A. **14**, p129; Kantor, Paul B. **17**, p99; Magnino, Joseph J., Jr. **6**, p219; McGill, Michael J. and Huitfeldt, Jennifer. **14**, p93; Rorvig, Mark E. **23**, p157; Shaw, Debora. **26**, p155; Smith, Linda C. **22**, p41; Summit, Roger K. and Firschein, Oscar. **9**, p285; Turtle, Howard, Penniman, W. David, and Hickey, Thomas. **16**, p55; Williams, Philip W. and Goldsmith, Gerry. **16**, p85.
Review
  Cuadra, Carlos A. **1**, p1
Rice, Ronald E.
  Rice, Ronald E. The Impacts of Computer-Mediated Organizational and Interpersonal Communication. **15**, p221
Richards, Pamela Spence
  Richards, Pamela Spence. Education and Training for Information Science in the Soviet Union. **27**, p267
Richmond, Phyllis A.
  Richmond, Phyllis A. Document Description and Representation. **7**, p73
Robbin, Alice
  Sy, Karen J. and Robbin, Alice. Federal Statistical Policies and Programs: How Good Are the Numbers? **25**, p3
Roderer, Nancy K.
  Palmour, Vernon E. and Roderer, Nancy K. Library Resource Sharing through Networks. **13**, p147
Rorvig, Mark E.
  Rorvig, Mark E. Psychometric Measurement and Information Retrieval. **23**, p157
Rosenberg, Victor
  Rosenberg, Victor. National Information Policies. **17**, p3
Rush, James E.
  Rush, James E. Handling Chemical Structure Information. **13**,.p209

Sable, Jerome
  Minker, Jack and Sable, Jerome. File Organization and Data Management. 2, p123
Salton, Gerard
  Salton, Gerard. Automated Language Processing. 3, p169
Samuelson, Kjell
  Samuelson, Kjell. International Information Transfer and Network Communication. 6, p277
Saracevic, Tefko
  Saracevic, Tefko, Braga, Gilda, and Quijano Solis, Alvaro. Information Systems in Latin America. 14, p249
Schipma, Peter B.
  Schipma, Peter B. Generation and Uses of Machine-Readable Data Bases. 10, p237
Schmierer, Helen F.
  Schmierer, Helen F. Bibliographic Standards. 10, p105
Scholarly
  Hills, Philip J. 18, p99
Schools
  Eisenberg, Michael B. and Spitzer, Kathleen. 26, p243
Schwartz, Candy
  Schwartz, Candy and Eisenmann, Laura M. Subject Analysis. 21, p37
Science
  Allen, Bryce L. 26, p3; Atherton, Pauline and Greer, Roger. 3, p329; Boyce, Bert R. and Kraft, Donald H. 20, p153; Caceres, Cesar A., Weihrer, AnnaLea, and Pulliam, Robert. 6, p325; Chartrand, Robert L. 11, p299; Farradane, J. 6, p399; Harmon, Glynn. 11, p347; Harvey, John F. 2, p419; Heilprin, Laurence B. 24, p343; Herner, Saul and Herner, Mary. 2, p1; Jahoda, Gerald. 8, p321; Keenan, Stella. 4, p273; Kinnucan, Mark T., Nelson, Michael J., and Allen, Bryce L. 22, p147; Menzel, Herbert. 1, p41; Preschel, Barbara M. and Woods, Lawrence J. 24, p267; Rath, Charla M. and Clement, John R.B. 23, p35; Richards, Pamela Spence. 27, p267; Shera, Jesse H. and Cleveland, Donald B. 12, p249; Shera, Jesse H. and McFarland, Anne S. 4, p439; Svenonius, Elaine and Witthus, Rutherford. 16, p291; Taylor, Robert S. 1, p15; Zunde, Pranas and Gehl, John. 14, p67
Sciences
  Vaupel, Nancy and Elias, Arthur. 16, p267
Scientific
  Lerner, Rita G., Metaxas, Ted, Scott, John T., Adams, Peter D., and Judd, Peggy. 18, p127
Scott, John T.
  Lerner, Rita G., Metaxas, Ted, Scott, John T., Adams, Peter D., and Judd, Peggy. Primary Publication Systems and Scientific Text Processing. 18, p127

Search
    Bates, Marcia J. **16**, p139; Climenson, W. Douglas. **1**, p107; Meadow, Charles T. and Meadow, Harriet R. **5**, p169; Shoffner, Ralph M. **3**, p137
Searching
    Mischo, William H. and Lee, Jounghyoun. **22**, p227
Secondary
    Bearman, Toni Carbo. **13**, p179; Neufeld, M. Lynne and Cornog, Martha. **18**, p151; Parkins, Phyllis V. and Kennedy, H.E. **6**, 247
Sector
    McDonald, Dennis D. **17**, p83
Sectors
    Berninger, Douglas E. and Adkinson, Burton W. **13**, p3
Segal, Jo An S.
    Segal, Jo An S. Networking and Decentralization. **20**, p203
Selective
    Housman, Edward M. **8**, p221
Senko, Michael E.
    Senko, Michael E. File Organization and Management Information Systems. **4**, p111
Services
    Aines, Andrew A. and Day, Melvin S. **10**, p3; Bearman, Toni Carbo. **13**, p179; Black, Donald V. and Fung, Margaret C. **18**, p307; Borko, Harold. **2**, p35; Burton, Sarah K. **16**, p247; Coyne, Joseph G., Carroll, Bonnie C. and Redford, Julia S. **18**, p231; Eisenberg, Michael B. and Spitzer, Kathleen. **26**, p243; Frank, Robyn C. **22**, p293; Gannett, Elwood K. **8**, p243; Griffiths, José-Marie. **17**, p269; Keenan, Stella. **4**, p273; Keren, Carl and Harmon, Larry. **15**, p289; Koenig, Michael E.D. **25**, p55; Marron, Beatrice and Fife, Dennis. **11**, p163; McCarn, Davis B. **13**, p85; McDonald, Dennis D. **17**, p83; Mick, Colin K. **14**, p37; Neufeld, M. Lynne and Cornog, Martha. **18**, p151; Parkins, Phyllis V. and Kennedy, H.E. **6**, p247; Raben, Joseph and Burton, Sarah K. **16**, p247; Rees, Alan M. **2**, p63; Simpson, G.S., Jr. and Flanagan, Carolyn. **1**, p305; Tibbo, Helen R. **26**, p287; Vaupel, Nancy and Elias, Arthur. **16**, p267
Set
    Bookstein, Abraham. **20**, p117
Shaffer, Clifford A.
    Shaffer, Clifford A. Data Representations for Geographic Information Systems. **27**, p135
Shank, Russell
    Olson, Edwin E., Shank, Russell, and Olsen, Harold A. Library and Information Networks. **7**, p279
Sharing
    Palmour, Vernon E. and Roderer, Nancy K. **13**, p147
Sharp, John R.
    Sharp, John R. Content Analysis, Specification, and Control. **2**, p87
Shaw, Debora
    Shaw, Debora. Human-Computer Interface for Information Retrieval. **26**, p155

Shaw, Ward
 Shaw, Ward and Culkin, Patricia B. Systems that Inform: Emerging Trends in Library Automation and Network Development. 22, p265
Shera, Jesse H.
 Shera, Jesse H. and Cleveland, Donald B. History and Foundations of Information Science. 12, p249;
 Shera, Jesse H. and McFarland, Anne S. Professional Aspects of Information Science and Technology. 4, p439
Sherrod, John
 Murdock, John and Sherrod, John. Library and Information Center Management. 11, p381;
 Sherrod, John. National Information Issues and Trends. 1, p337
Shoffner, Ralph M.
 Shoffner, Ralph M. Organization, Maintenance and Search of Machine Files. 3, p137
Sieck, Steven K.
 Sieck, Steven K. Business Information Systems and Databases. 19, p311
Silberman, Harry F.
 Silberman, Harry F. and Filep, Robert T. Information Systems Applications in Education. 3, p357
Simmons, Peter
 Simmons, Peter. Library Automation. 8, p167
Simmons, Robert F.
 Simmons, Robert F. Automated Language Processing. 1, p137
Simms, Robert L., Jr.
 Simms, Robert L., Jr. and Fuchs, Edward. Communications Technology. 5, p113
Simpson, G.S., Jr.
 Simpson, G.S., Jr. and Flanagan, Carolyn. Information Centers and Services. 1, p305
Smith, Diane Pirog
 Prywes, Noah S. and Smith, Diane Pirog. Organization of Information. 7, p103
Smith, Linda C.
 Smith, Linda C. Artificial Intelligence Applications in Information Systems. 15, p67;
 Smith, Linda C. Artificial Intelligence and Information Retrieval. 22, p41
Smith, Mona F.
 Freeman, Robert R. and Smith, Mona F. Environmental Information. 21, p241
Social
 Doctor, Ronald D. 27, p43; Preschel, Barbara M. and Woods, Lawrence J. 24, p267
Society
 Kochen, Manfred. 18, p277; Parker, Edwin B. 8, p345

Software
   Vigil, Peter. **21**, p63
Solving
   Mills, R.G. **2**, p233
Sources
   Ercegovac, Zorana. **27**, p173
Soviet Union
   Richards, Pamela Spence. **27**, p267
Sowizral, Henry A.
   Sowizral, Henry A. Expert Systems. **20**, p179
Sparck Jones, Karen
   Kay, Martin and Sparck Jones, Karen. Automated Language Processing. **6**, p141
Specification
   Baxendale, Phyllis. **1**, p71; Fairthorne, Robert A. **4**, p73; Sharp, John R. **2**, p87; Taulbee, Orrin E. **3**, p105
Spence, A. Michael
   Spence, A. Michael. An Economist's View of Information. **9**, p57
Spigai, Frances G.
   Spigai, Frances G. and Butler, Brett B. Micrographics. **11**, p59
   Spigai, Fran. Information Pricing. **26**, p39
Spitzer, Kathleen L.
   Eisenberg, Michael B. and Spitzer, Kathleen L. Information Technology and Services in Schools. **26**, p243
Spring, Michael B.
   Spring, Michael B. Information Technology Standards. **26**, p79
Spring, William C., Jr.
   Spring, William C., Jr. Applications in Medicine. **2**, p311
Standards
   Park, Margaret K. **12**, p59; Schmierer, Helen F. **10**, p105; Spring, Michael B. **26**, p79; Tannehill, Robert S., Jr. **18**, p61
State
   Hearle, Edward F.R., **5**, p325
Statistical
   Kinnucan, Mark T., Nelson, Michael J., and Allen, Bryce L. **22**, p147; Sy, Karen J. and Robbin, Alice. **25**, p3

Steinfield, Charles W.
   Steinfield, Charles W. Computer-Mediated Communication Systems. **21**, p167
Stern, Barrie T.
   Stern, Barrie T. Evaluation and Design of Bibliographic Data Bases. **12**, p3
Storage
   Goldstein, Charles M. **19**, p65; Kantor, Paul B. **17**, p99

Structure
   Lipscomb, Karen J., Lynch, Michael F., and Willett, Peter. 24, p189; Rush, James E. 13, p209
Structures
   Yang, Chung-Shu, 13, p125
Studies
   Ercegovac, Zorana. 27, p173; Hewins, Elizabeth T. 25, p145
Subject
   Lancaster, F. Wilfrid, Elliker, Calvin, and Connell, Tschera Harkness. 24, p35; Liston, David M., Jr. and Howder, Murray L. 12, p81; Schwartz, Candy and Eisenmann, Laura M. 21, p37; Travis, Irene L. and Fidel, Raya. 17, p123
Summit, Roger K.
   Summit, Roger K. and Firschein, Oscar. Document Retrieval Systems and Techniques. 9, p285
Surprenant, Thomas T.
   Surprenant, Thomas T. Global Threats to Information. 20, p3
Svenonius, Elaine
   Svenonius, Elaine and Witthus, Rutherford. Information Science as a Profession. 16, p291
Swanson, Rowena Weiss
   Swanson, Rowena Weiss. Design and Evaluation of Information Systems. 10, p43
Sy, Karen J.
   Sy, Karen J. and Robbin, Alice. Federal Statistical Policies and Programs: How Good Are the Numbers? 25, p3
System
   Baruch, Jordan J. 1, p255; Blumstein, Alfred. 7, p471; Wyllys, Ronald E. 14, p3
Systems
   Beard, Joseph J. 6, p369; Bearman, Toni Carbo. 13, p179; Bennett, John L. 7, p159; Black, Donald V. and Fung, Margaret C. 18, p307; Blumstein, Alfred. 7, p471; Borko, Harold, 2, p35; Bourne, Charles P. 1, p171; Brandhorst, Wesley T. and Eckert, Philip F. 7, p379; Burt, Patricia V. and Kinnucan, Mark T. 25, p175; Cleverdon, Cyril W. 6, p41; Coyne, Joseph G., Carroll, Bonnie C., and Redford, Julia S. 18, p231; Debons, Anthony and Montgomery, K. Leon. 9, p25; Drenth, Hilary, Morris, Anne, and Tseng, Gwyneth. 26, p113; Eastman, Caroline M. 20, p91; Frank, Robyn C. 22, p293; Gannett, Elwood K. 8, p243; Grattidge, Walter and Creps, John E., Jr. 13, p297; Griffiths, José-Marie. 17, p269; Hawkins, Donald T. 16, p171; Hearle, Edward F.R. 5, p325; Hersey, David F. 13, p263; Huffenberger, Michael A. and Wigington, Ronald L. 14, p153; Kantor, Paul B. 17, p99; Katter, Robert V. 4, p31; King, Donald W. 3, p61; Lancaster, F. Wilfrid and Gillespie, Constantine J. 5, p33; Lerner, Rita G., Metaxas, Ted, Scott, John T., Adams, Peter D., and Judd, Peggy. 18, p127; Levy, Richard P. and Cammarn, Maxine R. 3, p397; Luedke, James A., Jr.,

Kovacs, Gabor J., and Fried, John B. **12**, p119; Mailloux, Elizabeth. **24**, p239; Marron, Beatrice and Fife, Dennis **11**, p163; Martin, Thomas H. **8**, p203; McCarn, Davis B. **13**, p85; Mick, Colin K. **14**, p37; Neufeld, M. Lynne and Cornog, Martha. **18**, p151; Raben, Joseph and Burton, Sarah K. **16**, p247; Raben, Joseph and Widmann, R.L. **7**, p439; Raitt, David I. **20**, p55; Rees, Alan M. **2**, p63; Saracevic, Tefko, Braga, Gilda, and Quijano Solis, Alvaro. **14**, p249; Senko, Michael E. **4**, p111; Shaffer, Clifford A. **27**, p135; Shaw, Ward and Culkin, Patricia B. **22**, p265; Sieck, Steven K. **19**, p311; Silberman, Harry F. and Filep, Robert T. **3**, p357; Smith, Linda C. **15**, p67; Sowizral, Henry A. **20**, p179; Steinfield, Charles W. **21**, p167; Summit, Roger K. and Firschein, Oscar. **9**, p285; Swanson, Rowena Weiss. **10**, p43; Tate, F.A. **2**, p285; Tibbo, Helen R. **26**, p287; Tilley, Carolyn B. **25**, p313; Vaupel, Nancy and Elias, Arthur. **16**, p267; Vinsonhaler, John F. and Moon, Robert D. **8**, p277; Voges, Mickie A. **23**, p193; Wanger, Judith. **14**, p219; Weiss, Stanley D. **5**, p299

Tannehill, Robert S., Jr.
   Tannehill, Robert S., Jr. Bibliographic and Information-Processing Standards. **18**, p61
Tate, F.A.
   Tate, F.A. Handling Chemical Compounds in Information Systems. **2**, p285
Taulbee, Orrin E.
   Taulbee, Orrin E. Content Analysis, Specification, and Control. **3**, p105
Taylor, Robert S.
   Taylor, Robert S. Professional Aspects of Information Science and Technology. **1**, p15
Technical
   Griffin, Hillis L. **3**, p241
Techniques
   American Institute of Physics Staff. **2**, p339; Bates, Marcia J. **16**, p139; Belkin, Nicholas J. and Croft, W. Bruce. **22**, p109; Burt, Patricia V. and Kinnucan, Mark T. **25**, p175; Climenson, W. Douglas. **1**, p107; Marron, Beatrice and Fife, Dennis. **11**, p163; McCarn, Davis B. **13**, p85; McGill, Michael J. and Huitfeldt, Jennifer. **14**, p93; Summit, Roger K. and Firschein, Oscar. **9**, p285; Wyllys, Ronald E. **14**, p3
Technologies
   Doctor, Ronald D. **27**, p42; Goldstein, Charles M. **19**, p65
Technology
   Atherton, Pauline and Greer, Roger. **3**, p329; Ballou, Hubbard W. **8**, p121; Broadbent, Marianne and Koenig, Michael E.D. **23**, p237; Brumm, Eugenia. **26**, p197; Cawkell, Anthony E. **15**, p37; Chartrand, Robert L. **21**, p203; Dunn, Donald A. **10**, p165; Eisenberg, Michael B. and Spitzer, Kathleen. **26**, p243; Farradane, J. **6**, p399; Harvey, John F. **2**, p419; Herner, Saul and Herner, Mary. **2**, p1; Huskey, Harry D. **5**, p73; Keenan, Stella. **4**, p273; Keplinger, Michael S. **15**, p3; Long, Philip L. **11**, p211; Menzel, Herbert. **1**, p41; Nelson,

KEYWORD AND AUTHOR INDEX 423

    Carl E. 6, p77; Palmquist, Ruth A. 27, p3; Rath, Charla M. and Clement, John R.B. 23, p35; Shera, Jesse H. and McFarland, Anne S. 4, p439; Simms, Robert L., Jr. and Fuchs, Edward. 5, p113; Spring, Michael B. 26, p79; Taylor, Robert S. 1, p15; Thompson, Charles W.N. 10, p383; Tibbo, Helen R. 26, p287; Veaner, Allen B. 4, p175

Telecommunications
    Brimmer, Karl W. 17, p33

Teletext
    Veith, Richard H. 18, p3

Tenopir, Carol
    Tenopir, Carol. Full-Text Databases. 19, p215

Teplitz, Arthur
    Teplitz, Arthur. Microform and Reprography. 5, p87

Terrant, Seldon W.
    Terrant, Seldon W. Computers in Publishing. 15, p191;
    Terrant, Seldon W. The Computer and Publishing. 10, p273

Text
    Lerner, Rita G., Metaxas, Ted, Scott, John T., Adams, Peter D., and Judd, Peggy. 18, p127; Lesk, Michael. 19, p97; Tenopir, Carol. 19, p215

Theories
    Boyce, Bert R. and Kraft, Donald H. 20, p153

Theory
    Arnold, Stephen E. 25, p87

Thompson, Charles W.N.
    Thompson, Charles W.N. Technology Utilization. 10, p383

Threats
    Surprenant, Thomas T. 20, p3

Tibbo, Helen R.
    Tibbo, Helen R. Information Systems, Services, and Technology for the Humanities. 26, p287

Tighe, Ruth L.
    Miller, Ronald F. and Tighe, Ruth L. Library and Information Networks. 9, p173

Tilley, Carolyn B.
    Tilley, Carolyn B. Medical Databases and Health Information Systems. 25, p313

Tomberg, Alex
    Tomberg, Alex. European Information Networks. 12, p219

Toxicological
    Kissman, Henry M. and Wexler, Philip. 18, p185

Training
    Cooper, Marianne and Lunin, Lois F. 24, p295; Harmon, Glynn. 11, p347; Richards, Pamela Spence. 27, p267; Wanger, Judith. 14, p219

Transfer
    Lorenz, John G. 4, p379; Samuelson, Kjell. 6, p277

Translation
    Tucker, Allen B., Jr. and Nirenburg, Sergei. **19**, p129
Travis, Irene L.
    Travis, Irene L. and Fidel, Raya. Subject Analysis. **17**, p123
Trends
    Hammer, Donald P. **2**, p385; Shaw, Ward and Culkin, Patricia B. **22**, p265; Sherrod, John. **1**, p337
Tseng, Gwyneth
    Drenth, Hilary, Morris, Anne, and Tseng, Gwyneth. Expert Systems as Information Intermediaries. **26**, p113
Tucci, Valerie K.
    Tucci, Valerie K. Information Marketing for Libraries. **23**, p59
Tucker, Allen B., Jr.
    Tucker, Allen B., Jr. and Nirenburg, Sergei. Machine Translation: A Contemporary View. **19**, p129
Turn, Rein
    Turn, Rein. Privacy Protection. **20**, p27
Turtle, Howard
    Turtle, Howard, Penniman, W. David, and Hickey, Thomas. Data Entry/ Display Devices for Interactive Information Retrieval. **16**, p55

Unconventional
    Hollaar, Lee A. **14**, p129
Update
    Long, Philip L. **11**, p211
Use
    Gechman, Marvin C. **7**, p323; Hewins, Elizabeth T. **25**, p145; Wilde, Daniel U. **11**, p267; Williams, Martha E. **9**, p221
User (*see also* End-User)
    Bennett, John L. **7**, p159; Martin, Thomas H. **8**, p203; Mischo, William H. and Lee, Jounghyoun. **22**, p227
Uses
    Allen, Thomas J. **4**, p3; Crane, Diana. **6**, p3; Crawford, Susan. **13**, p61; Dervin, Brenda and Nilan, Michael. **21**, p3; Herner, Saul and Herner, Mary. **2**, p1; Lin, Nan and Garvey, William D. **7**, p5; Lipetz, Ben-Ami. **5**, p3; Martyn, John. **9**, p3; Menzel, Herbert. **1**, p41; Paisley, William J. **3**, p1; Schipma, Peter B. **10**, p237
Utilization
    Thompson, Charles W.N. **10**, p383

Value
    Griffiths, José-Marie. **17**, p269
van Dam, Andries
    van Dam, Andries and Michener, James C. Hardware Developments and Product Announcements. **2**, p187

Vaupel, Nancy
    Vaupel, Nancy and Elias, Arthur. Information Systems and Services in the Life Sciences. **16**, p267
Veaner, Allen B.
    Veaner, Allen B. Reprography and Microform Technology. **4**, p175
Veith, Richard H.
    Veith, Richard H. Videotex and Teletext. **18**, p3
Veneziano, Velma
    Veneziano, Velma. Library Automation: Data for Processing and Processing for Data. **15**, p109
Vickery, Brian C.
    Vickery, Brian C. Document Description and Representation. **6**, p113
Video
    Kletter, Richard C. and Hudson, Heather. **7**, p197
Videotex
    Veith, Richard H. **18**, p3
View
    Spence, A. Michael. **9**, p57; Tucker, Allen B., Jr. and Nirenburg, Sergei. **19**, p129
Vigil, Peter
    Vigil, Peter. The Software Interface. **21**, p63
Vinsonhaler, John F.
    Vinsonhaler, John F. and Moon, Robert D. Information Systems Applications in Education. **8**, p277
Visual
    Markey, Karen. **19**, p271
Vizine-Goetz, Diane
    O'Neill, Edward T. and Vizine-Goetz, Diane. Quality Control in Online Databases. **23**, p125
Voges, Mickie A.
    Voges, Mickie A. Information Systems and the Law. **23**, p193
Vrooman, Hugh T.
    Reed, Mary Jane Pobst and Vrooman, Hugh T. Library Automation. **14**, p193

Walker, Donald E.
    Walker, Donald E. Automated Language Processing. **8**, p69
Wanger, Judith
    Wanger, Judith. Education and Training for Online systems. **14**, p210
Warner, Amy J.
    Warner, Amy J. Natural Language Processing. **22**, p79
Wasserman, Paul
    Wasserman, Paul and Daniel, Evelyn. Library and Information Center Management. **4**, p405
Weihrer, Anna Lea
    Caceres, Cesar A., Weihrer, Anna Lea, and Pulliam, Robert. Information Science Applications in Medicine. **6**, p325

Weil, Ben H.
  Weil, Ben H. Copyright Developments. **10**, p359
Weiss, Stanley D.
  Weiss, Stanley D. Management Information Systems. **5**, p299
Wente, Van A.
  Wente, Van A. and Young, Gifford A. Current Awareness and Dissemination. **5**, p259
Werdel, Judith A.
  Adams, Scott and Werdel, Judith A. Cooperation in Information Activities through International Organizations. **10**, p303
Wexler, Philip
  Kissman, Henry M. and Wexler, Philip. Toxicological Information. **18**, p185
White, Howard D.
  White, Howard D. and McCain, Katherine W. Bibliometrics. **24**, p119
Widmann, R.L.
  Raben, Joseph and Widmann, R.L. Information Systems Applications in the Humanities. **7**, p439
Wigington, Ronald L.
  Huffenberger, Michael A. and Wigington, Ronald L. Database Management Systems. **14**, p153
Wilde, Daniel U.
  Wilde, Daniel U. Generation and Use of Machine-Readable Data Bases. **11**, p267
Willett, Peter
  Lipscomb, Karen J., Lynch, Michael F., and Willett, Peter. Chemical Structure Processing. **24**, p189
Williams, Martha E.
  Larson, Signe and Williams, Martha E. Computer Assisted Legal Research. **15**, p251;
  Williams, Martha E. Use of Machine-Readable Data Bases. **9**, p221
Williams, Philip W.
  Williams, Philip W. and Goldsmith, Gerry. Information Retrieval on Mini- and Microcomputers. **16**, p85
Wilson, John H., Jr.
  Wilson, John H., Jr. Costs, Budgeting, and Economics of Information Processing. **7**, p39
Witthus, Rutherford
  Svenonius, Elaine and Witthus, Rutherford. Information Science as a Profession. **16**, p291
Woods, Lawrence
  Preschel, Barbara M. and Woods, Lawrence J. Social Science Information. **24**, p267
Wooster, Harold
  Wooster, Harold. Biomedical Communications. **17**, p187

Writing
    Hjerppe, Roland. 21, p123
Wyllys, Ronald E.
    Wyllys, Ronald E. System Design—Principles and Techniques. 14, p3

Yang, Chung-Shu
    Yang, Chung-Shu. Design and Evaluation of File Structures. 13, p125
Young, Gifford A.
    Wente, Van A. and Young, Gifford A. Current Awareness and Dissemination. 5, p259

Zimmerman, Edward K.
    Zimmerman, Edward K. and Brimmer, Karl W. National Planning for Data Communications. 16, p3
Zunde, Pranas
    Zunde, Pranas and Gehl, John. Empirical Foundations of Information Science. 14, p67

About the Editor . . .

Professor Martha E. Williams assumed the Editorship of the *ANNUAL REVIEW OF INFORMATION SCIENCE AND TECHNOLOGY* with Volume 11 and has produced a series of books that provide unparalleled insights into, and overviews of, the multifaceted discipline of information science.

Professor Williams holds the positions of Director of the Information Retrieval Research Laboratory and Professor of Information Science in the Coordinated Science Laboratory (CSL) as well as Professor of Information Science in the Graduate School of Library and Information Science and affiliate of the Computer Science Department at the University of Illinois, Urbana-Champaign, Illinois. As a chemist and information scientist Professor Williams has brought to the Editorship a breadth of knowledge and experience in information science and technology.

She has served as a Director and Chairman of the Board of Engineering Information, Inc.; she is founding editor of *Computer-Readable Databases: A Directory and Data Sourcebook;* Editor of *Online Review* (Learned Information, Ltd., Oxford, England); and Program Chairman for the National Online Meetings, which are sponsored by *Online Review*. She was appointed by the Secretary of Health, Education and Welfare, Joseph Califano, to be a member of the Board of Regents of the National Library of Medicine (NLM) in 1978 and has served as Chairman of the Board. She has been a member of the Numerical Data Advisory Board of the National Research Council (NRC), National Academy of Sciences (NAS). She was a member of the Science Information Activities task force of the National Science Foundation (NSF), was chairman of the Large Database subcommittee of the NAS/NRC Committee on Chemical Information, and was chairman of the Gordon Research Conference on Scientific Information Problems in Research in 1980.

Professor Williams is a Fellow of the American Association for the Advancement of Science, Honorary Fellow of the Institute of Information Scientists in England, and recipient of the 1984 Award of Merit of the American Society for Information Science. She is a member of, has held offices in, and/or is actively involved in various committees of the American Association for the Advancement of Science (AAAS), the American Chemical Society (ACS), the Association for Computing Machinery (ACM), and the American Society for Information Science (ASIS). She has published numerous books and papers and serves on the editorial boards of several journals. She is the founder and President of Information Market Indicators, Inc., and consults for many governmental and commercial organizations.

ASIS and Its Members

For over 50 years the leading professional society for information professionals, the American Society for Information Science is an association whose diverse membership continues to reflect the frontiers and horizons of the dynamic field of information science and technology. ASIS owes its stature to the cumulative contributions of its members, past and present.

ASIS counts among its membership some 4000 information specialists from such fields as computer science, management, engineering, librarianship, chemistry, linguistics, and education. As was true when the Society was founded, ASIS membership continues to lead the information profession in the search for new and better theories, techniques, and technologies to improve access to information through storage and retrieval advances. And now, as then, ASIS and its members are called upon to help determine new directions and standards for the development of information policies and practices.

Individual Membership Application

New Member
Renewal

asis AMERICAN SOCIETY FOR INFORMATION SCIENCE

Please print or type in black ink.

Name (Last, First, Middle) _____ Day Phone ( ) _____ Ext. _____
Title _____
Organization _____
Mailing Address _____
City _____ State _____ Zipcode _____ Plus 4: _____
Province (Outside U.S.) _____ Country _____ Mail Code _____

Check One—The Above Address is My ☐ Work ☐ Home

Please select category of membership:

☐ Regular $95 $ _____

☐ Student $25 $ _____

I am a full-time student at _____
Faculty advisor's signature _____

Special Interest Group (SIG) Dues

☐ Check here if one free SIG selected.

Additional SIGs _____ x $6 each $ _____
Total Membership and SIG Dues $ _____
Contribution to ASIS Scholarship Fund $ _____
Contribution to ASIS Development Fund $ _____
Total Payment Enclosed $ _____ (US)

Chapter Membership: You will automatically become a member of the chapter serving your geographic area (if one exists). Information about your chapter and additional chapters you may want to join will be sent to you upon receipt of your membership application.

Check or money order enclosed (Payable to ASIS)
or charge my   ☐ VISA   ☐ Mastercard
Account # _____
Expiration Date _____
Signature _____

Because your ASIS membership is individual rather than organizational, your membership goes with you if you make a career move. All membership fees and contributions are tax-deductible to the full extent of the law in the United States. You will receive notification of your active membership when your application form is processed. Please allow 4-6 weeks for delivery. For new members, membership is for one year from the month in which dues are received. Membership fees are non-refundable.

Of the annual membership dues, $11 is payment for the *Bulletin*, $19 is payment for the *Journal*.

All ASIS members may select one SIG at no charge. You may join additional SIGs at $6 each. Please note *all* selections here. Enclose payment of $6 for the second and succeeding selections.

☐ Arts and Humanities (AH)
☐ Automated Language Processing (ALP)
☐ Biological and Chemical Information Systems (BC)
☐ Behavioral and Social Sciences (BSS)
☐ Classification Research (CR)
☐ Computerized Retrieval Services (CRS)
☐ Education for Information Science (ED)
☐ Foundations of Information Science (FIS)
☐ Human-Computer Interaction (HCI)
☐ Information Analysis and Evaluation (IAE)
☐ International Information Issues (III)
☐ Library Automation and Networks (LAN)
☐ Management (MGT)
☐ Medical Information Systems (MED)
☐ Numeric Data Bases (NDB)
☐ Office Information Systems (OIS)
☐ Personal Computers (PC)
☐ Information Generation and Publishing (PUB)
☐ Storage and Retrieval Technology (SRT)
☐ Technology, Information and Society (TIS)

Please mail this form with your payment to
American Society for Information Science
Ben Franklin Station
P.O. Box 554
Washington, DC 20044-0554

All other correspondence to ASIS Headquarters.

8720 Georgia Avenue, Suite 501, Silver Spring, MD 20910
Tel.: 301-495-0900 FAX 301-495-0810

WITHDRAWN
OWENS LIBRARY
N.W.M.S.U.